Fodor's

ESSENTIAL
HAWAII

Welcome to Hawaii

Little did we realize that the emergence of a novel coronavirus in early 2020 would abruptly bring almost all travel to a halt. Although our Fodor's writers around the world have continued working to bring you the best of the destinations they cover, we still anticipate that more than the usual number of businesses will close permanently in the coming months, perhaps with little advance notice. We don't expect things to return to "normal" for some time. As you plan your upcoming travels to Hawaii, please confirm that places are still open and let us know when we need to make updates by writing to us at editors@fodors.com.

TOP REASONS TO GO

★ **Beaches:** Every island claims its share of postcard-perfect strands.

★ **Resorts:** Spas, pools, lavish gardens, and golf courses make relaxing easy.

★ **Pearl Harbor:** This historic memorial site on Oahu is not to be missed.

★ **Napali Coast:** Kauai's jagged emerald-green coast makes an unforgettable excursion.

★ **Whale-Watching:** In winter humpback whales swim right off Maui's shores.

★ **Volcanoes National Park:** On the Big Island you can explore the world's most active volcano.

Contents

MAPS

Chapter 1

EXPERIENCE HAWAII

37 ULTIMATE EXPERIENCES

Hawaii offers terrific experiences that should be on every traveler's list. Here are Fodor's top picks for a memorable trip.

1 Explore Oahu's North Shore

Make a day of it when you head to the North Shore. Start off in Kaneohe and drive up Kamehameha Highway to Haleiwa, stopping along the way at fruit stands, shrimp trucks, beaches, world-famous surfing spots, and scenic overlooks. *(Ch. 3)*

2 Tour a Kona Coffee Plantation

Big Island farmers share their passion for farming genuine Kona coffee by offering free tours. Our favorite is Lions Gate Farm at mile marker 101 in Honaunau. (Ch. 5)

3 Be a Cowboy for a Day

Saddle up and get ready to ride the ranges, cliffs, and trails of the Big Island on horseback. It's one of the best ways to take in the island's beautiful scenery. (Ch. 5)

4 Go Mountain Tubing

A century ago, Lihue Plantation dug waterways to irrigate its fields. Now you can take a tubing tour via the waterways for a glimpse of Kauai's hidden interior. *(Ch. 6)*

5 Go Deep-Sea Fishing

The deep Pacific waters surrounding Kauai are teeming with fish. Charters, most of which depart from Lihue, visit the best spots and provide all the gear. *(Ch. 6)*

6 Experience Maui's Charm

Discovered by hippies in the 1970s, Paia continues to be a hip and happening place with galleries, eateries, antique stores, and, of course, surf shops. *(Ch. 4)*

7 Snorkel at Hanauma Bay

This Oahu nature preserve nestled in a volcanic crater with a vibrant reef is a phenomenal, family-friendly place to see colorful fish and other sea life. *(Ch. 3)*

8 Watch Lava Flow at Hawaii Volcanoes National Park

Witness the primal birth of living land from two eruption sites flowing from the Big Island's Kilauea Volcano, currently the world's most active volcano. *(Ch. 5)*

9 Watch for Whales

Humpback whales hang out in the AuAu Channel off Maui every winter, and boats leaving from Lahaina can be in the midst of these gentle giants within 15 minutes. *(Ch. 4)*

10 Learn to Surf

On Oahu, Waikiki is still a popular spot to try Hawaii's favorite sport, but White Plains has fewer crowds and great conditions for beginner surfers. *(Ch. 3)*

11 Attend a Luau

Guests are treated to Hawaiian-style storytelling, complete with hula dancing, traditional knife dancing, and fire poi ball throwing at traditional luaus.

12 Enjoy a Shave Ice on Oahu

Matsumoto's on the North Shore may be the most well-known, but we prefer Island Snow in Kailua. *(Ch. 3)*

13 Golf at Duffer's Paradise

The perfect storm of golf occurs on Maui, where stunning weather, gorgeous views, and amazing course layouts converge. *(Ch. 4)*

14 Visit a 5-Star Beach

The Big Island's most beautiful beaches, including Anaehoomalu Bay, Hapuna Beach, and Kaunaoa Beach, flank the Kohala Coast. *(Ch. 5)*

15 Visit Sacred Heiaus

Remains of sacred structures of the Kauai kingdom are found in Wailua along Route 580 between the mouth of the Wailua River and Mount Waialeale. *(Ch. 6)*

16 Hike Waimea Canyon

A vast canyon on Kauai's west side, this geologic wonder measures a mile wide, more than 10 miles long, and 3,567 feet deep. *(Ch. 6)*

17 Watch the Pros Surf at Waimea Bay

Oahu's Waimea Bay was integral to the early development of big wave surfing, and it's still a great place to watch the pros. You'll get the best views during the winter. *(Ch. 3)*

18 Relive History at Pearl Harbor

On Oahu, the World War II Valor in the Pacific National Monument preserves four different World War II sites at Pearl Harbor, including the the USS *Arizona* Memorial. *(Ch. 3)*

19 Explore Big Island Lava Tubes

The Thurston Lava Tube in Hawaii Volcanoes National Park is convenient. Though they require guides, the Kula Kai Caverns and Kilauea Caverns of Fire are fascinating. *(Ch. 5)*

20 Dive the Cathedrals of Lanai

These lava tubes comprise one of Maui's primo diving spots (technically off Lanai) boasting a variety of multicolored fish, eels, turtles, dolphins, and octopi. (Ch. 8)

21 Walk Down to Waipio Valley

This lush, waterfall-laden, Big Island valley—surrounded by sheer, fluted 2,000-foot cliffs—was once a favorite retreat for Hawaiian royalty. (Ch. 5)

22 Have a Plate Lunch

Everyone should try this Hawaiian lunch tradition: an entrée with white rice and a scoop of macaroni salad. It's an island favorite and bargain-priced. (Ch. 3)

23 Visit Iolani Palace

Oahu has the only royal residence in the U.S., and it introduces you to Hawaii's monarchical era, which ended with the 1893 overthrow of Queen Liliuokalani. (Ch. 3)

24 See the Sunrise

Haleakala National Park's Puu Ulaula Overlook is Maui's highest point and the best place to see the sunrise. (Ch. 4)

25 Relax on Kauai's Poipu Beach

Popular with tourists and locals, uncrowded Poipu Beach has calm waters ideal for snorkeling, and you might just spot an endangered Hawaiian monk seal. *(Ch. 6)*

26 Watch a Hula Show

If you want a more traditional, less touristy introduction to hula and Hawaiian music, go to the Kuhio Beach Hula Show on Oahu's Kuhio Beach. *(Ch. 3)*

27 Snorkel Molokini Crater

Tropical fish thrive at Molokini Crater, a partially submerged caldera about 3 miles off of Maui's southern coast that serves as a fortress against the waves. *(Ch. 4)*

28 The Road to Hana

One of the world's most famous drives, Maui's precarious road has more than 600 curves and crosses some 50 gulch-straddling bridges in just 52 coastline miles. *(Ch. 4)*

29 Helicopter Vistas

Kauai's interior is best seen via helicopter. Tours showcase the breathtaking scenery of places like Waimea Canyon and Waialeale Crater. *(Ch. 6)*

30 Kayak to Secret Falls

Kayaking Kauai's Wailua River, one of the few that's navigable in Hawaii, leads you into a mystical realm of lush rain forests, velvety green mountains, and secret, crystal-clear waterfalls. *(Ch. 6)*

31 Walk Through Waikiki

The best way to people-watch, shop, eat, and sightsee along Oahu's iconic Waikiki tourist strip is by foot. *(Ch. 3)*

32 Hike to the Green Sands Beach

It's worth the effort to drive to the end of South Point Road and hike to the Big Island's Papakolea Beach. Bring lots of water. *(Ch. 5)*

33 Historic Lahaina

Once an active Maui hub for whaling, pineapple, and sugar, Lahaina is a busy downtown with restaurants, shops, and galleries. *(Ch. 4)*

34 Hike a Bamboo Forest

On Maui, Haleakala National Park's 4-mile round-trip Pipiwai Trail is a dramatic realm of plunging waterfalls, archaic ferns, and an immense bamboo forest. *(Ch. 4)*

35 Coastal Sunset Sail

Kauai sunsets are sublime, and perhaps the best way to experience that magical hour of the day is by boat, facing stunning Napali Coast. *(Ch. 6)*

36 Stargaze on Maunakea

The sunset and stargazing at Maunakea's summit is outstanding. The visitor center offers free public stargazing four nights a week. *(Ch. 5)*

37 Visit Iao Valley

Central Maui's iconic, green-mantled natural spire rises 1,200 feet above a verdant valley; go early in the day before clouds obscure the views. *(Ch. 4)*

WHAT'S WHERE

1 Oahu. Honolulu and Waikiki are here—and it's a great big luau. The island has hot restaurants and lively nightlife as well as gorgeous white-sand beaches, knife-edged mountain ranges, and cultural sites, including Pearl Harbor.

2 Maui. The phrase *Maui no ka oi* means Maui is the best, the most, the tops. There's good reason for the superlatives. It's got a little of everything, perfect for families with divergent interests.

3 Big Island of Hawaii. It has two faces, watched over by snowcapped Maunakea and steaming Mauna Loa. The Kona side has parched, lava-strewn lowlands, and eastern Hilo is characterized by lush flower farms, waterfalls, and fresh lava forming daily.

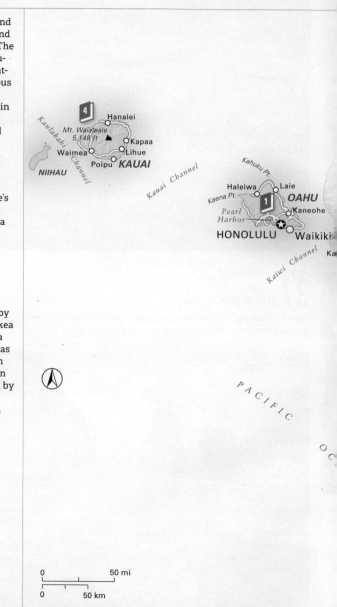

0   50 mi

0   50 km

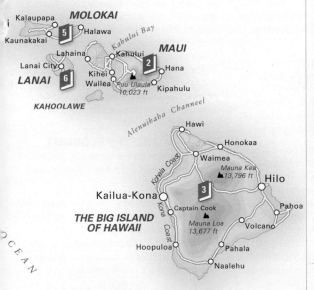

4 Kauai. This is the "Garden Island," and it's where you'll find the lush, green, folding sea cliffs of Napali Coast; the colorful and awesome Waimea Canyon; and more beaches per mile of coastline than any other Hawaiian island.

5 Molokai. It's the least changed, most laid-back of the Islands. Come here to ride a mule down a cliff to Kalaupapa Peninsula; to experience the Kamakou Preserve, a 2,774-acre wildlife refuge; and for plenty of peace and quiet.

6 Lanai. For years, there was nothing here except for pineapples and red-dirt roads. In 2012, Oracle billionaire Larry Ellison purchased 98% of the island, and it still attracts the well-heeled in search of privacy, with two upscale resorts, archery and shooting, four-wheel-drive excursions, and superb scuba diving.

Hawaii Today

Hawaiian culture and tradition have experienced a renaissance over the last few decades. There's been a real effort to revive traditions and to respect history as the Islands go through major changes. New resort developments often have a Hawaiian cultural expert on staff to ensure cultural sensitivity and to educate newcomers. Nonetheless, development itself remains the biggest issue for all Islanders, with land prices still skyrocketing, putting popular areas out of reach for locals. Traffic is becoming a problem on roads that were not designed to accommodate all the drivers (particularly on Oahu and Maui), and the Islands' limited natural resources are being seriously tapped while 90% of Hawaii's food and energy are still imported despite government efforts to increase sustainability.

SUSTAINABILITY

Kauai may be the leader with regard to sustainability. On some sunny days, the Kauai electric grid is more than 95% powered by alternative-energy sources. In fact, Kauai leads the state in alternative energy solutions, including hydro.

Much of Hawaii's open land has historically been used for mono-cropping of pineapple and sugarcane. Those businesses are all but gone on a grand scale. When the Maui Pinapple Company ceased production in 2009, a group of executives began the Maui Gold Pineapple Company with, 1,350 acres on the slopes of Mount Haleakala, where they still grow pineapples for export and local use.

Oahu is home to many of the restaurants and chefs leading the Hawaii Regional Cuisine food movement, with a focus on fresh, local ingredients. Chefs are expanding and riffing off Hawaiian

Regional Cuisine, taking it in new, international, eclectic, and refreshing directions.

BACK-TO-BASICS AGRICULTURE

Emulating how the Hawaiian ancestors lived and returning to their simple ways of growing and sharing a variety of foods have become statewide initiatives. Many locals buy all their fruit and produce from the numerous farmers' markets, which often feature exotic in-season crops at reasonable costs.

The seed of this movement is thriving with various farmers' markets and partnerships between restaurants and local farmers. Localized efforts such as the Hawaii Farm Bureau Federation are collectively aiding the organic and sustainable agricultural renaissance. From home-cooked meals to casual plate lunches to fine-dining cuisine, these sustainable trailblazers enrich the state's culinary tapestry. A recent "explosion" of food trucks on Kauai, Oahu, and Maui offering various cuisines also uplifts the overall quality of life.

TOURISM AND THE ECONOMY

The $17 billion tourism industry represents more than a third of Hawaii's state income.

One way the industry has changed has been to adopt more eco-conscious practices, as many residents feel that development shouldn't happen without regard for impact to local communities and their natural environment.

The belief that an industry based on the Hawaiians' *aloha* should protect, promote, and empower local culture and provide more entrepreneurial opportunities for local people has become more important to tourism businesses. More companies are incorporating authentic Hawaiiana into their programs and are aiming not only to provide a commercially viable tour but also to ensure that visitors leave feeling connected to his or her host.

The concept of *kuleana,* a word denoting both privilege and responsibility, is a traditional value. Having the privilege to live in such a sublime place comes with the responsibility to protect it.

SOVEREIGNTY

Political issues of sovereignty continue to divide Native Hawaiians, who have formed myriad organizations, each operating with a separate agenda and lacking one collectively defined goal. Ranging from achieving complete independence to solidifying a nation within a nation, existing sovereignty models remain fractured and their future unresolved.

The introduction of the Native Hawaiian Government Reorganization Act of 2009 (The Akaka Bill) attempted to set up a legal framework in which Native Hawaiians can attain federal recognition and coexist as a self-governed entity. Still held up in Congress, the bill has faced innumerable challenges through the years, including among Native Hawaiians who disagree about its merits and mission.

RISE OF HAWAIIAN PRIDE

After the overthrow of the monarchy in 1893, a process of Americanization began. Traditions were duly silenced in the name of citizenship. Teaching the Hawaiian language was banned from schools, and children were distanced from their local customs.

But Hawaiians are resilient people, and with the rise of the civil rights movement they began to reflect on their own national identity, bringing an astonishing renaissance of the Hawaiian culture to fruition.

The people rediscovered language, hula, chanting, and even the traditional Polynesian arts of canoe building and wayfinding (navigation by the stars without use of instruments). This cultural resurrection is now firmly established in today's Hawaiian culture, with a palpable pride that exudes from Hawaiians young and old.

LATEST ERUPTIONS

In May 2018, dramatic changes began happening at Kilauea Volcano on the Big Island of Hawaii. The collapse of the Puu Oo vent, which has been continuously erupting since 1983, preceded fissure eruptions in a remote neighborhood in Lower Puna, destroying dozens of homes. Meanwhile, back in Hawaii Volcanoes National Park, the lava lake at Halemaumau began receding quickly, creating ash plumes above the summit and steam explosions.

What to Eat and Drink in Hawaii

HAWAIIAN PLATE

The Hawaiian plate comprises the delicious, traditional foods of Hawaii, all on one heaping plate. You can find these combo meals anywhere from roadside lunch wagons to five-star restaurants. Get yours with the melt-in-your-mouth shredded kalua pig, pork, or chicken *laulau* (cooked in ti leaves) with *lomi* salmon (diced salmon with tomatoes and onions) on the side and the coconut-milk haupia for dessert. Most Hawaiian plates come with the requisite two scoops of white rice. Don't forget to try *poi*, or pounded and cooked taro. For an authentic plate, visit Helena's Hawaiian Food on Oahu; just be sure to get there early.

SHAVE ICE

Shave ice is simple in its composition—fluffy ice drizzled in Technicolor syrups. Shave ice traces its roots to Hawaii's plantation past. Japanese laborers would use the machetes from their field work to finely shave ice from large frozen blocks and then pour fruit juice over it.

POKE

In Hawaiian, *poke* is a verb that means to slice and cut into pieces. It perfectly describes the technique Hawaiians have used for centuries to prepare poke the dish. The cubed raw fish, most commonly ahi, or tuna, is traditionally tossed with Hawaiian sea salt, imu kohu, seaweed, inamona, or crushed, roasted kukui nuts. Today, there are countless varieties of poke across the Islands. It's a must try when visiting Hawaii. On Oahu, Ono Seafood, a no-frills, take-out eatery serves made-to-order poke.

MUSUBI

Musubi are Hawaii's answer to the perfect snack. Portable, handheld, and salty, musubi are a great go-to any time of day. The local comfort food is a slice of Spam encased in packed white rice and snugly wrapped with nori, or dried seaweed. Available everywhere, musubi are usually just a few dollars.

MAI TAI

When people think of a Hawaiian cocktail, the colorful Mai Tai often comes to mind. It's the unofficial drink to imbibe at a luau and refreshingly tropical. This potent concoction has a rum base and is traditionally made with orange curaçao, orgeat, fresh squeezed lime juice, and simple syrup.

MANAPUA

When *kamaaina*, or Hawaii residents, are invited to a potluck, business meeting, or even an impromptu party, you'll inevitably see a box filled with manapua.

Poke

Inside these airy white buns are pockets of sweet char siu pork. Head to Oahu's Chinatown in Honolulu, and you'll find Chinese restaurants with manapua on their menus, as well as manapua take-out places serving a variety of fillings. There's sweet potato, curry chicken, *lup cheong* (or Chinese sausage), even sweet flavors such as custard and ube, a purple yam popular in Filipino desserts.

SAIMIN

This only-in-Hawaii noodle dish is the culinary innovation of Hawaii plantation workers in the late 1800s who created a new comfort food with ingredients and traditions from their home countries.

LOCO MOCO

Loco moco is one of Hawaii's classic comfort-food dishes. The traditional loco moco consists of white rice topped with a hamburger patty and fried eggs and generously blanketed in rich, brown gravy. Cafe 100 in Hilo on Hawaii Island is renowned as the home of the loco moco. The 74-year-old café's original loco moco is one of the most popular, and at the amazing price of $4.35.

KONA COFFEE

In Kona, on Hawaii Island, coffee reigns supreme. There are roughly 600 coffee farms dotting the west side of the island, each producing flavorful coffee grown in the rich, volcanic soil. Kona coffee is typically harvested from August to December.

MALASADA

Malasadas are a beloved treat in Hawaii. The Portuguese pastries are about the size of a baseball and are airy, deep-fried, and dusted with sugar. In Honolulu, on Oahu, Lenard's Bakery is a well-known purveyor of these delicious desserts.

What to Buy in Hawaii

MACADAMIA NUT CANDY
Macadamia are native to Australia, but the gumball-sized nut remains an important crop in Hawaii. It was first introduced in the late 1880s as a windbreak for sugar cane crops. Today, mac nuts, as they are colloquially known, are a popular local food, especially in desserts. They are easily found at convenience and grocery stores.

LEI
As a visitor to Hawaii, you will likely receive a lei, either a shell, kukui nut, or the fragrant flower variety, as a welcome to the Islands. Kamaaina or Hawaii residents mark special occasions by gifting lei.

LAUHALA
The hala tree is most known for its long, thin leaves and the masterful crafts that are created from them. Lauhala weavers make baskets, hats, mats, jewelry, and more, using intricate patterns.

JEWELRY
Island-inspired jewelry is a unique and personalized gift. There are several styles from which to choose, including pieces featuring Tahitian pearls, shells like the dainty orange and pink sunrise shell, and gold Hawaiian heirloom necklaces and bangles with black Old English lettering.

ALOHA WEAR
Aloha wear in Hawaii has come a long way from the cheap fabrics with the too bright and kitsch patterns (although those still exist). Local designers have been creating stylish, modern Aloha shirts, dresses, and more with soft, sleek prints that evoke Island botanicals, heritage, and tradition. Hawaii residents sport Aloha wear for everything from work to weddings.

KONA COFFEE
Reminiscence about your wonderful Hawaii getaway each time you brew a cup of Kona coffee. Authentic Kona coffee is renowned throughout the world for its heady aroma and full-bodied flavor. Stores and cafés sell bags of varying sizes.

BIG ISLAND HONEY
With its temperate climate and bountiful foliage, honeybees love Hawaii. The island's unique ecosystem results in robust honey flavors, including the nutty macadamia nut blossom honey or the ohia lehua variety, made from the endemic tree.

KOA WOOD
If you're looking for an heirloom keepsake from the Islands, consider a Koa wood product. Grown only in Hawaii, the valuable Koa wood is some of the world's rarest and hardest wood. Hawaiians traditionally made surfboards and canoes from Koa trees.

HAWAIIAN SEA SALT
A long tradition of harvesting salt beds by hand continues today on the islands of Kauai and Molokai. The salt comes in various colors, including inky black and brick red; these distinctive colors come from the salt reacting and mixing with activated charcoal and alaea, or volcanic clay.

UKULELE
In Hawaiian, *ukulele* means "the jumping flea." The small instrument made its way to the Islands in the 1880s via Portuguese immigrants who brought with them the four-string, guitar-like machete. It is renowned as a solo instrument today, with artists like Jake Shimabukuro and Taimane Gardner popularizing it.

Flora and Fauna in Hawaii

KUKUI
The kukui, or candlenut, is Hawaii's state tree. Hawaiians had many uses for kukui. Oil was extracted from its nuts and burned as a light source and also rubbed on fishing nets to preserve them. The juice from the husk's fruit was used as a dye. The small kukui blossoms and nuts also had medicinal purposes.

PLUMERIA
This fragrant flower is named after Charles Plumier, the noted French botanist who discovered it in Central America in the late 1600s. Plumeria come in shades of white, yellow, pink, red, and orange. The hearty, plentiful blossoms are frequently used in lei.

GARDENIA
The gardenia is a favorite for lei makers because of its sweet smell. The plant is native to tropical regions throughout China and Africa, but there are also endemic gardenia in Hawaii. The nanu gardenia are found only in the Islands and have petite white blossoms.

HONU
The honu, or Hawaiian green sea turtle, is a magical sight. The graceful reptile is an endangered and protected species in Hawaii. It's easier to run across honu during a snorkeling or scuba diving excursion, but they occasionally can be spotted coming to the ocean's surface.

HUMPBACK WHALES
Each year, North Pacific humpback whales make the long journey to Hawaii from Alaska. With its warm waters, Hawaii's shores provide the ideal place for the marine mammals to mate, birth, and nurse their young. They arrive between November and May, and their presence is an anticipated event for many. You can see them up close during whale-watching boat tours.

MONK SEAL

Known as the *ilio holo I ka uaua*, or, "dog that runs in rough water," monk seals are endemic to Hawaii and critically endangered. Most of these mammals, which can grow more than seven feet long and weigh more than 600 pounds, live in remote, uninhabited Northwestern Hawaiian Islands.

TROPICAL FISH

Approximately 25% of the fish species in the Islands are endemic. Snorkeling in Hawaii is a unique, fun opportunity to see colorful fish, big and small. Interestingly, Hawaii's state fish, the tongue-twister *humuhumunukunukuapuaa*, or reef trigger, is not endemic to the state.

NENE GOOSE

Pronounced *nay-nay*, the endemic nene goose (the state bird) is the rarest in the world. Thanks to preservation efforts, the goose, which is a descendent of the Canadian goose, has been bred back from the edge of extinction and reintroduced into the wild.

HIBISCUS

In 1923, the Territory of Hawaii passed a law designating hibiscus as Hawaii's official flower. While there are more than 30 introduced species of the large, colorful flowers throughout the Islands, there are five endemic types. In Hawaiian, the endemic hibiscus has yellow blossoms and is known as mao hau hele, which means the "traveling green tree."

PIKAKE

These small, delicate blossoms are known for their hypnotic sweet scent. The jasmine flower was introduced from India and was a favorite of Princess Kaiulani. Pikake, which is the Hawaiian word for the blossom as well as peacock—another favorite of the princess—is the subject of many mele or Hawaiian songs.

What to Read and Watch

HAWAIIAN MYTHOLOGY, BY MARTHA BECKWITH

This exhaustive work of ethnology and folklore was researched and collected by Martha Beckwith over decades and published when she was 69. *Hawaiian Mythology* is a comprehensive look at the Hawaiian ancestral deities and their importance throughout history.

HAWAII'S STORY BY HAWAII'S QUEEN, BY LILIUOKALANI

This poignant book, by Queen Liliuokalani, chronicles the 1893 overthrow of the Hawaiian monarchy and her plea for her people. It's an essential read to understand the political undercurrent and the push for sovereignty that exists in the Islands more than 125 years later.

MARK TWAIN'S LETTERS FROM HAWAII, BY MARK TWAIN

In 1866, when Samuel Clemens was 31, he sailed from California and spent four months in Hawaii. He eventually mailed 25 letters to the *Sacramento Union* newspaper about his experiences. Along the way, Twain sheds some cultural biases as he visits the Kilauea Volcano, meets with Hawaii's newly formed legislators, and examines the sugar trade.

SHOAL OF TIME: A HISTORY OF THE HAWAIIAN ISLANDS, BY GAVAN DAWS

Perhaps the most popular book of this best-selling Honolulu author is *Shoal of Time*. Published in 1974, this account of modern Hawaiian history details the colonization of Hawaii and everything that was lost in the process.

MOLOKAI, BY ALAN BRENNERT

Alan Brennert's debut novel, set in the 1890s, follows a Hawaiian woman who contracts leprosy as a child and is sent to the remote, quarantined community of Kalaupapa on the island of Molokai where she then lives. The Southern California–based author was inspired to write the book during his visits to Hawaii.

THE DESCENDANTS

Based on the book by local author, Kaui Hart Hemmings, the film adaptation starring George Clooney and directed by Alexander Payne was filmed on Oahu and Kauai. It spotlights a contemporary, upper-class family in Hawaii as they deal with family grief and landholdings in flux.

50 FIRST DATES

The majority of this 2004 Drew Barrymore–Adam Sandler rom-com was shot on Oahu. While the plot is simultaneously cute and cheesy, *50 First Dates* highlights the beauty of Hawaii. You can pick out several picturesque island places, including the rolling Kualoa Ranch and Waimanalo, Makapuu, and Kaneohe Bay, all on Oahu's rustic East Side.

BLUE HAWAII

The 1961 musical features the hip-shaking songs and moves by Elvis Presley, who plays tour guide Chadwick Gates. Elvis famously sings *Ke Kali Nei Au*, or *The Hawaiian Wedding Song*, at the iconic and now-shuttered Coco Palms Resort on Kauai. (The resort has remained closed since 1992 following Hurricane Iniki.)

MOANA

The release of *Moana* in 2016 was celebrated by many in Hawaii and the Pacific for showcasing Polynesian culture. The now-beloved animated movie, which tells the story of the demigod Maui, features the voice talents of Aulii Cravalho and Dwayne Johnson. In 2018, *Moana* was re-recorded and distributed in Olelo Hawaii, or the Hawaiian language, with Cravalho reprising her role. It marked the first time a Disney movie was available in Hawaiian.

Choosing Your Island

You've decided to go to Hawaii, but should you stay put and relax on one island or try sampling more than one? If all you have is a week, it is probably best to stick to just one island. You traveled all this way, why spend your precious vacation time at car-rental counters, hotel check-in desks, and airports? But, with seven or more nights, a little island-hopping is a great way to experience the diversity of sights and experiences that are packed into this small state. Here are some of our favorite island-pairing itineraries for every type of trip.

FAMILY TRAVEL: OAHU AND MAUI

If you're traveling with children, Oahu and Maui have the most options.

Why Oahu: Oahu is by far the most kid-friendly island. For sea life, visit the Waikiki Aquarium and Sea Life Park or let the little ones get up close and personal with fish at Hanauma Bay. At Pearl Harbor, you can visit an aircraft carrier or, if the kids are at least four, a World War II submarine. Then there's the Honolulu Zoo and a slippery slide–filled water park, not to mention some very family-friendly and safe beaches. *Plan to spend 4 nights.*

Why Maui: Whales! Though you can see whales from any island between November and April, there's no better place than Maui. If your visit doesn't fall during peak whale-watching season, visit the Whalers Village Museum, the Hawaiian Islands Humpback Whale National Marine Sanctuary, or the Maui Ocean Center (to get an up-close look at some of Hawaii's smaller sea creatures). Away from the water, there's the Sugar Cane Train. *Plan to spend at least 3 nights.*

ROMANCE: MAUI AND KAUAI

If you're getting away for seclusion, romantic walks along the beach, and the pampering at world-class spas, consider Maui and Kauai.

Why Maui: You'll find waterfalls, salt-and-pepper sand beaches, and incredible views as you follow the twisting turning Road to Hana. The luxury resorts in Wailea or Kaanapali provide lots of fine dining and spa treatment options. And for those who want to start their day early, there's the drive up to Haleakala to see the sun rise—or for couples who prefer to sleep in, there's the arguably even more spectacular sunset from the summit. *Plan to spend 4 nights.*

Why Kauai: The North Shore communities of Hanalei and Princeville provide the opportunity to get away and indulge in some spectacular beaches, hiking, and helicopter rides. At Princeville, you can experience views straight out of *South Pacific* as well as excellent dining and spas at the St. Regis Hotel, while a drive to Kee Beach at the end of the road provides options for pulling over and grabbing a beach, all for just the two of you. *Plan to spend at least 3 nights.*

GOLF, SHOPPING, AND LUXURY: MAUI AND THE BIG ISLAND

For luxurious travel, great shopping, restaurants, and accommodations you can't beat Maui and the Big Island.

Why Maui: The resorts at Wailea and Kaanapali have endless options for dining, shopping, and spa treatments. And, the golf on Maui can't be beat with Kapalua, the Dunes at Maui Lani, and Makena Resort topping the list of spectacular courses. *Plan to spend 4 nights.*

Why the Big Island: In addition to having incredible natural scenery, the Big Island offers world-class resorts and golfing along the Kohala Coast. The Mauna Kea and Hapuna golf courses rank among the top in state while the courses at Mauna Lani Resort and Waikoloa Village allow the unusual experience of playing in and around lava flows. Gourmet dining and spa treatments are readily available at the top resorts, and you'll find shopping opportunities at King's Shops at Waikoloa Village as well as within many of the resorts themselves. Or, travel to Hawi or Waimea (Kamuela) for authentic island boutiques. *Plan to spend at least 3 nights.*

NATURAL BEAUTY AND PRISTINE BEACHES: THE BIG ISLAND AND KAUAI

Really want to get away and experience nature at its most primal? The Big Island is the place to start, followed by a trip to Kauai.

Why the Big Island: Home to 11 different climate zones, the Big Island is large enough to contain all the other Hawaiian Islands. There are countless options for those who want to get off the beaten track and get their hands (and feet) dirty—or sandy as the case may be. See lava flowing or steam rising from Kilauea. Visit beaches in your choice of gold, white, green, or black sand. Snorkel or dive just offshore from an ancient Hawaiian settlement. Or, hike through rain forests to hidden waterfalls. The choices are endless on this island. *Plan to spend at least 4 nights.*

Why Kauai: The Napali Coast is the main draw for those seeking secluded beaches and incredible scenery. If you're interested in hiking to otherwise inaccessible beaches along sheer sea cliffs, this is as good as it gets. Or, head up to Waimea Canyon to see the "Grand Canyon of the Pacific." Want waterfalls? Opaekaa Falls outside Lihue is one of the state's

most breathtaking. And there's no better place for bird-watching than Kilauea Point National Wildlife Refuge. *Plan to spend at least 3 nights.*

VOLCANIC VIEWS: THE BIG ISLAND AND MAUI

For those coming to Hawaii for the volcanoes, there are really only two options: the Big Island and Maui.

Why the Big Island: Start by flying into Hilo and head straight to Hawaii Volcanoes National Park and Kilauea Volcano. Plan to spend at least two days at Kilauea—you'll need time to really explore the caldera, drive to the end of Chain of Craters Road, and have some time for hiking in and around this active volcano. While eruptions are unpredictable (and more rare these days), helicopter companies can get you views of otherwise inaccessible lava flows. You can also make a visit up to the summit of Maunakea with a tour company. From here you'll see views not only of the observatories (Maunakea is one of the best places in the world for astronomy), but also Kilauea and Haleakala volcanoes, which loom in the distance. *Plan to spend at least 4 nights.*

Why Maui: Though all the islands in Hawaii were built from the same hot spot in Earth's crust, the only other island to have had volcanic activity in recorded history is Maui, at Haleakala. The House of the Sun (as Haleakala is known) has great hiking and camping opportunities. *Plan to spend 3 nights.*

The History of Hawaii

Hawaiian history is long and complex; a brief survey can put into context the ongoing renaissance of native arts and culture.

THE POLYNESIANS

Long before both Christopher Columbus and the Vikings, Polynesian seafarers set out to explore vast stretches of open ocean in double-hulled canoes. From western Polynesia, they traveled back and forth between Samoa, Fiji, Tahiti, the Marquesas, and the Society Isles, settling on the outer reaches of the Pacific, Hawaii, and Easter Island as early as AD 300. The golden era of Polynesian voyaging peaked around AD 1200, after which the distant Hawaiian Islands were left to develop their own unique cultural practices and subsistence in relative isolation.

The Islands' symbiotic society was deeply intertwined with religion, mythology, science, and artistry. Ruled by an *alii*, or chief, each settlement was nestled in an *ahupuaa*, a pie-shape land division from the uplands, where the alii lived, through the valleys and down to the shores where the commoners resided. Everyone contributed, whether it was by building canoes, catching fish, making tools, or farming land.

A UNITED KINGDOM

When the British explorer Captain James Cook arrived in 1778, he was revered as a god. With guns and ammunition purchased from Cook, the Big Island chief, Kamehameha the Great, gained a significant advantage over the other alii. He united Hawaii into one kingdom in 1810, bringing an end to the frequent interisland battles that dominated Hawaiian life.

Tragically, the new kingdom was beset with troubles. Native religion was abandoned, and *kapu* (laws and regulations) were eventually abolished. The European explorers brought foreign diseases with them, and within a short decades, the Native Hawaiian population was decimated.

New laws regarding land ownership and religious practices eroded the underpinnings of precontact Hawaii. Each successor to the Hawaiian throne sacrificed more control over the island kingdom. As Westerners permeated Hawaiian culture, Hawaii became more riddled with layers of racial issues, injustice, and social unrest.

MODERN HAWAII

In 1893, the last Hawaiian monarch, Queen Liliuokalani, was overthrown by a group of Americans and European businessmen and government officials, aided by an armed militia. This led to the creation of the Republic of Hawaii, and it became a U.S. territory for the next 60 years. The loss of Hawaiian sovereignty and the conditions of annexation have haunted the Hawaiian people since the monarchy was deposed.

Pearl Harbor was attacked in 1941, which pulled the United States immediately into World War II. Tourism, from its beginnings in the early 1900s, flourished after the war and naturally inspired rapid real estate development in Waikiki. In 1959, Hawaii officially became the 50th state. Statehood paved the way for Hawaiians to participate in the American democratic process, which was not universally embraced by Hawaiians. With the rise of the civil rights movement in the 1960s, Hawaiians began to reclaim their own identity, from language to hula.

Kids and Families

With dozens of adventures, discoveries, and fun-filled beach days, Hawaii is a blast with kids. Even better, the things to do here do not appeal only to small fry. The entire family, parents included, will enjoy surfing, discovering a waterfall in the rain forest, and snorkeling with sea turtles. And there are plenty of organized activities for kids that will free parents' time for a few romantic beach strolls.

CHOOSING A PLACE TO STAY

Condos: Condo and vacation rentals are a fantastic value for families vacationing in Hawaii. You can cook your own food, which is cheaper than eating out and sometimes easier (especially if you have a finicky eater in your group), and you'll get twice the space of a hotel room for about a quarter of the price. If you decide to go the condo route, be sure to ask about the size of the complex's pool (some try to pawn a tiny soaking tub off as a pool) and whether barbecues are available.

Resorts: All the big resorts make kids' programs a priority, and it shows. When you are booking your room, ask about "kids eat free" deals and the number of kids' pools at the resort. Also check out the size of the groups in the children's programs, and find out whether the cost of the programs includes lunch, equipment, and activities.

OCEAN ACTIVITIES

Hawaii is all about getting your kids outside—away from TV and video games. And who could resist the turquoise water; the promise of spotting dolphins or whales; and the fun of body boarding, snorkeling, or surfing?

On the Beach: Most people like being in the water, but toddlers and school-age kids are often completely captivated by Hawaii's beaches. The swimming pool at your condo or hotel is always an option, but don't be afraid to hit the beach with a little one in tow. There are several in Hawaii that are nearly as safe as a pool—completely protected bays with pleasant white-sand beaches. As always, use your judgment, and heed all posted signs and lifeguard warnings.

On the Waves: Surf lessons are a great idea for older kids, especially if Mom and Dad want a little quiet time. Beginner lessons are always on safe and easy waves and last anywhere from two to four hours.

The Underwater World: If your kids are ready to try snorkeling, Hawaii is a great place to introduce them to the underwater world. Even without the mask and snorkel, they'll be able to see colorful fish darting this way and that, and they may also spot turtles and dolphins at many of the island beaches.

LAND ACTIVITIES

In addition to beach experiences, Hawaii has rain forests, botanical gardens, aquariums (Oahu and Maui), and even petting zoos and hands-on children's museums that will keep your kids entertained and out of the sun for a day.

AFTER DARK

At night, younger kids get a kick out of luau, and many of the shows incorporate young audience members, adding to the fun. The older kids might find it all a bit lame, but there are a handful of new shows in the Islands that are more modern, incorporating acrobatics, lively music, and fire dancers. If you're planning on hitting a luau with a teen in tow, we highly recommend going the modern route.

HAWAIIAN CULTURAL TRADITIONS HULA, LEI, AND LUAU

HULA: MORE THAN A FOLK DANCE

Hula has been called "the heartbeat of the Hawaiian people" and also "the world's best-known, most misunderstood dance." Both are true. Hula isn't just dance. It is storytelling.

Chanter Edith McKinzie calls it "an extension of a piece of poetry." In its adornments, implements, and customs, hula integrates every important Hawaiian cultural practice: poetry, history, genealogy, craft, plant cultivation, martial arts, religion, protocol. So when 19th-century Christian missionaries sought to eradicate a practice they considered depraved, they threatened more than just a folk dance.

With public performance outlawed and private hula practice discouraged, hula went underground for a generation. The fragile verbal link by which culture was transmitted from teacher to student hung by a thread. Even increasing literacy did not help because hula's practitioners were a secretive and protected circle.

As if that weren't bad enough, vaudeville, Broadway, and Hollywood got hold of the hula, giving it the glitz treatment in an

unbroken line from "Oh, How She Could Wicky Wacky Woo" to "Rock-A-Hula Baby." Hula became shorthand for paradise: fragrant flowers, lazy hours. Ironically, this development assured that hundreds of Hawaiians could make a living performing and teaching hula. Many danced *auana* (modern form) in performance; but taught *kahiko* (traditional), quietly, at home or in hula schools.

Today, decades after the cultural revival known as the Hawaiian Renaissance, language immersion programs have assured a new generation of proficient chanters, songwriters, and translators. Visitors can see more, and more authentic, traditional hula than at any other time in the last 200 years.

Like the culture of which it is the beating heart, hula has survived.

Lei *poo*. Head lei. In *kahiko*, greenery only. In auana, flowers.

Face emotes appropriate expression. Dancer should not be a smiling automaton.

Shoulders remain relaxed and still, never hunched, even with arms raised. No bouncing.

Eyes always follow leading hand.

Lei. Hula is rarely performed without a shoulder lei.

Traditional hula skirt is loose fabric, smocked and gathered at the waist.

Arms and hands remain loose, relaxed, below shoulder level— except as required by interpretive movements.

Hip is canted over weight-bearing foot.

Knees are always slightly bent, accentuating hip sway.

Kupee. Ankle bracelet of flowers, shells, or foliage.

In kahiko, feet are flat. In auana, they may be more arched, but not tiptoes or bouncing.

BASIC MOTIONS

Speak or Sing

Moon or Sun

Grass Shack or House

Mountains or Heights

Love or Caress

At backyard parties, hula is performed in bare feet and street clothes, but in performance, adornments play a key role, as do rhythm-keeping implements such as the pahu drum and the *ipu* (gourd).

In hula *kahiko* (traditional style), the usual dress is multiple layers of stiff fabric (often with a pellom lining, which most closely resembles *kapa*, the paperlike bark cloth of the Hawaiians). These wrap tightly around the bosom but flare below the waist to form a skirt. In pre-contact times, dancers wore only kapa skirts. Men traditionally wear loincloths.

Monarchy-period hula is performed in voluminous muumuu or high-necked muslin blouses and gathered skirts. Men wear white or gingham shirts and black pants.

In hula *auana* (modern), dress for women can range from grass skirts and strapless tops to contemporary tea-length dresses. Men generally wear aloha shirts, but sometimes grass skirts over pants or even everyday gear.

SURPRISING HULA FACTS

■ Grass skirts are not traditional; workers from Kiribati (the Gilbert Islands) brought this custom to Hawaii.

■ In olden-day Hawaii, *mele* (songs) for hula were composed for every occasion—name songs for babies, dirges for funerals, welcome songs for visitors, celebrations of favorite pursuits.

■ Hula *mai* is a traditional hula form in praise of a noble's genitals; the power of the *alii* (royalty) to procreate gave mana (spiritual power) to the entire culture.

■ Hula students in old Hawaii adhered to high standards: scrupulous cleanliness, no sex, daily cleansing rituals, certain food prohibitions, and no contact with the dead. They were fined if they broke the rules.

WHERE TO WATCH

If you're interested in "the real thing," there are annual hula festivals on each island. Check the individual island visitors' bureaus websites at ⊕ *www.gohawaii.com*.

If you can't make it to a festival, there are plenty of other hula shows—at most resorts, many lounges, and even at certain shopping centers. Ask your hotel concierge for performance information.

ALL ABOUT LEI

Lei brighten every occasion in Hawaii, from birthdays to bar mitzvahs to baptisms. Creative artisans weave nature's bounty—flowers, ferns, vines, and seeds—into gorgeous creations that convey an array of heartfelt messages: "Welcome," "Congratulations," "Good luck," "Farewell," "Thank you," "I love you." When it's difficult to find the right words, a lei expresses exactly the right sentiment.

WHERE TO BUY THE BEST LEI

Most airports in Hawaii have lei stands where you can buy a fragrant garland upon arrival. Every florist shop in the Islands sells lei; you can also treat yourself to a lei while shopping for provisions at any supermarket or box store. And you'll always find lei sellers at crafts fairs and outdoor festivals.

LEI ETIQUETTE

■ To wear a closed lei, drape it over your shoulders, half in front and half in back. Open lei are worn around the neck, with the ends draped over the front in equal lengths.

■ Pikake, ginger, and other sweet, delicate blossoms are "feminine" lei. Men opt for cigar, crown flower, and ti leaf lei, which are sturdier and don't emit as much fragrance.

■ Lei are always presented with a kiss, a custom that supposedly dates back to World War II when a hula dancer fancied an officer at a U.S.O. show. Taking a dare from members of her troupe, she took off her lei, placed it around his neck, and kissed him on the cheek.

■ You shouldn't wear a lei before you give it to someone else. Hawaiians believe the lei absorbs your mana (spirit); if you give your lei away, you'll be giving away part of your essence.

	ORCHID Growing wild on every continent except Antarctica, orchids—which range in color from yellow to green to purple—comprise the largest family of plants in the world. There are more than 20,000 species of orchids, but only three are native to Hawaii—and they are very rare. The pretty lavender vanda you see hanging by the dozens at local lei stands has probably been imported from Thailand.
	MAILE Maile, an endemic twining vine with a heady aroma, is sacred to Laka, goddess of the hula. In ancient times, dancers wore maile and decorated hula altars with it to honor Laka. Today, "open" maile lei usually are given to men. Instead of ribbon, interwoven lengths of maile are used at dedications of new businesses. The maile is untied, never snipped, for doing so would symbolically "cut" the company's success.
	ILIMA Designated by Hawaii's Territorial Legislature in 1923 as the official flower of the island of Oahu, the golden ilima is so delicate it lasts for just a day. Five to seven hundred blossoms are needed to make one garland. Queen Emma, wife of King Kamehameha IV, preferred ilima over all other lei, which may have led to the incorrect belief that they were reserved only for royalty.
	PLUMERIA This ubiquitous flower is named after Charles Plumier, the noted French botanist who discovered it in Central America in the late 1600s. Plumeria ranks among the most popular lei in Hawaii because it's fragrant, hardy, plentiful, inexpensive, and requires very little care. Although yellow is the most common color, you'll also find plumeria lei in shades of pink, red, orange, and "rainbow" blends.
	PIKAKE Favored for its fragile beauty and sweet scent, pikake was introduced from India. In lieu of pearls, many brides in Hawaii adorn themselves with long, multiple strands of white pikake. Princess Kaiulani enjoyed showing guests her beloved pikake and peacocks at Ainahau, her Waikiki home. Interestingly, pikake is the Hawaiian word for both the bird and the blossom.
	KUKUI The kukui (candlenut) is Hawaii's state tree. Early Hawaiians strung kukui nuts (which are quite oily) together and burned them for light; mixed burned nuts with oil to make an indelible dye; and mashed roasted nuts to consume as a laxative. Kukui nut lei may not have been made until after Western contact, when the Hawaiians saw black beads from Europe and wanted to imitate them.

LUAU: A TASTE OF HAWAII

The best place to sample Hawaiian food is at a backyard luau. Aunts and uncles are cooking, the pig is from a cousin's farm, and the fish is from a brother's boat.

But even locals have to angle for invitations to those rare occasions. So your choice is most likely between a commercial luau and a Hawaiian restaurant.

Some commercial luau are less authentic; they offer little of the traditional diet and are more about umbrella drinks, spectacle, and fun.

For greater culinary authenticity, folksy experiences, and rock-bottom prices, visit a Hawaiian restaurant (most are in anonymous storefronts in residential neighborhoods). Expect rough edges and some effort negotiating the menu.

In either case, much of what is known today as Hawaiian food would be as foreign to a 16th-century Hawaiian as risotto or chow mien. The pre-contact diet was simple and healthy—mainly raw and steamed seafood and vegetables. Early Hawaiians used earth ovens and heated stones to cook seafood, taro, sweet potatoes, and breadfruit and seasoned their food with sea salt and ground kukui nuts. Seaweed, fern shoots, sweet potato vines, coconut, banana, sugarcane, and select greens and roots rounded out the diet.

Successive waves of immigrants added their favorites to the ti leaf–lined table. So it is that foods as disparate as salt salmon and chicken long rice are now Hawaiian—even though there is no salmon in Hawaiian waters and long rice (cellophane noodles) is Chinese.

AT THE LUAU: KALUA PORK

The heart of any luau is the *imu*, the earth oven in which a whole pig is roasted. The preparation of an imu is an arduous affair for most families, who tackle it only once a year or so, for a baby's first birthday or at Thanksgiving, when many Islanders prefer to imu their turkeys. Commercial luau operations have it down to a science, however.

THE ART OF THE STONE
The key to a proper imu is the *pohaku*, the stones. Imu cook by means of long, slow, moist heat released by special stones that can withstand a hot fire without exploding. Many Hawaiian families treasure their imu stones, keeping them in a pile in the backyard and passing them on through generations.

PIT COOKING
The imu makers first dig a pit about the size of a refrigerator, then lay down *kiawe* (mesquite) wood and stones, and build a white-hot fire that is allowed to burn itself out. The ashes are raked away, and the hot stones covered with banana and ti leaves. Well-wrapped in ti or banana leaves and a net of chicken wire, the pig is lowered onto the leaf-covered stones. Laulau (leaf-wrapped bundles of meats, fish, and taro leaves) may also be placed inside. Leaves—ti, banana, even ginger—cover the pig followed by wet burlap sacks (to create steam). The whole is topped with a canvas tarp and left to steam for the better part of a day.

OPENING THE IMU
This is the moment everyone waits for: The imu is unwrapped like a giant present and the imu keepers gingerly wrestle out the steaming pig. When it's unwrapped, the meat falls moist and smoky-flavored from the bone, looking just like Southern-style pulled pork, but without the barbecue sauce.

WHICH LUAU?
Most resort hotels have luau on their grounds that include hula, music, and, of course, lots of food and drink. Each island also has at least one "authentic" luau. For lists of the best luau on each island, visit the Hawaii Visitors and Convention Bureau website at ⊕ *www. gohawaii.com*.

MEA AI ONO: GOOD THINGS TO EAT.

LAULAU
Steamed meats, fish, and taro leaf in ti-leaf bundles: fork-tender, a medley of flavors; the taro resembles spinach.

Laulau

LOMI LOMI SALMON
Salt salmon in a piquant salad or relish with onions and tomatoes.

POI
Poi, a paste made of pounded taro root, may be an acquired taste, but it's a must-try during your visit.

Lomi Lomi Salmon

Consider: The Hawaiian Adam is descended from *kalo* (taro). Young taro plants are called "keiki"–children. Poi is the first food after mother's milk for many Islanders. Ai, the word for food, is synonymous with poi in many contexts.

Not only that, we love it. "There is no meat that doesn't taste good with poi," the old Hawaiians said.

But you have to know how to eat it: with something rich or powerfully flavored. "It is salt that makes the poi go in," is another adage. When you're served poi, try it with a mouthful of smoky kalua pork or salty lomi lomi salmon. Its slightly sour blandness cleanses the palate. And if you don't like it, smile and say something polite. (And slide that bowl over to a local.)

Poi

E HELE MAI AI! COME AND EAT!

Local-style Hawaiian restaurants tend to be inconveniently located in well-worn store-fronts with little or no parking, outfitted with battered tables and clattering Melmac dishes, but they personify aloha, invariably run by local families who welcome tourists who take the trouble to find them.

Many are cash-only operations and combination plates, known as "plate lunch," are a standard feature: one or two entrées, two scoops of steamed rice, one scoop of macaroni salad, and—if the place is really old-style—a tiny portion of coarse Hawaiian salt and some raw onions for relish.

Most serve some foods that aren't, strictly speaking, Hawaiian, but are beloved of ka-maaina, such as salt meat with watercress (preserved meat in a tasty broth), or *akubone* (skipjack tuna fried in a tangy vinegar sauce).

Weddings and Honeymoons

There's no question that Hawaii is one of the country's foremost honeymoon destinations. Romance is in the air here, and the white, sandy beaches, turquoise water, swaying palm trees, balmy tropical breezes, and brilliant sunshine put people in the mood for love. So it goes without saying that Hawaii has also become a popular wedding destination, especially as new resorts and hotels entice visitors, and same-sex marriage is legal. Once the knot is tied, why not stay for the honeymoon?

THE BIG DAY

Choosing the Perfect Place. You really have two choices to make: the ceremony location and where to have the reception. For the former, Hawaii boasts stunning beaches, sea-hugging bluffs, gardens, private residences, resort lawns, and, of course, places of worship. As for the reception, there are these same choices, as well as restaurants and even a luau. If you decide to go outdoors, make sure to have a backup plan for inclement weather.

Finding a Wedding Planner. If you're planning to invite more than an officiant and your loved one to your wedding ceremony, seriously consider a Hawaii-based wedding planner who can help select a location, design the floral scheme, and recommend a florist and photographer. They can also plan the menu and choose a restaurant, caterer, or resort, and suggest any Hawaiian traditions to incorporate into your ceremony.

Getting Your License. There's no waiting period in Hawaii, no residency or citizenship requirements, and no required blood test or shots. You can apply and pay the fee online; however, both partners must appear together in person before a marriage-license agent to receive the marriage license (the permit to get married) at the State Department of Health. You'll need proof of age—the legal age to marry is 18. Upon approval, a marriage license is immediately issued and costs $60. After the ceremony, your officiant will mail the marriage certificate to the state. Approximately four months later, you will receive a copy in the mail. For more detailed information, visit ⊕ *marriage.ehawaii.gov.*

Also—this is important—the person performing your wedding must be licensed by the Hawaii Department of Health, even if he or she is a licensed officiant. Be sure to ask.

Wedding Attire. In Hawaii, basically anything goes, from long, formal dresses with trains to white bikinis. For men, a pair of solid-colored slacks with a nice aloha shirt is appropriate. If you're planning a wedding on the beach, barefoot is the way to go.

Local Customs. The most obvious traditional Hawaiian wedding custom is the lei exchange, in which the bride and groom take turns placing a lei around the neck of the other—with a kiss. Bridal lei are usually floral, whereas the groom's is typically made of *maile,* a green leafy garland. Brides often also wear a *lei poo,* a circular floral headpiece.

THE HONEYMOON

Do you want champagne and strawberries delivered to your room each morning? A breathtaking swimming pool in which to float? A five-star restaurant in which to dine? Then a resort is the way to go. A small inn is also good if you're on a tight budget or don't plan to spend much time in your room. The lodging accommodations are almost as plentiful as the beaches.

Chapter 2

TRAVEL SMART

2

Updated by Karen Anderson,
Lehia Apana, Tiffany Hill, and
Charles E. Roessler

★ **CAPITAL:**
Honolulu

👫 **POPULATION:**
1,412,687

🗨 **LANGUAGE:**
Hawaiian and English

$ **CURRENCY:**
USD

☎ **AREA CODE:**
808

⚠ **EMERGENCIES:**
911

🚗 **DRIVING:**
On the right

⚡ **ELECTRICITY:**
200v/50 cycles; electrical
plugs have two round prongs

🕐 **TIME:**
6 hours behind New York

🌐 **WEB RESOURCES:**
www.gohawaii.org
www.hvcb.org

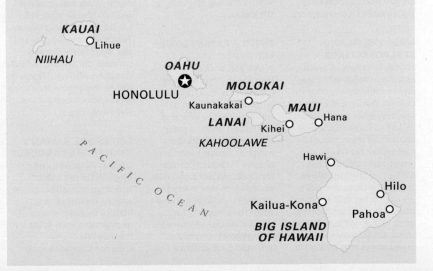

Know Before You Go

Do they really hand you a lei when you arrive? What are some common Hawaiian phrases? How can you help protect the coral? Traveling to Hawaii is an easy adventure, but we've got tips to make your trip seamless and more meaningful. Below are all the answers to FAQs about Hawaii.

COVID-19

All tourism to Hawaii shut down for several months in early 2020 due to COVID-19. It's likely that the impact to the local economy will continue into 2021.

DON'T CALL IT "THE STATES"

Hawaii was admitted to the Union in 1959, so residents can be somewhat sensitive when visitors refer to their own hometowns as "back in the States." Instead, refer to the contiguous 48 states as "the mainland." When you do, you won't appear to be such a *malihini* (newcomer).

WELCOME ISLAND-STYLE GREETINGS

Hawaii is a friendly place, and this is reflected in the day-to-day encounters with friends, family, and even business associates. Women will often hug and kiss one another on the cheek, and men will shake hands and sometimes combine that with a friendly hug. When a man and woman are greeting each other and are good friends, it is not unusual for them to hug and kiss on the cheek. Children are taught to call any elders "auntie" or "uncle," even if they aren't related; it's a way to show respect.

LOOK, BUT DON'T TOUCH

Help protect Hawaii's wildlife by loving it from a distance. Stay at least 10 feet away from turtles and 100 feet from monk seals, wherever you encounter them. Though they may not look it, corals are alive and fragile; harming them also harms the habitat for reef fish and other marine life. Avoid touching or stepping on coral, and take extra care when entering and exiting the water.

ENJOY A FRESH FLOWER LEI

When you walk off a long flight, nothing quite compares with a Hawaiian lei greeting. The casual ceremony ranks as one of the fastest ways to make the transition from the worries of home to the joys of your vacation. Though the tradition has created an expectation that everyone receives this floral garland when they step off the plane, the state of Hawaii cannot greet each of its more than 8 million annual visitors. If you've booked a vacation with a wholesaler or tour company, a lei greeting might be included in your package. If not, it's easy to arrange a lei greeting before you arrive at Kahului Airport with Alii Greeting Service ☎ *(808-877-7088;* ⊕ *www.aliigreeting-service.com).* An orchid and plumeria lei is considered standard and costs about $25 per person. You can also tuck a single flower behind your ear; a flower behind the left ear means you are in a relationship or unavailable, while the right ear indicates you are looking for love.

APPRECIATE THE HAWAIIAN LANGUAGE

While Hawaiian and English are both official state languages, the latter is used widely. Making the effort to learn some Hawaiian words can be rewarding, however. Hawaiian words you are most likely to encounter during your visit to the Islands are *aloha* (hello and good-bye), *mahalo* (thank you), *keiki* (child), *haole* (Caucasian or foreigner), *mauka* (toward the mountains), *makai* (toward the ocean), and *pau* (finished, all done). If you'd like to learn more Hawaiian words, check out ⊕ *www.wehewehe.org.*

LISTEN FOR HAWAII'S UNOFFICIAL LANGUAGE

Besides Hawaiian and English, there's a third (albeit unofficial) language spoken here. Hawaiian history includes waves of immigrants, each bringing their own language. To communicate with each other, they developed a dialect known as Pidgin English, or "Pidgin" for short. If you listen closely, you will know what is being said by the inflections and by the body language. For an informative and sometimes hilarious view of Pidgin, check out *Pidgin to da Max* by Douglas Simonson and *Fax to da Max* by Jerry Hopkins. Both are available at most local bookstores in the Hawaiiana sections and at variety stores. While it's nice to appreciate this unique language, it's not wise to emulate it, as it can be considered disrespectful.

BE MINDFUL OF LOCAL CUSTOMS

If you've been invited to the home of friends living in Hawaii (an ultimate compliment), bring a small gift and take off your shoes when you enter their house. Try to take part in a cultural festival during your stay in the Islands; there is no better way to get a glimpse of Hawaii's ethnic mosaic.

INSECTS AND PESTS

It's the tropics, so don't be surprised if you encounter an extra-large flying cockroach at night or the occasional mosquito buzzing around you during the day. Pack insect repellent and anti-itch spray. A rare but emerging disease in Hawaii, rat lungworm disease, can be contracted by accidental consumption of a slug or slug residue hidden in lettuce or other types of vulnerable produce. Never eat fruit that you pick up off the ground. Think twice about eating locally grown lettuce unless it was grown hydroponically. Rat lungworm disease is a devastating affliction.

CHECK THE WEATHER

Of all the islands in the Hawaiian Islands chain, the Big Island is the most diverse in terms of weather. The variety of elevations and the vast expanse of differing topography produce a range of weather patterns that can vary from one town to the next on any given day. Take, for example, the seaside enclave of Puako near Kawaihae in South Kohala. Here, it could be searing hot and windy one moment, while just a 15-minute drive up the highway in Waimea, it could be "sweater weather." Some areas of the Big Island are incredibly rainy, like the entire town of Hilo, while other areas stay relatively arid, such as the resort zones in South Kohala. At the higher elevations, such as in Volcano Village, it can get downright bonechilling, with temperatures dropping into the low 40s on some nights. Pack accordingly and bring layers.

On Maui, it seems there's a natural wonder around every corner. But don't be caught off guard by the pretty vistas—the environment can change in an instant, and with little or no warning. Strong ocean currents, flash flooding, and rockslides are a real threat, especially during extreme weather events. If you're hiking somewhere like Haleakala National Park, you'll want to check wind, rain, and snow conditions, as all three elements are common. The County of Maui offers safety tips for visitors, and it's a good idea to familiarize yourself with local conditions before heading out on any adventure. ⊕ *o.maui.hi.us/oceansafety*.

Kauai's environment can change in an instant, and with little or no warning. Strong ocean currents, flash floods (like those that ravaged the North Shore in 2018), and rockslides are a real threat, especially during extreme weather events. If you're hiking, you'll want to check wind and rain conditions. Hurricane season runs from June to November.

Getting Here

Air

Flying time to Oahu or Maui is about 10 hours from New York, 8 hours from Chicago, and 5 hours from Los Angeles.

All the major airline carriers serving Hawaii fly direct to Honolulu; some also offer nonstops to Maui, Kauai, and the Big Island, though most flights to the latter two come from the West Coast only. Honolulu International Airport, although open-air and seemingly more casual than most major airports, can be very busy. Allow extra travel time during busy mornings and afternoons.

Plants and plant products are subject to regulation by the Department of Agriculture, both on entering and leaving Hawaii. Upon leaving, you'll have to have your bags x-rayed and tagged at the airport's agricultural inspection station before you proceed to check-in. Pineapples and coconuts with the packer's agricultural inspection stamp pass freely; papayas must be treated, inspected, and stamped. All other fruits are banned for export to the U.S. mainland. Flowers pass except for gardenia, rose leaves, jade vine, and mauna loa. Also banned are insects, snails, soil, cotton, cacti, sugarcane, and all berry plants.

Bringing your dog or cat with you is a tricky process and not something to be done lightly. Hawaii is a rabies-free state and requires animals to pass strict quarantine rules, which you can find online at ⊕ *hdoa.hawaii.gov/ai/aqs/*. Most airlines do not allow pets to travel in the cabin on flights to Hawaii (though Alaska Airlines and Hawaiian Airlines are notable exceptions). If specific pre- and post-arrival requirements are met, most animals qualify for a five-day-or-less quarantine.

GETTING HERE

Big Island of Hawaii: The Big Island's two airports are in Kona and Hilo. Most people rent cars or get shuttle service from their resort (not usually for free). The approximate taxi rate is $3 for the initial 1/8th mile, plus $3 for each additional mile. SpeediShuttle serves the Kona Airport only.

Kauai: All commercial flights use the Lihue Airport. Taxis cost anywhere from $17–$20 to Wailua–Waipouli, $35–$41 to Poipu, or $72–$95 to Princeville–Haena.

Oahu: Honolulu International Airport is 20 minutes (40 during rush hour) from Waikiki. Car rental is mostly by van pickup across the street from baggage claim. An inefficient airport taxi system requires you to line up for a taxi wrangler who radios for cars ($40–$45 plus 60¢ per bag to Waikiki). Other options: TheBus ($2.75, one lap-size bag allowed), and the Roberts Hawaii Express Shuttle ($16 per person). Uber and Lyft also serve the airport.

Maui: Most visitors arrive at Kahului Airport in Central Maui and rent a car. If you don't want to drive yourself, SpeediShuttle costs $67 per couple to Kaanapali, $47 to Wailea. Taxis cost roughly $20 to Wailuku, to $79 to Kaanapali, $45 to Kihei, $69 to Lahaina, or $50 to Wailea.

Lanai and Molokai: Ferries and air taxis are available from Maui to Lanai (no ferry service to Molokai any longer); airport shuttles are available on Molokai, but not Lanai.

AIRPORTS

All of Hawaii's major islands have their own airports, but Honolulu's International Airport is the main stopover for most domestic and international flights. From Honolulu, there are flights to the

Neighbor Islands almost every half-hour from early morning until evening. In addition, some carriers offer nonstop service directly from the mainland to Maui, Kauai, and the Big Island on a limited basis.

BIG ISLAND OF HAWAII AIRPORTS

Those flying to the Big Island regularly land at one of two fields. Ellison Onizuka Kona International Airport at Keahole, on the west side, serves Kailua-Kona, Keauhou, the Kohala Coast, North Kohala, Waimea, and points south. Hilo International Airport is more appropriate for those planning visits based on the east side of the island.

Waimea-Kohala Airport, called Kamuela Airport by residents, is used primarily for private flights between islands, but has recently welcomed one commercial carrier with a single route.

HONOLULU/OAHU AIRPORT

Honolulu International Airport (HNL) is roughly 20 minutes (9 miles) west of Waikiki (40 minutes during rush hour), and is served by most of the major domestic and international carriers. To travel to other islands from Honolulu, you can depart from either the interisland terminal or the commuter-airline terminal, located in two separate structures adjacent to the main overseas terminal building. A free Wiki-Wiki shuttle bus operates between terminals.

KAUAI

On Kauai, visitors fly into Lihue Airport, on the East Side of the island. Visitor information booths are outside each baggage-claim area. Visitors will also find news- and lei stands, an HMS Host restaurant, and a Travel Traders gift shop at the airport.

MAUI AIRPORTS

Maui has two major airports. Kahului Airport handles major airlines and interisland flights; it's the only airport on Maui that has direct service from the mainland. Kapalua–West Maui Airport is served by Hawaiian and Mokulele airlines. If you're staying in West Maui and you're flying in from another island, you can avoid the hour drive from the Kahului Airport by flying into Kapalua–West Maui Airport. Hana Airport in East Maui is small; Mokulele Airlines offers daily flights between Kahului and Hana.

MOLOKAI AIRPORT

Molokai's Hoolehua Airport is small and centrally located, as is Lanai Airport. Both rural airports handle a limited number of flights per day. There's a small airfield at Kalaupapa on Molokai, and required visitor permits are available via tour companies listed on the National Park Service website ⊕ www.nps.gov. Visitors coming from the U.S. mainland to these islands must first stop in Oahu or Maui and change to an interisland flight.

LANAI AIRPORT

Lanai Airport has a federal agricultural inspection station, so guests departing to the mainland can check luggage directly.

FLIGHTS

Big Island of Hawaii: Serving Kona are Air Canada, Alaska Airlines, American Airlines, Delta Airlines, Hawaiian Airlines, Japan Airlines, Mokulele, United Airlines, Virgin Atlantic, and Westjet. Hawaiian, Mokulele, and United fly also into Hilo.

Kauai: Alaska Airlines, American Airlines, Delta, Hawaiian, and United Airlines all offer nonstop flights to Kauai from the mainland U.S.; all other Mainland flights require a connection in Honolulu.

Getting Here

Lanai and Molokai: No airlines fly nonstop to either island from the mainland U.S. All flights to Lanai are via Honolulu; you can take local flights to Molokai from the Big Island of Hawaii, Honolulu, or Maui.

Maui: Alaska Airlines, American Airlines, Delta, Hawaiian Airlines, United offer nonstop service from the U.S. mainland.

Oahu: From the U.S. mainland, Alaska Airlines, American, Delta, Hawaiian, and United are the primary U.S. carriers to serve Honolulu.

GETTING AROUND

Oahu: If you want to travel around the island on your own schedule, renting a car is a must. Heavy traffic toward downtown Honolulu begins as early as 6:30 am and lasts until 9 am. In the afternoon, expect traffic departing downtown to back up beginning around 3 pm until approximately 7 pm.

Maui: Driving from one point on Maui to another can take longer than the mileage indicates. It's 52 miles from Kahului Airport to Hana, but the drive can take three hours. As for driving to Haleakala, the 38-mile drive from the mountain's base to its summit will take you about two hours. Traffic on Maui's roads can be heavy, especially during the rush hours of 6 am to 8:30 am and 3:30 pm to 6:30 pm.

Big Island: It's a good idea to rent a car with four-wheel drive, such as a jeep, on the Big Island. Some of the island's best sights (and most beautiful beaches) are at the end of rough or unpaved roads. Most agencies make you sign an agreement that you won't drive on the path to Mauna Kea and its observatories. Keep in mind that while a good portion of the Saddle Road is smoothly paved, it is also remote, winding, and bumpy in certain areas, unlighted, and bereft of gas stations.

Kauai: A rental car is the best way to get to your hotel, though taxis and some hotel shuttles are available. From the airport it will take you about 15 to 25 minutes to drive to Wailua or Kapaa, 30 to 40 minutes to reach Poipu, and 45 minutes to an hour to get to Princeville or Hanalei. Kauai roads can have heavy traffic.

🚢 Boat

There is daily ferry service between Lahaina on Maui, and Manele Bay on Lanai, via Expeditions Lanai Ferry. The 9-mile crossing costs $60 round-trip ($40 for children) and takes about 45 minutes or so, depending on ocean conditions (which can make this trip a rough one).

There is no longer ferry service to Molokai.

🚌 Bus

BIG ISLAND OF HAWAII

Depending on where you're staying, you can take advantage of the affordable Hawaii County Mass Transit Agency's Hele-On Bus, which travels several routes throughout the island. Mostly serving local commuters, the Hele-On Bus costs $2 per person (students and senior citizens pay $1). Just wait at a scheduled stop and flag down the bus. A one-way journey between Hilo and Kona takes about four hours. There's regular service in and around downtown Hilo, Kailua-Kona, Waimea, North and South Kohala, Honokaa, and Pahoa. However, some routes are served only once a day so if you are planning on using the bus, be sure to study up carefully before assuming the bus serves your area.

Visitors staying in Hilo can take advantage of the Transit Agency's Shared Ride Taxi program, which provides door-to-door transportation in the area. A one-way fare is $2, and a book of 15 coupons can be purchased for $30. Visitors to Kona can also take advantage of free trolleys operated by local shopping centers.

KAUAI

On Kauai, the County Transportation Agency operates the Kauai Bus, which provides service between Hanalei and Kekaha. It also provides limited service to the airport and to Koloa and Poipu. The fare is $2 for adults, and frequent-rider passes are available.

MAUI

Maui Bus, operated by the tour company Roberts Hawaii, offers 13 routes in and between various Central, South, and West Maui communities. You can travel in and around Wailuku, Kahului, Lahaina, Kaanapali, Kapalua, Kihei, Wailea, Maalaea, the North Shore (Paia), and Upcountry (including Kula, Pukalani, Makawao, Haliimaile, and Haiku). The Upcountry and Haiku Islander routes include a stop at Kahului Airport. All routes cost $2 per boarding.

OAHU

Getting around by bus is an affordable option on Oahu, particularly in the most heavily touristed areas of Waikiki. In addition to TheBus and the Waikiki Trolley, Waikiki has brightly painted private buses, many of them free, that shuttle you to such commercial attractions as dinner cruises, garment factories, and the like.

You can travel around the island or just down Kalakaua Avenue for $2.75 on Honolulu's municipal transportation system, affectionately known as TheBus. It's one of the island's best bargains. Buses make stops in Waikiki every 10–15 minutes to take passengers to nearby shopping areas. Free transfers have been discontinued, but you can purchase a one-day pass for $5.50. Just ask the driver as you're boarding. Exact change is required, and dollar bills are accepted.

The Waikiki Trolley has five lines and dozens of stops that allow you to plan your own itinerary while riding on brass-trimmed, open-air buses that look like trolleys. The Historic Honolulu Tour (Red Line) travels between Waikiki and Chinatown and includes stops at the State Capitol, Iolani Palace, and the King Kamehameha statue. The Waikiki-Ala Moana Shopping Shuttle (Pink Line) runs from the T Galleria by DFS to Eggs 'n Things, stopping at various Waikiki locations and the Ala Moana Center. The Scenic Diamond Head Sightseeing Tour (Green Line) runs through Waikiki and down around Diamond Head. There's also a south shore coastline tour (Blue Line) and a line that runs to Aloha Stadium and Pearl Harbor (Purple Line). A one-day pass costs $23 to $45, four-day passes are $36.50 to $74, and seven-day passes are $41 to $79. All passes are discounted when purchased in advance.

Car

Technically, the Big Island of Hawaii is the only island you can completely circle by car, but each island offers plenty of sightseeing from its miles of roadways.

On Kauai, the 15-mile stretch of Napali Coast is the only part of the island's coastline that's not accessible by car.

Getting Here

Otherwise, one main road can get you from Barking Sands Beach on the West Side to Haena on the North Shore.

Traffic on Maui can be very bad branching out from Kahului to and from Paia, Kihei, and Lahaina. Parking along many streets is curtailed during these times, and towing is strictly practiced. Read curbside parking signs before leaving your vehicle, even at a meter.

Although Molokai and Lanai have fewer roadways, car rental is still worthwhile and will allow plenty of interesting sightseeing. A four-wheel-drive vehicle is best.

Oahu can be circled except for the roadless northwest-shore area around Kaena Point. Elsewhere, major highways follow the shoreline and traverse the island at two points. Rush-hour traffic (6:30 to 8:30 am and 3:30 to 6 pm) can be frustrating around Honolulu and the outlying areas, as many thoroughfares allow no left turns.

Asking for directions will almost always produce a helpful explanation from the locals, but you should be prepared for an Island term or two. Instead of using compass directions, remember that Hawaii residents refer to places as being either *mauka* (toward the mountains) or *makai* (toward the ocean) from one another.

GASOLINE
National chains like 76, 7-Eleven, and Shell are ubiquitous, and accept all major credit cards right at the pump or inside the station. Gasoline is generally more expensive than on the mainland United States (other than in California). Neighbor Islands have higher gasoline prices than Oahu.

ROAD CONDITIONS
It's difficult to get lost in most of Hawaii. Although their names may challenge a visitor's tongue, roads and streets are well marked; just watch out for the many one-way streets in Waikiki. Keep an eye open for the Hawaii Visitors and Convention Bureau's red-caped King Kamehameha signs, which mark attractions and scenic spots. Free publications containing high-quality road maps can be found on all islands. And, of course, a GPS or your passenger's smartphone are great options for finding your way around, too.

Many of Hawaii's roads are two-lane highways with limited shoulders—and yes, even in paradise, there is traffic, especially during the morning and afternoon rush hour. In rural areas, it's not unusual for gas stations to close early. If you see that your tank is getting low, don't take any chances; fill up when you see a station. In Hawaii, turning right on a red light is legal, except where noted. Use caution during heavy downpours, especially if you see signs warning of falling rocks. If you're enjoying views from the road or need to study a map, pull over to the side. Remember the aloha spirit when you are driving: allow other cars to merge; don't honk (it's considered extremely rude in the Islands); leave a comfortable distance between your car and the car ahead of you; use your headlights, especially during sunrise and sunset; and use your turn signals.

ROADSIDE EMERGENCIES
If you have an accident or car trouble, call the roadside assistance number on your rental car contract or AAA Help. If you find that your car has been broken into or stolen, report it immediately to your rental car company and they can assist you. Call 911 for any emergency.

RULES OF THE ROAD

Be sure to buckle up, as Hawaii has a strictly enforced mandatory seat-belt law for front- and backseat passengers. Children under four must be in a car seat (available from car-rental agencies), and children ages four to seven must be seated in a booster seat or child safety seat with restraint such as a lap and shoulder belt. Hawaii also prohibits texting or talking on the phone (unless you are over 18 and using a hands-free device) while driving. The highway speed limit is usually 55 mph. In-town traffic travels 25–40 mph. Jaywalking is not uncommon, so watch for pedestrians, especially in congested areas such as Waikiki and downtown Honolulu. Unauthorized use of a parking space reserved for persons with disabilities can net you a $250–$500 fine.

Hawaii's drivers are generally courteous, and you rarely hear a horn. People will slow down and let you into traffic with a wave of the hand. A friendly wave back is customary. If a driver sticks a hand out the window in a fist with the thumb and pinky sticking straight out, this is a good thing: it's the *shaka,* the Hawaiian symbol for "hang loose," and is often used to say "thanks."

CAR RENTAL

If you plan to do lots of sightseeing, it's best to rent a car. Even if all you want to do is relax at your resort, you may want to hop in the car to check out a popular restaurant. All the big national rental car agencies have locations throughout Hawaii. There also are several local rental car companies so be sure to compare prices before you book. While in the Islands, you can rent anything from an econobox to a Ferrari. On the Big Island, Lanai, and Molokai, four-wheel-drive vehicles are recommended for exploring off the beaten path. It's wise to make reservations far in advance and make sure that a confirmed reservation guarantees you a car, especially if visiting during peak seasons or for major conventions or sporting events.

Rates begin at about $30 to $40 a day for an economy car with air-conditioning, automatic transmission, and unlimited mileage, depending on your pickup location. This does not include the airport concession fee, general excise tax, rental vehicle surcharge, or vehicle license fee. When you reserve a car, ask about cancellation penalties and drop-off charges should you plan to pick up the car in one location and return it to another.

In Hawaii you must be 21 years of age to rent a car, and you must have a valid driver's license and a major credit card. Those under 25 will pay a daily surcharge of $10 to $30. Your unexpired mainland driver's license is valid for rental for up to 90 days. Request car seats and extras such as GPS when you make your reservation. Car seats and boosters range from about $10 to $15 per day.

Getting Here

Car Rental Resources

Automobile Associations

AAA	☎ 800/222–4357 for roadside assistance	⊕ www.aaa.com
National Automobile Club	☎ 650/294–7000	⊕ www.nacroadservice.com (CA residents only)

Local Agencies

Aloha Campers (Maui)	☎ 855/671–1122	⊕ www.alohacampers.com
Discount Hawaii Car Rental	☎ 800/292–1930	⊕ www.discounthawaiicarrental.com
Harper Car and Truck Rental (Big Island)	☎ 808/969-1478	⊕ www.harpershawaii.com
Hawaii Car Rental (Big Island, Maui, Oahu)	☎ 800/655–7989	⊕ www.hawaiicarrental.com
Hawaiian Discount Car Rentals (all but Lanai)	☎ 800/955–3142	⊕ www.hawaiidrive-o.com

Major Agencies

Alamo	☎ 888/233–8749	⊕ www.alamo.com
Avis	☎ 800/633–3469	⊕ www.avis.com
Budget	☎ 800/218–7992	⊕ www.budget.com
Dollar	☎ 800/800–5252	⊕ www.dollar.com
Enterprise	☎ 855/226–9289	⊕ www.enterprise.com
Hertz	☎ 800/654–3131	⊕ www.hertz.com
National Car Rental	☎ 888/826–6890	⊕ www.nationalcar.com
Thrifty	☎ 800/334–1705	⊕ www.thrifty.com

Essentials

Accommodations

Hawaii truly offers something for everyone. Are you looking for a luxurious oceanfront resort loaded with amenities, an intimate two-room bed and breakfast tucked away in a lush rain forest, a house with a pool and incredible views for your extended family, a condominium just steps from the 18th hole, or even a campsite at a national park? You can find all these and more throughout the Islands.

Most hotels and other lodgings require you to give your credit card details before they will confirm your reservation. Get confirmation in writing and have a copy of it handy when you check in. Be sure you understand the hotel's cancellation policy. Some places allow you to cancel without any kind of penalty—even if you prepaid to secure a discounted rate—if you cancel at least 24 hours in advance. Others require you to cancel a week in advance or penalize you the cost of one night. Small inns and bed and breakfasts are most likely to require you to cancel far in advance. Most hotels allow children under a certain age to stay in their parents' room at no extra charge, but others charge for them as adults; find out the cutoff age for discounts.

Hotel reviews have been shortened. For full information, visit www.Fodors.com.

BED-AND-BREAKFASTS

For many travelers, nothing compares to the personal service and guest interaction offered at bed and breakfasts. There are hundreds of them throughout the Islands; many even invite their guests to enjoy complimentary wine tastings and activities such as lei making and basket weaving. Each island's website also features a listing of member B&Bs that are individually owned.

CONDOMINIUM AND HOUSE RENTALS

Vacation rentals are perfect for couples, families, and friends traveling together who like the convenience of staying at a home away from home. Properties managed by individual owners can be found on online vacation-rental listing directories such as HomeAway, Vacation Rentals By Owners (VRBO), and Airbnb, as well as on the visitors bureau website for each island. There also are several Islands-based management companies with vacation rentals.

Compare companies, as some offer Internet specials and free night stays when booking. Policies vary, but most require a minimum stay, usually greater during peak travel seasons.

Communications

INTERNET

Major hotels and resorts offer Wi-Fi in rooms and/or lobbies. In some cases there will be an hourly or daily charge billed to your room.

Dining

Whether you're looking for a dinner for two in a romantic oceanfront dining room or a family get-together in a hole-in-the-wall serving traditional Hawaiian fare like *kalua* (cooked in an underground oven) pig, you'll find it throughout the Islands. When it comes to eating, Hawaii has something for every taste bud and every budget. With chefs using locally grown fruits and vegetables, vegetarians often have many exciting choices for their meals. And because Hawaii is a popular destination for families, restaurants almost always have a children's menu.

Essentials

When making a reservation at your hotel's dining room, ask about free or reduced-price meals for children.

MEALS AND MEALTIMES

Breakfast is usually served from 6 or 7 am to 9:30 or 10 am.

Lunch typically runs from 11:30 am to around 1:30 or 2 pm and will include salads, sandwiches, and lighter fare. The "plate lunch," a favorite of many locals, usually consists of an Asian protein—like shoyu chicken, seared ahi or teriyaki beef—served with two scoops of white rice and a scoop of macaroni or potato salad.

Dinner is usually served from 5 to 9 pm and, depending on the restaurant, can be a simple or lavish affair. Stick to the chefs' specials if you can, because they usually represent the best of the season. Poke (marinated raw tuna) is a local specialty and can often be found on pupu (appetizer) menus.

Meals in resort areas are pricey and only sometimes excellent. The restaurants we include are the cream of the crop in each price category. Unless otherwise noted, the restaurants listed are open daily for lunch and dinner.

For guidelines on tipping, see Tipping.

RESERVATIONS

Regardless of where you are, it's a good idea to make a reservation if you can. In some places, it's expected. We only mention reservations specifically when they are essential or when they are not accepted. For popular restaurants, book as far ahead as you can (often a month or more), and reconfirm as soon as you arrive. Large parties should always call ahead to check the reservations policy.

WINE, BEER, AND SPIRITS

Hawaii has a new generation of microbreweries, including on-site microbreweries at many restaurants. The drinking age in Hawaii is 21 years of age, and a photo ID must be presented to purchase alcoholic beverages. Bars are open until 2 am; venues with a cabaret license can stay open until 4 am. No matter what you might see in the local parks, drinking alcohol in public parks or on the beaches is illegal. It's also illegal to have open containers of alcohol in motor vehicles.

⊕ Health

Hawaii is known not only as the Aloha State, but also as the Health State. The life expectancy here is 82.4 years, the longest in the nation. Balmy weather makes it easy to remain active year-round, and the low-stress attitude seems to contribute to the general well-being. When visiting the Islands, however, there are a few health issues to keep in mind.

The Hawaii State Department of Health recommends that you drink 16 ounces of water per hour to avoid dehydration when hiking or spending time in the sun. Use sunblock, wear UV–reflective sunglasses, and protect your head with a visor or hat. If you're not acclimated to warm, humid weather, you should allow plenty of time for rest stops and refreshments. When visiting freshwater streams, be aware of the tropical disease leptospirosis, spread by animal urine and carried into streams and mud. Symptoms include fever, headache, nausea, and red eyes. If left untreated it can cause liver and kidney damage, respiratory failure, internal bleeding, and even death. To avoid this, don't swim or wade in freshwater streams or ponds if you have open sores and don't drink from any freshwater streams or ponds.

On the Islands, fog is a rare occurrence, but there can often be "vog," an airborne haze of gases released from volcanic vents on the Big Island. During certain weather conditions, such as "Kona Winds," the vog can settle over the Islands and wreak havoc with respiratory and other health conditions, especially asthma or emphysema. If susceptible, stay indoors and get emergency assistance if needed.

The Islands have their share of insects. Most are harmless but annoying, but Dengue fever, a mosquito-borne disease, has been reported in Oahu. When planning to spend time outdoors in hiking areas, wear long-sleeve clothing and pants, and use mosquito repellent containing DEET. In damp places you may encounter the dreaded local centipedes, which are brown and blue and measure up to eight inches long. Their painful sting is similar to those of bees and wasps. When camping, shake out your sleeping bag and check your shoes, as the centipedes like cozy places. When hiking in remote areas, always carry a first-aid kit.

COVID-19

A novel coronavirus brought all travel to a virtual standstill in the first half of 2020. Although the illness is mild in most people, some experience severe and even life-threatening complications. Once travel started up again, albeit slowly and cautiously, travelers were asked to be particularly careful about hygiene and to avoid any unnecessary travel, especially if they are sick.

Older adults, especially those over 65, have a greater chance of having severe complications from COVID-19. The same is true for people with weaker immune systems or those living with some types of medical conditions, including diabetes, asthma, heart disease, cancer, HIV/AIDS, kidney disease, and liver disease. Starting two weeks before a trip, anyone planning to travel should be on the lookout for some of the following symptoms: cough, fever, chills, trouble breathing, muscle pain, sore throat, new loss of smell or taste. If you experience any of these symptoms, you should not travel at all.

And to protect yourself during travel, do your best to avoid contact with people showing symptoms. Wash your hands often with soap and water. Limit your time in public places, and, when you are out and about, wear a cloth face mask that covers your nose and mouth. Indeed, a mask may be required in some places, such as on an airplane or in a confined space like a theater, where you share the space with a lot of people.

You may wish to bring extra supplies, such as disenfecting wipes, hand sanitizer (12-ounce bottles were allowed in carry-on luggage as of this writing), and a first-aid kit with a thermometer. Given how abruptly travel was curtailed in March 2020, it is wise to consider protecting yourself by purchasing a travel insurance policy that will reimburse you for any costs related to COVID-19-related cancellations.

Not all travel insurance policies protect against pandemic-related cancellations, so always read the fine print.

🧭 Tours

Even people in paradise have to work. Generally local business hours are weekdays 8–5. Banks are usually open Monday–Thursday 8:30–4 and until 6 on Friday. Some banks have Saturday-morning hours.

Essentials

Many self-serve gas stations stay open around the clock, with full-service stations usually open from around 7 am until 9 pm. U.S. post offices generally are open weekdays from 8 or 10 to 4:30 or 5 and Saturday from 9 to noon or 2. On Oahu, the Ala Moana post office is the only branch to stay open until 4:30 pm on Saturday. The main Honolulu International Airport facility is open until 4 pm on Saturday.

Most museums generally open their doors between 9 and 10 and stay open until 5 Tuesday to Saturday. Many museums operate with afternoon hours only on Sunday and close on Monday. Visitor-attraction hours vary, but most sights are open daily with the exception of major holidays such as Christmas. Check the local newspaper upon arrival for attraction hours and schedules if visiting over holiday periods. The local daily carries a listing of "What's Open/What's Not" for those time periods.

Stores in resort areas sometimes open as early as 8, with shopping-center opening hours varying from 9 to 10 on weekdays and Saturday, a bit later on Sunday. Bigger malls stay open until 9 weekdays and Saturday and close at between 5 and 7 on Sunday. Boutiques in resort areas may stay open as late as 11.

💲 Money

⇨ *Prices for sights are given for adults.* Substantially reduced fees are almost always available for children, students, and senior citizens.

📷 Packing

Hawaii is casual: sandals, bathing suits, and comfortable, informal clothing are the norm. In summer, synthetic slacks and shirts, although easy to care for, can be uncomfortably warm. Only a few upscale restaurants require a jacket for dinner. The aloha shirt is accepted dress in Hawaii for business and most social occasions. Shorts are standard daytime attire, along with a T-shirt or polo shirt. There's no need to buy expensive sandals on the mainland—here you can get flip-flops for a couple of dollars and off-brand sandals for $20. Golfers should remember that many courses have dress codes requiring a collared shirt. If you're not prepared, you can pick up appropriate clothing at resort pro shops. If you're visiting in winter or planning to visit a high-altitude area, bring a sweater or light- to medium-weight jacket. A polar fleece pullover is ideal.

One of the most important things to tuck into your suitcase is sunscreen. Hats and sunglasses offer important sun protection, too. All major hotels in Hawaii provide beach towels.

➕ Safety

Hawaii is generally a safe tourist destination, but it's still wise to follow common-sense safety precautions. Hotel and visitor-center staff can provide information should you decide to head out on your own to more remote areas. Don't leave any valuables in your rental car, not even in a locked trunk. Avoid poorly lighted areas, beach parks, and isolated areas after dark as a precaution.

When hiking, stay on marked trails, no matter how alluring the temptation might be to stray. Weather conditions can cause landscapes to become muddy, slippery, and tenuous, so staying on marked trails will lessen the possibility of a fall or getting lost. Be sure to heed flash flood watches or warnings. Never try to cross a stream, either on foot or in a vehicle, during these weather conditions.

Ocean safety is of the utmost importance when visiting an island destination. Don't swim alone, and follow the international signage posted at beaches that alerts swimmers to strong currents, man-of-war jellyfish, sharp coral, high surf, sharks, and dangerous shore breaks. At coastal lookouts along cliff tops, heed the signs indicating that waves can climb over the ledges. Check with lifeguards at each beach for current conditions, and if the red flags are up, indicating swimming and surfing are not allowed, don't go in. Waters that look calm on the surface can harbor strong currents and undertows.

$ Taxes

There's a 4.17% state sales tax on all purchases, including food. A hotel room tax of 10.25%, combined with the sales tax of 4.17%, equals a 14.42% rate added onto your hotel bill. A $5-per-day road tax is also assessed on each rental vehicle.

📍 Time

Hawaii is on Hawaiian standard time, six hours behind New York, and three hours behind Los Angeles.

When the U.S. mainland is on daylight saving time, Hawaii is not, so add an extra hour of time difference between the Islands and U.S. mainland destinations. You may also find that things generally move more slowly here. That has nothing to do with your watch—it's just the laid-back way called Hawaiian time.

💵 Tipping

As this is a major vacation destination and many of the people who work in the service industry rely on tips to supplement their wages, tipping is not only common, but expected. Consider a tip of 18% to 20% for excellent restaurant service, even at casual eateries. It's customary to tip all service folk at hotels and resorts, from valets to housekeepers. Keeping a stash of "singles" in your wallet or handbag makes this easy.

🧭 Tours

ADVENTURE STUDY TOURS

A tour of Kilauea—the most active volcano on earth—is even better when led by an actual geologist, volcanologist, retired ranger, or even botanist. Mother Nature does not offer a money-back guarantee, so keep in mind that seeing active lava cannot be promised.

Friends of Hawaii Volcanoes National Park
SPECIAL-INTEREST | With tours tailored to small groups or individuals, the Friends of Hawaii Volcanoes National Park offers custom tours with specialist guides who help you make fascinating discoveries and learn details about such geologic features as lava tubes, vents, and fumaroles. Tours are tailored to your interest and group size and last four to eight hours. Another option is to join the Friends and participate in their regular programs.

Essentials

☎ *808/985–7373* ⊕ *fhvnp.org* ✉ *From $325 for group of 1–6 people.*

BIKING TOURS

If you're a bicycling enthusiast, you've got exciting options on the Big Island. ■ **TIP→ Most airlines accommodate bikes as luggage, provided they're dismantled and boxed.**

Bicycle Adventures

ADVENTURE TOURS | Take a seven-day Hawaii tour that includes biking, hiking, snorkeling, sailing, and whale-watching. Accommodations, meals, and park admissions are included. ☎ *800/443–6060* ⊕ *www.bicycleadventures.com* ✉ *From $3,568.*

BIRD-WATCHING TOURS

More than 150 species of birds live in the Hawaiian Islands. For $5,450 per person double-occupancy, Field Guides has a three-island (Oahu, Kauai, and the Big Island), 10-day, guided bird-watching trip that includes accommodations, meals, ground transportation, and interisland air.

Victor Emanuel Nature Tours, the largest company in the world specializing in birding tours, has two 10-day fall Hawaii and spring Hawaii trips to Oahu, Kauai, and the Big Island that cost $4,895 (fall), including double-occupancy accommodations, meals, interisland air, ground transportation, and guided excursions.

GUIDED TOURS

One way to manage several Hawaiian Islands on the same trip is to take a guided tour that includes all your travel arrangements in the Islands, including hotels, interisland transfers, and some sightseeing.

Atlas Cruises & Tours

GUIDED TOURS | This escorted-tour operator, in business for more than 25 years, partners with major companies such as Collette, Globus, Tauck, and Trafalgar to offer a wide variety of travel experiences. Tours run 7–12 nights. ☎ *800/942–3301* ⊕ *www.atlastravelweb.com* ✉ *From $2,024.*

Globus

GUIDED TOURS | Founded in 1928 by a man who transported visitors across Lake Lugano, Switzerland, in a rowboat, this family-owned company grew to become the largest guided vacation operator in the world. Globus offers four Hawaii itineraries, running 9–12 nights; two include a 7-night cruise on Norwegian Cruise Lines. ☎ *866/755–8581* ⊕ *www. globusjourneys.com* ✉ *From $2,496.*

Tauck Travel

GUIDED TOURS | Begun in 1925 by Arthur Tauck with a tour through the back roads of New England, Tauck has since spread its offerings across the world. Its 11-night multi-island "Best of Hawaii" tour covers noteworthy sights such as Iao Valley and Haleakala National Park. ☎ *800/788–7885* ⊕ *www.tauck.com* ✉ *From $7,590.*

Trafalgar

GUIDED TOURS | This company prides itself on its "Insider Experiences," defined as visiting hidden places, meeting local people, and sharing traditions you may not discover on your own. Trafalgar offers several itineraries, running 7–12 nights. ☎ *866/513–1995* ⊕ *www.trafalgar.com* ✉ *From $2,605.*

YMT Vacations

GUIDED TOURS | Billing itself as the best choice in affordable travel, YMT offers a 13-day, four-island tour and a 12-day Hawaiian Islands cruise and tour. ☎ *877/322–6185* ⊕ *www.ymtvacations. com* ✉ *From $1,999.*

HIKING
Hawaii Forest and Trail
ECOTOURISM | This company offers two different bird-watching tours. The Endangered Native Habitat (Rainforest and Dryforest) Birding Adventure takes bird lovers to explore a cloud-misted rain forest on the slopes of Mauna Kea as well as a dry-forest habitat on Mauna Loa. Expert guides help you search native forests for amakihi, iiwi, elepaio, *apapane*, and the endangered *akiapolaau*.

The Hakalau Forest tour offers outstanding opportunities to spot the rarest endemic birds, allowing exclusive access to the highly restricted Hakalau National Wildlife Refuge. You may even see such thrilling sights as the highly endangered, bright orange *akepa* juvenile being fed by its parents. Walking sticks, binoculars, rain ponchos, and meals are provided. ☎ *800/464–1993* ⊕ *www.hawaii-forest. com* ✉ *From $189.*

Sierra Club Outings
SPECIAL-INTEREST | Various day hikes are offered to such popular areas as Kokee, Sleeping Giant, and Mahaulepu Coast. Check their website or the local newspaper, *The Garden Island,* for these types of local outings. ☎ *415/977–5500* ⊕ *sierra- clubkauai.org.*

Timberline Adventures
SPECIAL-INTEREST | ☎ *800/417–2453* ⊕ *www.timberline-adventures.com.*

Victor Emanuel Nature Tours
SPECIAL-INTEREST | This mainland-based tour company offers periodic bird-watching tours in Hawaii, usually in February and October. ☎ *800/328–8368* ⊕ *www. ventbird.com.*

◉ Trip Insurance

Comprehensive trip insurance is valuable if you're booking a very expensive or complicated trip (particularly to an isolated region) or if you're booking far in advance. Comprehensive policies typically cover trip cancellation and interruption, letting you cancel or cut your trip short because of illness, or, in some cases, acts of terrorism in your destination. Such policies might also cover evacuation and medical care. Some also cover you for trip delays because of bad weather or mechanical problems, as well as for lost or delayed luggage.

Always read the fine print of your policy to make sure that you're covered for the risks that most concern you. Compare several policies to be sure you're getting the best price and range of coverage available.

Hawaiian Vocabulary

Although an understanding of Hawaiian is by no means required on a trip to the Aloha State, a *malihini,* or newcomer, will find plenty of opportunities to pick up a few of the local words and phrases. Traditional names and expressions are widely used in the Islands. You're likely to read or hear at least a few words each day of your stay.

Simplifying the learning process is the fact that the Hawaiian language contains only seven consonants—*H, K, L, M, N, P, W,* and the silent *'okina,* or glottal stop, written '—plus one or more of the five vowels. All syllables, and therefore all words, end in a vowel. Each vowel, with the exception of a few diphthongized double vowels, such as *au* (pronounced "ow") or *ai* (pronounced "eye"), is pronounced separately. Thus *'Iolani* is four syllables (ee-oh-la-nee), not three (yo-la-nee). Although some Hawaiian words have only vowels, most also contain some consonants, but consonants are never doubled.

Pronunciation is simple. Pronounce *A* "ah" as in *father; E* "ay" as in *weigh; I* "ee" as in *marine; O* "oh" as in *no; U* "oo" as in *true.*

Consonants mirror their English equivalents, with the exception of *W.* When the letter begins any syllable other than the first one in a word, it is usually pronounced as a *V. 'Awa,* the Polynesian drink, is pronounced "ava," *'ewa* is pronounced "eva."

Almost all long Hawaiian words are combinations of shorter words; they are not difficult to pronounce if you segment them. *Kalaniana'ole,* the highway running east from Honolulu, is easily understood as *Kalani ana 'ole.* Apply the standard pronunciation rules—the stress falls on the next-to-last syllable of most two- or three-syllable Hawaiian words—and Kalaniana'ole Highway is as easy to say as Main Street.

Now about that fish. Try *humu-humu nuku-nuku āpu a'a.*

The other unusual element in Hawaiian language is the *kahakō,* or macron, written as a short line (¯) placed over a vowel. Like the accent (´) in Spanish, the kahakō puts emphasis on a syllable that would normally not be stressed. The most familiar example is probably *Waikīkī.* With no macrons, the stress would fall on the middle syllable; with only one macron, on the last syllable, the stress would fall on the first and last syllables. Some words become plural with the addition of a macron, often on a syllable that would have been stressed anyway. No Hawaiian word becomes plural with the addition of an *S,* since that letter does not exist in the language.

The Hawaiian diacritical marks are not printed in this guide.

PIDGIN

You may hear pidgin, the unofficial language of Hawai'i. It is a Creole language, with its own grammar, evolved from the mixture of English, Hawaiian, Japanese, Portuguese, and other languages spoken in 19th-century Hawai'i, and it is heard everywhere.

GLOSSARY

What follows is a glossary of some of the most commonly used Hawaiian words. Hawaiian residents appreciate visitors who at least try to pick up the local language.

'a'ā: rough, crumbling lava, contrasting with *pāhoehoe,* which is smooth.

'ae: yes.

aikane: friend.

āina: land.

akamai: smart, clever, possessing savoir faire.

akua: god.

ala: a road, path, or trail.

ali'i: a Hawaiian chief, a member of the chiefly class.

aloha: love, affection, kindness; also a salutation meaning both greetings and farewell.

'ānuenue: rainbow.

'a'ole: no.

'apōpō: tomorrow.

'auwai: a ditch.

auwē: alas, woe is me!

'ehu: a red-haired Hawaiian.

'ewa: in the direction of 'Ewa plantation, west of Honolulu.

hala: the pandanus tree, whose leaves (*lau hala*) are used to make baskets and plaited mats.

hālau: school.

hale: a house.

hale pule: church, house of worship.

hana: to work.

haole: foreigner. Since the first foreigners were Caucasian, *haole* now means a Caucasian person.

hapa: a part, sometimes a half; often used as a short form of *hapa haole,* to mean a person who is part-Caucasian.

hau'oli: to rejoice. *Hau'oli Makahiki Hou* means Happy New Year. *Hau'oli lā hānau* means Happy Birthday.

heiau: an outdoor stone platform; an ancient Hawaiian place of worship.

he mea iki or **he mea 'ole:** you're welcome.

holo: to run.

holoholo: to go for a walk, ride, or sail.

holokū: a long Hawaiian dress, somewhat fitted, with a yoke and a train. It was worn at court, and at least one local translates the word as "expensive mu'umu'u."

holomū: a post–World War II cross between a *holokū* and a mu'umu'u, less fitted than the former but less voluminous than the latter, and having no train.

honi: to kiss; a kiss. A phrase that some tourists may find useful, quoted from a popular hula, is *Honi Ka'ua Wikiwiki:* Kiss me quick!

honu: turtle.

ho'omalimali: flattery, a deceptive "line," bunk, baloney, hooey.

huhū: angry.

hui: a group, club, or assembly. A church may refer to its congregation as a *hui* and a social club may be called a *hui.*

hukilau: a seine; a communal fishing party in which everyone helps to drive the fish into a huge net, pull it in, and divide the catch.

hula: the dance of Hawai'i.

iki: little.

ipo: sweetheart. Commonly seen as "ku'uipo," or "my sweetheart."

ka: the. This is the definite article for most singular words; for plural nouns, the definite article is usually *nā.* Since there is no *S* in Hawaiian, the article may be your only clue that a noun is plural.

Hawaiian Vocabulary

kahuna: a priest, doctor, or other trained person of old Hawai'i, endowed with special professional skills that often included prophecy or other supernatural powers.

kai: the sea, saltwater.

kalo: the taro plant from whose root *poi* (paste) is made.

kamā'aina: literally, a child of the soil; it refers to people who were born in the Islands or have lived there for a long time.

kanaka: originally a man or humanity, it is now used to denote a male Hawaiian or part-Hawaiian, but is occasionally taken as a slur when used by non-Hawaiians. *Kanaka maoli* is used by some Native Hawaiian rights activists to embrace part-Hawaiians as well.

kāne: a man, a husband. If you see this word (or kane) on a door, it's the men's room.

kapa: also called by its Tahitian name, *tapa,* a cloth made of beaten bark and usually dyed and stamped with a repeat design.

kapakahi: crooked, cockeyed, uneven. You've got your hat on *kapakahi.*

kapu: keep out, prohibited. This is the Hawaiian version of the more widely known Tongan word *tabu* (taboo).

kēia lā: today.

keiki: a child; *keikikāne* is a boy, *keikiwahine* a girl.

kōkua: to help, assist. Often seen in signs like "Please *kōkua* and throw away your trash."

kona: the leeward side of the Islands, the direction (south) from which the *kona* wind and *kona* rain come.

kula: upland.

kuleana: a homestead or small plot of ground on which a family has been installed for some generations without necessarily owning it. By extension, *kuleana* is used to denote any area or department in which one has a special interest or prerogative. You'll hear it used this way: "If you want to hire a surfboard, see Moki; that's his *kuleana.*"

kupuna: grandparent; elder.

lā: sun.

lamalama: to fish with a torch.

lānai: a porch, a balcony, an outdoor living room.

lani: heaven, the sky.

lau hala: the leaf of the *hala,* or pandanus tree, widely used in handicrafts.

lei: a garland of flowers.

lōlō: feeble-minded, crazy.

luna: a plantation overseer or foreman.

mahalo: thank you.

mahina: moon.

makai: toward the ocean.

mālama: to take care of, preserve, protect

malihini: a newcomer to the Islands.

mana: the spiritual power that the Hawaiians believe inhabits all things and creatures.

manō: shark.

manuahi: free, gratis.

mauka: toward the mountains.

mauna: mountain.

mele: a Hawaiian song or chant, often of epic proportions.

Mele Kalikimaka: Merry Christmas (a transliteration from the English phrase).

Menehune: a Hawaiian pixie. The *Menehune* were a legendary race of little people who accomplished prodigious work, such as building fishponds and temples in the course of a single night.

moana: the ocean.

mu'umu'u: the voluminous dress in which the missionaries enveloped Hawaiian women. Culturally sensitive locals have embraced the Hawaiian spelling but often shorten the spoken word to "mu'u." Most English dictionaries include the spelling "muumuu."

nani: beautiful.

nui: big.

'ohana: family.

'ono: delicious.

pāhoehoe: smooth, unbroken, satiny lava.

palapala: document, printed matter.

pali: a cliff, precipice.

pānini: prickly pear cactus.

paniolo: a Hawaiian cowboy, a rough transliteration of *español,* the language of the Islands' earliest cowboys.

pau: finished, done.

pilikia: trouble. The Hawaiian word is much more widely used here than its English equivalent.

pū: large conch shell used as trumpet before start of luau and other special events.

puka: a hole.

pule: prayer, blessing. Often performed before a meal or event.

pupule: crazy, like the celebrated Princess Pupule. This word has replaced its English equivalent in local usage.

pu'u: volcanic cinder cone.

tūtū: grandmother

waha: mouth.

wahine: a female, a woman, a wife, and a sign on the ladies' room door; the plural form is *wāhine.*

wai: freshwater, as opposed to saltwater, which is *kai.*

wailele: waterfall.

wikiwiki: to hurry, hurry up (since this is a reduplication of *wiki,* quick, neither *W* is pronounced as a *V*).

Great Itineraries

Road Trip: Best of the Big Island in a Week

Experiencing the best of the Big Island requires some drive time, plus some downtime.

DAY 1: HISTORIC KAILUA VILLAGE

Start your first day in Kailua-Kona with a stroll around Historic Kailua Village. Eat breakfast or brunch at one of the ocean-front restaurants along Alii Drive. Stroll the seaside village's many gift stores, art galleries, and apparel boutiques. Historic landmarks include royal **Hulihee Palace** and the oldest Christian church in Hawaii, **Mokuaikaua Church.** In the afternoon, take a ride on the **Atlantis Submarine,** or take a sunset dinner sail with **Body Glove Cruises.**

Logistics: The village is walkable. There are paid and free lots behind the stores on the *mauka* (mountain) side of Alii Drive.

DAY 2: BEST KOHALA BEACHES

Head north to the beautiful sand beaches of the Kohala Coast. Check out **Anae-hoomalu Bay** in Waikoloa Beach Resort. Not only can you rent beach amenities including kayaks or stand-up paddle-boards, you'll also be near Queens' Mar-ketPlace with its restaurants and shops. For lunch, try **Lava Lava Beach Club,** right on the beach at Anaehoomalu Bay. Head north to Kawaihae and visit **Puukohola Heiau National Historic Site,** where King Kamehameha I oversaw the building of a great temple. On the way back, make a stop at **Hapuna Beach State Recreation Area.**

Logistics: Parking is easy at Waikoloa Beach Resort. Distance and time traveled: 35 miles one-way, 40 minutes one-way, starting in Kailua-Kona. Car, via Queen Kaahumanu Highway.

DAY 3: KEALAKEKUA BAY

In South Kona, **Kealakekua Bay State Historical Park** attracts visitors to this marine conservation district frequented by spinner dolphins. The **Captain James Cook Monument,** a white obelisk on a wharf, marks where the navigator was slain in 1779. Guided kayak tours are available, and snorkeling here is excellent. In the afternoon, visit the historic **St. Benedict Painted Church** and **Puuhonua O Honaunau National Historical Park.** On your way back north, stop at **Greenwell Farms** in Kealakekua for a Kona coffee farm tour.

Logistics: Take the lower bypass road from Keauhou or the upper road from Kailua-Kona, and head down Napoopoo Road to the end. Distance and time traveled: 44 miles round-trip, 35 minutes one-way, starting in Kailua-Kona. Car, via Highway 11.

DAY 4: HAWAII VOLCANOES NATIONAL PARK

It's a long drive from Kona to **Hawaii Volcanoes National Park,** so leave early to get to the park by 11 am. Begin at the **Kilauea Visitor Center,** where you can review maps, buy trail-guide booklets, or talk to the rangers. Stroll along a board-walk to the **sulfur banks** and **steam vents.** Along the way, stop at **Volcano Art Center** to view fantastic local art. Drive to the Steaming Bluffs and walk to an overlook with views of Halemaumau Crater and Kilauea Caldera. Then drive down Chain of Craters Road to visit **Thurston Lava Tube** and the adjacent **Kilauea Iki Trail.** Afterward, stop by **Volcano House** and eat lunch or dinner at **The Rim.**

Logistics: The park is open 24/7, but entrance fees are charged during normal visiting hours. Distance from Kailua-Kona one-way: 90 miles. Time traveled one-way: 2½ hours.

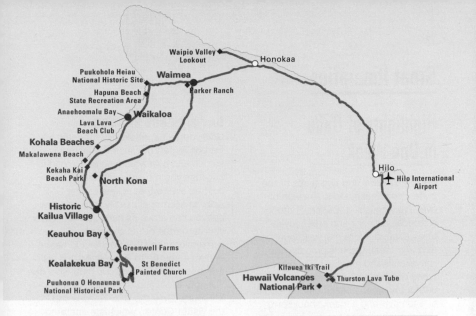

DAY 5: WAIMEA AND UPCOUNTRY

At the foothills of Maunakea, the small upcountry town is home to **Parker Ranch,** one of the country's largest privately owned cattle ranches. You can book several activities in town, including horseback riding and tours of two historic homes. Waimea has great restaurants, including **Merriman's** and **Big Island Brewhaus.** Not far from Waimea, **Waipio Valley** is a beautiful destination best explored by horseback or guided tour. The nearby town of **Honokaa** still feels like a slice of the old sugar plantation days.

Logistics: Waimea can be reached from Kona via the upper road, or up Kawaihae Drive from the lower road. Distance from Kailua-Kona: 39 miles one-way.

DAY 6: KEAUHOU BAY

Keauhou is just south of Kailua-Kona on Alii Drive. Here you'll find lots of recreational activities, including tennis, golf, and stand-up paddleboarding. **Keauhou Shopping Center** has movie theaters, restaurants, and cafés. The **Sheraton Kona Resort and Spa at Keauhou Bay** has the bayfront **Rays on the Bay,** open for dinner. One of the island's most popular activities is a nighttime manta ray tour with operators who depart nightly from Keauhou Harbor.

Tips

Book manta ray and snorkeling and kayaking tours in advance, as they are popular.

Plan your time at Hawaii Volcanoes National Park carefully so you see what you want.

Logistics: You'll need your car to drive around the area. Distance from Kailua-Kona: 5 miles one-way on Alii Drive. Time traveled one-way: 10 minutes.

DAY 7: NORTH KONA

Two of the best beaches near Kailua-Kona take some time to get to. **Kekaha Kai State Park—Mahaiula Side** is down a long gravel road that winds through a lava field on the way to a wonderful white-sand beach. About a 20-minute walk south across a lava field from Kekaha Kai State Park, **Makalawena Beach** is a true gem and worth the hike. If you go to Makalawena, pack lots of water, a shade umbrella, food, and sunscreen. End your trip with a great dinner.

Logistics: On Wednesday, the park is closed. Distance from Kailua-Kona: 17 miles one-way.

Great Itineraries

Highlights of Oahu in One Week

With the capital and two thirds of the state's population, Oahu is a vibrant, ever-evolving island. Cultural, outdoor, historical, culinary, and other adventures abound. From *mauka* (mountains) to *makai* (sea), Oahu is probably the Hawaiian island most likely to please all types of travelers—whether you're an outdoorsy type, a beach bum, a foodie, or a family—and a week should give you enough time to see the highlights. You can either use the bus or take taxis or rideshares while you're in Honolulu, but rent a car to get out of Waikiki and around the island for a true feel for all things Oahu in this one-week highlights itinerary.

DAY 1: WAIKIKI

You'll want to get your beach legs under you after that long flight to Oahu. Given the time difference between Hawaii and the rest of the U.S. (it's 6 hours earlier than the east coast, 3 hours earlier than the west coast), you'll probably be jet-lagged. Use your earlier rising to go grab coffee and head to Waikiki, Sans Souci, or Fort DeRussy Beach. You'll see locals on their morning jogs at Kapiolani Park and catching waves at their favorite shore break. Once caffeinated, hit Kalakaua Avenue on foot, the best way to shop and sightsee. Got kiddos in tow? Try the Waikiki Aquarium or the Honolulu Zoo. Get some refreshments with tea at the Moana Surfrider, the oldest hotel in Waikiki, or mai tais and *pupu* (hors d'oeuvres) at Duke's Waikiki (a better deal at lunch). In the afternoon, it's time for a surf lesson on the beginner-friendly waves of Waikiki. Finish your day with a surfside dinner at your restaurant of choice to watch the sunset.

DAY 2: PEARL HARBOR

Give yourself a whole day for Pearl Harbor, in part because the history is so rich and overwhelming and in part because you may be waiting in lines. Just be aware that tickets for the USS *Arizona* Memorial usually run out early, but you can arrive as early as 7 am. After your ferry ride out to the memorial, you can explore the USS *Bowfin* submarine or take a shuttle to Ford Island and visit the restored USS *Missouri* battleship (the "Mighty Mo") and the Pacific Aviation Museum. Only the USS *Arizona* and the Visitor Center, which are operated by the National Park Service, are free; the other sights are operated by private entities and charge admission. You won't be allowed to carry bags to any of the sights, so be sure that anything important fits in your pockets, though you can pay to store your bags near the Visitor Center. Head back to Waikiki for some late-afternoon beach time and a good dinner.

DAY 3: DOWNTOWN HONOLULU AND CHINATOWN

Cab or bus it to downtown Honolulu for a guided tour of the royal residence, Iolani Palace, where you'll get an excellent overview of Hawaii's monarchical era from the early 1800s through its overthrow in 1893. Next, take a walk between Honolulu Hale, Kawaiahao Church, Hawaiian Mission Houses Historic Site and Archives, the Hawaii State Capitol, Washington Place, the Kamehameha I statue, and Aliiolani Hale for historical highlights (several companies offer professionally guided walks of the area). Then, keep walking the half-mile through Honolulu's business district into Chinatown for lunch at one of its eclectic eateries. For Chinese food, Little Village Noodle House is always a good bet. Browse the shops, art galleries, and cultural sites like the Mauna

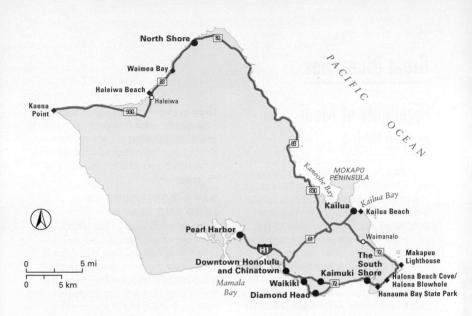

Kea Marketplace, Chinatown Cultural Plaza, Izumo Taisha Shrine, and Kuan Yin Temple.

DAY 4: DIAMOND HEAD AND KAIMUKI

Today you will go the opposite direction from downtown. Tours of Shangri La, the opulent waterfront home of heiress Doris Duke, with its Islamic art and architecture, book up well in advance, but it's well worth the effort to make an online reservation for a small surcharge. Shuttles to the Kahala home-turned-museum start and end at the Honolulu Museum of Art. After your tour, grab a to-go lunch from Diamond Head Market & Grill, and enjoy it at the picnic tables at Diamond Head State Monument and Park. Then hike the relatively easy 1½-hour trail up and down this dormant volcano. Finish the day with dinner in the foodie neighborhood of Kaimuki.

DAY 5: KAILUA AND SOUTH SHORE

Head to the Windward side for a stop in Kailua, a once sleepy suburb that's become a popular visitor spot. Go for a swim at quintessential Kailua Beach, then have lunch at Kalapawai Cafe & Deli or Kono's. Next, drive along the southeastern shore via Waimanalo, and choose your afternoon adventure: 1) do the easy, stroller-friendly hike at Makapuu Lighthouse with great whale-watching views in winter and spring; 2) snorkel at Hanauma Bay State Park, the pristine nature preserve where you'll have more space to swim with the fish if you arrive after the morning-to-midday rush; or 3) stop at Halona Blowhole and the *From Here to Eternity* Halona Beach Cove nearby.

DAY 6: NORTH SHORE

Explore Oahu's countryside with a drive to the North Shore. The beaches here are home to some of the world's most famous surf breaks. Each winter, surfers from around the globe converge to catch barreling waves of 15 feet or higher. Haleiwa is the biggest town on the North Shore and is filled with surf shops, charming boutiques, and restaurants. Grab lunch from Haleiwa Joe's or Uncle Bo's Haleiwa. If you can manage to wait in the long line, enjoying a treat at Matsumoto Shave Ice is a sweet way to end the day.

Great Itineraries

Highlights of Maui in One Week

Lounging beside the pool or napping on a sandy beach may fulfill your initial fantasy of a tropical Hawaiian vacation, but Maui has much more to offer: underwater encounters with rainbow-colored fish, an icy dip in a jungle waterfall, or a trek across the moonlike landscape of a dormant volcano. ⚠ **As a tropical island, Maui is susceptible to dangerous surf, flash flooding, and other natural hazards. Always check road, ocean, and wilderness advisories before venturing out.**

DAY 1: GETTING SETTLED

On your way out of Kahului Airport, stop at Costco, Target, or Walmart to pick up beach gear, sunscreen, food, and drink.

Once ensconced at your hotel or condo, unwind from your long flight by exploring the grounds, dozing by the pool, or splashing in the ocean—it's why you came to Maui, isn't it?

Logistics: Road signs will point you to the two main resort areas: Highway 311 (Maui Veterans Highway) to 31 (Piilani) south to Kihei and Wailea, and Highway 380 (Kuihelani) to 30 (Honoapiilani) west to Lahaina and Kapalua.

DAY 2: SURF, SAND AND ... FORE!

Head to the nearest beach for snorkeling, swimming and sunbathing, or surfing in the gentle waves of Cove Park in Kihei or Launiupoko in West Maui. If golf's more your game, hit the tournament-quality golf links in the resort areas; cheaper rates can be found at the scenic Waiehu, Waikapu, and Maui Lani courses in Central Maui. Spend the evening (it'll be cooler) visiting Lahaina town, which is packed with shops, restaurants, and art galleries.

Logistics: Many hotels and condos offer free shuttle service to golfing, shopping, and dining. Driving to Lahaina from South Maui, take Highway 310 (North Kihei Road) and turn left on Highway 30 (Honoapiilani).

DAY 3: ADVENTURE ON LAND AND SEA

Get a different view of the island—and discover what's beneath the surface—on a full- or half-day boat excursion to Molokini, a crescent-shaped islet that sits 3 miles off South Maui, or take a snorkeling, scuba diving, or dolphin- and whale-watching trip. If you prefer dry land, head to Maui Tropical Plantation in Waikapu, which offers tram tours and a country store; it's also the home base for Flyin Hawaiian Zipline and Maui Zipline's introductory course. Plan to be back early enough for a sunset luau at your resort or at Old Lahaina Luau.

Logistics: Boat tours leave from Maalaea Harbor in South Maui and Lahaina Harbor in West Maui. To get to the Maui Tropical Plantation from West Maui, follow Highway 30 (Honoapiilani) south to Waikapu; from South Maui, take Highway 310 (North Kihei Road) and turn right onto Highway 30.

DAY 4: HALEAKALA AND UPCOUNTRY

Sunrise at the 10,000-foot summit of this dormant volcano is so popular that the National Park Service now requires reservations (make yours as early as possible, up to 60 days in advance of your visit). To avoid the crush, consider planning your day in reverse. Start with some great body surfing at Baldwin Beach Park on the North Shore, followed by lunch in the former plantation town of Paia, home to charming boutiques and cafés. Once Upcountry, tour Surfing Goat Dairy, Ali'i Kula Lavender farm, or MauiWine, before heading to the Haleakala summit in the afternoon when the park is uncrowded. It's not sunrise, but the spectacular sunset vista encompasses at least three islands and the broad expanse separating Maui's two mountains.

Logistics: To reach Haleakala from South Maui, take Highway 311 (Maui Veterans Highway) out of Kihei to connect with Highway 36 (Hana) and then Highway 37 (Haleakala). From West Maui, follow Highway 30 (Honoapiilani) to 380 (Kuihelani), which connects with 36.

DAY 5: THE ROAD TO HANA
Today's the day to tackle the 600 curves of the Road to Hana (Highway 36/360). There aren't a lot of dining options in Hana, but many hotels offer picnic baskets for the road, or fill your cooler and gas tank in Paia, the last chance for provisions. Pause to stretch your legs at the Keanae Arboretum, picturesque Keanae Landing, or any of the roadside waterfalls. Approaching Hana town, turn into Waianapanapa State Park, with its rugged lava outcroppings, black-sand beach, trails, and caves with freshwater pools. There isn't much reason to stop in Hana town, except for lunch at the food trucks if you didn't bring your own, so continue on to the Kipahulu District of Haleakala National Park, site of the Pools of Oheo (nicknamed Seven Sacred Pools) and 400-foot Waimoku Falls. (Check for updates on closures due to flash flooding and landslides.) Don't leave Kipahulu without visiting the grave site of famed aviator Charles Lindbergh, who is buried at 19th-century Palapala Hoomau Church.

Logistics: Follow directions to Haleakala, but stay on Highway 36/360 (Hana).

DAY 6: BACK TO THE BEACH
A full day is needed to recover from a trek to Hana, so take it easy with a visit to the Maui Ocean Center, where you'll be mesmerized by the sharks, rays, and tuna circling the 750,000-gallon open-ocean tank. Then spend the rest of the day relaxing in the water or at the spa with lunch beside the pool.

Logistics: From South Maui, take Highway 31 (Piilani) to 310 (North Kihei Road), then head a short distance left on Highway 30 (Honoapiilani). From West Maui, head south on Highway 30 to Maalaea/Maui Ocean Center.

DAY 7: CENTRAL MAUI
Squeeze in a final session at the beach or pool before checking out of your hotel and heading to Central Maui to be closer to the airport. If you like history, Hale Hoikeike at the Bailey House features the island's largest collection of Hawaiian artifacts. Just five minutes up the road is Iao Valley State Park and one of the most photographed landmarks in Hawaii: Iao Needle. Eat like a local with lunch or an early dinner at Umi, Miko's, or A Saigon Cafe in Wailuku or Da Kitchen, Ichiban, or Tin Roof in Kahului. If there's still time, visit Kanaha Beach Park by Kahului Airport to watch world-class wind- and kite surfers or shop for gifts and souvenirs at the many malls.

Logistics: From South Maui, take Highway 311 (Maui Veterans Highway) all the way to 32 (Kaahumanu) in Kahului, then turn left toward Wailuku; from West Maui, Highway 30 (Honoapiilani) leads right into Wailuku town. Kahului Airport is a 10-minute drive from here.

Great Itineraries

Road Trip: The Best of Kauai in 8 Days

Kauai is small, but its major byways generally circumnavigate the island with no through-roads, so it can take more time than you expect to get around. Hiking Kalalau Trail, kayaking Wailua River, showering in a waterfall, watching whales at Kilauea Lighthouse, shopping for gifts at Koloa Town shops—there's so much to see and do. Rather than trying to check everything off your list in one fell swoop, choose your favorites and devote a full day to the experiences.

DAY 1: SETTLE IN ON THE EAST SIDE

The East Side of the island is a convenient area to make a home base. Stay here, and you'll have the easiest access to most of the island's top attractions. Fresh off a long flight, you'll likely just want to relax by the pool at your hotel/condo or hit **Kealia Beach** just north of funky Kapaa Town. The far end near the rock jetty is for safe swimming and easy body surfing. There are plenty of welcoming dining options around Kapaa, such as the **Lemongrass Grill** or **Hukilau Lanai,** for a fantastic first meal.

Logistics: Wailua/Kapaa traffic can be a nightmare, so avoid rush and midday times. It's 10 miles from the airport to Kapaa, but drive times can vary from 15 to 35 minutes. Kealia Beach is three minutes outside Kapaa and has plenty of parking.

DAY 2: TAKE IT ALL IN

For an incredible, and literal, overview of Kauai's beaches, forests, canyons, waterfalls, and ocean, take a morning helicopter trip with **Blue Hawaiian Helicopters** or **Jack Harter** out of Lihue. Images of the rolling verdant carpet far below will linger long in your memory. Afternoon is free for beach time or laid-back shopping in Kapaa Town. Or have lunch in Lihue and lounge on **Kalapaki Beach.**

Logistics: Lihue Airport to Kalapaki Bay is five minutes south of Lihue.

DAY 3: EAST SIDE OFFERINGS

Check out the Kapaa/Wailua area, which has a little something for everyone. Rent a bike at **Kauai Cycle** and coast along the Kauai Path (Ke Ala Hele Makalae), enjoying the ocean views and invigorating fresh air. Or take a moderate, 2-mile hike on the **Sleeping Giant Trail** for panoramic vistas of the entire East Side. Then get back on the main road for a few-minutes' drive up to **Opaekaa Falls,** one of the Wailua River's mightiest displays.

Logistics: From mid-Kapaa to the starting point of the Sleeping Giant Trail is 3 miles; just avoid rush hours.

DAY 4: SOUTH SIDE SIGHTS

Start with a hike on the **Mahaulepu Heritage Trail** for wondrous ocean-side views of pristine beaches and craggy ledges. A quick dip at **Poipu Beach Park** will refresh your limbs after your hike. Drive down Lawai Road to spot the **Spouting Horn,** Kauai's version of Old Faithful. Right next door is the **National Tropical Botanical Garden,** where you can tour beautiful grounds of exotic flora and learn about the biodiversity in Hawaii and the Pacific.

Logistics: The Mahaulepu Trail is about 10 minutes from Koloa Town. From there to Spouting Horn is about another 10-minute drive.

DAY 5: AT SEA ON NAPALI COAST

Choose your preferred watercraft (Zodiac for adventure rafting or catamaran for pleasure cruising) and depart from the boat harbor in Eleele for an unforgettable journey up breathtakingly scenic Napali Coast. Most trips are about four hours and usually include a light snack; some include drinks. Don't schedule anything too demanding afterwards, as you'll likely be tired, and you'll want to savor the memories of the sights you just beheld.

DAY 6: EXPLORE THE OTHER KAUAI

In the mountains of Kokee on the West Side, you'll enjoy the splendor of the mountains, the ocean, the sunlight, and the crisper air. Stop along the way at the scenic overlooks of **Waimea Canyon** and be dazzled by the interplay of light and shadow as the sun moves across this spectacular landscape. Hike the relatively short Canyon Trail to a divine waterfall. Have lunch at the **Kokee Lodge,** check out the **Kokee Museum** next door, and continue another 5 miles or so to the Kalalau Lookout.

Logistics: Drive up from Waimea and come down on the Kekaha side, which is more gradual. It's about 30 minutes straight up to the lodge, but scenic spots stretch it out.

DAY 7: NORTH SHORE PLAYGROUND

The North Shore's plentiful sights and activities include swimming, surfing, golf, tennis, botanical gardens, ziplining, hiking, and horseback riding. Visit **Limahuli Garden** in Hanalei, which features an ancient Hawaiian layout of a typical self-sufficient community, or **Na Aina Kai** with its artistic and working-farm focus. At the **Kilauea Lighthouse** behold the cliffs, exotic birds, and magnificent coastal view. Spend the rest of your day at **Hanalei Bay** swimming, taking a surf lesson, or just walking the 2-mile jewel of a crescent-shape beach. For the family, a round of golf at **Kauai Mini-Golf** in Kilauea can be joyful and instructive: the 18-hole layout reveals Hawaii's story through its landscaping.

Logistics: Limahuli is about a 10-minute drive past Hanalei. From there back to Kilauea is about a 20-minute drive on the main road.

DAY 8: HIKE THE KALALAU TRAIL

You've taken in magnificent Napali Coast from the sea; now experience it from land. This moderate trek offers incredible views peering straight down over the deep blue sea, a visit to a lovely beach, and a hike up a stream to a 300-foot waterfall. You won't be taking the arduous 11-mile journey of the entire coastal Kalalau Trail, so take your time and enjoy Kauai's scenery. Be sure to secure a parking permit before hitting the trail.

Logistics: It's 2 miles into Hanakapiai Beach. Allow an hour. The hike up the valley is also 2 miles—but plan on 90 minutes each way, as the trail cuts through jungle.

Contacts

Air

State of Hawaii Airports Division Offices. ☎ 808/836–6413 ⊕ www. hidot.hawaii.gov/airports.

AIRPORT INFORMATION Ellison Onizuka Kona International Airport at Keahole (KOA). ☎ 808/327–9520 ⊕ hawaii.gov/koa. **Daniel K. Inouye International Airport.** (HNL). ✉ 300 Rodgers Blvd., Airport Area ☎ 808/836–6411 ⊕ airports.hawaii.gov. **Hilo International Airport (ITO).** ☎ 808/961–9300 ⊕ hawaii. gov/ito. **Hana Airport (HNM).** ✉ 700 Alalele Rd., Hana ☎ 808/872–3830 ⊕ www.airports.hawaii. gov/hnm. **Kahului Airport (OGG).** ✉ 1 Keolani Pl., Kahului ☎ 808/872–3830 ⊕ www.airports.hawaii. gov/ogg. **Kapalua–West Maui Airport (JHM).** ✉ 4050 Honoapiilani Hwy, Lahaina ☎ 808/665–6108 ⊕ www.airports.hawaii. gov/jhm. **Lanai Airport (LNY).** ☎ 808/565–7942 ⊕ www.airports.hawaii. gov/lny. **Lihue Airport (LIH).** ☎ 808/246–1448 ⊕ www.hawaii.gov/ dot/airports. **Molokai Airport (MKK).** ✉ 3980 Airport Loop, Hoolehua ☎ 808/567–9660 ⊕ www. airports.hawaii.gov/mkk. **Waimea-Kohala Airport (MUE).** ☎ 808/887–8126 ⊕ hawaii.gov/mue.

MAINLAND AIRLINE CONTACTS Alaska Airlines. ☎ 800/252–7522 ⊕ www. alaskaair.com. **American Airlines.** ☎ 800/433–7300 ⊕ www.aa.com. **Delta Airlines.** ☎ 800/221–1212 for U.S. reservations, 800/241–4141 for international reservations ⊕ www.delta.com. **Hawaiian Airlines.** ☎ 800/367–5320 ⊕ www.hawaiia-nairlines.com. **Southwest.** ☎ 800/435–9792 ⊕ www. southwest.com. **United Airlines.** ☎ 800/864–8331 for U.S. reservations ⊕ www.united.com.

INTERISLAND AIRLINE CONTACTS Hawaiian Airlines. ☎ 800/367–5320 ⊕ www.hawaiianairlines. com. **Makani Kai Air.** ☎ 808/834–1111, 877/255–8532 ⊕ www.makanikaiair. com. **Mokulele Airlines.** ☎ 866/260–7070 ⊕ www. mokuleleairlines.com.

⛴ Boat and Ferry

Expeditions Lanai Ferry. ☎ 800/695–2624 ⊕ www. go-lanai.com.

🚌 Bus

Hele-On Bus. ☎ 808/961–8744 ⊕ www.heleonbus. org. **Kauai Bus.** ☎ 808/246–8110 ⊕ www.kauai.com/ kauai-bus. **Maui Bus.** ☎ 808/871–4838 ⊕ www. mauicounty.gov/bus.

TROLLEY CONTACTS Waikiki Trolley. ☎ 808/593–2822 ⊕ waikikitrolley.com.

⚠ Emergencies

AAA Help. ☎ 800/222–4357 ⊕ www.hawaii.aaa.com.

🛏 Lodging

Airbnb. ☎ 855/424–7262 ⊕ www.airbnb.com. **Hawaii's Best Bed & Breakfasts.** ☎ 808/885–4550 ⊕ www.bestbnb.com. **HomeAway.** ☎ 877/228–3145 ⊕ www.homeaway. com. **Vacation Rentals By Owner.** ⊕ www.vrbo.com.

📍 Visitor Information

Hawaii Beach Safety. ⊕ hawaiibeachsafety.com. **Hawaii Department of Land and Natural Resources.** ⊕ dlnr.hawaii.gov. **Hawaii Tourism Authority.** ⊕ www. gohawaii.com. **Island of Hawaii Visitors Bureau.** ☎ 800/648–2441 ⊕ www. gohawaii.com/islands/ hawaii-big-island. **Kauai Visitors Bureau.** ✉ 4334 Rice St # 101, Lihue ☎ 808/245–3971 ⊕ www.gohawaii. com/kauai. **Maui Visitors Bureau.** ⊕ www.gohawaii. com/islands/maui.

Oahu Visitors Bureau ⊕ www.gohawaii.com/ islands/oahu.

Chapter 3

OAHU

Updated by Powell Berger,
Marla Cimini, Cheryl Crabtree,
Trina Kudlacek, Anna Weaver

3

◎ Sights	🍴 Restaurants	🛏 Hotels	🛍 Shopping	🍸 Nightlife
★★★★★	★★★★★	★★★★★	★★★★★	★★★★★

WELCOME TO OAHU

TOP REASONS TO GO

★ **Waves:** Body board or surf some of the best breaks on the planet.

★ **Pearl Harbor:** Remember Pearl Harbor with a visit to the *Arizona* Memorial.

★ **Diamond Head:** Scale the crater whose iconic profile looms over Waikiki.

★ **Nightlife:** Raise your glass to the best party scene in Hawaii.

★ **The North Shore:** See Oahu's country-side—check out the famous beaches from Sunset to Waimea bays and hike to the remote tip of the island.

1 Honolulu and Pearl Harbor. The vibrant capital city holds the nation's only royal palace. It also encompasses Waikiki—dressed in lights at the base of Diamond Head—and Pearl Harbor.

2 West (Leeward) and Central Oahu. This rugged western side of the island is finding a new identity as a "second city" of suburban homes, golf courses, and resorts. Central Oahu is an integral part of Hawaii's rich cultural history.

3 North Shore. Best known for its miles of world-class surf breaks and green sea-turtle sightings, the North Shore is home to the legendary laid-back surf town of Haleiwa. This plantation area also boasts farms, restaurants, and hiking trails.

4 Windward (East) Oahu. The sleepy neighborhoods at the base of the majestic Koolau Mountains offer a respite from the bustling city. On the southeastern corner of Oahu, Honolulu's main bedroom communities crawl up the steep-sided valleys that flow into Maunalua Bay.

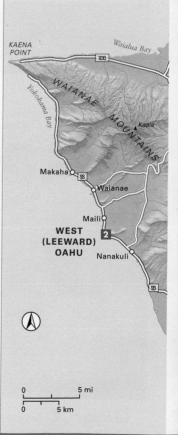

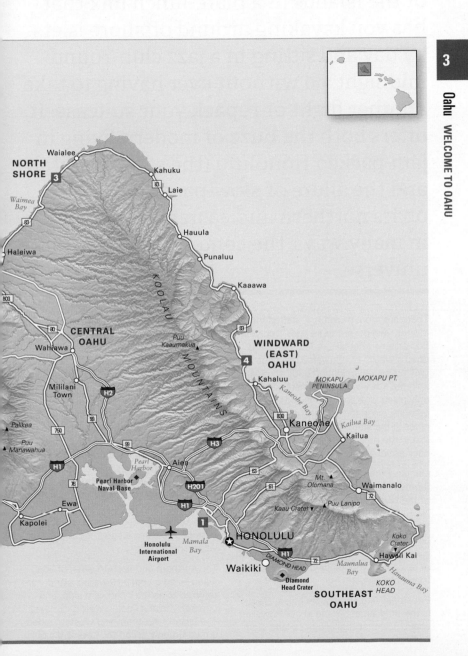

NORTH
SHORE **3**

Waialee

Kahuku

83 Laie

*Waimea
Bay*

83

Haleiwa

Hauula

Punaluu

803

Kaaawa

80

KOOLAU

CENTRAL
OAHU

Wahiawa

*Puu
Kaaumakua* ▲

83

4

WINDWARD
(EAST)
OAHU

Mililani
Town

H2

MOUNTAINS

Kahaluu

*MOKAPU
PENINSULA*

MOKAPU PT.

Palikea
▲

750

99

Kaneohe Bay

830

Kaneohe

Kailua Bay

*Puu
Manawahua* ▲

99

H3

Kailua

H1

*Pearl
Harbor*

Aiea

63

*Mt.
Olomana* ▲

78

H201

Pearl Harbor
Naval Base

61

Puu Lanipo ▲

Waimanalo

72

Ewa

H1

Kaau Crater ▼

*Koko
Crater* ▲

Kapolei

✈
Honolulu
International
Airport

*Mamala
Bay*

⊛ HONOLULU

H1

DIAMOND HEAD

72

Hawaii Kai

Waikiki

1

*Maunalua
Bay*

Hanauma Bay

*KOKO
HEAD*

Diamond
Head Crater

SOUTHEAST
OAHU

Oahu is one-stop Hawaii—all the allure of the Islands in a plate-lunch mix that has you kayaking around offshore islets by day and sitting in a jazz club 'round midnight, all without ever having to take another flight or repack your suitcase. It offers both the buzz of modern living in jam-packed Honolulu (the state's capital) and the allure of slow-paced island life on its northern and eastern shores. It is, in many ways, the center of the Hawaiian universe.

There are more museums, staffed historic sites, and guided tours here than you'll find on any other island. And only here does a wealth of renovated buildings and well-preserved neighborhoods so clearly spin the story of Hawaii's history. It's the only place to experience Islands-style urbanity, since there are no other true cities in the state. And yet you can get as lost in the rural landscape and be as laid-back as you wish.

Oahu is home to Waikiki, the most famous Hawaiian beach, as well as some of the world's most famous surf on the North Shore and Hawaii's best known historical site—Pearl Harbor. If it's isolation, peace, and quiet you want, Oahu might not be for you, but if you'd like a bit of spice with your piece of paradise, this island provides it.

Encompassing 597 square miles, Oahu is the third-largest island in the Hawaiian chain. Scientists believe the island was formed about 4 million years ago by three shield volcanoes: Waianae, Koolau, and the recently discovered Kaena. Recognized in mid-2014, Kaena is the oldest of the three and has long since been submerged 62 miles from Kaena Point on Oahu's northwestern side. Waianae created the mountain range on the western side of the island, whereas Koolau shapes the eastern side. Central Oahu is an elevated plateau bordered by the two mountain ranges, with Pearl Harbor to the south. Several of Oahu's most famous natural landmarks, including Diamond Head and Hanauma Bay, are tuff rings and cinder cones formed during a renewed volcanic stage (roughly 1 million years ago).

The northern and eastern sides of Oahu—and on each Hawaiian island—are referred to as the Windward side, and generally have a cooler, wetter climate. The island's southern and western sides are commonly called the Leeward side, and are typically warmer and more arid. The island's official flower, the little orange *ilima,* grows predominantly in the east, but lei throughout the island incorporate *ilima.* Numerous tropical fish call the reef at Hanauma Bay home, migrating humpback whales can be spotted off the coast past Waikiki and Diamond Head from December through April, spinner dolphins pop in and out of the island's bays, and the 15 islets off Oahu's eastern coast provide refuge for endangered seabirds.

Oahu is the most visited Hawaiian island because early tourism to Hawaii started here. It's also the most inhabited island today—69% of the state's population lives on Oahu—due to job opportunities and the island's military bases. Although Kilauea Volcano on Hawaii was a tourist attraction in the late 1800s, it was the building of the Moana Hotel on Waikiki Beach in 1901 and subsequent advertising of Hawaii to wealthy San Franciscans that really fueled tourism in the Islands. Oahu was drawing tens of thousands of guests yearly when, on December 7, 1941, Japanese Zeros appeared at dawn to bomb Pearl Harbor. Though tourism understandably dipped during the war (Waikiki Beach was fenced with barbed wire), the subsequent memorial only seemed to attract more visitors, and Oahu remains hugely popular with tourists—especially the Japanese—to this day.

Planning

Beaches

Tropical sun mixed with cooling trade winds and pristine waters make Oahu's shores a literal heaven on Earth. But contrary to many assumptions, the island is not one big beach. There are miles and miles of coastline without a grain of sand, so you need to know where you're going to fully enjoy the Hawaiian experience.

Much of the island's southern and eastern coast is protected by inner reefs. The reefs provide still coastline water but not much as far as sand is concerned. However, where there are beaches on the south and east shores, they are mind-blowing. In West Oahu and on the North Shore you can find the wide expanses of sand you would expect for enjoying the sunset. Sandy bottoms and protective reefs make the water an adventure in the winter months. Most visitors assume the seasons don't change a bit in the Islands, and they would be mostly right—except for the waves, which are big on the South Shore in summer and placid in winter. It's exactly the opposite on the north side, where winter storms bring in huge waves, but the ocean becomes glass-like come May and June.

Getting Here and Around

AIR

Honolulu International Airport (HNL) is roughly 20 minutes (9 miles) west of Waikiki (60 minutes during rush hour) and is served by most of the major domestic and international carriers, including Southwest. To travel to other islands from Honolulu, you can depart from either the interisland terminal or the commuter terminal, located in two separate structures adjacent to the main overseas terminal building. A free Wiki-Wiki shuttle bus operates between terminals.

CAR

You can get away without renting a car if you plan on staying in Waikiki. But if you want to explore the rest of the island, there's no substitute for having your own wheels. Avoid the obvious tourist cars—candy-color convertibles, for example—and never leave anything valuable inside, even if you've locked the car. A GPS will save you on phone data and guide you

Great Itineraries

To experience even a fraction of Oahu's charms, you need a minimum of four days and a bus pass or car. The following itineraries will take you to our favorite spots on the island.

First Day in Waikiki

You'll be up at dawn due to the time change and dead on your feet by afternoon due to jet lag. Have a dawn swim, change into walking gear, and head east along Kalakaua Avenue to Monsarrat Avenue toward Diamond Head. Either climb to the summit (about 1½ hours round-trip) or enjoy the view from the lookout. After lunch—there are plenty of options along Monsarrat—take a nap in the shade, do some shopping, or visit the nearby East Honolulu neighborhoods of Moiliili and Kaimuki, rife with small shops and quaint restaurants. End the day with an early and inexpensive dinner at a spot in one of these neighborhood.

Southeast and Windward Exploring

For sand, sun, and surf, follow H1 east to the keyhole-shaped Hanauma Bay for picture-perfect snorkeling, then round the southeast tip of the island with its windswept cliffs and the famous Halona Blowhole. Watch body surfers at Sandy Beach, or walk up the trail leading to the Makapuu Point Lighthouse. If you like, stop in at Sea Life Park. In Waimanalo, stop for a local-style plate lunch, or punch on through to Kailua, where there's intriguing shopping and good eating. Lounge at Lanikai Beach until sunset, then grab dinner at one of the area's many restaurants.

The North Shore

Hit H1 westbound and then H2 to get to the North Shore. You'll pass through pineapple fields before dropping down a scenic winding road to Waialua and Haleiwa. Stop in Haleiwa town to shop, enjoy shave ice, and pick up a guided dive or snorkel trip. On winding Kamehameha Highway, stop at famous big-wave beaches, take a dip in a cove with a turtle, and buy fresh island fruit from roadside stands.

Pearl Harbor

Pearl Harbor is almost an all-day investment. Be on the grounds by 7:30 am to line up for USS *Arizona* Memorial tickets. Clamber all over the USS *Bowfin* submarine. Finally, take the free trolley to see the "Mighty Mo" battleship. If it's Wednesday, Saturday, or Sunday, make the five-minute drive *mauka* (toward the mountains) for bargain-basement shopping at the sprawling Aloha Stadium Swap Meet.

Town Time

If you are interested in history, devote a day to Honolulu's historic sites. Downtown, see Iolani Palace, the Kamehameha Statue, and Kawaiahao Church. A few blocks east, explore Chinatown, gilded Kuan Yin Temple, and artsy Nuuanu with its galleries. On the water is the informative Hawaii Maritime Center. Hop west on H1 to the Bishop Museum, the state's anthropological and archaeological center. And 1 mile up Pali Highway is Queen Emma Summer Palace, whose shady grounds were a royal retreat. The Foster Botanical Garden is worth a visit for plant lovers.

through Oahu's sometimes-confusing streets.

If you are renting a car, reserve your vehicle in advance, especially when traveling during the holidays and summer breaks. This will not only ensure that you get a car but also that you get the best rates. Also, be prepared to pay for parking; almost all hotels in Honolulu (and many outside of Honolulu) charge for parking.

Except for one area around Kaena Point, major highways follow Oahu's shoreline and traverse the island at two points. Rush-hour traffic (6:30–9:30 am and 3:30–6 pm) can be frustrating around Honolulu and the outlying areas. Winter swells also bring traffic to the North Shore, as people hoping to catch some of the surfing action clog the two-lane Kamehameha Highway. Parking along many streets is curtailed during these times, and tow-away zones are strictly enforced. Read curbside signs before leaving your vehicle, even at a meter.

Asking for directions will almost always produce a helpful explanation from the locals, but you should be prepared for an island term or two. Instead of using compass directions, remember that Hawaii residents refer to places as being either *mauka* (toward the mountains) or *makai* (toward the ocean). Other directions depend on your location: in Honolulu, for example, people say to "go Diamond Head," which means toward that famous landmark, or to "go *ewa*," meaning in the opposite direction. A shop on the *mauka*–Diamond Head corner of a street is on the mountain side of the street on the corner closest to Diamond Head. It all makes perfect sense once you get the lay of the land.

Here are some average driving times—without traffic—that will help you plan your excursions.

Driving Times

Waikiki to Ko Olina	1 hour
Waikiki to Haleiwa	45 minutes
Waikiki to Hawaii Kai	25 minutes
Waikiki to Kailua	30 minutes
Waikiki to downtown Honolulu	10 minutes
Waikiki to airport	25 minutes
Kaneohe to Turtle Bay	1 hour
Hawaii Kai to Kailua	25 minutes
Haleiwa to Turtle Bay	20 minutes

Hotels

As in real estate, location matters. And although Oahu is just 44 miles long and 30 miles wide—meaning you can circle the entire island before lunch—it boasts neighborhoods and lodgings with very different vibes and personalities. If you like the action and choices of big cities, consider Waikiki, a 24-hour playground with everything from surf to karaoke bars. Those who want an escape from urban life look to the island's leeward or windward sides or to the North Shore, where the surf culture creates a laid-back atmosphere.

The majority of tourists who come to Oahu stay in Waikiki, but choosing accommodations in downtown Honolulu affords you the opportunity to be close to shopping and restaurants at Ala Moana Center, the largest shopping mall in the state. It also provides easy access to the airport.

If you want to get away from the bustle of the city, contemplate a stay on Oahu's Leeward Coast. Consider the Ko Olina resort area, about 20 minutes from the Honolulu International Airport and 40 minutes from Waikiki. Here, there are great golf courses and quiet beaches and coves that make for a relaxing getaway. But you'll need a car to get off the

86

Where to Stay on Oahu

Neighborhood	Local Vibe	Pros	Cons
Honolulu	Lodging options are limited in downtown Honolulu, but if you want an urban feel or to be near Chinatown, look no farther.	Access to a wide selection of art galleries, boutiques, and new restaurants as well as Chinatown.	No beaches within walking distance. If you're looking to get away from it all, this is not the place.
Waikiki	Lodgings abound in Waikiki, from youth hostels to five-star accommodations. The area is always abuzz with activity, and anything you desire is within walking distance.	You can surf in front of the hotels, wander miles of beach, and explore hundreds of restaurants and bars.	This is tourist central. Prices are high, and you are not going to get the true Hawaii experience.
Windward Oahu	More in tune with the local experience, here is where you'll find most of the island's B&Bs and enjoy the lush side of Oahu.	From beautiful vistas and green jungles, this side really captures the tropical paradise most people envision when dreaming of a Hawaiian vacation.	The lushness comes at a price—it rains a lot on this side. Also, luxury is not the specialty here; if you are looking to get pampered, stay elsewhere.
The North Shore	This is true country living, with one luxurious resort exception. It's bustling in the winter (when the surf is up) but pretty slow-paced in the summer.	Amazing surf and long stretches of sand truly epitomize the beach culture in Hawaii. Historic Haleiwa has enough stores to keep shopaholics busy.	There is no middle ground for accommodations; you're either in backpacker cabanas or $300-a-night suites. There is also zero nightlife, and traffic can get heavy during winter months.
West (Leeward) Oahu	This is the resort side of the rock; there is little outside of these resorts but plenty on the grounds to keep you occupied for a week.	Ko Olina's lagoons offer the most kid-friendly swimming on the island, and the golf courses on this side are magnificent. Rare is the rainy day out here.	You are isolated from the rest of Oahu, with little in the way of shopping or jungle hikes.

property if you want to explore the rest of the island.

Other, more low-key options are on Windward Oahu or the North Shore. Both regions are rustic and charming, with quaint eateries and coffee shops, local boutiques, and some of the island's best beaches. One of Oahu's premier resorts, Turtle Bay, is located here, too.

Nightlife

Oahu is the best of all the Islands for nightlife. The locals call it *pau hana,* but you might call it happy hour (the literal translation of the Hawaiian phrase is "done with work"). On weeknights, it's likely that you'll find the working crowd, still in their business-casual attire, downing chilled beers even before the sun goes down. Those who don't have to wake up in the early morning should change into a fresh outfit and start the evening closer to 10 pm.

On the weekends, it's typical to have dinner at a restaurant before hitting the clubs around 9:30. Some bar-hoppers start as early as 7, but partygoers typically don't patronize more than two establishments a night. That's because getting from one Oahu nightspot to the next usually requires transportation. Happily, cab services are plentiful, and rideshares like Uber and Lyft give Honolulu a San Francisco feel.

You can find a bar in just about any area on Oahu. Most of the clubs, however, are in Waikiki, near Ala Moana, and in Chinatown, near downtown Honolulu. The drinking age is 21 on Oahu and throughout Hawaii. Many bars will admit younger people but will not serve them alcohol. By law, all establishments that serve alcoholic beverages must close by 2 am, although you might get lucky and stumble into a secret all-night party. The only exceptions are those with a cabaret license, which can stay open until 4 am.

■TIP→ Some places have a cover charge of $5–$10, but with many establishments, getting there early means you don't have to pay.

Performing Arts

If all-night dancing isn't for you, Oahu also has a thriving arts and culture scene, with community-theater productions, stand-up comedy, outdoor concerts, film festivals, and chamber-music performances. Major Broadway shows, dance companies, rock stars, and comedians come through the Islands, too. Check local newspapers—the *Honolulu Star-Advertiser* or *Midweek*—for the latest events. Websites like ⊕ *www.frolichawaii.com* and ⊕ *www.honolulumagazine.com* also have great information.

DINNER CRUISES AND SHOWS
Several dinner cruises depart either from the piers adjacent to the Aloha Tower Marketplace in downtown Honolulu or from Kewalo Basin, near Ala Moana Beach Park, and head along the coast toward Diamond Head. There's usually a buffet-style dinner with a local flavor, dancing, drinks, and a sensational sunset. Except as noted, dinner cruises cost approximately $80 to $200, cocktail cruises $40 to $55. Some cruises offer discounts for online reservations. Most major credit cards are accepted. In all cases, reservations are essential. Check the websites for savings of up to 15%.

LUAU
The luau is an experience that everyone, both local and tourist, should have. Today's luau still offer traditional foods and entertainment, but there's often a fun, contemporary flair. With many, you can watch the roasted pig being carried out of its *imu,* a hole in the ground used for cooking food with heated stones.

Luau average around $100 per person—some are cheaper, others twice that amount—and are held around the island, not just in Waikiki. Reservations—and a camera—are a must.

Restaurants

Oahu is undergoing something of a renaissance at both ends of the dining spectrum. You can splurge on world-class contemporary cuisine at destination restaurants and explore local flavors at popular, very affordable holes in the wall. Whatever your taste and budget, you'll find places that pique your interest and palate.

You may wish to budget for a pricey dining experience at the very top of the restaurant food chain, where chefs Alan Wong, Roy Yamaguchi, George Mavroth- alassitis, Chris Kajioka, and others you've seen on the Food Network and Travel Channel put a sophisticated spin on local foods and flavors. Savor dishes that take cues from Japan, China, Korea, the Phil- ippines, the United States, and Europe, then are filtered through an Island sensi- bility. Take advantage of the location, and order the superb local fish—mahimahi, opakaka, ono, and opah.

Spend the rest of your food dollars where budget-conscious locals do: in plate- lunch places and small ethnic eateries, at roadside stands and lunch wagons, or at window-in-the-wall delis. Snack on a *musubi* (a handheld rice ball wrapped with seaweed and often topped with Spam), slurp shave ice with red-bean paste, or order Filipino pork adobo with two scoops of rice and macaroni salad.

Outside Honolulu and Waikiki there are fewer dining options, but restaurants tend to be filled with locals and are cheaper and more casual. Windward Oahu's dining scene has improved great- ly in recent years due to the visitors to Kailua and Lanikai beaches, so everything from plate lunches to Latin foods to creative regional offerings can be found there. Across the rest of the island,

the cuisine is mainly American—great if you're traveling with kids—but there are a handful of Italian and Asian places worth trying as well.

What It Costs in U.S. Dollars			
$	$$	$$$	$$$$
RESTAURANTS			
Under $17	$17–$26	$27–$35	Over $35
HOTELS			
Under $180	$180–$260	$261–$340	Over $340

Shopping

Eastern and Western traditions meet on Oahu, where savvy shoppers find luxury goods at high-end malls and scout tiny boutiques and galleries filled with pottery, blown glass, woodwork, and Hawaiian-print clothing by local artists. This blend of cultures is pervasive in the wide selection of spas as well. Hawaiian *lomilomi* and hot-stone massages are as omnipresent as the orchid and plumeria flowers decorating every treatment room.

Exploring downtown Honolulu, Kailua on the windward side, and the North Shore often yields the most original merchandise. Some of the small stores carry imported clothes and gifts from around the world—a reminder that, on this island halfway between Asia and the United States, shopping is a multicultural experience.

If you're getting a massage at a spa, there's a spiritual element to the *lomilomi* that calms the soul while the muscles release tension. During a hot-stone mas- sage, smooth rocks, taken from the earth with permission from Pele, the goddess of volcanoes, are heated and placed at focal points on the body. Others are covered in oil and rubbed over tired limbs, feeling like powerful fingers. For an alternative, refresh skin with mango scrubs so fragrant they seem edible. Savor the unusual sensation of bamboo tapped against the arches of the feet. Indulge in a scalp massage that makes the entire body tingle. Day spas provide additional options to the self-indulgent services offered in almost every major hotel on the island.

Tours

Guided tours are convenient; you don't have to worry about finding a parking spot or getting admission tickets. Most of the tour guides have taken special classes in Hawaiian history and lore, and many are certified by the state of Hawaii. On the other hand, you won't have the freedom to proceed at your own pace, nor will you have the ability to take a detour trip if something else catches your attention.

BUS AND VAN TOURS
Polynesian Adventure
BUS TOURS | This company leads tours of Pearl Harbor and other Oahu sights and also offers a circle-island tour by motor coach, van, or minicoach. ☎ *808/833–3000, 888/206–4531* ⊕ *www.polyad.com* ✉ *From $51.*

THEME TOURS
Discover Hawaii Tours
BUS TOURS | In addition to circle-island and other Oahu-based itineraries on motor- and minicoaches, this company can also get you from Waikiki to the lava flows of the Big Island or to Maui's Hana Highway and back in one day. ☎ *808/739–7911* ⊕ *www.discoverhawaiitours.com* ✉ *From $50.*

E Noa Tours
BUS TOURS | This outfitter's certified tour guides conduct circle-island, Pearl Harbor, helicopter, and shopping tours. ☎ *808/591–2561, 800/824–8804* ⊕ *www. enoa.com* ✉ *From $29.*

Visitor Information

CONTACTS Hawaii Visitors & Convention Bureau. ☎ *800/464–2924 for brochures* ⊕ *www.gohawaii.com.* **Oahu Visitors Bureau.** ☎ *800/464–2924* ⊕ *www.gohawaii.com/islands/oahu.*

Honolulu and Pearl Harbor

Here is Hawaii's only true metropolis, its seat of government, center of commerce and shipping, entertainment and recreation mecca, a historic site, and an evolving urban area—conflicting roles that engender endless debate and controversy. For the visitor, Honolulu is an everyman's delight: hipsters and scholars, sightseers and foodies, nature lovers and culture vultures all can find their bliss.

Once there was the broad bay of Mamala and the narrow inlet of Kou, fronting a dusty plain occupied by a few thatched houses and the great Pakaka *heiau* (shrine). Nosing into the narrow passage in 1794, British sea captain William Brown named the port Fair Haven. Later, Hawaiians would call it Honolulu, or "sheltered bay." As shipping traffic increased, the settlement grew into a Western-style town of streets and buildings, tightly clustered around the single freshwater source, Nuuanu Stream. Not until piped water became available in the early 1900s did Honolulu spread across the greening plain. Long before that, however, Honolulu gained importance when King Kamehameha I reluctantly abandoned his home on the Big Island to build a stately compound near the harbor in 1804 to better protect Hawaiian interests from the Western incursion.

Two hundred years later, the entire island is, in a sense, Honolulu—the City and County of Honolulu. The city has no official boundaries, extending across the flatlands from Pearl Harbor to Waikiki and high into the hills behind.

The main areas (Waikiki, Pearl Harbor, downtown, Chinatown) have the lion's share of the sights, but greater Honolulu also has a lot to offer. One reason to venture farther afield is the chance to glimpse Honolulu's residential neighborhoods. Types of classic Hawaiian homes include the tiny green-and-white plantation-era house, with its corrugated tin roof, two windows flanking a central door and small porch, and the breezy bungalow, with its swooping Thai-style roofline and two wings flanking screened French doors through which breezes blow into the living room. Note the tangled "Grandma-style" gardens and many *ohana* houses—small homes in the backyard of a larger home or built as apartments perched over the garage, allowing extended families to live together. Carports, which rarely house cars, are the island's version of rec rooms, where parties are held and neighbors sit to "talk story." Sometimes you see gallon jars on the flat roofs of garages or carports: these are pickled lemons fermenting in the sun. Also in the neighborhoods, you find the folksy restaurants and takeout spots favored by locals.

Waikiki and Diamond Head

Waikiki is approximately 3 miles east of downtown Honolulu.

A short drive from downtown Honolulu, Waikiki is Oahu's primary resort area. A mix of historic and modern hotels and condos front the sunny 2-mile stretch of beach, and many have clear views of Diamond Head. The area is home to much of the island's dining, nightlife, and shopping—from posh boutiques to hole-in-the-wall eateries to craft booths at the International Marketplace.

Waikiki was once a favorite retreat for Hawaiian royalty. In 1901, the Moana Hotel debuted, introducing Waikiki as an international travel destination. The region's fame continued to grow when Duke Kahanamoku helped popularize the sport of surfing, offering lessons to visitors at Waikiki. You can see Duke immortalized in a bronze statue, with a surfboard, on Kuhio Beach. Today there is a decidedly "urban resort" vibe here; streets are clean, gardens are manicured, and the sand feels softer than at beaches farther down the coast. At first glance, there isn't much of a local culture—it's mainly tourist crowds—but if you explore the neighborhood, you can still find the relaxed surf-y vibe and friendly "aloha spirit" that has drawn people here for more than a century.

Diamond Head Crater is perhaps Hawaii's most recognizable natural landmark. It got its name from sailors who thought they had found precious gems on its slopes; these later proved to be calcite crystals, a much more common mineral. Hawaiians saw a resemblance in the sharp angle of the crater's seaward slope to the oddly shaped head of the ahi fish and so called it Leahi, though later they Hawaiianized the English name to Kaimana Hila. It is commemorated in a widely known hula—*A ike i ka nani o Kaimana Hila, Kaimana Hila, kau mai i luna* ("We saw the beauty of Diamond Head, Diamond Head set high above").

The sprawling Kapiolani Park lies in the shadow of the Diamond Head Crater, which is just beyond the easternmost limits of Waikiki. King David Kalakaua established the park in 1887, named it after his queen, and dedicated it "to the use and enjoyment of the people." Kapiolani Park is a 500-acre expanse where you can go for a stroll, play all sorts of field sports, enjoy a picnic, see wild animals and tropical fish at the Honolulu Zoo and the Waikiki Aquarium, or hear live music at the Waikiki Shell or the Kapiolani Bandstand.

Bounded by the Ala Wai Canal on the north and west, the beach on the south, and the Honolulu Zoo to the east, Waikiki is compact and easy to walk around. TheBus runs multiple routes here from the airport and downtown Honolulu. By car, finding Waikiki from H1 can be tricky; look for the Punahou exit for the west end of Waikiki and the King Street exit for the eastern end.

For those with a Costco card, the cheapest gas on the island is at the three Costco stations. The one in Honolulu is on Arakawa Street, between Dillingham Boulevard and Nimitz Highway; the one in Waipio is at 94-1231 Ka Uka Boulevard; and the one in Kapolei is at 4589 Kapolei Parkway.

◉ Sights

Diamond Head State Monument and Park

NATURE SITE | Panoramas from this 760-foot extinct volcanic peak, once used as a military fortification, extend from Waikiki and Honolulu in one direction and out to Koko Head in the other, with surfers and windsurfers scattered like confetti on the cresting waves below. This 360-degree perspective is a great orientation for first-time visitors. On a clear day, look east past Koko Head to glimpse the outlines of the islands of Maui and Molokai.

To enter the park from Waikiki, take Kalakaua Avenue east, turn left at Monsarrat Avenue, head a mile up the hill, and look for a sign on the right. Drive through the tunnel to the inside of the crater. The ¾-mile trail to the top begins at the parking lot. Be aware that the hike to the crater is an upward ascent with numerous stairs to climb; if you aren't in the habit of getting occasional exercise, this might not be for you. At the top, you'll find a somewhat awkward scramble through a tunnel and bunker out into the open air, but the view is worth it.

Take bottled water with you to stay hydrated under the tropical sun, as there are no water stations along the hike. ■TIP→ To beat the heat and the crowds, rise early and make the hike before 8 am. As you walk, note the color of the vegetation: if the mountain is brown, Honolulu has been without significant rain for a while; but if the trees and undergrowth glow green, you'll know it's the wet season (winter) without looking at a calendar. This is when rare Hawaiian marsh plants revive on the floor of the crater. Keep an eye on your watch if you're here at day's end: the gates close promptly at 6 pm. ⊠ Diamond Head Rd. at 18th Ave., Diamond Head ☎ 808/587–0300 ⊕ dlnr.hawaii.gov/dsp/parks/oahu/diamond-head-state-monument ⊠ $1 per person, $5 per vehicle (cash only).

Honolulu Zoo

ZOO | FAMILY | The world definitely has bigger and better zoos, but this one, though showing signs of age, is 42 acres covered by well-paved, walkable trails and features a lush garden with tropical flowers. To get a glimpse of the endangered nene, the Hawaii state bird, check out the zoo's Kipuka Nene Sanctuary. A few highlights include a Japanese Giant Salamander habitat, and an ectotherm complex, which houses a Burmese python, elongated tortoises, and a giant African snail. Though many animals prefer to remain invisible—particularly the elusive big cats—the monkeys and elephants appear to enjoy being seen and are a hoot to watch. It's best to get to the zoo right when it opens, because the animals are livelier in the cool of the morning.

Children adore the petting zoo, where they can make friends with a llama or stand in the middle of a koi pond. There's an exceptionally good gift shop. On weekends, the Art on the Zoo Fence, on Monsarrat Avenue on the Diamond Head side outside the zoo, has affordable artwork by local contemporary artists.

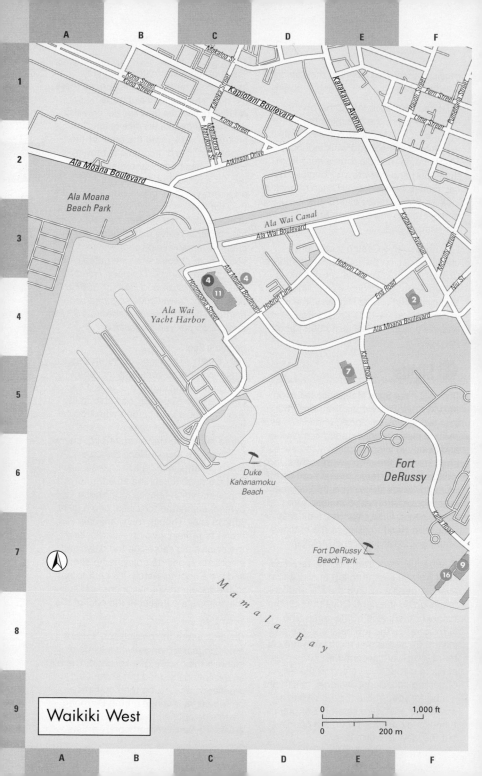

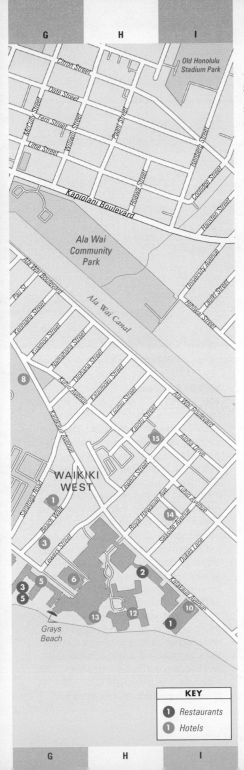

Restaurants ▼

1 Duke's Waikiki.............I8
2 Island Vintage Wine Bar................. H7
3 La Mer G7
4 100 Sails Restaurant & Bar........C4
5 Orchids.................. G8

Hotels ▼

1 The Breakers Hotel..... G6
2 DoubleTree by Hilton Alana - Waikiki Beach............ F4
3 Embassy Suites by Hilton Waikiki Beach Walk G7
4 The Equus C4
5 Halekulani Hotel G7
6 Halepuna Waikiki by Halekulani G7
7 Hilton Hawaiian Village Beach Resort............. E5
8 Luana Waikiki Hotel & Suites........... G5
9 Outrigger Reef Waikiki Beach Resort............. F7
10 Outrigger Waikiki Beach Resort.......................I8
11 Prince Waikiki............C4
12 The Royal Hawaiian, a Luxury Collection Resort, Waikiki H8
13 Sheraton Waikiki........ H8
14 Shoreline Hotel Waikiki I7
15 The Surfjack Hotel & Swim Club............. H6
16 Waikiki Shore F7

KEY

1 Restaurants
1 Hotels

Despite the steep climb, Diamond Head, an extinct volcanic crater on the eastern edge of Waikiki, is one of Honolulu's most popular hiking destinations.

Metered parking is available all along the *makai* (ocean) side of the park and in the lot next to the zoo—but it can fill up early. TheBus makes stops here along the way to and from Ala Moana Center and Sea Life Park (Routes 8 and 22). ✉ *151 Kapahulu Ave., Waikiki* ☎ *808/971–7171* ⊕ *www.honoluluzoo.org* 💲 *$19.*

Kapiolani Bandstand

ARTS VENUE | **FAMILY** | The Victorian-style Kapiolani Bandstand, which was originally built in the late 1890s, is Kapiolani Park's stage for community entertainment and concerts. Founded by King Kamehameha III in 1836, the Royal Hawaiian Band is the nation's only city-sponsored band, and performs free concerts at the bandstand as well as at Iolani Palace and the center stage at Ala Moana Center. Visit the band's website for concert dates, and check event-listing websites and the *Honolulu Star-Advertiser*—Oahu's local newspaper—for event information at the bandstand. ✉ *2805 Monsarrat Ave., Waikiki* ☎ *808/922–5331* ⊕ *www.rhb-music.com.*

Waikiki Aquarium

ZOO | **FAMILY** | This small yet fun attraction harbors more than 3,500 organisms and 500 species of Hawaiian and South Pacific marine life, including an endangered Hawaiian monk seal and a zebra shark. The Living Reef exhibit opened in 2019 and showcases a wall of diverse corals and fascinating reef environments found along Hawaii's shorelines. Check out exhibits on the Northwestern Hawaiian Islands (which explains the formation of the island chain) and Ocean Drifters (about various types of jellyfish). A 60-foot exhibit houses sea horses, sea dragons, and pipefish. A free self-guided mobile audio tour is available via your own smartphone. The aquarium offers activities of interest to adults and children alike, including a focus on the importance of being eco-friendly and keeping our oceans clean. ✉ *2777 Kalakaua Ave., Waikiki* ☎ *808/923–9741* ⊕ *www.waikikiaquarium.org* 💲 *$12.*

⚓ Beaches

The 2-mile strand called Waikiki Beach extends from Hilton Hawaiian Village on one end to Kapiolani Park and Diamond Head on the other. Although it's one contiguous piece of beach, it's as varied as the people that inhabit the Islands. Whether you're an old-timer looking to enjoy the action from the shade or a sports nut wanting to do it all, you can find every beach activity here without ever jumping in the rental car.

Plenty of parking exists on the west end at the Ala Wai Marina, where you can park in metered stalls around the harbor for $1 an hour. For parking on the east end, Kapiolani Park and the Honolulu Zoo also have metered parking for $1 an hour—more affordable than the $10 per hour the resorts want. ■TIP➔ If you're staying outside the area, our best advice is to park at either end of the beach and walk in.

Duke Kahanamoku Beach
BEACH—SIGHT | FAMILY | Named for Hawaii's famous Olympic swimming champion, Duke Kahanamoku, this is a hard-packed beach with the only shade trees on the sand in Waikiki. It's great for families with young children because it has both shade and the calmest waters in Waikiki, thanks to a rock wall that creates a semiprotected cove. The ocean clarity here is not as brilliant as most of Waikiki because of the stillness of the surf, but it's a small price to pay for peace of mind about youngsters. The beach fronts the Hilton Hawaiian Village Beach Resort and Spa. **Amenities:** food and drink; parking (fee); showers; toilets. **Best for:** sunset; walking. ⊠ 2005 Kalia Rd., Waikiki.

★ Fort DeRussy Beach Park
BEACH—SIGHT | FAMILY | This is one of the finest beaches on the south side of Oahu. A wide, soft, ultrawhite beachfront with gently lapping waves makes it a family favorite for running-jumping-frolicking fun. The new, heavily shaded grass grilling area, sand volleyball courts, and aquatic rentals make this a must for the active visitor. This area includes benches as well, if you just want to take a break. The beach fronts Hale Koa Hotel as well as Fort DeRussy. **Amenities:** food and drink; lifeguards; showers; toilets; water sports. **Best for:** swimming; walking. ⊠ 2161 Kalia Rd., Waikiki.

Kahaloa and Ulukou Beaches
BEACH—SIGHT | The beach widens back out here, creating the "it" spot for the bikini crowd—and just about everyone else. This is where you find most of the catamaran charters for a spectacular sail out to Diamond Head, as well as surfboard and outrigger canoe rentals for a ride on the rolling waves of the Canoes surf break. Beachgoers can also rent daily chairs and umbrellas in this area. Great music and outdoor dancing beckon the sand-bound visitor to the lively Duke's restaurant, where shirt and shoes not only aren't required, they're discouraged. The Royal Hawaiian Hotel and the Moana Surfrider are both on this beach. **Amenities:** food and drink; lifeguards; parking (fee); showers; toilets; water sports. **Best for:** partiers; surfing. ⊠ 2259 Kalakaua Ave., Waikiki.

Kuhio Beach Park
BEACH—SIGHT | FAMILY | Featuring a bronze statue of Duke Kahanamoku, the father of modern-day surfing, this lively beach is bordered by a landscaped walkway with a few benches and some shade. It's great for strolls and people-watching any time of day. Check out the Kuhio Beach hula mound Tuesday, Thursday, and Saturday at 6:30 (at 6 November–January) for free hula and Hawaiian-music performances and a torch-lighting ceremony at sunset. Surf lessons for beginners are available from the beach center every half hour. **Amenities:** food and drink; lifeguards; showers; toilets; water sports. **Best for:** surfing; walking. ⊠ 2461

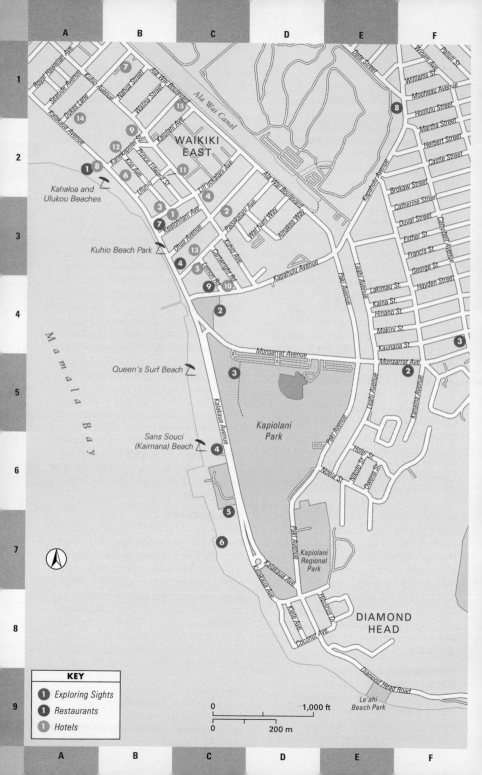

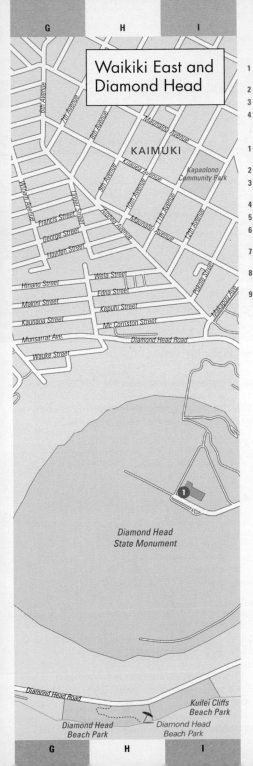

Waikiki East and Diamond Head

KAIMUKI

Kapaolono Community Park

Diamond Head State Monument

Diamond Head Road

Kuilei Cliffs Beach Park

Diamond Head Beach Park

Diamond Head Beach Park

Diamond Head Road

Sights ▼

1 Diamond Head State Monument and Park **I6**
2 Honolulu Zoo **C4**
3 Kapiolani Bandstand **C5**
4 Waikiki Aquarium........**C6**

Restaurants ▼

1 beachhouse at the moana...................**A2**
2 Bogart's Café.............**F5**
3 Diamond Head Market & Grill **F4**
4 d.k Steakhouse...........**C3**
5 Hau Tree Lanai...........**C7**
6 Michel's at the Colony Surf **C7**
7 Morimoto Asia Waikiki **B3**
8 Side Street Inn on Da Strip...............**E1**
9 Teddy's Bigger Burgers...........**C4**

Hotels ▼

1 Alohilani Resort Waikiki Beach...........**B3**
2 Aston at the Waikiki Banyan **C3**
3 Aston Waikiki Beach Tower............**B3**
4 Hilton Waikiki Beach **C2**
5 Hotel Renew..............**C3**
6 Hyatt Regency Waikiki Resort & Spa **B2**
7 Ilima Hotel **B1**
8 Moana Surfrider, A Westin Resort & Spa, Waikiki Beach...........**A2**
9 Ohana Waikiki East by Outrigger................**B2**
10 Queen Kapiolani Hotel.......................**C4**
11 Royal Grove Hotel **B2**
12 Sheraton Princess Kaiulani **B2**
13 Waikiki Beach Marriott Resort & Spa **C3**
14 Waikiki Beachcomber By Outrigger.............**A1**
15 Waikiki Sand Villa Hotel.................**C1**

Waikiki and Honolulu, looking west to Diamond Head, as seen from above

Kalakaua Ave., Waikiki ⊕ Go past Moana Surfrider Hotel to Kapahulu Ave. pier.

Queen's Surf Beach

BEACH—SIGHT | FAMILY | So named as it was once the site of Queen Liliuokalani's beach house, this beach is near the Waikiki Aquarium and draws a mix of locals and tourists of all ages—and it seems as if someone is always playing a steel drum. There are banyan trees for shade and volleyball nets for pros and amateurs alike. It's known as the area's premier body-boarding spot at the break called "The Wall" (as surfing is not allowed here). The water fronting Queen's Surf is also an aquatic preserve, providing the best snorkeling in Waikiki. **Amenities:** lifeguards; showers; toilets. **Best for:** swimming; walking. ⊠ *2598 Kalakaua Ave., Waikiki ⊕ Across from entrance to Honolulu Zoo.*

Sans Souci (Kaimana) Beach

BEACH—SIGHT | FAMILY | Located at the eastern end of Waikiki (across from the zoo), this small rectangle of sand is a good sunning spot for beach lovers of all ages. Usually quieter than the beaches in the heart of town, Sans Souci is favored by locals who wish to avoid the crowds while still enjoying the convenience of Waikiki. There are lifeguards here and children enjoy its shallow, safe waters, which are protected (for now) by the walls of the historic natatorium, an Olympic-size saltwater swimming arena that's been closed for decades. Serious swimmers and triathletes also swim in the channel here, beyond the reef. The New Otani Kaimana Beach Hotel is next door. **Amenities:** lifeguards; parking (fee); showers; toilets. **Best for:** swimming; walking. ⊠ *2776 Kalakaua Ave., Waikiki ⊕ Across from Kapiolani Park, between New Otani Kaimana Beach Hotel and Waikiki War Memorial Natatorium.*

🍴 Restaurants

As Honolulu's tourist hub, Waikiki is dense with restaurants. There are notable steak houses and grills in Waikiki as well, serving upscale American cuisine. But thanks to the many Japanese nationals who stay here, Waikiki is blessed with lots of cheap, filling, authentic Japanese food, particularly noodle houses. Plastic representations of food in the window outside are an indicator of authenticity and a help in ordering. It's not uncommon for a server to accompany a guest outside so that the selection can be pointed to.

beachhouse at the moana

$$$$ | MODERN HAWAIIAN | A truly lovely spot for elegant oceanfront dining, beachhouse serves upscale seafood and modern Hawaiian dishes in a picturesque setting on the veranda of the historical Moana Surfrider Resort, the oldest hotel in Waikiki. Avid fans say the views and romantic location are worth the price. **Known for:** oceanfront dining; gourmet dinners and afternoon tea; romantic setting. $ *Average main: $44* ✉ *Moana Surfrider Hotel, 2365 Kalakaua Ave., Waikiki* ☎ *808/921–4600* ⊕ *www.beachhousewaikiki.com.*

★ Bogart's Café

$$ | AMERICAN | With more than 20 years as a local favorite, Bogart's is an unassuming spot that's situated in a strip mall near Diamond Head and away from the bustle of Waikiki. Offering breakfast, lunch, and a newly introduced dinner service, it's an equally great spot for a bagel or açai bowl in the morning as for a sophisticated, post-sunset dinner. **Known for:** a local favorite for breakfast and lunch; great pasta dishes for dinner; a neighborhood staple. $ *Average main:* ✉ *3045 Monsarrat Ave., Waikiki* ☎ *808/739–0999* ⊕ *www.bogartscafe.com.*

Diamond Head Market & Grill

$ | AMERICAN | Just five minutes from Waikiki hotels is award-winning chef Kelvin Ro's one-stop food shop—indispensable if you have accommodations with a kitchen or if you want a quick grab-and-go meal. Join surfers, beachgoers, and Diamond Head hikers at the takeout window to order gourmet sandwiches and plates such as hand-shape burgers, portobello mushroom sandwiches, Korean kalbi ribs, and grilled ahi with wasabi-ginger sauce, rice, and salad. Grab-and-go selections include sandwiches, bentos, and salads. **Known for:** excellent desserts and scones; picnic fare for the beach; well-priced grab-and-go dinners. $ *Average main: $12* ✉ *3158 Monsarrat Ave., Diamond Head* ☎ *808/732–0077* ⊕ *www.diamondheadmarket.com.*

d.k Steakhouse

$$$$ | STEAKHOUSE | Honolulu has its share of national-chain steak houses, but D.K. Kodama's local steak house serves steaks free from hormones, antibiotics, and steroids straight from Oahu's first dry-aging room. **Known for:** addictive potatoes au gratin topped with Maui onions and Parmesan; local flavors, local ownership, and locally sourced produce and select meats; sunset views from outdoor tables. $ *Average main: $55* ✉ *Waikiki Beach Marriott Resort & Spa, 2552 Kalakaua Ave., Waikiki* ☎ *808/931–6280* ⊕ *www.dksteakhouse.com* ◷ *No lunch.*

Duke's Waikiki

$$$ | AMERICAN | FAMILY | Locals often take visiting friends and family from the mainland to this popular open-air hotel restaurant for the beachfront setting—it's right in front of the famed Canoes surf break in Waikiki—and bar scene and *pupu* (hors d'oeuvres) more than the food. Named for the father of modern surfing and filled with Duke Kahanamoku memorabilia, it offers a large salad bar and a crowd-pleasing menu that includes fish, prime rib, and *huli huli* (rotisserie). **Known for:** iconic local spot with great views, fun bar scene, and perfect location in Waikiki; Duke's on Sunday is so popular that musician Henry Kapono wrote a song about it (Duke's on Sunday); bar seating offers better service. $ *Average main: $28* ✉ *Outrigger Waikiki Beach Resort, 2335 Kalakaua Ave., Waikiki* ☎ *808/922–2268* ⊕ *www.dukeswaikiki.com.*

Hau Tree Lanai

$$$$ | **AMERICAN** | Countless anniversaries, birthdays, and family milestones have been celebrated under this spectacular *hau* tree, where it's said that even Robert Louis Stevenson found shade as he mused and wrote about Hawaii. Still today, diners are captivated by the shade, the beach views, the romantic setting, and a menu that delivers everything from eggs Benedict to a sizzling steak. **Known for:** the romantic beach dining spot folks dream about; spectacular views of the beach and water by day and by night; a solid menu, big portions, and attentive service. $ *Average main: $48* ⊠ *The New Otani Kaimana Beach Hotel, 2863 Kalakaua Ave., Waikiki* ☎ *808/921–7066* ⊕ *www.kaimana.com.*

★ Island Vintage Wine Bar

$$ | **WINE BAR** | Tucked away on the second floor of the Royal Hawaiian Center is a newly opened Island Vintage Wine Bar (a sister restaurant of the nearby bustling Island Vintage café). Stylish and sleek, this fun, cozy spot offers a selection of over 40 different wines by the glass from across the world. **Known for:** vending-machine style wines by the glass; a subdued happy hour; massive Wagyu burgers. $ *Average main: $25* ⊠ *Royal Hawaiian Center , 2301 Kalakaua Ave., Bldg. C, Level 2, Waikiki* ☎ *808/799–9463* ⊕ *www.islandvintagewinebar.com.*

La Mer

$$$$ | **FRENCH** | Well-regarded La Mer is one of the most romantic dining spots on Oahu, with spectacular views of Diamond Head. Featuring neoclassical French cuisine, the restaurant remains a popular "special occasion" restaurant, offering three prix-fixe options (with three-, four-, or seven courses). **Known for:** it doesn't get more romantic than this; an impressive wine list and a sommelier to match; a classy bar scene that includes the romance at a less staggering price. $ *Average main: $160* ⊠ *Halekulani Hotel, 2199 Kalia Rd., Waikiki* ☎ *808/923–2311* ⊕ *www.halekulani.com/la-mer-restaurant* ☉ *No lunch* 👔 *Jacket required.*

Michel's at the Colony Surf

$$$$ | **FRENCH** | Often called Waikiki's most romantic spot, Michel's is an old-school French favorite on Waikiki's tranquil Gold Coast, where you are paying for the spectacular beachside sunset views in addition to the delicious, classic French fare. It opened in 1962, so the ambience seems somewhat dated, with lots of wood and stone and bow-tied servers preparing things like lobster bisque and steak tartare tableside. **Known for:** the sound of the surf and live music most nights; classic French cuisine with some local twists; a pricy experience and a vibe that steps back in time. $ *Average main: $55* ⊠ *Colony Surf, 2895 Kalakaua Ave., Waikiki* ☎ *808/923–6552* ⊕ *www. michelshawaii.com* ☉ *No lunch.*

Morimoto Asia Waikiki

$$$$ | **JAPANESE FUSION** | Locals were surprised when chef Masahara Morimoto vacated the Modern for new digs at the renovated and rebranded Alohilani Resort (formerly the Pacific Beach Hotel), but loyalists have not been disappointed. The sleek space includes an open-air lanai and gorgeous bar, as well as a dining room designed for entertaining clients or celebrating with friends. **Known for:** attentive service and great food; casual elegance in a lovely spot in Waikiki; Asian fusion menu with enough classics to draw loyalists. $ *Average main: $41* ⊠ *Alohilani Resort, 2490 Kalakaua Ave., Waikiki* ☎ *808/922–0022* ⊕ *www.morimotoasiawaikiki.com.*

100 Sails Restaurant & Bar

$$$$ | **ECLECTIC** | **FAMILY** | After the top-to-bottom renovations of the Prince Hotel in 2017, the former Prince Court (known for its buffet and views) has become the 100 Sails, featuring a new take with the same commitment to great food and great views. Slightly more casual than its predecessor, the spacious and airy 100 Sails

continues the everything-you-can-imagine buffet tradition (with crab legs and prime rib, of course) along with plenty of à la carte small bites. **Known for:** international buffet for every meal; views and sunsets to rival any other Waikiki location; high-quality food and a huge selection. $ *Average main: $58* ✉ *Hawaii Prince Hotel Waikiki, 100 Holomoana St., Waikiki* ☎ *808/944–4494* ⊕ *www.princewaikiki. com/dining/honolulu-american-restaurant.*

Orchids

$$$$ | SEAFOOD | Perched along the seawall at historic Gray's Beach, Orchids in the luxe Halekulani resort is open all day—it's a locus of power breakfasters, ladies who lunch, celebrating families at the over-the-top Sunday brunch, and the gamut at dinner. The louvered walls are open to the breezes, sprays of orchids add color, the food is perfectly prepared, and the wine list is intriguing. **Known for:** island breezes, ocean sounds, and five-star service and food; lovely ocean views and live music at sunset; a menu with something for just about everyone. $ *Average main: $42* ✉ *Halekulani Hotel, 2199 Kalia Rd., Waikiki* ☎ *808/923– 2311* ⊕ *www.halekulani.com/dining/ orchids-restaurant.*

Side Street Inn on Da Strip

$$ | ECLECTIC | FAMILY | The original Hopaka Street pub is famous as the place where celebrity chefs gather after hours; this second location is also popular and situated on bustling Kapahulu Avenue, closer to Waikiki. Local-style bar food— salty panfried pork chops with a plastic tub of ketchup, lup cheong fried rice, and passion fruit–glazed ribs—are served in huge, shareable portions. **Known for:** portions that can seemingly feed you for a week; popular local spot with a crowd of regulars; sports-bar feel with lots of fried food. $ *Average main: $20* ✉ *614 Kapahulu Ave., Waikiki* ☎ *808/739–3939* ⊕ *www.sidestreetinn.com* ⊘ *No lunch.*

Teddy's Bigger Burgers

$ | BURGER | Modeled after 1950s diners, this local franchise serves classic moist and messy burgers, along with turkey and veggie burgers, as well as salads, and chicken breast and fish sandwiches. The fries are crisply perfect, and the shakes rich and sweet. **Known for:** messy burgers, great fries, and rich milk shakes; diner-style service, with food to go; dependable quick lunch across the island. $ *Average main: $11* ✉ *Waikiki Grand Hotel, 134 Kapahulu Ave., Waikiki* ☎ *808/926–3444* ⊕ *www.teddysbb.com.*

🛏 Hotels

Hotels in Waikiki range from superluxe resorts to the kind of small, beachy places where shirtless surfers hang out in the lobby. It's where the heart of the visitor action is on Oahu. Those traveling with families might want to take into consideration easy access to the beach, restaurants, and other activities, as parking in the area can sometimes be difficult and pricey. For those looking to be slightly removed from the scene, choose accommodations on the *ewa* (western) end of Waikiki.

★ Alohilani Resort Waikiki Beach

$$$ | HOTEL | Opened in 2018 in the center of Waikiki, the modern, stylish high-rise is across the street from the beach. **Pros:** new and modern; several restaurants in the hotel; great kid's club. **Cons:** resort fee is $45 per day; large hotel and can feel impersonal; you must cross the street for the beach. $ *Rooms from: $275* ✉ *2490 Kalakaua Ave., Waikiki* ☎ *808/922–1233* ⊕ *www.alohilaniresort. com* ⮡ *839 rooms* ⦿ *No meals.*

Aston at the Waikiki Banyan

$$ | RENTAL | FAMILY | Families and active travelers love the convenience and action of this hotel, just a block from Waikiki Beach, the aquarium, the zoo, and bustling Kalakaua Avenue. **Pros:** many rooms have great views with kitchens; walking

distance to shops, beach, restaurants, and activities; fabulous and massive recreation deck for the entire family. **Cons:** rooms are individually owned so conditions can vary greatly; resort fee is $25 per day; sharing hotel with residents. [$] *Rooms from: $200* ✉ *201 Ohua Ave., Waikiki* ☎ *808/922–0555, 877/997–6667 toll-free for reservations* 🌐 *www.aston-waikikibanyan.com* 🛏 *876 suites* 🍴 *No meals.*

Aston Waikiki Beach Tower

$$$$ | **RENTAL** | **FAMILY** | You'll find the elegance of a luxury all-suites condominium combined with the intimacy and service of a boutique hotel in the center of Waikiki. **Pros:** roomy suites with quality amenities; great private lanai and views; a recreation deck with something for everyone. **Cons:** no on-site restaurants; you must cross a busy street to the beach; space, amenities, and location don't come cheap. [$] *Rooms from: $699* ✉ *2470 Kalakaua Ave., Waikiki* ☎ *808/926-6400, 855/776–1766 toll-free* 🌐 *www.astonwaikikibeachtower.com* 🛏 *140 suites* 🍴 *No meals.*

The Breakers Hotel

$ | **RENTAL** | Despite an explosion of high-rise construction all around it, the Breakers continues to transport guests back to 1960s-era Hawaii in this small, low-rise complex about two blocks from the beach. **Pros:** intimate atmosphere with fabulous poolside courtyard; great location; a throwback to a different era. **Cons:** a bit worn down and dated; parking space is extremely limited (but free); showers only. [$] *Rooms from: $170* ✉ *250 Beach Walk, Waikiki* ☎ *808/923–3181, 800/923–7174 toll-free* 🌐 *www.breakers-hawaii.com* 🛏 *63 rooms* 🍴 *No meals.*

Doubletree by Hilton Alana - Waikiki Beach

$$ | **HOTEL** | A convenient location—10 minutes' walk from the Hawaii Convention Center—a professional staff, pleasant public spaces, and a 24-hour business center and small gym draw a global business clientele to this reliable chain hotel. **Pros:** walkable to the beach and Ala Moana mall; walk-in glass showers with oversize rain showerheads; heated outdoor pool and 24-hour fitness center. **Cons:** a 10-minute walk to the beach; little local flavor; resort fee is $30 per day. [$] *Rooms from: $230* ✉ *1956 Ala Moana Blvd., Waikiki* ☎ *808/941–7275* 🌐 *www.hilton.com* 🛏 *317 rooms* 🍴 *No meals.*

Embassy Suites by Hilton Waikiki Beach Walk

$$$ | **RESORT** | **FAMILY** | In a place where space is at a premium, this all-suites resort offers families and groups traveling together a bit more room to move about, with two 21-story towers housing one- and two-bedroom suites. **Pros:** no resort fee; spacious and modern rooms; complimentary hot breakfast and evening reception daily. **Cons:** no direct beach access; lobby feels more like a business hotel; property can seem busy and noisy. [$] *Rooms from: $319* ✉ *201 Beachwalk St., Waikiki* ☎ *800/362–2779 toll-free, 808/921–2345 direct to hotel* 🌐 *www.embassysuiteswaikiki.com* 🛏 *369 suites* 🍴 *Free Breakfast.*

The Equus

$ | **HOTEL** | **FAMILY** | This small, boutique hotel has been completely renovated with a Hawaiian country theme that pays tribute to Hawaii's polo-playing history. **Pros:** casual and fun atmosphere; attentive staff; nicely furnished rooms. **Cons:** busy, hectic area; must cross a major road to get to the beach; resort fee is $25 a day. [$] *Rooms from: $160* ✉ *1696 Ala Moana Blvd., Waikiki* ☎ *808/949–0061* 🌐 *www.equushotel.com* 🛏 *67 rooms* 🍴 *No meals.*

★ Halekulani Hotel

$$$$ | **RESORT** | The luxurious Halekulani exemplifies the translation of its name—the "house befitting heaven"—and from the moment you step into the lobby, the attention to detail and impeccable service wrap you in privilege at this prime beachfront location away from Waikiki's bustle. **Pros:** heavenly interior and exterior spaces; wonderful dining opportunities in-house; no resort fee. **Cons:** might feel a bit formal for Waikiki; pricey; beachfront here is narrow, with little room for sunbathing. ⓢ *Rooms from: $500* ✉ *2199 Kalia Rd., Waikiki* ☎ *808/923–2311 direct to hotel, 800/367–2343 reservations toll-free* ⊕ *www.halekulani.com* ⇆ *453 rooms* ⦿ *No meals.*

★ Halepuna Waikiki by Halekulani

$$$$ | **HOTEL** | Completely renovated and given a new name in late 2019, the former Waikiki Parc makes a contemporary statement, offering the same attention to detail in service and architectural design as its elegant sister hotel, the Halekulani, but without the beachfront location and higher prices. **Pros:** modern, new, and well-appointed; great access to Waikiki Beach and Beach Walk shopping and dining; no resort fee. **Cons:** no direct beach access; rooms can be small; swimming pool can get busy during prime time. ⓢ *Rooms from: $366* ✉ *2233 Helumoa Rd., Waikiki* ☎ *808/921–7272 direct to hotel, 800/422–0450 reservations toll-free* ⊕ *www.halepuna.com* ⇆ *297 rooms* ⦿ *No meals.*

Hilton Hawaiian Village Beach Resort

$$$ | **RESORT** | **FAMILY** | Location, location, location: this mega resort and convention destination sprawls over 22 acres on Waikiki's widest stretch of beach, with the green lawns of neighboring Fort DeRussy creating a buffer zone to the high-rise lineup of central Waikiki. **Pros:** activities and amenities can keep you and the kids busy for weeks; stellar spa; Friday-night fireworks. **Cons:** size of property can be overwhelming; resort fee is $50 per day; parking is expensive ($43 per day for self-parking). ⓢ *Rooms from: $310* ✉ *2005 Kalia Rd., Waikiki* ☎ *808/949–4321, 800/774–1500 toll-free* ⊕ *www. hiltonhawaiianvillage.com* ⇆ *4499 rooms* ⦿ *No meals.*

Hilton Waikiki Beach

$$ | **HOTEL** | Two blocks from Kuhio Beach, this 37-story high-rise, located on the Diamond Head end of Waikiki, is great for travelers who want to be near the action, but not right in it. **Pros:** central location; helpful staff; pleasant, comfortable public spaces. **Cons:** resort fee is $30 per day; very few rooms have views; older property that shows some wear. ⓢ *Rooms from: $219* ✉ *2500 Kuhio Ave., Waikiki* ☎ *808/922–0811 direct to hotel, 888/370–0980 toll-free* ⊕ *www.hiltonwaikikibeach. com* ⇆ *609 rooms* ⦿ *No meals.*

Hotel Renew

$ | **HOTEL** | Located a block from world-famous Waikiki Beach, this stylish boutique hotel is fresh from a 2019 redesign and is focused on wellness and renewal, a chic change from the big resorts that dominate the oceanfront here. **Pros:** free beach supplies, including towels, chairs, umbrellas, and snorkel gear; personalized, upscale service; close to zoo, aquarium, and beach. **Cons:** no pool; daily amenity fee of $25; rooms are on the small side. ⓢ *Rooms from: $159* ✉ *129 Paoakalani Ave., Waikiki* ☎ *808/687–7700, 877/997–6667 toll-free* ⊕ *www.hotelrenew.com* ⇆ *72 rooms* ⦿ *No meals.*

Hyatt Regency Waikiki Resort & Spa

$$$ | **RESORT** | **FAMILY** | This large high-rise hotel, where the lively atrium-style lobby is the focal point, is across the street from Kuhio Beach, but there's no resort between it and the Pacific Ocean. **Pros:** public spaces are open; elegant and very professional spa; kid-friendly and close to the beach. **Cons:** in a very busy and crowded part of Waikiki; on-site pool is quite small; resort fee is $45 per day. ⓢ *Rooms from: $300* ✉ *2424 Kalakaua Ave., Waikiki* ☎ *808/923–1234 direct to hotel, 800/633–7313 toll-free for reservations* ⊕ *www.hyattregencywaikiki.com* ⇆ *1230 rooms* ⦿ *No meals.*

Ilima Hotel

$ | **RENTAL** | Tucked away on a residential side street near Waikiki's Ala Wai Canal, this locally owned, 17-story, condominium-style hotel is a throwback to old Waikiki, offering large units that are ideal for families. **Pros:** free parking in Waikiki is a rarity; great value; free Wi-Fi. **Cons:** furnishings are dated; resort fee is $20 per day; no ocean views. [$] *Rooms from: $160* ✉ *445 Nohonani St., Waikiki* ☎ *808/923–1877, 800/801–9366* 🌐 *www.ilima.com* 🛏 *98 units* 🍴 *No meals.*

Luana Waikiki Hotel & Suites
$$ | **HOTEL** | **FAMILY** | At the entrance to Waikiki near Fort DeRussy is this welcoming hotel offering both rooms and condominium units, all with private lanai. **Pros:** coin-operated laundry facilities on-site; sundeck with barbecue grills; free yoga and folding bicycles. **Cons:** no direct beach access; resort fee is $25 per day; pool is small. [$] *Rooms from: $199* ✉ *2045 Kalakaua Ave., Waikiki* ☎ *808/955–6000 direct to hotel, 855/747-0755 toll-free* 🌐 *www.aquaaston.com* 🛏 *225 units* 🍴 *No meals.*

Moana Surfrider, A Westin Resort & Spa, Waikiki Beach
$$$$ | **RESORT** | This historic beauty—the oldest hotel in Waikiki—is still a wedding and honeymoon favorite, with a sweeping main staircase and Victorian furnishings in its historic (and expensive) Moana Wing; rooms in the 1950s-era Diamond Head Tower and Surfrider tower are more contemporary. **Pros:** elegant, historic property; best place on Waikiki Beach to watch hula and have a drink; can't beat the location. **Cons:** you'll likely dodge bridal parties in the lobby; resort fee is $37 per day; expensive parking ($35/day for self-parking across the street). [$] *Rooms from: $479* ✉ *2365 Kalakaua Ave., Waikiki* ☎ *808/922–3111, 866/716–8112 toll-free* 🌐 *www.moana-surfrider.com* 🛏 *791 rooms* 🍴 *No meals.*

Ohana Waikiki East by Outrigger
$$ | **HOTEL** | If you want to be in central Waikiki and don't want to pay beachfront lodging prices, consider the Ohana Waikiki East. **Pros:** close to the beach and reasonable rates; decent on-site eateries, including a piano bar; in the middle of the Waikiki action. **Cons:** some rooms with no lanai and very basic public spaces; an older property with signs of wear and tear; resort fee is $22 per day. [$] *Rooms from: $229* ✉ *150 Kaiulani Ave., Waikiki* ☎ *808/922–5353 direct to hotel, 866/956–4262 toll-free* 🌐 *www.ohanahotelsoahu.com* 🛏 *441 rooms* 🍴 *No meals.*

Outrigger Reef Waikiki Beach Resort
$$$ | **HOTEL** | **FAMILY** | With a prime oceanfront location, the Outrigger Reef offers an updated experience with an abundance of island flavor. **Pros:** on the beach; direct access to Waikiki Beach Walk; attentive staff. **Cons:** room decor is dated; views from nonoceanfront rooms are uninspiring; resort fee is $35 per day. [$] *Rooms from: $340* ✉ *2169 Kalia Rd., Waikiki* ☎ *808/923–3111 direct to hotel, 866/956–4262 toll-free, 800/688–7444* 🌐 *www.outriggerreef-onthebeach.com* 🛏 *669 rooms* 🍴 *No meals.*

Condo Comforts

The local **Foodland** grocery-store chain has two locations near Waikiki, one in Market City in Kaimuki (✉ *2939 Harding Ave., near intersection with Kapahulu Ave. and highway overpass,* ☎ *808/734–6303*, and the other in the Ala Moana Center (✉ *1450 Ala Moana Blvd.,* ☎ *808/949–5044*). A number of smaller convenience stores are in the middle of Waikiki. One of the best is **Coco Cove** (✉ *2284 Kalakaua Ave.,* ☎ *808/924-6677*), which also sells fresh poke, apparel, beach stuff, and tourist-oriented items.

Outrigger Waikiki Beach Resort

$$$$ | RESORT | FAMILY | Outrigger's star property sits on one of the finest sections of Waikiki Beach and is a visitor favorite for its array of cultural activities, live music, dining options, and bar scene. **Pros:** the best beach bar in Waikiki; shopping, activities, and services abound on the property; on-site coin-operated laundry. **Cons:** a busy property—many people use it as a throughway to the beach; resort fee is $35 per day; rooms are dated. [$] *Rooms from: $450* ✉ *2335 Kalakaua Ave., Waikiki* ☎ *808/923–0711, 808/956–4262, 800/442–7304 toll-free* 🌐 *www.outriggerwaikikihotel.com* 🛏 *525 rooms* 🍴 *No meals.*

Prince Waikiki

$$$$ | HOTEL | This slim, renovated high-rise offers luxury oceanfront rooms and suites overlooking the Ala Wai Yacht Harbor at the *ewa* (western) edge of Waikiki. **Pros:** fantastic views from all rooms; no resort fee; parking included. **Cons:** busy property; no beach access; rooms don't have lanai. [$] *Rooms from: $400* ✉ *100 Holomoana St., Waikiki* ☎ *888/977–4623 toll-free for reservations, 808/956–1111 direct to hotel* 🌐 *www.princewaikiki.com* 🛏 *563 rooms* 🍴 *No meals.*

Queen Kapiolani Hotel

$$$ | HOTEL | After a multimillion-dollar renovation in 2018, the Queen Kapiolani Hotel reopened with a contemporary look combined with a retro nod to the 1970s. **Pros:** incredible Diamond Head views; renovated in 2018; beach gear available at valet desk. **Cons:** resort fee is $40 per day; bathrooms are small and dated despite renovation; noise from pool bar can be bothersome. [$] *Rooms from: $280* ✉ *150 Kapahulu Ave., Waikiki* ☎ *808/650–7841* 🌐 *www.queenkapiolani.com* 🛏 *315 rooms* 🍴 *No meals.*

Royal Grove Hotel

$ | HOTEL | Two generations of the Fong family have put their heart and soul into the operation of this tiny (by Waikiki standards), pink, six-story, hotel that feels like a throwback to the days of boarding houses—an era in which rooms were outfitted for function, not style, and served up with a wealth of simple hospitality at a price that didn't break the bank. **Pros:** very economical Waikiki option; no resort fee; a throwback to another era. **Cons:** no air-conditioning in some rooms; rooms and property are very dated; no on-site parking. [$] *Rooms from: $150* ✉ *151 Uluniu Ave., Waikiki* ☎ *808/923–7691* 🌐 *www.royalgrovehotel.com* 🛏 *87 rooms* 🍴 *No meals.*

★ The Royal Hawaiian, a Luxury Collection Resort, Waikiki

$$$$ | RESORT | There's nothing like the iconic "Pink Palace of the Pacific," which is on 14 acres of prime Waikiki Beach and which has held fast to the luxury and grandeur that first defined it in the 1930s, when it became a favorite of the rich and famous. **Pros:** can't beat it for history; mai tais and sunsets are amazing; luxury in a prime location. **Cons:** resort fee is $38 per day; you'd better like pink; be prepared to share the luxury with brides and galas. [$] *Rooms from: $500* ✉ *2259 Kalakaua Ave., Waikiki* ☎ *808/923–7311, 866/716–8110 toll-free* 🌐 *www.royal-hawaiian.com* 🛏 *528 rooms* 🍴 *No meals.*

Sheraton Princess Kaiulani

$$$ | HOTEL | FAMILY | The Princess Kaiulani sits across the street from the regal Moana Surfrider, without some of the more elaborate amenities (such as a spa or a kid's club), but with rates that are considerably kinder to the wallet. **Pros:** in the heart of everything in Waikiki, with the beach right across the street; beach service with chairs, towels, fruit, and water available; great value for the location. **Cons:** lobby area can feel like Grand Central Station; pool closes at 7 pm; resort fee $33 per day. [$] *Rooms from: $289* ✉ *120 Kaiulani Ave., Waikiki* ☎ *808/922–5811, 866/716–8109 toll-free* 🌐 *www.princess-kaiulani.com* 🛏 *1040 rooms* 🍴 *No meals.*

Sheraton Waikiki

$$$$ | HOTEL | FAMILY | If you don't mind crowds, this enormous hotel that towers over its neighbors on Waikiki could be the place for you. **Pros:** location in the heart of everything; variety of on-site activities and dining options; swimming pools often ranked among the Islands' best. **Cons:** busy atmosphere clashes with laid-back Hawaiian style; resort fee is $35 per day; room sizes and views vary. $ *Rooms from: $409* ✉ *2255 Kalakaua Ave., Waikiki* ☎ *808/922–4422, 866/716–8109 toll-free for reservations* ⊕ *www.sheraton-waikiki. com* ➔ *1636 rooms* ❖ *No meals.*

Shoreline Hotel Waikiki

$$ | HOTEL | Situated right on the bustling Seaside Avenue in Waikiki, this 14-story, 1970s-era, modernist boutique hotel is another old dame that's been brought back to life as an urban-chic property. **Pros:** great location in the middle of bustling Waikiki; no resort fee; hipster decor a refreshing break from old-style Hawaiiana. **Cons:** if splashy colors everywhere aren't your thing, skip it; rooms are small and inconsistent, so ask about the details; pool very small. $ *Rooms from: $250* ✉ *342 Seaside Ave., Waikiki* ☎ *808/931–2444, 855/931–2444 toll-free* ⊕ *www.shorelinehotelwaikiki.com* ➔ *135 rooms* ❖ *No meals.*

The Surfjack Hotel & Swim Club

$$$ | HOTEL | Numerous Waikiki properties have transformed their mid-century digs into hip, 21st-century style, but none has done it as well as this 1960s-inspired boutique hotel with a surfing vibe. **Pros:** hipster, urban-chic vibe that works; retro, locally designed decor; Ed Kenney restaurant on-site. **Cons:** resort fee is $25 per day; far from the beach; rooms can be inconsistent. $ *Rooms from: $290* ✉ *412 Lewers St., Waikiki* ☎ *808/923–8882* ⊕ *www.surfjack.com* ➔ *112 rooms* ❖ *No meals.*

Hotel Cultural Programs 🛏

Hotels, especially in Waikiki, are fueling a resurgence in Hawaiian culture, thanks to repeat visitors who want a more authentic island experience. In addition to lei-making and hula-dancing lessons, you can learn how to strum a ukulele, listen to Grammy Award–winning Hawaiian musicians, watch a revered master *kumu* (teacher) share the art of ancient hula and chant, chat with a marine biologist about Hawaii's endangered species, learn about the island's sustainability efforts, or get a lesson in the art of canoe making.

Waikiki Beach Marriott Resort & Spa

$$$$ | RESORT | FAMILY | On the eastern edge of Waikiki, this flagship Marriott sits on about five acres across from Kuhio Beach and close to Kapiolani Park, the Honolulu Zoo, and the Waikiki Aquarium. **Pros:** stunning views of Waikiki; airy, tropical public spaces; unbeatable location. **Cons:** large impersonal hotel, sometimes confusing to navigate; Kalakaua Avenue can be noisy; resort fee is $37 per day. $ *Rooms from: $350* ✉ *2552 Kalakaua Ave., Waikiki* ☎ *808/922–6611, 800/367–5370 toll-free* ⊕ *www.marriottwaikiki. com* ➔ *1310 rooms* ❖ *No meals.*

Waikiki Beachcomber by Outrigger

$$ | HOTEL | FAMILY | Located almost directly across from the Royal Hawaiian Center and next door to the new and revamped International Market Place, the Beachcomber is a well-situated high-rise hotel for families as well as those looking for a boutique feel in the heart of the action. **Pros:** great beach views from some rooms; renovated and stylish; lovely pool area. **Cons:** very busy area in

the thick of Waikiki action; not beach-front; resort fee is $30 per day. $ Rooms from: $260 ⊠ 2300 Kalakaua Ave., Waikiki ☎ 808/922–4646, 877/418–0711 ⊕ www. waikikibeachcomber.com 🛏 496 rooms ◉ No meals.

Waikiki Sand Villa Hotel
$ | HOTEL | FAMILY | Families and those looking for an economical rate without sacrificing proximity to Waikiki's beaches, dining, and shopping return to the Waikiki Sand Villa year after year. Pros: fun bar; pool and foot spa great for lounging; no resort fee. Cons: the noise from the bar might annoy some; 10-minute walk to the beach; street noise from Ala Wai can get loud. $ Rooms from: $165 ⊠ 2375 Ala Wai Blvd., Waikiki ☎ 808/922–4744, 800/247–1903 toll-free ⊕ www.sandvilla-hotel.com 🛏 214 rooms ◉ No meals.

Waikiki Shore
$$ | RENTAL | FAMILY | Nestled between Fort DeRussy Beach Park and the Out-rigger Reef Resort, this is the only condo hotel directly on Waikiki Beach. Pros: right on the beach; great views from spacious private lanai; units available in different sizes. Cons: units can vary and some are dated; extra cleaning fee can be expensive; two management companies rent here, so ask questions when booking. $ Rooms from: $230 ⊠ 2161 Kalia Rd., Waikiki ☎ 808/952–4500 Castle reservations, 808/922–3871 Outrigger reservations local, 800/688–7444 Outrigger reservations toll-free ⊕ www.castleresorts.com 🛏 168 suites ◉ No meals.

⊙ Nightlife

★ Duke's Waikiki
BARS/PUBS | Making the most of its spot on Waikiki Beach, Duke's is a bustling destination featuring live music everyday. This laid-back bar-and-grill's surf theme pays homage to Duke Kahanamoku, who popularized the sport in the early 1900s. Contemporary Hawaiian musicians like Henry Kapono and Maunalua

have performed here, as have nationally known musicians like Jimmy Buffett. It's not unusual for surfers to leave their boards outside to step in for a casual drink after a long day on the waves. The cocktail menu is filled with island-style drinks: try a sunset sour or coconut mojito while watching the Waikiki waves. ⊠ Outrigger Waikiki, 2335 Kalakaua Ave., Suite 116, Waikiki ☎ 808/922–2268 ⊕ www.dukeswaikiki.com.

Hideout
BARS/PUBS | The Hideout is a mini-oasis on the outdoor lobby level of the Laylow Hotel, one of Waikiki's newer hotels. Technically, it's not a rooftop bar, but with a fire pit (surrounded by sand), tiki torches, comfy couches, and palm trees swaying overhead, it certainly exudes rooftop vibes. The Hideout has a full menu, but it's best to come here for some pre- or postdinner drinks and pupu (a few favorites are poke tacos and pork belly Brussels sprouts). And with a daily happy hour from 4:30 to 6:30 pm, it's easier on your wallet, too. Get the Lime in the Coconut, made with Old Lahaina rum, lime, coconut, and mango boba at the bottom of the martini glass. ⊠ Laylow Hotel, 2299 Kuhio Ave., Waikiki ☎ 808/628–3060 ⊕ www.hideoutwaikiki.com.

Hula's Bar and Lei Stand
DANCE CLUBS | Hawaii's oldest and best-known gay-friendly nightspot offers panoramic views of Diamond Head by day and high-energy club music by night. Check out the all-day happy hour, which starts at 10 am. There's an abundance of drink specials on weekends and discounted pitchers of beer and cocktails on Sunday. There are plenty of great food options, too, including nachos, tacos, pork sliders, and more. Celebrity patrons have included Elton John, Adam Lambert, and Dolly Parton. ⊠ Waikiki Grand Hotel, 134 Kapahulu Ave., 2nd fl., Waikiki ☎ 808/923–0669 ⊕ www.hulas.com.

★ Lewers Lounge

BARS/PUBS | A great spot for predinner drinks or postsunset cocktails, Lewers Lounge offers a relaxed but chic atmosphere in the middle of Waikiki. The menu features a selection of classic and contemporary cocktails. Some standouts include Chocolate Dreams (made with Van Gogh Dutch Chocolate Vodka) and the Lost Passion (featuring a rich blend of tequila, Cointreau, and fresh juices topped with champagne). Enjoy your libation with great nightly live jazz and tempting desserts, such as the hotel's famous coconut cake. Or just sit back and relax in the grand setting of the luxurious lounge, which is decked in dramatic drapes and cozy banquettes. ⊠ *Halekulani Hotel, 2199 Kalia Rd., Waikiki* ☎ *808/923–2311* ⊕ *www.halekulani.com.*

Lulu's Waikiki

BARS/PUBS | Even if you're not a surfer, you'll love this place's retro vibe and the unobstructed second-floor view of Waikiki Beach. The open-air setting, casual dining menu, and tropical drinks are all you need to help you settle into your vacation. The venue transforms from a nice spot for breakfast, lunch, or dinner (happy hour is 3 to 5 pm) to a bustling, high-energy club with live music lasting into the wee hours. ⊠ *Park Shore Waikiki Hotel, 2586 Kalakaua Ave., Waikiki* ☎ *808/926–5222* ⊕ *www.luluswaikiki.com.*

★ Mai Tai Bar at the Royal Hawaiian

BARS/PUBS | The bartenders here sure know how to mix up a killer mai tai. This is, after all, *the* establishment that first made the famous drink in the Islands. The pink umbrella–shaded tables at the outdoor bar are front-row seating for sunsets and also have an unobstructed view of Diamond Head. It's an ideal spot to soak in the island vibes just steps from the sand. Contemporary Hawaiian musicians hold jam sessions onstage nightly. ⊠ *Royal Hawaiian Hotel, 2259 Kalakaua Ave., Waikiki* ☎ *808/923–7311* ⊕ *www.royal-hawaiian.com.*

Moana Terrace

BARS/PUBS | FAMILY | Three floors up from busy Waikiki, this casual, open-air terrace by the Waikiki Beach Marriott Resort & Spa pool is where some of Hawaii's finest musicians play every evening. Check out the daily happy hour specials. Order a drink served in a fresh pineapple (and perhaps a light snack), and watch the sun dip into the Pacific. ⊠ *Waikiki Beach Marriott Resort & Spa, 2552 Kalakaua Ave., Waikiki* ☎ *808/922–6611* ⊕ *www.marriotthawaii.com.*

RumFire

BARS/PUBS | Locals and visitors head here for the convivial atmosphere, trendy decor, and the million-dollar view of Waikiki Beach and Diamond Head. Come early to get a seat for happy hour (3–5 pm daily). If you're feeling peckish, there's a menu of tasty, Asian-influenced small-plates. RumFire also features original cocktails, signature shots, and daily live music. On Friday and Saturday night, the bar gets even livelier once local DJs start spinning at 9:30. ⊠ *Sheraton Waikiki, 2255 Kalakaua Ave., Waikiki* ☎ *808/922–4422* ⊕ *www.rumfirewaikiki.com.*

Sky Waikiki

MUSIC CLUBS | Offering a bird's-eye view of the city and coastline, Sky Waikiki's rooftop bar sits 19 stories above the city, just below Top of Waikiki, the strip's iconic revolving restaurant (and is managed by the same company). From the couches on the welcoming, open-air lanai, you are treated to nearly 360-degree scenic views of Diamond Head, the Waikiki beaches, and the classic coral Royal Hawaiian hotel. It's one of the best spots to take in a Waikiki sunset. The bar offers happy hour drink specials daily, and the club inside exudes contemporary-LA chic every night. Resident DJs spin on Friday and Saturday night. Be sure to order the popular SkyTai cocktail as you enjoy the views. ⊠ *Waikiki Trade Center, 2270 Kalakaua Ave., Waikiki* ☎ *808/979–7590* ⊕ *www.skywaikiki.com.*

The Study

BARS/PUBS | It's tricky to find the Study at the Modern Honolulu—it's behind a huge, revolving bookcase in the lobby across from the registration desk. It's an uberchic space, with intimate alcoves and oversize sofas that are both hip and inviting. The bar features literary-theme cocktails with premium spirits, like the Great Gatsby, the Huckleberry Finn, and the War and Peace. This bar attracts a hip crowd, features live music every night, and has a great weeknight happy hour. ⊠ *The Modern Honolulu, 1775 Ala Moana Blvd., Waikiki* ☎ *808/450–3396 main/hotel number* ⊕ *www.themodernhonolulu.com/the-study.*

Tiki's Grill & Bar

BARS/PUBS | Tiki torches light the way to this fun restaurant and bar overlooking Kuhio Beach. A mix of locals and visitors heads here for happy hour and, later, to enjoy its kitschy cool, casual vibe. There's great nightly entertainment featuring contemporary Hawaiian musicians playing lively and popular cover tunes. The drinks menu is extensive and (not surprisingly) tiki-focused. Don't leave without sipping on the Lava Flow (rum, coconut milk, pineapple juice, strawberry puree) or noshing on the famous coconut shrimp, ahi poke, and macadamia-crusted fish of the day. And if you love the tiki vibe, you can purchase an array of whimsical merchandise, including the colorful tiki mugs. ⊠ *Aston Waikiki Beach Hotel, 2570 Kalakaua Ave., Waikiki* ☎ *808/923–8454* ⊕ *www.tikisgrill.com.*

✪ Performing Arts

DINNER CRUISES AND SHOWS

Magic of Polynesia

MAGIC | **FAMILY** | Hawaii's top illusionist, John Hirokawa, displays mystifying sleight of hand in this highly entertaining show, which incorporates contemporary hula and Islands music into its acts. It's held in the Waikiki Beachcomber by Outrigger's $7½-million showroom. Reservations are required for dinner (nightly at 5:45) and the show (at 7). Menu choices range from ginger sesame glazed chicken to a deluxe steak-and-lobster combo. Walk-ins are permitted if you just want the entertainment. The box office is open daily from noon to 9 pm. ⊠ *Waikiki Beachcomber by Outrigger, 2300 Kalakaua Ave., Waikiki* ☎ *808/971–4321* ⊕ *www.robertshawaii.com/oahu-tours/magic-of-polynesia* ⊡ *Show from $35 per person.*

LUAU

Royal Hawaiian Luau: Aha'aina

ARTS-ENTERTAINMENT OVERVIEW | With traditional island dancing and cultural demonstrations in a beachfront location, the Royal Hawaiian's Aha'aina luau is an entertaining show with hula, fire dancing, great music, and more. The buffet-style dinner includes Hawaiian-inspired specialties and luau favorites. A professional and upscale event, it takes place on the hotel's sprawling oceanfront lawn, a prime location. Luau options range from "cocktail and show" (1½-hour event) to "premium dinner and show" (three-hour event). This luau is scheduled for two nights a week (Monday and Thursday), so be sure to reserve in advance during the high season. ⊠ *The Royal Hawaiian, a Luxury Collection Resort, 2259 Kalakaua Ave., Waikiki* ☎ *808/921–4600* ⊕ *www.royal-hawaiianluau.com* ⊡ *From $85.*

✪ Shopping

There are two distinct types of shopping experiences for visitors: vast malls with the customary department stores and tiny boutiques with specialty items. Three malls in Honolulu provide a combination of the standard department stores and interesting shops showcasing original paintings and woodwork from local artists and craftsmen. Shoppers who know where to look in Honolulu will find everything from designer merchandise to unusual Asian imports.

Possibilities are endless, but a bit of scouting is usually required to get past the items you'll find in your own hometown. Industrious bargain hunters can detect the perfect gift in the sale bin of a slightly hidden store at every mall.

You'll find that shops stay open fairly late in Waikiki. Stores open at around 9 am and many don't close until 10 or even 11 pm.

CLOTHING
Newt at the Royal
CLOTHING | Newt is known for high-quality, handwoven Panama hats and tropical sportswear for men and women. ⊠ *The Royal Hawaiian Hotel, 2259 Kalakaua Ave., Waikiki* ☎ *808/923–4332* ⊕ *www. newtattheroyal.com.*

FOOD
★ Honolulu Cookie Company
FOOD/CANDY | Did someone say "free samples"? To really impress those back home, pick up a box of locally baked, gourmet cookies. Choose from dozens of delicious flavors of premium shortbread delights with a wide variety of sizes, all designed for travel. In addition to the location in the Royal Hawaiian Center, there are a number of these stores in Waikiki, so you probably won't be able to avoid them—even if you try. ⊠ *Royal Hawaiian Center, 2233 Kalakaua Ave., Waikiki* ☎ *808/931–8937.*

GIFTS
Sand People
GIFTS/SOUVENIRS | This cute shop stocks beach-inspired, easy-to-carry gifts, such as fish-shaped Christmas ornaments, Hawaiian-style notepads, frames, charms in the shape of flip-flops (known locally as "slippahs"), soaps, kitchen accessories, ceramic clocks, and other fun island-themed items. There's another branch in the International Marketplace, one in Kailua, as well as three each on Kauai and Maui. ⊠ *Moana Surfrider, 2369 Kalakaua, Waikiki* ☎ *808/924–6773.*

JEWELRY
Philip Rickard
JEWELRY/ACCESSORIES | The heirloom design collection of this famed jeweler highlights custom Hawaiian jewelry, particularly its Wedding Collection, which is often sought by celebrities. Made in many different gold colors and platinum, the jewelry features traditional Hawaiian scrolling patterns, enameled names, and inlays. ⊠ *International Market Place, 2330 Kalakaua Ave., Level 1, Banyan Court, #105, Waikiki* ☎ *808/924–7972* ⊕ *www. philiprickard.com.*

SHOPPING CENTERS
Royal Hawaiian Center
SHOPPING CENTERS/MALLS | An open and inviting facade has made this three-block-long center a garden of Hawaiian shops. There are more than 110 stores and restaurants, including the Apple Store and ABC stores, as well as local gems such as Oiwi Ocean Gear, Fighting Eel, Honolulu Cookie Company, and Koi Honolulu, a cool clothing boutique. Check out tropical Panama hats at Hawaiian Island Arts or offerings at Island Soap & Candleworks, while Royal Hawaiian Quilt offers handmade Hawaiian quilts, pillow covers, kitchen accessories, and more. A number of restaurants at all price points round out the dining options, along with the newly-opened Waikiki Food Hall, complimentary cultural classes, plus a theater and nightly outdoor entertainment. ⊠ *2201 Kalakaua Ave., Waikiki* ☎ *808/922–0588* ⊕ *www.royalhawaiiancenter.com.*

T Galleria by DFS, Hawaii
SHOPPING CENTERS/MALLS | It's all about designer brands here: Hermès, Cartier, Michael Kors, Dior, and Marc Jacobs are among the shops on the Waikiki Luxury Walk in this enclosed mall, as well as Hawaii's largest beauty and cosmetic store. The third floor caters to duty-free shoppers only and features an exclusive Watch Shop. ⊠ *330 Royal Hawaiian Ave., Waikiki* ☎ *808/931–2700* ⊕ *www.dfs. com/en/tgalleria-hawaii.*

Inexpensive Local Souvenirs

Hawaii can be an expensive place. If you are looking to bring someone a gift, consider the following, which can be found all over the island:

Locally published, Hawaii-theme books for children and adults can be found at places like **Na Mea Hawaii/ Native Books** and **Bookends Kailua.**

Try the coconut peanut butter from **North Shore Goodies.** Just when you thought peanut butter couldn't get any better, someone added coconut to it and made it even more delicious.

If you are a fan of plate lunches, **Rainbow Drive-In** has T-shirts with regular orders—"All rice," "Gravy all over," "Boneless"—printed on them. They come packed in an iconic plate lunch box.

Relive your memories of tea on the Veranda by purchasing Island Essence Tea, created by the **Moana Surfrider.**

Harvested from a salt farm on Molokai, **Hawaii Traditional Gourmet Sea Salts** come in a variety of flavors, including black lava, red alaea clay, and classic. They're colored to match their flavor, so they are beautiful as well as tasty.

Foodland makes insulated cooler bags that are decorated with uniquely local designs that go beyond tropical flowers and coconuts. Look for the pidgin or poke designs. **Whole Foods** Hawaii-theme reuseable totes are also very popular.

Made with all-natural, local ingredients, like kukui-nut oil, local flowers, herbs, even seaweed, indigenous bar soap is available online or in stores like **Blue Hawaii Lifestyle.**

2100 Kalakaua

SHOPPING CENTERS/MALLS | The ultimate destination for designer shopping in Hawaii is in an elegant town house–style center known as Luxury Row. Shops include Chanel, Coach, Tiffany & Co., Yves Saint Laurent, Bottega Veneta, Gucci, Hugo Boss, Miu Miu, and Montcler. ⊠ *2100 Kalakaua Ave., Waikiki* ☎ *808/922–2246* ⊕ *www.luxuryrow.com.*

Waikiki Beach Walk

SHOPPING CENTERS/MALLS | This open-air shopping center greets visitors at the west end of Waikiki's Kalakaua Avenue with 70 locally owned stores and restaurants. Get reasonably priced, fashionable resort wear for yourself at Mahina; find unique pieces by local artists at Under the Koa Tree; or buy local delicacies from the Poke Bar. Of course, you can pick up T-shirts, bathing suits, and casual beach attire here as well. And you can also browse Koa and sandalwood gifts at Martin & MacArthur in the nearby Outrigger Reef and Sheraton Waikiki hotels, as well as other locations. The mall also features free local entertainment on the outdoor-fountain stage at least once a week. ⊠ *226 Lewers St., Waikiki* ☎ *808/931–3591* ⊕ *www.waikikibeachwalk.com.*

Pearl Harbor

Pearl Harbor is approximately 9 miles west of downtown Honolulu, beyond Honolulu International Airport.

December 7, 1941. Every American then alive recalls exactly what he or she was doing when the news broke that the Japanese had bombed Pearl Harbor, the catalyst that brought the United States into World War II. Those who are younger have learned about the events of the fateful day, when more than 2,000 people died, and a dozen ships were sunk. Here, in what is still a key Pacific naval base, the attack is remembered every day by thousands of visitors. In recent years, the memorial has been the site of reconciliation ceremonies involving Pearl Harbor veterans from both sides. There are five distinct sights in Pearl Harbor, but only two are part of Pearl Harbor National Memorial. The others are privately operated. It's possible to make reservations for the national park sites at ⊕ *www. recreation.gov.*

◉ Sights

★ *Battleship Missouri* Memorial

MILITARY SITE | The Japanese signed their Terms of Surrender after World War II on the deck of the USS *Missouri,* which was commissioned in 1944 as the last battleship ever built. In 2017, the battleship underwent a $3.5-million renovation (now complete) to replace rusted steel and repaint its upper decks. It's the biggest preservation effort to the *Missouri* since it was dry-docked in 2009 for a $15.5-million top-to-bottom paint job. To begin your visit, pick up tickets online or at the Pearl Harbor Visitor Center. Then board a shuttle bus for the ride to Ford Island. Join a guided tour to learn more about the *Missouri's* long and dramatic history. Near the entrance are a gift shop and a lunch wagon and shave ice stand. ✉ *Ford Island, 63 Cowpens St., Pearl Harbor* ✣ *You cannot drive directly to the USS Missouri; you must take a shuttle bus from Pearl Harbor Visitor Center* ☎ *808/455–1600* ⊕ *ussmissouri.org* 🎫 *From $30* ⊙ *No bags allowed. Storage lockers available at main Pearl Harbor Visitor Center.*

Pearl Harbor Aviation Museum

MUSEUM | The Ford Island museum documents the history of aviation in the Pacific during World War II and is housed in hangars 37 and 79, which survived

the Japanese attack on Pearl Harbor on December 7, 1941. There are a number of interesting (sometimes interactive) displays, including the plane flown by President George H.W. Bush. You can purchase tickets online ahead of time, at the Pearl Harbor Visitor Center or at the museum itself after you get off the shuttle bus, which departs for the museum and the USS *Missouri* from the Pearl Harbor Visitor Center. ✉ *Ford Island, 319 Lexington Blvd., Pearl Harbor* ✣ *You cannot drive directly to the museum; you must take a shuttle bus to Ford Island from the Pearl Harbor Visitor Center* ☎ *808/441–1000* ⊕ *pearlharboraviation-museum.org* 🎫 *$25* ☞ *No bags allowed. Storage lockers available at main Pearl Harbor Visitor Center.*

★ Pearl Harbor Visitor Center

INFO CENTER | The Pearl Harbor Visitor Center reopened after a $58-million renovation and is now the gateway to the Pearl Harbor National Memorial and the starting point for visitors to this historic site. At the visitor center are interpretive exhibits in two separate galleries (*Road to War* and *Attack*) that feature photographs and personal memorabilia from World War II veterans. But there are other exhibits, a bookstore, and a Remembrance Circle, where you can learn about the people who lost their lives on December 7, 1941. Survivors are sometimes on hand to give their personal accounts and answer questions. The visitor center is also where you start your tour of the USS *Arizona* Memorial if you have secured a walk-in or reserved a timed ticket (reserve at ⊕ *www. recreation.gov).* ✉ *Pearl Harbor National Memorial, 1 Arizona Memorial Pl., Pearl Harbor* ☎ *808/954–8759, 866/332–1941 toll-free* ⊕ *pearlharborvisitorcenter.org* 🎫 *Free (timed-entry ticket fee $1)* ☞ *Advanced tickets can be reserved 60 days prior, 1 day prior, and on the day of your desired tour.*

Continued on page 119

USS *West Virginia* (BB48), 7 December 1941

PEARL HARBOR

December 7, 1941. Every American then alive recalls exactly what he or she was doing when the news broke that the Japanese had bombed Pearl Harbor, the catalyst that brought the United States into World War II.

Although it was clear by late 1941 that war with Japan was inevitable, no one in authority seems to have expected the attack to come in just this way, at just this time. So when the Japanese bombers swept through a gap in Oahu's Koolau Mountains in the hazy light of morning, they found the bulk of America's Pacific fleet right where they hoped it would be: docked like giant stepping stones across the calm waters of the bay named for the pearl oysters that once prospered there. More than 2,000 people died that day, including 49 civilians. A dozen ships were sunk.

And on the nearby air bases, virtually every American military aircraft was destroyed or damaged. The attack was a stunning success, but it lit a fire under America, which went to war with "Remember Pearl Harbor" as its battle cry. Here, in what is still a key Pacific naval base, the attack is remembered every day by thousands of visitors, including many curious Japanese, who for years heard little World War II history in their own country. In recent years, the memorial has been the site of reconciliation ceremonies involving Pearl Harbor veterans from both sides.

GETTING AROUND

Pearl Harbor is both a working military base and the most-visited Oahu attraction. Four distinct destinations share a parking lot and are linked by footpath, shuttle, and ferry.

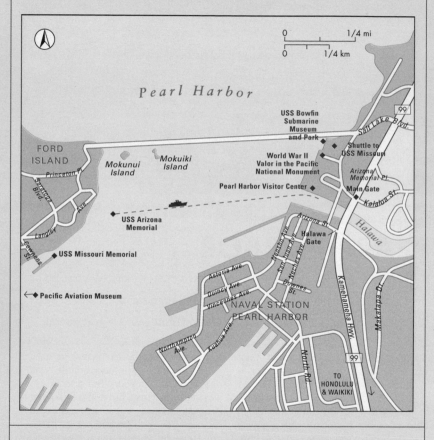

The visitor center is accessible from the parking lot. The *USS Arizona* Memorial itself is in the middle of the harbor; get tickets for the ferry ride at the visitor center. The USS *Bowfin* is also reachable from the parking lot. The USS *Missouri* is docked at Ford Island, a restricted area of the naval base. Vehicular access is prohibited. To get there, take a shuttle bus from the station near the *Bowfin*.

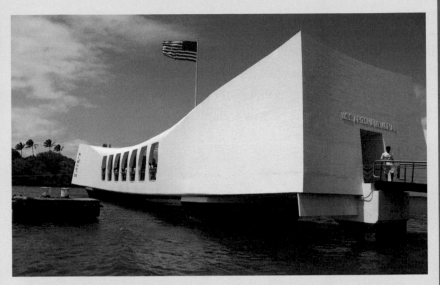

ARIZONA MEMORIAL

Snugged up tight in a row of seven battleships off Ford Island, the USS Arizona took a direct hit that December morning, exploded, and rests still on the shallow bottom where she settled.

The swooping, stark-white memorial, which straddles the wreck of the USS *Arizona*, was designed to represent both the depths of the low-spririted, early days of the war, and the uplift of victory.

A visit here begins at the Pearl Harbor Visitor Center, which recently underwent a $58 million renovation. High definition projectors and interactive exhibits were installed, and the building was modernized. From the visitor center, a ferry takes you to the memorial itself, and a new shuttle hub now gives access to sites that were previously inaccessible, like the USS *Utah* and USS Oklahoma.

A somber, contemplative mood descends upon visitors during the ferry ride to the *Arizona*; this is a place where 1,177 crewmen lost their lives.

Gaze at the names of the dead carved into the wall of white marble. Scatter flowers (but no lei—the string is bad for the fish). Salute the flag. Remember Pearl Harbor.

☎ *808/422–0561*
⊕ *www.nps.gov/valr*

USS *MISSOURI* (BB63)

Together with the Arizona Memorial, the Missouri's presence in Pearl Harbor perfectly bookends America's WWII experience that began December 7, 1941, and ended on the "Mighty Mo's" starboard deck with the signing of the Terms of Surrender.

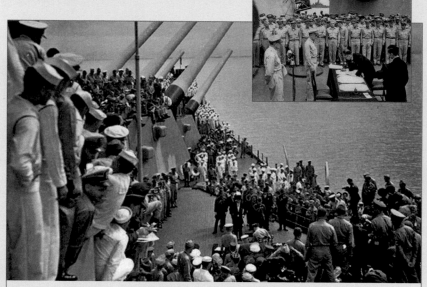

Surrender of Japan, USS Missouri, 2 September 1945

In the parking area behind the USS *Bowfin* Museum, board a shuttle for an eight-minute ride to Ford Island and the teak decks and towering superstructure of the *Missouri*. The last battleship ever built, the *Missouri* famously hosted the final act of WWII, the signing of the Terms of Surrender. The commission that governs this floating museum has surrounded her with buildings tricked out in WWII style with quonset huts serving as shaded eating areas for the nearby lunch wagon and a Victory Store housing a souvenir shop and covered with period mottos ("Don't be a blabateur").

■ TIP→ Definitely hook up with a tour guide (no additional charge) or audio tour—these add a great deal to the experience.

The *Missouri* is all about numbers: 209 feet tall, six 239,000-pound guns, capable of firing up to 23 miles away. Absorb these during the tour, then stop to take advantage of the view from the decks. The Mo is a work in progress, with only a handful of her hundreds of spaces open to view.

☎ *808/455-1600* or ☎ *877/644-4896*
⊕ *www.ussmissouri.org*

USS *BOWFIN* (SS287)

SUBMARINE MUSEUM & PARK

Launched one year to the day after the Pearl Harbor attack, the USS Bowfin sank 44 enemy ships during WWII and now serves as the centerpiece of a museum honoring all submariners.

Although the *Bowfin* no less than the *Arizona* Memorial commemorates the lost, the mood here is lighter. Perhaps it's the childlike scale of the boat, a metal tube just 16 feet in diameter, packed with ladders, hatches, and other obstacles, like the naval version of a jungle gym. Perhaps it's the World War II-era music that plays in the covered patio. Or it might be the museum's touching displays—the penciled sailor's journal, the Vargas girlie posters. Aboard the boat nicknamed "Pearl Harbor Avenger," compartments are fitted out as though "Sparky" was away from the radio room just for a moment, and "Cooky" might be right back to his pots and pans. The museum includes many artifacts to spark family conversations, among them a vintage dive suit that looks too big for Shaquille O'Neal.

A caution: The Bowfin could be hazardous for very young children; no one under four allowed.

☎ *808/423–1341*
⊕ *www.bowfin.org*

PACIFIC AVIATION MUSEUM PEARL HARBOR

This museum opened on December 7, 2006, as as a tribute to aviation in the Pacific. Located on Ford Island in Hangars 37 and 79, actual seaplane hangars that survived the Pearl Harbor attack, the museum is made up of a theater where a short film on Pearl Harbor kicks off the tour, an education center, a shop, and a restaurant. Exhibits—many of which are interactive and involve sound effects— include an authentic Japanese Zero in a diorama setting, vintage aircraft, and the chance to play the role of a World War II pilot using one of six flight simulators. Various aircrafts are employed to narrate the great battles: the Doolittle Raid on Japan, the Battle of Midway, Guadalcanal, and so on. The actual Stearman N2S-3 in which President George H. W. Bush soloed is housed in Hangar 79. ☎ *808/441–1000* ⊕ *www.pacificaviationmuseum.org* 🎫 *$25, $35 with the one-hour Legends of Pearl Harbor add-on, $10.50 extra for flight simulator*

PLAN YOUR PEARL HARBOR DAY LIKE A MILITARY CAMPAIGN

DIRECTIONS

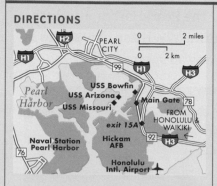

Take H–1 west from Waikiki to Exit 15A and follow signs. Or take TheBus route 20 or 47 from Waikiki. Beware high-priced private shuttles. It's a 30-minute drive from Waikiki.

WHAT TO BRING

Picture ID is required during periods of high alert; bring it just in case.

You'll be standing, walking, and climbing all day. Wear something with lots of pockets and a pair of good walking shoes. Carry a light jacket, sunglasses, hat, and sunscreen.

No purses, packs, or bags are allowed. Take only what fits in your pockets. Cameras are okay but without the bags. A private bag storage booth is located in the parking lot near the visitors' center ($5). Leave nothing in your car; theft is a problem despite bicycle security patrols.

HOURS

Hours are 7 am to 5 pm for the visitor center, though the attractions open at 8 am. The *Arizona* Memorial starts giving out tickets on a first-come, first-served basis at 7 am; the last tickets are given out at 3 pm. Spring break, summer, and holidays are busiest, and tickets sometimes run out by noon or earlier.

TICKETS

Arizona: Free. Add $7.50 for museum audio tours, and $1 if you reserve your ticket in advance online.

Aviation: From $25 adults, from $12 children. Add $10 for aviator's guided tour.

Missouri: $25 adults, $13 children. Add $25 for in-depth, behind-the-scenes tours.

Bowfin: $15 adults, $7 children. Children under 4 may go into the museum but not aboard the *Bowfin*.

A 1-day Passport to Pearl Harbor ticket includes all ships and exhibits, including the USS Arizona audio tour for $72 per adult, $35 per child; plus $1 per ticket for the reservation fee (buy at ⊕ www.recreation.gov).

KIDS

This might be the day to enroll younger kids in the hotel children's program. Preschoolers chafe at long waits, and attractions involve some hazards for toddlers. Older kids enjoy the *Bowfin* and *Missouri*, especially.

MAKING THE MOST OF YOUR TIME

Expect to spend at least half a day; a whole day is better if you're a military history buff.

At the *Arizona* Memorial, you'll get a ticket, be given a tour time, and then have to wait anywhere from 15 minutes to 3 hours. You must pick up your own ticket so you can't hold places. If the wait is long, skip over to the *Bowfin* to fill the time.

SUGGESTED READING

Pearl Harbor and the USS Arizona Memorial, by Richard Wisniewski. $5.95. 64-page magazine-size quick history.

Bowfin, by Edwin P. Hoyt. $14.95. Dramatic story of undersea adventure.

The Last Battleship, by Scott C. S. Stone. $11.95. Story of the Mighty Mo.

★ **USS** *Arizona* **Memorial**

MEMORIAL | The USS *Arizona*, which was destroyed by a Japanese bomber on December 7, 1941, lies precisely where she sank. Your visit begins prosaically—a line, a wait filled with shopping, visiting the museum, and strolling the grounds. You can reserve timed tickets online 60 days in advance or 1 day prior at ⊕ *www. recreation.gov* and skip the wait, which is advisable since this is one of Hawaii's busiest tourist sights, and tickets do sell out. When your tour starts, you watch a short documentary film, then board the ferry to the memorial. At the site, you may scatter flowers in memory of the dead (but no lei—the string is bad for the fish). ⊠ *Pearl Harbor National Memorial, Pearl Harbor* ☎ *808/422–3399* ⊕ *www. nps.gov/valr* ⊠ *Free (advanced reservation timed-entry tickets $1); museum audio tours $8; "deluxe" tour with extra smartphone and virtual reality center access $13; "passport" tour that also includes visiting the Bowfin, Missouri, and Pearl Harbor Aviation Museum $72. Arrive early for limited same-day tickets.*

USS *Bowfin* **Submarine Museum and Park**

MILITARY SITE | The USS *Bowfin* claimed to have sunk 44 enemy ships during World War II and now serves as the centerpiece of a museum honoring all submariners. The submarine, which has been preserved as a museum and is privately owned and operated, includes a good audio tour with admission. Children under four are not allowed on the boat due to safety considerations. ⊠ *11 Arizona Memorial Pl., Pearl Harbor* ☎ *808/423–1341* ⊕ *www.bowfin.org* ⊠ *$15* ⟳ *Tickets available in advance or on arrival.*

Downtown

Honolulu's past and present play a delightful counterpoint throughout the downtown area, which is approximately 6 miles east of Honolulu International Airport. Postmodern glass-and-steel office buildings look down on the Aloha Tower, built in 1926 and, until the early 1960s, the tallest structure in Honolulu. Hawaii's history is told in the architecture of these few blocks: the cut-stone, turn-of-the-20th-century storefronts of Merchant Street; the gracious, white-columned, American-Georgian manor that was the home of the Islands' last queen; the jewel-box palace occupied by the monarchy before it was overthrown; the Spanish-inspired, stucco and tile-roofed, Territorial Era government buildings- and the 21st-century glass pyramid of the First Hawaiian Bank Building.

To reach downtown Honolulu from Waikiki by car, take Ala Moana Boulevard to Alakea Street and turn right; three blocks up on the right, between South King and Hotel streets, there's a municipal parking lot in Alii Place. There are also public parking lots in buildings along Alakea, Smith, Beretania, and Bethel streets (Chinatown Gateway on Bethel Street is a good choice). The best parking downtown, however, is metered street parking along Punchbowl Street—when you can find it.

Another option is to take the highly popular and convenient TheBus to the Aloha Tower Marketplace, or take a trolley from Waikiki.

◉ Sights

★ **Honolulu Museum of Art**

MUSEUM | Originally built around the collection of a Honolulu matron who donated much of her estate to the museum, the academy is housed in a maze of courtyards, cloistered walkways, and quiet, low-ceiling spaces. There's an impressive permanent collection that includes the third-largest collection of Hiroshige's *ukiyo-e* Japanese prints in the country (donated by James Michener); Italian Renaissance paintings; and American and European art by Monet,

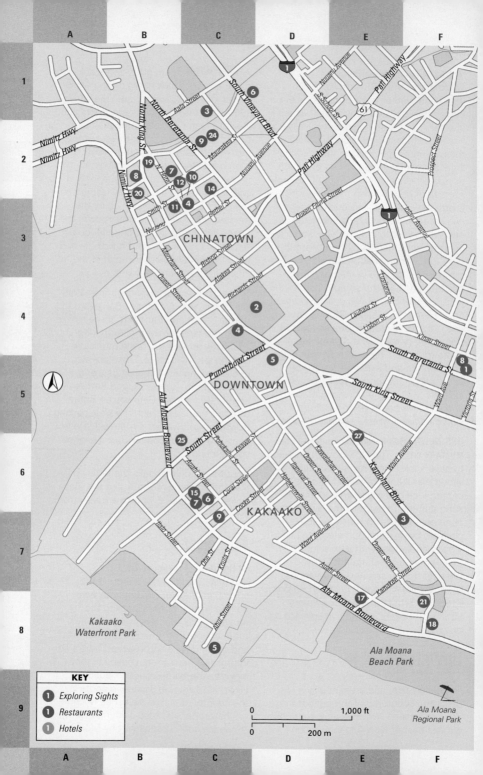

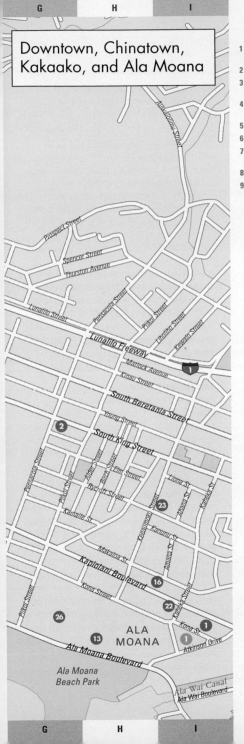

Downtown, Chinatown, Kakaako, and Ala Moana

Sights ▼

1 Honolulu
  Museum of Art...........F5
2 Iolani Palace D4
3 Izumo Taishakyo
  Mission of Hawaii C1
4 Kamehameha I
  Statue C4
5 Kawaiahao Church D5
6 Kuan Yin Temple C1
7 Maunakea
  Marketplace.............B2
8 Oahu Market B2
9 POW! WOW!
  Hawaiian Murals C7

Restaurants ▼

1 Akasaka....................I8
2 Bac Nam.................G6
3 Chef Chai F7
4 Fete.........................C3
5 53 by the Sea C8
6 Hank's Haute Dogs C6
7 Highway Inn
  Kakaako...................C6
8 Honolulu Museum
  of Art Café F5
9 Legend Seafood
  Restaurant................C2
10 Little Village
  Noodle House............C2
11 Livestock Tavern........B3
12 Lucky Belly C2
13 Mariposa H8
14 Mei Sum Chinese
  Dim Sum Restaurant C2
15 Moku Kitchen C6
16 MW Restaurant...........I8
17 Nobu Honolulu E8
18 Panya F8
19 Pho To Chau
  Restaurant...............B2
20 The Pig and
  the Lady..................B3
21 Scratch Kitchen
  & Meatery................F8
22 Shokudo Japanese
  Restaurant & Bar.........I8
23 Sorabol Korean
  Restaurant................I7
24 Terry's Place.............C2
25 Vino Italian Tapas
  & Wine Bar...............C6
26 Vintage Cave
  Honolulu G8
27 Yanagi Sushi.............E5

Hotels ▼

1 Ala Moana Hotel..........I8

Shangri La

The marriage of heiress Doris Duke to a much older man when she was 23 didn't last. But their around-the-world honeymoon did leave her with two lasting loves: Islamic art and architecture, which she first encountered on that journey; and Hawaii, where the honeymooners made an extended stay while Doris learned to surf and befriended islanders unimpressed by her wealth.

Today, visitors to her beloved Oahu home—where she spent most winters—can share both loves by touring her estate. The sought-after tours are coordinated by and begin at the Honolulu Museum of Art in downtown Honolulu. A short van ride then takes small groups on to the house itself, on the far side of Diamond Head. *For more information, see the listing in Southeast Oahu.*

van Gogh, and Whistler, among many others. The newer Luce Pavilion complex, nicely incorporated into the more traditional architecture of the place, has a traveling-exhibit gallery, a Hawaiian gallery, an excellent café, and a gift shop. The Doris Duke Theatre screens art films. This is also the jumping-off point for tours of Doris Duke's striking estate, which is now the Shangri La Museum of Islamic Art, Culture, and Design. If you wish to visit, you should reserve tickets well in advance. ⊠ *900 S. Beretania St., Downtown* ☎ *808/532–8700* ⊕ *www.honolulu-museum.org* ✉ *$20 (free 1st Wed. and 3rd Sun. of month)* ⊗ *Closed Mon.*

★ **Iolani Palace**

CASTLE/PALACE | America's only official royal residence was built in 1882 on the site of an earlier palace. It contains the thrones of King Kalakaua and his successor (and sister) Queen Liliuokalani. Bucking the stereotype of simple island life, the palace had electric lights even before the White House. Downstairs galleries showcase the royal jewelry, as well as a kitchen and offices that have been restored to the glory of the monarchy. The palace is open for guided tours or self-guided audio tours, and reservations are recommended. ■**TIP→ If you're set on taking a guided tour, call or book online for reservations a few days in advance.** Tours

are available only in the mornings and are limited. The palace gift shop and ticket office was formerly the Iolani Barracks, built to house the Royal Guard. ⊠ *364 S. King St., Downtown* ☎ *808/522–0832* ⊕ *www.iolanipalace.org* ✉ *$27 guided tour, $20 audio tour* ⊗ *Closed Sun. (except for monthly Kamaaina Sun.).*

Kamehameha I Statue

PUBLIC ART | Paying tribute to the Big Island chieftain who united all the warring Hawaiian Islands into one kingdom at the turn of the 18th century, this statue, which stands with one arm outstretched in welcome, is one of three originally cast in Paris by American sculptor T. R. Gould. The original statue, lost at sea and replaced by this one, was eventually salvaged and is now in Kapaau, on the Big Island, near the king's birthplace. Each year on the king's birthday (June 11), the more famous copy is draped in fresh lei that reach lengths of 18 feet and longer. A parade proceeds past the statue, and Hawaiian civic clubs, women in hats and impressive long *holoku* dresses, and men in sashes and cummerbunds honor the leader whose name means "The One Set Apart." ⊠ *417 S. King St., outside Aliiolani Hale, Downtown.*

Take a guided tour of Iolani Palace, America's only royal residence, built in 1882.

Kawaiahao Church

RELIGIOUS SITE | Fancifully called Hawaii's Westminster Abbey, this historic house of worship witnessed the coronations, weddings, and funerals of generations of Hawaiian royalty. Each of the building's 14,000 coral blocks was quarried from reefs offshore at depths of more than 20 feet and transported to this site. Interior woodwork was created from the forests of the Koolau Mountains. The upper gallery displays paintings of the royal families. The graves of missionaries and of King Lunalilo are adjacent. Services in English, with songs and prayers in Hawaiian, are held each Sunday. An all-Hawaiian service is held at 5 pm on the second and fourth Sunday of the month (Kawaiahao's affiliation is United Church of Christ). Although there are no guided tours, you can look around the church at no cost. ⊠ *957 Punchbowl St., at King St., Downtown* ☎ *808/469–3000* ⊕ *www.kawaiahao.org* ⌇ *Free.*

🍴 Restaurants

Bac Nam

$ | VIETNAMESE | Tam and Kimmy Huynh's menu is much more extensive than most, ranging far beyond the usual pho and *bun* (cold noodle dishes) found at many Vietnamese restaurants. The no-frills, hole-in-the-wall atmosphere is welcoming and relaxed at this go-to spot for locals, who swear it's the best in town. **Known for:** spring and summer rolls; limited free parking behind the restaurant; excellent crabmeat curry soup. Ⓢ *Average main: $12* ⊠ *1117 S. King St., Ala Moana* ☎ *808/597–8201* ⊙ *Closed Sun.*

Honolulu Museum of Art Café

$$ | AMERICAN | The Honolulu Museum of Art's cool courtyards and galleries filled with works by masters from Monet to Hokusai are well worth a visit and, afterward, so is this popular lunch restaurant. The open-air café is flanked by a burbling water feature and 8-foot-tall ceramic "dumplings" by artist Jun Kaneko—a tranquil setting in the shade of a 75-year-old monkeypod tree in which to eat your salad or sandwich. **Known for:** piadina pesto-caprese flatbread sandwich; limited but beautifully prepared menu of soups, salads, sandwiches, and mains; nice spot for Sunday brunch. $ *Average main: $18* ✉ *Honolulu Museum of Art, 900 S. Beretania St., Downtown* ☎ *808/532–8734* ⊕ *www.honolulumuseum.org/394-museum_cafe* ☾ *Closed Mon. No dinner.*

Yanagi Sushi

$$$ | JAPANESE | One of relatively few restaurants to serve the complete menu until 2 am (until 10 pm on Sunday), Yanagi is a full-service Japanese restaurant offering not only sushi and sashimi around a small bar, but also *teishoku* (combination menus), tempura, stews, and grill-it-yourself shabu-shabu. The fish can be depended on for freshness and variety. **Known for:** late-night happy hour; baked crabmeat volcano roll, spicy shrimp tempura roll, or live abalone sashimi; local favorite. $ *Average main: $28* ✉ *762 Kapiolani Blvd., Downtown* ☎ *808/597–1525* ⊕ *www.yanagisushi-hawaii.com.*

▼ Nightlife

★ Bar Leather Apron

BARS/PUBS | This James Beard Award–nominated bar at this intimate cocktail spot, oddly situated in the mezzanine of a downtown Honolulu office building, seats only six at the bar along with a few other tables. So you'll want to make reservations to enjoy bespoke cocktails that utilize only the finest liquors and ingredients. Owners Tom Park and Justin Park (no relation) have cultivated a reputation for their E Ho'o Pau Mai Tai made with a 5-year-old, raisin-infused El Dorado rum and another, 12-year-old El Dorado rum, as well as coconut water syrup, spiced orgeat, ohia blossom honey, lime, vanilla, and absinthe, and served up with a kiawe wood smoke presentation. The bar is closed on Sunday and Monday. ✉ *Topa Financial Center, 745 Fort St.,* *Mezzanine Level, Suite 127A, Downtown* ☎ *808/524–0808* ⊕ *www.barleatherapron.com.*

Murphy's Bar & Grill

BARS/PUBS | On the edge of Chinatown and the financial district, this bar has served drinks to such locals and visitors as King Kalakaua and Robert Louis Stevenson since the late 1800s. The kind of Irish pub you would find in Boston, Murphy's offers a break from all the tropical, fruit-garnished drinks found in Waikiki, and it's definitely the place to be on St. Patrick's Day. Friendly bartenders and waitstaff serve Guinness on tap, pub food favorites, and Irish specialties like corned beef and cabbage and shepherd's pie. If you time it right, you can try their incredible homemade pies, which are served only on Fridays and quickly sell out. ✉ *2 Merchant St., Downtown* ☎ *808/531–0422* ⊕ *www.murphyshawaii.com.*

⊕ Performing Arts

DINNER CRUISES AND SHOWS

Atlantis Cruises

ENTERTAINMENT CRUISE | The sleekly high-tech *Majestic*, designed to sail smoothly in rough waters, powers farther along Waikiki's coastline than its competitors. Enjoy seasonal whale-watching trips between January and March during the day or year-round sunset cocktail and dinner cruises aboard the 400-passenger boat. (Atlantis is also known for its submarine tours off Waikiki.) The boat's dining room is elegantly laid out, and the standard Hawaii buffet fare will fill you up while you enjoy a tropical cocktail, champagne, beer, or guava juice. Honeymooners and those celebrating anniversaries and birthdays—and even the occasional proposal—are the majority of passengers, and they add to the festive atmosphere along with the live Hawaiian music accompaniment. Make sure to head up to the top deck for the best view of Waikiki and the sunset. ■TIP➔ **For the** sunset cruise, if you plan on having two or more alcoholic beverages plus coffee, tea, or soda, it's worth purchasing the $25 drink package. ⊠ *1 Aloha Tower Rd., Pier 6, Downtown* ☎ *808/973–9800, 800/381–0237* ⊕ *majestichawaii.com* ✉ *From $66.*

Chinatown

Chinatown's original business district was made up of dry-goods and produce merchants, tailors and dressmakers, barbers, herbalists, and dozens of restaurants. The meat, fish, and produce stalls remain, but the mix is heavier now on gift and curio stores, lei stands, jewelry shops, and bakeries, with a smattering of noodle makers, travel agents, Asian-language video stores, and dozens of restaurants.

The name "Chinatown" here has always been a misnomer. Though three-quarters of Oahu's Chinese lived closely packed in these 25 acres in the late 1800s, even then the neighborhood was half Japanese. Today you hear Vietnamese and Tagalog as often as Mandarin and Cantonese, and there are voices of Japan, Singapore, Malaysia, Korea, Thailand, Samoa, and the Marshall Islands, as well.

Perhaps a more accurate name is the one used by early Chinese: Wah Fau (Chinese Port), signifying a landing and jumping-off place. Chinese laborers, as soon as they completed their plantation contracts, hurried into the city to start businesses here. It's a launching point for today's immigrants, too: Southeast Asian shops almost outnumber Chinese; stalls carry Filipino specialties like winged beans and goat meat; and in one tiny space, knife-wielding Samoans skin coconuts to order.

In the half century after the first Chinese laborers arrived in Hawaii in 1851, Chinatown was a link to home for the all-male cadre of workers who planned to return to China rich and respected. Merchants not only sold supplies, they held mail, loaned money, wrote letters, translated documents, sent remittances to families, served meals, offered rough bunkhouse accommodations, and were the center for news, gossip, and socializing.

Although much happened to Chinatown in the 20th century—beginning in January 1900, when almost the entire neighborhood was burned to the ground to halt the spread of bubonic plague—it remains a bustling, crowded, noisy, and odiferous place bent primarily on buying and selling and sublimely oblivious to its status as a National Historic District or the encroaching gentrification on nearby Nuuanu Avenue.

Chinatown occupies 15 blocks immediately north of downtown Honolulu—it's flat, compact, and very walkable.

◉ Sights

Izumo Taishakyo Mission of Hawaii
RELIGIOUS SITE | From Chinatown Cultural Plaza, cross a stone bridge to the Izumo Taishakyo Mission of Hawaii to visit the shrine established in 1906. It honors Okuninushi-no-Mikoto, a *kami* (god) who is believed in Shinto tradition to bring good fortune if properly courted (and thanked afterward). ⊠ *215 N. Kukui St., Chinatown* ✚ *At the canal* ☎ *808/538–7778* ⊕ *izumotaishahawaii.com.*

Kuan Yin Temple
RELIGIOUS SITE | A couple of blocks *mauka* (toward the mountains) from Chinatown is the oldest Buddhist temple in the Islands. Mistakenly called a goddess by some, Kuan Yin, also known as Kannon, is a *bodhisattva*—one who chose to remain on Earth doing good even after achieving enlightenment. Transformed from a male into a female figure centuries ago, she is credited with a particular sympathy for women. You will see representations of her all over the Islands: holding a lotus flower (beauty from the mud of human frailty), as at the temple; pouring out a pitcher of oil (like

mercy flowing); or as a sort of Madonna with a child. Visitors are permitted but be aware this is a practicing place of worship. ✉ *170 N. Vineyard Blvd., Chinatown* ✣ *Park at Foster Botanical Gardens.*

Maunakea Marketplace

MARKET | On the corner of Maunakea and Hotel streets is this busy plaza surrounded by shops and an air-conditioned indoor market and food court where you can buy fresh seafood and local produce in season or chow down on banana lumpia and fresh fruit smoothies and bubble tea (juices and flavored teas with tapioca balls inside). It gets packed every year for the annual Chinese Lunar New Year. ✉ *1120 Maunakea St., Chinatown* 🌐 *geyserholdings.com/maunakea.*

Oahu Market

MARKET | In this tenant-owned market founded in 1904, you'll find a taste of old-style Chinatown, where you might spot a whole butchered pig, head intact, on display and where glassy-eyed fish of every size and hue lie forlornly on ice. Bizarre magenta dragonfruit, ready-to-eat char siu and pork belly, and bins brimming with produce add to Oahu Market's color. You'll find some of the cheapest Oahu prices on fruits and vegetables in this and other Chinatown markets. ✉ *N. King St., Chinatown* ✣ *At Kekaulike St.*

🍴 Restaurants

Fete

$$ | **HAWAIIAN** | Fete slipped into its cozy brick-walled space amid the Chinatown culinary boom in 2016, and it's been packing in regulars ever since. Folks come for the burgers and specials at lunch; for dinner, try one of the pastas, locally sourced seafood, or to-die-for twice-fried Kauai chicken with grits and collard greens. **Known for:** Brooklyn-meets-Hawaii menu; great pau hana/happy hour menu; craft cocktails and extensive drink menu. [$] *Average main: $25* ✉ *2 N. Hotel St., Chinatown* ☎ *808/369–1390* 🌐 *fetehawaii.com.*

Legend Seafood Restaurant

$ | **CHINESE** | At this large Chinatown institution, the dim sum cart ladies stop at your table and show you their Hong Kong–style fare. This is a great place to try dim sum for the first time before going exploring. **Known for:** still-warm custard tarts; dim sum, reasonably priced by the dish; easy parking in the cultural plaza parking lot. [$] *Average main: $13* ✉ *Chinese Cultural Plaza, 100 N. Beretania St., Suite 108, Chinatown* ☎ *808/532–1868* 🌐 *www.legendseafoodhonolulu.com.*

Little Village Noodle House

$$ | **CHINESE** | Unassuming and budget-friendly, Little Village is so popular with locals that it expanded to the space next door. Considered some of the best Chinese food on Oahu, the extensive Pan-Asian menu is filled with crowd-pleasers like honey-walnut shrimp and crispy orange chicken. **Known for:** something for everyone on the menu; fun interior design with village decor; BYOB. [$] *Average main: $18* ✉ *1113 Smith St., Chinatown* ☎ *808/545–3008* 🌐 *www.littlevillagehawaii.com.*

★ Livestock Tavern

$$ | **MODERN AMERICAN** | Livestock Tavern scores big with its seasonal offerings of comfort foods, craft cocktails, and cowboy-minimalist decor. Although meat commands the menu, offerings like burrata, creative salads, sandwiches, and fish round out the possibilities. **Known for:** lively bar scene; go-to lunch spot; fresh-cut fries. [$] *Average main: $20* ✉ *49 N. Hotel St., Chinatown* ☎ *808/537–2577* 🌐 *www.livestocktavern.com* 🕒 *Closed Sun. No lunch Sat.*

Lucky Belly

$$ | **ASIAN** | A hip local crowd sips cocktails and slurps huge bowls of familiar noodle dishes with a modern twist at this popular fusion ramen bar. The service here is unpretentious and attentive if you eat in, but you can also order your food to go. **Known for:** steaming hot pot dishes; small but unique cocktail menu; "Belly Bowl" with smoked bacon, sausage, and pork belly. [$] *Average main: $17* ✉ *50 N. Hotel St., Chinatown* ☎ *808/531–1888* ⏲ *Closed Sun.*

Mei Sum Chinese Dim Sum Restaurant
$ | **CHINESE** | In contrast to the sprawling, noisy halls in which dim sum is generally served, Mei Sum is compact, shiny, and bright, not to mention a favorite of locals who work in the area. Be ready to guess and point at the color photos of dim sum favorites or the items on the carts as they come by, or ask fellow diners for suggestions. **Known for:** deep-fried garlic eggplant; house special garlic rice; dim sum made fresh daily. [$] *Average main: $11* ✉ *1170 Nuuanu Ave., Suite 102, Chinatown* ✣ *Next to post office* ☎ *808/531–3268* 🌐 *meisumdimsum.com.*

Pho To Chau Restaurant
$ | **VIETNAMESE** | Those people lined up on River Street know where to get bowls of steaming *pho* (Vietnamese beef noodle soup) with all the best trimmings. This hole-in-the-wall storefront was the go-to pho spot long before hipsters and foodies found Chinatown. **Known for:** no-frills service and sometimes a wait for food once seated; old school 1970s decor; large pho can be easily shared. [$] *Average main: $10* ✉ *1007 River St., Chinatown* ☎ *808/533–4549* 💳 *No credit cards* ⏲ *No dinner* ☞ *Cash only.*

Terry's Place
$$ | **BISTRO** | This country-style European bistro (formerly known as HASR Bistro) is in a quiet courtyard next to its sister wine shop. Owner Terry Kakazu brings her wine expertise to the menu of classic, elevated comfort food. **Known for:** small plates to share; extensive wine list; great place for groups and celebrations. [$] *Average main: $25* ✉ *31 N. Pauahi St., Chinatown* ☎ *808/533–4277* 🌐 *terrysplace808.com* ⏲ *Closed Sun. and Mon. No lunch.*

★ **The Pig and the Lady**
$$ | **MODERN ASIAN** | Chef Andrew Le's casual noodle house attracts downtown office workers by day and becomes a creative contemporary restaurant at night, pulling in serious chowhounds. Drawing on both his Vietnamese heritage and multicultural island flavors, the talented, playful Le is a wizard with spice and acid, turning out dishes of layered flavor. **Known for:** bahn mi sandwiches at lunch and pho all day; house-made soft-serve custards and sorbets, including unexpected flavors; Hanoi-style egg coffee. [$] *Average main: $20* ✉ *83 N. King St., Chinatown* ☎ *808/585–8255* 🌐 *www.thepigandthelady.com* ⏲ *Closed Sun. and Mon.*

🍸 Nightlife

The Dragon Upstairs
MUSIC CLUBS | Though it was once more cool and jazz-centric, The Dragon Upstairs remains a hole-in-the-wall bar to stop at for an eclectic mix of bands, open mikes, live karaoke, and comedy acts (there's usually a small cover charge for live bands). Tucked above Hank's Cafe Honolulu, this small venue is painted a deep red and decorated with dragons and Chinese theater masks. The bar menu is basic but adequate. It's closed Sunday. ✉ *1038 Nuuanu Ave., Chinatown* ☎ *808/526–1411.*

Encore Saloon
BARS/PUBS | Hawaii isn't a hotbed for quality Mexican cuisine, so when Encore opened in 2016, it was a welcome addition to Chinatown's already buzzing bar and restaurant scene. The mezcal-focused bar also serves good Mexican-inspired food, but its drinks menu is most impressive, offering more than 50 varieties of tequila and mezcal, both of which are distilled from agave. You can also get a traditional margarita here, as well as wine and canned beer. If you're hungry, order the pork carnitas burrito. The bar is closed on Sunday. ✉ *10 N. Hotel St.,*

Chinatown ☎ 808/367–1656 ⊕ encoresa-loon.com.

J. Dolan's

BARS/PUBS | This place bills itself as an Irish pub that serves New York–style pizza. The drinks and rotating beers on tap are just as popular as the pizza since they're reasonably priced by Honolulu standards. The classics are always on the menu in this *Cheers*-like bar, but J.J. Dolan's daily specials are toothsome and inventive. From downtown professionals to local families, these pies are crowd-pleasers. ✉ 1147 Bethel St., Chinatown ☎ 808/537–4992 ⊕ www.jdolans.com.

Manifest

BARS/PUBS | With exposed red brick, big skylights, and rotating exhibitions from local photographers and painters, Manifest Hawaii has an artist's loft feel to it. Café by day, and bar/club/music venue by night, Manifest has both a good cup of Joe and quality cocktails. It's closed on Sunday. ✉ 32 N. Hotel St., Chinatown ⊕ www.manifesthawaii.com.

The Tchin Tchin! Bar

BARS/PUBS | This chill Chinatown bar gets its name from the Chinese expression "qing, qing" (which means "please please"), often used as a toast; soldiers returning from the Chinese Opium Wars introduced it in France and throughout Europe. With an extensive wine menu—by the glass and the bottle—plus a selection of single malt bourbon, whiskey, and scotch, it's an ideal spot for a drink or tapas-style food. The bar's open-air rooftop lanai is the best place to sit, romantically lit with string lights and featuring a large living wall flourishing with ferns. The bar is closed on Sunday and Monday. ✉ 39 N. Hotel St., Chinatown ☎ 808/528–1888 ⊕ www.thetchintchinbar.com.

🛍 Shopping

Louis Pohl Gallery

ART GALLERIES | Stop in this gallery to browse modern works from some of Hawaii's finest artists. In addition to pieces by resident artists, there are monthly exhibitions by local and visiting artists. ✉ 1142 Bethel St., Suite A, Chinatown ☎ 808/521–1812 ⊕ www.louispohlgallery.com.

Kakaako

This 600-acre section of Honolulu between Ala Moana Center and downtown is in the middle of a decade-long redevelopment plan that began in 2012; it remains a neighborhood in transition. Now home to everything from ramshackle mechanic shops to the University of Hawaii's medical school, Kakaako's old warehouses and mom-and-pop storefronts are being replaced by gleaming luxury condos, shops, and restaurants. Many new condo buildings in the Ward/Kakaako area have already been finished, and others grow taller by the day or are about to break ground. It's also home to new big-box stores like T.J. Maxx, as well as smaller local boutiques. Every month seems to bring new happenings such as the Honolulu Night Market, a pop-up shopping event.

👁 Sights

POW! WOW! Hawaii Murals

PUBLIC ART | The POW! WOW! Worldwide art collective was founded in Hawaii in 2010 and has now spread to nearly 20 cities around the world. Its most visible form on Oahu are several blocks colorful, eclectic, and innovative murals on the sides of once-derelict looking warehouses and other buildings. Every year around Valentine's Day, artists from all over come to refresh and add new murals to the collection, and the event wraps up with a big food, art, and entertainment festival centered at the SALT at Kakaako complex. Grab a bite to eat, and wander around any time of the year to take in this unique street art. ✉ *Kakaako* ✣ *Murals are centered on Cooke, Auahi, and Pohukaina Sts.* ☎ *808/223–7462* 🌐 *powwowhawaii.com.*

🍴 Restaurants

53 by the Sea

$$$$ | CONTEMPORARY | Housed in a McVilla aimed at attracting a Japanese wedding clientele, this restaurant serves contemporary Continental food that focuses primarily on beautifully plated, well-prepared standards—albeit with a million-dollar view of Honolulu. Perched at water's edge, with famed surf break Point Panic offshore, 53 by the Sea uses its setting to great advantage—the crescent-shape dining room faces the sea, so even if you're not at a table nestled against the floor-to-ceiling windows, you have a fine view. **Known for:** odd villa decor that somehow works; free valet parking; wedding chapel on-site in case the mood strikes. [$] *Average main: $50* ✉ *53 Ahui St., Kakaako* ☎ *808/536–5353* 🌐 *53bythesea.com.*

Hank's Haute Dogs

$ | HOT DOG | FAMILY | Owner Hank Adaniya's idea of a hot dog involves things like a duck and foie gras sausage with truffle mustard and stone fruit compote. Originally a true hole-in-the-wall, the gentrified Hank's is still a tiny spot where you can go classic with the Chicago Dog, made with the traditional fixings (including neon-green relish), or gourmet with the butter-seared lobster sausage topped with garlic-relish aioli. **Known for:** 11 varieties of dogs daily, plus another five or so daily specials; fries, truffle fries, and onion rings to die for; part of Kakaako's SALT area. [$] *Average main: $9* ✉ *324 Coral St., Kakaako* ☎ *808/532–4265* 🌐 *www.hankshautedogs.com* ☞ *Remember to get parking validated.*

Highway Inn Kakaako

$ | MODERN HAWAIIAN | FAMILY | Highway Inn serves up what it does best: local favorites like Kalbi ribs, *kalua* (roasted in an underground oven) pork sliders, beef stew, and old-fashioned hamburger steaks. For those looking to try *poi* (the puddinglike dish made of pounded taro), this is a good spot. **Known for:** Kakaako location is in SALT complex; relatively close to the cruise terminal; signature combo plates. [$] *Average main: $16* ✉ *680 Ala Moana Blvd., Kakaako* ☎ *808/954–4955* 🌐 *myhighwayinn.com.*

Moku Kitchen

$$ | HAWAIIAN | FAMILY | In the hip SALT complex, Moku's draws locals, including both foodies and families, as well as visitors looking for authentic farm-to-table cuisine in a laid-back, urban setting. One of legendary chef Peter Merriman's restaurants, Moku focuses on upcountry farm fare cooked in the on-site rotisserie; locally sourced pizzas, salads, and sandwiches; and an impressive list of craft cocktails and beers. **Known for:** twice-daily happy hour (3–5:30 pm and 9–11 pm); impressive list of craft cocktails, wine, and beer, including the signature monkeypod mai tai; live music almost nightly. [$] *Average main: $20* ✉ *SALT at Our Kakaako, 660 Ala Moana Blvd., Kakaako* ☎ *808/591–6658* 🌐 *www.mokukitchen.com.*

Nobu Honolulu

$$$$ | JAPANESE FUSION | Always a local favorite, Nobu's move from Waikiki to a chic Ward high-rise has only made it better. Still anchored in its award-winning "New Style" Japanese cuisine, the restaurant serves up signature Nobu dishes found at all the restaurants along with original Hawaii options like Kurobuta pork belly and ahi poke. **Known for:** casual elegance at serious prices; black cod lacquered with sweet den miso and yellowtail sashimi with jalapeño; a bar scene that rarely disappoints. [$] *Average main: $38* ✉ *Waiea at Ward Village, 1118 Ala*

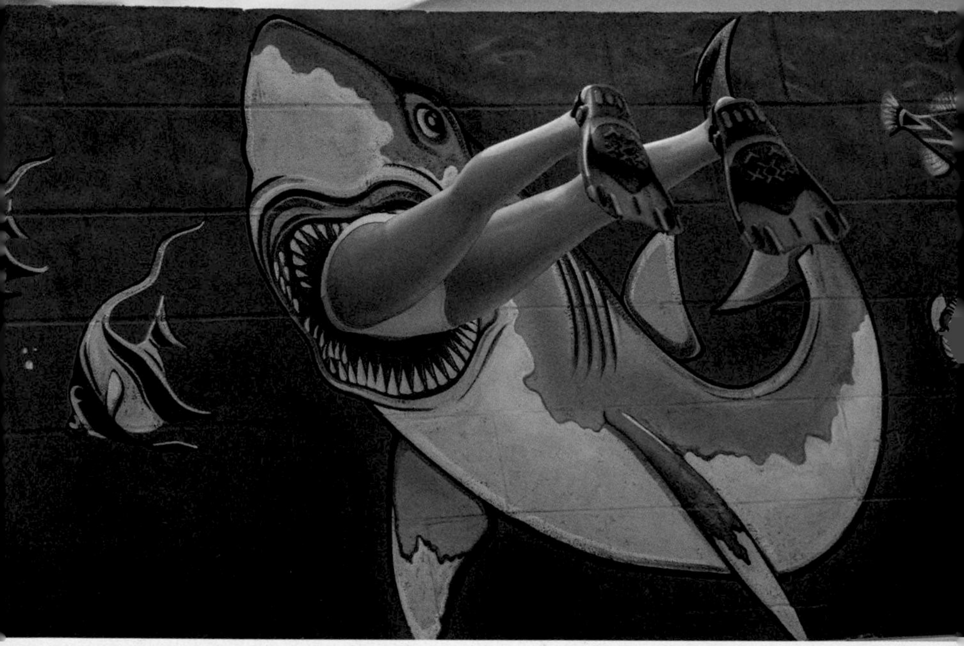

You won't soon forget the eye-popping murals the Pow! Wow! collective has painted on the buildings in the redeveloping Kakaako neighborhood.

Moana Blvd., Kakaako ☎ *808/237–6999* 🌐 *www.noburestaurants.com* 🕑 *No lunch.*

Panya

$$ | **ECLECTIC** | This easy-breezy café run by Hong Kong–born sisters Alice and Annie Yeung offers a crowd-pleasing menu of contemporary American (salads, sandwiches, pastas) and Asian (Thai-style steak salad, Japanese-style fried chicken, Singaporean seafood *laksa*), served in a disco-tinged space (there's also a full bar). They're also known for their pastries, dessert, and happy hour. **Known for:** French-style pastries and cakes; eclectic and extensive menu; Japanese cheesecake. [$] *Average main: $18* ✉ *1288 Ala Moana Blvd., Kakaako* ☎ *808/946–6388* 🌐 *panyabistro.com.*

Scratch Kitchen & Meatery

$$ | **MODERN AMERICAN** | Tucked into the chic South Shore Market in Kakaako's Ward Village, this former Chinatown spot has moved uptown with its hipster decor, open kitchen, and creative comfort food. It's popular for breakfast and brunch and has both small plates and generous entrées on its dinner menu. **Known for:** milk 'n' cereal pancakes; spicy (and good) chicken and waffles; large portions. [$] *Average main: $18* ✉ *South Shore Market at Ward Village, 1170 Auahi St., Kakaako* ✥ *Enter on side of building, along Queen St.* ☎ *808/589–1669* 🌐 *scratch-hawaii.com.*

Vino Italian Tapas & Wine Bar

$$ | **WINE BAR** | Vino has a lock on local oenophiles and pau hana time groups, who make a beeline for this wine bar and restaurant. Chef Keith Endo creates his take on contemporary Mediterranean-inspired cuisine, including house-made pastas, sausage and cheese, all paired with wines selected by the nationally recognized sommelier Chuck Furuya. **Known for:** regular wine-food pairing dinners; jumbo shrimp in a resonant cioppino sauce; great happy hour spot. [$] *Average main: $25* ✉ *Waterfront Plaza, 500 Ala Moana Blvd., Suite 6F, Kakaako* ☎ *808/524–8466* 🌐 *www.vinohawaii.com* 🕑 *Closed Mon. No lunch.*

Nightlife

Aloha Beer Co.

BREWPUBS/BEER GARDENS | At this cool brewpub, you order everything at the counter and then pick a spot to sit in either the industrial indoor taproom or the casual outdoor area. (The HI Brau Room upstairs, which has its own speak-easy-style entrance, is definitely worth checking out for unique cocktails, too.) With 12 beers on draft, including the Hop Lei IPA, Waimanalo Farmhouse, Froot Loops, and Portlock Porter, you can find something to your taste. If you're hungry, there's also pretty good food—snacking boards, hearty sandwiches, small plates, and steak frites—to nosh on. ⊠ *700 Queen St., Kakaako* ☎ *808/544–1605* ⊕ *www.alohabeer.com.*

★ Bevy

BARS/PUBS | Tucked at the end of a row of new boutiques in Kakaako, Bevy is urban, modern, and furnished with up-cycled materials (its benches are upholstered in denim jeans, and its table tops feature flattened wine boxes). Locals in the know go for artisan cocktails created by owner and award-winning mixologist Christian Self, who deftly concocts libations with obscure ingredients and complex flavors. One happy hour (4–7 pm) bright spot is the $1.50 oyster shooters. There's a live DJ on Friday and Saturday night, but the bar is closed on Sunday. (Next door is Taco-ako, Self's street taco lunch spot.) ⊠ *675 Auahi St., Kakaako* ☎ *808/594–7445* ⊕ *www.bevyhawaii.com.*

★ Waikiki Brewing Company

BREWPUBS/BEER GARDENS | This company not only brews its own quality craft beer but also serves delicious food. Although the original is still operational in Waikiki at 1945 Kalakaua Avenue, this second location opened in 2017. The brewery always offers nine beers on tap, including the Skinny Jeans IPA and the Hana Hou Hefe, to which orange peel and strawberry puree are added before fermentation.

You can also buy six-packs at the bar to go. What makes this location unique is that the chef smokes meat in-house using local kiawe wood, resulting in tender and flavorful beef brisket, pulled pork, chicken, and bratwurst. Accompanying barbecue sauces are made with Waikiki Brewing beer. ⊠ *831 Queen St., Kakaako* ☎ *808/591–0387* ⊕ *waikikibrewing.com.*

🛍 Shopping

Anne Namba Designs

CLOTHING | This designer combines the beauty of classic kimonos with contemporary styles to make unique pieces for career and evening. In addition to women's apparel, she designs a men's line. ⊠ *324 Kamani St., Kakaako* ☎ *808/589–1135* ⊕ *annenamba.com.*

Ala Moana

Ala Moana abuts Waikiki to the east (stopping at the Ala Wai Canal) and King Street to the north. Kakaako, Kewalo Basin Harbor, and the Blaisdell Center complex roughly mark its western edge. Probably its most notable attraction is the sprawling Ala Moana Center, jam-packed with almost any store you could wish for.

🏖 Beaches

Honolulu proper only has one beachna. Popular with locals, it hosts everything from Dragon Boat competitions to the Aloha State Games.

Ala Moana Regional Park (*Ala Moana Beach Park*)

BEACH—SIGHT | FAMILY | A protective reef makes Ala Moana essentially a ½-mile-wide saltwater swimming pool. Very smooth sand and no waves create a haven for families and stand-up paddle surfers. After Waikiki, this is the most popular beach among visitors, and the free parking area can fill up quickly on sunny weekend days. On the Waikiki side is a peninsula called Magic Island, with shady trees and paved sidewalks ideal for jogging. Ala Moana Beach Park (officially know as Ala Moana Regional Park) also has playing fields, tennis courts, and a couple of small ponds for sailing toy boats. The beach is for everyone, but only in the daytime; after dark it's a high-crime area, with lots of homeless people. **Amenities:** food and drink; lifeguards; parking (free); showers; toilets. **Best for:** swimming; walking. ✉ *1201 Ala Moana Blvd., Ala Moana.*

🍴 Restaurants

Akasaka

$$ | **JAPANESE** | Step inside this tiny sushi bar tucked between the strip clubs behind the Ala Moana Hotel, and you'll swear you're in an out-of-the-way Edo neighborhood in some indeterminate time. Don't be deterred by its dodgy neighbors or its reputation for inconsistent service. **Known for:** popular spot for late-night food; spicy tuna roll; no pretense, nothing fancy. [$] *Average main: $21* ✉ *1646 B Kona St., Suite B, Ala Moana* ☎ *808/942–4466.*

Chef Chai

$$$ | **FUSION** | This contemporary dining room in a condo building on the edge of Kakaako offers an eclectic, global fusion of seafood, meats, and creative starters and salads, with a focus on healthier options. Situated right across from Blaisdell Arena and Concert Hall, Chef Chai's is the go-to spot before and after the theater and concerts. **Known for:** early-bird and prix-fixe menu options that will leave you stuffed; ahi tartare with avocado mousse in miniwaffle cones; excellent desserts. [$] *Average main: $30* ✉ *Pacifica Honolulu, 1009 Kapiolani Blvd., Ala Moana* ☎ *808/585–0011* 🌐 *www.chefchai.com* ⏲ *Closed Mon.*

Mariposa

$$$ | **ASIAN** | Yes, the popovers and the wee cups of bouillon are there at lunch, but in every other regard, the menu at this Neiman Marcus restaurant departs from the classic model, incorporating a clear sense of Pacific place. The breezy, open-air veranda, with a view of Ala Moana Beach Park, twirling ceiling fans, and life-size hula-girl murals say Hawaii. **Known for:** extensive cocktail menu; corn chowder; lovely interiors reminiscent of Hawaii plantation days. [$] *Average main: $35* ✉ *Neiman Marcus, Ala Moana Center, 1450 Ala Moana Blvd., Ala Moana* ☎ *808/951–3420* 🌐 *neimanmarcushawaii.com/Restaurants/Mariposa.htm.*

★ MW Restaurant

$$$ | **HAWAIIAN** | The "M" and "W" team of husband-and-wife chefs Michelle Karr-Ueko and Wade Ueko bring together their collective experience (20 years alongside chef Alan Wong, a side step to the famed French Laundry, and some serious kitchen time at comfort food icon Zippy's) to create a uniquely local menu with a decidedly upscale twist. But don't overlook dessert. **Known for:** scrumptious desserts (save room); small bar that turns out nice craft cocktails; excellent fish dishes. [$] *Average main: $35* ✉ *1538 Kapiolani Blvd., Suite 107, Ala Moana* ✣ *Behind strip shopping center; walk down side to lights in back* ☎ *808/955–6505* 🌐 *www.mwrestaurant.com.*

Shokudo Japanese Restaurant & Bar

$$ | **JAPANESE** | With a soaring ceiling, crazy red mobile sculpture, contemporary Japanese grazing plates, fruity vodka "sodas," and hungry young people, Shokudo is a culinary house of fun ranging from new-wave fusion dishes to more traditional noodle bowls and sushi. Do get the signature honey toast for dessert—a hollowed-out loaf of Japanese sandwich bread stuffed with cubes of its toasted innards and vanilla ice cream that's drizzled with honey. **Known for:** honey toast for dessert; sushi pizza; popular, but losing charm for old-timers with hit-or-miss service. [$] *Average main: $21* ✉ *Ala Moana Pacific Center, 1585*

Kapiolani Blvd., Ala Moana ☎ *808/941–3701* 🌐 *www.shokudojapanese.com.*

Sorabol Korean Restaurant
$$ | **KOREAN** | Open 24 hours a day on weekends and until 1 am on weeknights, with a tiny parking lot and a maze of booths and private rooms, Sorabol offers a vast menu encompassing the entirety of day-to-day Korean cuisine, plus sushi. It's great for wee hour "grinds" (local slang for food): *bibimbap* (veggies, meats, and eggs on steamed rice), *kalbi* and *bulgogi* (barbecued meats), meat or fish *jun* (thin fillets battered with egg then fried), and kimchi pancakes. **Known for:** late-night dining; simple but good Korean food; inconsistent service. [$] *Average main: $24* ✉ *805 Keeaumoku St., Ala Moana* ☎ *808/947–3113* 🌐 *www.sorabolhawaii.com.*

★ Vintage Cave Honolulu
$$$$ | **CONTEMPORARY** | Vintage Cave is a luxurious, pricey, art-filled reinvention of what was once the brick-lined basement of Shirokyua department store. The restaurant now offers two options: the more casual, Italian-focused Vintage Cave Café (for mere mortals) and the ultraluxe French-Japanese fusion Vintage Cave Club for those seeking an over-the-top experience. **Known for:** an elaborate dining experience with attentive service; dress-to-impress, though a jacket is no longer mandatory for men; Wagyu beef. [$] *Average main: $300* ✉ *Ala Moana Shopping Center, 1450 Ala Moana Blvd., Suite 2250, Level B, Row D, Ala Moana* ☎ *808/441–1744* 🌐 *vintagecave.com.*

Hotels

Ala Moana Hotel
$$$ | **HOTEL** | A decent value in a pricey hotel market, this well-located hotel is connected to Oahu's largest mall, the Ala Moana Center, by a pedestrian ramp and is a 10-minute walk to Waikiki. **Pros:** great value (and no resort fee); refreshed pool deck, lobby, and a new Starbucks; quick walk to the beach, convention center, and shopping. **Cons:** outside the heartbeat of Waikiki; smaller and older rooms in Kona Tower; expensive parking. [$] *Rooms from: $269* ✉ *410 Atkinson Dr., Ala Moana* ☎ *808/955–4811, 866/488–1396* 🌐 *www.alamoanahotelhonolulu.com* 🛏 *1100 rooms* 🍴 *No meals.*

Nightlife

Makai Bar
BARS/PUBS | After a long day of shopping at Ala Moana Center, the fourth-floor Makai Bar (formerly known as the Mai Tai Bar) is a perfect spot to relax. There's live entertainment and happy hour specials for both food and drink. There's never a cover charge and no dress code. To avoid waiting in line, get here before 9 pm. ✉ *Ala Moana Center, 1450 Ala Moana Blvd., Ala Moana* 🌐 *instagram.com/themakaibar.*

Shopping

ARTS AND CRAFTS

'Auana Quilts (Hawaiian Quilt Collection)
CRAFTS | Traditional island comforters, wall hangings, pillows, bags, and other Hawaiian-print quilt accessories are the specialty here. There is also a store in the Royal Hawaiian Hotel and one on Waikiki Beach Walk. ✉ *Ala Moana Shopping Center, 1450 Ala Moana Blvd., Shop 1106, Ala Moana* ☎ *808/955–9550* 🌐 *hawaiian-quilts.com.*

Na Hoku
JEWELRY/ACCESSORIES | If you look at the wrists of *kamaaina* (local) women, you might see Hawaiian heirloom bracelets fashioned in either gold or silver and engraved in a number of Islands-inspired designs. Na Hoku sells these and other traditional Hawaiian jewelry along with an array of modern Island influenced styles in designs that capture the heart of the Hawaiian lifestyle in all its elegant diversity. There are a number of other Na Hoku locations on Oahu and the other

islands (as well as in the continental United States). ✉ *Ala Moana Center, 1450 Ala Moana Blvd., Shop 2006, Ala Moana* ☎ *808/946–2100* ⊕ *nahoku.com.*

BOOKS
★ Na Mea Hawaii
BOOKS/STATIONERY | In addition to Island-style clothing for adults and children, Hawaiian cultural items, and unusual artwork such as Niihau-shell necklaces, this boutique's book selection covers Hawaiian history and language and includes children's books set in the Islands. Na Mea also has daily classes on Hawaiian language, culture, and history. ✉ *Ward Village, 1200 Ala Moana Blvd., Suite 270, Ala Moana* ☎ *808/596–8885* ⊕ *nameahawaii.com.*

CLOTHING
Reyn Spooner
CLOTHING | This is a good place to buy the aloha-print fashions residents wear. Look for the limited-edition Christmas shirt, a collector's item manufactured each holiday season. Reyn Spooner has seven locations statewide and offers styles for men and children and, sometimes, limited-edition women's wear. ✉ *Ala Moana Shopping Center, 1450 Ala Moana Blvd., Shop 2247, Ala Moana* ☎ *808/949–5929* ⊕ *reynspooner.com.*

FOOD
Longs Drugs
FOOD/CANDY | For gift items in bulk, try one of the many outposts of Longs, the perfect place to stock up on chocolate-covered macadamia nuts, candies, cookies, island tea, and 100% Kona coffee—at reasonable prices—to carry home. ✉ *Ala Moana Shopping Center, 1450 Ala Moana Blvd., 2nd level, Ala Moana* ☎ *808/941–4010* ⊕ *alamoana-center.com/en/directory/longs-drugs-789.html.*

GIFTS
Blue Hawaii Lifestyle
GIFTS/SOUVENIRS | The Ala Moana store carries a large selection of locally made products, including soaps, honey, tea, salt, chocolates, art, and CDs. Every item, in fact, is carefully selected from various Hawaiian companies, artisans, and farms, from the salt fields of Molokai to the lavender farms on Maui to the single-estate chocolate on Oahu's North Shore. A café in the store serves healthy smoothies, panini, tea, and espresso. ✉ *Ala Moana Shopping Center, 1450 Ala Moana Blvd., Shop 2312, Ala Moana* ☎ *808/949–0808* ⊕ *bluehawaiilifestyle.com.*

SHOPPING CENTERS
Ala Moana Shopping Center
SHOPPING CENTERS/MALLS | The world's largest open-air shopping mall is five minutes from Waikiki by bus. More than 350 stores and 160 dining options (including multiple food courts) make up this 50-acre complex, which is a unique mix of national and international chains as well as smaller, locally owned shops and eateries—and everything in between. Shirokiya Japan Village Walk and the newer Lanai@Ala Moana are worth stopping at for a range of casual dining options in one spot. Thirty-five luxury boutiques in residence include Gucci, Louis Vuitton, and Christian Dior. All of Hawaii's major department stores are here, including the state's only Neiman Marcus and Nordstrom, plus Macy's, Target, and Bloomingdale's. ✉ *1450 Ala Moana Blvd., Ala Moana* ☎ *808/955–9517* ⊕ *alamoana-center.com.*

Ward Village
SHOPPING CENTERS/MALLS | Heading west from Waikiki toward downtown Honolulu, you'll run into a section of town with five distinct shopping-complex areas; there are more than 135 specialty shops and 40 eateries here. The Ward Entertainment Center features 16 movie screens, including a state-of-the-art, 3-D, big-screen auditorium, and all theaters having reclining chairs and access to an extended food menu and alcoholic beverages for those of age. The South Shore

Market is a contemporary collection of local shops and restaurants, plus T.J. Maxx and Nordstrom Rack. For distinctive Hawaiian gifts, such as locally made muumuu, koa-wood products, and Niihau shell necklaces, visit Martin & MacArthur and Na Mea Hawaii. Over at the Ward Gateway Center, the Ohana Hale Marketplace is worth a stop to visit 140 local small businesses including food stalls, apparel and accessories shops, and gift and craft stands. You can hop on TheBus or take a trolley from Waikiki. There's also free parking around the entire Ward Village, though sometimes you have to circle for awhile to find a spot. Valet parking is also available. ✉ *1050-1200 Ala Moana Blvd., Ala Moana* ☎ *808/591–8411* 🌐 *www.wardvillageshops.com.*

Makiki Heights

Makiki includes the more unassuming neighborhood where President Barack Obama grew up. Other highlights include the exclusive Punahou School he attended and the notable Central Union Church, as well as the Tantalus area overlook.

🍴 Restaurants

★ Honolulu Burger Co.

$ | BURGER | FAMILY | Owner Ken Takahashi retired as a nightclub impresario on the Big Island to become a real-life burger king. This modest storefront is the home of the locavore burger, made with range-fed beef, Manoa lettuce, tomatoes, and a wide range of toppings, all island-grown—and you can taste the difference. **Known for:** miso kutie burger topped with red miso glaze and Japanese cucumber slices; blue Hawaii burger with blue cheese and bacon; showing up at local farmers markets or its own food truck. [$] *Average main: $12* ✉ *1295 S. Beretania St., Makiki Heights* ☎ *808/626–5202* 🌐 *honoluluburgerco.com.*

Kalihi-Liliha-Palama

North of downtown Honolulu, just off H1, is the tightly packed neighborhood of Kalihi. It's home to large industrial pockets but also the stellar Bishop Museum, Lion Coffee headquarters, and great local eateries like Mitsu-Ken. Liliha-Kapalama is a sliver of land that runs from ocean to mountain (known as an *ahupuaa* in Hawaiian) and is presided over by famed Kamehameha Schools—which from its hillside perch looks down on this warren of modest homes and shops—and the Bishop Museum. There are also some great food establishments here including Helena's Hawaiian Food and Liliha Bakery (not to be missed for its *ono coco* puffs).

👁 Sights

★ Bishop Museum

MUSEUM | Founded in 1889 by Charles R. Bishop as a memorial to his wife, Princess Bernice Pauahi Bishop, the museum began as a repository for the royal possessions of this last direct descendant of King Kamehameha the Great. Today, it's the state's designated history and culture museum. Its five exhibit halls house almost 25 million items that tell the history of the Hawaiian Islands and their Pacific neighbors. The complex also features a 16,500-square-foot science adventure wing with a three-story simulated volcano at its center, where regular "lava melts" take place, much to the enjoyment of younger patrons. The renovated Pacific Hall (formerly Polynesian Hall) now focuses on the history of the entire Pacific region.

The Hawaiian Hall, with state-of-the art and often interactive displays, teaches about the Hawaiian culture. Spectacular Hawaiian artifacts—lustrous feather capes, bone fishhooks, the skeleton of a giant sperm whale, photography and crafts displays, and an authentic, well-preserved grass house—are

The Bishop Museum is Hawaii's state historical museum and the repository for the royal artifacts of the last surviving direct descendant of King Kamehameha the Great.

displayed inside a three-story, 19th-century, Victorian-style gallery. The building alone, with its huge Victorian turrets and immense stone walls, is worth seeing. Also check out the planetarium, daily tours, *lauhala*-weaving and science demonstrations, special exhibits, the Shop Pacifica, and the Bishop Museum Café, which serves *ono* (delicious) Hawaiian food by local restaurant Highway Inn. ⊠ *1525 Bernice St., Kalihi* ☎ *808/847–3511* ⊕ *www.bishopmuseum.org* ⊠ *$25 (parking $5).*

Nuuanu

Immediately *mauka* of Kalihi, off Pali Highway, are a renowned resting place and a carefully preserved home where royal families retreated during the doldrums of summer. Nuuanu Pali was the site of a famous battle that was key to King Kamehameha I's success in uniting all the Hawaiian Islands under his rule and becoming the Islands' first monarch. Nuuanu Valley is known for its lush, quiet beauty and has several notable cemeteries, churches, and embassies.

⊙ Sights

National Memorial Cemetery of the Pacific
CEMETERY | Nestled in the bowl of Puowaina, or Punchbowl Crater, this 112-acre cemetery is the final resting place for more than 50,000 U.S. war veterans and family members and is a solemn reminder of their sacrifice. Among those buried here is Ernie Pyle, the famed World War II correspondent who was killed by a Japanese sniper on Ie Shima, an island off the northwest coast of Okinawa. There are intricate stone maps providing a visual military-history lesson. Puowaina, formed 75,000–100,000 years ago during a period of secondary volcanic activity, translates as "Hill of Sacrifice." Historians believe this site once served as an altar where ancient Hawaiians offered sacrifices to their gods. ■ **TIP→ The entrance to the cemetery has unfettered views of Waikiki and Honolulu—perhaps the finest on Oahu.** ⊠ *2177 Puowaina Dr., Nuuanu*

☎ *808/532–3720* 🌐 *www.cem.va.gov/cem/cems/nchp/nmcp.asp* 🎫 *Free.*

Queen Emma Summer Palace

HOUSE | Queen Emma, King Kamehameha IV's wife, used this small but stately New England–style home in Nuuanu Valley as a retreat from the rigors of court life in hot and dusty Honolulu during the mid- to late-1800s. Hourlong guided tours highlight the residence's royal history and its eclectic mix of European, Victorian, and Hawaiian furnishings, most of which are original to the home. There are excellent examples of feathered-covered kahilis, umeke bowls, and koa-wood furniture. Visitors also learn how Queen Emma established what is today the largest private hospital in Hawaii, opened a school for girls, and ran as a widow for the throne, losing to King Kalakaua. A short drive away, you can visit the Royal Mausoleum in Nuuanu, where she, her husband, and their son, Albert, who died at age 4, are buried beside many other Hawaiian royals. Guided tours are offered Monday through Saturday at 10, 11, 1, and 2, and on Sunday at 11 and 1. ✉ *2913 Pali Hwy., Nuuanu* ☎ *808/595–3167* 🌐 *www.daughtersofhawaii.org* 🎫 *$10.*

Moiliili

Packed into the neighborhood of Moiliili are flower and lei shops, restaurants, and little stores selling Hawaiian and Asian goodies. Most places of interest are along King Street, between Isenberg and Waialae avenues.

🍴 Restaurants

★ Alan Wong's Restaurant Honolulu

$$$$ | **MODERN HAWAIIAN** | James Beard Award–winning Alan Wong is the undisputed king of Hawaiian regional cuisine, earning love and respect for his humble demeanor and practice as much as for his food. The "Wong Way," as it's not-so-jokingly called by his staff, includes an ingrained understanding of the aloha spirit, evident in the skilled but unstarched service and creative and playful interpretations of Islands cuisine. **Known for:** well-deserved awards and accolades, which line the walls; ginger-crusted onaga (red snapper); "The Coconut" haubia sorbet in chocolate shell. [$] *Average main: $43* ✉ *McCully Court, 1857 S. King St., 3rd fl., Moiliili* ☎ *808/949–2526* 🌐 *alanwongs.com* 🕓 *No lunch.*

★ Chef Mavro

$$$$ | **MODERN EUROPEAN** | Marseilles transplant George Mavrothalassitis, who took two hotel restaurants to the top of the ranks before opening this well-regarded restaurant in 1998, is passionate about the care he takes to draw out the truest and most concentrated flavors, to track down the freshest fish, to create one-of-a-kind wine pairings, and marry French technique with global flavors and local ingredients. The menu changes quarterly, every dish (including dessert) matched with a select wine. **Known for:** exquisite prix-fixe cuisine; a focus on innovative uses for the freshest produce; wine pairings unmatched on Oahu. [$] *Average main: $195* ✉ *1969 S. King St., Moiliili* ☎ *808/944–4714* 🌐 *chefmavro.com* 🕓 *No lunch.*

Imanas Tei

$$$ | **JAPANESE** | Nihonjin (Japanese nationals) and locals flock to this tucked-away, bamboo-ceilinged restaurant for its tasteful, simple decor and equally tasteful—and perfect—sushi, sashimi, *nabe* (hot pots prepared at the table), and grilled dishes. You assemble your meal dish by dish, and the cost can add up if you aren't careful. **Known for:** simple food that some feel is better than in Japan; long waits; traditional izakaya experience. [$] *Average main: $30* ✉ *2626 S. King St., Moiliili* ☎ *808/941–2626, 808/934–2727* 🕓 *Closed Sun. No lunch.*

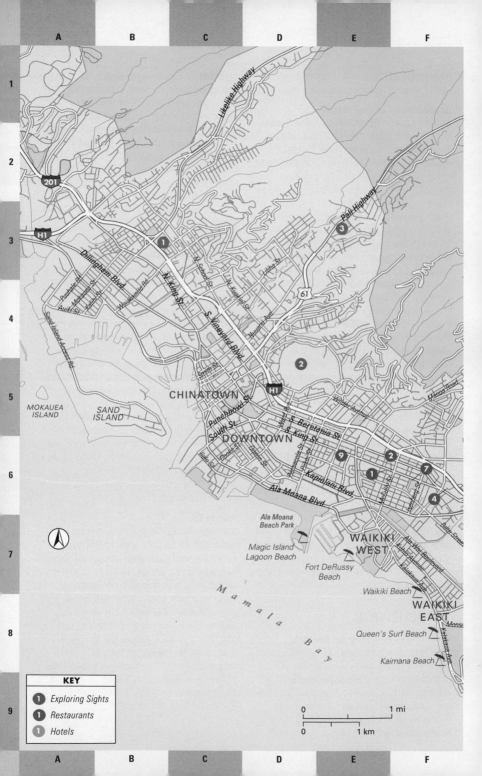

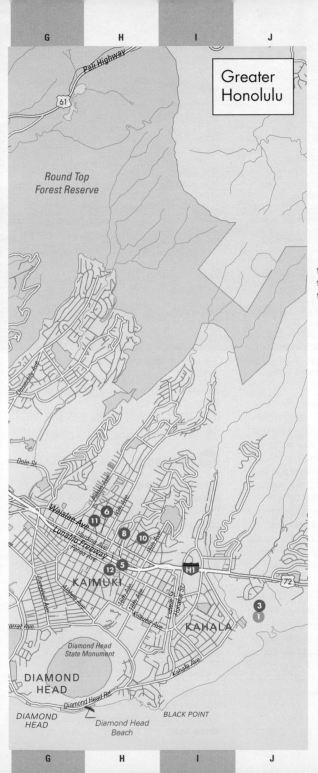

Greater Honolulu

Sights ▼

1 Bishop Museum **B3**
2 National Memorial
  Cemetery of the Pacific **D5**
3 Queen Emma Summer Palace **E3**

Restaurants ▼

1 Alan Wong's
  Restaurant Honolulu **E6**
2 Chef Mavro **F6**
3 Hoku's **J8**
4 Imanas Tei **F6**
5 Koko Head Cafe **H7**
6 Mud Hen Water **H7**
7 Peace Café **F6**
8 The Surfing Pig Hawaii **H7**
9 Sushi Sasabune **E6**
10 3660 on the Rise **H7**
11 Town **H7**
12 12th Avenue Grill **H7**

Hotels ▼

1 The Kahala Hotel & Resort **J8**

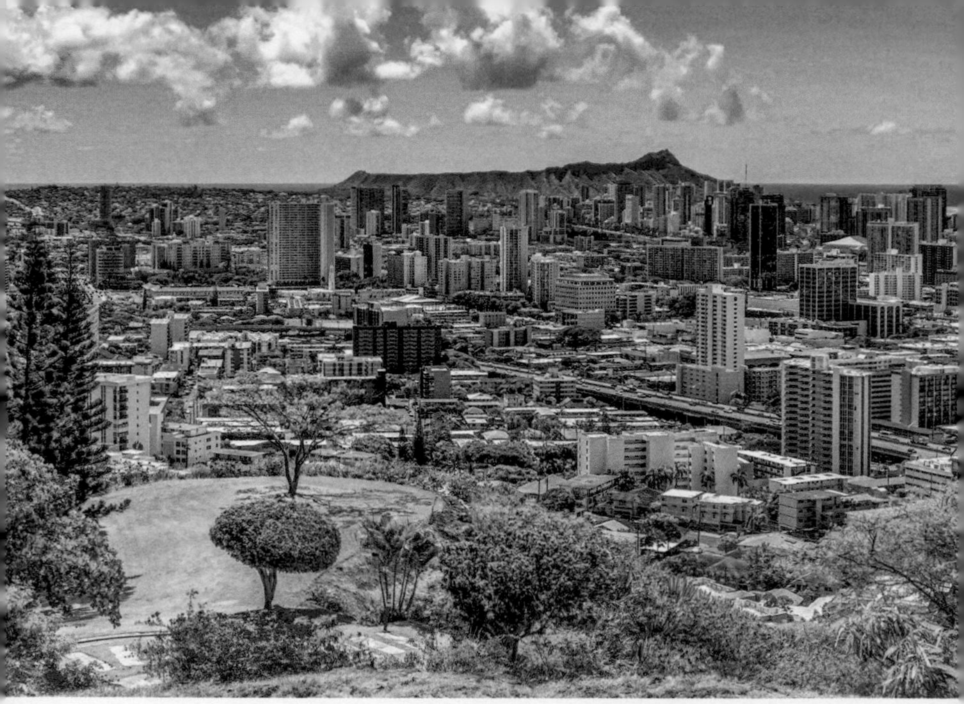

The Punch Bowl, yet another extinct volcanic crater, is home to the National Memorial Cemetery of the Pacific, the largest military cemetery in Hawaii.

Peace Café

$ | **VEGETARIAN** | This tranquil little storefront with a rustic country communal table is a nurturing sanctuary on a fast-food-loving island. Place your order at the counter, serve yourself fruit-infused water from a large glass beverage jar, and wait for your vegan plates, salads, and sandwiches. **Known for:** tempeh katsu; yogini plate (a mountain of brown rice, beans, greens, and seaweed); mellow and calming setting. [$] *Average main: $10* ✉ *2239 S. King St., Moiliili* ☎ *808/951–7555* 🌐 *peacecafehawaii.com* 🕑 *No dinner Sun.*

Sushi Sasabune

$$$$ | **JAPANESE** | Try to get a coveted seat at the counter, and prepare for an unforgettable sushi experience—if you behave. This is the home of Seiji Kumagawa—Honolulu's Sushi Nazi, who prefers that diners eat omakase-style, letting the chef send out his favorite choices, each priced individually (prices add up quickly). **Known for:** one of Honolulu's top sushi spots; fast service; no phone calls allowed in the restaurant. [$] *Average main: $150* ✉ *1417 S. King St., Moiliili* ☎ *808/947–3800* 🕑 *Closed Sun. and Mon. No lunch Sat.*

Shopping

Maui Divers Design Center

JEWELRY/ACCESSORIES | For a look into the harvesting and design of coral and black pearl jewelry, visit this shop and take a free tour at its adjacent factory near the Ala Moana Shopping Center. **■ TIP→ Avoid the "Pick a Pearl" option unless you're prepared to be upsold on a jewelry setting or two for the pearls "found" in your shells.** ✉ *1520 Liona St., Moiliili* ☎ *808/943–8350* 🌐 *mauidivers.com.*

Kapahulu

Walk just a few minutes from the eastern end of Waikiki, and you'll find yourself in this very local main drag of restaurants, bars, and shops (**Bailey's Antiques and Aloha Shirts** (✉ *517 Kapahulu Ave.*) is the place for rare, wearable collectibles). The original **Leonard's Bakery** (✉ *933 Kapahulu Ave.*) is where *malasadas* (Portuguese deep-fried doughnuts rolled in sugar) were first popularized.

Kaimuki

Ten minutes beyond Kapahulu, this commercial thoroughfare runs through an old neighborhood filled with cool old Craftsman bungalows (which are, alas, slowly being knocked down to make room for ticky-tacky boxes). Kaimuki has steadily been developing into a food mecca (challenged only by Chinatown), with a slew of award-winning restaurants and bars in a range of culinary styles. If you want to know what trends are happening in Hawaii food today, this is a neighborhood to visit. It may have the highest and most diverse concentration of eateries on the island, from an elevated barbecue spot and a shabu-shabu house to a chic, contemporary bistro and a nougat manufacturer.

🍴 Restaurants

★ Koko Head Cafe

$ | MODERN HAWAIIAN | When Lee Anne Wong, best known as a competitor on the first season of Bravo's *Top Chef,* moved to the Islands, foodies waited with bated breath for her first brick-and-mortar restaurant. And this is it: a lively and laid-back café in Kaimuki, where she took the concept of breakfast and flipped it, creating innovative dishes like Elvis's Revenge, a peanut butter-and-banana tempura sandwich with candied bacon. **Known for:** cornflake french toast; creative cocktail menu; crazy busy weekends. [$] *Average main: $13* ✉ *1145c 12th Ave., Kaimuki* ☎ *808/732–8920* 🌐 *kokoheadcafe.com* 🕒 *No dinner.*

Mud Hen Water

$$ | HAWAIIAN | The name of this restaurant perched on busy Waialae Avenue is the English translation of *Waialae* (meaning a gathering spot around a watering hole). Chef Ed Kenney (of Town, Kaimuki Superette, and Mahina & Sun's fame) explores modern interpretations of the Hawaiian foods he remembers from his childhood with an ever-changing locavore menu. **Known for:** small plates and snacks; beet poke; sorbetto and gelato. [$] *Average main: $17* ✉ *3452 Waialae Ave., Kaimuki* ☎ *808/737–6000* 🌐 *mudhenwater.com* 🕒 *Closed Mon.*

The Surfing Pig Hawaii

$$$ | BARBECUE | This fancier sibling of the island's three Kono's barbecue spots focuses on Americana-tinged-with-Hawaiian food and drinks served in a small, lofted eatery with a surfer-industrial vibe. Heaping portions of juicy smoked and grilled meats are the specialty, but The Surfing Pig also has several great fish appetizers and entrées. **Known for:** old-fashioned with bacon-infused bourbon, bacon garnish, and "smoking" cloche presentation; pork, beef, and porchetta slider trio; a strong brunch alternative in the neighborhood. [$] *Average main: $30* ✉ *3605 Waialae Ave., Kaimuki* ☎ *808/744–1992* 🌐 *thesurfingpighawaii.com.*

3660 on the Rise

$$$$ | MODERN HAWAIIAN | Named for its address on Honolulu's premier Waialae Avenue, this restaurant brought fresh dining to Kaimuki when it opened in 1992, inspiring a neighborhood dining renaissance. Loyalists swear by the steaks, crab cakes, and the signature dish, ahi katsu wrapped in *nori* (seaweed) and deep-fried with a wasabi-ginger butter sauce. **Known for:** special-occasion restaurant; good desserts; somewhat dated interior. [$] *Average main: $38* ✉ *3660 Waialae Ave., Kaimuki* ☎ *808/737–1177* 🌐 *3660ontherise.com* 🕒 *Closed Mon. No lunch.*

★ Town

$$ | **AMERICAN** | Town remains a hot spot for Honolulu's creative class and farm-to-table diners, a place where chef-owner Ed Kenney and his partner Dave Caldiero offer an eclectic menu that embraces Hawaii ingredients in unique ways, ranging from hand-cut pastas and refreshing, composed salads to clean preparations of fish and meat. The menu is constantly changing, reflecting what's fresh and available. **Known for:** eclectic menu that suits both meat eaters and vegetarians; trendy atmosphere; lunch option. [$] *Average main: $25* ✉ *3435 Waialae Ave., Kaimuki* ☎ *808/735–5900* 🌐 *www.townkaimuki.com.*

12th Avenue Grill

$$$ | **MODERN AMERICAN** | A local favorite since the doors opened, this award-winning American brasserie from chef-owner Kevin Hanney keeps surprising loyalists with an expanding menu and lively bar scene. The longtime favorite grilled pork chop is joined on the menu by other excellent meat and fish dishes and beautifully prepared soups, salads, and small plates. **Known for:** passion-fruit mochi cake with vanilla-ginger syrup; commitment to locally sourced ingredients; smoked ahi bruschetta. [$] *Average main: $28* ✉ *1120 12th Ave., Kaimuki* ☎ *808/732–9469* 🌐 *www.12thavegrill.com* ⏲ *No lunch.*

Kahala

Oahu's wealthiest neighborhood has streets lined with multimillion-dollar homes. At intervals along tree-lined Kahala Avenue are narrow lanes that provide public access to Kahala's quiet, narrow coastal beaches offering views of Koko Head. Kahala Mall includes restaurants, a movie theater, and a Whole Foods grocery store. Kahala is also the home of the private Waialae Country Club and golf course, site of the annual Sony Open PGA golf tournament in January.

🍴 Restaurants

Hoku's

$$$$ | **ASIAN FUSION** | Everything about this room speaks of quality and sophistication: the wall of windows with their beach views, the avant-garde cutlery and dinnerware, the solicitous staff, and the carefully constructed Euro-Pacific cuisine. The menu constantly changes, and new executive chef Jonathan Mizukami—along with chef du cuisine Eric Oto—is focusing even more on seasonal cuisine made with fresh, local ingredients (including herbs from the hotel's on-site herb garden). **Known for:** relaxed elegance in the grande dame of Hawaii's social scene; panoramic views from every table; setting and service that can outshine the food. [$] *Average main: $55* ✉ *The Kahala Hotel & Resort, 5000 Kahala Ave., Kahala* ☎ *808/739–8760* 🌐 *hokuskahala.com* ⏲ *No lunch.*

🛏 Hotels

★ The Kahala Hotel & Resort

$$$$ | **RESORT** | **FAMILY** | Hidden away in the upscale residential neighborhood of Kahala (on the other side of Diamond Head from Waikiki), this elegant oceanfront hotel, one of Hawaii's very first luxury resorts, has played host to celebrities, princesses, the Dalai Lama, and nearly every president since Lyndon Johnson. **Pros:** away from hectic Waikiki; top-notch Hoku's restaurant; heavenly spa. **Cons:** far from Waikiki; in a residential neighborhood, so not much to do within walking distance of hotel; small pool. [$] *Rooms from: $395* ✉ *5000 Kahala Ave., Kahala* ☎ *808/739–8888, 800/367–2525 toll-free* 🌐 *kahalaresort.com* 🛏 *338 rooms* 🍽 *No meals.*

Shopping

Kahala Mall

SHOPPING CENTERS/MALLS | This indoor mall has more than 100 stores and restaurants with a mix of both local and national retailers including Macy's, Reyn Spooner, an Apple store, Island Sole footwear, and T&C Surf. Don't miss homegrown boutiques, clothing stores, and galleries like Magnolia, Fighting Eel, Mahina, and SOHA Living. You can also browse local foods and products at Whole Foods. The recently renovated Kahala Theaters now has a full kitchen and bar and provides post-shopping entertainment. ✉ *4211 Waialae Ave., Kahala* ☎ *808/732–7736* ⊕ *www.kahalamallcenter.com.*

West (Leeward) and Central Oahu

The rugged Waianae and Kaala mountain ranges bisect the leeward side of the island from the central plateau. The queen of the range, Mount Kaala, is the highest peak on Oahu (4,003 feet) and dominates the landscape on all sides when clouds fail to obscure its majesty.

The tall mountains shield the western slopes from trade winds and heavy rain that falls to the north and east. The western side thus appears drier, and beaches are known for their pristine white sands and crystal-clear waters, excellent settings for snorkeling and diving. This geography (combined with flows from the western slopes of the parallel eastern Koolau range) also results in abundant water flows to the fertile central valley plains—where much of Oahu's delectable bounty originates.

The region's eastern portion edges Pearl Harbor and includes Aloha Stadium, Hawaii's Plantation Village, the Wet 'n Wild water park, and the Waikele Premium Outlets near Waipio. Kapolei, Oahu's

burgeoning "second city," lies due west of Pearl Harbor. It was a planned community, where, for years, the government has been trying to attract enough jobs to lighten inbound traffic to downtown Honolulu. A major mall and community center, Ka Makana Alii, opened here in 2017 to serve an expected influx of shoppers in the ensuing decades. Ko Olina—a lively, privately owned community centered on a golf course, several major resorts, and four man-made lagoons—occupies the southwestern tip of the island.

Some locals avoid Leeward and Central Oahu because of traffic that tends to bottleneck at the intersection of the H1, H2, and H3 freeways. But those who time their travels to avoid the traffic find great rewards throughout the region, especially the chance to explore the gorgeous and remote west coast beaches, including such far-flung Hawaiian communities of Nanakuli and Waianae and the end of the road at Keawaula, aka Yokohama Bay. A rest stop and a walk through the 3-acre maze at the Dole Plantation (the world's largest) near Wahiawa is well worth including in any Leeward excursion itinerary.

GETTING HERE AND AROUND

It's relatively easy to get to Leeward Oahu, which begins at folksy Waipahu and continues past Makakilo and Kapolei on H1 and Highway 93, Farrington Highway. It takes about a half-hour to get to Ko Olina from Waikiki, but rush hour traffic can create delays. A couple of cautions as you head to the leeward side: Highway 93 is a narrow, winding, two-lane road, notorious for accidents. There's an abrupt transition from an expansive freeway to a two-lane highway at Kapolei, and by the time you reach Nanakuli, it's a country road, so *slow down.* Also be aware of congestion between Ko Olina and Waianae during commuter hours.

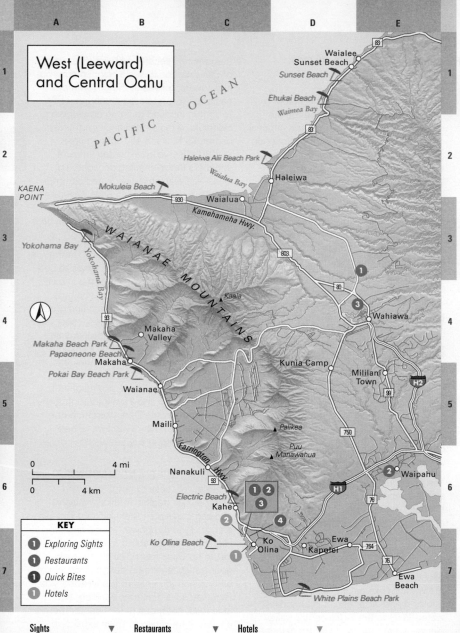

West (Leeward) and Central Oahu

PACIFIC OCEAN

KAENA POINT

Yokohama Bay

WAIANAE MOUNTAINS

Kaala

Waialee
Sunset Beach
Sunset Beach
Ehukai Beach
Waimea Bay

Haleiwa Alii Beach Park
Haleiwa
Waialua Bay
Waialua
Kamehameha Hwy.
Mokuleia Beach

Makaha Valley
Makaha Beach Park
Papaoneone Beach
Makaha
Pokai Bay Beach Park
Waianae
Maili

Kunia Camp
Mililani Town
Wahiawa

Palikea
Puu Manawahua

Nanakuli
Electric Beach
Kahe
Waipahu

Ko Olina Beach
Ko Olina
Kapolei
Ewa

Ewa Beach

White Plains Beach Park

0   4 mi
0   4 km

KEY

- ① Exploring Sights
- ① Restaurants
- ① Quick Bites
- ① Hotels

For Central Oahu, all sights are most easily reached by either the H1 or H2 freeway.

Kapolei

Kapolei is approximately 20 miles (30 minutes by car) west of downtown Honolulu and 12 miles (20 minutes by car) from Mililani; traffic can double or triple the driving time.

The planned community of Kapolei, where, for years, the government has been trying to attract enough jobs to lighten inbound traffic to downtown Honolulu, is often called Oahu's "Second City." It occupies much of 1800s business mogul James Campbell's 4,100-acre Ewa Plain estate, which once cultivated vast tracts of sugarcane and pineapple. Its first phases broke ground starting in the 1980s. Today, it is a thriving community with government centers, industrial parks, big box malls, businesses small and large, and the University of Hawaii West Oahu Campus. The Ko Olina complex to the west is officially part of the district and has a Kapolei zip code. The new elevated Honolulu Rail Transit line, scheduled to open in late 2020, will connect east Kapolei to Aloha Stadium in Honolulu.

◉ Sights

Hawaii's Plantation Village
MUSEUM | Starting in the 1800s, immigrants seeking work on the sugar plantations came to these Islands like so many waves against the shore. At this living museum 30 minutes from downtown Honolulu (without traffic), visit authentically furnished buildings, original and replicated, that re-create and pay tribute to the plantation era. See a Chinese social hall; a Japanese shrine, sumo ring, and saimin stand; a dental office; and historic homes. The village is open for guided tours only. ⊠ *Waipahu Cultural Gardens*

Park, 94-695 Waipahu St., Waipahu ☎ *808/677–0110* ⊕ *www.hawaiiplantationvillage.org* ⊠ *$15* ⊙ *Closed Sun.*

⚓ Beaches

White Plains Beach Park
BEACH—SIGHT | FAMILY | Concealed from the public eye for many years as part of the former Barbers Point Naval Air Station, this beach is reminiscent of Waikiki but without the condos and the crowds. It is a long, sloping beach with numerous surf breaks, but it is also mild enough at the shore for older children to play freely. It has views of Pearl Harbor and, over that, Diamond Head. Although the sand lives up to its name, the real joy of this beach comes from its history as part of a military property for the better part of a century. Expansive parking, great restroom facilities, and numerous tree-covered barbecue areas make it a great day-trip spot. As a bonus, a Hawaiian monk seal takes up residence here several months out of the year (seals are rare in the Islands). **Amenities:** lifeguards; parking (no fee); showers; toilets. **Best for:** surfing; swimming. ⊠ *Essex Rd. and Tripoli Rd., Kapolei* ✛ *Take Makakilo Exit off H1 West, then turn left. Follow it into base gates, make left. Blue signs lead to beach.*

🎭 Performing Arts

LUAU
Chief's Luau at Wet 'n' Wild Hawaii
ARTS-ENTERTAINMENT OVERVIEW | Chief Sielu and his *ohana* (family) perform at Wet 'n' Wild Hawaii waterpark. It's a top-rated luau with everything you'd expect from this island tradition: good food, rhythmic music, and interactive performances. The show ends with a high-energy fire-knife dance. The chef also heads the Fia Fia Luau at the Marriott in Ko Olina. ⊠ *Wet 'n' Wild Hawaii, 400 Farrington Hwy., Kapolei* ☎ *877/357–2480* ⊕ *www.chiefsluau.com* ⊠ *From $95.*

Germaine's Luau

THEMED ENTERTAINMENT | More than 3 million visitors have come to this luau, held about 45 minutes west of Waikiki in light traffic. Widely considered one of the most folksy and laid-back, Germaine's offers a tasty, multicourse, all-you-can-eat buffet. Admission includes the buffet and one drink to three drinks (depending on the package). It's held Tuesday to Sunday at 6. ✉ *91-119 Olai St., Kapolei* ☎ *808/202–2528* ⊕ *www.germainesluau. com* ✉ *From $85, transportation from $16.*

🛍 Shopping

Aloha Stadium Swap Meet & Marketplace

SHOPPING CENTERS/MALLS | This thrice-weekly outdoor bazaar attracts hundreds of vendors and even more bargain hunters. Every Hawaiian souvenir imaginable can be found here, from coral shell necklaces to bikinis, as well as a variety of ethnic wares, from Chinese brocaded dresses to Japanese pottery. There are also ethnic foods, silk flowers, and luggage in aloha floral prints. Shoppers must wade through the typical sprinkling of used and counterfeit goods to find value. Wear comfortable shoes, use sunscreen, and bring bottled water. The flea market takes place in the Aloha Stadium parking lot Wednesday and Saturday 8–3, Sunday 6:30–3. Admission is $1 per person ages 12 and up.

You can take either Uber or Lyft from your hotel. The Waikiki Trolley Purple Line also stops at the Swap Meet. For a cheaper but slower ride, take TheBus (⊕ *www. thebus.org*). You might also ask your hotel concierge about shared shuttle services. The new Hawaiian Rail trains will connect Aloha Stadium with Kapolei when they start running (scheduled for sometime in 2020). So you could shop at the swap meet and hop on the train to Ka Makana Alii to treasure-hunt even longer—all without a car! ✉ *Aloha Stadium, 99-500*

Salt Lake Blvd., Aiea ☎ *808/486–6704* ⊕ *www.alohastadiumswapmeet.net.*

Waikele Premium Outlets

SHOPPING CENTERS/MALLS | Armani Exchange, Calvin Klein, Coach, and Saks Fifth Avenue outlets anchor this discount destination of around 50 stores. You can take a shuttle from Waikiki for the 30-minute ride to the outlets for $18 round-trip, but the companies do change frequently. Reservations are recommended. ✉ *94-790 Lumiaina St., Waipahu* ☎ *808/676–5656* ⊕ *www.premiumoutlets.com/outlet/waikele.*

Ko Olina

24 miles west of downtown Honolulu.

For centuries, Hawaiian nobility rejuvenated at this pristine enclave on the island's southwestern shore. Today, Ko Olina is a major visitor hub, part of a decades-long master plan to attract jobs to the leeward side. The privately owned, 642-acre complex is a community unto itself, with one guarded public entrance/exit off Farrington Highway. It includes a golf course, three natural lagoons, a series of four man-made lagoons, three major resorts (each with a range of restaurants, shops, and activities), 4½ miles of walking paths, and a shopping area with additional restaurants and cafés. It's also home to the famed Paradise Cove Luau.

The lagoons are open to the public, but public parking is limited (first-come, first-served, sunrise to sunset). Come early (before 10 am) to nab one of the prized spots. If you park far away from your ultimate destination, you can hop aboard the free Ko Olina shuttle vans that circle the community every half-hour.

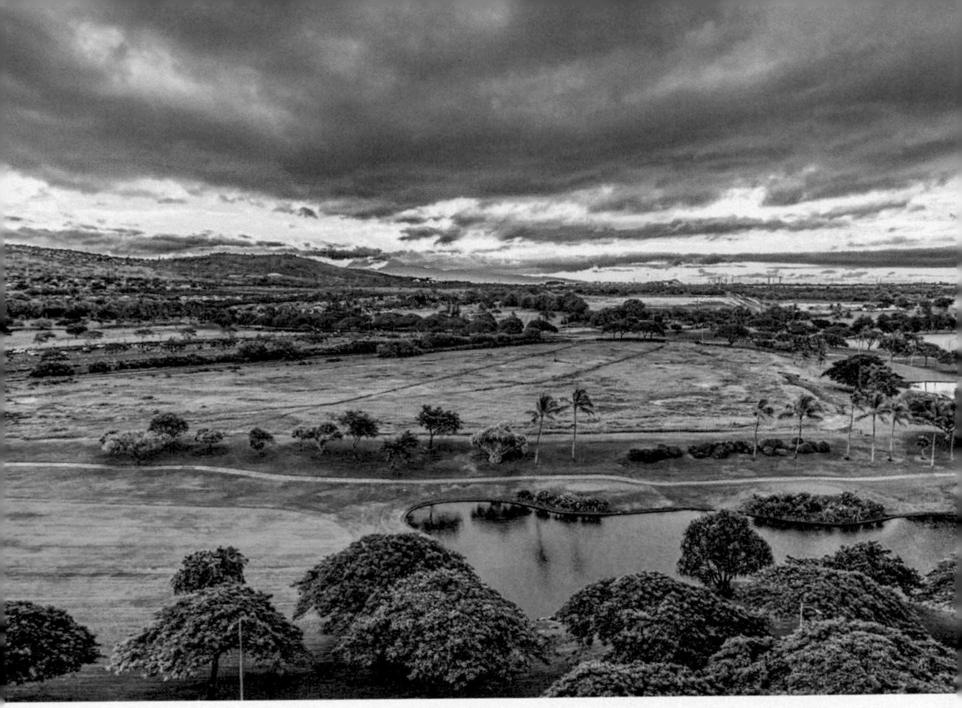

Ko Olina, a planned resort community on the island's southwestern shore, is the biggest tourist area on Leeward Oahu.

Beaches

Ko Olina Beach

BEACH—SIGHT | FAMILY | This is the best spot on the island if you have small kids. The resort area commissioned a series of four man-made lagoons, but, as it has to provide public beach access, you are the winner. Huge rock walls protect the lagoons, making them into perfect spots for the kids to get their first taste of the ocean without getting bowled over. The large expanses of seashore grass and hala trees that surround the semicircle beaches are made-to-order for nap time. A 1½-mile jogging track connects the lagoons. Due to its appeal for *keiki* (children), Ko Olina is popular, and the parking lot fills up quickly when school is out and on weekends, so try to get here before 10 am. The biggest parking lot is at the farthest lagoon from the entrance. There are actually three resorts here: Aulani (the Disney resort), Four Seasons Resort Oahu, and the Ko Olina Beach Villas Resort (which has a time-share section as well). **Amenities:** food and drink; parking (no fee); showers; toilets. **Best for:** sunset; swimming; walking. ✉ *92 Aliinui Dr., 23 miles west of Honolulu, Ko Olina* ✥ *Take Ko Olina exit off H1 West and proceed to guard shack.*

Restaurants

Ama Ama

$$$$ | MODERN HAWAIIAN | There's nothing "Mickey Mouse" about the food at the fine-dining restaurant of this Disney resort. Add to that the views of the Ko Olina lagoons and Pacific Ocean—and live music by top local performers Thursday–Sunday nights—and you have an evening worth the pretty penny. **Known for:** outstanding views and setting; consistently good food; hit-or-miss service. [$] *Average main: $44* ✉ *Aulani, a Disney Resort & Spa, 92-1185 Aliinui Dr., Ko Olina* ☎ *808/674–6200* 🌐 *www.disneyaulani.com/dining.*

Makahiki—The Bounty of the Islands

$$$$ | HAWAIIAN | FAMILY | The buffet restaurant at Disney's Aulani resort offers a wide variety of locally produced items, as well as familiar dishes from stateside and the rest of the world. You'll find sustainable Hawaiian seafood, Asian selections, familiar grilled meats and vegetables, and a kids' menu; an à la carte menu is also available. **Known for:** true reflection of Hawaii; wide array of food to please every member of the family; popular character breakfasts (which book up weeks in advance). $ *Average main: $57* ✉ *Aulani, a Disney Resort & Spa, 92-1185 Aliinui Dr., Ko Olina* ☎ *808/674–6200* ⊕ *www.disneyaulani.com/dining* ⊘ *No lunch.*

★ Mina's Fish House

$$$$ | SEAFOOD | Michael Mina, a James Beard Award winner, designed an exceptional line-to-table menu that celebrates the local catch to match the panoramic views spilling from indoor and lanai oceanfront tables. This might be the only restaurant in Hawaii (or the world) to have an on-site "fish sommelier," who guides you through the mind-boggling menu that includes a wide variety of cooking techniques, flavorings, and portions—from fillet to whole fish—and helps you choose the best matches for your particular palate. **Known for:** charbroiled Hawaiian seafood tower; Kona lobster dishes; daily happy hour. $ *Average main: $51* ✉ *Four Seasons Oahu Ko Olina Resort, 92-1001 Olani St., Ko Olina* ☎ *808/679–0079* ⊕ *www.michaelmina. net* ⊘ *No lunch weekdays.*

Monkeypod by Merriman Ko Olina

$$ | HAWAIIAN | Local farm-to-table guru Peter Merriman is known throughout Hawaii for his inventive and popular restaurants. Monkeypod at Ko Olina captures his creativity and locally inspired food mantra perfectly. **Known for:** lobster deviled eggs and fresh fish tacos; indoor/outdoor setting; life-changing strawberry cream pie. $ *Average main: $26* ✉ *Ko Olina Resort, 92-1048 Olani St., Ko Olina* ☎ *808/380–4086* ⊕ *www.monkeypodkitchen.com.*

🛏 Hotels

★ Aulani, A Disney Resort & Spa

$$$$ | RESORT | FAMILY | Disney's first property in Hawaii melds the Disney magic with breathtaking vistas, white sandy beaches, and sunsets that even Mickey stops to watch. **Pros:** tons to do on-site; family-friendly done right; Painted Sky: HI Style Studio. **Cons:** a long way from Waikiki; character breakfasts require advance reservation (book far in advance); areas and events can get really busy. $ *Rooms from: $524* ✉ *92-1185 Aliinui Dr., Kapolei* ☎ *714/520–7001, 808/674–6200, 866/443–4763* ⊕ *www.disneyaulani.com* 🛏 *832 rooms* ¶⊘¶ *No meals.*

★ Four Seasons Oahu at Ko Olina

$$$$ | RESORT | Oahu welcomed this luxurious new property to Ko Olina with great excitement—the first Four Seasons on the island, with nearly every room and suite in the 17-story hotel offering floor-to-ceiling windows and a private lanai, all with an ocean view. **Pros:** luxurious and exclusive; secluded, even in the Ko Olina complex; amenities and options abound. **Cons:** an hour from Waikiki; luxury doesn't come cheap; it doesn't always measure up to other Four Seasons. $ *Rooms from: $675* ✉ *92-1001 Olani St., in the Ko Olina complex, Ko Olina* ☎ *808/679–0079, 844/387–0308* ⊕ *www. fourseasons.com/oahu* 🛏 *371 rooms* ¶⊘¶ *No meals.*

🎭 Performing Arts

LUAU

Fia Fia Luau

THEMED ENTERTAINMENT | Just after sunset at the Marriott Ko Olina Beach Club, the charismatic Chief Sielu Avea leads the Samoan-based Fia Fia, an entertaining show that takes guests on the journey through the South Pacific. Every show is different and unscripted, but always a good look at Polynesian culture. It's the only recurring show with eight fire-knife dancers in a blazing finale. It's held on Tuesday at 4:30. Admission includes a buffet dinner. ⊠ *92-161 Waipahe Pl., Ko Olina* ☎ *808/679–4700, ⊕ www.marriott. com/hotels/hotel-information/restaurant/ hnlko-marriotts-ko-olina-beach-club* ⊠ *From $105.*

Paradise Cove Luau
THEMED ENTERTAINMENT | One of the largest shows on Oahu, the lively Paradise Cove Luau is held in the Ko Olina resort area, about 45 minutes from Waikiki (if there's light traffic). Drink in hand, you can stroll through the authentic village, learn traditional arts and crafts, and play local games. The stage show includes a fire-knife dancer, singing emcee, and both traditional and contemporary hula and other Polynesian dances. A finale dance features participation from the audience. Admission includes the buffet, activities, and the show. You pay extra for table service, box seating, and shuttle transport to and from Waikiki—the stunning sunsets are free. It starts daily at 5. ⊠ *92-1089 Alii Nui Dr., Ko Olina* ☎ *808/842–5911 ⊕ www.paradisecove. com* ⊠ *From $107; round-trip transportation from Waikiki $18.*

Waianae

9 miles north of Ko Olina.

Waianae refers to both the town and the western (leeward) shores of Oahu, from Ko Olina up to Yokohama Bay and the end of the road near Kaena Point. It's mostly rural, without tourist traps and few restaurants apart from fast food outlets, tiny cafés, and hole-in-the-wall poke shacks. Still, the Waianae coast is well worth a day trip, mostly to experience an area where "real" Hawaiians, descendants of natives who populated the coast centuries before the *haoles* arrived, live and play. The beaches boast crystal-clear

water. Turtles and dolphins swim near the shores, and when surf's up, Oahu's finest shredders show up to have fun and wow the watchers on the sand.

🔱 Beaches

Makaha Beach Park
BEACH—SIGHT | This beach provides a slice of local life most visitors don't see. Families string up tarps for the day, fire up hibachis, set up lawn chairs, get out the fishing gear, and strum ukulele while they "talk story" (chat). Legendary waterman Buffalo Keaulana can be found in the shade of the palms playing with his grandkids and spinning yarns of yesteryear. In these waters, Buffalo not only invented some of the most outrageous methods of surfing, but also raised his world-champion son Rusty. He also made Makaha the home of the world's first international surf meet in 1954, and it still hosts his Big Board Surfing Classic. With its long, slow-building waves, it's a great spot to try out longboarding. The swimming is generally decent in summer, but avoid the big winter waves. The only parking is along the highway, but it's free. **Amenities:** lifeguards; showers; toilets. **Best for:** surfing; swimming. ⊠ *84-450 Farrington Hwy., Waianae* ✛ *Go 32 miles west of Honolulu on the H1, then exit onto Farrington Hwy. The beach will be on your left.*

Wahiawa

Wahiawa is approximately 20 miles (30–35 minutes by car) north of downtown Honolulu, 20 miles (30 minutes by car) northeast of Ko Olina.

Oahu's central plain is a patchwork of old towns and new residential developments, military bases, farms, ranches, and shopping malls, with a few visit-worthy attractions and historic sites scattered about. Central Oahu encompasses the Moanalua Valley, residential Pearl City

In the summer, when the surf is calm, Makaha is a great snorkeling destination; in the winter, it's a popular surfing spot, especially for locals.

and Mililani, and the old plantation town of Wahiawa, on the uplands halfway to the North Shore.

James Dole first planted pineapples in the central plateau in the early 1900s, and the Dole Pineapple Plantation fields still border the northern limits of Wahiawa, a small town with a heavy military and working-class vibe. Lake Wilson (Wahiawa Reservoir) surrounds three sides of the town, and Highway 99 crosses two bridges (and several stoplights) to pass through. Wahiawa is the commercial hub for several military bases, including Schofield Barracks, Wheeler Army Airfield, and the U.S. Naval Computer and Telecommunications Area Master Station Pacific. The main drag—a five-block stretch of Highway 99 where traffic often slows to a snail's pace—was once a fast-food mecca but in recent years has given birth to a handful of decent cafés, restaurants, and an outpost of Black Sheep Cream Co., a popular Oahu ice creamery.

◉ Sights

Dole Plantation

COLLEGE | FAMILY | Pineapple plantation days are nearly defunct in Hawaii, but you can still celebrate Hawaii's famous golden fruit at this promotional center with exhibits, a huge gift shop, a snack concession, educational displays, and the world's second-largest maze. Take the self-guided Garden Tour, or hop aboard the Pineapple Express for a 20-minute train tour to learn a bit about life on a pineapple plantation. Kids love the more than 3-acre Pineapple Garden Maze, made up of 14,000 tropical plants and trees. If you do nothing else, stop by the cafeteria in the back for a delicious pineapple soft-serve Dole Whip. This is about a 40-minute drive from Waikiki, a suitable stop on the way to or from the North Shore. ⊠ 64-1550 Kamehameha Hwy., Wahiawa ☎ 808/621–8408 ⊕ www. doleplantation.com ☒ Plantation free, Pineapple Express $12, maze $9, garden tour $8.

Kukaniloko Birthstone State Monument
MEMORIAL | In the cool uplands of
Wahiawa is haunting Kukaniloko, where
noble chieftesses went to give birth to
high-ranking children. One of the most
significant cultural sites on the island,
the lava-rock stones here were believed
to possess the power to ease the labor
pains of childbirth. The site is marked by
approximately 180 stones covering about
a half acre. It's a 40- to 45-minute drive
from Waikiki. ⊠ *Kamehameha Hwy. and
Whitmore Ave., Wahiawa* ✛ *The north
side of Wahiawa town.*

The North Shore

*Approximately 35 miles (one hour by car)
north of downtown Honolulu, approximately 25 miles (one hour by car) from
Kualoa Regional Park (Chinaman's Hat) in
Windward Oahu.*

An hour from town and a world away in
atmosphere, Oahu's North Shore, roughly from Kahuku Point to Kaena Point, is
about small farms and big waves, tourist
traps, and otherworldly landscapes. Parks
and beaches, roadside fruit stands and
shrimp shacks, a bird sanctuary, and a
valley preserve offer a dozen reasons to
stop between the onetime plantation
town of Kahuku and the surf mecca of
Haleiwa.

Haleiwa has had many lives, from resort
getaway in the 1900s to plantation town
through the 20th century to its life today
as a surf and tourist magnet. Beyond
Haleiwa is the tiny village of Waialua; a
string of beach parks; an airfield where
gliders, hang gliders, and parachutists
play; and, at the end of the road, Kaena
Point State Recreation Area, which
offers a brisk hike, striking views, and
whale-watching in season.

Pack wisely for a day's North Shore
excursion: swim and snorkel gear, light
jacket and hat (the weather is mercurial,

especially in winter), sunscreen and sunglasses, bottled water and snacks, towels and a picnic blanket, and both sandals
and closed-toe shoes for hiking. A small
cooler is nice; you may want to pick up
some fruit or fresh corn. As always, leave
valuables in the hotel safe, and lock the
car whenever you park.

GETTING HERE AND AROUND
From Waikiki, the quickest route to the
North Shore is H1 east to H2 north, and
then the Kamehameha Highway past
Wahiawa. You'll hit Haleiwa in just under
an hour. The windward route (H1 east,
H3, Likelike or Pali Highway, through the
mountains, or Kamehameha Highway
north) takes at least 90 minutes to Haleiwa, but the drive is far prettier.

Waialua

30 miles northwest of Honolulu.

A tranquil, multicultural burg with sleepy
residential areas, uncrowded beach
parks, and small mom-and-pop businesses, Waialua provides refuge from
neighboring (and often tourist-choked)
Haleiwa. In the 1900s, Waialua Sugar
Company attracted workers from around
the world, and their descendants continue to live and work here. The former
sugar operation buildings now hold a
General Store and eclectic, trendy shops,
art studios, maker spaces for surfboard
shapers and other craftspeople, and a
coffee mill. Waialua is also the gateway to
a wild and scenic coastline that includes
Mokuleia Beach Park, Kaena Point State
Recreation Area, and Dillingham Airport,
where gliders and parachutists launch
and land.

👁 Sights

Kaena Point State Park
NATIONAL/STATE PARK | FAMILY | The name
means "the heat" and, indeed, this
windy barren coast lacks both shade

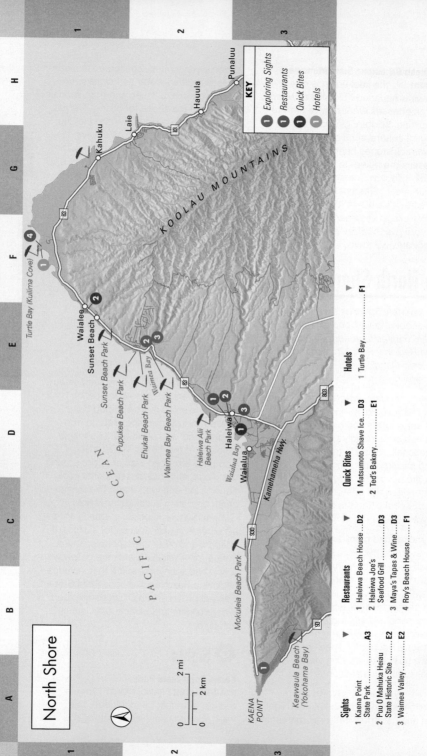

North Shore

KEY
- 1 Exploring Sights
- 1 Restaurants
- 1 Quick Bites
- 1 Hotels

KOOLAU MOUNTAINS

PACIFIC OCEAN

Turtle Bay (Kuilima Cove)

Mokuleia Beach Park

Keawaula Beach (Yokohama Bay)

KAENA POINT

Mokuleia Beach Park

Waialua

Haleiwa

Waialua Bay

Haleiwa Alii Beach Park

Waimea Bay Beach Park

Waimea Bay

Ehukai Beach Park

Pupukea Beach Park

Sunset Beach Park

Sunset Beach

Waialee

Kahuku

Laie

Hauula

Punaluu

Kamehameha Hwy.

Sights	▶
1 Kaena Point State Park	A3
2 Puu O Mahuka Heiau State Historic Site	E2
3 Waimea Valley	E2

Restaurants	▶
1 Haleiwa Beach House	D2
2 Haleiwa Joe's Seafood Grill	D3
3 Maya's Tapas & Wine	D3
4 Roy's Beach House	F1

Quick Bites	▶
1 Matsumoto Shave Ice	D3
2 Ted's Bakery	E1

Hotels	▶
1 Turtle Bay	F1

0   2 mi
0   2 km

and freshwater (or any man-made amenities). Pack water, wear sturdy closed-toe shoes, don sunscreen and a hat, and lock the car. The hike is along a rutted dirt road, mostly flat and nearly 3 miles long, (one-way) ending in a rocky, sandy headland. It is here that Hawaiians believed the souls of the dead met with their family gods, and, if judged worthy to enter the afterlife, leapt off into eternal darkness at Leinaakauane, just south of the point. In summer and at low tide, the small coves offer bountiful shelling; in winter, don't venture near the water. Rare native plants dot the landscape, and seabirds like the Laysan albatross nest here. If you're lucky, you might spot seals sunbathing on the rocks. From November through March, watch for humpbacks spouting and breaching. Binoculars and a camera are highly recommended. ✉ *69-385 Farrington Hwy., Waialua* ⊕ *dlnr.hawaii.gov/dsp/parks/oahu/ kaena-point-state-park.*

⊕ Beaches

Mokuleia Beach Park

BEACH—SIGHT | There is a reason why the producers of the TV show *Lost* chose this beach for their set. On the remote northwest point of the island, it is about 10 miles from the closest store or public restroom. Its beauty is in its lack of facilities and isolation—all the joy of being stranded on a deserted island without the trauma of the plane crash. The beach is wide and white, the waters bright blue (but a little choppy) and full of sea turtles and other marine life. Mokuleia is a great secret find; just remember to pack supplies and use caution, as there are no lifeguards. **Amenities:** parking (no fee). **Best for:** sunset, walking. ✉ *68-67 Farrington Hwy., Waialua* ⊕ *West of Haleiwa town center, across from Dillingham Airfield.*

Haleiwa

30 miles northwest of Honolulu, 3 miles northeast of Waialua.

North Shore's shopping, dining, and surf culture hub, Haleiwa has preserved and melded its historic plantation-era roots with a laid-back, 1960s-era vibe. During the 1920s, this seaside hamlet boasted a posh hotel at the end of a railroad line (both long gone), while the '60s saw hippies gathered here, followed by surfers from around the world. The town sits amid a picture-perfect setting on Waialua Bay, where the Anahulu River empties into the harbor. Haleiwa Alii Beach Park and Haleiwa Beach border the bay and provide endless opportunities for water sports and other activities.

Today, the streets of Historic Haleiwa Town reflect a fun mix of old and new, with charming general stores and contemporary boutiques, galleries, and eateries. Be sure to stop in at Liliuokalani Protestant Church, founded by missionaries in the 1830s. It's fronted by a large, stone archway built in 1910 and covered with night-blooming cereus. Also check out the historic Rainbow Bridge, whose iconic double arches appear on many local works of art.

⊕ Beaches

Haleiwa Alii Beach Park

BEACH—SIGHT | **FAMILY** | The winter waves are impressive here, but in summer, the ocean is like a lake, ideal for family swimming. The beach itself is big and often full of locals. Its broad lawn off the highway invites volleyball and Frisbee games and groups of barbecuers. This is also the opening break for the Triple Crown of Surfing, and the grass is often filled with art festivals or carnivals. **Amenities:** lifeguards; parking (no fee); showers; toilets. **Best for:** surfing; swimming. ✉ *66-167 Haleiwa Rd., Haleiwa* ⊕ *North of Haleiwa town center and past harbor.*

Kaena Point is remote and barren, but it's a beautiful place of religious significance: the ancient Hawaiians believed it was where the souls of the dead departed for the afterlife.

🍴 Restaurants

Haleiwa Beach House

$$ | AMERICAN | One of the newer restaurants on the North Shore takes full advantage of its epic views of the water and the glorious building it calls home (it was formerly occupied by longtime local icon Jameson's by the Sea). The menu is chock full of surf-and-turf options, from juicy burgers to grilled steaks, blackened fish to lobster and shrimp red Thai curry. **Known for:** view and setting that can't be beat; solid, reliable beef, seafood, salads, and kids options; craft beers on draft and a nice wine list. $ Average main: $25 ✉ 62-540 Kamemaheha Hwy, Haleiwa ☎ 808/637–3435 ⊕ www.haleiwabeach-house.com.

Haleiwa Joe's Seafood Grill

$$$ | AMERICAN | After the long drive to the North Shore, watching the boats and surfers come and go from the harbor while you enjoy a mai tai on Haleiwa Joe's open-air lanai may be just what you need. This casual little joint, just past the Anahulu Stream Bridge, rarely changes (and to some, that might feel dated), but regulars appreciate the familiarity;a more upscale Kaneohe location overlooks the lush Haiku Gardens. **Known for:** reliable food with a nice harbor setting; crunchy coconut shrimp; good daily fish specials. $ Average main: $27 ✉ 66-011 Kamehameha Hwy., Haleiwa ☎ 808/637–8005 ⊕ haleiwajoes.com.

Maya's Tapas & Wine

$$ | TAPAS | A cozy space with a slightly sophisticated (for the North Shore) vibe, Maya's serves up classic Spanish and Mediterranean dishes with Island twists. Here, seafood paella is made with local line-caught fish and shrimp, a burger combines Molokai venison and Kunoa beef, and hand-tossed flatbreads come with roasted local veggies and macadamia nut pesto. **Known for:** craft cocktails and sangria; savory paella and other specials; popular happy hour and Sunday brunch. $ Average main: $22 ✉ 66-250 Kamehameha Hwy., Unit D-101, Haleiwa ☎ 808/200–2964 ⊕ www.mayasta-pasandwine.com ⊗ No dinner Sun.

Malasadas 🍴

Malasadas are a contribution of the Portuguese, who came to the Hawaiian Islands to work on the plantations. Roughly translated, the name means "half-cooked," which refers to the origin of these deep-fried, heavily sugared treats said to have been created as a way to use up scraps of rich, buttery egg dough. They are similar to fluffy donuts and are offered in a multitude of flavors; some are fruit or cream-filled. A handful of bakeries specialize in them: **Leonard's** (✉ *933 Kapahulu Avenue*); **Kamehameha Bakery** (✉ *1284 Kalani Street, unit D-106*); and **Pipeline Bakery** (✉ *3632 Waialae Avenue*). Honolulu restaurants sometimes serve an upscale version stuffed with fruit puree, and they can usually be found at farmers markets, fairs, and carnivals. Eat them fresh and hot or not at all.

☕ Coffee and Quick Bites

Matsumoto Shave Ice

$ | CAFÉ | For a real slice of Haleiwa life, stop at Matsumoto Shave Ice, a family-run business in a building dating from 1910, for cool treats that are available in every flavor imaginable. For something different, order a shave ice with adzuki beans—the red beans are boiled until soft, mixed with sugar, and then placed in the cone with the ice on top. **Known for:** one of the most popular shave ice spots on Oahu; the Matsumoto with lemon, pineapple, and coconut syrup; house-made adzuki beans. [$] *Average main: $4* ✉ *66-111 Kamehameha Hwy., Suite 605, Haleiwa* ☎ *808/637–4827* 🌐 *www.matsumotoshaveice.com.*

🛍 Shopping

The Growing Keiki

CLOTHING | Frequent visitors return to this store year after year for a fresh supply of unique, locally made, Hawaiian-style clothing for youngsters. ✉ *66-051 Kamehameha Hwy., Haleiwa* ☎ *808/637–4544* 🌐 *www.thegrowingkeiki.com.*

★ Silver Moon Emporium

CLOTHING | The small boutique carries everything from Brighton jewelry and European designer wear to fashionable T-shirts, shoes, and handbags. Expect attentive and personalized yet casual service. The stock changes frequently, and there's always something wonderful on sale. No matter what your taste, you'll find something for everyday wear or special occasions. ✉ *North Shore Marketplace, 66-250 Kamehameha Hwy., Haleiwa* ☎ *808/637–7710.*

Pupukea

6 miles northeast of Haleiwa.

Pupukea is a tiny village that anchors the Seven Mile Miracle—the legendary stretch of North Shore coast that faithfully serves up some of the world's best barrels and perfectly shaped waves every winter. It's also home to Foodland, the only grocery store between Kahuku/Laie and Haleiwa, which means you're likely to rub elbows with seasoned professional surfers and visiting celebrities, along with slipper-clad locals, in the checkout line. Across the street are Shark's Cove and Three Tables, both excellent

While Waimea Bay is known for its big winter waves and surf culture, the Waimea Valley is an area of great historical significance. It's also known for its botanical specimens, including big tropical trees.

snorkeling and scuba sites when the winter swells abate. Banzai Pipeline and Sunset Beach are just a mile up the road. Drive up the hill behind Foodland to explore the sacred Puu o Mahuka Heiau, the largest shrine on the island.

◉ Sights

Puu o Mahuka Heiau State Historic Site

ARCHAEOLOGICAL SITE | Worth a stop for its spectacular views from a bluff high above the ocean overlooking Waimea Bay, this sacred spot is the largest heiau on the island and spans nearly 2 acres. At one time it was used as a *heiau luakini,* or a temple for human sacrifices. It's now on the National Register of Historic Places. Turn up the road at the Pupukea Foodland and follow the road up to the heiau. ⊠ *Pupukea Rd., ½ mile north of Waimea Bay, Pupukea* ✛ *From Rte. 83, turn right on Pupukea Rd. and drive 1 mile uphill* ⊕ *dlnr.hawaii.gov/dsp/parks/oahu/ puu-o-mahuka-heiau-state-historic-site.*

★ Waimea Valley

NATURE PRESERVE | FAMILY | Waimea may get lots of press for the giant winter waves in the bay, but the valley itself is a newsmaker and an ecological treasure in its own right. The local nonprofit is working to conserve and restore the natural habitat. Follow the Kamananui Stream up the valley through the 1,875 acres of gardens. The botanical collections here have more than 5,000 species of tropical flora, including a superb gathering of Polynesian plants. It's the best place on the island to see native species, such as the endangered Hawaiian moorhen. You can also see the restored Hale o Lono *heiau* (shrine) along with other ancient archaeological sites; evidence suggests that the area was an important spiritual center. Daily activities include botanical walking tours and cultural tours. At the back of the valley, Waihi Falls plunges 45 feet into a swimming pond. ■ **TIP→ Bring your board shorts—a swim is the perfect way to end your hike, although the pond can get crowded. Be sure to bring**

mosquito repellent, too; it can get buggy. ✉ *59-864 Kamehameha Hwy., Pupukea* ☎ *808/638–7766* ⊕ *www.waimeavalley. net* ☑ *$18.*

Beaches

Ehukai Beach Park

BEACH—SIGHT | What sets Ehukai apart is the view of the famous Banzai Pipeline. Here the winter waves curl into magnificent tubes, making it an experienced wave-rider's dream. It's also an inexperienced swimmer's nightmare. Spring and summer waves, on the other hand, are more accommodating to the average person, and there's good snorkeling. Except when the surf contests are going on, there's no reason to stay on the central strip. Travel in either direction from the center, and the conditions remain the same but the population thins out, leaving you with a magnificent stretch of sand all to yourself. **Amenities:** lifeguards; parking (no fee); showers; toilets. **Best for:** snorkeling; surfing. ✉ *59-337 Ke Nui Rd., Pupukea* ✛ *1 mile north of Foodland at Pupukea.*

★ Pupukea Beach Park (*Shark's Cove*)

BEACH—SIGHT | Surrounded by shady trees, Pupukea Beach Park is pounded by surf in the winter months but offers great diving and snorkeling in summer (March through October). The cavernous lava tubes and tunnels are great for both novice and experienced snorkelers and divers. It's imperative that you wear reef shoes at all times since there are a lot of sharp rocks. Sharp rocks also mean that this beach isn't the best for little ones. Some dive-tour companies offer round-trip transportation from Waikiki. Equipment rentals and dining options are nearby. **Amenities:** parking (no fee); showers; toilets. **Best for:** diving; snorkeling; swimming. ✉ *Pupukea* ✛ *3½ miles north of Haleiwa, across street from Foodland.*

Sunset Beach Park

BEACH—SIGHT | The beach is broad, the sand is soft, the summer waves are gentle—making for good snorkeling—and the winter surf is crashing. Many love searching this shore for the puka shells that adorn the necklaces you see everywhere. **Amenities:** lifeguards; parking (no fee); showers; toilets. **Best for:** snorkeling; sunset; surfing. ✉ *59-144 Kamehameha Hwy., Pupukea* ✛ *1 mile north of Ehukai Beach Park.*

★ Waimea Bay Beach Park

BEACH—SIGHT | Made popular in that old Beach Boys song "Surfin' U.S.A.," Waimea Bay Beach Park is a slice of big-wave heaven, home to king-size 25- to 30-foot winter waves. Summer is the time to swim and snorkel in the calm waters. The shore break is great for novice body surfers. Due to the beach's popularity, its postage-stamp parking lot is quickly filled, but it's also possible to park along the side of the road and walk in. **Amenities:** lifeguards; parking (no fee); showers; toilets. **Best for:** snorkeling; surfing; swimming. ✉ *61-31 Kamehameha Hwy., Pupukea* ✛ *Across from Waimea Valley, 3 miles north of Haleiwa.*

☕ Coffee and Quick Bites

Ted's Bakery

$ | **AMERICAN** | Sunburned tourists and salty surfers rub shoulders in their quest for Ted's famous chocolate *haupia* pie (layered coconut and dark chocolate puddings topped with whipped cream) and hearty plates—like garlic shrimp, gravy-drenched hamburger steak, and mahimahi. Parking spots and the umbrella-shaded tables are a premium, so be prepared to grab and go; if you can't get enough of that haupia goodness, Foodland and other grocery chains typically stock a selection of the famous pies as well. **Known for:** Ted's pies, which seem to show up at every Oahu pot luck; reliable all-day dining; plate lunches.

$ *Average main: $12* ✉ *59-024 Kamehameha Hwy., Pupukea* ☎ *808/638–8207* 🌐 *www.tedsbakery.com.*

Kahuku

Kawela Bay is 5½ miles northeast of Pupukea, Kahuku is about 9 miles northeast of Pupukea.

The Kahuku district, which stretches from Kahuku town to Kawela Bay, includes Kahuku Point, the northernmost point on Oahu. It's best known for fresh fruits and veggies from local farms (watch for farm stands along the highway), shrimp shacks, and exceptional high school football stars who go on to play at top-tier colleges and the NFL. Kahuku town is a collection of brand-name stores and tiny mom-and-pop shops amid modest residential neighborhoods filled with longtime island residents. Multimillion-dollar homes line the shores of the gated Kawela Bay community, but the public can access the beach off Kamehameha Highway at Kawela Camp. Park on the side of the road and walk about a quarter mile along a trail to get there.

Beaches

Turtle Bay (*Kuilima Cove*)
BEACH—SIGHT | FAMILY | Now known more for its namesake resort than its magnificent beach at Kuilima Cove, Turtle Bay is mostly passed over on the way to the better-known beaches of Sunset and Waimea. But for the average visitor with average swimming capabilities, this is a good place to be on the North Shore. The crescent-shape beach is protected by a huge sea wall. You can see and hear the fury of the northern swell while blissfully floating in cool, calm waters. The convenience of this spot is also hard to pass up—there is a concession selling sandwiches and sunblock right on the beach. The resort has free parking for beach guests. **Amenities:** food and drink; parking (no fee); showers; toilets. **Best for:** sunset; swimming. ✉ *57-20 Kuilima Dr., 4 miles north of Kahuku, Kahuku* ✣ *Turn into Turtle Bay Resort and follow signs to public parking lot and beach access spots.*

🍴 Restaurants

Roy's Beach House
$$$$ | MODERN HAWAIIAN | Loyalists of Roy Yamaguchi's iconic spots in Hawaii Kai and Waikiki are thrilled that he's also represented on the North Shore, in this rustic-beam-and-concrete-floor pavilion literally on the sand at Turtle Bay. All the favorites are served at this more beach-casual spot, from the miso butterfish to the beef short ribs, along with a more casual lunch menu. **Known for:** casual, romantic setting right on the beach; Roy's signature dishes; special-occasion celebrations. $ *Average main: $42* ✉ *Turtle Bay, 57-091 Kamehameha Hwy., Kahuku* ☎ *808/293–0801* 🌐 *www.roysbeachhouse.com.*

🛏 Hotels

★ Turtle Bay
$$$$ | RESORT | Sprawling over nearly 1,300 acres of natural landscape on the edge of Kuilima Point in Kahuku, the Turtle Bay resort boasts spacious guest rooms averaging nearly 500 square feet and with lanai that showcase stunning peninsula views. **Pros:** fabulous open public spaces in a secluded area of Oahu; beautiful two-level spa; excellent location for exploring the North Shore. **Cons:** very remote—even Haleiwa is a 20-minute drive; hefty resort fee; 24/7 resort living isn't for everyone. $ *Rooms from: $360* ✉ *57-091 Kamehameha Hwy., Kahuku* ☎ *808/293–6000, 800/203–3650, 866/827–5321 for reservations* 🌐 *www.turtlebayresort.com* 🛏 *535 rooms* 🍴 *No meals.*

If you're a snorkeler, head straight for Hanauma Bay, the best and most popular place to snorkel on Oahu.

Windward (East) Oahu

Looking at Honolulu's topsy-turvy urban sprawl, you would never suspect the windward side existed.

It's a secret Oahuans like to keep, so they can watch the awe on the faces of their guests when the car emerges from the tunnels through the mountains and they gaze for the first time on the panorama of turquoise bays and emerald valleys watched over by the knife-edged Koolau ridges. Jaws literally drop. Every time. And this just a 15-minute drive from downtown.

It's on this side of the island where many native Hawaiians live. Evidence of traditional lifestyles is abundant in crumbling fishponds, rock platforms that once were altars, taro patches still being worked, and throw-net fishermen posed stock-still above the water (though today, they're invariably wearing polarized sunglasses, the better to spot the fish).

Here the pace is slower, more oriented toward nature. Beachgoing, hiking, diving, surfing, and boating are the draws, along with a visit to the Polynesian Cultural Center and poking through little shops and wayside stores.

GETTING HERE AND AROUND

Keeping in mind there is really only one road that follows the windward coastline from Waikiki, you do have several options to get to this side. You can spend a day hugging the coast as you drive east and then turn north until you arrive at the home of the Polynesian Cultural Center, Laie. For this partial "circle island tour" first head east on the H1 interstate past Diamond Head until it becomes Kalanianaole Highway. Look for Kamehameha Highway once you get to Kaneohe and continue following this two-lane road all the way to the North Shore. Just as spectacular but a much more direct route is by taking the H1 Highway to either the Pali, Like Like, or H3 interstate across the mountains and through the tunnels to Kaneohe and beyond. While the Pali

When Doris Duke died in 1993, her estate, Shangri La, became a museum of Islamic culture and art. Tours leave from the Honolulu Museum of Art in downtown Honolulu.

Highway gives you the option of stopping to take in the view at the Pali Lookout, the H3 offers the most breathtakingly beautiful arrival to this side of the island.

Hawaii Kai

Driving southeast from Waikiki on busy, four-lane Kalanianaole Highway, you'll pass a dozen bedroom communities tucked into the valleys at the foot of the Koolau Range, with fleeting glimpses of the ocean from a couple of pocket parks. Suddenly, civilization falls away, the road narrows to two lanes, and you enter the rugged coastline of Koko Head and Ka Iwi.

This is a cruel coastline: dry, windswept, and with rocky shores and untamed waves that are notoriously treacherous. While walking its beaches, do not turn your back on the ocean, don't venture close to wet areas where high waves occasionally reach, and be sure to heed warning signs.

⊙ Sights

Halona Blowhole

VIEWPOINT | Below a scenic turnout along the Koko Head shoreline, this oft-photographed lava tube sucks the ocean in and spits it out. Don't get too close, as conditions can get dangerous. ■**TIP→ Look to your right to see the tiny beach below that was used to film the wave-washed love scene in** *From Here to Eternity*. In winter, this is a good spot to watch whales at play. Offshore, the island of Molokai calls like a distant siren, and every once in a while Lanai is visible in blue silhouette. Take your valuables with you, and lock your car, because this scenic location is overrun with tourists and therefore a hot spot for petty thieves. ⊠ *Kalanianaole Hwy., Hawaii Kai ⊹ 1 mile east of Hanauma Bay.*

Koko Crater Botanical Gardens

GARDEN | If you've visited any of Oahu's other botanical gardens, this one will stand in stark contrast. Inside the tallest tuff cone on Oahu, in one of the hottest and driest areas on the island, Koko Crater Botanical Garden allows visitors the opportunity to see dryland species of plants including baobab trees, cacti, plumeria, and bougainvillea. ■TIP→ Be sure to bring plenty of water, sunscreen, and a hat. This is the driest, hottest side of the island. ⊠ 7491 Kokonani St., Hawaii Kai ✛ Entrance at end of Kokonani St. ☎ 808/522-7066 ⊕ www.honolulu.gov/parks/hbg.html ⊐ Free.

Lanai Lookout
VIEWPOINT | A little more than half a mile past Hanauma Bay as you head toward Makapuu Point, you'll see a turnout on the ocean side with some fine views of the coastline. In winter, you'll have an opportunity to see storm-generated waves crashing against lava cliffs. This is also a popular place for winter whale-watching, so bring your binoculars, some sunscreen, and a picnic lunch, and join the small crowd scanning for telltale white spouts of water only a few hundred yards away. On clear days, you should be able to see the islands of Molokai and Lanai off in the distance, hence the name. ⊠ Kalanianaole Hwy., Hawaii Kai ✛ Just past Hanauma Bay.

★ Shangri La Museum of Islamic Art, Culture & Design
HOUSE | For more than 50 years, the home was a work in progress as Dories Duke traveled the world, buying art and furnishings and picking up ideas for her Mughal Garden, for the Playhouse in the style of a 17th-century Irani pavilion, and for the water terraces and tropical gardens. When she died in 1993, Duke left instructions that her home was to become a public center for the study of Islamic art. The house is open by guided tour only, and reservations are required. Book your spot as early as possible, as tours fill up very quickly. Tours take 2½ hours including transportation from the Honolulu Museum of Art (900 S. Beretania St., downtown Honolulu), where all tours begin. Children under eight are not admitted. ⊠ Hawaii Kai ☎ 808/532-3853 for Honolulu Museum of Art ⊕ www.shangrilahawaii.org ⊐ Tour $25 ($2 fee for online reservations, $2 for phone reservations) ⊗ Closed Sun.–Tues. and Sept.

Beaches

★ Hanauma Bay Nature Preserve
BEACH—SIGHT | FAMILY | Picture this as the world's biggest open-air aquarium. You go here to see fish, and fish you'll see. Due to their exposure to thousands of visitors every week, these fish are more like family pets than the skittish marine life you might expect. An old volcanic crater has created a haven from the waves where the coral has thrived. There's an educational center where you must watch a nine-minute video about the nature preserve before being allowed down to the bay. ■TIP→ The bay is best early in the morning (around 7), before the crowds arrive; it can be difficult to park later in the day.

Snorkel equipment and lockers are available for rent, and there's an entry fee for nonresidents. Smoking is not allowed, and the beach is closed on Tuesday. Wednesday to Monday, the beach is open 6 am–6 pm (until 7 pm June–August). There's a tram from the parking lot to the beach, or you can walk the short distance. Need transportation? Take TheBus each way from anywhere on the island. Alternatively, Hanauma Bay Tours runs snorkeling tours to Hanauma Bay, with equipment and transportation from Waikiki hotels. **Amenities:** food and drink; lifeguards; parking (fee); showers; toilets. **Best for:** snorkeling; swimming. ⊠ 7455 Kalanianaole Hwy., Hawaii Kai ☎ 808/768-6861 ⊕ www.honolulu.gov/cms-dpr-menu/site-dpr-sitearticles/1716-hanauma-bay-home.html ⊐ Nonresidents $8; parking $1; mask and snorkel from $12; tram from parking lot to beach $3 round-trip ⊗ Closed Tues.

3

Oahu WINDWARD (EAST) OAHU

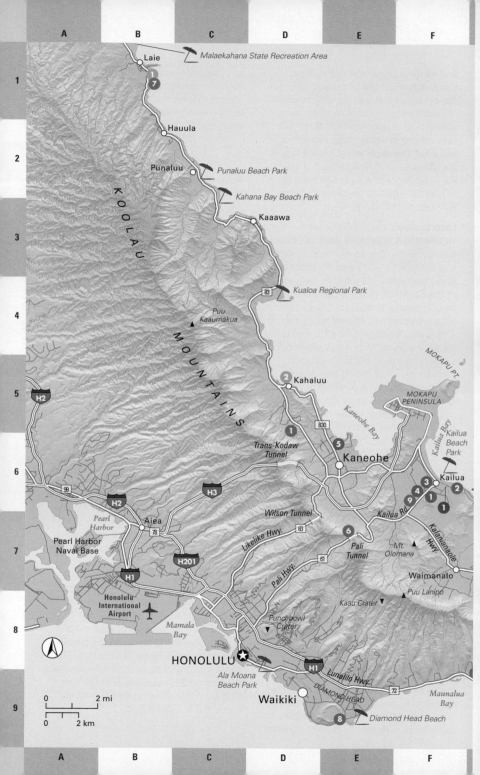

Malaekahana State Recreation Area

Laie

Hauula

Punaluu

Punaluu Beach Park

Kahana Bay Beach Park

Kaaawa

K O O L A U

Kualoa Regional Park

Puu
Kaaumakua

M O U N T A I N S

Kahaluu

MOKAPU PT.

MOKAPU
PENINSULA

Kaneohe Bay

Trans-Kodaw
Tunnel

Kaneohe

Kailua
Beach
Park

Kailua

H2

H2

Aiea

Pearl
Harbor

H3

Wilson Tunnel

Kailua Rd.

Pearl Harbor
Naval Base

Likelike Hwy.

Pali Hwy.

Pali
Tunnel

Mt.
Olomana

Kalanianaole Hwy.

Waimanalo

H201

H1

Honolulu
International
Airport

Puu Lanipo

Mamala
Bay

Punchbowl
Crater

Kaau Crater

HONOLULU

Ala Moana Beach Park

H1

Lunalilo Hwy.

DIAMOND HEAD

Maunalua
Bay

Waikiki

0   2 mi

0   2 km

Diamond Head Beach

Windward (East) Oahu

Sights ▼

1 Byodo-In Temple........ **D5**
2 Halona Blowhole **G9**
3 Koko Crater
  Botanical Gardens...... **G8**
4 Lanai Lookout **G9**
5 Makapuu Point.......... **H8**
6 Nuuanu Pali Lookout.... **E7**
7 Polynesian
  Cultural Center **B1**
8 Shangri La Museum
  of Islamic Art,
  Culture & Design......... **E9**
9 Ulupo Heiau
  State Historic Site **F6**

Restaurants ▼

1 Boots & Kimo's
  Homestyle Kitchen **F6**
2 Buzz's Lanikai **F6**
3 Cinnamon's
  Restaurant................ **F6**
4 Kalapawai Cafe
  & Deli..................... **F6**
5 Pah Ke's Chinese
  Restaurant................ **E5**
6 Roy's Hawaii Kai **G8**

Quick Bites ▼

1 Island Snow **F6**

Hotels ▼

1 Courtyard Oahu
  North Shore **B1**
2 Paradise Bay Resort ... **D5**

KEY

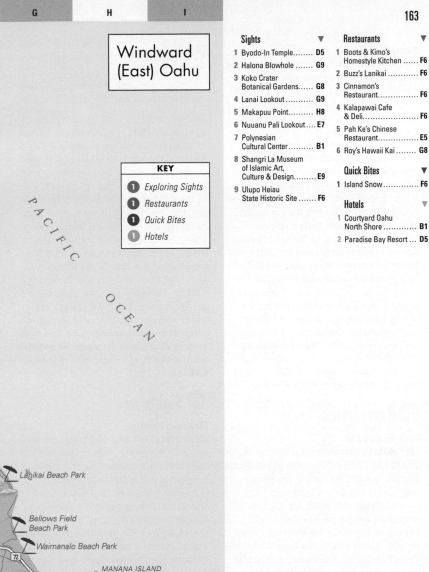

1 Exploring Sights
1 Restaurants
1 Quick Bites
1 Hotels

PACIFIC OCEAN

Lanikai Beach Park

Bellows Field
Beach Park

Waimanalo Beach Park

72

MANANA ISLAND
(RABBIT ISLAND)

Makapuu Beach Park
5

Sandy Beach Park
3 ▼ Koko Crater   2
6 Hawaii Kai
4   Halona Cove

Hanauma Bay
Nature Preserve
Hanauma Bay

KOKO
HEAD

Sandy Beach Park

BEACH—SIGHT | Probably the most popular beach with locals on this side of Oahu, the broad, sloping beach is covered with sunbathers there to watch the "Show" and soak up rays. The Show is a shore break that's like no other in the Islands. Monster ocean swells rolling into the beach combined with the sudden rise in the ocean floor causes waves to jack up and crash magnificently on the shore. Expert surfers and body boarders young and old brave this danger to get some of the biggest barrels you can find for body surfing. ⚠ **But keep in mind that the beach is nicknamed Break-Neck Beach for a reason: many neck and back injuries are sustained here each year.** Use extreme caution when swimming here, or just kick back and watch the drama unfold from the comfort of your beach chair. **Amenities:** lifeguards; parking (no fee); showers; toilets. **Best for:** walking. ✉ *7850 Kalanianaole Hwy., Hawaii Kai* ✥ *Makai (toward ocean) of Kalanianaole Hwy., 2 miles east of Hanauma Bay.*

🍴 Restaurants

Roy's Hawaii Kai

$$$ | **MODERN HAWAIIAN** | Roy Yamaguchi is one of the 12 founding chefs of Hawaiian regional cuisine, a culinary movement that put Hawaii on the food map back in 1991. Opened in 1988, his flagship restaurant across the highway from Maunalua Bay is still packed every night with food-savvy visitors mixing with well-heeled residents. **Known for:** spectacular sunset views and a tiki torch–lit lanai and bar area; small and large portions available for many dishes; signature menu items like blackened ahi with a cultlike following. [$] *Average main: $34* ✉ *Hawaii Kai Corporate Plaza, 6600 Kalanianaole Hwy., Hawaii Kai* ☎ *808/396–7697* 🌐 *www.royshawaii.com* 🕒 *No lunch.*

Waimanalo

14 miles northeast of Honolulu, 11 miles north of Hawaii Kai.

This modest little seaside town flanked by chiseled cliffs is worth a visit. Home to more Native Hawaiian families than Kailua to the north or Hawaii Kai to the south, Waimanalo's biggest draws are its beautiful beaches, offering glorious views to the windward side. Bellows Beach is great for swimming, body surfing, and camping, and Waimanalo Beach Park is also safe for swimming. Down the side roads, as you head *mauka* (toward the mountains), are little farms that grow a variety of fruits and flowers. Toward the back of the valley are small ranches with grazing horses. **■ TIP→ If you see any trucks selling corn, and you're staying at a place where you can cook it, be sure to get some in Waimanalo. It may be the sweetest you'll ever eat, and prices are the lowest on Oahu.**

👁 Sights

Makapuu Point

VIEWPOINT | This spot has breathtaking views of the ocean, mountains, and the windward Islands. The point of land jutting out in the distance is Mokapu Peninsula, site of a U.S. Marine base. The spired mountain peak is Mt. Olomana. On the long pier is part of the Makai Undersea Test Range, a research facility that's closed to the public. Offshore is Manana Island (Rabbit Island), a picturesque cay said to resemble a swimming bunny with its ears pulled back. Nestled in the cliff face is the **Makapuu Lighthouse,** which became operational in 1909 and has the largest lighthouse lens in America. The lighthouse is closed to the public, but near the Makapuu Point turnout you can find the start of a paved mile-long road (it's closed to vehicular traffic). Hike up to the top of the 647-foot bluff for a closer view of the lighthouse and, in

Did You Know?

Windward Oahu's Makapuu Beach is protected by Makapuu Point, but currents are still strong so be cautious when in the water.

winter, to do some whale-watching. ⊠ *Ka Iwi State Scenic Shoreline, Kalanianaole Hwy., Waimanalo* ✛ *At Makapuu Beach* ⊕ *dlnr.hawaii.gov/dsp/hiking/oahu/ makapuu-point-lighthouse-trail.*

☺ Beaches

★ Bellows Field Beach Park
BEACH—SIGHT | Bellows is the same beach as Waimanalo, but it's under the auspices of the military, making it more friendly for visitors—though that also limits public access to weekends. The park area is excellent for camping, and ironwood trees provide plenty of shade. ■**TIP→ The beach is best before 2 pm. After 2, trade winds bring clouds that get hung up on steep mountains nearby, causing overcast skies.** There are no food concessions, but McDonald's and other takeout options are right outside the entrance gate. **Amenities:** lifeguards; parking (no fee); showers; toilets. **Best for:** solitude; swimming; walking. ⊠ *520 Tinker Rd., Waimanalo* ✛ *Enter on Kalanianaole Hwy. near Waimanalo town center.*

Makapuu Beach Park
BEACH—SIGHT | A magnificent beach protected by Makapuu Point welcomes you to the windward side. Hang gliders circle above, and the water is filled with body boarders. Just off the coast you can see Bird Island, a sanctuary for aquatic fowl, jutting out of the blue. The currents can be heavy, so check with a lifeguard if you're unsure of safety. Before you leave, take the prettiest (and coldest) outdoor shower available on the island. Being surrounded by tropical flowers and foliage while you rinse off that sand will be a memory you will cherish from this side of the rock. **Amenities:** lifeguards; parking (no fee); showers; toilets. **Best for:** sunrise; walking. ⊠ *41-095 Kalanianaole Hwy., Waimanalo* ✛ *Across from Sea Life Park, 2 miles south of Waimanalo.*

Waimanalo Beach Park
BEACH—SIGHT | FAMILY | One of the most beautiful beaches on the island, Waimanalo is a local pick, busy with picnicking families and active sports fields. Expect a wide stretch of sand; turquoise, emerald, and deep blue seas; and gentle shore-breaking waves that are fun for all ages. Theft is an occasional problem, so lock your car. **Amenities:** lifeguards; parking (no fee); showers; toilets. **Best for:** sunrise; swimming; walking. ⊠ *41-849 Kalanianaole Hwy., Waimanalo* ✛ *South of Waimanalo town center.*

Kailua

13 miles northeast of Honolulu, 6 miles north of Waimanalo.

Upscale Kailua is the most easily accessed town on the windward side. With two of Oahu's best beaches, Kailua town also offers great shopping and dining opportunities in its central core. You could easily spend a day visiting the stunning beaches, kayaking, exploring a hidden *heiau* (shrine), picnicking, or dining out with locals.

◉ Sights

Ulupo Heiau State Historic Site
ARCHAEOLOGICAL SITE | Although they may look like piles of rocks to the uninitiated, *heiau* are sacred stone platforms for the worship of the gods and date from ancient times. *Ulupo* means "night inspiration," referring to the legendary Menehune, a mythical race of diminutive people who are said to have built the heiau under the cloak of darkness. Find this spot, with signs near the heiau also explaining Kailua's early history, tucked next to the Windward YMCA. ⊠ *Kalanianaole Hwy. and Kailua Rd., Kailua* ✛ *Behind Windward YMCA* ⊕ *dlnr.hawaii.gov/dsp/parks/oahu/ ulupo-heiau-state-historic-site.*

Beaches

★ Kailua Beach Park

BEACH—SIGHT | FAMILY | A cobalt-blue sea and a wide continuous arc of powdery sand make Kailua Beach Park one of the island's best beaches, illustrated by the crowds of local families who spend their weekend days here. This is like a big Lanikai Beach, but a little windier and a little wider, and a better spot for spending a full day. Kailua Beach has calm water, a line of palms and ironwoods that provide shade on the sand, and a huge park with picnic pavilions where you can escape the heat. This is the "it" spot if you're looking to try your hand at windsurfing or kiteboarding. You can rent kayaks nearby at Kailua Beach Adventures (130 Kailua Road) and take them to the Mokulua Islands for the day. **Amenities:** lifeguards; parking (no fee); showers; toilets; water sports. **Best for:** swimming; walking; windsurfing. ✉ *437 Kawailoa Rd., Kailua* ✣ *Near Kailua town, turn right on Kailua Rd. After Kalapawai Market, cross bridge, then turn left into beach parking lot.*

Lanikai Beach Park

BEACH—SIGHT | Think of the beaches you see in commercials: peaceful jade-green waters, powder-soft white sand, families and dogs frolicking mindlessly, and offshore islands in the distance. It's an ideal spot for camping out with a book. Though the beach hides behind multimillion-dollar houses, by state law there is public access every 400 yards. Street parking is available but difficult to find (and prohibited on holiday weekends). **■TIP→ Look for walled or fenced pathways every 400 yards, leading to the beach. Be sure not to park in the marked bike/jogging lane.** There are no shower or bathroom facilities here—but you'll find both a two-minute drive away at Kailua Beach Park. **Amenities:** none. **Best for:** sunrise; swimming; walking. ✉ *974 Mokulua Dr., Kailua* ✣ *Past Kailua Beach Park.*

Restaurants

Boots & Kimo's Homestyle Kitchen

$ | AMERICAN | Sometimes you wait an hour for a table here since the restaurant's fervent followers come back again and again for the banana pancakes topped with thick macadamia-nut sauce. And it's no wonder: brothers Ricky and Jesse Kiakona treat their guests like family. **Known for:** macadamia nut pancakes; long lines of patient regulars; new location offering a nicer waiting area (but still the long waits). [$] *Average main: $13* ✉ *151 Hekili St., Suite 102, Kailua* ☎ *808/263–7929* 🌐 *www.bootsnkimos.com* 🕓 *No dinner.*

Buzz's Lanikai

$$$ | STEAKHOUSE | Virtually unchanged since owners Bobby Lou and Buzz opened it in 1967, this neighborhood institution opposite Kailua Beach Park is filled with the aroma of grilling steaks and plumeria blooms. Sadly, Buzz has passed on, but you can now enjoy a predinner drink on Stan's Deck, a salute to Bobby Lou's second husband. **Known for:** local institution; the views from the lanai at lunch; excellent fruity beach cocktails. [$] *Average main: $35* ✉ *413 Kawailoa Rd., Kailua* ☎ *808/261–4661* 🌐 *www.buzzsoriginalsteakhouse.com.*

Cinnamon's Restaurant

$ | AMERICAN | Known for uncommon variations on common breakfast themes (pancakes, eggs Benedict, French toast, home fries, and eggs), this neighborhood favorite is tucked into a hard-to-find Kailua office park (call for directions). Local-style lunch plates are good, but the main attraction is breakfast. **Known for:** endless variations on pancakes, eggs Benedict, and waffles; cinnamon rolls (of course); long waits. [$] *Average main: $14* ✉ *315 Uluniu St., Kailua* ☎ *808/261–8724* 🌐 *www.cinnamons808.com.*

Kalapawai Cafe & Deli

$$ | ECLECTIC | This one-stop, green-and-white, Mediterranean-leaning café, wine bar, bakery, and gourmet deli is the creation of the Dymond family, two generations of restaurateurs who have shaken up the windward food scene. Come in on your way to the beach for a cup of coffee and bagel, and stop back for a gourmet pizza or bruschetta (how does eggplant confit, sweet peppers, honey, and goat cheese sound?) for lunch or a candlelight dinner at night. **Known for:** signature dishes by night; good coffee and sandwiches by day; impressive wine list for such a small spot. $ *Average main: $19* ⊠ *750 Kailua Rd., Kailua* ☎ *808/262–3354* ⊕ *www.kalapawaimarket.com.*

☕ Coffee and Quick Bites

Island Snow

$ | HAWAIIAN | This hole in the wall has been creating shave ice perfection in its tiny original spot since 1979, but when two young girls named Obama discovered the luscious flavors in 2008, it was really put on the map. A favorite spot for both locals and storied visitors (and these days lots of regular tourists), they make a mean shave ice, whether you stick with standard flavors like cherry or go for lilikoi guava with a snowcap on top. **Known for:** the best shave ice on the windward side; the Obama girls, who grew up on this stuff (look for their photos on the wall); long lines of local kiteboarders and surfers. $ *Average main: $5* ⊠ *130 Kailua Rd., Kailua* ☎ *808/263–6339* ⊕ *islandsnow.com.*

▼ Nightlife

Boardrider's Bar & Grill

BARS/PUBS | Tucked away in Kailua Town, Boardrider's has long been the place for local bands to strut their stuff. Look for live music—reggae to rock and roll—every Friday and Saturday night. The space includes a pool table, dartboards, and eight TVs for watching the game. ⊠ *201-A Hamakua Dr., Kailua* ☎ *808/261–4600.*

🛍 Shopping

★ Bookends

BOOKS/STATIONERY | Shop for gifts, or just take a break with the family at this independent bookstore, which feels more like a small-town library, welcoming browsers to linger for hours. It sells new and secondhand books, and its large children's section is filled with both books and toys. ⊠ *600 Kailua Rd., Kailua* ☎ *808/261–1996.*

★ Global Village

CLOTHING | Tucked into a tiny strip mall near Maui Tacos, this boutique features clothing, accessories, gifts, and handcrafted jewelry from the islands and around the globe. ⊠ *Kailua Village Shops, 539 Kailua Rd., No. 104, Kailua* ☎ *808/262–8183* ⊕ *www.globalvillagehawaii.com.*

★ Under a Hula Moon

HOUSEHOLD ITEMS/FURNITURE | Exclusive tabletop items and Pacific home decor, such as shell wreaths, shell night-lights, Hawaiian beach sheets, frames, and unique one-of-a-kind gifts with an Islands influence, define this eclectic shop. ⊠ *Kailua Shopping Center, 600 Kailua Rd., Kailua* ☎ *808/261–4252.*

Kaneohe

11 miles northeast of Oahu, 6 miles west of Kailua.

The largest community on Oahu's windward side, Kaneohe (meaning "bamboo man" in Hawaiian) is a sprawling community with malls, car dealerships, and a few worthwhile restaurants. At the base of the Koolau Mountains, Kaneohe sees a lot more rain than neighboring Kailua and is the greener for it. Kaneohe doesn't see a lot of tourists, but there are two

Windward Oahu Villages

Tiny villages—generally consisting of a sign, store, a beach park, possibly a post office, and not much more—are strung along Kamehameha Highway on the windward side. Each has something to offer. In **Waiahole**, look for fruit stands and an ancient grocery store. In **Kaaawa**, there's a convenience store–gas station. In **Punaluu**, get a plate lunch at Keneke's, or visit venerable Ching General Store. Kim Taylor Reece's photo studio, featuring haunting portraits of hula dancers, is between Punaluu and Hauula. **Hauula** has the gallery of fanciful landscape artist Lance Fairly; the Shrimp Shack; Hauula Gift Shop & Art Gallery, formerly yet another Ching Store, now a clothing shop where sarongs wave like banners; and, at Hauula Kai Shopping Center, Tamura's Market, with excellent seafood and the last liquor before Mormon-dominated Laie.

worthwhile sights, which take advantage of their proximity to the mountains—the Byodo-In Temple and Hoomaluhi Botanical Garden.

 ## Sights

★ Byodo-In Temple
RELIGIOUS SITE | Tucked away in the back of the Valley of the Temples cemetery is a replica of the 11th-century Temple at Uji in Japan. A 2-ton, carved-wood statue of the Buddha presides inside the main building. Next to the temple are a meditation pavilion and gardens set dramatically against the sheer, green cliffs of the Koolau Mountains. You can ring the 5-foot, 3-ton brass bell for good luck and feed some of the hundreds of koi, ducks, and swans that inhabit the garden's 2-acre pond. Or, you can enjoy the peaceful surroundings and just relax. Call ahead to schedule a guided tour. ✉ 47-200 Kahekili Hwy., Kaneohe ☎ 808/239–9844 ⊕ www.byodo-in.com ☜ $4 (cash only).

★ Nuuanu Pali Lookout
VIEWPOINT | This panoramic perch looks out to expansive views of Windward Oahu. It was in this region that King Kamehameha I drove defending forces over the edges of the 1,200-foot-high cliffs, thus winning the decisive battle for control of Oahu. From here, views stretch from Kaneohe Bay to a small island off the coast called Mokolii ("little lizard," also known as Chinaman's Hat). Temperatures at the summit are several degrees cooler than in warm Waikiki, so bring a jacket along. Hang on tight to any loose possessions, and consider wearing pants; it gets extremely windy at the lookout, which is part of the fun. And be sure to lock your car in the pay-to-park lot; break-ins have occurred here (this wayside is in the most trafficked state park in Hawaii). ✉ Pali Hwy., Kaneohe ✛ at very top of Pali Hwy. ⊕ hawaiistateparks.org/parks/oahu/nu%-CA%BBuanu-pali-state-wayside/ ☜ Free ☞ Parking $3 per car.

Beaches

Kahana Bay Beach Park
BEACH—SIGHT | FAMILY | Local parents often bring their children here to wade in safety in the very shallow, protected waters. This pretty beach cove, surrounded by mountains, has a long arc of sand that is great for walking and a cool, shady grove of tall ironwood and pandanus trees that is ideal for a picnic. An ancient Hawaiian fishpond, which was in use

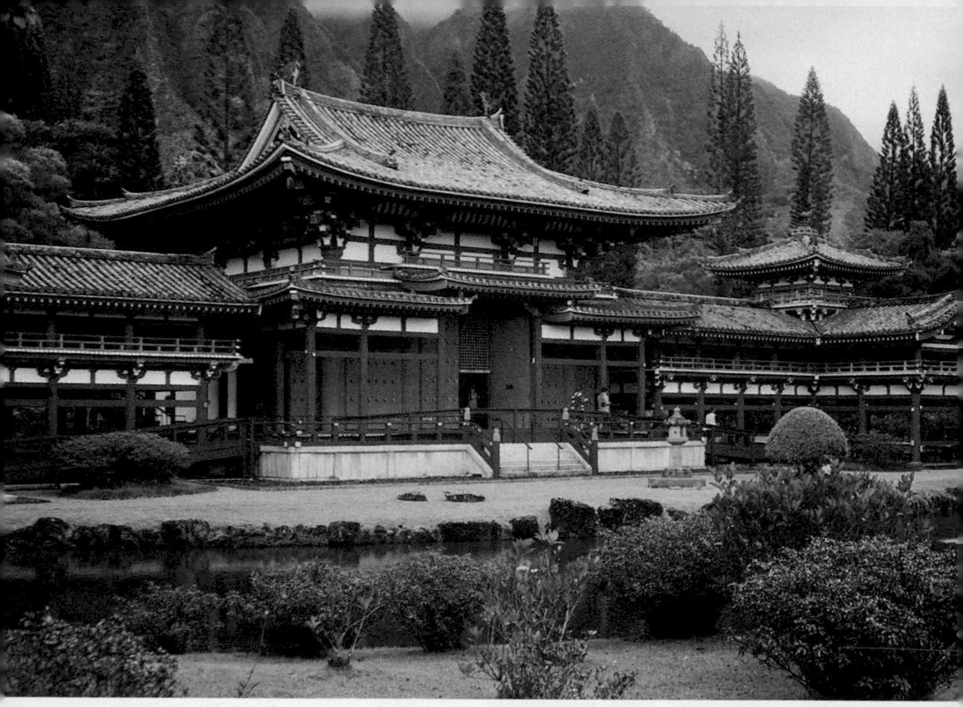

The Byodo-In Temple on the windward side of Oahu is a replica of an 11th-century temple in Japan.

until the 1920s, is visible nearby. The water here is not generally a clear blue due to the runoff from heavy rains in the valley. **Amenities:** parking (no fee); showers; toilets. **Best for:** swimming; walking. ✉ *52-201 Kamehameha Hwy., Kaneohe* ✢ *North of Kualoa Park.*

🍴 Restaurants

Pah Ke's Chinese Restaurant

$ | **CHINESE** | If you happen to be on the windward side at dinner time, this out-of-the-ordinary Chinese restaurant—named for the local pidgin term for Chinese (literally translated, this is "Chinese's Chinese Restaurant")—is a good option. Ebullient owner and chef Raymond Siu, a former hotel pastry chef, focuses on healthier cooking techniques and local ingredients. **Known for:** dependable spot for the family; house specials that are usually better than standard menu fare; a big dining room with bright lights and not much atmosphere. [$] *Average main: $12* ✉ *46-018 Kamehameha Hwy., Kaneohe* ☎ *808/235–4505* 🌐 *www.pahke.com.*

🛏 Hotels

Paradise Bay Resort

$$$ | **RESORT** | Located right on picturesque Kaneohe Bay amidst the junglelike fauna of the windward side, this resort offers apartment-style units ranging from cozy studios to spacious two-bedroom suites with breathtaking views of the majestic Koolau Mountains; there's also one stand-alone cottage in a remote area not generally frequented by tourists. **Pros:** local, authentic experience; beautiful views over the bay; pet-friendly (but $25 per night charge). **Cons:** remote location not near most other attractions; neighborhood is a bit run-down; rental car a necessity (but parking included in $35 nightly resort fee). [$] *Rooms from: $300* ✉ *47-039 Lihikai Dr., Kaneohe* ☎ *800/735–5071, 808/239–5711* 🌐 *www.paradisebayresort.com* 🛏 *46 rooms* 🍽 *Free Breakfast.*

Kaaawa

14 miles north of Kaneohe, 23 miles northeast of Honolulu.

Less a village than a collection of homes and bookended by its elementary school and fire station, Kaaawa consists of little more than a post office, bus stop, gas station, and, of course, a beach park.

Beaches

Kualoa Regional Park

BEACH—SIGHT | Grassy expanses border a long, narrow stretch of sand with spectacular views of Kaneohe Bay and the Koolau Mountains, making Kualoa one of the island's most beautiful picnic, camping, and beach areas. Dominating the view is an islet called Mokolii, better known as Chinaman's Hat, which rises 206 feet above the water. You can swim in the shallow areas of this rarely crowded beach year-round. The one drawback is that it's usually windy here, but the wide-open spaces are ideal for kite flying. **Amenities:** lifeguards; showers; toilets. **Best for:** solitude; swimming. ✉ *49-479 Kamehameha Hwy., Kaaawa* ✣ *North of Waiahole.*

Laie

10 miles north of Kaaawa, 33 miles north of Honolulu.

Visiting Laie—over an hour by car and a world away from bustling Waikiki and Honolulu—is like taking a trip to another island. Home to a Mormon temple and the Mormon-founded Polynesian Cultural Center, Laie is a "dry town."

Sights

★ Polynesian Cultural Center

ARTS VENUE | **FAMILY** | Re-created individual villages showcase the lifestyles and traditions of Hawaii, Tahiti, Samoa, Fiji, the Marquesas Islands, New Zealand, and Tonga. Focusing on individual islands within its 42-acre center, 35 miles from Waikiki, the Polynesian Cultural Center was founded in 1963 by the Church of Jesus Christ of Latter-day Saints. It houses restaurants, hosts luau, and demonstrates cultural traditions such as hula, fire dancing, and ancient customs and ceremonies. The Hukilau Marketplace carries Polynesian handicrafts. There are multiple packages available, from basic admission to an all-inclusive deal. Every May, the PCC hosts the World Fireknife Dance Competition, an event that draws the top fire-knife dance performers from around the world. Get tickets for that event in advance. **■ TIP→ If you're staying in Honolulu, see the center as part of a van tour so you won't have to drive home late at night after the two-hour evening show.** ✉ *55-370 Kamehameha Hwy., Laie* ☎ *800/367–7060* 🌐 *www.polynesia.com* 🎟 *From $70* 🕒 *Closed Sun.*

Hotels

Courtyard Oahu North Shore

$$$ | **HOTEL** | This property offers reliable and affordable accommodations close to the Polynesian Cultural Center and a short drive to some of the North Shore's most iconic beaches and surfing spots. **Pros:** best bet for North Shore exploring; reliable, modern, and clean; near the beach. **Cons:** a long drive to the rest of Oahu's attractions; no alcohol served in the hotel or nearby establishments; a car is needed, and parking is not free. [$] *Rooms from: $270* ✉ *55-400 Kamehameha Hwy., Laie* ☎ *808/293–4900* 🌐 *www.marriott.com/hotels/travel/hnloa-courtyard-oahu-north-shore* 🛏 *144 rooms* 🍴 *No meals.*

Kualoa Point is in Kualoa Regional Park in Kaaawa, a beautiful but windy area overlooking Kaneohe Bay and the towering Koolau Mountains.

🏛 Performing Arts

DINNER CRUISES AND SHOWS

Ha: Breath of Life

DANCE | The Polynesian Cultural Center's long-running nightly show, *Ha: Breath of Life,* is a story of love, respect, and responsibility. *Ha,* which means "breath" in Hawaiian, follows the central character of Mana from his birth to the birth of his own child. The performances highlight ancient Hawaiian, Polynesian, Samoan, and Tahitian culture, music, and dance, including fire-knife dancers, and with more than 100 performers. Performances are Monday–Saturday at 7:30 pm. ✉ *Polynesian Cultural Center, 55-370 Kamehameha Hwy., Laie* ☎ *800/367–7060* ⊕ *www.habreathoflife.com* ✉ *From $89.95.*

LUAU

★ Polynesian Cultural Center Alii Luau

THEMED ENTERTAINMENT | Although this elaborate luau has the sharpest production values, there is no booze allowed (it's a Mormon-owned facility in the heart of Laie—Mormon country). It's held amid the seven re-created villages at the Polynesian Cultural Center in the North Shore town of Laie, about a 1½-hour drive from Honolulu. The luau—considered one of the most authentic on the island—includes the *Ha: Breath of Life* show that has long been popular with both residents and visitors. Rates vary depending on activities and amenities that are included (personalized tours, reserved seats, or table service, for example). Waikiki transport is available. It's held Monday–Saturday at 5. ✉ *Polynesian Cultural Center, 55-370 Kamehameha Hwy., Laie* ☎ *808/293–3333, 800/367–7060* ⊕ *www. polynesia.com* ✉ *From $119.95.*

Activities and Tours

From snorkeling on the North Shore to kayaking to small islands off Kailua Beach to stand-up paddleboarding in Waikiki—when you're on Oahu, there's always a reason to get wet. You can swim with native fish in a protected bay, surf waves in an outrigger canoe, take to the skies in a parasail above Diamond Head, or enjoy panoramic views of Waikiki aboard a 45-foot catamaran. Diving into the ocean—whether in a boat, on a board, or with your own finned feet—is a great way to experience Oahu.

But, as with any physical activity, heed the warnings. The ocean is unpredictable and unforgiving, and it can be as dangerous as it can be awe-inspiring. But if you respect it, it can offer you the kind of memories that last well after your vacation.

Aerial Tours

Taking an aerial tour of the Islands opens up a world of perspective. Look down from the sky at the outline of the USS *Arizona*, where it lies in its final resting place below the waters of Pearl Harbor, or get a glimpse of the vast carved expanse of a volcanic crater—here are views only seen by an "eye in the sky." Don't forget your camera.

Blue Hawaiian Helicopters
FLYING/SKYDIVING/SOARING | This company stakes its claim as Hawaii's largest helicopter company, with tours on all the major Islands and more than two-dozen choppers in its fleet. The 45-minute Oahu tour seats up to six passengers and includes narration from your friendly pilot along with sweeping views of Waikiki, the beautiful Windward Coast, and the North Shore. If you like to see the world from above or are just pinched for time and want to get a quick overview of the whole island without renting a car, this is the way to go. Discounts are available if you book online in advance. ⊠ *99 Kaulele Pl., Airport Area* ☎ *808/831–8800, 800/745–2583* ⊕ *www.bluehawaiian.com* ⊠ *From $284.*

Magnum Helicopters
FLYING/SKYDIVING/SOARING | For the adventurous, this Magnum PI doors-off helicopter tour offers sweeping views of Keehi Lagoon through urban Honolulu and the harbor, including the Aloha Tower and Waikiki Beach. Soar past and over Diamond Head Crater and up the scenic coast by Makapuu Lighthouse, Sandy Beach, and over Windward Oahu's iconic Lanikai and Kailua beaches. The breathtaking finale takes you inland to Sacred Falls, known for its stunning, 1,000-foot falls and its starring role in Jurassic Park, before returning to the airport via North Shore surf spots and a bird's-eye view of Pearl Harbor and the USS *Arizona* Memorial. ⊠ *130 Iolana Pl., Airport Area* ☎ *808/833–4354* ⊕ *www.magnumhelicopters.com* ⊠ *From $269.*

The Original Glider Rides
FLYING/SKYDIVING/SOARING |"Mr. Bill" has been offering piloted glider (sailplane) rides over the northwest end of Oahu's North Shore since 1970. Piloted scenic rides for one or two passengers are in sleek, bubble-top, motorless aircraft with aerial views of mountains, shoreline, coral pools, windsurfing sails, and, in winter, humpback whales. Seeking more thrills? You can also take a more acrobatic ride or take control yourself in a mini lesson. Flights run 15–60 minutes long and depart continuously, daily 10–5. Reservations are requested. ⊠ *Dillingham Airfield, 69-132 Farrington Hwy., Waialua* ☎ *808/637–0207* ⊕ *www.honolulusoaring.com* ⊠ *From $85.*

Paradise Helicopters
FLYING/SKYDIVING/SOARING | Paradise offers tours on several islands, with Oahu tours departing from two helipads: Kalaeloa (at

the Ko Olina resorts on the west side) and Turtle Bay Resort on the North Shore. Kalaeloa options range from a one-hour scenic tour over Diamond Head to a two-hour island circle (daytime and sunset) to specialized trips that focus on WW II history. Turtle Bay choices include several 1½-hour North Shore adventures, offering scenic vistas of beaches as well as inland waterfalls. ☎ 866/300–2294 ⊕ paradise-copters.com ⊠ From $295.

Boat Tours and Charters

Being on the water can be the best way to enjoy the Islands. Whether you want to see the fish in action or experience how they taste, there is a tour for you.

For a sailing experience in Oahu, you need go no farther than the beach in front of your hotel in Waikiki. Strung along the sand are several beach catamarans that will provide you with one-hour rides during the day and 90-minute sunset sails. Look for $35 for day sails and $49–$120 for sunset rides. ■TIP➔ Feel free to haggle, especially with the smaller boats. Some provide drinks for free, some charge for them, and some let you pack your own, so keep that in mind when pricing the ride. Or choose to go the ultraluxe route and charter a boat for a day or week. These run from less than $100 per person per day to over $1,000. (see Deep-Sea Fishing).

Hawaii Nautical

BOATING | With two locations—one in Waikiki and one on the Waianae Coast—this outfit offers a wide variety of cruise options, including guaranteed-sighting dolphin and whale-watching (in season), gourmet dinners, lunches, snorkeling, scuba diving, and sunset viewing. Three-hour cruises, including lunch and two drinks, depart from the Kewalo Basin Harbor just outside Waikiki. (The company's Port Waikiki Cruises sail from the Hilton Pier off the Hilton Hawaiian Village in Waikiki.) For those interested in leaving from the Waianae Coast, snorkel tours are available from the Waianae Boat Harbor on Farrington Highway (85-471 Farrington Hwy.). Prices include all gear, food, and two alcoholic beverages. The dock in the Waianae Boat Harbor is a little more out of the way, but this is a much more luxurious option than what is offered in Waikiki. Both morning and afternoon snorkel tours include stops for observing dolphins from the boat and visit to a snorkel spot well populated with fish. All gear, snacks, sandwiches, and two alcoholic beverages make for a more complete experience. Pickup in Ko Olina is free. ⊠ Kewalo Basin Harbor, 1125 Ala Moana Blvd., Waikiki ☎ 808/234–7245 ⊕ www.hawaiinautical.com ⊠ From $97.

Maitai Catamaran

BOATING | Taking off from the stretch of sand behind the Sheraton Waikiki, this 44-foot cat is the fastest and sleekest on the beach. There are a variety of tours to choose from, including a sunset sail and a snorkel excursion. If you have a need for speed and want a more upscale experience, this is the boat for you. ⊠ Sheraton Waikiki, 2255 Kalakaua Ave., Waikiki ⊹ On beach behind hotel ☎ 808/922–5665, 800/462–7975 ⊕ www. maitaicatamaran.net ⊠ From $39.

Star of Honolulu Cruises

BOATING | FAMILY | Founded in 1957, this company's fleet includes two family-friendly vessels. The 232-foot Star of Honolulu, which casts off at Pier 8 in the Aloha Tower harbor (1 Aloha Tower Dr., downtown Honolulu) offers seasonal whale-watching as well as sunset gourmet dinner cruises with live entertainment. Some cruises even teach you how to string lei, play ukulele, or dance hula. Moored at the Waianae Boat Harbor (85-491 Farrington Hwy., Waianae ⊕ www.dolphin-star.com), the 65-foot Dolphin Star catamaran, offers either dolphin-viewing or snorkeling cruises with optional barbecue lunches.

Take a helicopter tour for a unique perspective of the island.

Because of its size, this cat provides a comfortable way for three generations of family members to enjoy the water together. Transportation from all hotels on the island can be arranged. ⊠ *Honolulu* ☎ *808/983–7827, 800/334–6191* ⊕ *www.starofhonolulu.com* ✉ *From $42.*

Tradewind Charters

BOATING | This company's half-day private excursions can include sailing, snorkeling, reef fishing, sunset dinner cruises, or whale-watching excursions and can accommodate from 2 to 49 people. Traveling on these luxury yachts not only gets you away from the crowds but also gives you the opportunity to take the helm if you wish. The cruises may include snorkeling at an exclusive anchorage, as well as hands-on snorkeling and sailing instruction. All charters are for the full ship. ⊠ *Kewalo Basin Harbor, 1125 Ala Moana Blvd., Ala Moana* ☎ *808/227–4956, 800/829–4899* ⊕ *www.tradewind-charters.com* ✉ *From $495.*

Body Boarding and Body Surfing

Body boarding (or sponging) has long been a popular alternative to surfing for a couple of reasons. First, the start-up cost is much less—a usable board can be purchased for $30–$40 or can be rented on the beach for $5 an hour. Second, it's a whole lot easier to ride a body board than to tame a surfboard. All you have to do is paddle out to the waves, then turn toward the beach as the wave approaches and kick like crazy.

Most grocery and convenience stores sell body boards. Though these boards don't compare to what the pros use, beginners won't notice a difference in their handling on smaller waves.

Though they are not absolutely necessary for body boarding, fins do give you a tremendous advantage when you're paddling. If you plan to go out into bigger surf, we would also suggest getting a leash, which reduces the chance you'll lose your board. The smaller, sturdier versions of dive fins used for body boarding sell for $25–$60 at surf and sporting-goods stores. Most beach stands don't rent fins with the boards, so if you want them you'll probably need to buy them.

Body surfing requires far less equipment—just a pair of swim fins with heel straps—but it can be a lot more challenging to master. Typically, surf breaks that are good for body boarding are good for body surfing.

If the direction of the current or dangers of the break are not readily apparent to you, don't hesitate to ask a lifeguard for advice.

BEST SPOTS

Body boarding and body surfing can be done anywhere there are waves, but due to the paddling advantage surfers have over spongers, it's usually more fun to go to surf breaks exclusively for body boarding.

Bellows Beach. On Oahu's windward side, Bellows Field Beach has shallow waters and a consistent break that makes it an ideal spot for body boarders and body surfers. (Surfing isn't allowed between the two lifeguard towers.) But take note: the Portuguese man-of-war, a blue jellyfishlike invertebrate that delivers painful and powerful stings, is often seen here. ⊠ *41-043 Kalanianaole Hwy., Waimanalo.*

Kuhio Beach Park. This beach is an easy spot for first-timers to check out the action. The Wall, a break near the large pedestrian walkway called Kapahulu Groin, is the quintessential body boarding spot. The soft, rolling waves make it perfect for beginners. Even during summer's south swells, it's relatively tame because of the outer reefs. ⊠ *Waikiki Beach, between the Sheraton Moana Surfrider Hotel and the Kapahulu Groin, Honolulu.*

Makapuu Beach. With its extended waves, Makapuu Beach is a sponger's dream. If you're a little more timid, go to the far end of the beach to **Keiki's,** where the waves are mellowed by Makapuu Point. Although the main break at Makapuu is much less dangerous than Sandy's, check out the ocean floor—the sands are always shifting, sometimes exposing coral heads and rocks. Always check (or ask lifeguards about) the currents, which can get pretty strong. ⊠ *41-095 Kalanianaole Hwy., across from Sea Life Park.*

Sandy Beach. The best spot—and arguably one of the most dangerous—on the island for advanced body boarding is Sandy Beach, located on Oahu's eastern shore. Dubbed one of the most treacherous shore breaks in the nation, the break can be extremely dangerous even when it's small. As lifeguards will attest, there are more neck injuries suffered here than at any other surf break in the United States. It's awesome for the advanced, but know its danger before paddling out. ⊠ *8800 Kalanianaole Hwy., 2 miles east of Hanauma Bay, Honolulu.*

Waimanalo Beach Park. With the longest sand beach on Oahu's windward side, Waimanalo Bay has a shallow sandbar at the water's edge that provides good waves for body boarding and body surfing. It's an ideal break for novices because of its soft waves. Like Walls in Waikiki, this area is protected by an outer reef. And like Bellows, it's favored by the dangerous Portuguese man-of-war. ⊠ *Aloiloi St., Waimanalo.*

EQUIPMENT

There are more than 30 rental spots along Waikiki Beach, all offering basically the same prices. But if you plan to body board for more than just an hour, we would suggest buying an inexpensive board for $20–$40 at an ABC Store—there are more than 30 in the Waikiki area—and giving it to a kid at the end of your vacation. It will be more cost-effective for you, and you'll be passing along some aloha spirit in the process.

Deep-Sea Fishing

Fishing isn't just a sport in Hawaii, it's a way of life. A number of charter boats with experienced crews can take you on a sportfishing adventure throughout the year. Sure, the bigger yellowfin tuna (ahi) are generally caught in summer, and the coveted spearfish are more frequent in winter, but you can still hook them any day of the year. You can also find dolphin-fish (mahimahi), wahoo (ono), skipjacks, and the king—Pacific blue marlin—ripe for the picking on any given day. The largest marlin ever caught, weighing in at 1,805 pounds, was reeled in along Oahu's coast.

When choosing a fishing boat in the Islands, keep in mind the immensity of the surrounding ocean. Look for veteran captains who have decades of experience. Better yet, find those who care about Hawaii's fragile marine environment. Many captains now tag and release their catches to preserve the state's fishing grounds.

The general rule for the catch is an even split with the crew. Unfortunately, there are no "freeze-and-ship" providers in the state, so unless you plan to eat the fish while you're here, you'll probably want to leave it with the boat. Most boats do offer mounting services for trophy fish; ask your captain.

Prices vary greatly, but expect to pay from around $65 per person for a spot on a boat with more than 20 people to $2,000 for an overnight trip for up to 6 people. Besides the gift of fish, a gratuity of 10%–20% is standard, but use your own discretion depending on how you feel about the overall experience.

BOATS AND CHARTERS
Maggie Joe Sport Fishing
FISHING | The oldest sportfishing company on Oahu boasts landing one of the largest marlins ever caught out of Kewalo Basin. With a fleet of three boats, including the 53-foot custom *Maggie Joe* (which can hold up to 15 anglers and has air-conditioned cabins, hot showers, and cutting-edge fishing equipment), they offer a variety of offshore fishing packages. A marine taxidermist can mount the monster you reel in. Half-day exclusives on the 41-foot *Sea Hawk* or the 38-foot *Ruckus* can accommodate up to six people and are the cheapest options for daytime fishing. The larger *Maggie Joe* embarks on three-quarter or full-day (but not half-day) sails. ✉ *Kewalo Basin, 1025 Ala Moana Blvd., Ala Moana* ☎ *808/591–8888, 877/806–3474* ⊕ *www.maggiejoe.com* ☑ *From $190.*

Magic Sportfishing
FISHING | This 50-foot Pacifica fishing yacht, aptly named *Magic,* boasts a slew of sportfishing records, including some of the largest marlins caught in local tournaments and the most mahimahi hooked during a one-day charter. This yacht is very comfortable, with twin diesel engines that provide a smooth ride, air-conditioning, and a cozy seating area. The boat can accommodate up to six passengers and offers both shared and full charters, inviting both skilled anglers and first-timers to experience deep-sea fishing in Hawaii. ✉ *Kewalo Basin Harbor, 1125 Ala Moana Blvd., Slip G, Ala Moana* ☎ *808/596–2998* ⊕ *www.magicsportfishing.com* ☑ *From $220 per person for a shared charter; from $1,190 for a private charter.*

Sashimi Fun Fishing
FISHING | With a luxury, 74-foot boat for sport fishing, a 65-footer for bottom fishing, and a 100-foot double-decker for dinner cruises, Sashimi Fun Fishing offers a variety of water activities. Choose a midnight shark hunt, head out in search

of marlin, bottom fish near shore, or relax and enjoy live entertainment on the *Prince Kuhio's* sunset steak-and-seafood dinner cruise. Rates can include hotel transportation. ✉ *Kewalo Basin Harbor, 1025 Ala Moana Blvd., Ala Moana* ☎ *808/955–3474* ⊕ *www.808955fish.com* ⊕ *www.princekuhiocruises.com* 🍴 *From $63 per person for shared trips; $69 for dinner cruises.*

Golf

Unlike on the other Hawaiian Islands, the majority of Oahu's golf courses are not associated with hotels and resorts. In fact, of the island's three dozen–plus courses, only five are tied to lodging; none is in the tourist hub of Waikiki.

Municipal courses are a good choice for budget-conscious golfers but are more crowded and are not always maintained to the same standard as the private courses. Your best bet is to call the day you want to play and inquire about walk-on availability. Greens fees are standard at city courses: walking rate $66 for visitors, riding cart $20 for 18 holes, pull carts $4.

Greens fees listed here are the highest course rates per round on weekdays and weekends for U.S. residents. (Some courses charge non–U.S. residents higher prices.) Discounts are often available for resort guests and for those who book tee times online. Twilight fees are usually offered; call individual courses for information.

WAIKIKI

Ala Wai Municipal Golf Course

GOLF | Just across the Ala Wai Canal from Waikiki, this municipal golf course is said to host more rounds than any other U.S. course—up to 500 per day. Not that it's a great course, just really convenient. The best bet for a visitor is to show up and expect to wait at least an hour or call up to three days in advance for a tee-time

reservation. When reserving, the automated system will ask for an ID code—simply enter your phone number and give that number and your tee time when checking in. The course itself is flat; Robin Nelson did some redesign work in the 1990s, adding mounding, trees, and a lake. The Ala Wai Canal comes into play on several holes on the back nine, including the treacherous 18th. There's also an on-site restaurant and bar. ✉ *404 Kapahulu Ave., Waikiki* ☎ *808/733–7387 for starter's office, 808/738–4652 for pro shop, 808/296–2000 for reservations only* ⊕ *www.honolulu.gov/des/golf/ala-wai.html* 🏌 *$66* 🕴 *18 holes, 5861 yards, par 70.*

SOUTHEAST OAHU

Hawaii Kai Golf Course

GOLF | The **Championship Golf Course** (William F. Bell, 1973) winds through a Honolulu suburb at the foot of Koko Crater. Homes (and the liability of a broken window) come into play on many holes, but they are offset by views of the nearby Pacific and a crafty routing of holes. With several lakes, lots of trees, and bunkers in all the wrong places, Hawaii Kai really is a "championship" golf course, especially when the trade winds howl. Greens fees for this course include a mandatory cart. The **Executive Course** (1962), a par-54 track, is the first of only three courses in Hawaii built by Robert Trent Jones Sr. Although a few changes have been made to his original design, you can find the usual Jones attributes, including raised greens and lots of risk-reward options. You may walk or use a cart on this course for an additional fee. ✉ *8902 Kalanianaole Hwy., Hawaii Kai* ☎ *808/395–2358* ⊕ *hawaiikaigolf.com* 🍴 *Championship Course $150, Executive Course $50* 🕴 *Championship Course: 18 holes, 6207 yards, par 72. Executive Course: 18 holes, 2196 yards, par 54.*

WINDWARD OAHU
Koolau Golf Club

GOLF | Koolau Golf Club is marketed as the toughest golf course in Hawaii and one of the most challenging in the country. Dick Nugent and Jack Tuthill (1992) routed 10 holes over jungle ravines that require at least a 110-yard carry. The par-4 18th may be the most difficult closing hole in golf. The tee shot from this hole's regular tees must carry 200 yards of ravine, 250 from the blue tees. The approach shot is back across the ravine, 200 yards to a well-bunkered green. Set at the windward base of the Koolau Mountains, the course is as much beauty as beast. Kaneohe Bay is visible from most holes, orchids and yellow ginger bloom, the shama thrush (Hawaii's best singer since Don Ho) chirps, and waterfalls flute down the sheer, green mountains above. The greens fee includes a (required) cart. ✉ 45-550 Kionaole Rd., Kaneohe ☎ 808/236-4653 ⊕ www.koolaugolfclub.com ✇ $165 ⚑ 18 holes, 7310 yards, par 72.

Olomana Golf Links

GOLF | Bob and Robert L. Baldock are the architects of record for this layout, but so much has changed since it opened in 1969 that they would recognize little of it. A turf specialist was brought in to improve fairways and greens, tees were rebuilt, new bunkers added, and mangroves cut back to make better use of natural wetlands. But what really puts Olomana on the map is that this is where wunderkind Michelle Wie learned the game. A cart is required at this course and is included in the greens fee. ✉ 41-1801 Kalanianaole Hwy., Waimanalo ☎ 808/259-7926 ⊕ www.olomanalinks. com ✇ $59 for 9 holes, $105 for 18 holes ⚑ 18 holes, 6306 yards, par 72.

★ Royal Hawaiian Golf Club

GOLF | In the cool, lush Maunawili Valley, Pete and Perry Dye created what can only be called target jungle golf. In other words, the rough is usually dense jungle, and you may not hit a driver on three of the four par 5s, or several par 4s, including the perilous 18th that plays off a cliff to a narrow green protected by a creek. Mt. Olomana's twin peaks tower over the course. ■TIP→ The back nine wanders deep into the valley and includes an island green (par-3 11th) and perhaps the loveliest inland hole in Hawaii (par-4 12th). ✉ 770 Auloa Rd., at Luana Hills Rd., Kailua ☎ 808/262-2139 ⊕ royalhawaiiangc.com ✇ $160 ⚑ 18 holes, 5541 yards, par 72.

NORTH SHORE
Turtle Bay Resort & Spa

GOLF | When the Lazarus of golf courses, the **Fazio Course** (George Fazio, 1971), rose from the dead in 2002, Turtle Bay on Oahu's rugged North Shore became a premier golf destination. Two holes had been plowed under when the **Palmer Course** (Arnold Palmer and Ed Seay, 1992) was built, while the other seven lay fallow, and the front nine remained open. Then new owners came along and re-created holes 13 and 14 using Fazio's original plans, and the Fazio became whole again. It's a terrific track with 90 bunkers. The gem at Turtle Bay, though, is the Palmer. The front nine is mostly open as it skirts Punahoolapa Marsh, a nature sanctuary, while the back nine plunges into the wetlands and winds along the coast. The short par-4 17th runs along the rocky shore, with a diabolical string of bunkers cutting diagonally across the fairway from tee to green. Carts are required for both courses and are included in the greens fees. ✉ 57-049 Kuilima Dr., Kahuku ☎ 808/293-8574 ⊕ www.turtlebaygolf. com ✇ Fazio Course: $69 for 9 holes, $129 for 18 holes. Palmer Course: $99 for 9 holes, $199 for 18 holes ⚑ Fazio Course: 18 holes, 6600 yards, par 72. Palmer Course: 18 holes, 7200 yards, par 72.

CENTRAL OAHU
Royal Kunia Country Club

GOLF | At one time, the PGA Tour considered buying the Royal Kunia Country Club and hosting the Sony Open here. It's that good. ■TIP➔ Every hole offers fabulous views from Diamond Head to Pearl Harbor to the nearby Waianae Mountains. Robin Nelson's eye for natural sight lines and his dexterity with water features add to the visual pleasure. Carts are required and are included in the greens fee. ✉ 94-1509 Anonui St., Waipahu ☎ 808/688–9222 ⊕ www.royalkuniacc.com ⚑ From $85 ⛳ 18 holes, 6507 yards, par 72.

Waikele Country Club

GOLF | Outlet stores are not the only bargain in Waikele. The adjacent, daily-fee golf course offers a private club–like atmosphere and a terrific Ted Robinson (1992) layout. Robinson's water features are less distinctive here but define the short par-4 4th hole—with a lake running down the left side of the fairway and guarding the green—and the par-3 17th, which plays across a lake. The par-4 18th is a terrific closing hole, with a lake lurking on the right side of the green. Carts are required and are included in the greens fee. ✉ 94-200 Paioa Pl., Waipahu ☎ 808/676–9000 ⊕ www.golfwaikele.com ⚑ $170 ⛳ 18 holes, 6261 yards, par 72.

WEST (LEEWARD) OAHU
Coral Creek Golf Course

GOLF | On the Ewa Plain, 4 miles inland, Coral Creek is cut from ancient coral left from when this area was still underwater. Robin Nelson (1999) did some of his best work in making use of the coral—and of some dynamite, blasting out portions to create dramatic lakes and tee and green sites. They could just as easily call it Coral Cliffs, because of the 30- to 40-foot cliffs Nelson created. They include the par-3 10th green's grotto and waterfall and the vertical drop-off on the right side of the par-4 18th green. An ancient creek meanders across the course, but there's not much water, just enough to be a babbling nuisance. Carts are required and are included in the greens fee. ✉ 91-1111 Geiger Rd., Ewa Beach ☎ 808/441–4653

⊕ www.coralcreekgolfhawaii.com ⚑ $75 for 9 holes, $150 for 18 holes ⛳ 18 holes, 6347 yards, par 72.

Ko Olina Golf Club

GOLF | Hawaii's golden age of golf-course architecture came to Oahu when Ko Olina Golf Club opened in 1989. Ted Robinson, king of the water features, went splash-happy here, creating nine lakes that come into play on eight holes, including the par-3 12th, where you reach the tee by driving behind a Disney-like waterfall. Tactically, though, the most dramatic is the par-4 18th, where the approach is a minimum 120 yards across a lake to a two-tiered green guarded on the left by a cascading waterfall. Today Ko Olina has matured into one of Hawaii's top courses. You can niggle about routing issues—the first three holes play into the trade winds (and the morning sun), as do two consecutive par 5s on the back nine play—but Robinson does enough solid design to make those of passing concern. ■TIP➔ The course provides free transportation from Waikiki hotels. ✉ 92-1220 Aliinui Dr., Ko Olina ☎ 808/676–5300 ⊕ www.koolinagolf.com ⚑ $115 for 9 holes, $225 for 18 holes ⛳ 18 holes, 6432 yards, par 72.

Hiking

The trails of Oahu cover a full spectrum of environments: desert walks through cactus, slippery paths through bamboo-filled rain forest, and scrambling rock climbs up ancient volcanic calderas. The only thing you won't find is an overnighter, as even the longest of hikes won't take you more than half a day. In addition to being short in length, many of the prime hikes are within 10 minutes of downtown Waikiki, meaning that you won't have to spend your whole day getting back to nature.

BEST SPOTS
Diamond Head Crater
HIKING/WALKING | Every vacation has requirements that must be fulfilled, so that when your neighbors ask, you can say, "Yeah, did it." Climbing Diamond Head is high on that list of things to do on Oahu. It's a moderately easy hike if you're in good physical condition, but be prepared to climb many stairs along the way. Also be sure to bring a water bottle, because it's hot and dry. Only a mile up, a clearly marked trail with handrails scales the inside of this extinct volcano. At the top, the fabled final 99 steps take you up to the pillbox overlooking the Pacific Ocean and Honolulu. It's a breathtaking view and a lot cheaper than taking a helicopter ride for the same photo op. Last entry for hikers is 4:30 pm. ⊠ *Diamond Head Rd. at 18th Ave., Diamond Head* ⊹ *Enter on east side of crater; there's limited parking inside, so most park on street and walk in* ☎ *808/587–0300* ⊕ *dlnr.hawaii.gov/dsp/parks/oahu/diamond-head-state-monument* ⌲ *$1 per person, $5 to park.*

★ Kaena Point Trail
HIKING/WALKING | Kaena Point is one of the island's last easily accessible pockets of nature left largely untouched. For more than a quarter century, the state has protected nearly 60 acres of land at the point, first as a nature preserve and, more recently, as an ecosystem restoration project for endangered and protected coastal plants and seabirds. The uneven 5-mile trail around the point can be entered from two locations—Koawaula Beach (aka Yokohama Bay) at the end of Farrington Highway on Oahu's western coastline, or Mokuleia at the same highway's northern coast endpoint. It's a rugged coastline hike without much shade, so bring lots of water and sunscreen (or better yet, start early!). ■**TIP**➔ **Keep a lookout for the Laysan albatrosses; these enormous birds have recently returned to the area. Don't be surprised if they come in for a closer look**

at you, too. ⊠ *81-780 Farrington Hwy., Waianae* ⊹ *Take Farrington Hwy. to its end at Yokohama. Hike in on old 4x4 trail* ⊕ *dlnr.hawaii.gov/dsp/hiking/oahu/kaena-point-trail.*

Makapuu Lighthouse Trail
HIKING/WALKING | For the less adventurous hiker and anyone looking for a great view, this paved trail that runs up the side of Makapuu Point in Southeast Oahu fits the bill. Early on, the trail is surrounded by lava rock but, as you ascend, foliage—the tiny white *koa haole* flower, the cream-tinged spikes of the *kiawe,* and, if you go early enough, the stunning night-blooming *cereus*—begins taking over the barren rock. At the easternmost tip of Oahu, where the island divides the sea, this trail gives you a spectacular view of the cobalt ocean meeting the land in a cacophony of white caps. To the south are several tide pools and the lighthouse, while the eastern view looks down upon Manana (Rabbit) and Kaohikaipu islets, two bird sanctuaries just off the coast. The 2-mile round-trip hike is a great break on a circle-island trip. From late December to early May, this is a great perch to see migrating humpback whales. ■**TIP**➔ **Be sure not to leave valuables in your car, as break-ins, even in the parking lot, are common.** ⊠ *Makapuu Lighthouse Rd., Hawaii Kai* ⊹ *Take Kalanianaole Hwy. to base of Makapuu Point, then look for parking lot* ⊕ *dlnr.hawaii.gov/dsp/hiking/oahu/makapuu-point-lighthouse-trail.*

★ Manoa Falls Trail
HIKING/WALKING | Travel up into the valley beyond Honolulu to make the Manoa Falls hike. Though only a mile long, this well-trafficked path, visited by an estimated 100,000 hikers a year, passes through so many different ecosystems that you feel as if you're in an arboretum—and you're not far off. (The beautiful Lyon Arboretum is right near the trailhead, if you want to make another stop.) Walk among the elephant ear ape plants, ruddy fir trees, and a bamboo forest straight

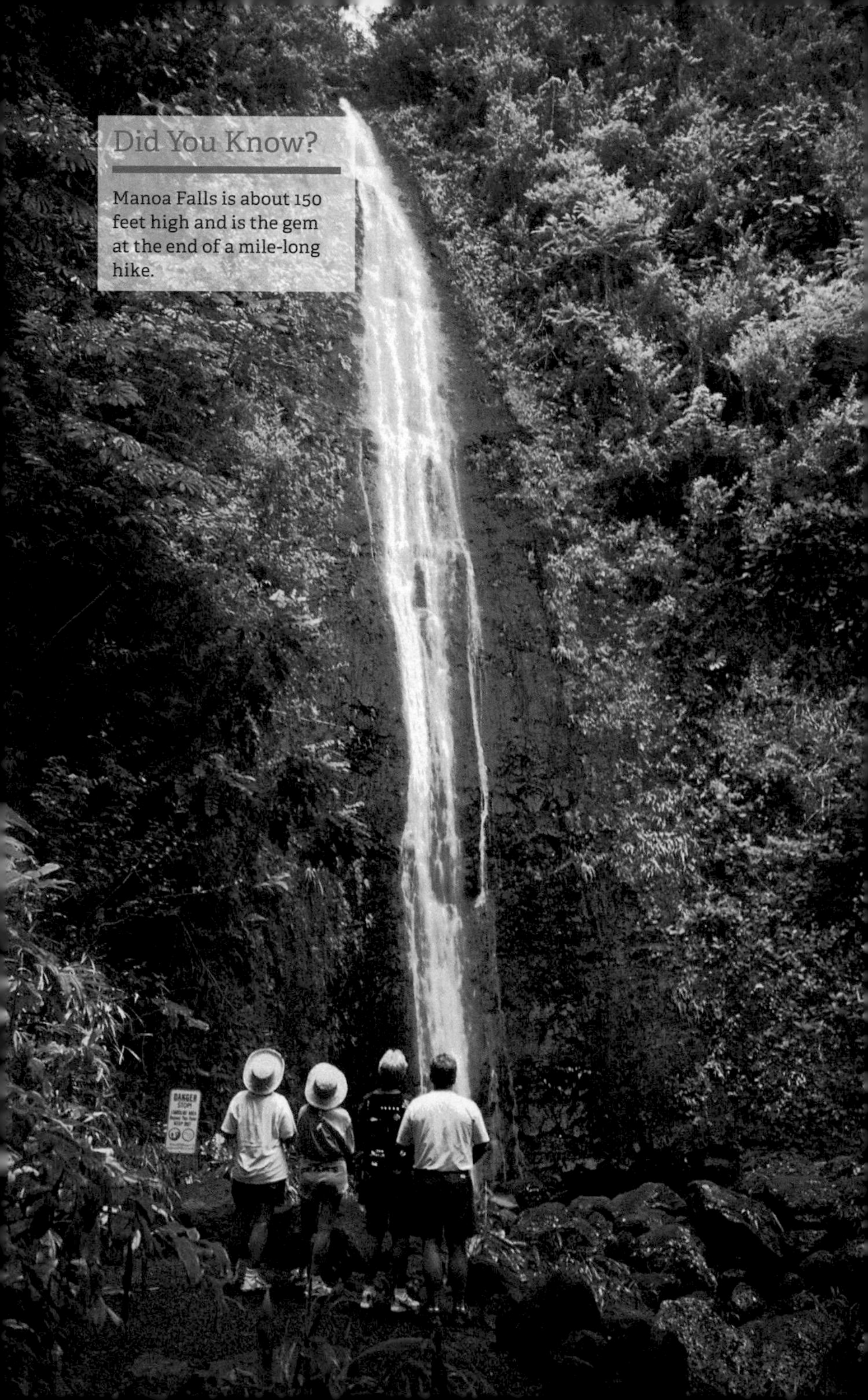

Did You Know?

Manoa Falls is about 150 feet high and is the gem at the end of a mile-long hike.

out of China. At the top is a 150-foot waterfall, which can be an impressive cascade or, if rain has been sparse, little more than a trickle. This hike is more about the journey than the destination; make sure you bring some mosquito repellent because they grow 'em big up here. ⚠ The trail is undergoing renovations, which were supposed to finish in the first half of 2020 but which have been extended, so there are sometimes unscheduled and unexpected closures. ✉ *3998 Manoa Rd., Manoa* ✛ *West Manoa Rd. is behind Manoa Valley in Paradise Park. Take West Manoa Rd. to end, park on side of road or in parking lot for a small fee, follow trail signs* ⊕ *www.hawaiitrails.org/trails/#/ trail/manoa-falls-trail/225.*

GOING WITH A GUIDE

Hawaii Nature Center

HIKING/WALKING | FAMILY | A good choice for families, the center in upper Makiki Valley conducts a number of programs for both adults and children. There are guided hikes into tropical settings that reveal hidden waterfalls and protected forest reserves. They don't run tours every day, so it's a good idea to get advance reservations. ✉ *2131 Makiki Heights Dr., Makiki Heights* ☎ *808/955–0100* ⊕ *www.hawaiinaturecenter.org.*

Oahu Nature Tours

HIKING/WALKING | Guides explain the native flora and fauna and history that are your companions on the various walking and hiking tours of the North Shore, Diamond Head, and Windward Oahu. The company also offers much more expensive private birding tours, perfect for those interested in spotting one of Hawaii's native honeycreepers. Tours include pickup at centralized Waikiki locations and are discounted if booked online in advance. ☎ *808/924–2473* ⊕ *www. oahunaturetours.com* ✉ *From $36.*

Horseback Riding

Happy Trails Hawaii

HORSEBACK RIDING | FAMILY | Take a guided horseback ride above the North Shore's Waimea Bay along trails that offer panoramic views from Kaena Point to the famous surfing spots. Groups are no larger than 10, and instruction is provided. The rides are particularly family-friendly, and children six and older are welcome. You can take either a 1½- or a 2-hour ride, which includes a 15-minute minilesson. Reservations are required. ✉ *59-231 Pupukea Rd., Pupukea* ✛ *Go 1 mile mauka (toward mountain) up Pupukea Rd.; the office is on right* ☎ *808/638–7433* ⊕ *www.happytrailshawaii.com* ✉ *From $99.*

Kualoa Ranch

HORSEBACK RIDING | FAMILY | This 4,000-acre working ranch across from Kualoa Beach Park on Windward Oahu offers two-hour trail rides in the breathtaking Kaaawa Valley, which was the site of such movie back lots as *Jurassic Park, Godzilla,* and *50 First Dates,* as well as numerous television shows, including *Lost.* There is an hour-long option, but it doesn't take you into the valley. Instead, this tour takes you to the scenic northern section of the ranch with its WWII-era bunkers. Kualoa has other activities—bus, boat, and Jeep tours; electric mountain bike tours; kayak adventure tours; ATV trail rides; canopy zipline tours; and children's activities—that may be combined for full-day package rates. The minimum age for horseback rides is 10. ✉ *49-479 Kamehameha Hwy., Kaneohe* ☎ *800/231–7321, 808/237–7321* ⊕ *www. kualoa.com* ✉ *From $88.*

Turtle Bay Stables

HORSEBACK RIDING | FAMILY | Trail rides follow the 12-mile-long coastline and even step out onto sandy beaches fronting this luxe resort on Oahu's fabled North Shore. The stables here are part of the resort but can be utilized by nonguests.

The 4,000-acre Kualoa Ranch may look familiar to you; a popular film site, it's been featured in several *Jurassic Park* movies, as well as other films and TV shows (you can take a film sites tour of the ranch).

The sunset ride is a definite must. A basic trail ride lasts 45 minutes and visits filming sites for ABC's *Lost* and the film *Pirates of the Caribbean.* ✉ *Turtle Bay Resort, 57-091 Kamehameha Hwy., Kahuku* ☎ *808/293–6024* ⊕ *www.turtlebayresort.com/things-to-do/sports-recreation/horse-riding* 🖼 *From $86.*

Kayaking

Kayaking is an easy way to explore the ocean—and Oahu's natural beauty—without much effort or skill. It offers a vantage point not afforded by swimming or surfing and a workout you won't get lounging on a catamaran. Even novices can get in a kayak and enjoy the island's scenery.

The ability to travel long distances can also get you into trouble. ■ TIP➜ **Experts agree that rookies should stay on the windward side.** Their reasoning is simple: if you get tired, break or lose an oar, or just plain pass out, the onshore winds will eventually blow you back to the beach.

The same cannot be said for the offshore breezes of the North Shore and West Oahu.

Kayaks are specialized: some are better suited for riding waves while others are designed for traveling long distances. Your outfitter can address your needs depending on your skill level. Sharing your plans with your outfitter can lead to a more enjoyable—and safer—experience. Expect to pay from $35 for a half-day single rental to $139 for a guided kayak tour with lunch. Some kayaking outfitters also rent stand-up paddleboards (⇨ *see Stand-Up Paddling*).

BEST SPOTS

If you want to try your hand at surfing kayaks, **Bellows Field Beach** (near Waimanalo Town Center, entrance on Kalanianaole Highway) on the windward side and **Mokuleia Beach** (across from Dillingham Airfield) on the North Shore are two great spots. Hard-to-reach breaks, the ones that surfers exhaust themselves trying to reach, are easily accessed by kayak. The buoyancy of the kayak also allows you to catch the wave earlier and get out in front of the white wash. One reminder on these spots: if you're a little green, stick to Bellows Field Beach with those onshore winds. Generally speaking, you don't want to be catching waves where surfers are; in Waikiki, however, pretty much anything goes.

The perennial favorite of kayakers is **Lanikai Beach,** on the island's windward side. Tucked away in an upscale residential area, this award-winning beach has become a popular spot for amateur kayakers because of its calm waters and onshore winds. More adventurous paddlers can head to the Mokulua Islands, two islets less than 1 mile from the beach. You can land on Moku Nui, which has surf breaks and small beaches great for picnicking. Take a dip in Queen's Bath, a small saltwater swimming hole.

For something a little different, try the Kahana River on the island's windward side, which empties into the ocean at **Kahana Bay Beach Park.** The river may not have the blue water of the ocean, but the majestic Koolau Mountains, with waterfalls during rainy months, make for a picturesque backdrop. It's a short jaunt, about 2 miles round-trip from the beach, but it's tranquil and packed with rain-forest foliage. Bring mosquito repellent.

EQUIPMENT, LESSONS, AND TOURS
Go Bananas
KAYAKING | Staffers make sure that you rent the appropriate kayak for your abilities and can also outfit your rental car with soft racks to transport your boat to the beach. (Racks are included in the rental fee.) You can rent either a single or double kayak. The store also carries clothing and kayaking accessories and rents stand-up paddleboards. (There's a second location in Aiea, which is closer to the North Shore.) ⊠ 799 Kapahulu Ave., Kapahulu ☎ 808/737–9514 ⊕ www.gobananaskayaks.com ⊠ From $35.

Kailua Beach Adventures
KAYAKING | One of the best places for beginners to rent kayaks is Kailua Beach, and Kailua Beach Adventures has an ideal location just across the street. The company offers two- and five-hour guided kayak tours (the longer tour includes lunch, time for kayaking, and time for the beach). More adventurous visitors can rent a kayak (double or single for a half or full day) and venture to the Mokulua Islands off Lanikai. You can also rent snorkeling equipment, stand-up paddleboards, and bikes. (Discounts are given if booked online.) ⊠ Kailua Beach Shopping Center, 130 Kailua Rd., Kailua ☎ 808/262–2555 ⊕ www.kailuasailboards.com ⊠ From $59 for rental, $139 for tours.

Twogood Kayaks Hawaii
KAYAKING | The outfitter offers kayak rentals (single or double), lessons, and guided tours. Guides are trained in the history, geology, and birds of the area. Fully guided kayak excursions are either 2½ or 5 hours and include lunch, snorkeling gear, and transportation to and from Waikiki. For those who want to create their own itinerary, owner Bob Twogood offers custom "Elite" tours. The outfitter has also recently added rental bikes as well as guided hikes to its offerings. ⊠ 134B Hamakua Dr., Kailua ☎ 808/262–5656 ⊕ www.twogoodkayaks.com ⊠ Rentals from $60, tours from $115.

Scuba Diving

Not all of Hawaii's beauty is above water. What lurks below can be just as magnificent.

Although snorkeling provides adequate access to this underwater world, nothing gives you the freedom—or depth, quite literally—as scuba.

The diving on Oahu is comparable with any you might do in the tropics, but its uniqueness comes from the isolated environment of the Islands. There are literally hundreds of species of fish and marine life that you can find only in this chain. In fact, about 25% of Hawaii's marine life can be seen here only—nowhere else in the world. Adding to the singularity of diving off Oahu is the human history of the region. Military activities and tragedies of the 20th century filled the waters surrounding Oahu with wreckage that the ocean creatures have since turned into their homes.

Although instructors certified to license you in scuba are plentiful in the Islands, we suggest that you get your PADI certification before coming, as a week of classes may be a bit of a commitment on a short vacation. Expect to pay around $100 for a two-tank boat dive (provided that you are certified). ■TIP→ You can go on short, shallow introductory dives without the certification, but the best dives require it and cost a bit more.

BEST SPOTS

Hanauma Bay Nature Preserve. On Oahu's southeast shore, about 30 minutes drive east of Waikiki, Hanauma Bay Nature Preserve is home to more than 250 different species of fish, of which a quarter can be found nowhere else in the world. This has made this volcanic crater bay one of the most popular dive sites in the state. It's a long walk from the parking lot to the beach—even longer lugging equipment—so consider hooking up with a licensed dive-tour operator. Preservation efforts have aided the bay's delicate ecosystem, so expect to see various butterfly fish, surgeonfish, tangs, parrot fish, and endangered Hawaiian sea turtles. ⊠ 7455 Kalanianaole Hwy., Hawaii Kai ☎ 808/396–4229 $7.50 per person and $1 parking.

Hundred Foot Hole. Once an ancient Hawaiian fishing ground reserved for royalty, the Hundred Foot Hole is a cluster of volcanic boulders that have created ledges, caves, and a large open-ended cavern perfect for diving. Accessible from shore, this spot near Diamond Head attracts octopus, manta rays, and the occasional white-tip shark. ⊠ Off Diamond Head, Honolulu.

Mahi Waianae. Hawaii's waters are littered with shipwrecks, but one of the most intact and accessible is the Mahi Waianae, a 165-foot minesweeper that was sunk in 1982 off the Waianae Coast. It lies upright in about 90 feet of calm and clear water, encrusted in coral and patrolled by white spotted eagle rays and millet seed butterfly fish. The wreck serves as an artificial reef for such Hawaii aquatic residents as blue-striped snappers, puffer fish, lionfish, moray eels, and octopus. Visibility averages about 100 feet, making this one of the most popular dives on the island. ⊠ Waianae.

Maunalua Bay. The bay stretches about 7 miles, from Portlock Point to Black Point on Oahu's southeastern shore. Teeming with marine life, this spot has several accessible dive sites of varying difficulty. The shallow-water Turtle Canyon is home to endangered Hawaiian green sea turtles. Fantasy Reef is another shallow dive with three plateaus of volcanic rock lined with coral that is home to fish, eels, and sea turtles. In about 85 feet of water, Baby Barge is an easy-to-penetrate sunken vessel encrusted in coral. An advanced dive, the wreck of a Vought F4U Corsair gives you a close-up look at garden eels and stingrays. ⊠ Southeast Oahu.

Sharks Cove. Oahu's best shore dive is accessible only during the summer months. Sharks Cove, on Oahu's North Shore, churns with monster surf during the winter, making this popular snorkeling and diving spot extremely dangerous. In summer, the cavernous lava tubes and tunnels are great for both novices and experienced divers. Some dive-tour companies offer round-trip transportation from Waikiki. ⊠ Haleiwa.

Three Tables. A short walk from Sharks Cove is Three Tables, named for a trio of flat rocks running perpendicular to shore. There are lava tubes to the right of these rocks that break the surface and then extend out about 50 feet. Although this area isn't as active as Sharks Cove, you can still spot octopus, moray eels, parrot fish, green sea turtles, and the occasional shark. ⊠ *Haleiwa.*

EQUIPMENT, LESSONS, AND TOURS

Aaron's Dive Shop
SCUBA DIVING | This friendly and well-equipped dive shop caters to everyone. Take an "introductory" dive if you're not certified; get certified; or sign up for an offshore day or night dive excursion if you're experienced. In addition to organized group dives, the company's "Dive Concierge" can arrange private charters for those who want a completely customized experience. Snorkelers can go along on many dives as well. ⊠ *307 Hahani St., Kailua* ☎ *808/262–2333* ⊕ *aaronsdiveshop.com* ⊴ *From $140 for 2-tank dive.*

Surf 'N Sea
SCUBA DIVING | The North Shore headquarters for all things water-related is also great for diving. One interesting perk: upon request, their dive guides can shoot a video of you diving. It's hard to see facial expressions under the water, but it still might be fun for those who want to prove that they took the plunge. Two-tank shore dives are the most economical choice (prices for noncertified divers are higher), but the company also offers boat dives, and in the summer, night dives are available for only slightly more. ⊠ *62-595 Kamehameha Hwy., Haleiwa* ☎ *800/899–7873* ⊕ *www.surfnsea.com* ⊴ *From $120 (2-tank shore dives).*

Snorkeling

If you can swim, you can snorkel. And you don't need any formal training, either.

Snorkeling is a favorite pastime for both visitors and residents and can be done anywhere there's enough water to stick your face in. You can pick up a mask and snorkel at a corner ABC store for around $35, including fins, and get going on your own or pay up to $175 for a luxurious snorkel cruise including lunch and drinks. Each spot will have its great days depending on the weather and time of year, so consult with the purveyor of your gear for tips on where the best viewing is that day. Keep in mind that the North Shore should be attempted only when the waves are calm, namely in the summertime.

Make sure you put plenty of sunscreen on your back (or better yet, wear a T-shirt) because once you start gazing below, your head may not come back up for hours.

BEST SPOTS

Electric Beach. On the western side of the island, directly across from the electricity plant—hence the name—Electric Beach is a haven for tropical fish, making it a great snorkeling spot. The expulsion of hot water from the plant raises the temperature of the ocean, attracting Hawaiian green sea turtles, spotted moray eels, and spinner dolphins. Although visibility is not always the best, the crowds are small and the fish are guaranteed. ⊠ *Farrington Hwy., 1 mile west of Ko Olina Resort, Kapolei.*

Hanauma Bay Nature Preserve. What Waimea Bay is to surfing, Hanauma Bay in Southeast Oahu is to snorkeling. Easily the most popular snorkeling spot on the island, it's home to more than 250 different species of marine life. Due to the protection of the narrow mouth of the cove and the prodigious reef, you will be hard-pressed to find a place you will feel safer while snorkeling. ⊠ *7455 Kalanianaole Hwy., Honolulu* ☎ *808/396–4229* *$7.50 per person and $1 parking.*

Queen's Surf Beach. On the edge of Waikiki, Queen's Surf is a marine reserve located between Kapahulu Groin and the Waikiki Aquarium. It's not as chock-full of fish as Hanauma Bay, but it has its share of colorful reef fish and the occasional Hawaiian green sea turtle. Just yards from shore, it's a great spot for an escape if you're stuck in Waikiki and have grown weary of watching the surfers. ⊠ *Kalakaua Ave., Honolulu.*

Sharks Cove. Great shallows protected by a huge reef make Sharks Cove on the North Shore a prime spot for snorkelers, even young ones, in the summer. You'll find a plethora of critters, from crabs to octopus, in water that's no more than waist deep. When the winter swells come, this area can turn treacherous. ⊠ *Kamehameha Hwy., across from Foodland, Haleiwa.*

EQUIPMENT AND TOURS
Hanauma Bay Snorkeling Excursions
SNORKELING | If you're going to Hanauma Bay, you have three options: take a chance with limited parking spaces at the park, take TheBus, or contact Hanauma Bay Snorkeling Excursions. They provide transportation to and from Waikiki hotels, equipment, and instruction on how to use the equipment for a reasonable price that does not include the $7.50 park entrance fee. ☎ *808/306–3393* ⊕ *www. hanaumabaysnorkel.com* ☎ *From $25.*

Snorkel Bob's
SNORKELING | This place has all the stuff you'll need—and more—to make your water adventures more enjoyable. Bob makes his own gear and is active in protecting reef fish species. Feel free to ask the staff about good snorkeling spots, as the best ones can vary with weather and the seasons. You can either rent or buy gear (and reserve it in advance

online). ⊠ *700 Kapahulu Ave., Kapahulu* ☎ *808/735–7944, 800/262–7725* ⊕ *www. snorkelbob.com* ☎ *Rentals from $38 per wk.*

Spas

Excellent day and resort spas can be found throughout Oahu, primarily in the resorts of Waikiki but also downtown and on the North Shore. Individual treatments and day packages offer a wide choice of rejuvenating therapies, some of which are unique to the Islands. Try the popular *lomilomi* massage with kukui-nut oil (*lomi* meaning to rub, knead, and massage using palms, forearms, fingers, knuckles, elbows, knees, feet, even sticks). Add heated *pohaku* (stones) placed on the back to relieve sore muscles, or choose a facial using natural ingredients such as coconut, mango, papaya, ti leaf, Hawaiian honey, or ginger. Many full-service spas offer couples' private treatment rooms, fitness suites, yoga, and hydrotherapy pools.

HONOLULU
WAIKIKI
Mandara Spa at the Hilton Hawaiian Village Beach Resort & Spa
SPA/BEAUTY | From its perch in the Kalia Tower, Mandara Spa, an outpost of the chain that originated in Bali, overlooks the mountains, ocean, and downtown Honolulu. Fresh Hawaiian ingredients and traditional techniques headline an array of treatments. Try an exotic upgrade, such as reflexology or a Balinese body polish. Or relieve achy muscles with a traditional Thai poultice massage. The delicately scented, candlelit foyer can fill up quickly with robe-clad conventioneers, so be sure to make a reservation. There are spa suites for couples, a private infinity pool, and a boutique. ⊠ *Hilton Hawaiian Village Beach Resort & Spa, 2005 Kalia Rd., 3rd and 4th fl., Kalia Tower, Waikiki* ☎ *808/945–7721* ⊕ *www.mandaraspa. com.*

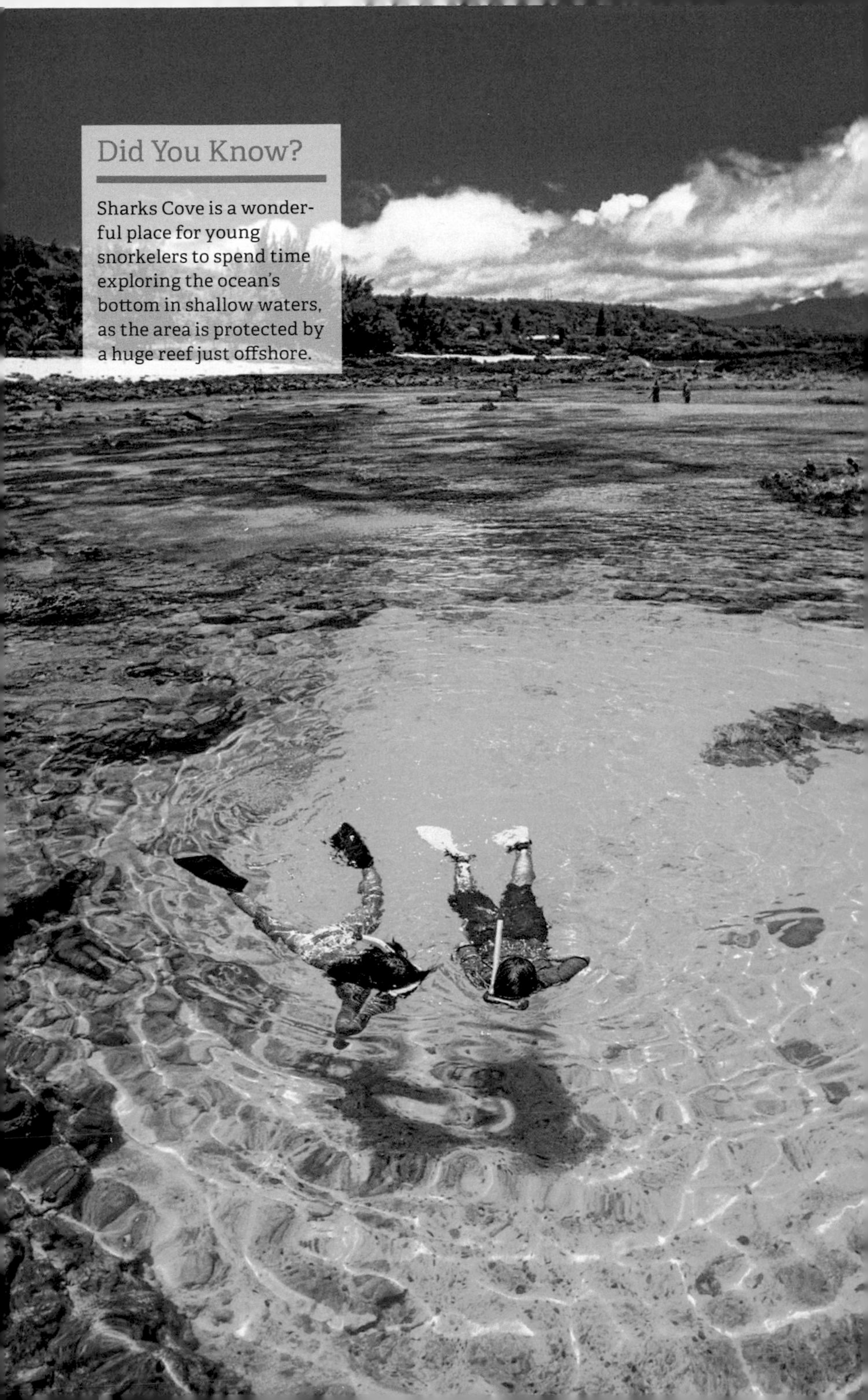

Did You Know?

Sharks Cove is a wonderful place for young snorkelers to spend time exploring the ocean's bottom in shallow waters, as the area is protected by a huge reef just offshore.

Na Hoola Spa at the Hyatt Regency Waikiki Resort & Spa

SPA/BEAUTY | Na Hoola is the premier resort spa in Waikiki, with 16 treatment rooms sprawling across 10,000 square feet and two floors of the Hyatt on Kalakaua Avenue. Arrive early for your treatment to enjoy the postcard views of Waikiki Beach. Four packages identified by Hawaii's native healing plants—noni, kukui, awa, and kalo—combine various body, face, and hair treatments; the spa also has luxurious packages that last three to six hours. The Kele Kele body wrap employs a self-heating mud wrap to release tension and stress. The small exercise room is for use by hotel guests only. ⊠ *Hyatt Regency Waikiki Resort & Spa, 2424 Kalakaua Ave., Waikiki* 🕾 *808/923–1234, 808/237–6330 for reservations* ⊕ *www.nahoolaspawaikiki.com.*

★ SpaHalekulani

SPA/BEAUTY | SpaHalekulani mines the traditions and cultures of the Pacific Islands with massages and body and facial therapies. Try the Samoan Nonu, which uses warm stones and healing nonu gel to relieve muscle tension. The exclusive line of bath and body products is scented by maile, lavender orchid, or coconut passion. Facilities are specific to treatment but may include Japanese furo bath or steam shower. ⊠ *Halekulani Hotel, 2199 Kalia Rd., Waikiki* 🕾 *808/931–5322* ⊕ *www.halekulani.com/living/spahalekulani.*

The Spa at Trump Waikiki

SPA/BEAUTY | The Spa at Trump offers private changing and showering areas for each room, creating an environment of uninterrupted relaxation. No matter what treatment you choose, it is inspired by "personal intention," such as purify, balance, heal, revitalize, or calm, to elevate the senses throughout your time there. Don't miss the signature gemstone treatments, which feature products by Shiffa; or treat yourself to a Naturally Yours facial to emerge with younger-looking skin. The Healing Hawaiian Ocean Ritual is one of the most popular massages to begin—or end—your day. ⊠ *Trump International Hotel Waikiki, 223 Saratoga Rd., Waikiki* 🕾 *808/683–7466* ⊕ *www.trumpwaikikihotel.com.*

ALA MOANA
Hoala Salon and Spa

SPA/BEAUTY | This Aveda concept spa has everything from Vichy showers to hydrotherapy rooms to customized aromatherapy. They'll even touch up your makeup for free before you leave. ⊠ *Ala Moana Shopping Center, 3rd fl., 1450 Ala Moana Blvd., Ala Moana* 🕾 *808/947–6141* ⊕ *www.hoalasalonspa.com.*

THE NORTH SHORE
★ Nalu Kinetic Spa at Turtle Bay

SPA/BEAUTY | Luxuriate at the ocean's edge in this 11,000-square-foot spa at the Turtle Bay resort. Try one of the spa's signature treatments, including a coconut-lava shell massage or a ginger-lime sugar scrub followed by a coconut-argan oil infusion. There are private spa suites, an outdoor treatment cabana that overlooks the surf, and a lounge area and juice bar. Spa guests may also join fitness classes for a fee. ⊠ *Turtle Bay, 57-091 Kamehameha Hwy., Kahuku* 🕾 *808/447–6868* ⊕ *www.nalukineticspa.com.*

WEST (LEEWARD) OAHU
Laniwai—A Disney Spa

SPA/BEAUTY | At this spa, every staff member—or "cast member," as they call themselves—is extensively trained in Hawaiian culture and history to ensure they are projecting the right *mana,* or energy, in their work. To begin each treatment, you select a special *pohaku* with words of intent, then cast it into a reflective pool. Choose from about 150 spa therapies, and indulge in Kula Wai, the only outdoor hydrotherapy garden on Oahu—with private vitality pools, a reflexology path, six different "rain" showers, whirlpool jet spas, and more. ⊠ *Aulani, A Disney Resort & Spa, 92-1185 Aliinui Dr., Ko Olina* 🕾 *808/674–6300* ⊕ *disneyaulani.com/spa-fitness.*

Stand-Up Paddling

From the lakes of Wisconsin to the coast of Lima, Peru, stand-up paddleboarding (or SUP, for short) is taking the sport of surfing to the most unexpected places. Still, the sport remains firmly rooted in the Hawaiian Islands.

Back in the 1960s, Waikiki beach boys would paddle out on their longboards using a modified canoe paddle. It was longer than a traditional paddle, enabling them to stand up and stroke. It was easier this way to survey the ocean and snap photos of tourists learning how to surf. Eventually it became a sport unto itself, with professional contests at world-class surf breaks and long-distance races across treacherous waters.

Stand-up paddleboarding is easy to learn—though riding waves takes some practice—and most outfitters on Oahu offer lessons for all skill levels starting at about $55. It's also a great workout; you can burn off yesterday's dinner buffet, strengthen your core, and experience the natural beauty of the island's coastlines all at once. Once you're ready to head out on your own, half-day rentals start at $50.

If you're looking to learn, go where there's already a SUP presence. Avoid popular surf breaks, unless you're an experienced stand-up paddle surfer, and be wary of ocean and wind conditions. You'll want to find a spot with calm waters, easy access in and out of the ocean, and a friendly crowd that doesn't mind the occasional stand-up paddleboarder.

BEST SPOTS

Ala Moana Beach Park. About a mile west of Waikiki, Ala Moana is the most SUP-friendly spot on the island. In fact, the state installed a series of buoys in the flat-water lagoon to separate stand-up paddlers and swimmers. There are no waves here, making it a great spot to learn, but beware of strong trade winds, which can push you into the reef.

Anahulu Stream. Outfitters on the North Shore like to take SUP beginners to Anahulu Stream, which empties into Waialua Bay near the Haleiwa Boat Harbor. This area is calm and protected from winds, plus there's parking at the harbor, and surf shops nearby rent boards.

Waikiki. There are a number of outfitters on Oahu's South Shore that take beginners into the waters off Waikiki. **Canoes,** the surf break fronting the Duke Kahanamoku statue, and the channels between breaks are often suitable for people learning how to maneuver their boards in not-so-flat conditions. But south swells here can be deceptively menacing, and ocean conditions can change quickly. Check with lifeguards before paddling out, and be mindful of other surfers in the water.

White Plains. If you've got a car with racks, you might want to venture to White Plains, a fairly uncrowded beach about 27 miles west of Waikiki. It's a long, sandy beach with lots of breaks, and plenty of room for everyone. There are lifeguards, restrooms, and lots of parking, making this a great spot for beginners and those just getting comfortable in small waves.

EQUIPMENT AND LESSONS
Hawaiian Watersports
WATER SPORTS | FAMILY | Paddle off the shore of picturesque Kailua Beach. This safety-conscious outfitter offers both equipment rentals and 90-minute and 3-hour group or individual lessons. A one-stop shop for water sports, they also offer kiteboarding, surfing, and windsurfing lessons as well as kayak tours and equipment rentals. Discounts are available online if you book ahead. ⊠ 171 Hamakua Dr., Kailua ☎ 808/262–5483 ⊕ www.hawaiianwatersports.com ☎ Rentals from $59.

This surfer is doing a stellar job of riding the infamous Banzai Pipeline on Oahu's North Shore.

Paddle Core Fitness

WATER SPORTS | Paddling is a way of life for Reid Inouye, who now shares his passion for the sport with students. (He's also the publisher of *Standup Paddle Magazine*.) His company offers introductory classes as well as fitness programs for serious paddlers. Lessons and workout programs are held in the flat waters of Ala Moana Beach, where there's a designated area for paddling, and you can have either group or private lessons. ⊠ *Ala Moana Beach Park, Ala Moana Blvd., Ala Moana* ☎ *808/200–0574* ⊕ *www.paddlecorefitness.com* ✉ *Workout programs from $25, lessons from $135.*

Submarine Tours

Atlantis Submarines

TOUR—SPORTS | This is the underwater adventure for the unadventurous. Not fond of swimming, but want to see what you've been missing? Board this high-tech 64-passenger vessel for a ride past shipwrecks, turtle breeding grounds, and coral reefs. The tours, which depart from the pier at the Hilton Hawaiian Village, are available in several languages. (Discounts are available if booked online.) ⊠ *Hilton Hawaiian Village Beach Resort & Spa, 2005 Kalia Rd., Honolulu* ☎ *808/973–9800, 800/381–0237 for reservations* ⊕ *www.atlantisadventures. com* ✉ *From $133.*

Surfing

Perhaps no word is more associated with Hawaii than surfing. Every year the best of the best gather on Oahu's North Shore to compete in their version of the Super Bowl: the prestigious Vans Triple Crown of Surfing. The pros dominate the waves for a month, but the rest of the year belongs to folks just trying to have fun.

Oahu is unique because it has so many famous spots: Banzai Pipeline, Waimea Bay, Kaiser Bowls, and Sunset Beach. These spots, however, require experience. Nonetheless, with most dependable sets and access to lessons, Waikiki is still a great place for beginners to learn or for novice surfers to catch predictable waves. Group lessons on Waikiki Beach start at $50, but if you really want to fine-tune your skills, you can pay up to $500 for a daylong private outing with a former pro.

The island also has miles of coastline with surf spots that are perfect for everyday surfers. But remember this surfer's credo: when in doubt, don't go out. If you're unsure about conditions, stay on the beach and talk to locals to get more info about surf breaks before trying yourself.

⚠ If you don't want to run the risk of a confrontation with local surfers, who can be very territorial about their favorite breaks, try some of the alternate spots listed below. They may not have the name recognition, but the waves can be just as great.

BEST SPOTS
Makaha Beach Park. If you like to ride waves, try Makaha Beach on Oahu's west side. It has legendary, interminable rights that allow riders to perform all manner of stunts: from six-man canoes with everyone doing headstands to Bullyboards (oversize body boards) with whole families along for the ride. Mainly known as a longboarding spot, it's predominantly local but respectful to outsiders. Use caution in winter, as the surf can get huge. It's not called Makaha—which means "fierce"—for nothing. ⊠ 84-369 Farrington Hwy., Waianae.

Sunset Beach. If you want to impress your surfing buddies back home, catch a wave at the famous Sunset Beach on Oahu's North Shore. Two of the more manageable breaks are **Kammie Land** (or Kammie's) and **Sunset Point.** For the daring, Sunset is part of the Vans Triple Crown of Surfing for a reason. Thick waves and long rides await, but you're going to want to have a thick board and a thicker skull. Surf

etiquette here is a must, as it's mostly local. ⊠ 59-104 Kamehameha Hwy., 1 mile north of Ehukai Beach Park, Haleiwa.

Ulukou Beach. In Waikiki you can paddle out to **Populars,** a break at Ulukou Beach. Nice and easy, Populars—or Pops—never breaks too hard and is friendly to both newbies and veterans. It's one of the best places to surf during pumping south swells, as this thick wave breaks in open ocean, making it more rideable. The only downside is the long paddle out to the break from Kuhio Beach, but that keeps the crowds manageable. ⊠ Waikiki Beach, in front of the Sheraton Waikiki hotel, Honolulu.

White Plains Beach. Known among locals as "mini Waikiki," the surf at White Plains breaks in numerous spots, preventing the logjams that are inevitable at many of Oahu's more popular spots. It's a great break for novice to intermediate surfers, though you do have to keep a lookout for wayward boards. From the H1, take the Makakilo exit. ⊠ Off H1, Kapolei.

EQUIPMENT AND LESSONS
Aloha Beach Services
SURFING | It may sound like a cliché, but there's no better way to learn to surf than from a beach boy in Waikiki. And there's no one better than Harry "Didi" Robello, a second-generation beach boy and owner of Aloha Beach Services. Learn to surf in an hour-long group lesson, a semiprivate lesson, or with just you and an instructor. You can also rent a board here. ⊠ 2365 Kalakaua Ave., on beach near Moana Surfrider, Waikiki ☎ 808/922–3111 ⊕ www.alohabeachservices.com 🏄 Lessons from $50, board rentals from $20.

Faith Surf School
SURFING | Professional surfer Tony Moniz started his own surf school in 2000, and since then, he and his wife, Tammy, have helped thousands of people catch their first waves in Waikiki. The 90-minute group lessons include all equipment and are the cheapest option. You can pay

more (sometimes a lot more) for semiprivate lessons with up to three people or for private lessons. You can also book an all-day surf tour with Moniz, riding waves with him at his favorite breaks. ⊠ *Outrigger Waikiki Beach Resort, 2335 Kalakaua Ave., Waikiki* 🕾 *808/931–6262* ⊕ *www.faithsurfschool.com* ✉ *Lessons from $65, board rental from $20.*

Surf 'N Sea

SURFING | This is a one-stop shop for surfers (and other water-sports enthusiasts) on the North Shore. Rent a short or long board by the hour or for a full day. Two-hour group lessons are offered, as are four- to five-hour surf safaris for experienced surfers. ⊠ *62-595 Kamehameha Hwy., Haleiwa* 🕾 *800/899–7873* ⊕ *www.surfnsea.com* ✉ *Lessons from $85, rentals from $35 per day.*

Whale-Watching

December is marked by the arrival of snow in much of America, but in Hawaii it marks the return of the humpback whale. These migrating behemoths move south from their North Pacific homes during the winter months for courtship and calving, and they put on quite a show. Watching males and females alike throwing themselves out of the ocean and into the sunset awes even the saltiest of sailors. Newborn calves riding gently next to their 2-ton mothers will stir you to your core. These gentle giants can be seen from the shore as they make a splash, but there is nothing like having your boat rocking beneath you in the wake of a whale's breach.

Wild Side Specialty Tours

WHALE-WATCHING | Boasting a marine-biologist/naturalist crew, this company takes you to undisturbed snorkeling areas. Along the way you may see dolphins and turtles. The company promises a sighting of migrating whales year-round on some itineraries. Tours may depart as early as 8 am from Waianae, so it's important to plan ahead. The three-hour deluxe wildlife tour is the most popular option. ⊠ *Waianae Boat Harbor, 85-471 Farrington Hwy., Waianae* 🕾 *808/306–7273* ⊕ *www.sailhawaii.com* ✉ *From $175.*

Chapter 4

MAUI

Updated by Lehia Apana and
Laurie Lyons-Makaimoku

◉ Sights	🍴 Restaurants	🛏 Hotels	🛍 Shopping	🍸 Nightlife
★★★★★	★★★☆☆	★★★☆☆	★★★☆☆	★★☆☆☆

WELCOME TO MAUI

TOP REASONS TO GO

★ **The Road to Hana:** Each curve of this legendary cliff-side road pulls you deeper into the lush green rain forest of Maui's eastern shore.

★ **Haleakala National Park:** Explore the lava bombs, cinder cones, and silverswords at the gasp-inducing, volcanic summit of Haleakala, the House of the Sun.

★ **Hookipa Beach:** On Maui's North Shore, the world's top windsurfers will dazzle you as they maneuver above the waves like butterflies shot from cannons.

★ **Waianapanapa State Park:** Head to East Maui and take a dip at the stunning black-sand beach or in the cave pool where an ancient princess once hid.

★ **Resorts, Resorts, Resorts:** Opulent gardens, pools, restaurants, and golf courses make Maui's resorts some of the best in the Islands.

1 West Maui. This leeward, sunny area is ringed by resorts and condominiums in areas such as Kaanapali and Kapalua. Also on the coast is the busy, tourist-oriented town of Lahaina.

2 South Shore. The leeward side of Maui's eastern half is what most people mean when they say South Shore. This popular area is sunny and warm year-round.

3 Central Maui. Between Maui's two mountain areas is Maui's county seat of Wailuku and the commercial center of Kahului (and the airport).

4 Upcountry. Island residents affectionately call the regions climbing up the slope of Haleakala Crater Upcountry.

5 North Shore. The North Shore has no large resorts, just plenty of picturesque small towns like Paia and Haiku.

6 Road to Hana. The island's northeastern, windward side is largely one great rain forest, traversed by the stunning Road to Hana.

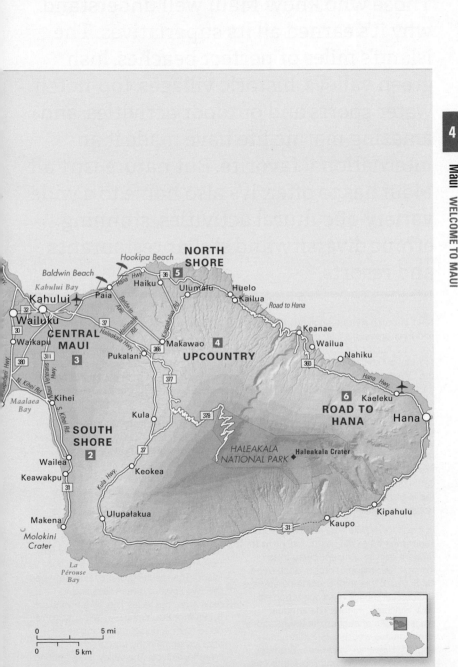

NORTH SHORE

Hookipa Beach

Baldwin Beach

Kahului Bay

Kahului

Wailuku

Paia

Haiku

Ulumalu

Huelo

Kailua

Road to Hana

Keanae

Wailua

Nahiku

Waikapu

CENTRAL MAUI

Makawao

UPCOUNTRY

Pukalani

Maalaea Bay

Kihei

Kula

Kaeleku

ROAD TO HANA

Hana

SOUTH SHORE

Wailea

Keawakpu

Keokea

HALEAKALA NATIONAL PARK

Haleakala Crater

Kipahulu

Makena

Molokini Crater

Ulupalakua

Kaupo

La Pérouse Bay

0   5 mi

0   5 km

Those who know Maui well understand why it's earned all its superlatives. The island's miles of perfect beaches, lush green valleys, historic villages, top-notch water sports and outdoor activities, and amazing marine life have made it an international favorite. But nature isn't all Maui has to offer: it's also home to a wide variety of cultural activities, stunning ethnic diversity, and stellar restaurants and resorts.

Maui is much more than sandy beaches and palm trees; it's a land of water and fire. Puu Kukui, the 5,788-foot interior of Mauna Kahalawai, also known as the "West Maui Mountains," is one of Earth's wettest spots—an annual rainfall of 400 inches has sculpted the land into impassable gorges and razor-sharp ridges. On the opposite side of the island, the blistering lava fields at Ahihi-Kinau receive scant rain. Just above this desert-like landscape, *paniolo* (cowboys) herd cattle on rolling fertile ranchlands. On the island's rugged east side is the lush tropical Hawaii of travel posters.

In small towns like Paia and Hana you can see remnants of the past mingling with modern-day life. Ancient *heiau* (plat-forms, often made of stone, once used as places of worship) line busy roadways. Old coral-and-brick missionary homes now welcome visitors. The antique smokestacks of sugar mills tower above communities where the children blend English, Hawaiian, Japanese, Chinese, Portuguese, Filipino, and more into one colorful language. Hawaii is a melting pot like no other. Visiting an eclectic mom-and-pop shop—such as Makawao's T. Komoda Store & Bakery—can feel like stepping into another country or back in time. The more you look here, the more you find.

At 729 square miles, Maui is the second-largest Hawaiian Island, but it offers more miles of swimmable beaches than any of its neighbors. Despite rapid growth over the past few decades, the local population still totals less than 200,000.

GEOLOGY
Maui is made up of two volcanoes, one now extinct and the other dormant but that erupted long ago, joined into one island. The resulting depression between the two is what gives the island its nickname, the Valley Isle. West Maui's 5,788-foot Puu Kukui was the first volca-no to form, a distinction that gives that area's mountainous topography a more weathered look. The Valley Isle's second

volcano is the 10,023-foot Haleakala, where desertlike terrain abuts tropical forests.

HISTORY

Maui's history is full of firsts—Lahaina was the first capital of Hawaii and the first destination of the whaling industry (early 1800s), which explains why the town still has that seafaring vibe. Lahaina was also the first stop for missionaries on Maui (1823). Although they suppressed aspects of Hawaiian culture, the missionaries did help invent the Hawaiian alphabet and built a printing press—the first west of the Rockies—that rolled out the news in Hawaiian, as well as, not surprisingly, Hawaii's first Bibles. Maui also boasts the first sugar plantation in Hawaii (1849) and the first Hawaiian luxury resort (1946), now called the Travaasa Hana.

ON MAUI TODAY

In the mid-1970s savvy marketers saw a way to improve Maui's economy by promoting the Valley Isle to golfers and luxury travelers. The strategy worked well; Maui's visitor count is about 2.6 million annually. Impatient traffic now threatens to overtake the ubiquitous aloha spirit, development encroaches on agricultural lands, and county planners struggle to meet the needs of a burgeoning population. But Maui is still carpeted with an eyeful of green, and for every tailgater there's a local on "Maui time" who stops for each pedestrian and sunset.

Planning

Getting Here and Around

AIR

Maui has two major airports. Kahului Airport handles major airlines and interisland flights; it's the only airport on Maui that has direct service from the mainland. Kapalua–West Maui Airport is served by Hawaiian and Mokulele airlines. If you're staying in West Maui and you're flying in from another island, you can avoid the hour drive from the Kahului Airport by flying into Kapalua–West Maui Airport. Hana Airport in East Maui is small; Mokulele Airlines flies twice per day between Kahului and Hana.

Service to Maui changes regularly, so it's best to check when you are ready to book. Alaska Airlines offers nonstop flights from Anchorage, Bellingham, WA; Oakland; Portland, OR; Sacramento; San Diego; and Seattle. American Airlines flies from Dallas, Los Angeles, and Phoenix. Hawaiian Airlines has nonstop service from Los Angeles, Oakland, Portland, San Francisco, and Seattle; it also offers the only nonstop flight from JFK to Honolulu. United's nonstop flights leave from Chicago, Denver, Los Angeles, and San Francisco. Delta has flights from Los Angeles, Salt Lake City, and Seattle. Virgin flies nonstop from Los Angeles and San Francisco. In addition to offering competitive rates and online specials, all have frequent-flyer programs that will entitle you to rewards and upgrades the more you fly.

CAR

Should you plan to do any sightseeing on Maui, it's best to rent a car. Even if all you want to do is relax at your resort, you may want to hop in the car to check out one of the island's popular restaurants.

Many of Maui's roads are two lanes, so allow plenty of time to return your vehicle to the airport. Traffic can be bad during morning and afternoon rush hours, especially between Kahului and Paia, Kihei, and Lahaina. Give yourself about 3½ hours before departure time to return your vehicle.

Make sure you've got a GPS or a good map. Free visitor publications containing high-quality road maps can be found at airports, hotels, and shops.

Great Itineraries

Maui's landscape is incredibly diverse, offering everything from underwater encounters with eagle rays to treks across moonlike terrain. Although daydreaming at the pool or on the beach may fulfill your initial island fantasy, Maui has much more to offer. The following one-day itineraries will take you to our favorite spots on the island.

Beach Day in West Maui

West Maui has some of the island's most beautiful beaches, though many of them are hidden by megaresorts. If you get an early start, you can begin your day snorkeling at Slaughterhouse Beach (in winter, D.T. Fleming Beach is a better option as it's less rough). Then spend the day beach hopping through Kapalua, Napili, and Kaanapali as you make your way south. You'll want to get to Lahaina before dark so you can spend some time exploring the historic whaling town before choosing a restaurant for a sunset dinner.

Focus on Marine Life on the South Shore

Start your South Shore trip early in the morning, and head out past Makena into the rough lava fields of rugged La Perouse Bay. At the road's end there are areas of the Ahihi-Kinau Marine Preserve open to the public (others are closed indefinitely) that offer good snorkeling. If that's a bit too far afield for you, there's excellent snorkeling at Polo Beach. Head to the right (your right while facing the ocean) for plenty of fish and beautiful coral. Head back north to Kihei for lunch, and then enjoy the afternoon learning more about Maui's marine life at the outstanding Maui Ocean Center at Maalaea.

Haleakala National Park, Upcountry, and the North Shore

If you don't plan to spend an entire day hiking in the crater at Haleakala National Park, this itinerary will at least allow you to take a peek at it. Get up early, and head straight for the summit of Haleakala (if you're jet-lagged and waking up in the middle of the night, you may want to get there in time for sunrise). Bring water, sunscreen, and warm clothing; it's freezing at sunrise. Plan to spend a couple of hours exploring the various lookout points in the park. On your way down the mountain, turn right on Makawao Avenue, and head into the little town of Makawao. You can have lunch here, or make a left on Baldwin Avenue and head downhill to the North Shore town of Paia, which has a number of great lunch spots and shops to explore. Spend the rest of your afternoon at Paia's main strip of sand, Hookipa Beach.

The Road to Hana

This cliff-side driving tour through rain-forest canopy reveals Maui's lushest and most tropical terrain. It will take a full day to explore this part of the North Shore and East Maui, especially if you plan to make it all the way to Oheo Gulch. You'll pass through communities where old Hawaii still thrives and where the forest runs unchecked from the sea to the summit. To really soak in the magic of this place, consider staying overnight in Hana town. Spend a full day winding toward Hana, hiking and exploring along the way, and the next day traveling leisurely back to civilization.

Hawaii residents refer to places as being either *mauka* (toward the mountains) or *makai* (toward the ocean).

Hawaii has a strict seat-belt law. All passengers, regardless of age, in the front and back seat must wear a seat belt. The fine for not wearing a seat belt is $102. Jaywalking is also common, so pay careful attention to pedestrians. Turning right on a red light is legal in the state, except where noted. Your unexpired mainland driver's license is valid for rental cars for up to 90 days.

Driving from one point on Maui to another can take longer than the mileage indicates. It's 52 miles from Kahului Airport to Hana, but the drive will take you about three hours if you stop to smell the flowers, which you certainly should do. As for driving to Haleakala, the 38-mile trip from sea level to the summit will take about two hours. The roads are narrow and winding; you must travel slowly. Kahului is the transportation hub—the main airport and largest harbor are here. Traffic on Maui's roads can be heavy, especially from 6 am–8:30 am and 3:30 pm–6:30 pm. Here are average driving times.

Hotels

Maui is well known for its lovely resorts, some of them very luxurious; many cater to families. But there are other options, including abundant and convenient apartment and condo rentals for all budgets. The resorts and rentals cluster largely on Maui's sunny coasts, in West Maui and the South Shore. For a different, more local experience, you might spend part of your time at a small bed-and-breakfast. Check Internet sites and ask about discounts and packages. *Hotel reviews have been shortened. For full information, visit Fodors.com.*

Driving Times

Kahului to Wailea	17 miles/30 mins
Kahului to Kaanapali	25 miles/45 mins
Kahului to Kapalua	36 miles/1 hr 15 mins
Kahului to Makawao	13 miles/25 mins
Kapalua to Haleakala	73 miles/3 hrs
Kaanapali to Haleakala	62 miles/2 hrs 30 mins
Wailea to Haleakala	54 miles/2 hrs 30 mins
Kapalua to Hana	88 miles/5 hrs
Kaanapali to Hana	77 miles/5 hrs
Wailea to Hana	69 miles/4 hrs 30 mins
Wailea to Lahaina	20 miles/45 mins
Kapalua to Lahaina	12 miles/20 mins

Restaurants

There's a lot going on for a place the size of Maui, from ethnic holes-in-the-wall to fancy oceanfront fish houses. Much of it is excellent, but some of it is overpriced and touristy. Choose menu items made with products that are abundant on the island, including local fish. Local cuisine is a mix of foods brought by ethnic groups since the late 1700s, blended with the foods Native Hawaiians have enjoyed for centuries. For a food adventure, take a drive into Central Maui and eat at one of the "local" spots recommended here.

What It Costs in U.S. Dollars

$	$$	$$$	$$$$
RESTAURANTS			
Under $18	$18–$26	$27–$35	Over $35
HOTELS			
Under $181	$181–$260	$261–$340	Over $340

Where to Stay in Maui

	Local Vibe	Pros	Cons
West Maui	Popular and busy, West Maui includes the picturesque, touristy town of Lahaina and the upscale resort areas of Kaanapali and Kapalua.	A wide variety of shops, water sports, and historic sites provide plenty to do. To relax, there are great beaches and brilliant sunsets.	Traffic is usually congested; parking is hard to find; beaches can be crowded.
South Shore	The protected South Shore of Maui offers diverse experiences and accommodations, from comfortable condos to luxurious resorts—and golf, golf, golf.	Many beautiful beaches; sunny weather; great snorkeling.	Numerous strip malls; crowded with condos; there can be lots of traffic.
Upcountry	Country and chic come together in farms, ranches, and trendy towns on the cool, green slopes of Haleakala.	Cooler weather at higher elevations; panoramic views of nearby islands; distinctive shops, boutiques, galleries, and restaurants.	Fewer restaurants; no nightlife; can be very dark at night and difficult to drive for those unfamiliar with roads and conditions.
North Shore	A hub for surfing, windsurfing, and kiteboarding. When the surf's not up, the focus is on shopping: Paia is full of galleries, shops, and hip eateries.	Wind and waves are terrific for water sports; colorful small towns to explore without the intrusion of big resorts.	Weather inland may not be as sunny as other parts of the island, and coastal areas can be windy; little nightlife; most stores in Paia close early, around 6 pm.
Road to Hana and East Maui	Remote and rural, laid-back and tropical Hana and East Maui are special places to unwind.	Natural experience; rugged coastline and lush tropical scenery; lots of waterfalls.	Accessed by a long and winding road; no nightlife; wetter weather; few places to eat or shop.

Visitor Information

The Hawaii Visitors and Convention Bureau (HVCB) has plenty of general and vacation-planning information for Maui and all the Islands, and it offers a free official vacation planner.

INFORMATION Maui Visitors Bureau.
⊕ *www.gohawaii.com/islands/maui.*

West Maui

Separated from the remainder of the island by steep *pali* (cliffs), West Maui has a reputation for attitude and action. Once upon a time, this was the haunt of whalers, missionaries, and the kings and queens of Hawaii. Today, the main drag, Front Street, is crowded with T-shirt and trinket shops, art galleries, and restaurants. Farther north is Kaanapali, Maui's first planned resort area. Its first hotel, the Sheraton, opened in 1963. Since then, massive resorts, luxury condos, and a shopping center have sprung up along the white-sand beaches, with championship golf courses across the road. A few miles farther up the coast is the ultimate in West Maui luxury, the resort area of Kapalua. In between, dozens of strip malls line both the *makai* (toward the sea) and *mauka* (toward the mountains) sides of the highway. There are gems here, too, like Napili Bay and its jaw-dropping crescent of sand.

Lahaina

27 miles west of Kahului; 4 miles south of Kaanapali.

Lahaina is a bustling waterfront town packed with visitors from around the globe. Some may describe the area as tacky, with too many T-shirt vendors and not enough mom-and-pop shops, but this historic town houses some of Hawaii's best restaurants, boutiques, cafés, and galleries. ■ **TIP→ If you spend Friday afternoon exploring Front Street, hang around for Art Night, when the galleries stay open late and offer entertainment, including artists demonstrating their work.**

Sunset cruises and other excursions depart from Lahaina Harbor. At the southern end of town, an important archaeological site—Mokuula—is currently being researched, excavated, and restored. This was once a spiritual and political center, as well as a home to Maui's chiefs.

It's about a 45-minute drive from Kahului Airport to Lahaina (take Route 380 to Route 30), depending on the traffic on this heavily traveled route. Traffic can be slow around Lahaina, especially 4–6 pm. Shuttles and taxis are available from Kahului Airport. The Maui Bus Lahaina Islander route runs from Queen Kaahumanu Center in Kahului to the Wharf Cinema Center on Front Street, Lahaina's main thoroughfare.

◉ Sights

Baldwin Home Museum

HISTORIC SITE | If you want some insight into 19th-century life in Hawaii, this informative museum is an excellent place to start. Begun in 1834 and completed the following year, the coral-and-stone house was originally home to missionary Dr. Dwight Baldwin and his family. The building has been carefully restored to reflect the period, and many of the original furnishings remain: you can view the family's grand piano, carved four-poster bed, and most interestingly, Dr. Baldwin's dispensary. Also on display is the "thunderpot"—learn how the doctor single-handedly inoculated 10,000 Maui residents against smallpox. ■ **TIP→ Admission includes an orientation by the docent, or come Friday at dusk for a special candlelight tour every half hour.** ⊠ *120 Dickenson St., Lahaina* ☎ *808/661–3262* ⊕ *www.lahainarestoration.org* ⌖ *$7, includes admission to Wo Hing Museum.*

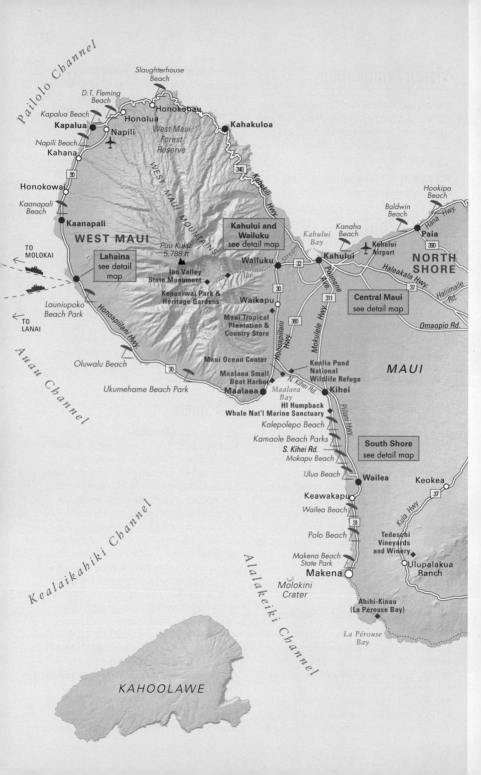

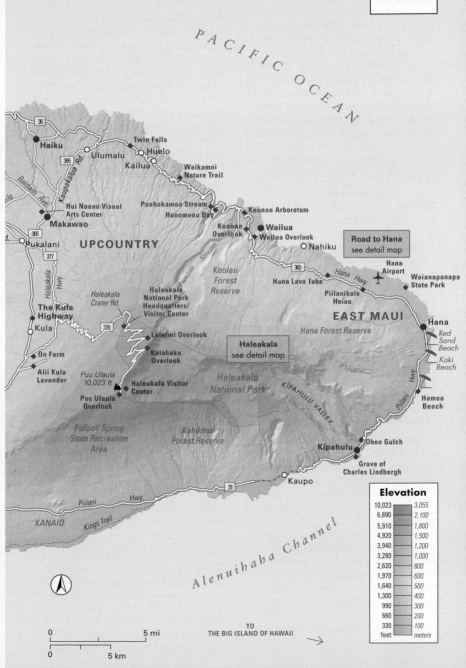

Maui

PACIFIC OCEAN

36 **Haiku**
365 Ulumalu ○ Twin Falls ○ Huelo
Kailua
Waikamoi
Nature Trail

Hui Noeau Visual
Arts Center
Makawao

Puahokamoa Stream
Honomanu Bay
Keanae Arboretum

Keanae
Overlook

Wailua
Wailua Overlook
○ Nahiku

Road to Hana
see detail map

Hana
Airport

Waianapanapa
State Park

360 Hana Hwy.

Hana Lava Tube

Piilanihale
Heiau

EAST MAUI

Hana Forest Reserve

Hana
Red
Sand
Beach
Koki
Beach

Koolau
Forest
Reserve

UPCOUNTRY

77 **Pukalani**
377

365

Baldwin Ave.
Kaupakalua Rd.

Haleakala
National Park
Headquarters/
Visitor Center

Haleakala Hwy.

**The Kula
Highway**

Haleakala
Crater Rd.

378

Leleiwi Overlook

Kalahaku
Overlook

○ **Kula**

On Farm

Alii Kula
Lavender

Puu Ulaula
10,023 ft
Haleakala Visitor
Center
Puu Ulaula
Overlook

Haleakala
see detail map

Haleakala
National Park

Hamoa
Beach

Piilani Hwy.

Polipoli Spring
State Recreation
Area

Kahikinui
Forest Reserve

KIPAHULU VALLEY

Oheo Gulch

Kipahulu

Grave of
Charles Lindbergh

31 ○ Kaupo

Piilani Hwy.

KANAIO

Kings Trail

Alenuihaha Channel

Elevation

feet	meters
10,023	3,055
6,890	2,100
5,910	1,800
4,920	1,500
3,940	1,200
3,280	1,000
2,620	800
1,970	600
1,640	500
1,300	400
990	300
660	200
330	100
feet	meters

0 ___ 5 mi
0 ___ 5 km

TO
THE BIG ISLAND OF HAWAII →

Banyan Tree

LOCAL INTEREST | Planted in 1873, this massive tree is the largest of its kind in the United States and provides a welcome retreat and playground for visitors and locals, who rest and play music under its awesome branches. ■ **TIP→ The Banyan Tree is a popular and hard-to-miss meeting place if your party splits up for independent exploring.** It's also a terrific place to be when the sun sets—mynah birds settle in here for a screeching symphony, which is an event in itself. ⊠ *Front St. between Hotel St. and Canal St., Lahaina* ⊕ *www.lahainarestoration.org.*

Hale Paahao (Old Prison)

HISTORIC SITE | Lahaina's jailhouse is a reminder of rowdy whaling days. Its name literally means "stuck-in-irons house," referring to the wall shackles and ball-and-chain restraints. The compound was built in the 1850s by convict laborers out of blocks of coral that had been salvaged from the demolished waterfront fort. Most prisoners were sent here for desertion, drunkenness, or reckless horse riding. Today, a figure representing an imprisoned old sailor tells his recorded tale of woe. There are also interpretive signs for the botanical garden and whale boat in the yard. ⊠ *Wainee St. and Prison St., Lahaina* ⊕ *www.lahainarestoration. org* ⊠ *Free.*

Holy Innocents Episcopal Church

RELIGIOUS SITE | Built in 1927, this beautiful open-air church is decorated with paintings depicting Hawaiian versions of Christian symbols (including a Hawaiian Madonna and child), rare or extinct birds, and native plants. At the afternoon services, the congregation is typically dressed in traditional clothing from Samoa and Tonga. Anyone is welcome to slip into one of the pews, carved from native woods. Queen Liliuokalani, Hawaii's last reigning monarch, lived in a large grass house on this site as a child. ⊠ *561 Front St., near Mokuhina St., Lahaina* ☎ *808/661–4202* ⊕ *www. holyimaui.org* ⊠ *Free.*

Martin Lawrence Galleries

ART GALLERIES | In business since 1975, Martin Lawrence displays the works of such world-renowned artists as Picasso, Erté, and Chagall in a bright and friendly gallery. There are also modern and pop art pieces by Keith Haring, Andy Warhol, and Japanese creative icon Takashi Murakami. ⊠ *790 Front St., at Lahainaluna Rd., Lahaina* ☎ *808/661–1788* ⊕ *www. martinlawrence.com.*

★ Old Lahaina Courthouse

GOVERNMENT BUILDING | The Lahaina Arts Society, Lahaina Vistor Center, and Lahaina Heritage Museum occupy this charming old government building in the center of town. Wander among the terrific displays and engage with an interactive exhibit about Lahaina's history, pump the knowledgeable visitor center staff for tips—be sure to ask for the walking-tour brochure covering historic Lahaina sites—and stop at the theater with a rotating array of films about everything from whales to canoes. Erected in 1859 and restored in 1999, the building has served as a customs and court house, governor's office, post office, vault and collector's office, and police station. On August 12, 1898, its postmaster witnessed the lowering of the Hawaiian flag when Hawaii became a U.S. territory. The flag now hangs above the stairway. ■ **TIP→ There's a public restroom in the building.** ⊠ *648 Wharf St., Lahaina* ☎ *808/667–9193 for Lahaina Visitor Center, 808/661–3262 for Lahaina Heritage Museum* ⊕ *www.lahainarestoration.org* ⊠ *Free.*

★ Waiola Church and Wainee Cemetery

CEMETERY | Immortalized in James Michener's *Hawaii,* the original church from the early 1800s was destroyed once by fire and twice by fierce windstorms. Repositioned and rebuilt in 1954, the church was renamed Waiola ("water of life") and has been standing proudly ever

Once a whaling center, Lahaina Harbor bustles with tour boats, fishing vessels, and pleasure craft.

since. The adjacent cemetery was the region's first Christian cemetery and is the final resting place of many of Hawaii's most important monarchs, including Kamehameha the Great's wife, Queen Keopuolani, who was baptized during her final illness. ✉ *535 Wainee St., Lahaina* ☎ *808/661–4349* ⊕ *www.waiolachurch. org* ✉ *Free.*

★ Wo Hing Museum

MUSEUM | Smack-dab in the center of Front Street, this eye-catching Chinese temple reflects the importance of early Chinese immigrants to Lahaina. Built by the Wo Hing Society in 1912, the museum contains beautiful artifacts, historic photo displays of Dr. Sun Yat-sen, and a Taoist altar. Don't miss the films playing in the rustic cookhouse next door—some of Thomas Edison's first films, shot in Hawaii circa 1898, show Hawaiian wranglers herding steer onto ships. Ask the docent for some star fruit from the tree outside, for an offering or for yourself.
■**TIP→ If you're in town in late January or early February, this museum hosts a nice**

Chinese New Year festival. ✉ *858 Front St., Lahaina* ☎ *808/661–5553* ⊕ *www. lahainarestoration.org* ✉ *$7, includes admission to Baldwin Home.*

🔺 Beaches

The beaches in West Maui are legendary for their glittering aquamarine waters backed by long stretches of golden sand. Reef fronts much of the western shore, making the underwater panorama something to behold. A few tips: parking can be challenging in resort areas; look for the blue "Shoreline Access" signs to find limited parking and a public path to the beach; and watch out for *kiawe* thorns when you park off-road, because they can puncture tires—and feet.

There are a dozen roadside beaches to choose from on Route 30, of which we like these best.

Launiupoko Beach Park

BEACH—SIGHT | FAMILY | This is the beach park of all beach parks: both a surf break and a beach, it offers a little something

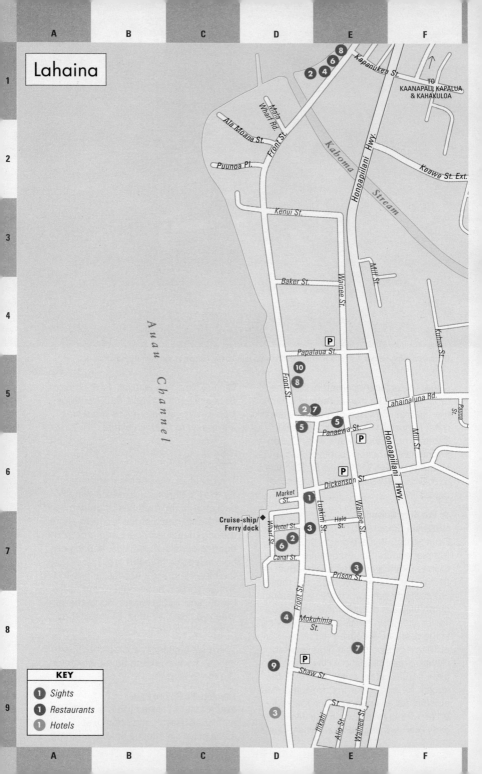

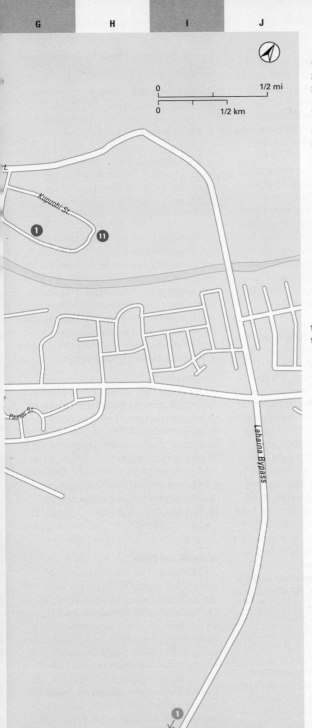

0   1/2 mi
0   1/2 km

Kupuohi St.

Paunau St.

Lahaina Bypass

for everyone with its inviting stretch of lawn, soft white sand, and gentle waves. The shoreline reef creates a protected wading pool, perfect for small children. Outside the reef, beginner surfers will find good longboard rides. From the long sliver of beach, you can enjoy superb views of neighbor islands, and, land side, of deep valleys cutting through West Maui's mountain. Because of its endless sunshine and serenity—not to mention such amenities as picnic tables and grills—Launiupoko draws a crowd on the weekends, but there's space for everyone (and overflow parking across the street). **Amenities:** parking (no fee); showers; toilets. **Best for:** partiers; sunset; surfing; swimming. ✉ *Rte. 30, Lahaina* ✣ *At mile marker 18.*

Olowalu

BEACH—SIGHT | More an offshore snorkel and stand-up paddling spot than a beach, Olowalu is also a great place to watch for turtles and whales in season. The beach is literally a pullover from the road, which can make for some unwelcome noise if you're looking for quiet. The entrance can be rocky (reef shoes help), but if you've got your snorkel gear it's a 200-yard swim to an extensive and diverse reef. Shoreline visibility can vary depending on the swell and time of day; late morning is best. Except for during a south swell, the waters are usually calm. You can find this rocky surf break a half mile north of mile marker 14. Snorkeling here is along pathways that wind among coral heads. Note: this is a local hangout and can be unfriendly at times. **Amenities:** none. **Best for:** snorkeling. ✉ *Rte. 30, Olowalu* ✣ *Look for mile marker 14, south of Olowalu General Store.*

🍴 Restaurants

Beautiful West Maui encompasses the area from tiny Olowalu, with its famous mom-and-pop Olowalu General Store, full of local-style *bentos* (box lunches), all the way north to the ritzy Kapalua Resort, with its glitzy annual wine-and-food festival. In between are Lahaina, the historic former capital of Hawaii, with its myriad restaurants on and off Front Street, and the resort area of Kaanapali. Have some fun checking out restaurants in the nooks and crannies of Kahana, Honokowai, and Napili, north of Kaanapali. All over the west side you'll find a rainbow of cuisines in just about every price category.

Walking Tours 👁

Lahaina's side streets are best explored on foot. Both the Baldwin Home Museum and the Lahaina Visitor Center offer self-guided walking-tour brochures with a map for $2 each. The historic trail map is easy to follow; it details three short but enjoyable loops of the town.

Alchemy Maui

$ | **ECLECTIC** | This no-frills cafe by Valley Isle Kombucha is part kombucha tasting room, part casual eatery. Try one of the many kombucha flavors on tap, which is crafted in small batches using local ingredients, and comes in flavors like guava pineapple and Kula strawberry. **Known for:** kombucha on tap; fresh and local ingredients; vegetarian and vegan options. [$] *Average main: $15* ✉ *157 Kupuohi St., Lahaina* ☎ *808/793–2115* 🌐 *www.valleyislekombucha.com* 🕒 *Closed Sun.*

Aloha Mixed Plate

$ | **HAWAIIAN** | This longtime Lahaina oceanfront classic is run by the same group of wonderful folks who bring you Old Lahaina Luau. This is the place to try a "plate lunch"—a protein served in Asian-style preparation, along with two scoops of rice and macaroni salad—and also features Hawaiian favorites like laulau, kalua pork, and poi from the restaurant's own farm. **Known for:** Hawaiian cuisine; oceanfront setting; alii or kalua pig plate. [$] *Average main: $11* ✉ *1285*

Front St., Lahaina ☎ *808/661–3322* 🌐 *www.alohamixedplate.com.*

Down the Hatch

$$ | AMERICAN | Located steps from Lahaina Harbor, this casual restaurant serves top-notch seafood with Southern flair. The shrimp po'boy, mahi mahi tacos and fish 'n' chips are perennial favorites, and a daily happy hour from 2 to 6 pm is one of the longest on the island. **Known for:** expansive seafood menu; happy hour; live music. [$] *Average main: $21* ✉ *Wharf Cinema Center, 658 Front St., Lahaina* ☎ *808/661–4900* 🌐 *dthmaui.com.*

Frida's Mexican Beach House

$$$$ | MEXICAN FUSION | No matter the cuisine, serial restaurateur Mark Ellman always delivers, as he does yet again with this oceanfront eatery along Front Street. The setting is reason enough to dine here, but the food—specializing in Latin-inspired dishes—attracts diners all on its own, and 40 varieties of tequila dominate the bar. **Known for:** grilled Spanish octopus; oceanfront setting; selection of tequila and mezcal. [$] *Average main: $37* ✉ *1287 Front St., Lahaina* ☎ *808/661–1278* 🌐 *www.fridasmaui.com.*

★ Gerard's

$$$$ | FRENCH | Classically trained French chef Gerard Reversade, who started as an apprentice in acclaimed Paris restaurants when he was just 14, has for more than three decades remained true to his Gascony roots. He cooks *his* way, utilizing island ingredients in such dishes as escargots *forestière* (with garlic and mushrooms), chilled cucumber soup, and the ahi tartare with taro chips; the wine list is first-class, and the dessert list is extensive. **Known for:** fine French cuisine; impeccable service; world-class wine list. [$] *Average main: $45* ✉ *The Plantation Inn, 174 Lahainaluna Rd., Lahaina* ☎ *808/661–8939* 🌐 *www.gerardsmaui.com* ⏲ *No lunch.*

Free Beach Access

All of the island's beaches are free and open to the public—even those that grace the backyards of fancy hotels. Some of the prettiest beaches are often hidden by buildings; look for the blue "Shoreline Access" signs that indicate public rights-of-way through condominiums, resorts, and other private properties.

Honu Seafood & Pizza

$$$$ | ECLECTIC | This oceanfront fish house and pizza restaurant is the work of celebrity chef Mark Ellman. Much of the seafood comes from New England and the Pacific Northwest, and the pizzas are cooked in a wood-fired brick oven (is there any other way?). **Known for:** unparalleled ocean views with sea turtle sightings; fantastic selection of craft beers and cocktails; gluten-free options. [$] *Average main: $36* ✉ *1295 Front St., Lahaina* ☎ *808/667–9390* 🌐 *www.honumaui.com.*

Lahaina Grill

$$$$ | AMERICAN | At the top of many "best restaurants" lists, this expensive upscale bistro is about as fashionably chic as it gets on Maui, and the interior is as pretty as the patrons. The Cake Walk (servings of Kona lobster crab cake, sweet Louisiana rock-shrimp cake, and seared ahi cake), bufala salad with locally grown tomatoes, and Kona-coffee-roasted rack of lamb are a few of the classics customers demand; the full menu—including dessert—is available at the bar. **Known for:** romantic ambience; downtown location; veal chops and seared lion paw scallops. [$] *Average main: $48* ✉ *127 Lahainaluna Rd., Lahaina* ☎ *808/667–5117* 🌐 *www.lahainagrill.com* ⏲ *No lunch.*

★ Mala Ocean Tavern

$$$$ | MODERN HAWAIIAN | The menu at this oceanfront standout is influenced by the Middle East, the Mediterranean, Italy, Bali, and Thailand. There's a focus on ingredients that promote local sustainability, and the cocktails and wine list are great, too. **Known for:** seared ahi bruschetta; whole wok-fried fish; oceanfront setting. $ *Average main: $38* ⊠ *1307 Front St., Lahaina* ☎ *808/667–9394* ⊕ *www.malaoceantavern.com.*

Pacific'O

$$$$ | MODERN HAWAIIAN | Sophisticated outdoor dining on the beach (yes, truly *on* the beach) and creative Island cuisine using local, fresh-caught fish and greens and veggies grown in the restaurant's own Upcountry O'o Farm (and, quite possibly, picked that very morning)—this is the Maui dining experience you've been dreaming about. Start with the award-winning appetizer of prawn-and-basil wontons, move on to any of the fantastic fresh fish dishes, and for dessert, finish with the banana pineapple *lumpia* served hot with homemade ice cream. **Known for:** beachfront dining; in-house produce; exceptional wine list. $ *Average main: $38* ⊠ *505 Front St., Lahaina* ☎ *808/667–4341* ⊕ *www.pacificomaui.com.*

Sale Pepe

$$ | ITALIAN | Aromas from a wood-fired oven lure you into this cozy Italian restaurant set just off of Front Street, and the wine list tempts you to stay awhile. Quality is paramount here—the flour, mozzarella, San Marzano tomatoes, and olive oil are imported directly from Italy—and chef-owner Michele Bari (also from Italy) honed his skills at the prestigious Scuola Italiana Pizzaioli (International School of Pizza) in Venice. **Known for:** attached wine bar, A Fianco; salumi and house-made focaccia; brick-oven pizzas. $ *Average main: $22* ⊠ *878 Front St., Units 7 and*

Island Hopping 👁

If you have a week or more on Maui, consider taking a day or two for a trip to Molokai or Lanai. Tour operators such as Trilogy offer day-trip packages to Lanai that include snorkeling and a van tour. Ferries to both islands have room for your golf clubs and mountain bike. (Avoid ferry travel on a blustery day.) If you prefer to travel to Molokai or Lanai by air and don't mind 4- to 12-seaters, you can take a small air taxi. Book with Pacific Wings (⇨ *see Air Travel in Travel Smart Hawaii*).

8, Lahaina ☎ *808/667–7667* ⊕ *www.salepepemaui.com* ⊗ *Closed Sun.*

★ Star Noodle

$ | ASIAN | This local favorite—despite its industrial park location—is one of Maui's most popular restaurants. A communal table in the center of the room (there are smaller tables around the perimeter) sets the scene for menu-musts like the ahi avo, shrimp tempura, and noodle dishes like the Lahaina fried soup that's served with fat chow fun, pork, and bean sprouts. **Known for:** steamed pork buns; shared, small-plate dining; house-made noodles. $ *Average main: $13* ⊠ *286 Kupuohi St., Lahaina* ☎ *808/667–5400* ⊕ *www.starnoodle.com.*

🛏 Hotels

Lahaina doesn't have a huge range of accommodations, but it does make a great headquarters for active families or those who want to avoid spending a bundle on resorts. One major advantage is the proximity of restaurants, shops, and activities—everything is within walking distance. It's a business district, however, and won't provide the same peace and quiet as resorts or secluded vacation rentals. Still, Lahaina has a nostalgic charm, especially early in the morning before the streets have filled with visitors and vendors.

★ Ho'oilo House

$$$$ | B&B/INN | A luxurious intimate getaway without resort facilities, this stunning, 2-acre B&B in the foothills of West Maui's mountain, just south of Lahaina town, exemplifies quiet perfection. **Pros:** friendly, on-site hosts; beautiful furnishings; gazebo for special events. **Cons:** not good for families with younger children; three-night minimum; far from shops and restaurants. [$] *Rooms from: $369* ✉ *138 Awaiku St., Lahaina* ☎ *808/667–6669* 🌐 *www.hooilohouse.com* 🛏 *6 rooms* 🍴 *Free breakfast.*

Lahaina Inn

$ | B&B/INN | An antique jewel in the heart of town, this two-story timbered building will transport romantics back to the turn of the 20th century. **Pros:** easy walking distance to shops, restaurants, and attractions; lovely antique style; price is right. **Cons:** rooms are small, especially bathrooms; some street noise; two stories, no elevator. [$] *Rooms from: $135* ✉ *127 Lahainaluna Rd., Lahaina* ☎ *808/661–0577, 800/222–5642* 🌐 *www.lahainainn.com* 🛏 *12 units* 🍴 *No meals.*

Lahaina Shores Beach Resort

$$ | RENTAL | You really can't get any closer to the beach than this seven-story rental property that offers panoramic ocean and mountain views and fully equipped kitchens. **Pros:** right on the beach; historical sites, attractions, and activities are a short walk away; no additional costs and no resort fee. **Cons:** older property; no posh, resort-type amenities; no restaurant on-site. [$] *Rooms from: $250* ✉ *475 Front St., Lahaina* ☎ *808/661–4835, 866/934–9176* 🌐 *www.lahainashores.com* 🛏 *199 rooms* 🍴 *No meals.*

Nightlife

Cheeseburger in Paradise

BARS/PUBS | A chain joint on Front Street, this place is known for—what else?—big beefy cheeseburgers, not to mention a great turkey burger. It's a casual place to start your evening, as they have live music (usually classic or contemporary rock) until 9:30 pm. The second-floor balcony gives you a bird's-eye view of Lahaina's Front Street action. ✉ *811 Front St., Lahaina* ☎ *808/661–4855* 🌐 *www.cheeseburgernation.com.*

Cool Cat Café

BARS/PUBS | You could easily miss this casual 1950s-style diner while strolling through Lahaina. Tucked in the second floor of the Wharf Cinema Center, its semi-outdoor area plays host to rockin' local music nightly until 9:30 pm. The entertainment lineup covers jazz, contemporary Hawaiian, and traditional island rhythms. It doesn't hurt that the kitchen dishes out specialty burgers, fish that's fresh from the harbor, and delicious homemade sauces from the owner's family recipes. ✉ *658 Front St., Lahaina* ☎ *808/667–0908* 🌐 *www.coolcatcafe.com.*

★ Slack Key Show: Masters of Hawaiian Music

MUSIC CLUBS | Grammy-winning musician George Kahumoku Jr. hosts this program on Wednesday, which features a rotating lineup of the Islands' finest slack-key artists as well as other traditional forms of Hawaiian music. The setup at Aloha Pavilion is humble, but you'll enjoy these beloved musicians in an intimate setting. ✉ *Napili Kai Beach Resort, 5900 Lower Honoapiilani Rd., Lahaina* ☎ *808/669–3858* 🌐 *www.slackkeyshow.com* 🎫 *$38 in advance, $45 at the door.*

Kaanapali and Nearby

4 miles north of Lahaina.

As you drive north from Lahaina, the first resort community you reach is Kaanapali, a cluster of high-rise hotels framing a world-class white-sand beach. This is part of West Maui's famous resort strip and is a perfect destination for families and romance seekers wanting to be in the center of the action. A little farther up the road lie the condo-filled beach towns of Honokowai, Kahana, and Napili, followed by Kapalua. Each boasts its own style and flavor, though most rely on a low-key beach vibe for people wanting upscale vacation rentals.

Shuttles and taxis are available from Kahului and West Maui airports. Resorts offer free shuttles between properties, and some hotels also provide complimentary shuttles into Lahaina. In the Maui Bus system the Napili Islander begins and ends at Whalers Village in Kaanapali and stops at most condos along the coastal road as far north as Napili Bay.

◉ Sights

Kaanapali

BEACH—SIGHT | The theatrical look of Hawaii tourism—planned resort communities where luxury homes mix with high-rise hotels, fantasy swimming pools, and a theme-park landscape—began right here in the 1960s, when clever marketers built this sunny shoreline into a playground for the world's vacationers. Three miles of uninterrupted white-sand beach and placid water form the front yard of this artificial utopia, with its many tennis courts and two championship golf courses.

In ancient times, the area near Sheraton Maui was known for its bountiful fishing (especially lobster) and its seaside cliffs. The sleepy fishing village was washed away by the wave of Hawaii's new economy: tourism. Puu Kekaa (today incorrectly referred to as Black Rock) was a *leina a ka uhane,* a place in ancient Hawaii believed to be where souls leaped into the afterlife. ⊠ *Kaanapali.*

Beaches

Kaanapali Beach

BEACH—SIGHT | If you're looking for quiet and seclusion, this is not the beach for you. But if you want lots of action, spread out your towel here. Stretching from the northernmost end of the Sheraton Maui Resort & Spa to the Hyatt Regency Maui Resort & Spa at its southern tip, Kaanapali Beach is lined with resorts, condominiums, restaurants, and shops. Ocean activity companies launch from the shoreline fronting Whalers Village, making it one of Maui's best people-watching spots. A concrete pathway weaves along the length of this 3-mile-long beach, leading from one astounding resort to the next.

The drop-off from Kaanapali's soft sugary sand is steep, but waves hit the shore with barely a rippling slap. The landmark promontory known as Puu Kekaa (nicknamed "Black Rock") was traditionally considered a *leina a ka uhane,* or jumping-off place for spirits. It's easy to get into the water from the beach to enjoy the prime snorkeling among the lava-rock outcroppings. ■**TIP→ Strong rip currents are often present near Puu Kekaa; always snorkel with a companion.**

Throughout the resort, blue "Shoreline Access" signs point the way to a few free-parking stalls and public rights-of-way to the beach. Kaanapali Resort public beach parking can be found between the Hyatt and the Marriott, between the Marriott and the Kaanapali Alii, next to Whalers Village, and at the Sheraton. You can park for a fee at most of the large hotels and at Whalers Village. The merchants in the shopping village will validate your parking ticket if you make a purchase. **Amenities:** parking (no fee); showers; toilets. **Best for:** snorkeling; sunset; swimming; walking. ⊠ *Honoapiilani Hwy., Kaanapali* ✛ *Follow any of the 3 Kaanapali exits.*

★ Napili Beach

BEACH—SIGHT | **FAMILY** | Surrounded by sleepy condos, this round bay is a turtle-filled pool lined with a sparkling white crescent of sand. Sunbathers love this beach, which is also a terrific sunset spot. The shore break is steep but gentle, so it's great for body boarding and body surfing. It's easy to keep an eye on kids here as the entire bay is visible from everywhere. The beach is right outside the Napili Kai Beach Resort, a popular local-style resort for honeymooners and families, only a few miles south of Kapalua. **Amenities:** showers; toilets. **Best for:** sunset; surfing; swimming. ⊠ *5900 Lower Honoapiilani Hwy., Napili* ✛ *Look for Napili Pl. or Hui Dr.*

🍴 Restaurants

CJ's Deli & Diner

$ | **AMERICAN** | Chef Christian Jorgensen left fancy hotel kitchens behind to open a casual place serving simple, delicious food—mango-glazed ribs, burgers, and classic Reuben sandwich—at reasonable prices including a vegan menu and kombucha on tap. If you're staying in a condo, the Chefs to Go service is a great alternative to picking up fast food (run-of-the-mill and usually lousy) as everything is prepped and comes with easy cooking instructions. **Known for:** filling, affordable food; mochiko chicken plate (a traditional Hawaiian fried chicken dish); casual atmosphere with Wi-Fi. $ *Average main: $12* ⊠ *Fairway Shops, 2580 Kekaa Dr., Kaanapali* ☎ *808/667–0968* ⊕ *www. cjsmaui.com.*

Hula Grill

$$$ | **MODERN HAWAIIAN** | **FAMILY** | A bustling, family-oriented spot on Kaanapali Beach, this restaurant designed to look like a sprawling '30s beach house serves large dinner portions with an emphasis on fresh local fish. But if you're just in the mood for an umbrella-adorned cocktail and some tasty, more casual fare, head to the popular Barefoot Bar, where you can wiggle your toes in the sand. **Known for:** macadamia nut-crusted fresh catch; location along Kaanapali boardwalk; classic cocktails and lively bar scene. $ *Average main: $29* ⊠ *Whalers Village shopping center, 2435 Kaanapali Pkwy., Kaanapali* ☎ *808/667–6636* ⊕ *www. hulagrillkaanapali.com.*

Japengo

$$$$ | **ASIAN** | Located inside the Hyatt Regency, this spot offers stunning ocean views and a gorgeous glassed-in sushi bar. The views aside, it's the food that makes Japengo worth a visit, as the award-winning sashimi-style hamachi and watermelon is delicious, the fresh local fish is well prepared—as are the sushi and hand rolls—and the desserts are amazing. **Known for:** ocean views from the bar and live Hawaiian and acoustic entertainment; dishes offered in half-portions at half-price; the flaming piña colada crème. $ *Average main: $38* ⊠ *Hyatt Regency Maui Resort & Spa, 200 Nohea Kai Dr., Kaanapali* ☎ *808/667-4727* ⊕ *www.hyatt.com/en-US/hotel/ hawaii/hyatt-regency-maui-resort-and-spa/ oggrm/dining* ⊘ *No lunch.*

Pulehu, an Italian Grill

$$$$ | **ITALIAN** | This restaurant proves that good food doesn't need to be complicated, using many local Maui products to do what the Italians do best: craft simple, delicious food that lets the ingredients shine. Must-haves include the panfried gnocchi Genovese, risotto-crusted fresh catch, and the deconstructed tiramisu. **Known for:** lobster risotto; porcini-dusted

lamb chops; excellent selection of Italian wines. $ *Average main: $36* ⊠ *The Westin Kaanapali Ocean Resort Villas, 6 Kai Ala Dr., Kaanapali* ☎ *808/667–3254* ⊕ *www.pulehurestaurantmaui.com* ⊘ *Closed Tues. and Wed. No lunch.*

★ Roy's Kaanapali

$$$$ | MODERN HAWAIIAN | Roy Yamaguchi is a James Beard Award–winning chef and the granddaddy of East-meets-West cuisine. His eponymous Maui restaurant, located next to the golf course clubhouse near Kaanapali's main entrance, features signature dishes like fire-grilled, Szechuan-spiced baby back ribs, Roy's original blackened ahi, and hibachi-style grilled salmon, as well as an exceptionally user-friendly wine list. **Known for:** classic Hawaiian regional cuisine; golf course setting; hot chocolate soufflé. $ *Average main: $42* ⊠ *2990 Kaanapali Pkwy., Kaanapali* ☎ *808/669–6999* ⊕ *www. royshawaii.com.*

Son'z Steakhouse

$$$$ | STEAKHOUSE | To enter the steakhouse, you descend a grand staircase into an amber-lighted dining room with soaring ceilings and a massive artificial lagoon complete with swans, ducks, waterfalls, and tropical gardens. Chef Geno Sarmiento's classic menu features favorites like the bone-in rib eye and Tomahawk steaks, and lighter appetites like the must-try black and blue ahi starter; the wine selection is one of Kaanapali's best. **Known for:** 100% USDA-certified-prime steaks; popular bar and happy hour; private, lagoon-front setting. $ *Average main: $40* ⊠ *Hyatt Regency Maui, 200 Nohea Kai Dr., Kaanapali* ☎ *808/667–4506* ⊕ *www.sonzsteakhouse.com* ⊘ *No lunch.*

Tiki Terrace

$$ | MODERN HAWAIIAN | Executive chef Tom Muromoto is a local boy who loves to cook modern, upscale Hawaiian food, and he augments the various fresh fish dishes on his menu with items influenced by Hawaii's ethnic mix. This casual, open-air restaurant is the only place on Maui—maybe in Hawaii—where you can have a Native Hawaiian combination plate that is as healthful as it is authentic. **Known for:** seafood lawalu (food wrapped in green ti leaves); Hawaiian laulau (pork wrapped in leaves that's cooked until tender); Native Hawaiian plate. $ *Average main: $26* ⊠ *Kaanapali Beach Hotel, 2525 Kaanapali Pkwy., Kaanapali* ☎ *808/667–0124* ⊕ *www. kbhmaui.com* ⊘ *No lunch.*

🛏 Hotels

With its long stretch of beach lined with luxury resorts, shops, and restaurants, Kaanapali is a playground. Expect top-class service here, as well as everything you could want a few steps from your room, including the calm waters of sun-kissed Kaanapali Beach. Wandering along the beach path between resorts is a recreational activity unto itself. Weather is dependably warm, and for that reason as well as all the others, Kaanapali is a popular—at times, downright crowded—destination.

Hyatt Regency Maui Resort & Spa

$$$$ | RESORT | FAMILY | Splashing waterfalls, swim-through grottoes, a lagoon-like swimming pool, and a 150-foot waterslide "wow" guests of all ages at this bustling Kaanapali resort; spacious standard rooms are another draw. **Pros:** nightly Drums of the Pacific luau and the must-see rooftop astronomy Tour of the Stars; contemporary restaurant and bar; water wonderland will thrill families. **Cons:** can be difficult to find a space in self-parking; popular resort might not offer the most peaceful escape; daily resort and parking fees. $ *Rooms from: $559* ⊠ *200 Nohea Kai Dr., Kaanapali* ☎ *808/661–1234* ⊕ *www.hyattregency-maui.com* ⇥ *810 rooms* ⦿ *No meals.*

Kaanapali Alii

$$$$ | **RENTAL** | Amenities like daily maid service, an activities desk, a small store with complimentary DVDs for guests to borrow, and a 24-hour front-desk service—and no pesky resort fees—make this a winning choice for families and those wanting to play house on Maui's most stunning shores. **Pros:** large comfortable units on the beach; quiet compared to other hotels in the resort; free parking. **Cons:** parking can be crowded during high season; no on-site restaurant; small pools can get crowded. [$] *Rooms from: $585* ✉ *50 Nohea Kai Dr., Kaanapali* ☎ *808/667–1400, 877/713–2844* 🌐 *www.kaanapalialii.com* 🛏 *264 units* 🍴 *No meals.*

★ **Kaanapali Beach Hotel**

$$ | **HOTEL** | This charming beachfront hotel is full of aloha—locals say it's one of the few resorts on the island where you can get a true Hawaiian experience as the entire staff takes part in the hotel's Pookela program, which teaches guests about the history, traditions, and values of Hawaiian culture. **Pros:** no resort fee; friendly staff; weekly Legends of Kaanapali luau. **Cons:** property is older than neighboring modern resorts; fewer amenities than other places along this beach; daily parking fee. [$] *Rooms from: $250* ✉ *2525 Kaanapali Pkwy., Kaanapali* ☎ *808/661–0011, 800/262–8450* 🌐 *www.kbhmaui.com* 🛏 *432 rooms* 🍴 *No meals.*

★ **Maui Eldorado Kaanapali**

$ | **RENTAL** | The Kaanapali Golf Course's fairways wrap around this fine, well-priced, two-story condo complex that boasts spacious studios, one- and two-bedroom units with fully equipped kitchens, and access to a stocked beach cabana on a semiprivate beach. **Pros:** privileges at the Kaanapali Golf Courses; Wi-Fi in all units; friendly staff. **Cons:** not right on beach; some distance from attractions of the Kaanapali Resort; no housekeeping but checkout cleaning fee. [$] *Rooms from: $150* ✉ *2661 Kekaa Dr., Kaanapali* ☎ *808/661–0021* 🌐 *www.mauieldorado.com* 🛏 *204 units* 🍴 *No meals.*

Royal Lahaina Resort

$$ | **RESORT** | Built in 1962, this grand property on the uncrowded, sandy shore in North Kaanapali has hosted millionaires and Hollywood stars, and today it pleases families and budget seekers as well as luxury travelers with a variety of lodging styles. **Pros:** on-site luau nightly; variety of lodgings and rates; tennis ranch with 11 courts and a pro shop. **Cons:** older property; daily self-parking fee; evening luau noise can be loud. [$] *Rooms from: $239* ✉ *2780 Kekaa Dr., Kaanapali* ☎ *808/661–3611, 800/447–6925, 808/386–8083 Reservations* 🌐 *www.royallahaina.com* 🛏 *447 units* 🍴 *No meals.*

Sheraton Maui Resort & Spa

$$$$ | **RESORT** | Set among dense gardens on Kaanapali's best stretch of beach, the Sheraton offers a quieter, more low-key atmosphere than its neighboring resorts, and sits next to and on top of Puu Kekaa, the site of a nightly torch-lighting and cliff-diving ritual. **Pros:** free shuttle to Lahaina and shopping malls; great snorkeling right off the beach; Maui Nui luau three times a week. **Cons:** extensive property can mean a long walk from your room to lobby, restaurants, and beach; daily resort and parking fees; beach subject to seasonal erosion. [$] *Rooms from: $659* ✉ *2605 Kaanapali Pkwy., Kaanapali* ☎ *808/661–0031, 866/500–8313* 🌐 *www.marriott.com/hnmsi* 🛏 *508 units* 🍴 *No meals.*

The Westin Maui Resort & Spa

$$$$ | **RESORT** | **FAMILY** | This 12-acre beachfront paradise offers a setting that is both beautiful and calming. **Pros:** free shuttle to Lahaina town; activity programs for all ages; one adults-only pool. **Cons:** daily resort and parking fees; a lot going on; crowded pool and common areas. [$] *Rooms from: $669* ✉ *2365 Kaanapali Pkwy., Kaanapali* ☎ *808/667–2525,*

866/716–8112 ⊕ *www.westinmaui.com*
↪ *770 rooms* ⦿ *No meals.*

🎭 Performing Arts

★ Hula Girl

ENTERTAINMENT CRUISE | FAMILY | This custom catamaran is one of the slickest and best-equipped boats on the island, complete with a VIP lounge by the captain's fly bridge. The initial cost doesn't include the cooked-to-order meals, but guests can choose from a relatively extensive menu that includes filet mignon, daily fish specials, and crème brûlée. If you're willing to splurge a little for live music, an onboard chef, and upscale service, this is your best bet. From mid-December to early April the cruise focuses on whale-watching. Check-in is in front of Leilani's restaurant at Whalers Village. ⊠ *2435 Kaanapali Pkwy., Kaanapali* ☎ *808/665–0344, 808/667–5980* ⊕ *www. sailingmaui.com* 🍽 *$90.*

Teralani Sailing Charters

ENTERTAINMENT CRUISE | These catamarans are modern, spotless, and laid out nicely for dining and lounging. They head back shortly after sunset, which means there's plenty of light to savor dinner and the view. During whale-watching season, the best seats are the corner booths by the stern of the boat. Catered by local fave Pizza Paradiso, the meal outdoes most dinner-cruise spreads. The trip departs from Kaanapali Beach in front of Leilani's at Whalers Village. ⊠ *2435 Kaanapali Pkwy., Kaanapali* ☎ *808/661–7245* ⊕ *www.teralani.net* 🍽 *$102.*

LUAU

Drums of the Pacific Luau

THEMED ENTERTAINMENT | FAMILY | By Kaanapali Beach, this luau shines in every category—convenient parking, well-made food, smooth-flowing buffet lines, and a nicely paced program that touches on Hawaiian, Samoan, Tahitian, Fijian, Tongan, and Maori cultures. Some guests get tickled by the onstage audience hula tutorial. The finale features three fire-knife dancers. You'll feast on delicious Hawaiian delicacies like *huli huli* chicken (grilled chicken marinated in a pineapple/soy sauce mixture), *lomilomi* salmon (tossed in a salad with tomatoes and Maui onions), and Pacific ahi *poke* (pickled raw tuna, tossed with herbs and seasonings). The dessert spread consists of chocolate, pineapple, and coconut indulgences. An open bar offers beer, wine, and standard tropical mixes. ⊠ *Hyatt Regency Maui, 200 Nohea Kai Dr., Kaanapali* ☎ *808/667–4727* ⊕ *www.drumsofthe-pacificmaui.com* 🍽 *$123–$158.*

🛍 Shopping

★ Whalers Village

SHOPPING CENTERS/MALLS | FAMILY | Chic Whalers Village boasts wonderful oceanfront restaurants and shops in the heart of Kaanapali. Upscale haunts include Louis Vuitton and Tourneau, and beautyphiles can get their fix at Sephora. Elegant home accessories at Martin and MacArthur and Totally Hawaiian Gift Gallery are perfect Hawaii-made souvenirs, while the many great surf and swimwear shops will prepare you for a day at the beach. Kids will fall in love with the whimsical two-story climbing structure at the lower courtyard. The outdoor mall also offers free weekly entertainment, lei-making classes, and hula lessons; check their website for a complete schedule. ⊠ *2435 Kaanapali Pkwy., Kaanapali* ☎ *808/661–4567* ⊕ *www.whalersvillage.com.*

Kapalua and Kahakuloa

Kapalua is 10 miles north of Kaanapali; 36 miles west of Kahului.

Upscale Kapalua is north of the Kaanapali resorts, past Napili, and is a hideaway for those with money who want to stay incognito. Farther along the Honoapiilani Highway is the remote village of Kahakuloa, a reminder of Old Hawaii.

On the north end of West Maui, remote Kahakuloa is a reminder of old Hawaii.

Shuttles and taxis are available from Kahului and West Maui airports. The Ritz-Carlton, Kapalua, has a resort shuttle within the Kapalua Resort.

Sights

Kahakuloa

MOUNTAIN—SIGHT | Drive past Kapalua and discover the wild side of West Maui. Tiny Kahakuloa village at the north end of Honoapiilani Highway is a relic of pre-jet-travel Maui. Remote villages similar to Kahakuloa were once tucked away in several valleys in this area. Many residents still grow taro and live in the old Hawaiian way. Driving this route is not for the faint of heart: the road weaves along coastal cliffs, and there are lots of blind curves; it's not wide enough for two cars to pass in places, so one of you (most likely you) will have to reverse on this nail-biter of a "highway." ⚠ **Watch out for stray cattle, roosters, and falling rocks.** True adventurers will find terrific snorkeling and swimming along this drive, as well as some good hiking trails, a labyrinth, and excellent banana bread. ⊠ *Kahakuloa.*

Kapalua

BEACH—SIGHT | Beautiful and secluded, Kapalua is West Maui's northernmost resort community. First developed in the late 1970s, the resort now includes the Ritz-Carlton, posh residential complexes, two golf courses, and the surrounding former pineapple fields. The area's distinctive shops and restaurants cater to dedicated golfers, celebrities who want to be left alone, and some of the world's richest folks. In addition to golf, recreational activities include hiking and snorkeling. Mists regularly envelop the landscape of tall Cook pines and rolling fairways in Kapalua, which is cooler and quieter than its southern neighbors. The beaches here, including Kapalua and D.T. Fleming, are among Maui's finest. ⊠ *Kapalua.*

Beaches

D.T. Fleming Beach

BEACH—SIGHT | **FAMILY** | Because the current can be quite strong, this charming, mile-long sandy cove is better for sunbathing than for swimming or water sports. Still, it's one of the island's most popular beaches. It's a perfect spot to watch the spectacular Maui sunsets, and there are picnic tables and grills. Part of the beach runs along the front of the Ritz-Carlton, Kapalua—a good place to grab a cocktail and enjoy the view. **Amenities:** lifeguards; parking (no fee); showers; toilets. **Best for:** sunset; walking. ✉ *Rte. 30, Kapalua* ✥ *About 1 mile north of Kapalua.*

★ Kapalua Bay Beach

BEACH—SIGHT | **FAMILY** | Over the years, Kapalua has been recognized as one of the world's best beaches, and for good reason: it fronts a pristine bay that is good for snorkeling, swimming, and general lazing. Just north of Napili Bay, this lovely sheltered shore often remains calm late into the afternoon, although currents may be strong offshore. Snorkeling is easy here, and there are lots of colorful reef fish. This popular area is bordered by the Kapalua Resort, so don't expect to have the beach to yourself. Walk through the tunnel from the parking lot at the end of Kapalua Place to get here. **Amenities:** parking (no fee); showers; toilets. **Best for:** snorkeling; sunset; swimming. ✉ *Rte. 30, Kapalua* ✥ *Turn onto Kapalua Pl.*

Mokuleia Bay (Slaughterhouse Beach)

BEACH—SIGHT | The island's northernmost beach is part of the Honolua-Mokuleia Marine Life Conservation District. "Slaughterhouse" is the surfers' nickname for what is officially Mokuleia. Weather permitting, this is a great place for body surfing and sunbathing. Concrete steps and a railing help you get down the cliff to the sand. The next bay over, Honolua, has no beach but offers one of the best surf breaks in Hawaii. Competitions are sometimes held there; telltale signs are cars pulled off the road and parked in the old pineapple field. **Amenities:** none. **Best for:** sunset; surfing. ✉ *Rte. 30, Kapalua* ✥ *At mile marker 32.*

Restaurants

The Gazebo Restaurant

$ | **DINER** | Breakfast is the reason to seek out this restaurant located poolside at the Napili Shores Resort. The food is standard diner fare, but the portions are big, the prices are low, and many folks think the pancakes—with either pineapple, bananas, macadamia nuts, or white chocolate chips—are the best in West Maui. **Known for:** ocean views with breakfast; create-your-own pancakes; enormous omelets. [$] *Average main: $12* ✉ *Napili Shores Maui, 5315 Lower Honoapiilani Hwy., Napili* ☎ *808/669–5621* ⏲ *No dinner.*

★ Merriman's Maui

$$$$ | **MODERN HAWAIIAN** | Perched above the postcard-perfect Kapalua Bay, this is the place to impress your date, as Chef Peter Merriman highlights the Islands' bounty by using fresh seafood and ingredients from local farms. With so many tempting creations—macadamia nut–crusted mahi or the Kahua Ranch rack of lamb—consider the duo option, which features two smaller-size entrées on one plate. **Known for:** panoramic ocean views; exceptional wine list; fire pit on the outdoor lanai. [$] *Average main: $44* ✉ *One Bay Club Pl., Kapalua* ☎ *808/669–6400* ⏲ *No lunch.*

Pizza Paradiso

$ | **ITALIAN** | When it opened in 1995 this was an over-the-counter pizza place, but it's evolved over the years into a local favorite, serving Italian, Mediterranean, and Middle Eastern comfort food as well as pizza. **Known for:** chicken Parmesan; gelato; pizzas with local Maui produce. [$] *Average main: $14* ✉ *Honokowai*

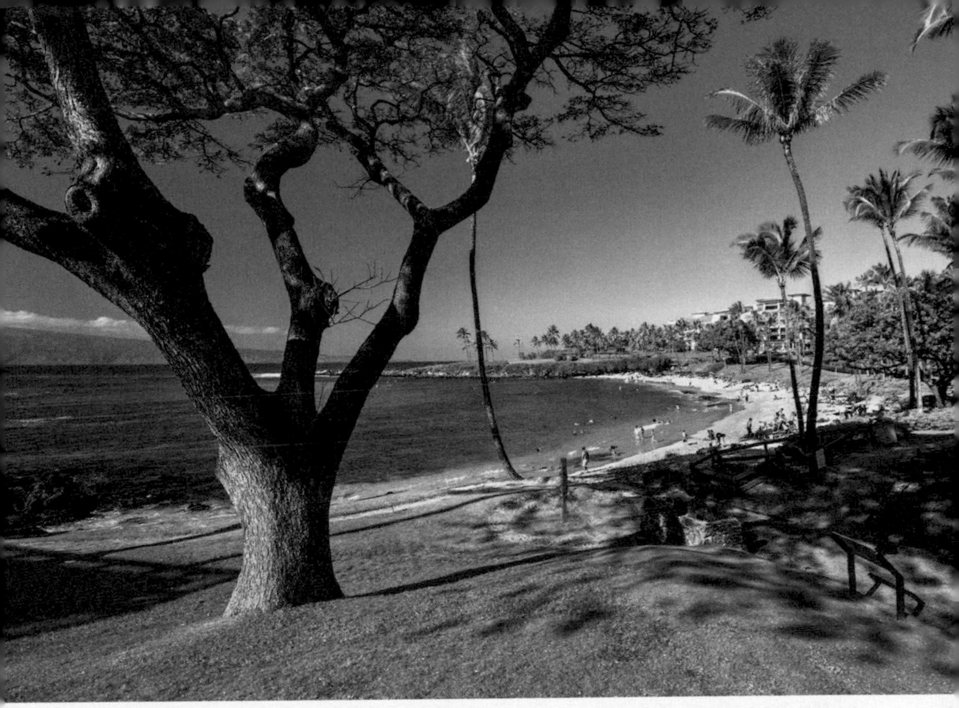

Sheltered Kapalua Bay Beach is ideal for snorkeling and swimming.

Marketplace, 3350 Lower Honoapiilani Hwy., Honokowai ☎ *808/667–2929* 🌐 *www.pizzaparadiso.com.*

★ Sansei Seafood Restaurant & Sushi Bar
$$ | ASIAN | With locations on three islands, Sansei takes sushi, sashimi, and contemporary Japanese food to a new level. If you're a fish or shellfish lover, this is the place for you. **Known for:** award-winning Shrimp Dynamite (tempura shrimp with a garlic masago aioli); panko-crusted ahi sashimi; late-night sushi specials. [$] *Average main: $26* ✉ *600 Office Rd., Kapalua* ☎ *808/669–6286* 🌐 *www.sansei-hawaii.com* 🕓 *No lunch.*

Hotels

The neighborhoods north of Kaanapali—Honokowai, Mahinahina, Kahana, Napili, and finally, Kapalua—blend almost seamlessly into one another along Lower Honoapiilani Highway. Each has a few shops and restaurants and a secluded bay or two to call its own. Many visitors have found a second home here, at one of the condominiums nestled between beach-access roads and groves of mango trees. You won't get the stellar service of a resort (except at Kapalua), but you'll be among the locals here, in a relatively quiet part of the island. Be prepared for a long commute, though, if you're planning to do much exploring elsewhere on the island. Kapalua is the area farthest north, but well worth all the driving to stay at the elegant Ritz-Carlton, which is surrounded by misty greenery and overlooks beautiful D.T. Fleming Beach.

Honua Kai Resort & Spa
$$$$ | RENTAL | FAMILY | Two high-rise towers contain these individually owned, eco-friendly (and family-friendly) units combining the conveniences of a condo with the full service of a hotel. **Pros:** large spacious rooms with full kitchens; upscale appliances and furnishings; beautiful, well-maintained grounds. **Cons:** sometimes windy; housekeeping every other day; beach is small and rocky, not

good for swimming. $ *Rooms from: $514* ✉ *130 Kai Malina Pkwy., Honokowai* ☎ *808/662–2800, 855/718–5789* 🌐 *www.honuakai.com* 🛏 *628 units* 🍴 *No meals.*

Mahina Surf

$$ | RENTAL | Of the many condo complexes lining the ocean-side stretch of Honoapiilani Highway, this one offers friendly service, a saline oceanfront pool, and affordable units—some with million-dollar views. **Pros:** oceanfront barbecues; resident turtles hang out on the rocks below; no hidden fees. **Cons:** rocky shoreline rather than a beach; no housekeeping (and cleaning fee for stays fewer than seven nights); minimum three-night stay. $ *Rooms from: $195* ✉ *4057 Lower Honoapiilani Hwy.* ☎ *808/669–6068, 800/367–6086* 🌐 *www.mahinasurf.com* 🛏 *56 units* 🍴 *No meals.*

The Mauian on Napili Bay

$$ | RENTAL | If you're looking for a low-key place with a friendly staff, this small, delightful beachfront property on Napili Bay may be for you. **Pros:** reasonable rates; located on one of Maui's top swimming and snorkeling beaches; free parking and no resort fees. **Cons:** small units; some may find motel-like design reduces privacy; few amenities. $ *Rooms from: $229* ✉ *5441 Lower Honoapiilani Hwy., Napili* ☎ *808/669–6205* 🌐 *www.mauian.com* 🛏 *44 rooms* 🍴 *No meals.*

★ Montage Kapalua Bay

$$$$ | RESORT | FAMILY | This luxury resort caters to well-heeled travelers who want the comfort and privacy of a residential-style suite combined with resort service and amenities—think elegantly furnished one- to four-bedroom units with gourmet kitchens, in-unit washers/dryers, and the largest lanai to be found. **Pros:** prime snorkeling; great kids clubs for children and teens; large, well-appointed rooms. **Cons:** pricey daily parking and resort fees; large property means lots of walking; far from other Maui attractions. $ *Rooms from: $1200* ✉ *1 Bay Dr., Kapalua* ☎ *808/662–6600* 🌐 *www.montagehotels.com/kapaluabay* 🛏 *50 units* 🍴 *No meals.*

★ Napili Kai Beach Resort

$$$ | RESORT | FAMILY | Spread across 10 beautiful acres along one of the best beaches on Maui, the family-friendly Napili Kai with its "old Hawaii" feel draws a loyal following to its island-style rooms that open onto private lanai. **Pros:** weekly kids' hula performances and Hawaiian slack-key guitar concert; fantastic swimming and sunning beach; no resort fees. **Cons:** not as modern as other resorts in West Maui; beach subject to periodic erosion; parking spaces tight for some. $ *Rooms from: $340* ✉ *5900 Lower Honoapiilani Hwy., Napili* ☎ *808/669–6271, 800/367–5030* 🌐 *www.napilikai.com* 🛏 *163 units* 🍴 *No meals.*

Papakea Resort

$$ | RENTAL | FAMILY | All studios and one- and two-bedroom units at this casual, oceanfront condominium complex face the ocean and, because the units are spread out among 11 low-rise buildings on about 13 acres of land, there is built-in privacy and easy parking. **Pros:** large rooms; lovely garden landscaping; complimentary activities include yoga, putting greens, lei making, and tennis lessons. **Cons:** no beach in front of property; pool can get crowded; busy, family-oriented property. $ *Rooms from: $235* ✉ *3543 Lower Honoapiilani Hwy., Honokowai* ☎ *808/669–4848, 888/671–5309* 🌐 *www.astonatpapakea.com* 🛏 *364 units* 🍴 *No meals.*

★ The Ritz-Carlton, Kapalua

$$$$ | RESORT | This notable hillside property features luxurious service and upscale accommodations along with an enhanced Hawaiian sense of place. **Pros:** spa, golf, walking trails, and many other activities; AAA 4-Diamond Banyan Tree restaurant will please locavores; many cultural and recreational programs. **Cons:** can be windy on grounds and at pool; far from major attractions such as Haleakala; daily parking and resort fees. $ *Rooms from: $549* ⊠ *1 Ritz-Carlton Dr., Kapalua* ☎ *808/669–6200, 800/262–8440* ⊕ *www.ritzcarlton.com/kapalua* ⤳ *466 units* ǁ○ǀ *No meals.*

Sands of Kahana

$$$ | **RENTAL** | Meandering gardens, spacious rooms, and an on-site restaurant distinguish this large condominium complex—units on the upper floors benefit from the height, with unrivaled ocean views stretching away from private lanais. **Pros:** restaurant on premises; fitness center, tennis courts, and sand volleyball court; one-, two-, and three-bedroom units available. **Cons:** may be approached about buying a time-share unit; street-facing units can get a bit noisy; property a bit dated. $ *Rooms from: $319* ⊠ *4299 Lower Honoapiilani Hwy., Kahana* ☎ *808/669–0400 property phone, 800/332–1137 for vacation rentals (Sullivan Properties)* ⊕ *www.sandsofkahanaresort.com* ⤳ *196 units* ǁ○ǀ *No meals.*

Westin Nanea Ocean Villas

$$$$ | **RESORT** | **FAMILY** | It's rare to find a resort that so thoroughly incorporates authentic Hawaiian cultural symbols and traditions into its design, but this deluxe beachfront property in North Kaanapali carries this commitment into its native landscaping and Puuhonua O Nanea cultural center that hosts artifacts, displays, activities, and talks. **Pros:** "zero-entry" family pool with sandy bottom and water slide; great location for snorkeling and water sports; free shuttle to Lahaina town and other Westin resorts. **Cons:** may be pitched to join time-share club; outside main Kaanapali resort; limited dining options. $ *Rooms from: $939* ⊠ *45 Kai Malina Pkwy., Kaanapali* ☎ *808/662–6300* ⊕ *www.westinnanea.com* ⤳ *390 units* ǁ○ǀ *No meals.*

▼ Nightlife

Alaloa Lounge

MUSIC CLUBS | When ambience weighs heavy on the priority list, this spot at the Ritz-Carlton, Kapalua, might just be the ticket. Nightly performances range from jazz to island rhythms, and the menu includes locally inspired cocktails and a fantastic lobster roll. Step onto the lanai for that plumeria-tinged tropical air and gaze at the deep blue of the Pacific. ⊠ *The Ritz-Carlton, Kapalua, 1 Ritz-Carlton Dr., Kapalua* ☎ *808/669–6200* ⊕ *www.ritzcarlton.com.*

The South Shore

Blessed by more than its fair share of sun, the southern shore of Haleakala was an undeveloped wilderness until the 1970s, when the sun worshippers found it. Now restaurants, condos, and luxury resorts line the coast from the world-class aquarium at Maalaea Harbor through working-class Kihei to lovely Wailea, a resort community rivaling its counterpart, Kaanapali, on West Maui. Farther south, the road disappears and unspoiled wilderness still has its way.

Sandy beach fronts nearly the entire southern coastline of Maui. The farther south, the better the beaches get. Kihei has excellent beach parks in town, with white sand, plenty of amenities, and paved parking lots. Good snorkeling can be found along the beaches' rocky borders. As good as Kihei is, Wailea is better. The beaches are cleaner, and the views more impressive. You can take a mile-long walk on a shore path from Ulua to near Polo Beach. Look for blue "Shore-line Access" signs for parking along the main thoroughfare, Wailea Alanui Drive. ■ **TIP→ Break-ins have been reported at many parking lots, so don't leave valuables in the car.** As you head to Makena, the terrain gets wilder; bring lunch, water, and sunscreen.

Maui's Top Beaches

The leeward shores of West and South Maui have calm beaches and some great snorkeling, but experienced surfers and windsurfers gravitate to the windward (North Shore and East Maui) beaches that face the open ocean. Here are some of our favorites.

Best for Families

Baldwin Beach, the North Shore. The long, shallow, calm end closest to Kahului is safe even for toddlers—with adult supervision, of course.

Kamaole III, the South Shore. Sand, gentle surf, a playground, a volleyball net, and barbecues all add up to great family fun.

Napili Beach, West Maui. Kids will love the turtles that snack on the *limu* (seaweed) growing on the lava rocks. This sometimes crowded crescent-shape beach offers sunbathing, snorkeling, swimming, body surfing, and startling sunsets.

Best Offshore Snorkeling

Olowalu, West Maui. The water remains shallow far offshore, and there's plenty to see.

Ulua, the South Shore. It's beautiful, and the kids can enjoy the tide pools while the adults experience the excellent snorkeling.

Best Surfing

Honolua Bay, West Maui. One bay over from Slaughterhouse (Mokuleia) Beach north of Kapalua you can find one of the best surf breaks in Hawaii.

Best Sunsets

Kapalua Bay, West Maui. The ambience here is as stunning as the sunset.

Keawakapu, the South Shore. Most active beachgoers enjoy this gorgeous spot before midafternoon, when the wind picks up, so it's never crowded at sunset.

Best for Seeing and Being Seen

Kaanapali Beach, West Maui. Backed by resorts, condos, and restaurants, this is not the beach for solitude. But the sand is soft, the waters are gentle, and the action varies from good snorkeling at Black Rock (Kekaa) to people-watching in front of Whalers Village—not for nothing is this section called "Dig Me Beach."

Wailea Beach, the South Shore. At this beach fronting the ultraluxurious Four Seasons and Grand Wailea resorts, you never know who might be hiding in that private cabana.

Best Setting

Makena (Oneloa), South Shore. Don't forget the camera for this beauty, a state park away from the Wailea resort area. Finding this long, wide stretch of golden sand and translucent offshore water is worth the effort. The icing on the cake is that this long beach is never crowded. Use caution for swimming, because the steep onshore break can get big.

Waianapanapa State Park, East Maui. This rustic black-sand beach will capture your heart—it's framed by lava cliffs and backed by bright-green beach *naupaka* bushes. Ocean currents can be strong, so enjoy the views and cool off in one of two freshwater pools. Get an early start, because your day's destination is just shy of Hana.

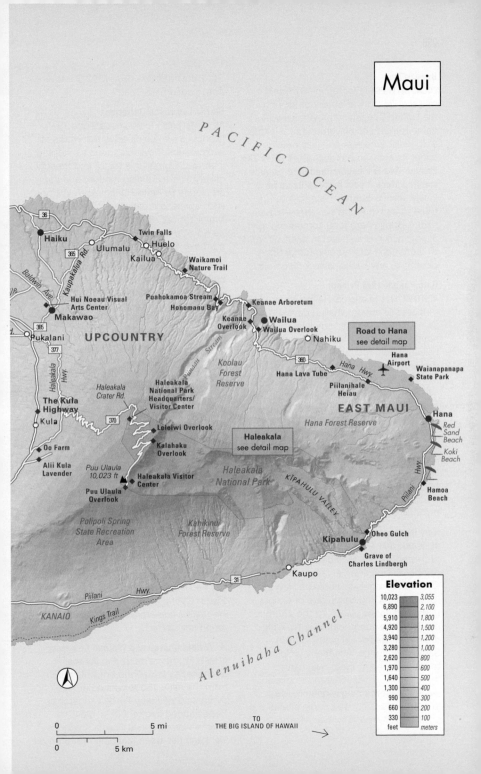

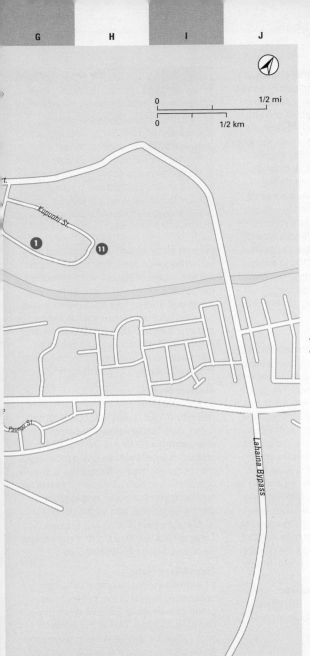

linguine pescatore; weekly nightlife. $ Average main: $28 ✉ 1188 Makawao Ave., Makawao ☎ 808/572–0220 🌐 www.casanovamaui.com.

Grandma's Coffee House

$ | **AMERICAN** | If you're taking a drive through gorgeous Upcountry, this is a great place to stop for a truly homegrown cup of coffee and a snack. The baked goods are fabulous, and the variety of menu items for breakfast and lunch is vast. **Known for:** generous portions; coffee roasted on-site; idyllic country location. $ *Average main: $12* ✉ *9232 Kula Hwy., Keokea* ☎ *808/878–2140* 🌐 *www.grandmascoffee.com.*

Haliimaile General Store

$$$$ | **MODERN HAWAIIAN** | Chef-restaurateur Beverly Gannon's first restaurant remains a culinary destination after more than a quarter century, serving classic dishes like Bev's "Famous" Crab Pizza and Asian duck, brie, and grape quesadilla; there are daily and nightly specials as well. The big, rambling former plantation store has two dining rooms: sit in the front to be seen and heard; head on back for some quiet and privacy. **Known for:** Bev Gannon's classic recipes; exquisite dining and specialty cocktails in an unlikely location; Hawaii regional cuisine. $ *Average main: $40* ✉ *900 Haliimaile Rd., Haliimaile* ✛ *Take exit on the left halfway up Haleakala Hwy.* ☎ *808/572–2666* 🌐 *www.hgsmaui.com.*

Kula Bistro

$$ | **ITALIAN** | Dishing up home-style comfort food with an Italian accent, this out-of-the-way eatery is worth the drive to scenic Kula, no matter when you arrive. Start the day with their crab cake Benedict, grab any one of their outstanding panini around lunchtime, or come for dinner, when a dizzying array of choices await, including favorites such as vodka pomodoro with seafood, vegetable lasagna, and filet mignon. **Known for:** BYOB; family and group friendly; impressive dessert lineup. $ *Average main: $25* ✉ *4566 Lower Kula Rd., Kula* ☎ *808/871–2960* 🌐 *www.kulabistro.com* ⏲ *No breakfast Mon.*

★ Polli's Mexican Restaurant

$ | **MEXICAN** | A Makawao staple since 1981, Polli's is set in the town's only intersection. The margaritas are legendary, and the enormous fajitas, burritos, and enchiladas ensure you'll never leave hungry; there are vegetarian options, too. **Known for:** mango margaritas; generous portions; house-made salsa and guacamole. $ *Average main: $16* ✉ *1202 Makawao Ave., Makawao* ☎ *808/572–7808* 🌐 *www.pollismexicanrestaurant.com.*

Hotels

★ The Banyan Tree Bed and Breakfast Retreat

$ | **B&B/INN** | **FAMILY** | If a taste of rural Hawaii life in plantation days coupled with quiet time and privacy is what you crave, you can find it at this 2-acre property: it's awash in tropical foliage, dotted with banyan trees, and has a 50-foot, saltwater pool and in-ground spa that afford views of Maui's northern coast and Molokai. **Pros:** one cottage and the pool are outfitted for travelers with disabilities; free on-site parking; you can walk to quaint Makawao town for dining and shopping. **Cons:** cottages have pretty basic furniture and few amenities; some daytime traffic noise; not all units have air-conditioning. $ *Rooms from: $175* ✉ *3265 Baldwin Ave., Makawao* ☎ *808/572–9021* 🌐 *www.bed-breakfast-maui.com* 🛏 *7 cottage suites* 🍴 *Free breakfast.*

Hale Hookipa Inn

$ | **B&B/INN** | A handsome, 1924, Craftsman-style house in the heart of Makawao town is on both the Hawaii and the National Historic Registers, and provides a great base for excursions to Haleakala, Hana, or North Shore beaches. **Pros:** genteel rural setting; price includes buffet breakfast with organic fruit from the garden; charming architecture and decor. **Cons:** a 20-minute drive to the nearest beach; this is not the sun, sand, and surf surroundings of travel posters; no food allowed in rooms. $ *Rooms from: $140* ✉ *32 Pakani Pl., Makawao* ☎ *808/281-2074* ⊕ *www.maui-bed-and-breakfast. com* ⤳ *4 units* ♒ *Free breakfast.*

▼ Nightlife

Casanova Italian Restaurant & Deli

BARS/PUBS | Casanova sometimes brings big acts and electronic dance music DJs from the mainland. Most Friday and Saturday nights attract a hip local scene with live bands and eclectic DJs spinning house, funk, and world music. Wednesday is Ladies Night (i.e., ladies get in free), which can be on the smarmy side. For everyone else, there's a $10 cover. ✉ *1188 Makawao Ave., Makawao* ☎ *808/572–0220* ⊕ *www.casanovamaui. com.*

★ Charley's Restaurant & Saloon

BARS/PUBS | The closest thing to country Maui has to offer, Charley's is a down-home dive bar in the heart of Paia. In addition to country music, it hosts reggae, house, Latin soul, and jazz nights, as well as one-off events with sought-after DJs. Live bands are featured throughout the week, and, despite its robust nightly offerings—or because of them?—Charley's is also known for its great breakfasts. ✉ *142 Hana Hwy., Paia* ☎ *808/579–8085* ⊕ *www.charleysmaui.com.*

Stopwatch Bar & Grill

BARS/PUBS | This friendly dive bar hosts karaoke nights on Thursday and Saturday, and books favorite local musicians on Sunday from 6 to 8 pm. ✉ *1127 Makawao Ave., Makawao* ☎ *808/572–1380* ⊕ *www. stopwatchbarandgrill.com.*

🛍 Shopping

Designing Wahine Emporium

CLOTHING | At this Upcountry haven for Hawaiian merchandise and Balinese imports, you can find endless gift options like authentic aloha shirts, jams and jellies, children's clothes and books, bath and beauty products, and home decor crafted from wood. ✉ *3640 Baldwin Ave., Makawao* ☎ *808/573–0990.*

Maui Master Jewelers

JEWELRY/ACCESSORIES | The shop's exterior is as rustic as all the old buildings of Makawao and belies the elegance of the handcrafted jewelry displayed within. The store has added a diamond collection to its designs. ✉ *3655 Baldwin Ave., Makawao* ☎ *808/573–5400* ⊕ *www.mauimasterjewelers.com* ⊙ *Closed Sun.*

Pink By Nature

CLOTHING | Owner Desiree Martinez knows what the modern bohemian wants to wear. She keeps her rustic store stocked with local jewelry and feminine pieces from Indah, Bella Dahl, and Novella Royale. Versatile plaid shirts from Rails are popular, as are the selections of Samudra bags and Lovely Bird hats. An equally stylish men's and home branch is located a few shops down. ✉ *3663 Baldwin Ave., Makawao* ☎ *808/572–9576* ⊕ *www.pinkbynaturemaui.com.*

Viewpoints Gallery

ART GALLERIES | This friendly gallery is co-owned by local artists and offers eclectic paintings, sculptures, photography, ceramics, and glass, along with locally made jewelry and quilts. Located along a cozy courtyard, its free monthly exhibits feature artists from various disciplines. ✉ *3620 Baldwin Ave., Makawao* ☎ *808/572–5979* ⊕ *www.viewpointsgallerymaui.com.*

The North Shore

Blasted by winter swells and wind, Maui's North Shore draws water-sports thrill seekers from around the world. But there's much more to this area of Maui than coastline. Inland, a lush, waterfall-fed Garden of Eden beckons. In forested pockets, wealthy hermits have carved out a little piece of paradise for themselves.

North Shore action centers on the colorful town of Paia and the windsurfing mecca of Hookipa Beach. It's a far cry from the more developed resort areas of West Maui and the South Shore. Paia is also a starting point for one of the most popular excursions in Maui, the Road to Hana. Waterfalls, phenomenal views of the coast and the ocean, and lush rain forest are all part of the spectacular 55-mile drive into East Maui.

You won't find any large resorts or condominium complexes along the North Shore, yet there's a variety of accommodations from the surf town of Paia, through tiny Kuau, and along the rain-forested Hana Highway through Haiku. Some are oceanfront but not necessarily beachfront (with sand); instead, look for tropical gardens overflowing with ginger, bananas, papayas, and nightly bug symphonies. Some have breathtaking views or the type of solitude that seeps in, easing your tension before you know it. You may encounter brief powerful downpours, but that's what makes this part of Maui green and lush. You'll need a car to enjoy staying on the North Shore.

Paia

9 miles east of Kahului; 4 miles west of Haiku.

At the intersection of Hana Highway and Baldwin Avenue, Paia has eclectic boutiques that supply everything from high fashion to hemp-oil candles. Some of Maui's best shops for surf trunks, Brazilian bikinis, and other beachwear are here. Restaurants provide excellent people-watching opportunities and an array of dining and takeout options, from flatbread to fresh fish. The abundance is helpful because Paia is the last place to snack before the pilgrimage to Hana and the first stop for the famished on the return trip.

This little town on Maui's North Shore was once a sugarcane enclave, with a mill, plantation camps, and shops. The old sugar mill finally closed, but the town continues to thrive. In the 1970s, Paia became a hippie town, as dropouts headed for Maui to open boutiques, galleries, and unusual eateries. In the 1980s, windsurfers—many of them European—discovered nearby Hookipa Beach and brought an international flavor to Paia. Today this historic town is hip and happening.

Route 36 (Hana Highway) runs directly though Paia; 4 miles east of town, follow the sign to Haiku, a short detour off the highway. You can take the Maui Bus from the airport and Queen Kaahumanu Shopping Center in Kahului to Paia and on to Haiku.

🔄 Beaches

Many of the people you see jaywalking in Paia sold everything they owned to come to Maui and live a beach bum's life. Beach culture abounds on the North Shore. But these folks aren't sunbathers; they're big-wave riders, windsurfers, or kiteboarders, and the North Shore is their challenging sports arena. Beaches here face the open ocean and tend to be rougher and windier than beaches elsewhere on Maui—but don't let that scare you off. On calm days, the reef-speckled waters are truly beautiful and offer a quieter and less commercial beachgoing experience than the leeward shore. Be

sure to leave your car in a paved parking area so that it doesn't get stuck in soft sand.

Baldwin Beach

BEACH—SIGHT | FAMILY | A local favorite, this approximately 1-mile stretch of comfortable golden sand is a good place to stretch out, jog, or swim, although the waves can sometimes be choppy and the undertow strong. Don't be alarmed by those big brown blobs floating beneath the surface; they're just pieces of seaweed awash in the surf. You can find shade along the beach beneath the ironwood trees. Though there is a pavilion, it's not the safest place to hang out. Instead, take your picnics to the treeline and enjoy visits from friendly birds and dogs. There are picnic tables, grills, and a large playing field as well.

The long, shallow pool at the Kahului end of the beach is known as Baby Beach. Separated from the surf by a flat reef wall, this is where ocean-loving families bring their kids (and sometimes puppies) to practice a few laps. Take a relaxing stroll along the water's edge from one end of Baldwin Beach to Baby Beach and enjoy the scenery. The view of the West Maui Mountains is hauntingly beautiful. **Amenities:** lifeguard; parking (no fee); showers; toilets. **Best for:** swimming; walking. ✉ *Hana Hwy., Paia* ✥ *About 1 mile west of Baldwin Ave.*

★ Hookipa Beach

BEACH—SIGHT | To see some of the world's finest windsurfers, hit this beach along the Hana Highway. It's also one of Maui's hottest surfing spots, with waves that can reach 20 feet. Hookipa is not necessarily a good swimming beach; however, there are a few spots that have protected reef areas that provide a shore break and places to play in the water, so getting wet isn't completely out of the question. It's also not the place to learn windsurfing, but it's great for hanging out and watching the pros. There are picnic tables and grills, though the pavilion area isn't particularly inviting. **Amenities:** lifeguard; parking (no fee); showers; toilets. **Best for:** surfing; windsurfing. ✉ *Hana Hwy, Paia* ✥ *At mile marker 9, about 2 miles east of Paia.*

Kanaha Beach

BEACH—SIGHT | Windsurfers, kiteboarders, joggers, and picnicking families like this long, golden strip of sand bordered by a wide grassy area with lots of shade that is within walking distance of Kahului Airport. The winds pick up in the early afternoon, making for the best kiteboarding and windsurfing conditions—if you know what you're doing, that is. The best spot for watching kiteboarders is at the far left end of the beach. A picnic paired with surf-watching makes a great option for a farewell activity before getting on a departing flight. **Amenities:** lifeguard; parking (no fee); showers; toilets. **Best for:** walking; windsurfing. ✉ *Amala Pl., Kahului* ✥ *From Kaahumanu Ave., turn makai onto Hobron St., then right onto Amala Pl. Drive just over a mile through an industrial area and take any of 3 entrances into Kanaha.*

🍴 Restaurants

Café des Amis

$ | ECLECTIC | The menu at this budget-friendly café features Mediterranean and Indian dishes, and the food is fresh and tasty. Expect flavors and preparations not easily obtainable at other island eateries, with a nice selection of sweet and savory crepes, Indian wraps, and salads with cocktails, wine, and beer to complement. **Known for:** delicious, good-value food like the chicken, avocado, and mozzarella crepe; vegetable curry; excellent people-watching. [$] *Average main: $16* ✉ *42 Baldwin Ave., Paia* ☎ *808/579–6323* 🌐 *www.cdamaui.com.*

Cafe Mambo

$ | **ECLECTIC** | Paia is one of Maui's most interesting food towns, and this colorful, airy, and brightly painted hangout is right in the thick of things. The menu features everything from burgers and fish to Mediterranean tastes, and aside from the great, well-priced food, the people-watching is fascinating. **Known for:** kalua duck quesadilla; vegetable tagine and vegan options; locally inspired tapas. $ *Average main: $16* ✉ *30 Baldwin Ave., Paia* ☎ *808/579–8021* ⊕ *www.cafemambomaui.com.*

Flatbread Company

$$ | **PIZZA** | **FAMILY** | This Vermont-based company marched right into Paia in 2007 and instantly became a popular restaurant and a valued addition to the community as it gives back to local nonprofits. The bustling restaurant uses organic, local, sustainable products, including 100% organically grown wheat for the made-fresh-daily dough, and it's a good spot to take the kids. **Known for:** Mopsy's Kalua Pork Pizza served with kiawe-smoked free-range pork shoulder and homemade organic mango barbecue sauce; small but lively bar and jam-packed Tuesday benefit nights; wood-fired, clay-oven pizzas;. $ *Average main: $22* ✉ *89 Hana Hwy., Paia* ☎ *808/579–8989* ⊕ *www.flatbreadcompany.com.*

★ Paia Fishmarket Restaurant

$ | **SEAFOOD** | If you're okay with communal picnic tables, or taking your meal to a nearby beach, this place in funky Paia town serves, arguably, the best fresh fish for the best prices on this side of the island. Four preparations are offered and, on any given day, there are at least four to six fresh fishes from which to choose; there are burgers, chicken, and pasta for the non-fish fans. **Known for:** delectable side dishes; grilled opah; local fish and local beer at low, local prices. $ *Average main: $15* ✉ *100 Hana Hwy., Paia* ☎ *808/579–8030* ⊕ *www.paiafishmarket.com.*

🛏 Hotels

Paia Inn

$$$ | **B&B/INN** | Located in the former plantation town of Paia, along Hana Highway, this chic inn with Southeast Asian influences is surprisingly quiet and includes oceanfront accommodations. **Pros:** unique and varied shops and dining just steps away in funky beach town; well-maintained property; excellent new on-site restaurant. **Cons:** some rooms are very small; limited on- and off-site parking; lots of street action. $ *Rooms from: $299* ✉ *93 Hana Hwy., Paia* ☎ *808/579–6000, 800/721–4000* ⊕ *www.paiainn.com* ⇨ *10 units* ⭍ *No meals.*

🛍 Shopping

★ Mana Foods

FOOD/CANDY | At this bustling health food store you can stock up on local fish and grass-fed beef for your barbecue. You'll find the best selection of organic produce on the island, as well as a great bakery and deli. The health and beauty room has a dizzying selection of products that promise to keep you glowing. ✉ *49 Baldwin Ave., Paia* ☎ *808/579–8078* ⊕ *www.manafoodsmaui.com.*

Paia Gelato

FOOD/CANDY | **FAMILY** | Fresh gelato made with locally sourced ingredients is the draw here. Try Surfing Goat Dairy's Lilikoi Quark flavor and thank us later (there is also a large dairy-free selection of gelato). You'll also find jams, jellies, and dressings from Jeff Gomes, coffees from Maui Coffee Roasters, and picnic box lunches from Hana Lunch Co. ✉ *99C Hana Hwy., Paia* ☎ *808/579–9201* ⊕ *www.paiagelato.com.*

★ Maui Crafts Guild

ART GALLERIES | One of the island's only artist cooperatives, Maui Crafts Guild is crammed with treasures. Resident artists produce lead-glazed pottery, basketry, glass and feather art, photography,

Above the rain forests of Haiku are views of the Pacific.

ceramics, and pressed-flower art. The prices are surprisingly low. ✉ *120 Hana Hwy., Paia* ☎ *808/579–9697* ⊕ *www.mauicraftsguild.com.*

★ Maui Girl

CLOTHING | This is *the* place on Maui for swimwear, cover-ups, beach hats, and sandals. Maui Girl designs its own suits, which have been spotted in *Sports Illustrated* fashion shoots and on celebrities. Tops and bottoms can be purchased separately, increasing your chances of finding the perfect fit. ✉ *12 Baldwin Ave., Paia* ☎ *808/579–9266* ⊕ *www.maui-girl.com.*

Maui Hands

ART GALLERIES | This gallery shows work by more than 300 local artists: exquisite woodwork, lovely ceramics, authentic Niihau shell lei, wave metal etchings, and whimsical clay figures. There are locations in Lahaina, Makawao, and at the Hyatt Regency Maui in Kaanapali. At each location, the gallery offers a unique Artists in Residence program that connects the public to the artists at local "talk story" sessions each month. ✉ *84 Hana Hwy., Paia* ☎ *808/579–9245* ⊕ *www.mauihands.com.*

Haiku

13 miles east of Kahului; 4 miles east of Paia.

At one time this area centered on a couple of enormous pineapple canneries. Both have been transformed into rustic warehouse malls. Because of the post office next door, Old Haiku Cannery earned the title of town center. Here you can try eateries offering everything from plate lunches to vegetarian dishes to juicy burgers and fantastic sushi. Follow windy Haiku Road to Pauwela Cannery, the other defunct factory-turned-hangout. This jungle hillside is a maze of flower-decked roads that seem to double back on themselves.

Haiku is a short detour off Hana Highway (Route 36) just past Hookipa Beach Park on the way to Hana. Haiku Road turns into Kokomo Road at the post office.

 Restaurants

★ Colleen's at the Cannery

$$ | AMERICAN | You'd never guess what's inside by the nondescript exterior and the location in an old pineapple cannery-cum-strip-mall, but this is one of Maui's most overlooked and underrated restaurants. Popular with locals for breakfast and lunch, at night during dinner is when the candles come out and it's time for martinis and fresh fish; you'll feel like you're at a hip urban eatery. **Known for:** excellent food featuring Upcountry's best produce; specialty artisan pizzas and enormous salads; eggs Benedict and bloody Marys. $ *Average main: $20 ⊠ Haiku Cannery Marketplace, 810 Haiku Rd., Haiku-Pauwela ☎ 808/575–9211 ⊕ www.colleensin-haiku.com.*

Nuka

$$ | ASIAN FUSION | This off-the-beaten-path izakaya-style Japanese eatery is worth the trek to sleepy Haiku. Diners flock here for the eclectic menu that includes everything from specialty French fries and fusion sushi rolls to sashimi and some of the best tempura around—all based on what's fresh from local farmers and fishermen. **Known for:** hard to get a table (no reservations); homemade green tea and black sesame ice cream; exceptional sushi and sashimi. $ *Average main: $18 ⊠ 780 Haiku Rd., Haiku-Pauwela ☎ 808/575–2939 ⊕ www.nukamaui. com ☻ Closed daily 1:30–4:30 pm. No lunch on weekends.*

Kuau

 Restaurants

Mama's Fish House

$$$$ | SEAFOOD | Set in an intimate location on the beach, Mama's has been *the* Maui destination for special occasions for almost four decades. A path of gecko-shape stones leads to an ever-changing fantasyland of Hawaiian kitsch, where savvy servers can explain the various fish types and preparations, and you'd be wise to heed their recommendation; the fish is so fresh that the daily menu lists who caught it that morning. **Known for:** Polynesian Black Pearl dessert; exceptionally fresh fish; ambience and romance. $ *Average main: $50 ⊠ 799 Poho Pl., Kuau ☎ 808/579–8488 ⊕ www. mamasfishhouse.com.*

Hotels

★ The Inn at Mama's Fish House

$$$ | RENTAL | FAMILY | Nestled in gardens adjacent to one of Maui's most popular dining spots (Mama's Fish House) and fronting a small beach known as Kuau Cove, these well-maintained studios, suites, and one- and two-bedroom cottages have been recently renovated with high-end appliances and furnishings and decorated with local artwork to provide contemporary beach house luxury. **Pros:** daily maid service; free parking and Wi-Fi; near Hookipa Beach and Paia town shops and restaurants. **Cons:** restaurant can get crowded during the evening; limited swimming at beach; not a full-service hotel with concierge. $ *Rooms from: $300 ⊠ 799 Poho Pl., Kuau ☎ 808/579–9764, 800/860–4852 ⊕ www.innatmamas.com ⇌ 12 units ◎ No meals.*

Road to Hana

The Road to Hana is a 55-mile journey into the unspoiled heart of Maui. Tracing a centuries-old path, the road begins as a well-paved highway in Kahului and ends in the tiny rustic town of Hana on the island's rain-gouged windward side, spilling into a backcountry rarely visited by humans. Many travelers venture beyond Hana to **Ohe'o Gulch** in East Maui, where you can cool off in basalt-lined pools and waterfalls.

This drive is a Hawaii pilgrimage for those eager to experience what glossy

Tips on Driving the Road to Hana

If you're prone to motion sickness be aware that the Road to Hana has its fair share of twists and turns. Drive with your window down to allow in the fresh air—tinged with the aroma of guava and ginger.

With short stops, the drive from Paia to Hana should take you between two and three hours one-way. Lunching in Hana, hiking, and swimming can easily turn the round-trip into a full-day outing, especially if you continue past Hana to the Oheo Gulch and Kipahulu. If you go that far, you might consider continuing around the "back side" for the return trip. The scenery is completely different, and you'll end up in beautiful Upcountry Maui.

Because there's so much scenery to take in—including abundant waterfalls and beaches—we recommend staying overnight in Hana. It's worth taking time to enjoy the full experience without being in a hurry. Try to plan your trip for a day that promises fair sunny weather—although the drive can be even more beautiful when it's raining, the roads become more hazardous.

During high season (January–March and summer), the Road to Hana tends to develop trains of cars, with everyone in a line of six or more driving as slowly as the first car. The solution: leave early (dawn) and return late (dusk). If you find yourself playing the role of locomotive, pull over and let the other drivers pass. You can also let someone else take the turns for you—several companies offer van tours.

Basic Road Tips

■ Common courtesy in Hawaii dictates that slower drivers should pull over for faster drivers. Please don't try to zoom through this winding road.

■ When approaching one-lane bridges, it is local custom for about five cars to go in one direction at a time. If you happen to be the sixth car, stop before entering the bridge and let drivers traveling in the other direction pass.

■ Instead of stopping in the middle of the road or on a bridge to snap photos, park at a turnoff and carefully walk back to the waterfall to take your photos.

■ Although rain makes the drive more beautiful, with gushing waterfalls and rainbows, it also makes the roads slick. Drive slowly and cautiously on wet roads.

■ Just after Haiku the mile markers start at zero again.

magazines consider the "real" Hawaii. To most, the lure of Hana is its timelessness, and paired with the spectacular drive (which brings to life the old adage: the journey *is* the destination), this is one of Hawaii's best experiences. The Road to Hana is also, undoubtedly, one of the most beautiful drives on the planet.

The challenging part of the road takes only an hour and a half, but the drive begs to be taken at a leisurely pace. You'll want to slow the passage of time to take in foliage-hugged ribbons of road and roadside banana-bread stands, to swim beneath a waterfall, and to absorb the lush Maui tropics in all their glory. You'll also want to stop often and let the driver enjoy the view, too.

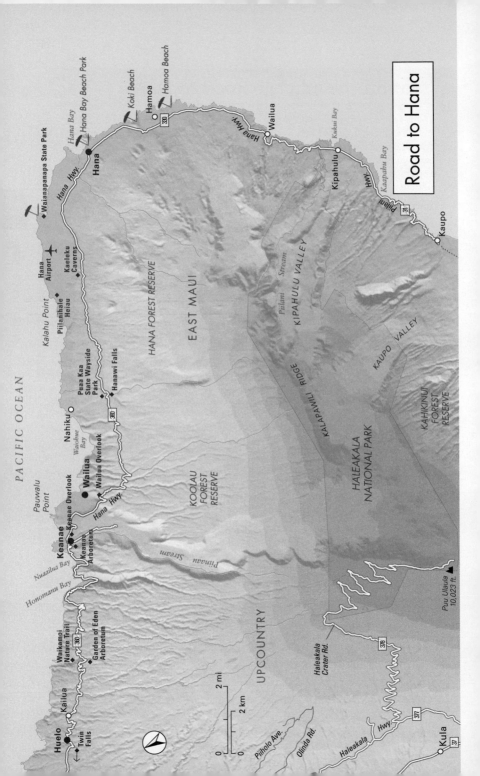

Road to Hana

PACIFIC OCEAN

EAST MAUI

HANA FOREST RESERVE

KOOLAU FOREST RESERVE

HALEAKALA NATIONAL PARK

KAHIKINUI FOREST RESERVE

UPCOUNTRY

KIPAHULU VALLEY

KAUPO VALLEY

KALAPAWILI RIDGE

Hana
Hana Bay
Hana Bay Beach Park
Waianapanapa State Park
Koki Beach
Hamoa
Hamoa Beach
360
Wailua
Hana Hwy.
Kipahulu
Kukui Bay
Hwy.
Kaapahu Bay
31
Kaupo
Hana Hwy.
Hana Airport
Kaeleku Caverns
Piilanihale Heiau
Kalahu Point
Nahiku
Puaa Kaa State Wayside Park
Hanawi Falls
360
Wailua
Wailua Overlook
Waiohue Bay
Keanae
Keanae Overlook
Keanae Arboretum
Nuaailua Bay
Honomanu Bay
Pauwalu Point
Pinaau Stream
Palani Stream
Puu Ulaula
10,023 ft.
Haleakala Crater Rd.
378
Huelo
Kailua
Twin Falls
Waikamoi Nature Trail
360
Garden of Eden Arboretum
Piiholo Ave.
Olinda Rd.
Haleakala Hwy.
377
37
Kula

2 mi
2 km
0

Huelo, Kailua, and Nearby

10 miles east of Haiku.

As the Road to Hana begins its journey eastward, the slopes get steeper, and the Pacific Ocean pops into view. The first waterfall you see, Twin Falls, is around mile marker 2, and farther up the road is the Koolau Forest Reserve. Embedded in the forest are two townships, Huelo and Kailua, both of which are great places to pull over and take in the dramatic landscape.

Just after Haiku, the mile markers on the Hana Highway change back to 0. The towns of Huelo and Kailua are at mile markers 5 and 6. To reach the townships, follow the signs toward the ocean side of the road.

Sights

The following sites are arranged geographically by mile marker en route to Hana.

Twin Falls

BODY OF WATER | Keep an eye out for the Twin Falls Farm Stand just after mile marker 2 on the Hana Highway. Stop here and treat yourself to some fresh sugarcane juice. If you're feeling adventurous, follow the path beyond the stand to the paradisiacal waterfalls known as Twin Falls. Although it's still private property, the "no trespassing" signs have been replaced by colorfully painted arrows pointing toward the easily accessible falls. Several deep, emerald pools sparkle beneath waterfalls and offer excellent (and a little cold) swimming and photo opportunities. In recent years, this natural attraction has become a tourist hot spot. Although the attention is well deserved, those who wish to avoid crowds may want to keep driving. ⊠ *Hana Hwy., past mile marker 2, Haiku-Pauwela.*

Huelo

TOWN | When you see the colorful mailboxes on the *makai* (toward the ocean) side of the road just past mile marker 4 on the Hana Highway, follow the windy road to the rural area of Huelo—a funky community that includes a mix of off-the-grid inhabitants and vacation rentals. The town features two picturesque churches, one of which is Kaulanapueo Church, constructed in 1853 out of coral blocks. If you linger awhile, you may meet local residents and learn about a rural lifestyle you might not have expected to find on the Islands. The same can be said for nearby Kailua (mile marker 6). ■TIP→ **When you're back up on Hana Highway, pull into the Huelo Lookout Fruit Stand for yummy smoothies and killer views of the Pacific below.** ⊠ *Hana Hwy., near mile marker 4, Huelo.*

Waikamoi Nature Trail

TRAIL | Slightly after the town of Huelo, the Hana Highway enters the Koolau Forest Reserve. Vines wrap around street signs, and waterfalls are so abundant that you don't know which direction to look. A good start is between mile markers 9 and 10, where the Waikamoi Nature Trail sign beckons you to stretch your car-weary limbs. A short (if muddy) trail leads through tall eucalyptus trees to a coastal vantage point with a picnic table. Signage reminds visitors: "Quiet, Trees at Work" and "Bamboo Picking Permit Required." *Awapuhi,* or Hawaiian shampoo ginger, sends up fragrant shoots along the trail. ■TIP→ **The area has picnic tables and a restroom.** ⊠ *Hana Hwy., between mile markers 9 and 10.*

Keanae, Wailua, and Nearby

13 miles east of Kailua.

Officially, Keanae is the halfway point to Hana, but for many, this is where the drive offers the most rewarding vistas.

Tropical Delights

The drive to Hana wouldn't be as enchanting without a stop or two at one of the countless fruit and flower (and banana bread) stands by the highway. Every so often a thatch hut tempts passersby with apple bananas (a smaller, firmer variety), *lilikoi* (passion fruit), avocados, or star fruit just plucked from the tree. Leave a few dollars in the can for the folks who live off the land. Huge bouquets of tropical flowers are available for a handful of change, and some farms will ship.

One standout is **Aunty Sandy's Banana Bread Stand**, in the blink-and-you'll-miss-it community of Keanae. This legendary banana-bread shop is just past the coral-and-lava-rock church. Aunty Sandy's sweet loaves lure locals and tourists alike, but be sure to arrive early, because once the stand runs out, you'll have to scurry back up the main road to the **Halfway to Hana Fruit Stand** to find a tasty replacement.

The greenery seems to envelop the skinny road, forcing drivers to slow to a crawl as they "ooh" and "aah" at the landscape. Keanae itself isn't much of a stunner—save the banana-bread shack at the bottom of the road—but the scenery as your car winds through these tropics makes the white-knuckle parts of the drive worth it. Around the village of Wailua, one of the most fiercely native Hawaiian regions on the island, there seem to be waterfalls at every turn.

◉ Sights

The following sites are arranged geographically by mile marker en route to Hana.

★ Garden of Eden Arboretum

GARDEN | Just beyond mile marker 10 on the Hana Highway, the Garden of Eden Arboretum offers interpretive trails through 26 acres of manicured gardens. Anyone with a green thumb will appreciate the care and attention given to the more than 500 varieties of tropical plants—many of them native. Trails lead to views of the lovely Puohokamoa Falls and provide a glimpse into the botanical wonders that thrive in this lush region. Be sure to stop by the gift shop on the way out for a wide variety of gifts made by local artisans and to hang out with the ducks and peacocks. ✉ *10600 Hana Hwy., past mile marker 10, Haiku-Pauwela* ☎ *808/572–9899* ⊕ *www.mauigardenofeden.com* ⌑ *$15.*

Keanae Arboretum

GARDEN | Here you can add to your botanical education or enjoy a challenging hike into the forest. Signs help you learn the names of the many plants and trees now considered native to Hawaii. The meandering Piinaau Stream adds a graceful touch to the arboretum and provides a swimming pond when there is enough water. You can take a fairly rigorous hike from the arboretum if you can find the trail at one side of the large taro patch. Be careful not to lose the trail once you're on it. A lovely forest waits at the end of the 25-minute hike. ✉ *Hana Hwy., past mile marker 16, Keanae* ⌑ *Free.*

Keanae Overlook

TOWN | Near mile marker 17 along the Hana Highway, you can stop at the Keanae Overlook. From this observation point you can take in the patchwork effect the taro patches create against the dramatic backdrop of the ocean. In the other direction there are awesome views of Haleakala through the foliage. This is a great spot for photos, but it is not recommended that you fly your drones over the inhabited areas. ⊠ *Hana Hwy., near mile marker 17, Keanae.*

Wailua Overlook

SCENIC DRIVE | From the parking lot on the side of the Hana Highway near mile marker 20, you can see Wailua Canyon in one direction and Wailua Village in the other. Photos are spectacular in the morning light of the verdant expanse below. Also from your perch, you can see Wailua Village's landmark 1860 church, which allegedly constructed of coral that washed up onto the shore during a storm. You'll want to take photos, but flying a drone over the populated area is strongly discouraged. ⊠ *Hana Hwy., near mile marker 20, Wailua (Maui County).*

Puaa Kaa State Wayside Park

BODY OF WATER | For a leg-stretching break, visitors will find a respite and real bathrooms at this small roadside park. This is one of the few places on the highway with plenty of parking, so take some time to linger and enjoy the short hike to a small waterfall and pool across the highway from the bathrooms. There are also picnic tables and friendly cats to welcome you. ⊠ *Hana Hwy., Wailua (Maui County)* ⊹ *½ mile past mile marker 22.*

Hanawi Falls

BODY OF WATER | At mile marker 24 of the Hana Highway, just as you approach the bridge, look toward the mountains to catch a glimpse of Hanawi Falls. This lush spring-fed stream travels 9 miles to the ocean, and the waterfalls are real crowd-pleasers, even when rains have been light. The best views are from the bridge. ⚠ **It is not safe to hike to the falls, and you must cross private property to get there. We strongly advise against this.** ⊠ *Hana Hwy., near mile marker 24, Keanae.*

Hana and Nearby

15 miles east of Keanae.

Even though the "town" is little more than a gas station, a post office, and a general store, the relaxed pace of life that Hana residents enjoy will likely have you in its grasp. Hana is one of the few places where the slow pulse of the island is still strong. The town centers on its lovely circular bay, dominated on the right-hand shore by a *puu* (volcanic cinder cone) called Kauiki. A short trail here leads to a cave, the birthplace of Queen Kaahumanu. Two miles beyond town, another puu presides over a loop road that passes Hana's two best beaches—Koki and Hamoa. The hill is called Ka Iwi O Pele (Pele's Bone). Offshore here, at tiny Alau Island, the demigod Maui supposedly fished up the Hawaiian Islands.

Although sugar was once the mainstay of Hana's economy, the last plantation shut down in the 1940s. In 1946, rancher Paul Fagan built the Hotel Hana-Maui (now the Travassa Hana) and stocked the surrounding pastureland with cattle. Now it's the ranch and its hotel that put food on most tables. It's pleasant to stroll around this beautifully rustic property. In the evening, while local musicians play in the lobby bar, their friends jump up to dance hula. The cross you can see on the hill above the hotel was put there in memory of Fagan.

⊙ Sights

The following sites are listed geographically by mile marker en route to Hana.

Kaeleku Caverns

CAVE | If you're interested in spelunking, take the time to explore Kaeleku Caverns (aka Hana Lava Tube), just after mile marker 31 on the Hana Highway. The site is a mile down Ulaino Road. The friendly folks at the cave give a brief orientation and promptly send nature enthusiasts into Maui's largest lava tube, accented by colorful underworld formations. You can take a self-guided, 30- to 40-minute tour daily 10:30–4 for $11.95 per person. LED flashlights are provided. For those who don't want to explore the caverns, this still makes for a great stop to check out the world's only red ti leaf maze on the grounds. ⊠ *205 Ulaino Rd., off Hana Hwy., past mile marker 31, Hana* ☎ *808/248–7308* ⊕ *www.mauicave.com* ▤ *$11.95.*

Piilanihale Heiau

ARCHAEOLOGICAL SITE | This temple, the largest *heiau* in Polynesia, was built for a great 16th-century Maui king named Piilani and his heirs. Hawaiian families continue to maintain and protect this sacred site as they have for centuries, and they have not been eager to turn it into a tourist attraction. However, there is now a brochure, so you can tour the property yourself. The heaiu is situated within the 122-acre **Kahanu Garden,** a federally funded research center focusing on the ethnobotany of the Pacific. ⊠ *650 Ulaino Rd., Hana* ✛ *To get here, turn left onto Ulaino Rd. at Hana Hwy. mile marker 31; the road turns to gravel; continue 1½ miles* ☎ *808/248–8912* ⊕ *www. ntbg.org* ▤ *$10 self-guided, $30 guided* ◷ *Closed Sun.*

★ Waianapanapa State Park

BEACH—SIGHT | Home to one of Maui's few black-sand beaches and freshwater caves for adventurous swimmers to explore, this park is right on the ocean. It's a lovely spot to picnic, hike, or swim. To the left you'll find the volcanic sand beach, picnic tables, and cave pools; to the right is an ancient trail that snakes along the ocean past blowholes, sea arches, and archaeological sites. Bird lovers could linger for hours watching the comings and goings of seabirds on the ocean outcroppings. The tide pools here turn red several times a year. Scientists say it's explained by the arrival of small shrimp, but legend claims the

color represents the blood of Popoalaea, said to have been murdered in one of the caves by her husband, Chief Kakae. In either case, the dramatic landscape is bound to leave a lasting impression. There is a private cemetery on the grounds of the park, so be mindful to keep out of this area. ∎**TIP**➔ **With a permit, you can stay in a state-run cabin or campsite for a steal. It's wise to book as early as possible, as these spots book up quickly.** ⊠ *Hana Hwy., near mile marker 32, Hana* ☎ *808/984–8109* ⊕ *www.hawaiistateparks.org* ▤ *Free.*

🏖 Beaches

East Maui's and Hana's beaches will literally stop you in your tracks—they're that beautiful. Black sand stands out against pewter skies and lush tropical foliage, creating picture-perfect scenes that seem too breathtaking to be real. Rough conditions often preclude swimming, but that doesn't mean you can't explore the shoreline.

★ Hamoa Beach

BEACH—SIGHT | **FAMILY** | Why did James Michener describe this stretch of salt-and-pepper sand as the most "South Pacific" beach he'd come across, even though it's in the North Pacific? Maybe it was the perfect half-moon shape, speckled with the shade of palm trees. Perhaps he was intrigued by the jutting black coastline, often outlined by rain showers out at sea, or the pervasive lack of hurry he felt here. Whatever it was, many still feel the lure. The beach can be crowded, yet it is nonetheless relaxing. Early mornings and late afternoons are best for swimming. At times the churning surf might intimidate swimmers, but the body surfing can be great. Though there are beach chairs and a pavilion at the beach, they are strictly for the use of Travaasa Hana guests. Hamoa is half a mile past Koki Beach on Haneoo Loop Road, 2 miles south of Hana town. **Amenities:**

showers; toilets. **Best for:** surfing; swimming. ✉ *Haneoo Loop Rd., Hana.*

Koki Beach

BEACH—SIGHT | You can tell from the trucks parked alongside the road that this is a favorite local surf spot. ■ **TIP→ Swimming is not recommended here, as there are no lifeguards, and the rip currents are powerful.** Look for awesome views of the rugged coastline and a sea arch on the left end. *Iwa,* or white-throated frigate birds, dart like pterodactyls over the offshore Alau Islet. Though it's not a swimming beach, the grassy area and picnic tables are cozy and allow visitors to watch the surfers navigate the waves, while the small red-sand beach is good for walks if the tide allows. **Amenities:** picnic tables **Best for:** surfing. ✉ *Haneoo Loop Rd., Hana* ✣ *About 2 miles south of Hana town.*

★ Waianapanapa State Park

BEACH—SIGHT | This black volcanic-pebble beach fringed with green beach vines and palms will remain in your memory long after your visit. Swimming here is both relaxing and invigorating. Strong currents bump smooth stones up against your ankles, while seabirds flit above a black, jagged sea arch, and fingers of white foam rush onto the beach. There are picnic tables and grills. At the edge of the parking lot, a sign tells you the sad story of a doomed Hawaiian princess. Stairs lead through a tunnel of interlocking Polynesian *hau* (a native tree) branches to an icy cave pool—the secret hiding place of the ancient princess (you can swim in this pool, but beware of mosquitoes). In the other direction a dramatic 3-mile coastal path continues past sea arches, blowholes, cultural sites, and even a ramshackle fishermen's shelter, all the way to Hana town. **Amenities:** parking (no fee); showers; toilets. **Best for:** swimming; walking. ✉ *Hana Hwy., Hana* ✣ *Near mile marker 32* ☎ *808/984–8109* 🌐 *www.hawaiistateparks.org.*

🍴 Restaurants

★ Hana Fresh Farm Stand

$ | AMERICAN | Directly in front of (and associated with) Hana Health, you'll find rows of tables laden with delicious and organic fresh salads and entrées worthy of any chic farm-to-table restaurant. Fresh fish plates, poke bowls, panini, and wraps are just a few of the always-changing choices, and best of all, the produce comes from the restaurant's own farm, directly behind the health center. **Known for:** freshly made salads and hot panini; fish kebabs; locally grown coffee and fresh fruit smoothies. [$] *Average main: $12* ✉ *4590 Hana Hwy., Hana* ✣ *Located between mile markers 34 and 35* ☎ *808/248–7515* 🌐 *www.hanafresh.org* 🕒 *No breakfast or dinner; closed Sat.–Sun.*

🛏 Hotels

★ Bamboo Inn on Hana Bay

$$ | B&B/INN | A thatched-roof gate opens to the courtyard of this informal Balinese-inspired guesthouse with a sweeping view of Hana Bay. The ground-floor studio has a private outdoor shower and the other two units have private whirlpool hot tubs on their second-floor decks. **Pros:** fall asleep to the sound of waves lapping at the rocky coast; close to town center; light breakfast included. **Cons:** limited mobile service, Wi-Fi available only in courtyard; no air-conditioning; no nightlife in this early-to-bed, early-to-rise town. [$] *Rooms from: $250* ✉ *4869 Uakea Rd., Hana* ☎ *808/248–7718* 🌐 *www.bambooinn.com* 🛏 *3 rooms* 🍽 *Free Breakfast.*

★ Hana Kai Maui

$$ | RENTAL | Perfectly situated on Hana Bay, this two-story "condotel" has an excellent reputation for cleanliness and visitor hospitality—and the ocean views are stunning. **Pros:** 10-minute walk to Hana Bay; one-night rentals are accepted under some conditions;

Hamoa Beach is one of Maui's most beautiful stretches of sand.

daily housekeeping. **Cons:** no nightlife or excitement in Hana town; no elevator; no air-conditioning or TV. $ *Rooms from: $250* ⊠ *4865 Uakea Rd., Hana* ☎ *808/248–8426, 800/346–2772* ⊕ *www.hanakaimaui.com* ⇲ *17 units* ⦿| *No meals.*

Travaasa Hana
$$$$ | **RESORT** | A destination in itself, this secluded and quietly luxurious property still delivers the tropical Hawaii of your dreams; for additional peace and privacy, splurge with a stay in the Ocean Bungalows set on sprawling lawns overlooking the rugged coastline. **Pros:** no resort or parking fees; no-tipping policy for everything except dining; truly unique property in a special place. **Cons:** spotty mobile service; oceanfront but no sandy beach (however, free shuttle to Hamoa Beach with chair setups); no nightlife in Hana. $ *Rooms from: $525* ⊠ *5031 Hana Hwy., Hana* ☎ *808/359–2401, 888/820–1043* ⊕ *www.travaasa.com/hana* ⇲ *76 units* ⦿| *No meals.*

👜 Shopping

★ Hana Coast Gallery
ART GALLERIES | One of the most well-curated galleries on the island, this 3,000-square-foot facility has handcrafted koa furniture, marble sculptures, photography, and jewelry on consignment from local artists as well as artists from across Polynesia. ⊠ *Travaasa Hana, 5031 Hana Hwy., Hana* ☎ *808/248–8636, 800/637–0188* ⊕ *www.hanacoast.com.*

East Maui

East Maui defies definition. Part hideaway for renegades, part escape for celebrities, this funky stretch of Maui surprises at every turn. You might find a smoothie shop that powers your afternoon bike ride, or a hidden restaurant–artist gathering off a backcountry road serving organic cuisine that could have been dropped in from San Francisco. Farms are abundant, and the dramatic beauty seems to get better the farther you get from Hana. This route leads through stark ocean vistas rounding the back side of Haleakala and into Upcountry. If you plan to meander this way, be sure to check the weather and road conditions.

Kipahulu and Nearby

11 miles east of Hana.

Most know Kipahulu as the resting place of Charles Lindbergh. Kipahulu devotes its energy to staying under the radar. There is not much for tourists, save an organic farm, a couple of cafés, and astounding natural landscapes. Maui's wildest wilderness might not beg for your tourist dollars, but it is a tantalizing place to escape just about everything.

To access Kipahulu from Hana, continue on Hana Highway, also known as 330, for 11 miles southeast. You can also reach the area from Upcountry's Highway 37, which turns into Highway 31, though this route can take up to two hours and is a bit rough on your rental car.

◉ Sights

Grave of Charles Lindbergh
CEMETERY | Many people travel the mile past Oheo Gulch to see the grave of Charles Lindbergh. The world-renowned aviator chose to be buried here because he and his wife, writer Anne Morrow Lindbergh, spent a lot of time living in the area in a home they'd built. He was buried here in 1974, next to Palapala Hoomau Congregational Church. The simple one-room church sits on a bluff over the sea, with the small graveyard on the ocean side and gorgeous views. Since this is a churchyard, be considerate and leave everything exactly as you found it. Next to the churchyard on the ocean side is a small county park, a good place for a peaceful picnic. ⊠ *Palapala Hoomau Congregational Church, Piilani Hwy., Kipahulu.*

Maui's Best Omiyage 🍴

Omiyage is the Japanese term for food souvenirs.

- Lavender-salt seasoning from **Alii Kula Lavender**
- Maui-grown pineapples from **Maui Gold Pineapple Company**
- Peaberry beans from **Maui Coffee Company**
- Nicky Beans from **Maui Coffee Roasters**
- Jeff's Jams and Jellies from **Paia Gelato**
- Hot Sauces from **HI Spice**

Kaupo Road
SCENIC DRIVE | Also called Piilani Highway, this road winds through what locals say is one of the last parts of real Maui. It goes all the way around Haleakala's back side through Ulupalakua Ranch and into Kula. The desert-like area, with its grand vistas, is unlike anything else on the island. This road has a reputation for being treacherous, and while narrow sections and steep cliffs can be intimidating for some drivers, recent road improvements have made this a much smoother ride. ⚠ **Some car-rental agencies call the area off-limits for their passenger cars, and they won't come to your rescue if you need emergency assistance. However, four-wheel drive isn't necessary.** The small communities around East Maui cling tenuously to the old ways—please be respectful of that if you do pass this way. Between Kipahulu and Kula may be a mere 38 miles, but the twisty road makes the drive take up to two hours. If you must drive this road at night, keep an eye out for free-range cattle crossing your path. ■TIP→ **Fill up on gas and food**

Food Shopping for Renters

Condo renters in search of food and takeout meals should try these great places around Maui.

West Maui

Foodland Farms This large supermarket combines the best of gourmet selections and local products with all the familiar staples you need to stock your vacation kitchen. It also makes an excellent *poke* (seafood salad). ⊠ *Lahaina Gateway Shopping Center, 345 Keawe St., Lahaina* ☎ *808/662–7088* ⊕ *www.foodland.com.*

South Shore

Safeway Find everything you could possibly need at this 24-hour supermarket, located in the Piilani Village Shopping Center. There's also a deli, prepared-foods and seafood section, and bakery. ⊠ *277 Piikea Ave., Kihei* ☎ *808/891–9120* ⊕ *www.safeway.com.*

Times Supermarket Watch for the parking lot barbecue on Wednesday and Friday, when chicken, teriyaki beef, steak, and shrimp are served plate lunch–style outside this supermarket. Hawaiian plates are served up on Thursday. ⊠ *1310 S. Kihei Rd., Kihei* ⊕ *www.timessupermarkets.com.*

Central Maui

Safeway Located a minute from Kahului Airport, this gigantic 24-hour supermarket has all the essentials, and then some. The deli, prepared-foods and seafood sections, and bakery are all fantastic. There's a good wine selection, tons of produce, and a flower shop where you can treat yourself to a fresh lei. ⊠ *1090 Hookele St., Kahului* ☎ *808/359–2970* ⊕ *www. safeway.com.*

Whole Foods Market This busy supermarket carries local organic produce, and the seafood, bakery, beer and wine, and meat offerings are exceptional. The pricey prepared foods—including pizza, sushi, a salad bar, Asian bowls, and Mexican fare—attract crowds. ⊠ *70 E. Kaahumanu Ave., Kahului* ⊕ *www.wholefoodsmarket.com.*

Upcountry

Foodland This branch of the local supermarket chain at the Pukalani Terrace Center is a full-service store with prepared foods, a deli, fresh sushi, local produce, and a good seafood section in addition to the usual fare. On Friday and Saturday, the store sets up a grill in the parking area to barbecue tender steak and teriyaki beef. ⊠ *55 Pukalani St., Pukalani* ☎ *808/572–0674.*

Pukalani Superette Stop at this family-owned store on your way up or down Haleakala for fresh Maui-grown produce and meat, flowers, and chocolate *haupia* (coconut) cream pies. ⊠ *15 Makawao Ave., Pukalani* ☎ *808/572–7616* ⊕ *www.pukalanisuperette.com.*

---

before departing, as the only stop out here is Kaupo Store, which hawks a few pricey necessities.

★ Oheo Gulch

BODY OF WATER | One branch of Haleakala National Park runs down the mountain from the crater and reaches the sea here, 10 miles past Hana at mile marker 42 on the Hana Highway, where a basalt-lined stream cascades from one pool to the next. Some tour guides still incorrectly call this area Seven Sacred Pools, but in truth there are more than seven, and they've never been considered sacred.

⚠ **While you may be tempted to take a dip, know that the pools are often closed because of landslides and flash flooding. If you see a closure notice, take it seriously, as people have died here.** The place gets crowded, as most people who drive the Hana Highway make this their last stop. It's best to get here early to soak up the solace of these waterfalls. ■**TIP→ The $30 entrance fee per car is good for three days and includes entry to Haleakala Volcano.** ✉ *Piilani Hwy., 10 miles south of Hana, Hana.*

Activities and Tours

Aerial Tours

Helicopter flight-seeing excursions can take you over the West Maui Mountains, Haleakala Crater, or the island of Molokai. This is a beautiful, thrilling way to see the island, and the *only* way to see some of its most dramatic areas and waterfalls. Tour prices usually include a digital video of your trip so you can relive the experience at home. Prices run from about $210 for a half-hour flight to more than $350 for a 75-minute tour with an ocean or cliffside landing. Discounts may be available online or, if you're willing to chance it, by calling at the last minute.

Tour operators come under sharp scrutiny for passenger safety and equipment maintenance. Don't be shy; ask about a company's safety record, flight paths, age of equipment, and level of operator experience. Generally, though, if it's still in business, it's doing something right.

Air Maui Helicopters

TOUR—SPORTS | Priding itself on a perfect safety record, Air Maui provides 45- to 75-minute flights covering the waterfalls of the West Maui Mountains, Haleakala Crater, Hana, and the spectacular sea cliffs of Molokai. Prices range from $220 for a West Maui/Molokai or Hana/ Haleakala tour to $353 for a 75-minute tour with ocean or cliffside landings. Discounts are available online. Charter flights are also available. ✉ *1 Kahului Airport Rd., Hangar 110, Kahului* ☎ *877/238–4942, 808/877–7005* ⊕ *www.airmaui.com.*

Sunshine Helicopters

TOUR—SPORTS | Take a tour of Maui in Sunshine's FXStar or WhisperStar aircraft. Prices start at $260 for 45 minutes, with discounts offered online. First-class seating is available for an additional fee. Sunshine also offers tours that combine helicopter flights with either a horseback ride or submarine adventure. Charter flights can be arranged. A pilot-narrated digital record of your actual flight is available for purchase. ✉ *Kahului Airport Rd. , Hangar 107, Kahului* ☎ *808/270–3999, 866/501–7738* ⊕ *www.sunshinehelicopters.com.*

Biking

Long distances and mountainous terrain keep biking from being a practical mode of travel on Maui. Still, painted bike lanes enable cyclists to travel all the way from Makena to Kapalua, and you'll see hardy souls battling the trade winds under the hot Maui sun.

Several companies offer guided bike tours down Haleakala. This activity is a great way to enjoy an easy, gravity-induced bike ride, but it isn't for those not confident on a bike. The ride is inherently dangerous due to the slope, sharp turns, and the fact that you're riding down an actual road with cars on it. That said, the guided bike companies take every safety precaution. A few companies offer unguided (or, as they like to say, "self-guided") tours where they provide you with the bike and transportation to the mountain and then you're free to descend at your own pace. Most companies offer discounts for Internet bookings.

Haleakala National Park no longer allows commercial downhill bicycle rides within its boundaries. As a result, tour amenities and routes differ by company. Ask about sunrise viewing from the Haleakala summit (be prepared to leave *very* early in the morning), if this is an important feature for you. Some lower-price tours begin at the 6,500-foot elevation just outside the national park boundaries, where you will be unable to view the sunrise over the crater. Weather conditions on Haleakala vary greatly, so a visible sunrise can never be guaranteed. Also, mornings are downright cold at the summit, so be sure to dress in layers and wear closed-toe shoes.

Each company has age and weight restrictions, and pregnant women are discouraged from participating, although they are generally welcome in the escort van. Reconsider this activity if you have difficulty with high altitudes, have recently been scuba diving, or are taking medications that may cause drowsiness.

BEST SPOTS
Thompson Road
BICYCLING | Street bikers will want to head out to scenic Thompson Road. It's quiet, gently curvy, and flanked by gorgeous views on both sides. Because it's at a higher elevation, the air temperature is cooler and the wind lighter. The coast back down toward Kahului on the Kula Highway is worth the ride up. ⊠ *Kula Hwy., off Rte. 37, Keokea.*

EQUIPMENT AND TOURS
★ Bike It Maui
BICYCLING | Small and family-owned, this company offers predawn and early morning guided tours that take riders from the 6,500-foot elevation of Haleakala down 22 miles of stunning scenery to Makawao town. The price of $140 includes transfers from your hotel. Riders must be at least 12 and weigh no more than 260 pounds. ⊠ *Kula* ☎ *808/878–3364,* ⊕ *www.bikeitmaui.com.*

★ Cruiser Phil's Volcano Riders
BICYCLING | In the downhill bicycle industry since 1983, "Cruiser" Phil Feliciano offers a New Dawn Sunrise Experience ($163) and morning tours ($147) that include hotel transfers, coffee and snacks, and a guided 26-mile ride down the mountain. Participants should be between 13 and 65, at least 5 feet tall, weigh less than 250 pounds, and have ridden a bicycle in the past year. Feliciano also offers structured independent bike tours ($109) and van-only tours ($96). Discounts are available for online bookings. ⊠ *58-A Amala Pl., Kahului* ☎ *808/893–2332, 877/764–2453* ⊕ *www.cruiserphil.com.*

Haleakala Bike Company
BICYCLING | If you're thinking about a Haleakala bike trip, consider Haleakala Bike Company. Meet at the Old Haiku Cannery and take the van shuttle to the summit. Along the way you can learn about the history of the island, the volcano, and other Hawaiiana. Food is not included, but there are several spots along the way down to stop, rest, and eat. The simple, mostly downhill route takes you right back to the cannery where you started. HBC also offers bike sales, rentals, and services, as well as van tours. Tour prices run $85–$160, with discounts available for online bookings. ⊠ *810 Haiku Rd., Suite 120, Haiku-Pauwela* ☎ *808/575–9575, 888/922–2453* ⊕ *www.bikemaui.com.*

Island Biker
BICYCLING | Maui's premier bike shop for rentals, sales, and service offers standard front-shock bikes, road bikes, and full-suspension mountain bikes. Daily rental rates run $60–$75, and weekly rates are $210–$250. The price includes a helmet, pump, water bottle, cages, tire-repair kit, and spare tube. Car racks are $5 per day (free with weekly rentals). The staff can suggest routes appropriate for mountain or road biking. ⊠ *415 Dairy*

Rd., Kahului ☎ *808/877–7744* ⊕ *www. islandbikermaui.com.*

Krank Cycles

BICYCLING | Krank Cycles is located in Upcountry Maui, close to the Makawao Forest Reserve. They offer full-day and weekly rentals of high-end road and mountain bikes. Owner Moose will provide you with maps and trail reports, in addition to your rental bike. ✉ *1120 Makawao Ave., Makawao* ☎ *808/572–2299* ⊕ *www.krankmaui.com.*

West Maui Cycles

BICYCLING | Serving the island's west side, West Maui Cycles offers cruisers for $15 per day, hybrids for $35 per day, and performance road bikes for $45–$130 per day. Per day rates are discounted for longer-term rentals. Sales and service are available. ✉ *1087 Limahana Pl., No. 6, Lahaina* ☎ *808/661–9005* ⊕ *www. westmauicycles.com.*

Body Boarding and Body Surfing

Body surfing and "sponging" (as body boarding is called by the regulars; "boogie boarding" is another variation) are great ways to catch some waves without having to master surfing—and there's no balance or coordination required. A body board (or "sponge") is softer than a hard fiberglass surfboard, which means you can ride safely in the rough-and-tumble surf zone. If you get tossed around—which is half the fun—you don't have a heavy surfboard nearby to bang your head on but you do have something to hang onto. Serious spongers invest in a single short-clipped fin to help propel them into the wave.

BEST SPOTS

In West Maui, **D.T. Fleming Beach** offers great surf almost daily along with some nice amenities: ample parking, restrooms, a shower, grills, picnic tables,

and a daily lifeguard. Caution is advised, especially during winter months, when the current and undertow can get rough.

Between Kihei and Wailea on the South Shore, **Kamaole III** is a good spot for body surfing and body boarding. It has a sandy floor, with 1- to 3-foot waves breaking not too far out. It's often crowded late in the day, especially on weekends when local kids are out of school. Don't let that chase you away; the waves are wide enough for everyone.

If you don't mind public nudity (officially illegal but practiced nonetheless), Puu Olai **(aka Little Beach)** on the South Shore is the best break on the island for body boarding and body surfing. The shape of the sandy shoreline creates waves that break a long way out and tumble into shore. Because it's sandy, you only risk stubbing a toe on the few submerged rocks. Don't try body boarding at neighboring Oneloa **(aka Big Beach)**—waves will slap you onto the steep shore. To get to Little Beach, take the first entrance to Makena State Beach Park; climb the rock wall at the north end of the beach.

On the North Shore, **Paia Bay** has waves suitable for spongers and body surfers. The beach is just before Paia town, beyond the large community building and grass field.

EQUIPMENT

Most condos and hotels have body boards available to guests—some in better condition than others (beat-up boards work just as well for beginners). You can also pick up a body board from any discount shop, such as Target or Longs Drugs (now owned by CVS), for upward of $30.

Auntie Snorkel

WATER SPORTS | You can rent decent body boards here for $5.95 a day or $19 a week. ✉ *2439 S. Kihei Rd., Kihei* ☎ *808/298–3021* ⊕ *www.auntiesnorkel. com.*

West Maui Sports and Fishing Supply

WATER SPORTS | This old country store has been around since 1987 and has some of the best prices on the west side. Surfboards go for $15 a day or $70 a week. Snorkel and fishing gear, beach chairs, and umbrellas are also available. ☒ *843 Wainee St., Lahaina* ☎ *808/661–6252* ⊕ *www.westmauisports.com.*

Deep-Sea Fishing

If fishing is your sport, Maui is your island. In these waters you'll find ahi, *aku* (skipjack tuna), barracuda, bonefish, *kawakawa* (bonito), mahimahi, Pacific blue marlin, ono, and *ulua* (jack crevalle). You can fish year-round, and you don't need a license.

Plenty of fishing boats run out of Lahaina and Maalaea harbors. If you charter a private boat, expect to spend in the neighborhood of $700 to $1,000 for a thrilling half day in the swivel seat. You can share a boat for much less if you don't mind close quarters with a stranger who may get seasick, drunk, or worse: lucky! Before you sign up, you should know that some boats keep the catch. Most will, however, fillet a nice piece for you to take home. And if you catch a real beauty, you might even be able to have it professionally mounted. ■**TIP→ Because boats fill up fast during busy seasons, make reservations before coming to Maui.**

You're expected to bring your own lunch and beverages in unbreakable containers. (Shop the night before; it's hard to find snacks at 6 am.) Boats supply coolers, ice, and bait. A 7% tax is added to the cost of a trip, and a 10%–20% tip for the crew is suggested.

BOATS AND CHARTERS
Die Hard Sportfishing

FISHING | Captain Fuzzy Alboro runs a highly recommended operation on the 33-foot *Die Hard.* Check-in times vary between 10 pm and 3 am, depending on the moon's location, and trips range from 4 to 8 hours. He takes a minimum of four and a maximum of six people. For a six-hour charter, the cost is $250 for a shared boat or $1,320 for a private charter. ☒ *Lahaina Harbor, 654 Wharf St., Slip 9, Lahaina* ☎ *808/344–5051* ⊕ *www. diehardsportfishing.com.*

Finest Kind Sportfishing

FISHING | An 1,118-pound blue marlin was reeled in by the crew aboard *Finest Kind,* a lovely 37-foot Merritt kept so clean you'd never guess the action it's seen. Captain Dave has been around these waters for about 40 years, long enough to befriend other expert fishers. This family-run company operates three boats and specializes in skilled trolling. Shared charters start at $200 for four hours and go up to $350 for a full day. Private trips run $800–$1,500. No bananas on board, please; the captain thinks they're bad luck for fishing. ☒ *Lahaina Harbor, Slip 7, Lahaina* ☎ *877/688–0999* ⊕ *www.finest-kindsportfishing.com.*

Golf

Maui's natural beauty and surroundings offer some of the most jaw-dropping gold course vistas imaginable; add a variety of challenging, well-designed layouts and it's easy to explain the island's popularity with golfers. Holes run across small bays, past craggy lava outcrops, and up into cool forested mountains. Most courses have mesmerizing ocean views, some close enough to feel the salt in the air. Although many of the courses are affiliated with resorts (and therefore a little pricier), the general-public courses are no less impressive. Playing on Lanai is another option.

Greens Fees: Golf can be costly on Maui. Greens fees listed here are the highest course rates per round on weekdays and weekends for U.S. residents. (Some courses charge non-U.S. residents higher prices.) Rental clubs may or may not be

Did You Know?

Lush vegetation and stunning views of the crystalline ocean make golfing on Maui a memorable experience.

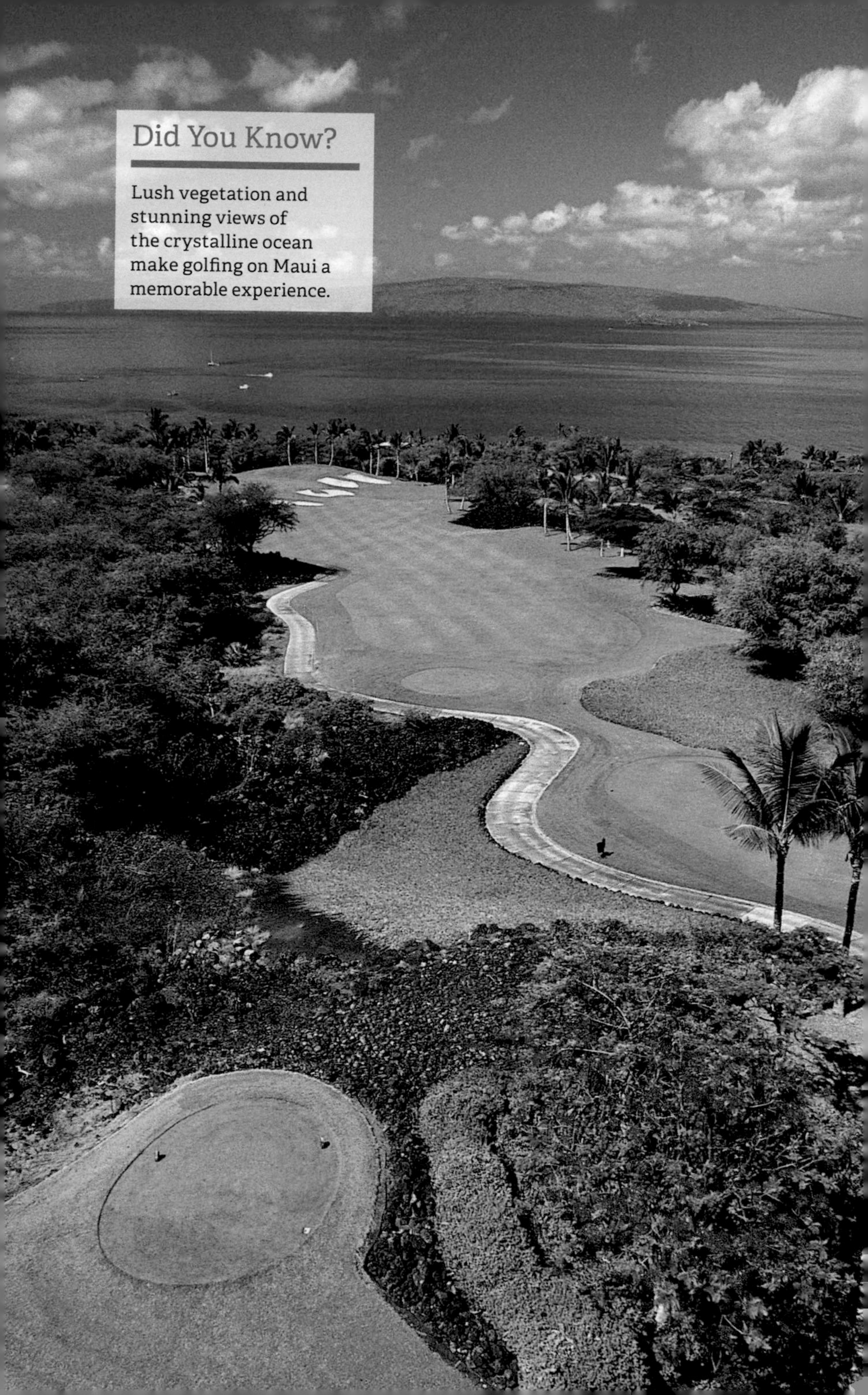

Tips for Golfing on Maui

Golf is golf and Hawaii is part of the United States, but island golf nevertheless has its own quirks. Here are a few tips to make your golf experience in the Islands more pleasant.

■ Sunscreen: Buy it, apply it (we're talking a minimum of 30 SPF). The subtropical rays of the sun are intense, even in December. Good advice is to apply sunscreen, at a minimum, on the 1st and 10th tees.

■ Stay hydrated. Spending four-plus hours in the sun and heat means you'll perspire away considerable fluids and energy.

■ All resort courses and many daily-fee courses provide rental clubs. In many cases, they're the latest lines from top manufacturers. This is true both for men and women, as well as for left-handers, which means you don't have to schlep clubs across the Pacific.

■ Pro shops at most courses are well stocked with balls, tees, and other accoutrements, so even if you bring your own bag, it needn't weigh a ton.

■ Come spikeless—few Hawaii courses still permit metal spikes. Also, most of the resort courses require a collared shirt.

■ Maui is notorious for its trade winds. Consider playing early or at twilight if you want to avoid the breezes, and remember that although they will frustrate you at times and make club selection difficult, you may well see some of your longest drives ever.

■ In theory you can play golf in Hawaii 365 days a year, but there's a reason the Hawaiian Islands are so green: an umbrella and light jacket can come in handy.

■ Unless you play a muni or certain daily-fee courses, plan on taking a cart. Riding carts are mandatory at most courses and are included in the greens fee.

included with the greens fee. Discounts are often available for resort guests, for twilight tee times, and for those who book online.

■TIP➔ Resort courses, in particular, offer more than the usual three sets of tees, so bite off as much or as little challenge as you like. Tee it up from the tips, and you can end up playing a few 600-yard par 5s and see a few 250-yard forced carries.

★ The Dunes at Maui Lani

GOLF | Robin Nelson is at his minimalist best here, creating a bit of British links in the middle of the Pacific. Holes run through ancient, lightly wooded sand dunes, 5 miles inland from Kahului Harbor. Thanks to the natural humps and slopes of the dunes, Nelson had to move very little dirt and created a natural beauty. During the design phase he visited Ireland, and not so coincidentally the par-3 3rd looks a lot like the Dell at Lahinch: a white dune on the right sloping down into a deep bunker and partially obscuring the right side of the green—just one of several blind to semiblind shots here. ✉ 1333 Maui Lani Pkwy., Kahului ☎ 808/873–0422 ⊕ www. dunesatmauilani.com 🖃 $95 ⚑ 18 holes, 6841 yards, par 72.

Kaanapali Golf Courses

GOLF | The Royal Kaanapali (North) Course (1962) is one of three in Hawaii designed by Robert Trent Jones Sr., the godfather of modern golf architecture. The greens average a whopping 10,000 square feet, necessary because of the often-severe undulation. The par-4 18th hole (into the prevailing trade breezes, with out-of-bounds on the left and a lake on the right) is notoriously tough. Designed by Arthur Jack Snyder, the Kaanapali Kai (South) Course (1976) shares similar seaside-into-the-hills terrain, but it is rated a couple of strokes easier, mostly because putts are less treacherous. ⊠ *2290 Kaanapali Pkwy., Lahaina* ☎ *808/661–3691, 866/454–4653* ⊕ *www.kaanapaligolfcourses.com* ✉ *Royal Kaanapali (North) Course $255, Kaanapali Kai (South) Course $205* 🏌. *Royal Kaanapali (North) Course: 18 holes, 6700 yards, par 71; Kaanapali Kai (South) Course: 18 holes, 6400 yards, par 70.*

★ Kapalua Golf

GOLF | Perhaps Hawaii's best-known golf resort and the crown jewel of golf on Maui, Kapalua hosts the PGA Tour's first event each January: the Sentry Tournament of Champions at the **Plantation Course**. On this famed course, Ben Crenshaw and Bill Coore (1991) tried to incorporate traditional shot values in a nontraditional site, taking into account slope, gravity, and the prevailing trade winds. The par-5 18th hole, for instance, plays 663 yards from the back tees (600 yards from the resort tees). The hole drops 170 feet in elevation, narrowing as it goes to a partially guarded green, and plays downwind and down-grain. Despite the longer-than-usual distance, the slope is great enough and the wind at your back usually brisk enough to reach the green with two well-struck shots—a truly unbelievable finish to a course that will challenge, frustrate, and reward the patient golfer.

The **Bay Course** (Arnold Palmer and Francis Duane, 1975) is the more traditional of Kapalua's courses, with gentle rolling fairways and generous greens. The most memorable hole is the par-3 5th hole,

with a tee shot that must carry over a turquoise inlet of Oneloa Bay. Each of the courses has a separate clubhouse. ⊠ *2000 Plantation Club Dr., Kapalua* ☎ *808/669–8044, 877/527–2582* ⊕ *www.golfatkapalua.com* ✉ *Plantation Course $329, Bay Course $229* 🏌. *Plantation Course: 18 holes, 7411 yards, par 73. Bay Course: 18 holes, 6600 yards, par 72.*

Kapalua Golf Academy

GOLF | Along with 23 acres of practice turf, an 18-hole putting course, and a 3-hole walking course, the Kapalua Golf Academy offers individual lessons, corporate clinics, golf schools, daily clinics, and custom off-site instruction. ⊠ *1000 Office Rd., Kapalua* ☎ *808/665–5455, 877/527–2582* ⊕ *www.golfatkapalua.com.*

Pukalani Country Club

GOLF | At 1,110 feet above sea level, Pukalani (Bob Baldock, 1980) provides one of the finest vistas in all Hawaii. Holes run up, down, and across the slopes of Haleakala. The trade winds tend to come up in the late morning and afternoon. This, combined with frequent elevation change, makes club selection a test. The fairways tend to be wide, but greens are undulating and quick. ⊠ *360 Pukalani St., Pukalani* ☎ *808/572–1314* ⊕ *www.pukalanigolf.com* ✉ *$89* 🏌. *18 holes, 6962 yards, par 72.*

Wailea Blue Course

GOLF | Wailea's original course, the Blue Course (1971), nicknamed "The Grand Lady of Wailea," is operated from a separate clubhouse from the Gold and Emerald courses, its newer siblings. Here, judging elevation change is key. Fairways and greens tend to be wider and more forgiving than on the newer courses, and they run through colorful flora that includes hibiscus, wiliwili, bougainvillea, and plumeria. ⊠ *100 Wailea Ike Dr., Wailea* ☎ *808/875–7450, 888/328–6284* ⊕ *www.waileagolf.com* ✉ *$190* 🏌. *18 holes, 6765 yards, par 71.*

★ Wailea Golf Club

GOLF | Wailea is the only Hawaii resort to offer three different courses: Gold, Emerald, and Blue—the latter at a different location with a separate pro shop. Designed by Robert Trent Jones Jr. (Gold and Emerald) and Arthur Jack Snyder (Blue), these courses share similar terrain, carved into the leeward slopes of Haleakala. Although the ocean does not come into play, its beauty is visible on almost every hole. ■TIP→ Remember, putts break dramatically toward the ocean.

Jones refers to the **Gold Course** at Wailea (1994) as the "masculine" course. It's all trees and lava, and regarded as the hardest of the three courses. The trick here is to note even subtle changes in elevation. The par-3 8th, for example, plays from an elevated tee across a lava ravine to a large, well-bunkered green framed by palm trees, the blue sea, and tiny Molokini. The course demands strategy and careful club selection. The **Emerald Course** (1994) is the "feminine" layout with lots of flowers and bunkering away from greens. Although this may seem to render the bunker benign, the opposite is true. A bunker well in front of a green disguises the distance to the hole. Likewise, the Emerald's extensive flower beds are dangerous distractions because of their beauty. The Gold and Emerald courses share a clubhouse, practice facility, and 19th hole. ✉ 100 Wailea Golf Club Dr., Wailea ☎ 808/875–7450, 888/328–6284 ⊕ www.waileagolf.com 🏌 Gold Course $250, Emerald Course $250 🏌. Gold Course: 18 holes, 7078 yards, par 72; Emerald Course: 18 holes, 6825 yards, par 72.

Hang Gliding and Paragliding

If you've always wanted to know what it feels like to fly, hang gliding or paragliding might be your perfect Maui adventure. You'll get open-air, bird's-eye views of the Valley Isle that you'll likely never forget. And you don't need to be a daredevil to participate.

LESSONS AND TOURS

Hanggliding Maui

HANG GLIDING/PARAGLIDING/PARASAILING | Armin Engert will take you on an instructional powered hang-gliding trip out of Hana Airport in East Maui. With more than 13,000 hours in the air and a perfect safety record, Armin flies you over Maui's most beautiful coast. A 30-minute flight lesson costs $190, a 45-minute lesson costs $250, and a 60-minute lesson is $310. Snapshots of your flight from a wing-mounted camera cost an additional $40, and a 34-minute DVD of the flight from a wing-mounted camera is available for $80. Reservations are required. ✉ Hana Airport, Alalele Pl., off Hana Hwy., Hana ☎ 808/264-3287 ⊕ www.hanggliding maui.com.

Proflyght Paragliding

HANG GLIDING/PARAGLIDING/PARASAILING | This is the only paragliding outfit on Maui to offer solo, tandem, and instruction at Polipoli Spring State Recreation Area. The leeward slope of Haleakala lends itself to paragliding with breathtaking scenery and air currents that increase during the day. Polipoli creates tremendous thermals that allow you to peacefully descend 3,000 feet to land. Tandem instruction prices run $115–$225. Solo paragliding certification is also available. ✉ 1100 Waipoli Rd., Kula ☎ 808/874–5433 ⊕ www.paraglidemaui.com.

Hiking

Hikes on Maui include treks along coastal seashore, verdant rain forest, and alpine desert. Orchids, hibiscus, ginger, heliconia, and anthuriums grow wild on many trails, and exotic fruits like mountain apple, *lilikoi* (passion fruit), and strawberry guava provide refreshing snacks for hikers. Note, though that much of what you see in lower-altitude forests is alien, brought to Hawaii at one time or another by someone hoping to improve on nature. Plants like strawberry guava may be tasty, but they grow over native plants and have become problematic weeds.

The best hikes get you out of the imported landscaping and into the truly exotic wilderness. Hawaii possesses some of the world's rarest plants, insects, and birds. Pocket field guides are available at most grocery or drug stores and can really illuminate your walk. If you watch the right branches quietly, you can spot the same honeycreepers or happy-face spiders scientists have spent their lives studying.

BEST SPOTS
HALEAKALA NATIONAL PARK
★ **Haleakala Crater**

HIKING/WALKING | Undoubtedly the best hiking on the island is at Haleakala Crater. If you're in shape, do a day hike descending from the summit along **Keoneheehee Trail** (aka Sliding Sands Trail) to the crater floor. You might also consider spending several days here amid the cinder cones, lava flows, and all that loud silence. Entering the crater is like landing on a different planet. In the early 1960s, NASA actually brought moon-suited astronauts here to practice what it would be like to "walk on the moon." Tent camping and cabins are available with permits. On the 30 miles of trails you can traverse black sand and wild lava formations, follow the trail of blooming *ahinahina* (silverswords), and take in tremendous views of big sky and burned-red cliffs.

The best time to go into the crater is in the summer months, when the conditions are generally more predictable. Be sure to bring layered clothing—and plenty of warm clothes if you're staying overnight. It may be scorching hot during the day, but it gets mighty chilly after dark. Bring your own drinking water, as potable water is available only at the two visitor centers. Overnight visitors must get a permit at park headquarters before entering the crater. *Moderate to difficult.* ⌂ *Haleakala Crater Rd., Makawao* ☎ *808/572–4400* ⊕ *www.nps.gov/hale* ☞ *$25 park entrance fee per vehicle (good for 3 days).*

OHEO GULCH
A branch of Haleakala National Park, Oheo Gulch is famous for its pools (the area is sometimes called the Seven Sacred Pools). Truth is, there are more than seven pools, and there's nothing sacred about them. A former owner of the Travaasa Hotel Hana started calling the area Seven Sacred Pools to attract the masses to sleepy old Hana. His plan worked, and the name stuck, much to the chagrin of many Mauians.

The best time to visit the pools is in the morning, before the crowds and tour buses arrive. Start your day with a vigorous hike. Oheo has some fantastic trails to choose from, including our favorite, the Pipiwai Trail. When you're done, nothing could be better than going to the pools, lounging on the rocks, and cooling off in the freshwater reserves. (Keep in mind, however, that the park periodically closes the pools to swimming when the potential for flash flooding exists.)

You can find Oheo Gulch on Route 31, 10 miles past Hana town. To visit, you must pay the $25-per-car national park fee, which is valid for three days and can be used at Haleakala's summit as well. For information about scheduled orientations and cultural demonstrations, be sure to visit Haleakala National Park's Kipahulu

Visitor Center, 10 miles past Hana. Note that there is no drinking water here.

★ Pipiwai Trail

HIKING/WALKING | This 2-mile trek upstream leads to the 400-foot Waimoku Falls, pounding down in all its power and glory. Following signs from the parking lot, head across the road and uphill into the forest. The trail borders a sensational gorge and passes onto a boardwalk through a mystifying forest of giant bamboo. This stomp through muddy and rocky terrain takes around three hours to fully enjoy. Although this trail is never truly crowded, it's best done early in the morning before the tours arrive. Be sure to bring mosquito repellent. *Moderate.* ✉ *Hana Hwy., Hana* ✛ *Near mile marker 42* ⊕ *www.nps.gov/hale* 🎫 *$25 park entrance fee per vehicle (good for 3 days).*

IAO VALLEY STATE MONUMENT
★ Iao Needle Lookout Trail & Ethnobotanical Loop

HIKING/WALKING | Anyone (including grandparents) can handle this short walk from the parking lot at Iao Valley State Monument. On your choice of two paved walkways, you can cross the Iao Stream and explore the junglelike area. Ascend the stairs up to the Iao Needle for spectacular views of Central Maui. Be sure to stop at the lovely Kepaniwai Heritage Gardens, which commemorate the cultural contributions of various immigrant groups. *Easy.* ✉ *Trailhead: Iao Valley State Monument parking lot, Rte. 32, Wailuku* ⊕ *www.dlnr.hawaii.gov/dsp/parks/maui/iao-valley-state-monument* 🎫 *$5 parking per car.*

THE SOUTH SHORE AND WEST MAUI
Hoapili Trail (King's Trail)

HIKING/WALKING | A challenging hike through eye-popping scenery in southwestern Maui is this 5½-mile coastal trail beyond the Ahihi-Kinau Natural Area Reserve. Named after a bygone king, it follows the shoreline, threading through the remains of ancient villages. King Hoapili created an islandwide road, and this wide path of stacked lava rocks is a marvel to look at and walk on. (It's not the easiest surface for the ankles and feet, so wear sturdy shoes.) This is brutal territory with little shade and no facilities, and extra water is a must. To get here, follow Makena Road to La Perouse Bay. The trail can be a challenge to find—walk south along the ocean through the *kiawe* trees, where you'll encounter numerous wild goats (don't worry—they're gentle), and past a scenic little bay. The trail begins just around the corner to the left. *Difficult.* ✉ *Trailhead: La Perouse Bay, Makena Rd., Makena.*

Kapalua Resort

HIKING/WALKING | The resort offers free access to miles of hiking trails as a self-guided experience. Trail information and maps are available at the Kapalua Village Center. The Village Walking Trails offer a network of exercise opportunities on former golf cart paths, including the 3.6-mile Lake Loop, which features sweeping views and a secluded lake populated with quacking ducks. The Coastal Trail provides views of the ocean and wildlife as it crosses the golden sand dunes of Oneloa Bay and past Ironwood Beach and the Ritz-Carlton, Kapalua, to its terminus at D.T. Fleming Beach Park. Sightings of green sea turtles, dolphins, and humpback whales (in season) are likely, along with nesting seabirds called *uaua kani*. Guided 1½ mile hikes on the coastal trail that include tide pool exploration are available for $99 through the Jean-Michel Cousteau Ambassadors of the Environment program at the Ritz-Carlton, Kapalua. ✉ *2000 Village Rd., corner of Office Rd., Kapalua* ☎ *808/665–4386 Kapalua Village Center concierge, 808/665-7292 Jean-Michel Cousteau Ambassadors of the Environment* ⊕ *www.kapalua.com.*

GOING WITH A GUIDE
★ Friends of Haleakala National Park

HIKING/WALKING | This nonprofit offers overnight trips into the volcanic crater. The purpose of your trip, the service work itself, isn't too much—mostly native planting, removing invasive plants, and light cabin maintenance. But participants are asked to check the website to learn more about the trip and certify readiness for service work. A knowledgeable guide accompanies each trip, taking you to places you'd otherwise miss and teaching you about the native flora and fauna. ☎ 808/876–1673 ⊕ www.fhnp.org.

★ Hike Maui

HIKING/WALKING | Started in 1983, the area's oldest hiking company remains extremely well regarded for waterfall, rain-forest, and crater hikes led by enthusiastic, highly trained guides who weave botany, geology, ethnobotany, culture, and history into the outdoor experience. Prices run $95–$259 for excursions lasting 3–11 hours (discounts for booking online). Hike Maui supplies day packs, rain gear, mosquito repellent, first-aid supplies, bottled water, snacks, lunch for the longer trips, and transportation to and from the site. Hotel transfers are available for most hikes (extra fee may apply). ⊠ Kahului ☎ 808/879–5270, 866/324–6284 ⊕ www.hikemaui.com.

Sierra Club

HIKING/WALKING | One great avenue into the island's untrammeled wilderness is Maui's chapter of the Sierra Club. Join one of the club's hikes into pristine forests, along ancient coastal paths, to historic sites, and to Haleakala Crater. Some outings require volunteer service, but most are just for fun. Bring your own food and water, rain gear, sunscreen, sturdy shoes, and a suggested donation of $5 for hikers over age 14 ($3 for Sierra Club members). This is a true bargain. ⊕ www.mauisierraclub.org.

Horseback Riding

GOING WITH A GUIDE
Mendes Ranch

HORSEBACK RIDING | Family-owned and run, Mendes operates out of the beautiful ranch land of Kahakuloa on the windward slopes of the West Maui Mountains. Morning and afternoon trail rides lasting 1½ hours ($110) are available. Cowboys take you cantering up rolling pastures into the lush rain forest, and then you'll descend all the way down to the ocean for a photo op with a dramatic backdrop. Don't expect a Hawaiian cultural experience here—it's all about the horses and the ride. ⊠ 3530 Kahekili Hwy., Wailuku ☎ 808/244–7320 for office, 800/871–5222 for reservations ⊕ www.mendesranch.com.

Kayaking

Kayaking is a fantastic and eco-friendly way to experience Maui's coast up close. Floating aboard a "plastic Popsicle stick" is easier than you might think, and allows you to cruise out to vibrant, living coral reefs and waters where dolphins and even whales roam. Kayaking can be a leisurely paddle or a challenge of heroic proportions, depending on your ability, the location, and the weather.
■TIP→ Although you can rent kayaks independently, we recommend hiring a guide.

An apparently calm surface can hide extremely strong ocean currents. Most guides are naturalists who will steer you away from surging surf, lead you to pristine reefs, and point out camouflaged fish, like the stalking hawkfish. Not having to schlep your gear on top of your rental car is a bonus. A half-day tour runs around $75.

If you decide to strike out on your own, tour companies will rent kayaks for the day with paddles, life vests, and roof racks, and many will meet you near your chosen location. Ask for a map of good entries and plan to avoid paddling back to shore against the wind (schedule extra time for the return trip regardless). Read weather conditions, bring binoculars, and take a careful look from the bay before heading in. For beginners, get there early in the day before the trade wind kicks in, and try sticking close to the shore. When you're ready to snorkel, secure your belongings in a dry pack on board and drag your kayak by its bowline behind you. (This isn't as hard as it sounds.)

BEST SPOTS

Makena Landing is an excellent starting point for a South Shore adventure. Enter from the paved parking lot or the small sandy beach a little south. The shoreline is lined with million-dollar mansions. The bay itself is virtually empty, but the right edge is flanked with brilliant coral heads and juvenile turtles. If you round the point on the right, you come across Five Caves, a system of enticing underwater arches. In the morning you may see dolphins, and the arches are havens for lobsters, eels, and spectacularly hued butterfly fish.

In West Maui, past the steep cliffs on the Honoapiilani Highway, there's a long stretch of inviting coastline that includes **Ukumehame Beach.** This is a good spot for beginners; entry is easy, and there's much to see in every direction. Pay attention if trade winds pick up from the late morning onward; paddling against them can be challenging. If you want to snorkel, the best visibility is farther out at Olowalu Beach. Watch for sharp kiawe thorns buried in the sand on the way into the water. Water shoes are recommended.

EQUIPMENT AND TOURS
Kelii's Kayak Tours
KAYAKING | One of the highest-rated kayak outfitters on the island, Kelii's offers kayaking trips and combo adventures where you can also surf, snorkel, or hike to a waterfall. Leading groups of up to eight

people, the guides show what makes each reef unique. Trips are available on the island's north, south, and west shores. ✉ *1993 S. Kihei Rd., Suite 12, Kihei* ☎ *808/874–7652,* ⊕ *www.keliiskayak.com.*

★ South Pacific Kayaks
KAYAKING | These guys pioneered recreational kayaking on Maui, so they know their stuff. Guides are friendly, informative, and eager to help you get the most out of your experience; we're talking true, fun-loving, kayak geeks who will maneuver away from crowds when exploring prime snorkel spots. South Pacific stands out as adventurous *and* environmentally responsible, plus their gear and equipment are well maintained. They offer a variety of trips leaving from both West Maui and South Shore locations. ✉ *95 Halekuai St., Kihei* ☎ *808/875–4848,* ⊕ *www.southpacifickayaks.com* 🛶 *From $74.*

Parasailing

Parasailing is an easy exhilarating way to earn your wings: just strap on a harness attached to a parachute, and a powerboat pulls you up and over the ocean from a launching dock or a boat's platform. ■TIP→ **Parasailing is limited to West Maui, and "thrill craft"—including parasails—are prohibited in Maui waters during humpback-whale calving season, December 15–May 15.**

LESSONS AND TOURS
West Maui Parasail
HANG GLIDING/PARAGLIDING/PARASAILING | Soar at 800 feet above the ocean for a bird's-eye view of Lahaina, or be daring at 1,200 feet for smoother rides and even better views. The captain will be glad to let you experience a "toe dip" or "freefall" if you request it. Hour-long trips departing from Lahaina Harbor and Kaanapali Beach include 8- to 10-minute flights and run from $90 for the 800-foot ride to $100 for the 1,200-foot ride.

Observers pay $45 each. ■TIP→ No para-sailing during whale season. ✉ Lahaina Harbor, Slip 15, Lahaina ☎ 808/661–4060 ⊕ www.westmauiparasail.com.

Rafting

The high-speed, inflatable rafts you find on Maui are nothing like the raft that Huck Finn used to drift down the Mississippi. While passengers grip straps, these rafts fly, skimming and bouncing across the sea. Because they're so maneuverable, they go where the big boats can't—secret coves, sea caves, and remote beaches. Two-hour trips run around $50, half-day trips upward of $100. ■TIP→ Although safe, these trips are not for the faint of heart. If you have back or neck problems or are pregnant, you should reconsider this activity.

TOURS
Blue Water Rafting
BOATING | One of the few ways to get to the stunning Kanaio Coast (the roadless southern coastline beyond Ahihi-Kinau), this rafting tour begins conveniently at the Kihei Boat Ramp on the South Shore. Dolphins, turtles, and other marine life are the highlight of this adventure, along with majestic sea caves, lava arches, and views of Haleakala. The Molokini stop is usually timed between the bigger catamarans, so you can enjoy the crater without the usual massive crowd. If conditions permit, you'll be able to snorkel the back wall, which has much more marine life than the inside. ✉ Kihei Boat Ramp, S. Kihei Rd., Kihei ☎ 808/879–7238 ⊕ www.bluewaterrafting.com ⌸ From $60.

Ocean Riders
BOATING | Start the day with a spectacular view of the sun rising above the West Maui Mountains, then cross the Auau Channel to Lanai's Kaiolohia (commonly referred to as Shipwreck Beach). After a short swim at a secluded beach, this tour circles Lanai, allowing you to view the island's 70 miles of remote coast. The "back side" of Lanai is one of Hawaii's unsung marvels, and you can expect to stop at three protected coves for snorkeling. You might chance upon sea turtles, monk seals, and a friendly reef shark, as well as rare varieties of angelfish and butterfly fish. Guides are knowledgeable and slow down long enough for you to marvel at sacred burial caves and interesting rock formations. Sit toward the back bench if you are sensitive to motion sickness. Tours include snorkel gear, a fruit breakfast, and a satisfying deli lunch. ✉ Mala Wharf, Front St., Lahaina ☎ 808/661–3586 ⊕ www.mauioceanriders.com ⌸ From $149.

★ Redline Rafting
WATER SPORTS | This company's raft tours begin with a trip to Molokini Crater for some snorkeling. If weather permits, the raft explores the crater's back wall, too. There's a quick stop at La Perouse Bay to spot dolphins, and then it's off to Makena for more underwater fun and a deli lunch. The rafts provide great seating, comfort, and shade. Whale-watching excursions are $49, and snorkel trips are $135. ✉ Kihei Boat Ramp, 2800 S. Kihei Rd., Kihei ☎ 808/201–7450 ⊕ www.redlinerafting.com.

Sailing

With the islands of Molokai, Lanai, Kahoolawe, and Molokini a stone's throw away, Maui waters offer visually arresting backdrops for sailing adventures. Conditions can be fickle, so some operations throw in snorkeling or whale-watching, and others offer sunset cruises. Winds are consistent in summer but variable in winter, and afternoons are generally windier throughout the year. Prices range from around $40 for two-hour trips to $80 for half-day excursions. ■TIP→ You won't be sheltered from the elements on the trim racing boats, so be sure to bring a hat that won't blow away, a light jacket, sunglasses, and sunscreen.

BOATS AND CHARTERS
Paragon Sailing Charters

SAILING | If you want to snorkel and sail, this is your boat. Many snorkel cruises claim to sail but actually motor most of the way—Paragon is an exception. Both Paragon vessels (one catamaran in Lahaina, the other in Maalaea) are shipshape, and crews are accommodating and friendly. Its mooring in Molokini Crater is particularly good, and tours will often stay after the masses have left. The Lanai trip includes a picnic lunch at Manele Bay, snorkeling, and a quick afternoon blue-water swim. Extras on the trips to Lanai include mai tais, sodas, dessert, and champagne. Hot and cold appetizers come with the sunset sail, which departs daily from Lahaina Harbor. Sunset sail starts at $85, snorkel at $125. ✉ *Maalaea Harbor, Maalaea* ☎ *808/244–2087,* ⊕ *www.sailmaui.com.*

★ Trilogy Excursions

SAILING | With more than four decades of experience and some good karma from their reef-cleaning campaigns, Trilogy has a great reputation in the community. It's one of only two companies that sail, rather than motor, to Molokini Crater. A two-hour sail starts at $75. The sunset trip includes appetizers, beer, wine, champagne, margaritas, and mai tais. Tours depart from Lahaina Harbor; Maalaea Harbor; and, in West Maui, in front of the Kaanapali Beach Hotel. ✉ *Lahaina Harbor, 675 Wharf St., Lahaina* ☎ *808/874–5649, 888/225–6284* ⊕ *www. sailtrilogy.com.*

Scuba Diving

Maui has been rated one of the top 10 dive spots in the United States. It's common to see huge sea turtles, eagle rays, and small reef sharks, not to mention many varieties of angelfish, parrotfish, eels, and octopuses. Most of the species are unique to this area, making it unlike other popular dive destinations. In addition, the terrain itself is different from other dive spots. Here you can find ancient and intricate lava flows full of nooks where marine life hide and breed. Although the water tends to be a bit rougher—not to mention colder—divers are given a great thrill during humpback-whale season, when you can actually hear whales singing underwater. Be sure to check conditions before you head out.

Some of the finest diving spots in all of Hawaii lie along the Valley Isle's western and southwestern shores. Dives are best in the morning, when visibility can hold a steady 100 feet. If you're a certified diver, you can rent gear at any Maui dive shop simply by showing your PADI or NAUI card. Unless you're familiar with the area, however, it's probably best to hook up with a dive shop for an underwater tour. Tours include tanks and weights and start around $130. Wet suits and buoyancy compensators are rented separately, for an additional $15–$30. Shops also offer introductory dives ($100–$160) for those who aren't certified. ■TIP➜ **Before signing on with any outfitter, it's a good idea to ask a few pointed questions about your guide's experience, the weather outlook, and the condition of the equipment.**

BEST SPOTS

Honolua Bay, a marine preserve in West Maui, is alive with many varieties of coral and tame tropical fish, including large ulua, kahala, barracuda, and manta rays. With depths of 20–50 feet, this is a popular summer dive spot, good for all levels. ■TIP➜ **High surf often prohibits winter dives.**

On the South Shore, one of the most popular dive spots is **Makena Landing** (also called Nahuna Point, Five Graves, or Five Caves). You can revel in underwater delights—caves, ledges, coral heads, and an outer reef home to a large green–sea turtle colony called Turtle Town.

Snorkelers can see adorable green sea turtles around Maui.

■TIP→ Entry is rocky lava, so be careful where you step. This area is for more experienced divers.

Three miles offshore from Wailea on the South Shore, **Molokini Crater** is world-renowned for its deep, crystal clear, fish-filled waters. A crescent-shape islet formed by the eroding top of a volcano, the crater is a marine preserve ranging 10–80 feet deep. The numerous tame fish and brilliant coral within the crater make it a popular introductory dive site. On calm days, the back side of Molokini Crater (called Back Wall) can be a dramatic sight for advanced divers, with visibility of up to 150 feet. The enormous drop-off into the Alalakeiki Channel offers awesome seascapes, black coral, and chance sightings of larger fish and sharks.

Some of the southern coast's best diving is at **Ahihi Bay,** part of the Ahihi-Kinau Natural Area Reserve. The area frequently closes due to shark sightings; call ahead before visiting. The area is best known for its "Fishbowl," a small cove right beside the road, next to a hexagonal house. Here you can find excellent underwater scenery, with many types of fish and coral. **■TIP→ Be careful of the rocky-bottom entry (wear reef shoes if you have them).** The Fishbowl can get crowded, especially in high season. If you want to steer clear of the crowds, look for a second entry ½ mile farther down the road—a gravel parking lot at the surf spot called Dumps. Entry into the bay here is trickier, as the coastline is all lava.

Formed from the last lava flow two centuries ago, **La Perouse Bay** brings you the best variety of fish—more than any other site. The lava rock provides a protective habitat, and all four types of Hawaii's angelfish can be found here. To dive the spot called Pinnacles, enter anywhere along the shore, just past the private entrance to the beach. Wear your reef shoes, as entry is sharp. To the right, you'll be in the Ahihi-Kinau Natural Area Reserve; to the left, you're outside. Look for the white sandy bottom with massive coral heads. Pinnacles is for experienced divers only.

EQUIPMENT, LESSONS, AND TOURS

Extended Horizons

DIVING/SNORKELING | This eco-friendly dive boat stands apart by being the only commercial vessel on Maui to run on 100% locally made biodiesel. Its popular Lanai charter has divers swimming through dramatic archways and lava structures, while other trips venture along West Maui. Shore and night dives are also available. Tours are run by enthusiastic and professional guides who are keen at not only identifying underwater creatures, but also interpreting their behavior. ✉ *Mala Boat Ramp, Lahaina* ☎ *808/667–0611* ⊕ *www.extendedhorizons.com* 💲 *From $129.*

Maui Dive Shop

SCUBA DIVING | Maui Dive Shop offers scuba charters, diving instruction, and equipment rental at its Kihei location. Excursions go to Molokini, Shipwreck Beach, and Cathedrals on Lanai. Intro dives are done offshore. Night dives, scooter dives, and customized trips are available, as are full SSI and PADI certificate programs. ✉ *1455 S. Kihei Rd., Kihei* ☎ *808/879–3388, 800/542–3483* ⊕ *www. mauidiveshop.com.*

★ Mike Severns Diving

SCUBA DIVING | This popular and reliable company has been around for more than four decades and takes groups of up to 12 certified divers, with two dive masters, to both popular and off-the-beaten-path dive sites. Marine biologists or naturalists offer informative briefings, and boat trips leave from Kihei Boat Ramp and go wherever conditions are best: the Molokini Marine Life Conservation District, Molokini Crater's Back Wall, Makena, or beyond La Perouse Bay. ✉ *Kihei Boat Ramp, S. Kihei Rd., Kihei* ☎ *808/879–6596* ⊕ *www.mikeseverns-diving.com* 💲 *Dives from $139 (BYO gear) or $159 (gear included); charters from $1,908.*

Snorkeling

There are two ways to approach snorkeling—by land or by sea. At around 7 am daily, a parade of boats heads out to Lanai or to Molokini Crater, that ancient cone of volcanic cinder off the coast of Wailea. Boat trips offer some advantages—deeper water, seasonal whale-watching, crew assistance, lunch, and gear. But much of Maui's best snorkeling is found just steps from the road. Nearly the entire leeward coastline from Kapalua south to Ahihi-Kinau offers opportunities to ogle fish and turtles. If you're patient and sharp-eyed, you may glimpse eels, octopuses, lobsters, eagle rays, and even a rare shark or monk seal. ■TIP➔ **Visibility is best in the morning, before the trade winds pick up.**

BEST SPOTS

Snorkel sites here are listed from north to south, starting at the northwest corner of the island.

Just north of Kapalua, the **Honolua Bay Marine Life Conservation District** has a superb reef for snorkeling. ■TIP➔ **Bring a fish key with you, as you're sure to see many species of triggerfish, filefish, and wrasses.** The coral formations on the right side of the bay are particularly dramatic, with pink, aqua, and orange varieties. On a lucky day, you might even be snorkeling with a pod of dolphins nearby. Take care entering the water; there's no beach, and the rocks and concrete ramp can be slippery. The northeast corner of this windward bay periodically gets hammered by big waves in winter. Avoid the bay then, as well as after heavy rains.

Minutes south of Honolua Bay, dependable **Kapalua Bay** beckons. As beautiful above the water as it is below, Kapalua is exceptionally calm, even when other spots get testy. Needle and butterfly fish dart just past the sandy beach, which is why it's sometimes crowded. ■TIP➔ **The** sand can be particularly hot here—watch your toes!

Black Rock, in front of the Sheraton Maui Resort & Spa at the northernmost tip of **Kaanapali Beach,** is great for snorkelers of any skill level. The entry couldn't be easier—dump your towel on the sand and in you go. Beginners can stick close to shore and still see lots of action. Advanced snorkelers can swim to the tip of Black Rock to see larger fish and eagle rays. One of the underwater residents here is a turtle whose hefty size earned him the name Volkswagen. He sits very still, so you have to look closely. Equipment can be rented on-site. Parking, in a small lot adjoining the hotel, is the only hassle.

Along Honoapiilani Highway there are several favorite snorkel sites, including the area just out from the cemetery at **Hanakaoo Beach Park.** At depths of 5 and 10 feet, you can see a variety of corals, especially as you head south toward Wahikuli Wayside Park.

South of Olowalu General Store, the shallow coral reef at **Olowalu** is good for a quick underwater tour, but if you're willing to venture out about 50 yards, you'll have easy access to an expansive coral reef with abundant turtles and fish—no boat required. Swim offshore toward the pole sticking out of the reef. Except for during a south swell, this area is calm, and good for families with small children. Boats sometimes stop here (they refer to this site as Coral Gardens) when conditions in Honolua Bay are not ideal. During low tide, be extra cautious when hovering above the razor-sharp coral.

The snorkeling is excellent down the coastline between Kihei and Makena on the South Shore. ■TIP➜ **The best spots are along the rocky fringes of Wailea's beaches—Mokapu, Ulua, Wailea, and Polo—off Wailea Alanui Drive.** Find one of the public parking lots sandwiched between Wailea's luxury resorts (look for a blue sign reading "Shoreline Access" with an arrow pointing to the lot), and enjoy the sandy entries, the calm waters with relatively good visibility, and the variety of fish. Of the four beaches, Ulua has the best reef. You may listen to snapping shrimp and parrotfish nibbling on coral.

In South Maui, the end of the paved section of Makena Road is where you'll find the **Ahihi-Kinau Natural Area Reserve.** Despite its lava-scorched landscape, the area is very popular, especially with sharks, which leads to frequent closures. Call ahead to make sure it's open. It's difficult terrain and the area does sometimes get crowded, but it's worth a visit to experience outstanding treasures, such as the sheltered cove known as the Fish Bowl. ■TIP➜ **Be sure to bring water: this is a hot and unforgiving wilderness.**

Between Maui and neighboring Kahoolawe you'll find the world-famous **Molokini Crater.** Its crescent-shape rim acts as a protective cove from the wind and provides a sanctuary for birds and colorful marine life. Most snorkeling tour operators offer a Molokini trip, and it's not unusual for your charter to share this dormant volcano with five or six other boats. The journey to this sunken crater takes more than 90 minutes from Lahaina, an hour from Maalaea, and less than half an hour from the South Shore.

EQUIPMENT

Most hotels and vacation rentals offer free use of snorkel gear. Beachside stands fronting the major resort areas rent equipment by the hour or day. If you're squeamish about using someone else's gear (or need a prescription lens), pick up your own at any discount shop. Costco and Longs Drugs have better prices than ABC stores; dive shops have superior equipment.

Continued on page 298

SNORKELING IN HAWAII

Molokini Crater

The waters surrounding the Hawaiian Islands are filled with life—from giant manta rays cruising off the Big Island's Kona Coast to humpback whales giving birth in the waters around Maui. Dip your head beneath the surface to experience a spectacularly colorful world: pairs of milletseed butterflyfish dart back and forth, redlipped parrotfish snack on coral algae, and spotted eagle rays flap past like silent spaceships. Sea turtles bask at the surface while tiny wrasses give them the equivalent of a shave and a haircut. The water quality is typically outstanding; many sites afford 30-foot-plus visibility. On snorkel cruises, you can often stare from the boat rail right down to the bottom.

Certainly few destinations are as accommodating to every level of snorkeler as Hawaii. Beginners can tromp in from sandy beaches while more advanced divers descend to shipwrecks, reefs, craters, and sea arches just offshore. Because of Hawaii's extreme isolation, the island chain has fewer fish species than Fiji or the Caribbean—but many of the fish that live here exist nowhere else. The Hawaiian waters are home to the highest percentage of endemic fish in the world.

The key to enjoying the underwater world is slowing down. Look carefully. Listen. You might hear the strange crackling sound of shrimp tunneling through coral, or you may hear whales singing to one another during winter. A shy octopus may drift along the ocean's floor beneath you. If you're hooked, pick up a waterproof fishkey from Long's Drugs. You can brag later that you've looked the Hawaiian turkeyfish in the eye.

Picasso Triggerfish	Milletseed Butterflyfish*	Yellow Tang
Moorish Idol	Hawaiian Whitespotted Toby*	Saddleback Wrasse*
Redlip Parrotfish	Hawaiian Turkeyfish*	Zebra Moray Eel
Stocky Hawkfish	Green Sea Turtle (Honu)	Spotted Eagle Ray

*endemic to Hawaii

POLYNESIA'S FIRST CELESTIAL NAVIGATORS: HONU

Honu is the Hawaiian name for two native sea turtles, the hawksbill and the green sea turtle. Little is known about these dinosaur-age marine reptiles, though snorkelers regularly see them foraging for *limu* (seaweed) and the occasional jellyfish in Hawaiian waters. Most female honu nest in the uninhabited Northwestern Hawaiian Islands, but a few sociable ladies nest on Maui and Big Island beaches. Scientists suspect that they navigate the seas via magnetism—sensing the earth's poles. Amazingly, they will journey up to 800 miles to nest—it's believed that they return to their own birth sites. After about 60 days of incubation, nestlings emerge from the sand at night and find their way back to the sea by the light of the stars.

SNORKELING

Many of Hawaii's reefs are accessible from shore.

The basics: Sure, you can take a deep breath, hold your nose, squint your eyes, and stick your face in the water in an attempt to view submerged habitats . . . but why not protect your eyes, retain your ability to breathe, and keep your hands free to paddle about when exploring underwater? That's what snorkeling is all about.

Equipment needed: A mask, snorkel (the tube attached to the mask), and fins. In deeper waters (any depth over your head), life jackets are advised.

Steps to success: If you've never snorkeled before, it's natural to feel a bit awkward at first, so don't sweat it. Breathing through a mask and tube, and wearing a pair of fins take getting used to. Like any activity, you build confidence and comfort through practice.

If you're new to snorkeling, begin by submerging your face in shallow water or a swimming pool and breathing calmly through the snorkel while gazing through the mask.

Next you need to learn how to clear water out of your mask and snorkel, an essential skill since splashes can send water into tube openings and masks can leak. Some snorkels have built-in drainage valves, but if a tube clogs, you can force water up and out by exhaling through your mouth. Clearing a mask is similar: lift your head from water while pulling forward on mask to drain. Some masks have built-in purge valves, but those without can be cleared underwater by pressing the top to the forehead and blowing out your nose (charming, isn't it?), allowing air to bubble into the mask, pushing water out the bottom. If it sounds hard, it really isn't. Just try it a few times and you'll soon feel like a pro.

Now your goal is to get friendly with fins—you want them to be snug but not too tight—and learn how to propel yourself with them. Fins won't help you float, but they will give you a leg up, so to speak, on smoothly moving through the water or treading water (even when upright) with less effort.

Flutter stroking is the most efficient underwater kick, and the farther your foot bends forward the more leg power you'll be able to transfer to the water and the farther you'll travel with each stroke. Flutter kicking movements involve alternately separating the legs and then drawing them back together. When your legs separate, the leg surface encounters drag from the water, slowing you down. When your legs are drawn back together, they produce a force pushing you forward. If your kick creates more forward force than it causes drag, you'll move ahead.

Submerge your fins to avoid fatigue rather than having them flailing above the water when you kick, and keep your arms at your side to reduce drag. You are in the water—stretched out, face down, and snorkeling happily away—but that doesn't mean you can't hold your breath and go deeper in the water for a closer look at some fish or whatever catches your attention. Just remember that when you do this, your snorkel will be submerged, too, so you won't be breathing (you'll be holding your breath). You can dive head-first, but going feet-first is easier and less scary for most folks, taking less momentum. Before full immersion, take several long, deep breaths to clear carbon dioxide from your lungs.

If your legs tire, flip onto your back and tread water with inverted fin motions while resting. If your mask fogs, wash condensation from lens and clear water from mask.

TIPS FOR SAFE SNORKELING

■ Snorkel with a buddy and stay together.

■ Plan your entry and exit points prior to getting in the water.

■ Swim into the current on entering and then ride the current back to your exit point.

■ Carry your flippers into the water and then put them on, as it's difficult to walk in them, and rocks may be slippery.

■ Make sure your mask fits properly and is not too loose.

■ Pop your head above the water periodically to ensure you aren't drifting too far out, or too close to rocks.

■ Think of the water as someone else's home—don't take anything that doesn't belong to you, or leave any trash behind.

■ Don't touch any sea creatures; they may sting.

■ Wear a T-shirt over your swimsuit to help protect you from being fried by the sun.

■ When in doubt, don't go without a snorkeling professional; try a guided tour.

■ Don't go in if the ocean seems rough.

Green sea turtle (Honu)

■TIP→ Don't shy away from asking for instructions; a snug fit makes all the difference in the world. A mask fits if it sticks to your face when you inhale deeply through your nose. Fins should cover your entire foot (unlike diving fins, which strap around your heel).

Maui Dive Shop

SNORKELING | You can rent pro gear (including optical masks, body boards, and wet suits) at their Kihei location. Pump these guys for weather info before heading out; they'll know better than last night's news forecaster, and they'll give you the real deal on conditions. ⊠ *1455 S. Kihei Rd., Kihei* ☎ *808/879–3388* ⊕ *www. mauidiveshop.com.*

Snorkel Bob's

SNORKELING | Here you can rent fins, masks, and snorkels, and Snorkel Bob's will throw in a carrying bag, map, and snorkel tips for as little as $9 per week. Avoid the circle masks and go for the split-level ($30 per week) or premium snorkel package ($38 per week); it's worth the extra money. There are seven Snorkel Bob's locations on Maui, including Kihei, Wailea, Lahaina, Kahana, and Napili. ⊠ *5425 C Lower Honoapiilani Hwy., Napili* ☎ *808/669–9603* ⊕ *www. snorkelbob.com.*

SNORKELING TOURS

The same boats that offer whale-watching, sailing, and diving also offer snorkeling excursions. Trips usually include visits to two locales, lunch, gear, instruction, and possible whale or dolphin sightings. Some captains troll for fish along the way.

Molokini Crater, a crescent about 3 miles offshore from Wailea, is the most popular snorkel cruise destination. You can spend half a day floating above the fish-filled crater for about $80. Some say it's not as good as it's made out to be, and that it's too crowded, but others consider it to be one of the best spots in Hawaii. Visibility is generally outstanding, and the fish are incredibly tame. Your second stop will be somewhere along the leeward coast, either Turtle Town near Makena or Coral Gardens toward Lahaina. ■TIP→ On blustery mornings, there's a good chance the waters will be too rough to moor in Molokini Crater, and you'll end up snorkeling somewhere off the shore, where you could have driven for free.

If you've tried snorkeling and are tentatively thinking about scuba, you may want to try "snuba," a cross between the two. With snuba, you dive 20 feet below the surface, only you're attached to an air hose from the boat. Many boats now offer snuba (for an extra fee of $45–$65) as well as snorkeling.

Snorkel cruises vary—some serve mai tais and steaks whereas others offer beer and cold cuts. You might prefer a large ferryboat to a smaller sailboat, or vice versa. Be sure you know where to go to board your vessel; getting lost in the harbor at 6 am is a lousy start. ■TIP→ Bring sunscreen, an underwater camera (they're double the price on board), a towel, and a cover-up for the windy return trip. Even tropical waters get chilly after hours of swimming, so consider wearing a rash guard. Wet suits can usually be rented for a fee.

Alii Nui Maui

SNORKELING | On this 65-foot luxury catamaran, you can come as you are (with a bathing suit, of course); towels, sunblock, and all your gear are provided. Because the owners also operate Maui Dive Shop, snorkel and dive equipment are top-of-the-line. Wet-suit tops are available to use for sun protection or to keep extra warm in the water. The boat, which holds a maximum of 60 people, is nicely appointed. A morning snorkel sail (there's a diving option, too) heads to Turtle Town or Molokini Crater and includes a continental breakfast, lunch, and post-snorkel alcoholic drinks. The three-, five-, or six-hour snorkel trip offers transportation from your hotel. Videography and huka (similar to snuba) are available for a fee. ✉ *Maalaea Harbor, Slip 56, Maalaea* ☎ *800/542–3483, 808/875–0333* ⊕ *www. aliinuimaui.com* ✉ *From $109.*

Maui Classic Charters

SNORKELING | FAMILY | Hop aboard the *Four Winds II*, a 55-foot, glass-bottom catamaran (great fun for kids), for one of the most dependable snorkel trips around. You'll spend more time than other charter boats at Molokini Crater and enjoy turtle-watching on the way home. The trip includes optional snuba ($62 extra), continental breakfast, barbecue lunch, beer, wine, and soda. With its reasonable price, the trip can be popular and crowded. The crew works hard to keep everyone happy, but if the trip is fully booked, you will be cruising with more than 100 new friends. For a more intimate experience, opt for the *Maui Magic*, Maalaea's fastest PowerCat, which holds fewer people than some of the larger vessels. ✉ *Maalaea Harbor, Slips 55 and 80, Maalaea* ☎ *808/879–8188, 800/736–5740* ⊕ *www.mauiclassiccharters.com* ✉ *From $52.*

Teralani Sailing Charters

SNORKELING | Choose between a standard snorkel trip with a deli lunch or a top-of-the-line excursion that's an hour longer and includes two snorkel sites and a barbecue-style lunch. The company's cats could hold well over 100 people, but 49 is the maximum per trip. The boats are kept in pristine condition. Freshwater showers are available, as is an open bar after the second snorkel stop. A friendly crew provides all your gear, a flotation device, and a quick course in snorkeling. During whale season, only the premier trip is available. Boarding is right off Kaanapali Beach fronting Whalers Village. ✉ *Kaanapali Beach, Kaanapali* ☎ *808/661–7245* ⊕ *www.teralani.net* ✉ *From $122.*

★ **Trilogy Excursions**

SNORKELING | Many people consider a trip with Trilogy Excursions to be a highlight of their vacation. Maui's longest-running operation has comprehensive offerings, with six beautiful 54- to 65-foot sailing vessels at three departure sites. All excursions are staffed by energetic crews who will keep you well fed and entertained with local stories and corny jokes. A full-day catamaran cruise to Lanai includes a continental breakfast and barbecue lunch, a guided tour of the island, a "Snorkeling 101" class, and time to snorkel in the waters of Lanai's Hulopoe Marine Preserve (Trilogy Excursions has exclusive commercial access). The company also offers Molokini Crater and Olowalu snorkel cruises that are top-notch. Tours depart from Lahaina Harbor; Maalaea Harbor; and, in West Maui, in front of the Kaanapali Beach Hotel. ✉ *Kaanapali* ☎ *808/874–5649, 888/225–6284* ⊕ *www.sailtrilogy.com* ✉ *From $125.*

Spas

WEST MAUI

The Ritz-Carlton Spa, Kapalua

SPA/BEAUTY | At this gorgeous 17,500-square-foot spa, you enter a blissful maze where floor-to-ceiling riverbed stones lead to serene treatment rooms, couples' *hales* (cabanas), and a rain forest–like grotto with a Jacuzzi, dry cedar sauna, and eucalyptus steam rooms. Hang out in the coed waiting area, where sliding-glass doors open to a whirlpool overlooking a taro-patch garden. Exfoliate any rough spots with an alaea salt (Hawaiian red sea salt) scrub, then wash off in a private outdoor shower garden before indulging in a lomilomi massage. High-end beauty treatments include advanced oxygen technology to tighten and nourish mature skin. The boutique has a highly coveted collection of organic, local, and high-end beauty products, fitness wear, and Maui-made Nina Kuna jewelry and natural skin-care lines. ✉ *The Ritz-Carlton, Kapalua, 1 Ritz-Carlton Dr., Kapalua* ☎ *808/669–6200, 800/262–8440* ⊕ *www.ritzcarlton.com* ☞ *$190 for 50-min massage, $350 spa packages.*

★ Spa Montage Kapalua Bay

SPA/BEAUTY | This spa's grand entrance opens onto an airy, modern beach house with panoramic island and ocean views. With amenities including a movement studio, fitness center, coed infinity pool, and outdoor hydrotherapy circuits, you can easily spend a day meandering about the spa's expansive layout without feeling cooped up. The spa menu includes therapies that incorporate local ingredients harvested from nearby Mauna Kahalawai (West Maui's mountain) and calming ingredients from the sea. ✉ *1 Bay Dr., Kapalua* ☎ *808/665–8282* ⊕ *www.montagehotels.com/spamontage/kapaluabay* ☞ *$215 for 60-min massage.*

SOUTH SHORE

Awili Spa and Salon, Andaz Maui at Wailea Resort

SPA/BEAUTY | At Awili Spa and Salon's apothecary or blending bar (*awili* means "to mix"), consultants assist in creating your personalized oils made from local ingredients. Set aside an extra hour to fully indulge in the blending bar, or opt for ready-made concoctions. The cool, soothing interior of this spa is an extension of the minimalist, monochromatic style of the Andaz Maui at Wailea Resort. Relaxation lounges are stocked with thoughtful amenities like tea, coconut shortbread cookies, and housemade granola. ✉ *Andaz Maui at Wailea Resort, 3550 Wailea Alanui Dr., Wailea* ☎ *808/573–1234* ⊕ *www.andazmaui.com* ☞ *$190 for 60-min massage.*

Spa & Wellness Center at Four Seasons Resort Maui

SPA/BEAUTY | Thoughtful gestures like fresh flowers beneath the massage table, organic ginger tea in the relaxation room, and your choice of music ease your mind and muscles before the treatment even begins. Shop for sustainable and organic beauty products like ISUN and Oshan Essentials, or book an appointment at the Ajne blending bar to customize a scent according to your body chemistry. For the ultimate indulgence, reserve one of the seaside open-air *hale hau* (traditional thatch-roof houses). Taking wellness to heart, the spa partnered with a clinical nutritionist, Dr. Mark Emerson, who gives a complimentary consultation and then designs a wellness program befitting the guest's health goals. Offerings include noninvasive laser body shaping treatments, indoor or outdoor fitness activities, and a nourishing menu created by the hotel's culinary team. ✉ *Four Seasons Resort Maui at Wailea, 3900 Wailea Alanui Dr., Wailea* ☎ *808/874–8000* ⊕ *www.fourseasons.com/maui* ☞ *$195 for 50-min massage.*

Willow Stream Spa, Fairmont Kea Lani

SPA/BEAUTY | This spa makes meticulous use of Hawaii's natural elements to replenish your Zen. Give a full hour to enjoy the fascinating amenities, two if you plan to work out. At the mud bar, small bowls of volcanic ash eucalyptus clay or white lavender and taro clay can be applied to the body before you head to the steam room. From there, rinse off in a high-tech shower that combines color, sound, and hydrotherapy to mimic different types of Hawaiian rain. A heated stone bench awaits to deepen the relaxation before the treatment. The spa has advanced technology like a state-of-the-art vichy shower which combines chromatherapy and hydrotherapy or LED light and microcurrent electric pulse to tighten the skin. ✉ *4100 Wailea Alanui, Wailea* ☎ *808/875–2229* ⊕ *www.fairmont-kea-lani.com* ☞ *$199 for 60-min Stress Relaxation massage.*

ROAD TO HANA

The Spa at Travaasa Hana

SPA/BEAUTY | A bamboo gate opens into an outdoor sanctuary with a lava-rock basking pool and hot tub. At first glimpse, this spa seems to have been organically grown, not built. Ferns still wet from Hana's frequent downpours nourish the spirit as you rest with a cup of Hawaiian herbal tea, take an invigorating dip in the cold plunge pool, or have a therapist stretch your limbs as you soak in the warm waters of the aquatic therapy pool. Luxurious skin-care treatments feature organic products from Epicuren and Honua Skincare, and body treatments incorporate organic Maui-made Ala Lani Bath and Body products. ⊠ *Travaasa Hana, 5031 Hana Hwy., Hana* ☎ *808/820–1043* ⊕ *www.travaasa.com/hana* ⌕ *$175 for 60-min massage, $500 spa package; prices reflect gratuity.*

Stand-Up Paddling

Also called stand-up paddle surfing or paddleboarding, stand-up paddling is the "comeback kid" of surf sports; you stand on a longboard and paddle out with a canoe oar. While stand-up paddling requires even more balance and coordination than regular surfing, it is still accessible to just about every skill level. Most surf schools now offer stand-up paddle lessons. Advanced paddlers can amp up the adrenaline with a downwind coastal run that spans almost 10 miles from North Shore's Maliko Gulch to Kahului Harbor, sometimes reaching speeds up to 30 mph.

The fun thing about stand-up paddling is that you can enjoy it whether the surf is good or the water is flat. However, as with all water sports, it's important to read the environment and be attentive. Look at the sky, and assess the wind by how fast the clouds are moving. Note where the whitecaps are going, and always point the nose of your board perpendicular to the wave. ■TIP➜ **Because of the size and speed of a longboard, stand-up paddling can be dangerous, so lessons are highly recommended, especially if you intend to surf.**

LESSONS
Stand-Up Paddle Surf School
WATER SPORTS | Maui's first school devoted solely to stand-up paddling was founded by the legendary Maria Souza, the first woman to surf the treacherous waves of Peahi (nicknamed "Jaws") on Maui's North Shore. Although most surf schools offer stand-up paddling, Maria's classes are in a league of their own. They include a proper warm-up with a hula-hoop and balance ball and a cool-down with yoga. A private session is $199. Locations vary depending on conditions. ⊠ *Kihei* ☎ *808/579–9231* ⊕ *www.standuppaddlesurfschool.com.*

Surfing

Maui's coastline has surf for every level of waterman or-woman. Waves on leeward-facing shores (West and South Maui) tend to break in gentle sets all summer long. Surf instructors in Kihei and Lahaina can rent you boards, give you onshore instruction, and then lead you out through the channel, where it's safe to enter the surf. They'll shout encouragement while you paddle like mad for the thrill of standing on water—most will give you a helpful shove. These areas are great for beginners; the only danger is whacking a stranger with your board or stubbing your toe against the reef.

The North Shore is another story. Winter waves pound the windward coast, attracting water champions from every corner of the world. Adrenaline addicts are towed in by Jet Ski to a legendary, deep-sea break called Jaws. Waves here periodically tower upward of 40 feet. The only spot for viewing this phenomenon (which happens just a few times a year) is on private property. So, if you hear the surfers next to you crowing about Jaws "going off," cozy up, and get them to take you with them.

Whatever your skill, there's a board, a break, and even a surf guru to accommodate you. A two-hour lesson is a good intro to surf culture.

You can get the wave report each day by checking page 2 of the *Maui News,* logging on to the Glenn James weather site (⊕ *www.hawaiiweathertoday.com*), or by calling ☎ *808/871–5054* (for the weather forecast) or ☎ *808/877–3611* (for the surf report).

BEST SPOTS

On the South Shore, beginners can hang ten at Kihei's **Cove Park,** a sometimes crowded but reliable 1- to 2-foot break. Boards can easily be rented across the street or in neighboring Kalama Park's parking lot. The only bummer is having to balance the 9-plus-foot board on your head while crossing busy South Kihei Road.

For advanced wave riders, **Hookipa Beach Park** on the North Shore boasts several well-loved breaks, including "Pavilions," "Lanes," "the Point," and "Middles." Surfers have priority until 11 am, when windsurfers move in on the action.

■ TIP→ **Competition is stiff here. If you don't know what you're doing, consider watching.**

Long- or shortboarders in West Maui can paddle out at **Launiupoko State Wayside.** The east end of the park has an easy break, good for beginners.

Also called Thousand Peaks, **Ukumehame** is one of the better beginner spots in West Maui. You'll soon see how the spot got its name—the waves here break again and again in wide and consistent rows, allowing lots of room for beginning and intermediate surfers.

Good surf spots in West Maui include "Grandma's" at **Papalaua Park,** just after the *pali* (cliff), where waves are so easy a grandma could ride 'em; **Puamana Beach Park** for a mellow longboard day; and **Lahaina Harbor,** which offers an excellent inside wave for beginners (called Break-wall), as well as the more advanced outside (a great lift if there's a big south swell).

EQUIPMENT AND LESSONS

Surf camps are becoming increasingly popular, especially with women. One- or two-week camps offer a terrific way to build muscle and self-esteem simultaneously.

Big Kahuna Adventures

SURFING | Rent soft-top longboards here for $25 for two hours or $35 for the day. Weekly rates are $125. This company also offers surf lessons starting at $69 per person and rents kayaks, stand-up paddleboards, plus snorkel and beach gear. Look for the Big Kahuna truck at Kalama Park; lessons take place at Cove Park. ⊠ *1794 S. Kihei Road, #9, Kihei* ☎ *808/875–6395* ⊕ *www.bigkahunaadventures.com.*

Goofy Foot

SURFING | Surfing "goofy foot" means putting your right foot forward. They might be goofy, but we like the right-footed gurus here. This shop is just plain cool and only steps away from "Breakwall," a great beginner's spot in Lahaina. A two-hour class with five or fewer students is $85, and you're guaranteed to be standing by the end or it's free. A private two-hour lesson is $170. ⊠ *505 Front St., Suite 123, Lahaina* ☎ *808/244–9283* ⊕ *www.goofyfootsurfschool.com.*

★ Hi-Tech Surf Sports

SURFING | Hi-Tech has some of the best boards, advice, and attitude around. It rents even its best surfboards—choose from longboards, shortboards, and hybrids—starting at $25 per day. There's another shop in Paia, and a third location in Kihei across the street from Cove Park, a popular surf spot for beginners. ⊠ *425 Koloa St., Kahului* ☎ *808/877–2111* ⊕ *www.surfmaui.com.*

★ Maui Surf Clinics

SURFING | FAMILY | Instructors here will get even the shakiest novice riding with the school's beginner program. A two-hour group lesson (up to five students) is $85. Private lessons with the patient and meticulous instructors are $170 for two hours. The company provides boards, rash guards, and water shoes, all in impeccable condition—and it's tops in the customer-service department. ✉ *505 Front St., Suite 201, Lahaina* ☎ *808/244- 7873* ⊕ *www.mauisurfclinics.com.*

Maui Surfer Girls

SURFING | Maui Surfer Girls started in 2001 with surf camps for teen girls, but quickly branched out to offer surfing lessons year-round. Located away from the crowds, Maui Surfer Girls specializes in private lessons and small groups, and their ratio of four students per instructor is the smallest in the industry. The highly popular summer camps are now open to women of all ages. ✉ *Lahaina* ☎ *808/670- 3886* ⊕ *www.mauisurfergirls.com.*

Whale-Watching

From December into May whale-watching becomes one of the most popular activities on Maui. During the season *all* outfitters offer whale-watching in addition to their regular activities, and most do an excellent job. Boats leave the wharves at Lahaina and Maalaea in search of humpbacks, allowing you to enjoy the awe-inspiring size of these creatures in closer proximity. From November through May, the Pacific Whale Foundation sponsors the Maui Whale Festival, a variety of whale-related events for locals and visitors; check the calendar at ⊕ *www. mauiwhalefestival.org.*

As it's almost impossible *not* to see whales in winter on Maui, you'll want to prioritize: is adventure or comfort your aim? If you desire close encounters with the giants of the deep, pick a smaller boat that promises sightings. Those who think "green" usually prefer the smaller, quieter vessels that produce the least amount of negative impact to the whales' natural environment. For those wanting to sip mai tais as whales cruise by, stick with a sunset cruise ($40 and up) on a boat with an open bar and *pupu* (Hawaiian tapas). ■**TIP→ Afternoon trips are generally rougher because the wind picks up, but some say this is when the most surface action occurs.**

Every captain aims to please during whale season, getting as close as legally possible (100 yards). Crew members know when a whale is about to dive (after several waves of its heart-shape tail) but can rarely predict breaches (when the whale hurls itself up and almost entirely out of the water). Prime viewing space (on the upper and lower decks, around the railings) is limited, so boats can feel crowded even when half full. If you don't want to squeeze in beside strangers, opt for a smaller boat with fewer bookings. Don't forget to bring sunscreen, sunglasses, a light long-sleeve cover-up, and a hat you can secure. Winter weather is less predictable and at times can be extreme, especially as the wind picks up. Arrive early to find parking.

BEST SPOTS

The northern end of **Keawakapu Beach** on the South Shore seems to be a whale magnet. Situate yourself on the sand or at the nearby restaurant and watch mamas and calves. From mid-December to mid-April, the Pacific Whale Foundation has naturalists at Ulua Beach and at the scenic viewpoint at **Papawai Point Lookout.** Like the commuting traffic, whales can be spotted along the pali of West Maui's Honoapiilani Highway all day long. Make sure to park safely before craning your neck out to see them.

Humpback whale calves are plentiful in winter; this one is breaching off West Maui.

BOATS AND CHARTERS
Maui Adventure Cruises

WHALE-WATCHING | Whale-watching from this company's raft puts you right above the water surface and on the same level as the whales. You'll forgo the cocktail in your hand but you won't have to deal with crowds, even if the vessel is at max capacity with 36 people. The whales can get up close if they like, and when they do it's absolutely spectacular. These rafts can move with greater speed than a catamaran, so you don't spend much time motoring between whales or pods. Refreshments are included. Prices are $49 for adults and $39 for kids 5–12 years old (children younger than 5 are not admitted). ⊠ *Lahaina Harbor, Slip 11, Lahaina* ☎ *808/661–5550* ⊕ *www. mauiadventurecruises.com.*

Pacific Whale Foundation

WHALE-WATCHING | FAMILY | With a fleet of 10 boats, this nonprofit organization pioneered whale-watching back in 1979. The crew (including a certified marine biologist) offers insights into whale behavior and suggests ways for you to help save marine life worldwide. One of the best things about these trips is the underwater hydrophone that allows you to listen to the whales sing. Trips meet at the organization's store, which sells whale-theme and local souvenirs. You'll share the boat with about 100 people in stadium-style seating. If you prefer a smaller crowd, book their eco-friendly raft cruises instead. ⊠ *Maui Harbor Shops, 300 Maalaea Rd., Suite 211, Maalaea* ☎ *808/650–7056* ⊕ *www. pacificwhale.org.*

Windsurfing

Windsurfing, invented in the 1950s, found its true home at Hookipa on Maui's North Shore in 1980. Seemingly overnight, windsurfing pros from around the world flooded the area. Equipment evolved, amazing film footage was captured, and a new sport was born.

The Humpback's Winter Home

The humpback whales' attraction to Maui is legendary, and seeing them December–May is a highlight for many visitors. More than half the Pacific's humpback population winters in Hawaii, especially in the waters around the Valley Isle, where mothers can be seen just a few hundred feet offshore, training their young calves in the fine points of whale etiquette. Watching from shore, it's easy to catch sight of whales spouting, or even breaching—when they leap almost entirely out of the sea, slapping back onto the water with a huge splash.

At one time, there were thousands of the huge mammals, but a history of overhunting and marine pollution reduced the world population to about 1,500. In 1966, humpbacks were put on the endangered-species list. Hunting or harassing whales is illegal in the waters of most nations, and in the United States boats and airplanes are restricted from getting too close. The jury is still out, however, on the effects of military sonar testing on the marine mammals.

Marine biologists believe the humpbacks (much like humans) keep returning to Hawaii because of its warmth. Having fattened themselves in subarctic waters all summer, the whales migrate south in the winter to breed, and a rebounding population of thousands cruise Maui waters. Winter is calving time, and the young whales probably couldn't survive in the frigid Alaskan waters. No one has ever seen a whale give birth here, but experts know that calving is their main winter activity because the 1- and 2-ton youngsters suddenly appear while the whales are in residence.

The first sighting of a humpback whale spout each season is exciting for locals on Maui. A collective sigh of relief can be heard: "Ah, they've returned." In the not-so-far distance, flukes and flippers can be seen rising above the ocean's surface. It's hard not to anthropomorphize the tail waving; it looks like such an amiable gesture. Each fluke is uniquely patterned, like a human's fingerprint, and is used to identify the giants as they travel halfway around the globe and back.

4

Maui ACTIVITIES AND TOURS

If you're new to the action, you can get lessons from the experts islandwide. For a beginner, the best thing about windsurfing is that (unlike surfing) you don't have to paddle. Instead, you have to hold on like heck to a flapping sail as it whisks you into the wind. Needless to say, you're going to need a little coordination and balance to pull this off. Instructors start you out on a beach at Kanaha, where the big boys go. Lessons range from two-hour introductory classes to five-day advanced "flight school."

BEST SPOTS

After **Hookipa Bay** was discovered by windsurfers four decades ago, this windy North Shore beach 10 miles east of Kahului gained an international reputation. The spot is blessed with optimal wave-sailing wind and sea conditions, and it offers the ultimate aerial experience.

In summer, the windsurfing crowd heads to **Kalepolepo Beach** on the South Shore. Trade winds build in strength, and by afternoon a swarm of dragonfly-sails can be seen skimming the whitecaps, with Mauna Kahalawai (often called the West Maui Mountains) as a backdrop.

A great site for speed, **Kanaha Beach Park** is dedicated to beginners in the morning hours, before the waves and wind really get roaring. After 11 am, the professionals choose from their quiver of sails the size and shape best suited for the day's demands. This beach tends to have smaller waves and forceful winds—sometimes sending sailors flying at 40 knots. If you aren't ready to go pro, this is a great place for a picnic while you watch from the beach. To get here, use any of the three entrances on Amala Place, which runs along the shore just north of Kahului Airport.

EQUIPMENT AND LESSONS
Action Sports Maui

WINDSURFING | The quirky, friendly professionals here will meet you at Kanaha Beach Park on the North Shore, outfit you with your sail and board, and guide you through your first "jibe," or turn. They promise your learning time for windsurfing will be cut in half. Lessons begin at 9 am every day except Sunday and cost $125 for a 2½-hour class. Three- and five-day courses cost $350 and $595, respectively. ⊠ *96 Amala Pl., Kahului* ☎ *808/283–7913* ⊕ *www.actionsportsmaui.com.*

★ Hawaiian Sailboarding Techniques

WINDSURFING | Considered one of Maui's finest windsurfing schools, Hawaiian Sailboarding Techniques brings you quality instruction by skilled sailors. Founded by Alan Cadiz, an accomplished World Cup Pro, the school sets high standards for a safe, quality windsurfing experience. Intro classes start at $125 for 2½ hours, gear included. The company is inside Hi-Tech Surf Sports, which offers excellent equipment rentals. ⊠ *Hi-Tech Surf Sports, 425 Koloa St., Kahului* ☎ *808/871–5423* ⊕ *www.hstwindsurfing.com.*

Zipline Tours

★ Flyin' Hawaiian Zipline

ZIP LINING | These guys have the longest line in the state (a staggering 3,600 feet), as well as the most unique course layout. You build confidence on the first line, then board a four-wheel-drive vehicle that takes you 1,500 feet above the town of Waikapu to seven more lines that carry you over 11 ridges and nine valleys. The total distance covered is more than 2½ miles, and the views are astonishing. The price ($185) includes water and snacks. You must be able to hike over steep, sometimes slippery terrain while carrying a 10-pound metal trolley. ⊠ *Waikapu* ☎ *808/463–5786* ⊕ *www.flyinhawaiianzipline.com.*

★ Piiholo Ranch Zipline

ZIP LINING | Four- to seven-line zipline courses are on this gorgeous 900-acre family ranch, with prices starting at $140. Access to the fifth and longest line is via a four-wheel-drive vehicle to the top of Piiholo Hill, where you are treated to stunning bicoastal views. Guides do a good job of weaving Hawaiian culture into the adventure. You must be able to climb three steep suspension bridges while hefting a 12-pound trolley over your shoulder. For those who fear heights, cheaper rates are available to follow along on foot. For the ultimate adventure, try the Zipline/Waterfall Hike ($238), for which the company has partnered with Hike Maui, the oldest land company in Hawaii. Piiholo offers significant discounts for online bookings. ⊠ *Piiholo Rd., Makawao* ☎ *800/374–7050* ⊕ *www.piiholozipline.com.*

Chapter 5

THE BIG ISLAND OF HAWAII

Updated by
Karen Anderson and
Kristina Anderson

👁 Sights	🍴 Restaurants	🧳 Hotels	👜 Shopping	🍸 Nightlife
★★★★★	★★★☆☆	★★★☆☆	★★★☆☆	★★☆☆☆

WELCOME TO THE BIG ISLAND OF HAWAII

TOP REASONS TO GO

★ **Hawaii Volcanoes National Park:** Explore newly made land and beaches, lava tubes, steam vents, and giant craters.

★ **Waipio Valley:** Experience a real-life secret garden, the remote spot known as the Valley of the Kings.

★ **Kealakekua Bay:** Watch spinner dolphins near the Captain Cook Monument, then go snorkeling over the fabulous coral reefs.

★ **The heavens:** Stargaze through high-tech telescopes on snow-topped Maunakea.

★ **Hidden beaches:** Discover one of the Kohala Coast's lesser-known gems.

1 Kailua-Kona and the Kona Coast. This seaside town houses a busy waterfront. South Kona is the place to taste samples of world-famous Kona Coffee.

2 The Kohala Coast and Waimea. The sparkling coast is home to long, white-sand beaches. In Waimea, ranches sprawl across the cool, upland hills of the area, known as *paniolo* (cowboy) country.

3 The Hamakua Coast. This area is home to waterfalls, ancient hidden valleys, rain forests, and the stunning Waipio Valley.

4 Hilo. Known as the City of Rainbows for all its rain, Hilo is what many consider the "real" Hawaii.

5 Hawaii Volcanoes National Park, Puna, and Kau. Don't miss Halemaumau Crater. The Puna district has the quirky, hippie town of Pahoa and the island's most recent lava flows. Round the southernmost part of the island to Kau for two of the Big Island's most unusual beaches.

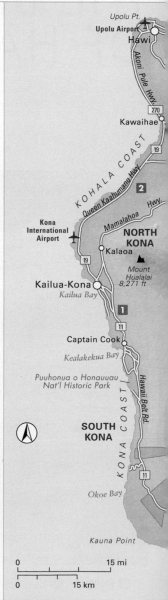

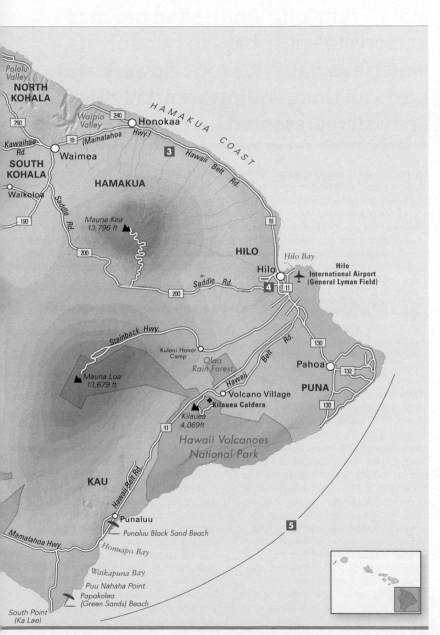

Nicknamed "The Big Island," Hawaii Island is a microcosm of Hawaii the state. From long white-sand beaches and crystal-clear bays to rain forests, waterfalls, valleys, exotic flowers, and birds, all things quintessentially Hawaii are well represented here.

An assortment of happy surprises also distinguishes the Big Island from the rest of Hawaii—an active volcano (Kilauea) oozing red lava and creating new earth every day, the clearest place in the world to view stars in the night sky (Maunakea), and some seriously good coffee from the famous Kona district, as well as from neighboring Kau.

Home to eight of the world's 13 sub-climate zones, this is the land of fire (thanks to active Kilauea volcano) and ice (compliments of not-so-active Maunakea, topped with snow and expensive telescopes). At just under a million years old, Hawaii is the youngest of the main Hawaiian Islands. Three of its five volcanoes are considered active: Mauna Loa, Hualalai, and Kilauea. The Southeast Rift Zone of Kilauea has been spewing lava regularly since January 3, 1983; another eruption began at Kilauea's summit caldera in March 2008, the first since 1982. Back in 1984, Mauna Loa's eruptions crept almost to Hilo, and it could fire up again any minute—or not for years. Hualalai last erupted in 1801, and geologists say it will definitely do so again within 100 years. Maunakea is currently considered dormant but may very well erupt again. Kohala, which last erupted some 120,000 years ago, is inactive, but on volatile Hawaii Island, you can never be sure.

AGRICULTURE

In the 19th- and mid-20th centuries, sugar was the main agricultural and economic staple of all the Islands, but especially the Big Island. The drive along the Hamakua Coast, from Hilo or Waimea, illustrates diverse agricultural developments on the island. Sugarcane stalks have been replaced by orchards of macadamia-nut trees, eucalyptus, and specialty crops from lettuce to strawberries. Macadamia-nut orchards on the Big Island supply 90% of the state's yield, while coffee continues to be big business, dominating the mountains above Kealakekua Bay. Orchids keep farmers from Honokaa to Pahoa afloat, and small organic farms produce meat, fruits, vegetables, and even goat cheese for high-end resort restaurants.

HISTORY

Hawaii's history is deeply rooted in its namesake island, which was home to the first Polynesian settlements and has the state's best-preserved *heiau* (temples) and *puuhonua* (refuges). Kamehameha, the greatest king in Hawaiian history and the man credited with uniting the Islands, was born here, raised in Waipio Valley, and died peacefully in Kailua-Kona. The other man who most affected Hawaiian history, Captain James Cook, spent the bulk of his time in the Islands here, docked in Kealakekua Bay. (He landed first on Kauai, but had little contact with the residents there.) Thus it was here that Western influence was first felt, and from here that it spread to the rest of Hawaii.

Planning

Getting Here and Around

AIR

Flying time to the Big Island is about 10 hours from New York; eight hours from Chicago; five hours from Los Angeles, Seattle, San Francisco, Oakland, Portland, and San Diego; and 15 hours from London, not including layovers. Some of the major airline carriers serving Hawaii fly direct to the Big Island, allowing you to bypass connecting flights out of Honolulu and Maui. If you're a more spontaneous traveler, island-hopping flights depart daily every 90 minutes or so.

Serving Kona are Air Canada, Alaska Airlines, American Airlines, Delta Airlines, Hawaiian Airlines, Japan Airlines, Mokulele, Southwest, United Airlines, Virgin Atlantic, and Westjet. Hawaiian Airlines, Mokulele, Southwest, and United fly into Hilo. Airlines schedule flights seasonally, meaning the number of daily flights—and sometimes the carriers themselves—vary according to demand.

Should you wish to visit neighboring islands, Hawaiian Airlines, Mokulele, and Southwest offer regular service. Prices for interisland flights have increased quite a bit in recent years, while flight schedule availability has been reduced. Mokulele also serves Waimea. Planning ahead is your best bet.

Big Island Air, in addition to offering air tours of the Big Island, offers charter service between all the Islands via a Cessna Caravan. Nine passengers can ride comfortably, and the charter has plenty of room for luggage.

Those flying to the Big Island regularly land at one of two fields. Ellison Onizuka Kona International Airport at Keahole, on the west side, serves Kailua-Kona, Keauhou, the Kohala Coast, North Kohala, Waimea, and points south. There are Visitor Information Program (VIP) booths by all baggage-claim areas to assist travelers. Additionally, the airport offers news and lei stands, Laniakea by Centerplate (a café), and a small gift and sundries shop. A modernization project launched in 2017 (and still ongoing at this writing) aims to join the two terminals (now separate) so that baggage and passenger screening can be streamlined and retail options enhanced.

Waimea-Kohala Airport, called Kamuela Airport by residents, is used primarily for private flights between islands but has recently welcomed one commercial carrier with a single route.

CAR

It's essential to rent a car when visiting the Big Island. As the name suggests, it's a very big island, and it takes a while to get from one destination to another.

Fortunately, when you circle the island by car, you are treated to miles and miles of wondrous vistas of every possible description. In addition to using standard compass directions such as east and west, Hawaii residents often refer to places as being either *mauka* (toward the mountains) or *makai* (toward the ocean).

It's difficult to get lost along the main roads of the Big Island. Although their names may challenge the visitor's tongue, most roads are well marked; in rural areas look for mile marker numbers. Free publications containing basic road maps are given out at car rental agencies, but if you are doing a lot of driving, invest about $4 in the standard Big Island map available at local retailers. GPS might be unreliable in remote areas.

⚠ **Driving the roads on the Big Island can be dangerous, as there's no margin for error**

Great Itineraries

Yes, the Big Island is big, and yes, there's a lot to see. If you're short on time, consider flying into one airport and out from the other. That will give you the opportunity to see both sides of the island without ever having to backtrack. If you'd prefer to spend your last few days near the beach, go from east to west; if hiking through rain forests and showering in waterfalls sounds like a better way to wrap up the trip, move from west to east. Or, head straight for Hawaii Volcanoes National Park and briefly visit Hilo before traveling the Hamakua Coast route and making your new base in Kailua-Kona.

Hike Volcanoes

Devote a full day to exploring Hawaii Volcanoes National Park. Head out on the Kilauea Iki trail—a moderately challenging, 4-mile loop near Thurston Lava Tube—by late morning, then visit the lava tube itself. Grab lunch at a nearby restaurant in Volcano Village, or plan ahead and pack your own picnic. Then drive to the Steaming Bluffs and walk to an overlook with views of Halemaumau Crater and Kilauea Caldera.

Black and Green Sand

Check out some of the unusual beaches you'll find only on the Big Island. Start with a hike into Green Sands Beach near South Point. When you've had your fill, hop back in the car and head south about half an hour to Punaluu Black Sand Beach, the favorite nesting place of endangered Hawaiian turtles.

Majestic Waterfalls and Valley of the Kings

Take a day to enjoy the splendors of the Hamakua Coast—almost any gorge you see on the road may indicate a waterfall waiting to surprise you. For a sure bet, head to beautiful Waipio Valley. Book a horseback, hiking, or four-wheel-drive tour, or walk on in yourself (just keep in mind that it's an arduous hike back up—a 25% grade for a little over a mile).

Once in the valley, take your first right to get to the black-sand beach. Pause to reflect here—the ancient Hawaiians believed this was where souls crossed over to the afterlife. Regardless of your beliefs, there is something unmistakably mystical about this place.

Waterfalls abound in the valley, depending on the amount of recent rainfall. Hike left until you reach the end of the beach; the spot is gorgeous and worthy of a million photos.

Sun and Stars

Spend the day lounging on a Kohala Coast beach (Hapuna, Kaunaoa—also known as Maunakea—or Kua Bay), then catch a one-of-a-kind island sunset from Maunakea's summit. For the safest, most comfortable experience, book a turnkey summit tour. Or stop in at the Onizuka Center for International Astronomy, a visitor center located at about 9,000 feet. If you have a 4WD (check with your rental car company for permission), you can join their free summit tour at 1 pm on weekends and return to the center to use the free telescopes for evening stargazing. Helpful U.H. Hilo astronomy students will guide you.

to avoid a head-on collision. Distracted drivers are all too common. Most roads and main highways are two lanes with no shoulders; if there is a shoulder to access, it might be riddled with rocks, debris, and potholes. Speeding and illegal passing are frequent occurrences along winding, remote roads. In addition, most roads are not well lit at night. Fatalities can happen at a moment's notice, whether on the main highway from the airport to the resorts, the Saddle Road, the upper road from Waimea to Hawi, or on the Hawaii Belt Road that wraps around the island. During Ironman week, cyclists pose additional potential hazards on all roads in West Hawaii. Use extreme caution when driving on the Big Island, and of course, do not drive after drinking.

The rerouted and repaved Saddle Road, now known as the Daniel K. Inouye Highway, is a nice shortcut across the middle of the island. This is especially convenient if you are staying on the west side of the island and wish to visit the east side (or vice versa). Hazardous conditions such as fog and speeding are common.

Before you embark on your day trip, it's a good idea to know how long it will take you to get to your destination. Some areas, like downtown Kailua-Kona and Waimea, can become congested at certain times of day. For those traveling to South Kona, a bypass road between Keauhou and Kealakekua alleviates congestion considerably during rush hour. In general, you can expect the following average driving times.

Beaches

Don't believe anyone who tells you that the Big Island lacks beaches. It's just one of the myths about Hawaii's largest island that has no basis in fact. It's not so much that the Big Island has fewer beaches than the other islands, just that there's more island, so getting to the beaches can be slightly less convenient.

Island Driving Times

Kailua-Kona to Kealakekua Bay	14 miles/25 min
Kailua-Kona to Kohala Coast	32 miles/40 min
Kailua-Kona to Waimea	40 miles/1 hr
Kailua-Kona to Hamakua Coast	53 miles/1 hr, 40 min
Kailua-Kona to Hilo	75 miles/2½ hrs
Kohala Coast to Waimea	16 miles/20 min
Kohala Coast to Hamakua Coast	29 miles/55 min
Hilo to Volcano	30 miles/40 min

That said, there are plenty of those perfect white-sand stretches you think of when you hear "Hawaii," and the added bonus of black- and green-sand beaches, thanks to the relative young age of the island and its active volcanoes. New beaches appear and disappear regularly, created and destroyed by volcanic activity. In 1989, a black-sand beach, Kamoamoa, formed when molten lava shattered as it hit cold ocean waters; it was enjoyed for a few years before it was closed by new lava flows in 1992. It's part of the ongoing process of the volcano's creation-and-change dynamic.

Hawaii's largest coral reef systems lie off the Kohala Coast. Waves have battered them over millennia to create abundant white-sand beaches on the northwest side of the island. Black-, mixed-, and green-sand beaches lie in the southern regions and along the coast nearest the volcano. On the eastern side of the island, beaches tend to be of the rocky-coast–surging-surf variety, but there are still a few worth visiting, and this is where the Hawaii shoreline is at its most picturesque.

Hotels

Even among locals, there is an ongoing debate about which side of the Big Island is "better," so don't worry if you're having a tough time deciding where to stay. Our recommendation? Do both. Each side offers a different range of accommodations, restaurants, and activities.

Some locals like to say that the east is "more Hawaiian," but we argue that King Kamehameha himself made Kailua-Kona his final home during his sunset years. Another reason to try a bit of both: your budget. You can justify splurging on a stay at a Kohala Coast resort for a few nights because you'll spend the rest of your time paying one-third that rate at a cozy cottage in Volcano or a vacation rental on Alii Drive. And although food at the resorts is very expensive, you don't have to eat every meal there. Condos and vacation homes can be ideal for a family trip or for a group of friends looking to save money and live like *kamaainas* (local residents) for a week or two. Many of the homes also have private pools and hot tubs, lanai, ocean views, and more—you can go as budget or as high-end as you like.

If you choose a bed-and-breakfast, inn, or an out-of-the-way hotel, explain your expectations fully to the proprietor and ask plenty of questions before booking. Be clear about your travel and location needs. Some places require stays of two or three days.

Hotel reviews have been shortened. For full information, visit Fodors.com.

CONDOS AND VACATION RENTALS

Renting a condo or vacation house gives you much more living space than the average hotel, plus the chance to meet more people (neighbors are usually friendly), lower nightly rates, and the option of cooking or barbecuing rather than eating out. When booking, remember that most properties are individually owned, with rates and amenities that differ substantially depending on the place. Some properties are handled by rental agents or agencies, while many are handled directly through the owner. The following is a list of our favorite booking agencies for various lodging types throughout the island. Be sure to call and ask questions before booking.

CONTACTS Big Island Villas. ☎ 808/936–3870, 808/443–6991 ⊕ www.bigislandvillas.com. **Hawaiian Beach Rentals.** ☎ 844/261–0464 ⊕ www.hawaiianbeachrentals.com. **Hawaii Vacation Rentals.** ☎ 808/882–7000 ⊕ www.vacationbigisland.com. **Keauhou Property Management.** ☎ 808/326–7053 ⊕ www.konacondo.net. **Kolea Vacations.** ☎ 888/565–3244 ⊕ www.koleavacations.com. **Kona Coast Vacations.** ☎ 808/329–2140 ⊕ www.konacoastvacations.com. **Kona Hawaii Vacation Rentals.** ☎ 808/326-4137 ⊕ www.konahawaii.com. **Kona Vacation Rentals.** ☎ 886/456-4252 ⊕ www.konarentals.com. **Knutson and Associates.** ☎ 808/329–1010 ⊕ www.konahawaiirentals.com. **South Kohala Management.** ☎ 808/883–8500 ⊕ www.southkohala.com.

Nightlife

If you're the sort of person who doesn't come alive until after dark, you might be a little lonely on the Big Island. Blame it on the sleepy plantation heritage. People did their cane raising in the morning, thus very limited late-night fun. Still, there are a few lively bars on the island, a handful of great local playhouses, half a dozen or so movie houses (including those that play foreign and independent films), and plenty of musical entertainment to keep you happy.

Where to Stay on the Big Island

	Local Vibe	Pros	Cons
Kailua-Kona	A bustling little village; Alii Drive brims with hotels and condo complexes.	Plenty to do, day and night; everything within easy walking distance of most hotels; many grocery stores in the area.	More traffic than anywhere else on the island; limited number of beaches; traffic noise on Alii Drive.
South Kona and Kau	Popular Kealakekua Bay has plenty of B&Bs and vacation rentals, with a few more farther south in Kau.	Kealakekua Bay is popular for kayaking and snorkeling and has some good restaurants; Captain Cook and Kainaliu have coffee farms.	Vog (volcano fog) from Kilauea often settles here; few sandy beaches; Kau is quite remote.
The Kohala Coast	Home to most of the Big Island's major resorts. Blue sunny skies prevail here, along with the island's best beaches.	Beautiful beaches; high-end shopping and dining; lots of activities for adults and children.	Pricey; long driving distances to Volcano, Hilo, and Kailua-Kona.
Waimea	Though it seems a world away, Waimea is only about a 15- to 20-minute drive from the Kohala Coast.	Beautiful scenery, *paniolo* (cowboy) culture; home to some exceptional local restaurants.	Can be cool and rainy year-round; nearest beaches are a 20-minute drive away.
The Hamakua Coast	A nice spot for those seeking peace, tranquility, and an alternative to the tropical-beach-vacation experience.	Close to Waipio Valley; foodie and farm tours in the area; good spot for honeymooners.	Beaches are an hour's drive away; convenience shopping is limited.
Hilo	Hilo is the wet and lush, eastern side of the Big Island. It's less touristy than the west side and retains much local charm.	Proximity to waterfalls, rain-forest hikes, museums, and botanical gardens; good B&B options.	The best white-sand beaches are on the other side of the island; noise from coqui frogs can be distracting at night.
Puna	Puna doesn't attract as many visitors as other regions, so you'll find good deals on rentals and B&Bs here.	A few black-sand beaches; off the beaten path and fairly wild; hot ponds; lava has flowed into the sea here in years past.	Few dining and entertainment options; no resorts or resort amenities; noisy coqui frogs at night.
Hawaii Volcanoes National Park and Vicinity	There are any number of enchanting B&B inns in fern-shrouded Volcano Village, near the park.	Good location for nighttime lava-watching; great for hiking, nature tours, and bike riding; close to Hilo and Puna.	Just a few dining options; not much nightlife; can be cold and wet.

Performing Arts

Many resorts have bars and late-night activities and events, and they keep pools and gyms open late so there's something to do after dinner.

And let's not forget the luau. These fantastic dance and musical performances are combined with some of the best local food on the island and are plenty of fun for the whole family.

Restaurants

Hawaii is a melting pot of cultures, and nowhere is this more apparent than in its cuisine. From luau and "plate lunches" to sushi and steak, there's no shortage of interesting flavors and presentations. Between star chefs and myriad local farms, the Big Island restaurant scene is becoming a destination for foodies. Food writers are praising the chefs of the Big Island for their ability to turn the local bounty into inventive blends inspired by the island's cultural heritage. This is a welcome shift from years past, in which many foods were imported and uninspired, and it's a happy trend for visitors, who get to taste juicy, flavorful Waimea tomatoes, handmade Hamakua goat cheese, locally raised beef, or even island-grown wine. Whether you're looking for a quick snack or a multicourse meal, you can find the best that the island has to offer at farmers' markets, restaurants, and cafés.

Resorts along the Kohala Coast have long invested in culinary programs offering memorable dining experiences that include inventive entrées, spot-on wine pairings, and customized chef's table options. But great food on the Big Island doesn't begin and end with the resorts. A handful of chefs have retired from the fast-paced hotel world and opened their own small bistros in upcountry Waimea or other places off the beaten track. Unique and wonderful restaurants have cropped up in Hawi, Kainaliu, and Holualoa, and on the east side of the island in Hilo.

What It Costs			
$	$$	$$$	$$$$
RESTAURANTS			
Under $17	$17–$26	$27–$35	Over $35
HOTELS			
Under $180	$180–$260	$261–$340	Over $340

Shopping

Residents like to complain that there isn't a lot of great shopping on the Big Island, but unless you're searching for winter coats, you can find plenty to deplete your pocketbook.

Dozens of shops in Kailua-Kona offer a range of souvenirs from far-flung corners of the globe and plenty of local coffee and foodstuffs to take home to everyone you left behind. Housewares and artworks made from local materials (lauhala, coconut, koa, and milo wood) fill the shelves of small boutiques and galleries throughout the island. Upscale shops in the resorts along the Kohala Coast carry high-end clothing and accessories, as do a few boutiques scattered around the island. Galleries and gift shops, many showcasing the work of local artists, fill historical buildings in Waimea, Kainaliu, Holualoa, and Hawi. Hotel shops generally offer the most attractive and original resort wear, but, as with everything else at resorts, the prices run higher than elsewhere on the island.

Spas

High prices are entirely too common at the island's resort spas, but a handful of unique experiences are worth every penny. Beyond the resorts, the Big Island is also home to independent massage therapists and day spas that offer similar treatments for lower prices, albeit usually in a slightly less luxurious atmosphere. In addition to the obvious relaxation benefits of any spa trip, the Big Island's spas have done a fantastic job incorporating local traditions and ingredients into their menus. Massage artists work with coconut or *kukui* (candlenut) oil, hot-stone massages are conducted with volcanic stones, and ancient healing techniques such as *lomilomi*—a massage technique with firm, constant movement—are staples at every island spa.

Tours

Kona Historical Society

SELF-GUIDED | The society, based in Kealakekua, sells a 24-page *Historic Kailua Village Map* booklet ($15) with a map and more than 40 historical photos. You can take a self-guided walking tour to learn more about the village's fascinating past. Order the booklet online before you travel so you have the guidebook in hand for your tour. ⊠ *81-6551 Mamalahoa Hwy., Kealakekua* ☎ *808/323–3222* ⊕ *www.konahistorical.org.*

Visitor Information

CONTACTS Island of Hawaii Visitors Bureau. ☎ *800/648–2441* ⊕ *www.gohawaii.com/islands/hawaii-big-island.*

Kailua-Kona and the Kona Coast

Kailua-Kona is about 7 miles south of the Kona airport.

More laid-back than the tonier Kohala Coast, the Kona Coast and its largest town, Kailua-Kona, are great if you are looking to get away from the crowds along the island's more famous white-sand beaches.

Except for the rare deluge, the sun shines year-round. Mornings offer cooler weather, smaller crowds, and more birds singing in the banyan trees; you'll see tourists and locals out running on Alii Drive, the town's main drag, by about 5 am every day. Afternoons sometimes bring clouds and light rain, but evenings often clear up so you can enjoy cool drinks, brilliant sunsets, gentle trade winds, and lazy hours spent gazing out over the ocean. Though there are better beaches north of town on the Kohala Coast, Kailua-Kona is home to a few gems, including a fantastic snorkeling beach (Kahaluu) and a tranquil bay perfect for kids (Kamakahonu Beach, in front of the Courtyard King Kamehameha's Kona Beach Hotel).

The south Kona Coast is quiet and relatively rural. Much of the farmland is in leasehold status, which explains why this part of the Big Island has remained rather untouched by development. Tour one of the coffee farms to find out what the big deal is about Kona coffee, and enjoy a free sample while you're at it. A 20-minute drive off the highway from Captain Cook leads to beautiful Kealakekua Bay, where Captain James Cook arrived in 1778, dying here not long after. Hawaiian spinner dolphins frolic in the bay, now a Marine Life Conservation District, nestled alongside high green cliffs that jut dramatically out to sea. Snorkeling is superb here, so you may want to bring your gear and spend an hour or so exploring the coral reefs. The bay is normally extremely calm. ■**TIP→ One of the best ways to spend a morning is to kayak in the pristine waters of Kealakekua Bay, paddling over to see the spot where Cook died. Guided tours are your best bet, and you'll likely see plenty of dolphins along the way.**

North of Kona International Airport, along Mamalahoa Highway, brightly colored bougainvilleas stand out in relief against

Kailua-Kona is the capital of Big Island.

miles of jet-black lava fields stretching from the mountain to the sea. Sometimes visitors liken it to landing on the moon when they first see it. True, the dry barren landscape may not be what you'd expect to find on a tropical island, but it's a good reminder of the island's evolving volcanic nature.

Kailua-Kona

Kailua-Kona is about 7 miles south of the Kona airport.

The largest town on the Kona Coast, lively Kailua-Kona offers plenty to accommodate the needs of locals and visitors, but it also has some signficant historic sites. Scattered among the shops, restaurants, and condo complexes of Alii Drive are Ahuena Heiau, a temple complex restored by King Kamehameha the Great and the spot where he spent his last days (he died here in 1819); the last royal palace in the United States (Hulihee Palace); and a battleground dotted with the graves of ancient Hawaiians who

fought for their way of life and lost. It was also here in Kailua-Kona that Kamehameha's successor, King Liholiho, broke with the ancient *kapu* (roughly translated as "forbidden," it was the name for the strict code of conduct that islanders were compelled to follow) system by publicly sitting and eating with women. The following year, on April 4, 1820, the first Christian missionaries came ashore here, changing life in the Islands forever.

Most first-time visitors to the island are startled by touching down on the seemingly endless black lava fields that make up the airport area and immediate surroundings. However, just a 10-minute drive on Queen Kaahumanu Highway heading south takes you into the seaside town of Kailua-Kona and nearby retail centers. To get to town, take a right onto Palani Road, and a left on Kuakini, and find one of the free lots along Kuakini Highway. You can park and walk right to the village and the seawall. You can also get to the restaurant row area by taking Kuakini Highway and turning right into the Coconut Grove Marketplace's vast free lot. From there, you can reach oceanfront establishments such as Bongo Ben's, Humpy's Big Island Alehouse, and Island Lava Java. Alii Drive, the town's main street, runs north and south along the water and is popular for walking, with plenty of shops and restaurants. Sunsets here are spectacular.

⊙ Sights

★ Holualoa

TOWN | Hugging the hillside along the Kona Coast, the artsy village of Holualoa is 3 miles up winding Hualalai Road from Kailua-Kona. Galleries here feature all types of artists—painters, woodworkers, jewelers, gourd makers, and potters—working in their studios in back and selling their wares up front. Look for frequent town-wide events such as art strolls and block parties. Then relax with a cup of coffee in one of the many cafés or stores. Formerly the exclusive domain of coffee plantations, Holualoa still boasts quite a few coffee farms offering free tours and inviting cups of Kona. ⊠ *Holualoa* ⊕ *www.holualoahawaii.com.*

Hula Daddy Kona Coffee

FARM/RANCH | On a walking tour of this working coffee farm (by advance reservation only), visitors can witness the workings of a small plantation, pick and pulp their own coffee beans, watch a roasting demonstration, and have a tasting. The gift shop carries whole beans and logo swag including bags, T-shirts, and mugs. Coffee brewing workshops and one-on-one tours with a master roaster are also offered. ⊠ *74-4944 Mamalahoa Hwy., Holualoa* ☎ *808/327–9744, 888/553–2339* ⊕ *www.huladaddy.com* ⊠ *From $15* ⊙ *Closed weekends.*

★ Hulihee Palace

CASTLE/PALACE | On the National Register of Historic Places, this lovely two-story oceanfront home, surrounded by jewel-green grass and elegant coco palms

and fronted by an elaborate wrought-iron gate, is one of only three royal palaces in America (the other two are in Honolulu). The royal residence was built by Governor John Adams Kuakini in 1838, a year after he completed Mokuaikaua Church. During the 1880s, it served as King David Kalakaua's summer palace.

Built of lava rock and coral lime mortar, it features vintage koa furniture, weaving, European crystal chandeliers, giant four-poster beds, royal portraits, tapa cloth, feather work, and Hawaiian quilts. After the overthrow of the Hawaiian monarchy in 1893, the property fell into disrepair. Set to be torn down for a hotel, it was rescued in 1920 by the Daughters of Hawaii, a nonprofit organization dedicated to preserving the culture and royal heritage of the Islands. The organization oversees and operates the site to this day. ⊠ *75-5718 Alii Dr., Kailua-Kona* ☎ *808/329–1877* ⊕ *www.daughtersofhawaii.org* ⊠ *$8 self-guided tour, $10 guided.*

Kailua Pier

MARINA | Though most fishing boats use Honokohau Harbor in Kailua-Kona, this pier dating from 1918 is still a hub of ocean activity. Outrigger canoe teams practice and race, shuttles transport cruise ship passengers to and from town, and tour boats depart from these docks daily. Along the seawall, children and old-timers cast their lines. For youngsters, a bamboo pole and hook are easy to come by, and plenty of locals are willing to give pointers. September brings the world's largest long-distance canoe race, while in October, 1,700 elite athletes leave from the pier to swim 2.4 miles as part of the famous Ironman World Championship triathlon. ⊠ *Alii Dr., Kailua-Kona* ✛ *Across from Courtyard King Kamehameha's Kona Beach Hotel* ⊠ *Free.*

★ Kamakahonu and Ahuena Heiau

ARCHAEOLOGICAL SITE | In the early 1800s, King Kamehameha the Great built a large

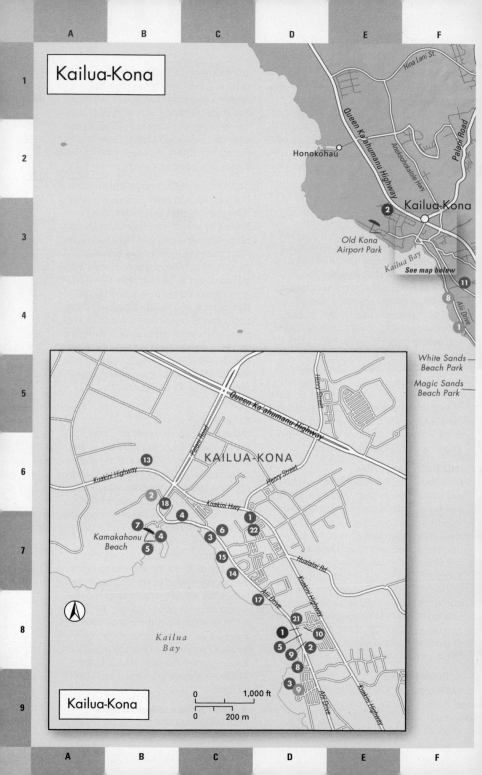

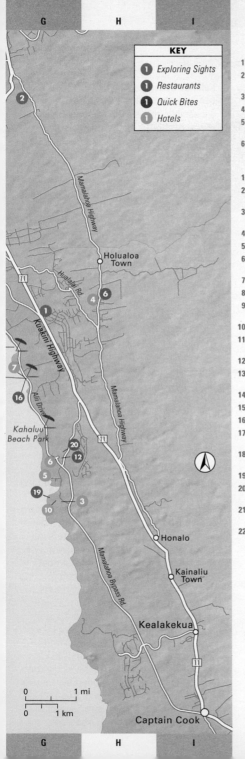

KEY

1 Exploring Sights
1 Restaurants
1 Quick Bites
1 Hotels

Sights ▼

1 Holualoa G4
2 Hula Daddy Kona
   Coffee G1
3 Hulihee Palace........... C7
4 Kailua Pier............... B7
5 Kamakahonu and
   Ahuena Heiau........... B7
6 Mokuaikaua Church..... C7

Restaurants ▼

1 Big Island Grill............ C7
2 Bongo Ben's
   Island Café D8
3 Don the Beachcomber
   at Royal Kona Resort... D9
4 The Fish Hopper C7
5 Foster's Kitchen.......... D8
6 Holuakoa
   Gardens and Cafe H4
7 Honu's on the Beach ... B7
8 Huggo's D8
9 Humpy's Big Island
   Alehouse................. D8
10 Island Lava Java........ D8
11 Jackie Rey's
    Ohana Grill.............. F4
12 Kenichi Pacific.......... G6
13 Kona Brewing Co.
    Pub and Brewery....... B6
14 Kona Inn Restaurant ... C7
15 Kona Taeng On Thai..... C7
16 Magics Beach Grill..... G5
17 Mi's Waterfront
    Bistro.................... D8
18 Quinn's
    Almost by the Sea B6
19 Rays on the Bay G6
20 Sam Choy's
    Kai Lanai................ G6
21 Thai Rin
    Restaurant and Bar..... D8
22 TK Noodle House........ C7

Quick Bites ▼

1 Kanaka Kava D8
2 Ultimate Burger.......... E3

Hotels ▼

1 Aston Kona
   by the Sea F4
2 Courtyard
   King Kamehameha's
   Kona Beach Hotel B6
3 Holua Resort at
   Mauna Loa Village...... G7
4 Holualoa Inn............. H4
5 Kanaloa at Kona
   by Outrigger G6
6 Kona Coast Resort...... G6
7 Kona Magic Sands G5
8 Kona Tiki Hotel F4
9 Royal Kona Resort...... D9
10 Sheraton Kona
    Resort and Spa at
    Keauhou Bay............ G7

royal compound at Kamakahonu, the bay fronting what is now the Courtyard King Kamehameha's Kona Beach Hotel. Today it is one of the most revered and historically significant sites in all of Hawaii. Kamakahonu, meaning "eye of the turtle," was named for a prominent turtle-shaped rock there, covered in cement when the hotel and pier were built. The Ahuena Heiau, a stunning *heiau* (temple), was dedicated to Lono, the Hawaiian god of peace and prosperity. It was also used as a seat of government.

Today the compound features a scaled-down replica of the temple and is a National Historic Landmark. It sustained some damage in the 2011 tsunami and has been repaired. You can't go inside the *heiau*, but you can view it from the beach or directly next door at the hotel's luau grounds. ⊠ *75-5660 Palani Rd., Kailua-Kona* ⊕ *www.nps.gov/places/kamakahonu. htm.*

★ Mokuaikaua Church

RELIGIOUS SITE | Site of the first Christian church in the Hawaiian Islands, this solid lava-rock structure, completed in 1837, is mortared with burned lime, coral, and *kukui* (candlenut) oil and topped by an impressive steeple. The ceiling and interior were crafted of timbers harvested from a forest on Hualalai and held together with wooden pegs, not nails. Inside, behind a panel of gleaming koa wood, rests a model of the brig *Thaddeus* as well as a koa-wood table crafted by Henry Boshard, pastor for 43 years. The gift shop is open most mornings, and a talk is given by the church historian Sundays at noon. Within the sanctuary, you may also encounter Aloha Greeters, who love to share the history of Mokuaikaua with visitors. The church still holds services and hosts community events, so please be respectful when entering the building. ⊠ *75-5713 Alii Dr., Kailua-Kona* ☎ *808/329–0655* ⊕ *www.mokuaikaua. org* ⚑ *Free.*

☺ Beaches

Kahaluu Beach Park

BEACH—SIGHT | Shallow and easily accessible, this salt-and-pepper beach is one of the Big Island's most popular swimming and snorkeling sites, thanks to the fringing reef that helps keep the waters calm, visibility high, and reef life—especially *honu* (green sea turtles) and colorful fish—plentiful. Because it is so protected, it's great for first-time snorkelers. Outside the reef, very strong rip currents can run, so caution is advised. Never hand-feed the unusually tame reef fish here; it upsets the balance of the reef. ■**TIP→ Experienced surfers find good waves beyond the reef, and scuba divers like the shore dives—shallow ones inside the breakwater, deeper ones outside.** Snorkel equipment and boards are available for rent nearby, and surf schools operate here. Kahaluu was a favorite of the Hawaiian royal family. **Amenities:** food and drink; lifeguards; parking (no fee); showers; toilets. **Best for:** snorkeling; surfing; swimming. ⊠ *78-6720 Alii Dr., Kailua-Kona* ✛ *5½ miles south of Kailua-Kona, across from Beach Villas* ☎ *808/961–8311* ⚑ *Free.*

Kamakahonu Beach

BEACH—SIGHT | **FAMILY** | This is where King Kamehameha spent his final days—the restored Ahuena Heiau sits on a platform across from the sand. Adjacent to Kailua Pier, the scenic crescent of white sand is one of the few beaches in downtown Kailua-Kona. The water here is almost always calm and the beach clean, making this a perfect spot for kids. For adults, it's a great place for swimming, stand-up paddling (SUP), watching outrigger teams practice, or enjoying a lazy beach day. It can get crowded on weekends. Snorkeling can be good north of the beach, and snorkeling, SUP, and kayaking equipment can be rented nearby. There's lots of grass and shade, and free parking in county lots is a short stroll away. **Amenities:** food and drink; showers;

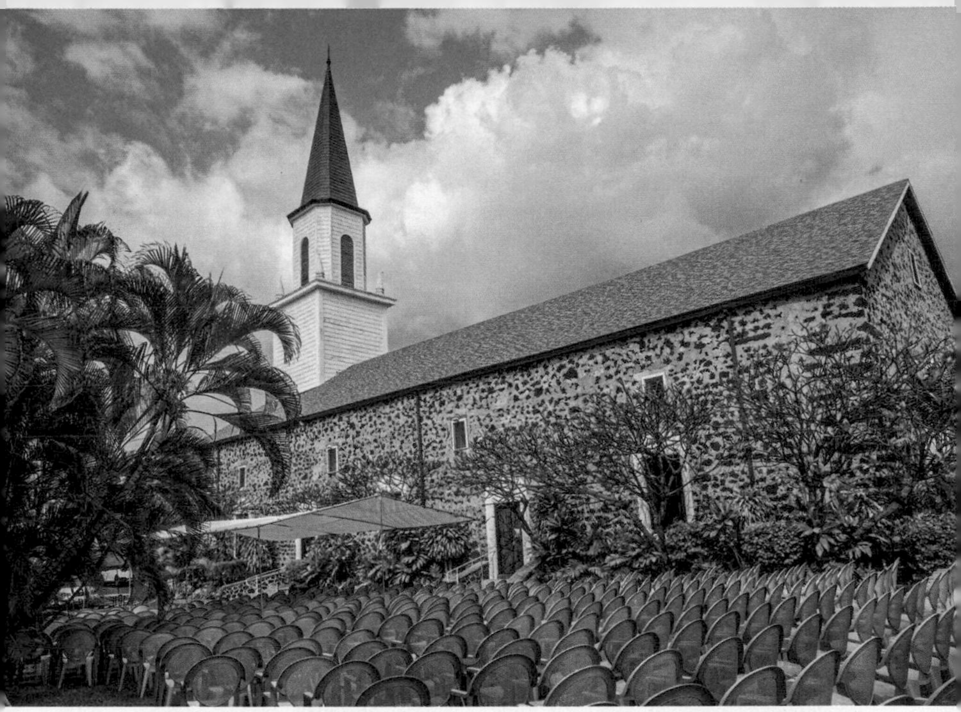

Mokuaikaua Church in Kailua-Kona, completed in 1837, was the first Christian church in the Hawaiian Islands.

toilets; water sports. **Best for:** snorkeling; swimming. ✉ *75-5660 Palani Rd., at Alii Dr., Kailua-Kona* 🎟 *Free.*

🍴 Restaurants

Big Island Grill

$ | **HAWAIIAN** | **FAMILY** | A local-style Hawaiian restaurant, this place looks like an old coffee shop—it's large and nondescript inside, with booths, basic tables, and bingo-hall chairs. Local families love it for the huge portions of pork chops, *loco moco* (meat, rice, and eggs smothered in gravy), and an assortment of fish specialties at very reasonable prices; "Biggie's" also serves a decent breakfast. **Known for:** authentic local vibe; Sunday breakfast; popularity with large groups and families. [$] *Average main: $15* ✉ *75-5702 Kuakini Hwy., Kailua-Kona* ☎ *808/326–1153* 🕓 *No lunch or dinner Sun.*

★ Bongo Ben's Island Café

$ | **AMERICAN** | At the entry of this super-casual, oceanfront diner with views of Kailua Bay, menus printed on the giant bongos tell the story. Offering great deals on a plethora of breakfast, lunch, and dinner items, the open-air restaurant bakes its own breads, cinnamon rolls, desserts, pizza crust, and hamburger buns on-site. **Known for:** early opening hours for breakfast; prime rib night and other weekly specials; discounts on morning and happy hour cocktails. [$] *Average main: $15* ✉ *75-5819 Alii Dr., Kailua-Kona* ☎ *808/329–9203* 🌐 *www.bongobens.com.*

Don the Beachcomber at Royal Kona Resort

$$ | **HAWAIIAN** | The "original home of the mai tai," Don the Beachcomber features an open-air, retro, tiki-bar setting with the absolute best view of Kailua Bay in town. Service can be slow, but the coconut prawns are worth the wait, as is the New York steak paired with bacon-wrapped shrimp. **Known for:** slow-roasted prime rib; dining on the water's edge; Don's Mai Tai Bar with menu items and 10 types of mai tais. [$] *Average main: $25* ✉ *Royal Kona Resort, 75-5852 Alii Dr., Kailua-Kona* ☎ *808/329–3111* 🌐 *www.royalkona.com* 🕓 *No lunch. No dinner Sun.–Wed.*

The Fish Hopper

$$ | SEAFOOD | FAMILY | With a bayside view in the heart of Historic Kailua Village, the open-air Hawaii location of the popular Monterey, California, restaurant has an expansive menu for breakfast, lunch, and dinner. Inventive fresh-fish specials as well as simple fish-and-chips and clam chowder are what the original is known for. **Known for:** award-winning clam chowder; tropical oceanfront dining; signature Volcano flaming cocktail. $ *Average main: $24* ⊠ *75-5683 Alii Dr., Kailua-Kona* ☏ *808/326–2002* ⊕ *www.fishhopper. com.*

★ Foster's Kitchen

$$ | AMERICAN | Ocean breezes flow through this open-air, bayfront restaurant on Alii Drive, known for a quality menu infused with Cajun and island influences; almost all dishes are made to order and feature non-GMO, hormone-free, or USDA certified organic ingredients. A must-try is the seafood pesto puff pastry on the appetizer menu, and for dinner, the steak house pasta (creamy mushroom pasta topped with a New York strip steak) is a good bet. **Known for:** scratch-made food and cocktails; live entertainment nightly; two happy hours daily. $ *Average main: $23* ⊠ *75-5805 Alii Dr., Kailua-Kona* ☏ *808/326–1600* ⊕ *www. fosterskitchen.com.*

Holuakoa Gardens and Cafe

$$ | AMERICAN | This respected slow-food restaurant features fine dining in a lush, open-air setting beneath the shade of an old monkeypod tree. The proprietors, top chefs from the Bay Area, strive to use all local and organic ingredients for such dinner entrées as handcrafted house gnocchi or Mediterranean seafood stew. **Known for:** farm-to-table cuisine; adjacent coffeehouse lounge; biodynamic and organic wines. $ *Average main: $25* ⊠ *76-5900 Old Government Rd., Holualoa* ☏ *808/322–2233* ⊕ *www.holuakoagardens.com* ☾ *No dinner Sun.*

Honu's on the Beach

$$$ | HAWAIIAN | Featuring alfresco dining near the sand, this is one of the few truly beachfront restaurants in Historic Kailua Village and is part of Courtyard King Kamehameha's Kona Beach Hotel. The venue offers prime views of Kailua Pier and the historic grounds of Kamakahonu Bay, as well as a menu dominated by Hawaii regional cuisine, highlighted by Hawaii ranchers' "natural" New York steak, fresh catch of the day, and sushi. **Known for:** views of sacred temple; daily breakfast buffet; tiki torches and inviting firepits at night. $ *Average main: $28* ⊠ *Courtyard King Kamehameha's Kona Beach Hotel, 75-5660 Palani Rd., Kailua-Kona* ☏ *808/329–2911* ⊕ *www. marriott.com* ☾ *No lunch.*

Huggo's

$$$$ | HAWAIIAN | A Kona icon since 1969, family-owned Huggo's is one of the few restaurants in town with prices and atmosphere comparable to the splurge restaurants at the Kohala Coast resorts. Dinner offerings sometimes fall short, considering the prices, but the *pupus* (appetizers) and small plates are usually a good bet. **Known for:** dining at the water's edge; landmark Kona restaurant; nightlife hot spot. $ *Average main: $36* ⊠ *75-5828 Kahakai Rd., off Alii Dr., Kailua-Kona* ☏ *808/329–1493* ⊕ *www.huggos.com.*

Humpy's Big Island Alehouse

$ | AMERICAN | This place is usually packed for a reason: the more than 36 craft brews on tap, plus an upstairs and downstairs bar with plenty of outdoor seating. Take in the oceanfront view with amazing sunsets while chowing down on stone-baked pizza, fresh salads, fish-and-chips, fish tacos, burgers, stone-baked subs, and lots of appetizers. **Known for:** largest selection of craft beer on the island; great crab cakes; good nightlife (for Kona). $ *Average main: $15* ⊠ *Coconut Grove MarketPlace, 75-5815 Alii Dr., Kailua-Kona* ☏ *808/324–2337* ⊕ *humpys-kona.com.*

Island Lava Java

$$ | AMERICAN | With cocktail bars both upstairs and downstairs, oceanfront Island Lava Java serves eggs Benedict for breakfast, fresh fish tacos for lunch, and pasta, steak, and seafood for dinner, plus towering, fresh bistro salads. There are also pizzas, sandwiches, and plenty of choices for both vegetarians and meat eaters. **Known for:** large portions using mostly local organic ingredients; bar with extensive cocktail menu; 100% Kona coffee. $ Average main: $20 ⊠ Coconut Grove MarketPlace, 75-5801 Alii Dr., Kailua-Kona ☎ 808/327–2161 ⊕ www. islandlavajava.com.

★ Jackie Rey's Ohana Grill

$$ | AMERICAN | FAMILY | The brightly decorated, open-air restaurant is a favorite lunch and dinner destination of visitors and residents, thanks to generous portions and a nice variety of chef's specials, steaks, and seafood dishes. Meals pair well with selections from Jackie Rey's well-rounded wine list. **Known for:** strong local following; great-value lunch menu with ribs and fish-and-chips; $5 happy hour. $ Average main: $23 ⊠ Pottery Terrace, 75-5995 Kuakini Hwy., Kailua-Kona ☎ 808/327–0209 ⊕ www.jackiereys.com ☉ No lunch weekends.

Kenichi Pacific

$$$ | JAPANESE | With black-lacquer tables and lipstick-red banquettes, Kenichi offers a more sophisticated dining atmosphere than what's normally found in Kona. This is where residents go when they feel like splurging on top-notch sushi, steak, and Asian-fusion cuisine. **Known for:** upscale dining at much less than resort prices; happy hour discounts on sushi; cheaper lounge menu of small plates. $ Average main: $30 ⊠ Keauhou Shopping Center, 78-6831 Alii Dr., Suite D-125, Kailua-Kona ☎ 808/322–6400 ⊕ www.kenichirestaurants.com ☉ No lunch.

★ Kona Brewing Co. Pub and Brewery

$ | AMERICAN | FAMILY | An ultrapopular destination with an outdoor patio, Kona Brewing offers an excellent, varied menu, including famous brews, pulled-pork quesadillas, gourmet pizzas, and a killer spinach salad with Gorgonzola cheese and macadamia nuts. The sampler tray offers four of the 10 available microbrews. **Known for:** Longboard Lager and other famous brews made on-site; live music; money-saving beer sampler. $ Average main: $12 ⊠ 74-5612 Pawai Pl., Kailua-Kona ✦ Off Kaiwi St. at end of Pawai Pl. ☎ 808/329–2739 ⊕ www. konabrewingco.com.

Kona Inn Restaurant

$$ | AMERICAN | This vintage open-air restaurant at the historical Kona Inn Shopping Village offers a beautiful oceanfront setting on Kailua Bay. It's a great place to have a mai tai and some appetizers later in the day, or to enjoy a calamari sandwich, clam chowder, or salad at lunch. **Known for:** sunset-watching spot; nice bar and lounge at all times; inconsistent food at dinner. $ Average main: $20 ⊠ Kona Inn Shopping Village, 75-5744 Alii Dr., Kailua-Kona ☎ 808/329–4455 ⊕ www. windandsearestaurants.com.

Kona Taeng On Thai

$ | THAI | A hidden gem, the open-air eatery is on the second floor of an oceanfront shopping center. Patrons can watch the scene below on bustling Alii Drive while enjoying freshly prepared Thai specialties, including plenty of vegetarian options and delicious Thai iced tea. **Known for:** uncrowded, spacious layout; open air on Alii Drive; large portions. $ Average main: $11 ⊠ Kona Inn Shopping Center, 75-5744 Alii Dr. , #208, 2nd fl., Kailua-Kona ☎ 808/329–1994.

Magics Beach Grill

$$$ | HAWAIIAN | In a vintage building dating from 1965, Magics offers an exhilarating oceanfront location overlooking the famous Disappearing Sands Beach, also known as Magic Sands. From

fried *ulu* (breadfruit) wedges in umami truffle oil aioli to griddled crab cakes and shoyu-and-coconut-braised pork belly, the eclectic menu features intriguing choices as well as family-friendly options. **Known for:** sunset beach views; spicy dragonfruit margarita; great happy hour 2–4 pm. $ *Average main: $33* ✉ *77-6452 Alii Dr., Kailua-Kona* ☎ *808/ 662–4427* ⊕ *magicsbeachgrill.com.*

Mi's Waterfront Bistro

$$ | ITALIAN | Overlooking Kailua Bay in Waterfront Row, this steady presence in the Kona dining scene offers a reliable, consistent menu. The restaurant's husband-and-wife owners prepare homemade pastas and focaccia daily and also offer some delicious specials such as lasagna and risotto. **Known for:** waterfront views; herb-cheese ravioli; good desserts. $ *Average main: $18* ✉ *75-5770 Alii Dr., Kailua-Kona* ☎ *808/323–3880* ⊕ *www.miswaterfrontbistro.com.*

★ Quinn's Almost by the Sea

$ | AMERICAN | FAMILY | With the bar in the front and the dining patio in the back, Quinn's may seem like a bit of a dive at first glance, but this venerable restaurant serves up the best darn cheeseburger and fries in town. The menu has many other tasty options, such as fish-and-chips and beef tenderloin tips. **Known for:** strong cocktails; comfort food like meatballs; old Kona vibe. $ *Average main: $15* ✉ *75-5655 Palani Rd., Kailua-Kona* ☎ *808/329–3822* ⊕ *www.quinnsalmostbythesea.com.*

★ Rays on the Bay

$$ | SOUTH PACIFIC | The Sheraton Kona's signature restaurant overlooks Keauhou Bay, offering nighttime views of native manta rays that appear nightly beneath the balcony. The stellar dinner menu includes fresh-catch seafood, island-raised beef, and farm-fresh salads, plus tantalizing appetizers like kampachi (yellowtail) sashimi, pork pot stickers, and poke. **Known for:** spectacular bayfront location; late-night dining; live music nightly. $ *Average main: $25* ✉ *Sheraton Kona Resort and Spa, 78-128 Ehukai St., Keauhou* ☎ *808/930–4949* ⊕ *www.raysonthebaykona.com* ⊘ *No lunch.*

Sam Choy's Kai Lanai

$$ | HAWAIIAN | FAMILY | Perched above a shopping center with a coastline view, celebrity chef Sam Choy's namesake restaurant includes a bar that looks like a charter-fishing boat and granite-topped tables with ocean views from every seat. Along with reasonably priced entrées, highlighted by Sam's trio of fish served with shiitake mushroom cream sauce, they also offer an ahi salad (served with deep-fried flour tortilla chips) for a refreshing choice. **Known for:** limited parking for such a popular place; family friendly with a kid's menu; happy hour at the Short Bait Bar. $ *Average main: $22* ✉ *Keauhou Shopping Center, 78-6831 Alii Dr., Suite 1000, Kailua-Kona* ☎ *808/333–3434* ⊕ *www.samchoyskailanai.com.*

Thai Rin Restaurant and Bar

$$ | THAI | This low-key oceanfront restaurant on Alii Drive offers an excellent selection of Thai food at decent prices. Everything is cooked to order, and the menu is brimming with choices, including five curries, a green-papaya salad, and deep-fried fish. **Known for:** great views with both indoor and outdoor seating; appetizer platters for sharing; convenience to village shops. $ *Average main: $18* ✉ *75-5799 Alii Dr., Kailua-Kona* ☎ *808/329–2929* ⊕ *kona123.com/thairin.html.*

TK Noodle House

$ | ASIAN FUSION | Former resort chef TK Keosavang serves up inventive Asian fusion cuisine with the emphasis on noodles. Generous portions are beautifully plated, like the crispy pork belly sauté with Chinese greens and garlic sauce, and noodle soups and abundant salads don't disappoint. **Known for:** ample parking; seafood yentafo soup; shabu-shabu table option. $ *Average main: $12* ⊠ *75 Hanama Pl., Kailua-Kona* ⊹ *Near Big Island Grill* ☎ *808/327–0070* ⊕ *www. cheftk.com.*

☕ Coffee and Quick Bites

Kanaka Kava

$ | HAWAIIAN | This is a popular local hangout, and not just because the kava drink makes you mellow. The Hawaiian proprietors also serve traditional Hawaiian food, including fresh poke, bowls of pulled *kalua* (earth oven–baked) pork, healthy organic greens, *opihi* (limpets), and traditional Hawaiian *laulau* (pork or chicken wrapped in taro leaves and steamed). **Known for:** kava served in coconut cups; Hawaiian specialties like fresh fish and laulau; squid luau (the leaf from a taro plant). $ *Average main: $12* ⊠ *Coconut Grove Marketplace, 75-5803 Alii Dr., Space B6, Kailua-Kona* ☎ *808/327–1660.*

Ultimate Burger

$ | DINER | FAMILY | Located in the Office Max shopping complex in Kailua-Kona, this excellent burger joint may look like a chain, but it's an independent, locally owned and operated eatery that serves 100% organic, grass-fed Big Island beef on buns locally made. Be sure to order a side of seasoned Big Daddy fries served with house-made aioli dipping sauce. **Known for:** organic, hormone-free ingredients; supporting local farmers and ranchers; excellent French fries. $ *Average main: $8* ⊠ *Kona Commons Shopping Center, 74-5450 Makala Blvd., Kailua-Kona* ☎ *808/329–2326* ⊕ *www. ultimateburger.net.*

Hotels

Aston Kona by the Sea

$$$$ | RENTAL | FAMILY | Complete modern kitchens, tiled lanai, and washer-dryer units are found in every suite of this comfortable oceanfront condo complex with a

---

Kona Condo Comforts 🍴

The **Safeway** at Crossroads Shopping Center (⊠ *75-1000 Henry St., Kailua-Kona* ☎ *808/329–2207*) offers an excellent inventory of groceries and produce, although prices can be steep.

For pizza, **Kona Brewing Co. Pub and Brewery** (⊠ *75-5629 Kuakini Hwy., accessed through the Kona Old Industrial Park, Kailua-Kona* ☎ *808/329–2739*) is the best bet, if you can pick it up. Otherwise, for delivery, try **Domino's** (☎ *808/329–9500*).

---

welcoming entry lobby and reception area that feels like a hotel. **Pros:** oceanfront location; lobby and activities desk; ocean-fed saltwater pool next to the property. **Cons:** no beach access (2 miles away); not walking distance to Kailua Village; individually owned units, so prices may vary. $ *Rooms from: $359* ⊠ *75-6106 Alii Dr., Kailua-Kona* ☎ *808/327–2300, 877/997–6667* ⊕ *www.astonhotels.com* ⤶ *86 units* ⭕ *No meals.*

Courtyard King Kamehameha's Kona Beach Hotel

$$$ | HOTEL | FAMILY | Right on the beach in the heart of Historic Kailua Village, this landmark hotel offers good vibrations and authentic local hospitality—all for less than the price of a Kohala Coast resort. **Pros:** central location; historical ambience; on-site restaurant and poolside bar. **Cons:** most rooms have partial ocean views; some rooms face the parking lot; pricey buffet. $ *Rooms from: $335* ⊠ *75-5660 Palani Rd., Kailua-Kona* ☎ *808/329–2911* ⊕ *marriott.com* ⤶ *452 rooms* ⭕ *No meals.*

★ Holualoa Inn

$$$$ | **B&B/INN** | Six spacious rooms and suites—plus two vintage, one-bedroom cottages perfect for honeymooners—are available at this 30-acre coffee-country estate, a few miles above Kailua Bay in the heart of the artists' village of Holualoa. **Pros:** within walking distance of art galleries and cafés; everything necessary for hosting a wedding or event; luxurious, Zen-like vibe. **Cons:** not kid friendly; non-heated swimming pool; no dinners. [$] *Rooms from: $440* ✉ *76-5932 Mamalahoa Hwy., Holualoa* ☎ *808/324–1121, 800/392–1812* 🌐 *www.holualoainn.com* 🛏 *8 rooms* 🍴 *Free breakfast.*

Holua Resort at Mauna Loa Village

$$$ | **RESORT** | Tucked away by Keauhou Bay amid a plethora of coconut trees, this well-maintained enclave of blue-roofed villas offers lots of amenities, including an 11-court tennis center (with a center court, pro shop, and lights), swimming pools, hot tubs, fitness center, manicured gardens, waterfalls, and covered parking. **Pros:** tennis center; upscale feeling; walking distance to major resort restaurants. **Cons:** no beach; partial ocean views; no on-site restaurant. [$] *Rooms from: $323* ✉ *78-7190 Kaleiopapa St., Kailua-Kona* ☎ *808/324–1550* 🌐 *www.shellhospitality.com* 🛏 *73 units* 🍴 *No meals.*

Kanaloa at Kona by Outrigger

$$ | **RENTAL** | The 18-acre grounds provide a peaceful and verdant background for this low-rise condominium complex bordering the Keauhou-Kona Country Club and within a five-minute drive of the nearest beaches (Kahaluu and Magic Sands). **Pros:** within walking distance of Keauhou Bay; three pools with hot tubs; shopping center and restaurants nearby. **Cons:** no restaurant on property; mandatory cleaning fee at check-in; air-conditioning available only by paying a daily fee. [$] *Rooms from: $259* ✉ *78-261 Manukai St., Kailua-Kona* ☎ *808/322–9625, 808/322–7222, 800/688–7444* 🌐 *www.outrigger.com* 🛏 *63 units* 🍴 *No meals.*

Kona Coast Resort

$$ | **RENTAL** | **FAMILY** | Just below Keauhou Shopping Center, this resort offers furnished condos on 21 acres with pleasant ocean views and a host of on-site amenities, including two swimming pools, beach volleyball, a cocktail bar, barbecue grills, a hot tub, tennis courts, a fitness center, hula classes, equipment rentals, and children's activities. **Pros:** all rooms updated in 2018; good amenities for kids; away from the bustle of downtown Kailua-Kona. **Cons:** some units have parking lot views; not on the beach; time-share salespeople. [$] *Rooms from: $220* ✉ *78-6842 Alii Dr., Keauhou* ☎ *808/324–1721* 🌐 *www.shellhospitality.com* 🛏 *268 units* 🍴 *No meals.*

Kona Magic Sands

$$ | **RENTAL** | Cradled between a lovely grass park and Magic Sands Beach Park, this condo complex is great for swimmers, surfers, and sunbathers. **Pros:** adjacent to popular Magic Sands Beach Park; affordable studio units; oceanfront view from all units. **Cons:** studios only; some units are dated; popular complex, but you have to book through a third-party site. [$] *Rooms from: $180* ✉ *77-6452 Alii Dr., Kailua-Kona* ☎ *808/329–9393, 800/622–5348* 🛏 *15 units* 🍴 *No meals.*

Kona Tiki Hotel

$ | **HOTEL** | This three-story, walk-up, budget hotel about a mile south of downtown Kailua Village, with modest, pleasantly decorated rooms—all of which have lanai right next to the ocean—is simply the best deal in town. **Pros:** friendly staff; oceanfront lanai on every room; free parking and continental breakfast. **Cons:** only one studio has a kitchen (others have fridges only); no TV in rooms; parking can be a challenge. [$] *Rooms from: $169* ✉ *75-5968 Alii Dr., Kailua-Kona* ☎ *808/329–1425* 🌐 *www.konatikihotel.com* 🛏 *16 rooms* 🍴 *Free breakfast.*

Royal Kona Resort

$$ | RESORT | FAMILY | If you're on a budget, this is a great option—the location is central; the bar, lounge, pool, and restaurant are right on the water; and the rooms feature contemporary Hawaiian decor with Polynesian accents. **Pros:** convenient location; waterfront pool; restaurant and bar with great views. **Cons:** can be crowded; $18 per day parking fee; grounds have dated feel. $ *Rooms from: $189* ⊠ *75-5852 Alii Dr., Kailua-Kona* ☎ *808/329–3111, 800/222–5642* ⊕ *www. royalkona.com* ⊃ *430 rooms* ¶○¶ *No meals.*

Sheraton Kona Resort and Spa at Keauhou Bay

$$$ | RESORT | FAMILY | What this big concrete structure lacks in intimacy, it makes up for with its beautifully manicured grounds, historical sense of place, stylish interiors, and stunning location on Keauhou Bay. Many rooms have great views of the bay and feel like they're right on the water, and each is decorated in a modern Polynesian style. **Pros:** cool pool; manta rays on view nightly; resort style at lower price. **Cons:** no beach; long walk from parking area; Wi-Fi can be spotty. $ *Rooms from: $290* ⊠ *78-128 Ehukai St., Keauhou* ☎ *808/930–4900* ⊕ *marriott. com* ⊃ *484 rooms* ¶○¶ *No meals.*

▶ Nightlife

BARS

★ Ola Brew

BARS/PUBS | An exciting start-up, this employee-owned brewing company offers an enticing and creative array of beers, ales, ciders, and hard seltzers. Ola Brew is committed to community investing with sponsorships and support of local farmers and merchants. Take a barstool at a picture window facing the main brewing operation and enjoy a fresh, on-tap draft and an appetizer. They sometimes host musicians or food trucks on the street out front or do

trivia nights. The taproom menu features reasonably priced salads, flatbreads, and poke bowls. Brewery tours start daily at 1. ⊠ *74-5598 Luhia St., Kailua-Kona* ☎ *808/339–3599* ⊕ *www.olabrewco.com.*

CLUBS

★ Gertrude's Jazz Bar

MUSIC CLUBS | You know you're in the right place when you climb the stairs to this little gem and notice that the steps are painted like piano keys. With a location in the heart of town, including a perfect view of Kailua Bay, this open-air club features an incredible variety of music (jazz, Latin, country, classical) and special events such as dance lessons, art nights, wine tastings, and themed dress-up parties. One of the owners is a renowned jazz musician and plays with his own group or with guest musicians. The tapas menu is straightforward and a tad overpriced. A small cover charge helps pay the musicians a living wage. ⊠ *75-5699 Alii Dr., Kailua-Kona* ☎ *808/327–5299* ⊕ *gertrudesjazzbar.com.*

Huggo's on the Rocks

PIANO BARS/LOUNGES | Jazz, Island, and classic-rock bands perform here nightly, and outside you may see people dancing in the sand. The food can miss, but the location, on the waterfront by the Royal Kona Resort, doesn't get better. Happy hour is 3 to 6. ⊠ *75-5824 Kahakai Rd., at Alii Dr., Kailua-Kona* ☎ *808/329–1493* ⊕ *www.huggosontherocks.com.*

Laverne's Sports Bar

DANCE CLUBS | On weekends, live concerts are on tap. Sometimes Hawaiian and island music headliners perform here, such as local recording artists Anuhea or Rebel Souljahz. Local musicians with followings also draw their "groupies." After 10, DJs spin tunes on the ocean-breeze-cooled dance floor. ⊠ *Coconut Grove Marketplace, 75-5819 Alii Dr., Kailua-Kona* ☎ *808/331–2633* ⊕ *www.laverneskona.com.*

🎭 Performing Arts

FESTIVALS

★ King Kamehameha Day Celebration Parade

FESTIVALS | Each summer on the Saturday nearest to King Kamehameha Day (June 11), at least 100 regal riders on horseback parade through Historic Kailua Village, showing off the colorful flora and aloha spirit of Hawaii. The traditional royal *pau* riders (women dressed in long skirts) include a queen and princesses representing the major Hawaiian Islands. A cultural festival with live music and a *houlaulea* (local fundraiser) always follow on the historic grounds of Hulihee Palace, Hawaii Island's only royal palace. This spectacular free event is one of the highlights of summer. ⊠ *Historic Kailua Village, Alii Dr., Kailua-Kona* ⊕ *www.konaparade.org.*

★ Kona Brewers Festival

FESTIVALS | At this lively annual celebration in early March by Kailua Pier, 70 types of ales and lagers by Hawaii and mainland craft brewers are showcased, along with culinary contributions by Hawaii Island chefs. There's also live "Blues and Brews" music, an art auction, a home brewers competition, a 5k run/walk, fashion shows, and a golf tournament. The multiday event is a community fundraiser and local favorite, but you must be 21 to attend. ■TIP➜ **Get tickets early online, as this event always sells out.** ⊠ *Courtyard King Kamehameha's Kona Beach Hotel, 75-5660 Palani Rd., Kailua-Kona* ☎ *808/331–3033* ⊕ *www.konabrewersfestival.com.*

★ Kona Coffee Cultural Festival

FESTIVALS | Held over 10 days in early November, on the Kona side, the longest-running food festival in Hawaii celebrates world-renowned Kona coffee. The highly anticipated festival includes coffee contests, serious cupping (tasting) competitions, a lecture series, label contests, farm tours, and a colorful community parade featuring the newly crowned Miss Kona Coffee. During the Holualoa Village Coffee and Art Stroll, you can meet artists and sample estate coffees. ⊠ *Kailua-Kona* ☎ *808/323–2006* ⊕ *www.konacoffeefest.com.*

LUAU

Haleo Luau at the Sheraton Kona Resort and Spa at Keauhou Bay

CULTURAL FESTIVALS | On the graceful grounds of the Sheraton Kona Resort and Spa at Keauhou Bay, this popular luau (Monday and Friday evening) takes you on a journey of song and dance, celebrating the historic Keauhou region, birthplace of King Kamehameha III. Before the show, you can participate in workshops on topics ranging from coconut-frond weaving to poi ball techniques. The excellent buffet is a feast of local favorites, including *kalua* (earth oven–baked) pig, poi, ahi poke, chicken long rice, fish, and mango chutney. Generous mai tai refills are a plus, and a highlight is the dramatic fire-knife dance finale. ⊠ *Sheraton Kona Resort and Spa at Keauhou Bay, 78-128 Ehukai St., Kailua-Kona* ☎ *808/930–4900* ⊕ *marriott.com* 💲 *$109.*

Island Breeze Luau

CULTURAL FESTIVALS | With traditional dancing showcasing the interconnected Polynesian roots of Hawaii, Samoa, Tahiti, and New Zealand, the "We Are *Ohana* (family)" luau is not a hokey tourist-trap event. These performers take their art seriously, and it shows. The historic oceanfront location—on the Courtyard King Kamehameha's Kona Beach Hotel's luau grounds and directly next to the king's former royal compound and Ahuena Heiau—adds to the authenticity. The bounty of food includes *kalua* (earth oven–baked) pig cooked. The hotel validates parking. ⊠ *75-5660 Palani Rd., Kailua-Kona* ☎ *866/482–9775* ⊕ *www.islandbreezeluau.com* 💲 *$114.*

Continued on page 334

BIRTH OF THE ISLANDS

How did the volcanoes of the Hawaiian Islands evolve here, in the middle of the Pacific Ocean? The ancient Hawaiians believed that the volcano goddess Pele's hot temper was the key to the mystery; modern scientists contend that it's all about plate tectonics and one very hot spot.

Plate Tectonics & the Hawaiian Question: The theory of plate tectonics says that the Earth's surface is comprised of plates that float around slowly over the planet's molten interior. The vast majority of earthquakes and volcanic eruptions occur near plate boundaries—the San Francisco earthquakes in 1906 and 1989, for example, were the result of activity along the nearby San Andreas Fault, where the Pacific and North American plates meet. Hawaii, more than 1,988 miles from the nearest plate boundary, is a giant exception. For years scientists struggled to explain the island chain's existence—if not a fault line, what caused the earthquakes and volcanic eruptions that formed these islands?

What's a hotspot? In 1963, J. Tuzo Wilson, a Canadian geophysicist, argued that the Hawaiian volcanoes must have been created by small concentrated areas of extreme heat beneath the plates. Wilson hypothesized that there is a hotspot beneath the present-day position of the Big Island. Its heat produced a persistent source of magma by partly melting the Pacific Plate above it. The magma, lighter than the surrounding solid rock, rose through the mantle and crust to erupt onto the sea floor, forming an active seamount. Each flow caused the seamount to grow until it finally emerged above sea level as an island volcano. Plausible so far, but why then, is there not one giant Hawaiian island?

HAWAIIAN CREATION MYTH

Holo Mai Pele, often played out in hula, is the Hawaiian creation myth. Pele sends her sister Hiiaka on an epic quest to fetch her lover Lohiau. Overcoming many obstacles, Hiiaka reaches full goddess status and falls in love with Lohiau herself. When Pele finds out, she destroys everything dear to her sister, killing Lohiau and burning Hiiaka's ohia groves. Each time lava flows from a volcano, ohia trees sprout shortly after, in a constant cycle of destruction and renewal.

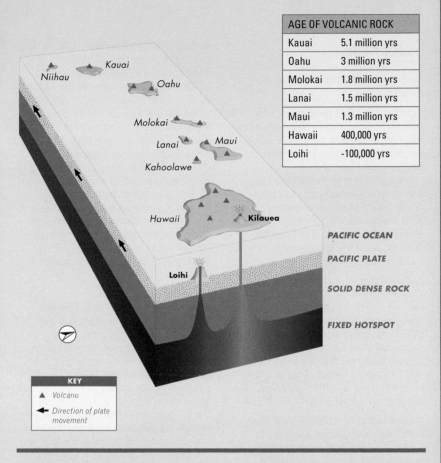

AGE OF VOLCANIC ROCK	
Kauai	5.1 million yrs
Oahu	3 million yrs
Molokai	1.8 million yrs
Lanai	1.5 million yrs
Maui	1.3 million yrs
Hawaii	400,000 yrs
Loihi	-100,000 yrs

PACIFIC OCEAN

PACIFIC PLATE

SOLID DENSE ROCK

FIXED HOTSPOT

KEY

▲ Volcano

← Direction of plate movement

Volcanoes on the Move: Wilson further suggested that the movement of the Pacific Plate itself eventually carries the island volcano beyond the hotspot. Cut off from its magma source, the island volcano becomes dormant. As the plate slowly moved, one island volcano would become extinct just as another would develop over the hotspot. After several million years, there is a long volcanic trail of islands and seamounts across the ocean floor. The oldest islands are those farthest from the hotspot. The exposed rocks of Kauai, for example, are about 5.1 million years old, but those on the Big Island are less than .5 million years old, with new volcanic rock still being formed.

An Island on the Way: Off the coast of the Big Island, the volcano known as Loihi is still submerged but erupting. Scientists long believed it to be a retired seamount volcano, but in the 1970s they discovered both old and new lava on its flanks, and in 1996 it erupted with a vengeance. It is believed that several thousand years from now, Loihi will be the newest addition to the Hawaiian Islands.

South Kona

Kealakekua is 14 miles south of Kailua-Kona.

Between its coffee plantations, artsy havens, and Kealakekua Bay—one of the most beautiful spots on the Big Island—South Kona has plenty of activities to occupy a day. Bring a swimsuit and snorkel gear, and hit Kealakekua Bay first thing in the morning. You'll beat the crowds, have a better chance of a dolphin sighting, and see more fish. After a morning of swimming or kayaking, head to one of the homey cafés in nearby Captain Cook to refuel.

The meandering road leading to Kealakekua Bay is home to a historic painted church, as well as coffee-tasting spots and several reasonably priced B&Bs with great views. The communities surrounding the bay (Kealakekua and Captain Cook) are brimming with local and transplanted artists. They're great places to shop for gifts or antiques, have some coffee, or take an afternoon stroll.

Several coffee farms around the Kona coffee-belt area welcome visitors to watch all or part of the coffee-production process, from harvest to packaging. Some tours are self-guided, and most are free, with the exception of the Kona Coffee Living History Farm.

To get to Kealakekua Bay, follow the signs off Highway 11, and park at Napoopoo Beach. It's not much of a beach (it used to be before Hurricane Iniki washed it away in 1992), but it provides easy access into the water.

◉ Sights

★ Captain James Cook Monument
MEMORIAL | On February 14, 1779, famed English explorer Captain James Cook was killed here during an apparent misunderstanding with local residents. He had chosen Kealakekua Bay as a landing place in November 1778. Arriving during the celebration of Makahiki, the harvest season, Cook was welcomed at first. Some Hawaiians saw him as an incarnation of the god Lono. Cook's party sailed away in February 1779, but a freak storm forced his damaged ship back to Kealakekua Bay. Believing that no god could be thwarted by a mere rainstorm, the Hawaiians were not so welcoming this time. The theft of a longboat brought Cook and an armed party ashore to reclaim it. Shots were fired, daggers and spears were thrown, and Captain Cook fell, mortally wounded. A 27-foot-high obelisk marks the spot where he died. ⊠ *Captain Cook* ⊕ *dlnr.hawaii.gov/dsp/parks/hawaii.*

Greenwell Farms
FARM/RANCH | FARMILY | The Greenwell family played a significant role in the cultivation of the first commercial coffee in the Kona area (as well as the first grocery store). Depending on the season, the 20-minute walking tour of this working farm takes in various stages of coffee production, including a look at the 100-year-old coffee trees. No reservations are required. Sample a cup of their famous Kona coffee at the end; the gift shop stays open until 5. ⊠ *81-6581 Mamalahoa Hwy., Kealakekua* ✛ *Ocean side, between mile markers 112 and 111* ☎ *808/323-2295* ⊕ *www.greenwell-farms.com* ⊠ *Free.*

★ Kealakekua Bay State Historical Park
NATIONAL/STATE PARK | One of the most beautiful spots in the state, this underwater marine reserve has dramatic cliffs that surround super-deep, crystal-clear, turquoise water chock-full of stunning coral pinnacles and tropical fish. The protected dolphins that frequent the sanctuary should not be disturbed, as they use the bay to escape predators and sleep. There's very little sand at west-facing **Napoopoo Beach,** but this is a nice easy place to enter the water and swim, as it's well protected from currents. At times,

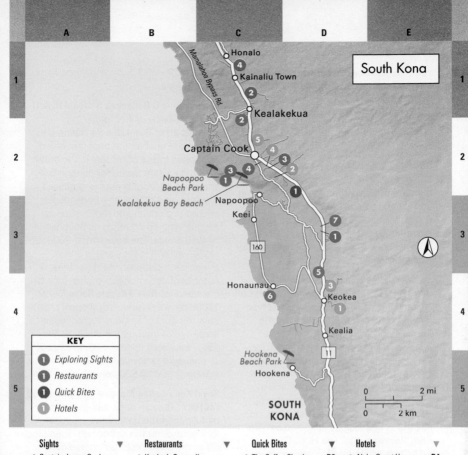

South Kona

	A	B	C	D	E

Honalo
4
Kainaliu Town
2
Kealakekua
2
5
Captain Cook 4
3 4 3
3 1 2
Napoopoo 1
Beach Park
Kealakekua Bay Beach Napoopoo
Keei
160
Honaunau 5
6 3
Keokea 1
Kealia
Hookena 11
Beach Park
Hookena
SOUTH
KONA

Manalahoa Bypass Rd

7
1

KEY
- 1 Exploring Sights
- 1 Restaurants
- 1 Quick Bites
- 1 Hotels

0 — 2 mi
0 — 2 km

Sights ▼
1 Captain James Cook Monument................**C2**
2 Greenwell Farms.........**C2**
3 Kealakekua Bay State Historical Park **C2**
4 Kona Coffee Living History Farm **C2**
5 Lions Gate Farms **D3**
6 Puuhonua O Honaunau National Historical Park **C4**
7 Royal Kona Coffee Museum and Coffee Mill...............**D3**

Restaurants ▼
1 Kaaloa's Super J's Authentic Hawaiian Food..........**D3**
2 Keei Cafe at Hokukano.................**C1**
3 Manago Hotel Restaurant...............**C2**
4 Teshima's Restaurant...............**C1**

Quick Bites ▼
1 The Coffee Shack.......**D2**

Hotels ▼
1 Aloha Guest House.....**D4**
2 Kaawa Loa Plantation.................**C2**
3 Kane Plantation Guesthouse..............**D4**
4 Manago Hotel............**C2**
5 Mermaid Dreams Bed and Breakfast.......**C2**

you may feel tiny jellyfish stings. There are no lifeguards, but there are bathrooms, a pavilion, shower, and (limited) parking. The **Captain James Cook Monument**, marking where the explorer died, is at the northern edge of the bay. Stay at least 300 feet from the shoreline along the cliffs, which have become unstable during recent earthquakes. A limited number of tour operators offer snorkeling and kayaking tours here, a good and very popular option. ⊠ *Beach Rd. off Government Rd. from Puuhonua Rd. (Hwy. 160), Captain Cook* ⊕ *dlnr.hawaii.gov/dsp/parks/hawaii* 🖾 *Free.*

★ Kona Coffee Living History Farm

HISTORIC SITE | On the National Register of Historic Places, this perfectly preserved farm was completely restored by the Kona Historical Society. It includes a 1913 farmhouse first homesteaded by the Uchida family and is surrounded by coffee trees, a Japanese bathhouse, a *kuriba* (coffee-processing mill), and a *hoshidana* (traditional drying platform). Caretakers still grow, harvest, roast, and sell the coffee exactly as they did more than 100 years ago. The H. N. Greenwell Store Museum is located on the same property. ⊠ *82-6199 Mamalahoa Hwy., mile marker 110, Captain Cook* 🕿 *808/323–2006* ⊕ *www.konahistorical. org* 🖾 *$15* ☉ *Closed weekends.*

★ Lions Gate Farms

FARM/RANCH | For a century, three generations have grown coffee on this pretty farm with spectacular ocean views in the heart of Honaunau. The coffee is processed in a mill that dates from 1942. Tours given by the friendly proprietors proudly show visitors how coffee and macadamia nuts are cultivated and harvested. The farmers also sell packaged coffee, nuts, and jams and jellies from this year's harvest and are passionate about producing only the best estate-grown Kona coffee. ⊠ *84-5085 Mamalahoa Hwy., mile marker 105, Honaunau*

🕿 *808/989–4883* ⊕ *www.coffeeofkona. com* 🖾 *Free.*

★ Puuhonua O Honaunau National Historical Park (*Place of Refuge*)

HISTORIC SITE | The 420-acre National Historical Park has the best preserved *puuhonua* (place of refuge) in the state. Providing a safe haven for noncombatants, *kapu* (taboo) breakers, defeated warriors, and others, the *puuhonua* offered protection and redemption for anyone who could reach its boundaries, by land or sea. The oceanfront, 960-foot stone wall still stands and is one of the park's most prominent features. A number of ceremonial temples, including the restored **Hale o Keawe Heiau** (circa 1700), have served as royal burial chambers. An aura of ancient sacredness and serenity still imbues the place. ⊠ *Rte. 160, Honaunau* ✛ *About 20 miles south of Kailua-Kona* 🕿 *808/328–2288* ⊕ *www. nps.gov/puho* 🖾 *$20 per vehicle.*

Royal Kona Coffee Museum and Coffee Mill

FACTORY | Take an easy, self-guided tour by following the descriptive plaques located around the coffee mill. Then stop off at the small museum to see coffee-making relics, peruse the gift shop, and watch an informational film. Visitors are also invited to enjoy the beautiful views as well as stroll through a real lava tube on the property. ⊠ *83-5427 Mamalahoa Hwy., Captain Cook* ✛ *Next to the tree house* 🕿 *808/328–2511* ⊕ *www. royalkonacoffee.com* 🖾 *Free* ☉ *Closed weekends.*

🏖 Beaches

★ Kealakekua Bay Beach

BEACH—SIGHT | Gorgeous and undeveloped, this area offers extraordinary vistas and protected swimming. The shoreline is rocky, but the area is surrounded by high green cliffs, creating calm conditions for superb swimming, snorkeling, and diving (beware of jellyfish). Protected Hawaiian spinner dolphins come to rest and escape predators during the day. Captain James Cook first landed in Hawaii here in 1778, but when he returned a year later, he was killed in a skirmish with Hawaiians, now marked by a monument on the north end of the bay. Rocky but walkable trails lead to Hikiau Heiau, a sacred place for the Hawaiian people. Please proceed respectfully and do not walk on it or enter it. Parking is very limited. ⚠ **Be aware of the off-limits area (in case of rockfalls) marked by orange buoys.** **Amenities:** parking (no fee); showers; toilets. **Best for:** snorkeling; swimming. ✉ *Kealakekua Bay State Historical Park, Napoopoo Rd. off Hwy. 11, just south of mile marker 111, Kealakekua* ☎ *808/961–9544.*

🍴 Restaurants

★ Kaaloa's Super J's Authentic Hawaiian Food

$ | HAWAIIAN | It figures that the best *laulau* (pork or chicken wrapped in taro leaves and steamed) in West Hawaii can be found at a roadside hole-in-the-wall rather than at an expensive resort luau; in fact, this humble family-run eatery was featured on the Food Network's *The Best Thing I Ever Ate*. Plate lunches to go include tender chicken or pork *laulau*, steamed for up to 10 hours. **Known for:** tasty kalua pig and cabbage; friendly and welcoming proprietors; plate lunches with chicken or pork laulau. [$] *Average main: $9* ✉ *83-5409 Mamalahoa Hwy., between mile markers 106 and 107, Honaunau* ☎ *808/328–9566* 🕒 *Closed Sun.*

Keei Cafe at Hokukano

$$ | ECLECTIC | This nicely appointed restaurant, just 15 minutes south of Kailua-Kona, serves delicious dinners with Brazilian, Asian, and European flavors highlighting fresh ingredients from local farmers. Favorites are the Brazilian seafood chowder or peanut-miso salad, followed by pasta primavera smothered with a basil-pesto sauce. **Known for:** most upscale restaurant in South Kona; live dinner music; cash-only place. [$] *Average main: $20* ✉ *79-7511 Mamalahoa Hwy., Kealakekua* ✣ *½ mile south of Kainaliu* ☎ *808/322–9992* 🌐 *www.keeicafe.net* 💳 *No credit cards* 🕒 *Closed Sun. and Mon. No lunch.*

Manago Hotel Restaurant

$ | HAWAIIAN | FAMILY | The historic Manago Hotel is like a time warp, complete with a vintage neon sign, Formica tables, and old photos. T-shirts brag (and it's not false advertising) that the restaurant has the best grilled pork chops in the world, and the fresh fish is excellent as well, especially the ono and ahi. **Known for:** one of the only places in Kona serving opelu, a local fish; mains come with a variety of side dishes; local hospitality. [$] *Average main: $10* ✉ *82-6155 Mamalahoa Hwy., Captain Cook* ☎ *808/323–2642* 🌐 *www.managohotel.com* 🕒 *Closed Mon.*

Teshima's Restaurant

$ | JAPANESE | FAMILY | It doesn't look like much, either inside or out, but Teshima's has been a *kamaaina* (local) favorite since 1929 for a reason. Locals gather at this small landmark restaurant whenever they're in the mood for fresh sashimi, puffy shrimp tempura, or *hekka* (beef and vegetables cooked in an iron pot). **Known for:** excellent tempura combos; long-standing family-owned establishment; authentic local flavor. [$] *Average main: $15* ✉ *79-7251 Mamalahoa Hwy., Honalo* ☎ *808/322–9140* 🌐 *www.teshimarestaurant.com.*

☕ Coffee and Quick Bites

The Coffee Shack

$ | AMERICAN | Visitors enjoy stopping here before or after a morning of snorkeling at Kealakekua Bay, and for good reason: the views of the Honaunau Coast from this roadside restaurant are stunning. This place is best for breakfast or a quick bite, as overpriced lunch plates can miss; but if you're in the mood for a Hawaiian smoothie, iced honey-mocha latte, scone, or homemade luau bread, it's worth the stop. **Known for:** scenic views of South Kona coastline; house-baked bread; its own brand of Kona coffee. Ⓢ *Average main: $12* ✉ *83-5799 Mamalahoa Hwy., Captain Cook* ☎ *808/328–9555* ⊕ *www.coffeeshack.com* ☾ *No dinner.*

Hotels

Aloha Guest House

$$ | B&B/INN | In the hills above Puuhonu O Honaunau National Historical Park, this guesthouse offers quiet elegance, complete privacy, and ocean views from every room. **Pros:** eco-conscious option; full breakfast; views of the South Kona coastline. **Cons:** remote location up a bumpy 1-mile dirt road; 40 minutes from downtown; four-wheel drive recommended. Ⓢ *Rooms from: $236* ✉ *Old Tobacco Rd. off Hwy. 11, near mile marker 104, Honaunau* ☎ *808/328–8955* ⊕ *www.alohaguesthouse.com* 🛏 *5 rooms* ⑪ *Free breakfast.*

★ Kaawa Loa Plantation

$$ | B&B/INN | Proprietors Mike Martinage and Greg Nunn operate a grand yet reasonably priced B&B, on a 5-acre coffee farm above Kealakekua Bay, in a home that features a 2,000-square-foot wraparound veranda with excellent views of the bay and the entire Honaunau Coast. **Pros:** gracious and friendly hosts; excellent breakfast; Hawaiian steam room. **Cons:** not within walking distance of bay; some rooms share a bath; slightly steep turnoff. Ⓢ *Rooms from: $209* ✉ *82-5990 Napoopoo Rd., Captain Cook* ☎ *808/323–2686* ⊕ *www.kaawaloaplantation.com* 🛏 *5 rooms* ⑪ *Free breakfast.*

Kane Plantation Guesthouse

$$$ | B&B/INN | The former home of late legendary artist Herb Kane, this luxury boutique guesthouse occupies a 16-acre avocado farm overlooking the South Kona coastline. **Pros:** sauna, hot tub, massage therapy room; upscale amenities; beautiful artwork. **Cons:** not on the beach; off the beaten track; 25 minutes to downtown. Ⓢ *Rooms from: $325* ✉ *84-1120 Telephone Exchange Rd., off Hwy. 11, Honaunau* ✛ *¼ mile past mile marker 105, south of Captain Cook* ☎ *808/328–2416* ⊕ *www.kaneplantationhawaii.com* 🛏 *3 suites* ⑪ *Free breakfast.*

Manago Hotel

$ | HOTEL | If you want to escape the touristy thing but still be close to the water and attractions like Kealakekua Bay and Puuhonua O Honaunau National Historical Park, this historical hotel is a good option. **Pros:** local color; rock-bottom prices; terrific on-site restaurant. **Cons:** not the best sound insulation between rooms; cheapest rooms share a community bath; some rooms have highway noise. Ⓢ *Rooms from: $75* ✉ *81-6155 Mamalahoa Hwy., Captain Cook* ☎ *808/323–2642* ⊕ *www.managohotel.com* 🛏 *64 rooms* ⑪ *No meals.*

Mermaid Dreams Bed and Breakfast

$ | B&B/INN | "Aloha" is the operative word at this mermaid-themed B&B a 10-minute drive from Kealakekua Bay; self-proclaimed mermaid herself, hostess/proprietor Heather Reynolds takes guests on morning mermaid swims in the bay, where they can learn to swim while wearing a tail (she even has mermaid tails for rent if you need one). **Pros:** gracious hosts; beautifully landscaped grounds; fireside lounge outside for evening cocktails. **Cons:** not on the beach; no children under age 13; two-night minimum stay. Ⓢ *Rooms from: $177* ✉ *81-1031 Keopuka Mauka Rd., Kealakekua* ☎ *808/649–9911* ⊕ *www.mermaiddreamsbedandbreakfast.com* 🛏 *5 rooms* ⑪ *Free breakfast.*

Nightlife

★ Korner Pocket

BARS/PUBS | A favored haunt of the South Kona crowd, Korner Pocket is tucked in the back of an office plaza. But don't

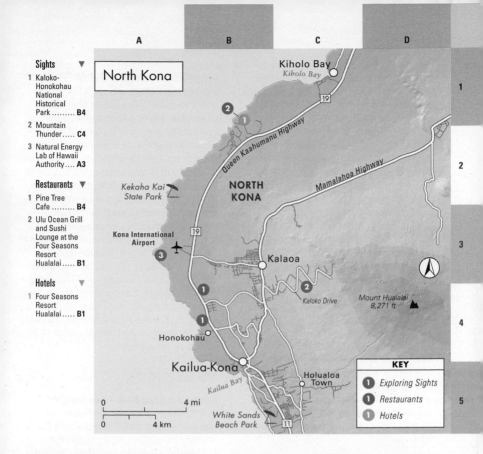

North Kona

Kiholo Bay
Kiholo Bay

19

Queen Kaahumanu Highway

Mamalahoa Highway

NORTH KONA

Kekaha Kai State Park

19

Kona International Airport

Kalaoa

Kaloko Drive

Mount Hualalai
8,271 ft

Honokohau

Kailua-Kona

Kailua Bay

Holualoa Town

11

White Sands Beach Park

0 — 4 mi
0 — 4 km

KEY
1 *Exploring Sights*
1 *Restaurants*
1 *Hotels*

let that deter you. They serve fantastic, affordable food, ranging from scrumptious burgers to a killer prime rib. Popular local bands frequently perform, with no cover, and everyone gets up to dance. You can also play pool. It's the only place open late down south. ✉ *81-970 Halekii St., Kealakekua* ☎ *808/322–2994.*

North Kona

The North Kona district is characterized by vast lava fields, dotted with turnoff points to some of the most beautiful beaches in the world. Most of the lava flows here originate from the last eruptions of Hualalai, in 1800 and 1801, although some flows by the resorts hail from Mauna Loa. The stark black lavascapes contrast spectacularly with luminous azure waters framed by coco

palms and white-sand beaches. Some of the turnoffs will take you to state parks with parking lots and bathrooms, while others are simply a park-on-the-highway-and-hike-in adventure.

Head north from Kona International Airport, and follow Highway 19 along the coast. Take caution driving at night between the airport and where resorts begin on the Kohala Coast; it's extremely dark, and there are few road signs or traffic lights on this two-lane road. Wild donkeys may appear on the roadway without warning.

◉ Sights

Kaloko–Honokohau National Historical Park
NATIONAL/STATE PARK | FAMILY | The trails at this sheltered, 1,160-acre coastal park near Honokohau Harbor, just north of

Kailua-Kona, are popular with walkers and hikers. The free park is a good place to observe Hawaiian archaeological history and intact ruins, including a *heiau* (temple), house platforms, ancient fishponds, and numerous petroglyphs, along a boardwalk. The park's wetlands provide refuge to waterbirds, including the endemic Hawaiian stilt and coot. Two beaches here are good for swimming, sunbathing, and sea turtle spotting: **Aiopio,** a few yards north of the harbor, is small and calm, with protected swimming areas (good for kids), while **Honokohau Beach** is a ¾-mile stretch with ruins of ancient fishponds, also north of the harbor. Of the park's three entrances, the middle one leads to a visitor center with helpful rangers and lots of information. Local docents with backgrounds in geology or other subjects give nature talks. To go directly to the beaches, take the harbor road north of the Gentry retail center, park in the gravel lot, and follow the signs. ⊠ *74-425 Kealakehe Pkwy., off Hwy. 19 near airport, Kailua-Kona* ☎ *808/329–6881* ⊕ *www.nps.gov/kaho* ≊ *Free.*

Mountain Thunder

FARM/RANCH | This coffee producer offers hourly "bean-to-cup" tours, including a tasting and access to the processing plant, which shows dry milling, sizing, coloring, sorting, and roasting. For $10, take the lava tube/nature walk in the cloud forest ecosystem. There's a small retail store where you can purchase coffee and souvenirs. Remember that afternoon rains are common at this elevation, so bring an umbrella and sturdy shoes. ⊠ *73-1944 Hao St., Kailua-Kona* ☎ *808/325–5566* ⊕ *www.mountainthunder.com* ≊ *Free.*

Natural Energy Lab of Hawaii Authority

COLLEGE | Just south of Kona International Airport, a large, mysterious group of buildings with a large photovoltaic (solar) panel installation resembles a top-secret military station, but it's actually the site of the Natural Energy Lab of Hawaii Authority, NELHA for short, and administered by the Friends of NELHA. Here, scientists, researchers, and entrepreneurs make use of a cold, deep-sea pipeline to develop and market everything from desalinated, mineral-rich drinking water and super-nutritious algae products to energy-efficient air-conditioning systems and environmentally friendly aquaculture techniques. Seahorses, abalone, *kampachi*, Dungeness crab, and Maine lobsters are also raised here. Start your visit at the gateway building and take the Seas the Day tour to learn about the Ocean Science and Technology Park, the Ocean Conservation tour, or the Sustainable Aquaculture tour. ⊠ *73-4485 Kahilihili St., Kailua-Kona* ☎ *808/329–8073* ⊕ *www.energyfuturehawaii.org* ≊ *$49* ⊗ *Closed weekends.*

⊕ Beaches

Kekaha Kai State Park—Kua Bay Side

BEACH—SIGHT | On the northernmost stretch of the park's coastline, this lovely beach is on an absolutely beautiful bay. The water is crystal clear, deep aquamarine, and peaceful in summer, but the park's paved entrance, amenities, and parking lot make it very accessible and, as a result, often crowded. Fine white sand sits in stark contrast to old black lava flows, and there's little shade—bring umbrellas as it can get hot. Rocky shores on either side protect the beach from winds in the afternoon. Gates open daily from 8 to 7. ⚠ **In winter, surf can get very rough, and often the sand washes away. Amenities:** parking (no fee); showers; toilets. **Best for:** surfing; swimming. ⊠ *Hwy. 19, north of mile marker 88, Kailua-Kona* ✛ *Across from Veterans Cemetery* ≊ *Free.*

★ Kekaha Kai State Park—Mahaiula Side

BEACH—SIGHT | It's slow going down a 1.8-mile, bumpy but paved road off Highway 19 to this beach park, but it's worth it. This state park encompasses three

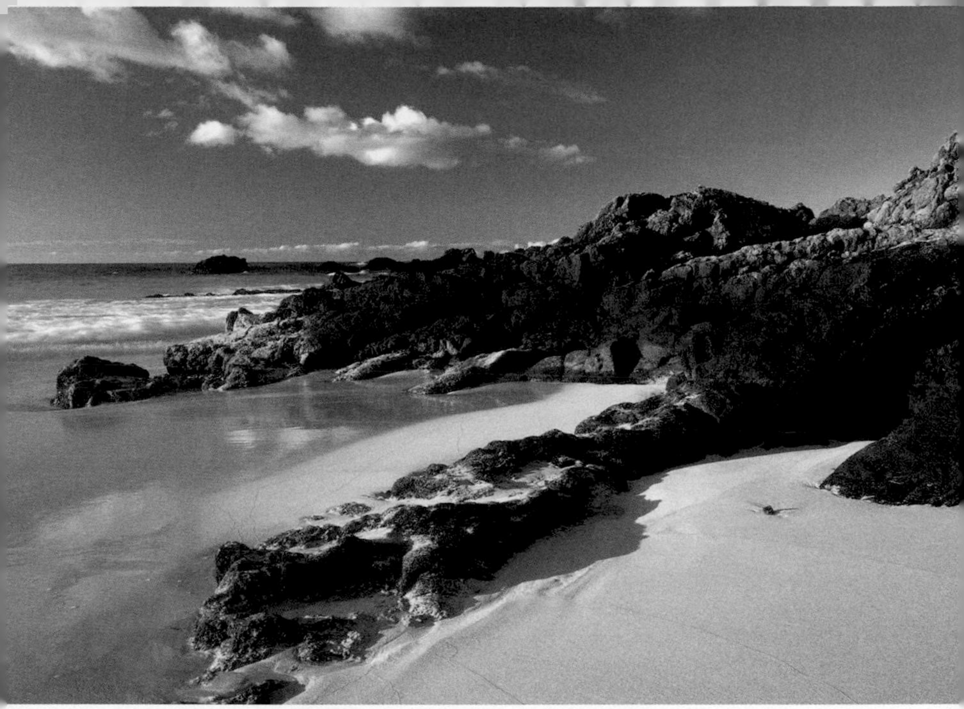

Kua Bay is protected from wind by the rocky shores that surround it.

beaches: from south to north, **Mahaiula**, **Makalawena**, and **Kua Bay**, which has its own entrance. Mahaiula and Makalawena are beautiful, wide expanses of white-sand beach with dunes. Makalawena has great swimming and body boarding. (Note: Makalawena, sandwiched between the two state parks, is private property and falls under the jurisdiction of Kamehameha Schools Bishop Estates.) From Makalawena, a 4½-mile trail leads to Kua Bay. If you're game, work your way on foot to the top of Puu Kuili, a 342-foot-high cinder cone with a fantastic coastline view. However, be prepared for the heat and bring lots of water, as none is available. Gates at the highway entrance close promptly at 7, so you need to leave the lot by 6:30. ⚠ **Watch out for rough surf and strong currents. Amenities:** toilets. **Best for:** swimming. ✉ *Hwy. 19, Kailua-Kona* ✣ *Turnoff is about 2 miles north of Kona International Airport* ☎ *808/327–4958, 808/974–6200* 🎟 *Free.*

🍴 Restaurants

Pine Tree Cafe

$ | **HAWAIIAN** | **FAMILY** | Named for a popular nearby surf spot, the café offers local classics such as *loco moco* (meat, rice, and eggs smothered in gravy), alongside new inventions like crab curry bisque. The fresh-fish plate is decent, and all meals are served with fries or rice and macaroni salad. **Known for:** early-morning breakfast; fresh fish; popularity with locals. [$] *Average main: $12* ✉ *Kohanaiki Plaza, 73-4354 Mamalahoa Hwy. (Hwy. 11), Kailua-Kona* ☎ *808/327–1234.*

★ Ulu Ocean Grill and Sushi Lounge at the Four Seasons Resort Hualalai

$$$$ | **MODERN HAWAIIAN** | Casual elegance takes center stage at the resort's flagship oceanfront restaurant, one of the most upscale restaurants on the Big Island. Breakfast can be à la carte or buffet, but nighttime is when the magic happens, with diverse menu choices—roasted beet salad, flame-grilled prime New York steak, Kona lobster, shrimp pad Thai, and

more—that make deciding what to order a challenge. **Known for:** sushi lounge; ingredients sourced from 160 local purveyors; impressive wine list. $ *Average main: $45* ✉ *Four Seasons Resort Hualalai, 72-100 Kaupulehu Dr., Kailua-Kona* 📞 *808/325–8000* ⊕ *www.fourseasons.com* ⊗ *No lunch.*

Hotels

★ Four Seasons Resort Hualalai

$$$$ | **RESORT** | **FAMILY** | Beautiful views everywhere, polished wood floors, custom furnishings and linens in warm earth and cool white tones, and Hawaiian fine artwork make this oceanfront resort a peaceful retreat. **Pros:** beautiful location; gourmet restaurants; renowned service. **Cons:** not the best beach among the resorts; quite pricey; 20-minute drive to Kailua-Kona. $ *Rooms from: $950* ✉ *72-100 Kaupulehu Dr., Kailua-Kona* 📞 *808/325–8000, 888/340–5662* ⊕ *www.fourseasons.com/hualalai* ⇥ *243 rooms* ⊗ *No meals.*

🛍 Shopping

ARTS AND CRAFTS
★ Hula Lamps of Hawaii

CRAFTS | Located near Costco in the Kaloko Light Industrial complex, this one-of-a-kind shop features the bronze creations of artist Charles Moore. Inspired by the vintage hula-girl lamps of the 1930s, Moore creates art pieces sought by visitors and residents alike. Mix and match with an array of hand-painted lampshades. ✉ *73-5613 Olowalu St., Suite 2, Kailua-Kona* ⊹ *Near Costco on upper road* 📞 *808/326–9583* ⊕ *www.hulalamps.com.*

Just Ukes

LOCAL SPECIALTIES | As the name suggests, this place is all about ukeleles—from music books to T-shirts and accessories like cases and bags. The independently owned shop carries a variety of ukuleles ranging from low-priced starter instruments to high-end models made of koa

and mango. ✉ *Kona Inn Shopping Village, 75-5744 Alii Dr., Kailua-Kona* 📞 *808/769–5101* ⊕ *justukes.com.*

★ Kimura's Lauhala Shop

CRAFTS | Originally a general store built in 1914, this shop features handmade products crafted by local lauhala weavers. Among the offerings are hats, baskets, containers, and mats, many of which are woven by the proprietors. Owner Alfreida Kimura-Fujita was born in the house behind the shop, and her daughter Renee is also an accomplished weaver. ✉ *77-996 Hualalai Rd., Holualoa* 📞 *808/324–0053.*

CLOTHING AND SHOES
Mermaids Swimwear

CLOTHING | Local residents know that Mermaids is the best place in Kona to buy fashion-forward ladies' swimwear, sandals, hats, sunglasses, and other stylish beach accessories. The owner's husband, Tony, is a famous surfboard maker whose World Core surf shop is just around the corner. ✉ *Kona Inn Shopping Village, 75-5744 Alii Dr., Kailua-Kona* 📞 *808/329–6677.*

FOOD AND WINE
★ Kona Wine Market

WINE/SPIRITS | Near Costco, this long-time local wineshop carries both local and imported varietals (with more than 600 high-end wines), specialty liquors, 150 craft beers, gourmet foods, and even cigars. As a bonus, the market delivers wine and gift baskets to hotels and homes. ✉ *73-5613 Olowalu St., Kailua-Kona* 📞 *808/329–9400* ⊕ *www.konawinemarket.com.*

★ Mrs. Barry's Kona Cookies

FOOD/CANDY | Since 1980, Mrs. Barry and her family have been serving yummy home-baked cookies, including macadamia nut, white chocolate–macadamia nut, oatmeal raisin, and coffee crunch. Packaged in beautiful gift boxes or bags, the cookies make excellent gifts for family back home. Stop by on your way to Costco or the airport and pick up a bag or two or three. Ah heck, just ask Mrs. Barry to ship your stash instead. ⊠ 73-5563 Maiau St., Kailua-Kona ✛ By Costco in the Kaloko Light Industrial Area ☎ 808/329–6055 ⊕ www.konacookies. com.

★ Westside Wines

WINE/SPIRITS | Tucked away in a small downtown Kona retail center below Longs, this nifty gourmet wine and spirits shop offers restaurant-quality "wine list" wines at affordable prices. It's also the place to find large-format craft beers, French Champagne, single-malt Scotches, organic vodka, small-batch bourbon, rye whiskey, fresh bread, and artisan cheese from around the world. George Clooney's Casamigos tequila is the store's house tequila. A certified wine specialist, proprietor Alex Thropp was one of the state's top wholesale wine reps for decades. Wine tastings take place Friday and Saturday afternoons from 3 to 6. ⊠ 75-5660 Kopiko St., #4, Kailua-Kona ✛ Below Longs Drugs in Kopiko Plaza ☎ 808/329–1777.

HOUSEWARES
The Spoon Shop

HOUSEHOLD ITEMS/FURNITURE | Williams-Sonoma has nothing on this excellent gourmet kitchenware store that brims with every manner of accoutrement for the avid cook. There's a great selection of gourmet seasonings, olive oils (try the truffle-infused olive oil!), dressings, and condiments. If you're planning a party or reception during your stay in paradise, the Spoon Shop has items for every occasion. Cooking classes with guest chefs take place weekly in the store's high-end demo kitchen. ⊠ 73-4976 Kamanu St., #105, Kailua-Kona ✛ Near Home Depot in New Industrial Area ☎ 808/887–7666 ⊕ www.thespoon-shopkona.com.

MARKETS
Alii Gardens Marketplace

OUTDOOR/FLEA/GREEN MARKETS | The outdoor stalls at this mellow, park-like market, open daily except Monday, offer tropical flowers, produce, soaps, kettle corn, coffee, coconut postcards, cookies, jewelry, koa wood, clothing, antiques and collectibles, handmade lei, silk flowers, and kitschy crafts. The homemade barbecue is a real hit. A food kiosk also serves shave ice, fish tacos, coconut water, fresh-fruit smoothies, and hamburgers. Free parking and Wi-Fi are available. ⊠ 75-6129 Alii Dr., Kailua-Kona ✛ 1½ miles south of Kona Inn Shopping Village ⊕ alii-gardens-marketplace.business.site.

Keauhou Farmers Market

OUTDOOR/FLEA/GREEN MARKETS | FAMILY | Held in the parking lot at Keauhou Shopping Center, this cheerful market is the place to go on Saturday morning for live music, local produce (much of it organic), goat cheese, honey, island-raised meat, flowers, macadamia nuts, fresh-baked pastries, Kona coffee, and plenty of local color. ⊠ Keauhou Shopping Center, 78-6831 Alii Dr., Kailua-Kona ⊕ www. keauhoufarmersmarket.com.

Kona Inn Farmers' Market

OUTDOOR/FLEA/GREEN MARKETS | An awesome florist creates custom arrangements while you wait at this touristy farmers' market near the ocean. There are more than 40 vendors with lots of crafts for sale, as well as some of the best prices on fresh produce and orchids in Kona. The market is held in a parking lot at the corner of Hualalai Road and Alii Drive, Wednesday to Sunday 7 to 4. Parking is free. ⊠ 75-7544 Alii Dr., Kailua-Kona.

SHOPPING CENTERS
Coconut Grove Marketplace

SHOPPING CENTERS/MALLS | The meandering oceanfront marketplace includes gift shops, cafés, restaurants (Outback Steakhouse, Humpy's Big Island Alehouse, Bongo Ben's, Lava Java, Foster's

Kitchen, Fumi's Kitchen), sports bars, sushi, boutiques, Jack's Diving Locker, a running store, and several art galleries. At night, locals gather to watch outdoor sand volleyball games held in the courtyard or grab a beer and enjoy live music. This place is always hopping, and it has the biggest free parking lot in downtown Kailua-Kona. ⊠ *75-5795–75-5825 Alii Dr., Kailua-Kona* ⊕ *www.thecoconutgrove-marketplace.com.*

Crossroads Shopping Center

SHOPPING CENTERS/MALLS | The in-town shopping center includes a Safeway with an excellent deli section for on-the-go snacks, as well as a Walmart, where visitors can find affordable Hawaii souvenirs, including aloha wear, discounted Kona coffee, and macadamia nuts. For a quick meal, there's a Denny's, a Subway, and a Domino's, as well as a small sushi restaurant. The Laulima Food Patch offers fresh salads and local-style specialties. Sakura is known for Japanese and other Asian plates. ⊠ *75-1000 Henry St., Kailua-Kona* ☎ *808/329–4822.*

Kaloko Light Industrial Park

SHOPPING CENTERS/MALLS | Located south of the airport, this large retail complex includes Costco, the best place to stock up on food if you're staying at a vacation rental. Kona Wine Market and the Spoon Shop feature gourmet finds, and Mrs. Barry's Kona Cookies sells beautifully packaged, delicious "souvenirs." ⊠ *Off Hwy. 19 and Hina Lani St., near Kona airport, Kailua-Kona.*

Keauhou Shopping Center

SHOPPING CENTERS/MALLS | About 5 miles south of Kailua Village, this neighborhood shopping center includes KTA Superstore, Longs Drugs, Kona Stories bookstore, and a multiplex movie theater. Kenichi Pacific, an upscale sushi restaurant, and Peaberry & Galette, a café that serves excellent crepes, are favorite eateries, joined by Bianelli's Pizza and Sam Choy's Kai Lanai, which is perched above the center. You can also grab a quick bite at Los Habaneros, Subway, or L&L Hawaiian Barbecue. ⊠ *78-6831 Alii Dr., Kailua-Kona* ☎ *808/322–3000* ⊕ *www. keauhoushoppingcenter.com.*

Kona Commons

SHOPPING CENTERS/MALLS | This downtown center features a Ross Dress for Less (for suitcases, shoes, swimsuits, and aloha wear) and Hawaiian Island Creations (for a great selection of surf gear, clothing, and accessories). Food and drink options include fast-food standbys like Dairy Queen, Subway, and Panda Express, as well as Ultimate Burger, for local beef and delicious homemade fries, and Genki Sushi, where the goods are delivered via conveyer belt. ■ TIP→ **Across the street, Target has fresh-flower lei for a fraction of the cost of local florists.** ⊠ *75-5450 Makala Blvd., Kailua-Kona* ⊕ *www.konacommons.com.*

Kona Inn Shopping Village

SHOPPING CENTERS/MALLS | Originally a hotel, the Kona Inn was built in 1928 to woo a new wave of wealthy travelers. As newer condos and resorts opened along the Kona and Kohala Coasts, it was transformed into a low-rise, outdoor shopping village with clothing boutiques, spas, art galleries, gift shops, an ice cream shop, a crystal store, and island-style eateries. Broad lawns with coconut trees on the ocean side provide a lovely setting for an afternoon picnic. The open-air Kona Canoe Club restaurant is a favorite for burgers. The iconic Kona Inn is best for drinks and appetizers, rather than full dinners. ⊠ *75-5744 Alii Dr., Kailua-Kona.*

The Kohala Coast and Waimea

The Kohala Coast is about 32 miles north of Kailua-Kona.

If you had only a weekend to spend on the Big Island, this is probably where you'd want to be. The Kohala Coast is a mix of the island's best beaches and swankiest hotels yet is not far from ancient valleys and temples, waterfalls, and funky artist enclaves.

The Kohala Coast is home to almost all of the Big Island's megaresorts. Dotting the coastline are manicured lawns and golf courses, restaurants, and destination spas. But the real attraction here is the area's glorious beaches. On a clear day, you can see Maui, and during the winter months, numerous glistening humpback whales cleave the waters just offshore. Many visitors to the Big Island check in here and rarely leave the area. If you're looking to be pampered and lounge on the beach or by the pool all day with an umbrella drink in hand, this is where you need to be. You can still see the rest of the island since most of the hiking and adventure-tour companies offer pickups at the Kohala Coast resorts, and many of the hotels have connections to car-rental agencies (though the number of cars is limited, and you will need to book ahead).

Rounding the northern tip of the island, the arid coast shifts rather suddenly to green villages and hillsides, leading to lush Pololu Valley in North Kohala, as the hot sunshine along the coast gives way to cooler temperatures. In this area are the quaint sugar-plantation towns turned artsy villages of Hawi and Kapaau. New galleries are interspersed with charming reminders of old Hawaii—wooden board-walks, quaint local storefronts, ice cream shops, delicious neighborhood restaurants, friendly locals, and a delightfully slow pace. There's great shopping for everything from antiques and designer beachwear to authentic Hawaiian crafts.

A short drive from the resorts, Waimea's upcountry, pastoral countryside is sprinkled with well-tended, vintage homes with picket fences and flower beds. There's a gentle *paniolo* (Hawaiian cowboy) vibe thoughout the town, which boasts a number of excellent restaurants worth seeking out.

GETTING HERE AND AROUND

Two days is sufficient time for experiencing each unique side of Kohala—one day for the resort perks, including the beach, the spa, the golf, and the restaurants; one day for hiking and admiring the waterfalls and valleys of North Kohala, coupled with a wander around Hawi and Kapaau. In addition, don't miss a quick drive up to explore the rustic town of Waimea, with its restaurants, galleries, and bucolic scenery.

The best way to explore the valleys of North Kohala is with a hiking tour. Look for one that includes lunch, maybe a zipline, and a dip in one of the area's waterfall pools.

The Kohala Coast and Waimea are most accessible from the Ellison Onizuka Kona International Airport. South Kohala is a roughly 30-minute drive from the airport, while it's double that to either Hawi or Waimea.

While some resort guests enjoy staying at a resort for their entire trip (shopping and restaurants are within walking distance), others appreciate having a rental car to sightsee and explore the island's wide diversity at their own pace. There are many rental options at the airport, but if you change your mind mid-trip and want to rent a car, the rental companies operate a satellite office from the Fairmont Orchid Hotel and one in Waikoloa Village.

VISITOR INFORMATION
CONTACTS North Kohala Welcome Center.
✉ *55-3393 Akoni Pule Hwy., Hawi ✛ Just past the "Welcome to Kohala" sign* ☎ *808/889–5523* ⊕ *www.northkohala.org.*

Waikoloa

25 miles north of Ellison Onizuka Kona International Airport.

Waikoloa is a region known for its two large resort properties (one a bit outlandish), excellent golf, and eclectic

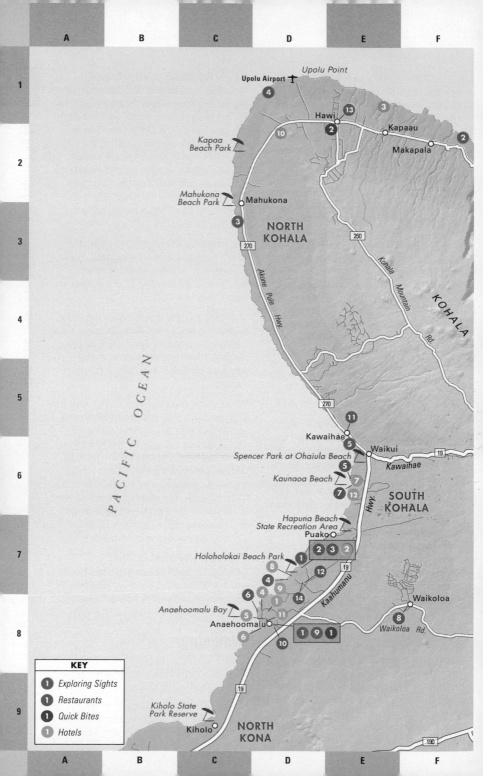

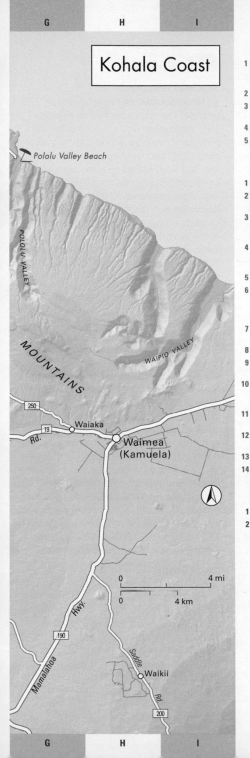

Kohala Coast

Pololu Valley Beach

POLOLU VALLEY

MOUNTAINS

WAIPIO VALLEY

250

19

Waiaka

Rd.

Waimea
(Kamuela)

0   4 mi
0   4 km

190

Mamalahoa

Hwy.

Saddle

Rd.

Waikii

200

shopping at both the Kings' Shops and Queens' MarketPlace. Sushi, local grills, food courts, and pricey restaurants all combine to give you abundant eating choices in Waikoloa. The natural gem here is the stunning, classically tropical Anaehoomalu Bay, once the site of royal fishponds and today an ideal spot to soak up some sun, explore along the trails, or try windsurfing. Waikoloa Village, a few miles inland and up the hill to the northeast, offers golf and rental condos for a fraction of the cost of the big resorts.

Beaches

★ Anaehoomalu Bay

BEACH—SIGHT | **FAMILY** | This gorgeous, expansive stretch of white sand, classically fringed with coco palms, fronts the Waikoloa Beach Marriott and is a perfect spot for swimming, windsurfing, snorkeling, and diving. Unlike some Kohala Coast beaches near hotel properties, this one is very accessible to the public and offers plenty of free parking. The bay is well protected, so even when the surf is rough or the trade winds are blasting, it's fairly calm here. (Mornings are calmest.) Snorkel gear, kayaks, and body boards are available for rent at the north end. **■ TIP→ Locals will appreciate your efforts to use the proper name rather than simply its nickname, "A-Bay."**

Behind the beach are two ancient Hawaiian fishponds, **Kuualii** and **Kahapapa,** that once served ancient Hawaiian royalty. A walking trail follows the coastline to the Hilton Waikoloa Village next door, passing by tide pools, ponds, and a turtle sanctuary where sea turtles can often be spotted sunbathing on the sand. Footwear is recommended for the trail. **Amenities:** food and drink; parking (no fee); showers; toilets; water sports. **Best for:** snorkeling; sunset; swimming; walking. ✉ *69-275 Waikoloa Beach Dr., Waikoloa* ✣ *Just south of Waikoloa Beach Marriott; turn left at Kings' Shops* 🎟 *Free.*

Restaurants

★ A-Bay's Island Grill

$ | **MODERN HAWAIIAN** | Beachy yet upscale, the restaurant has an in-house beer sommelier who advises on the perfect pairing with your food choice, which can range from fresh catch, steak, burgers, and sandwiches to crab cakes and escargots. This sports bar offers a 24-tap digital beer tower and 10 TV screens. **Known for:** fish tacos; one of the only restaurants on the Kohala Coast open until midnight; great tapas menu. [$] *Average main: $14* ✉ *Kings' Shops, 250 Waikoloa Beach Dr., Waikoloa* ☎ *808/209–8494* 🌐 *www.a-bays.com.*

KPC (Kamuela Provision Company) at the Hilton Waikoloa Village

$$$$ | **MODERN HAWAIIAN** | The breezy lanai has the most spectacular view of the leeward coast of any restaurant on the Big Island, and it's the perfect accompaniment to the elegant yet down-to-earth Hawaii regional cuisine and specialty cocktails. Entrées are on the pricey side, but the ginger-steamed *monchong* (a deep-water Hawaiian fish) is a winner, and the Keahole lobster chowder does not disappoint. **Known for:** specialty cocktails, such as the Island Passion mango martini; the island's best sunset dinner spot; decadent Kona Coffee Mud Slide dessert. [$] *Average main: $50* ✉ *Hilton Waikoloa Village, 69-425 Waikoloa Beach Dr., Waikoloa* ☎ *808/886–1234* 🌐 *www.hiltonwaikoloavillage.com* 🕒 *No lunch.*

Pueo's Osteria

$$$ | **ITALIAN** | Hidden in a shopping center in residential Waikoloa Village, this late-night destination serves dinner from 5 until midnight (*pueo* means "owl" in Hawaiian, and refers to the restaurant's "night owl" concept). Renowned executive chef James Babian (Four Seasons Hualalai, Fairmont Orchid) serves up multiregional Italian offerings that combine farm-fresh ingredients with fine imported Italian products like prosciutto from

Parma. **Known for:** Early Owl specials daily from 5 to 6 pm; late-night bar menu until 1 am; Tuscan-inspired dining room. [$] *Average main: $27* ✉ *Waikoloa Village Highlands Center, 68-1845 Waikoloa Rd., Waikoloa* ✣ *Near Subway* ☎ *808/339–7566* 🌐 *www.pueososteria.com* 🕑 *No lunch.*

Roy's Waikoloa Bar and Grill
$$$$ | **MODERN HAWAIIAN** | **FAMILY** | One of celebrity chef Roy Yamaguchi's Hawaii restaurants, this reliable, albeit pricey, place overlooks the lake at the Kings' Shops and is, granted, not an ocean-front setting. The three-course, prix-fixe meal is a good bet, as is blackened ahi; the macadamia nut–crusted Hawaiian fish with Kona lobster cream sauce is a melt-in-your-mouth encounter. **Known for:** great appetizers to share; extensive list of wines by the glass; outstanding kids' menu. [$] *Average main: $40* ✉ *Kings' Shops at Waikoloa Village, 69-250 Waikoloa Beach Dr., Waikoloa* ☎ *808/886–4321* 🌐 *www.roysrestaurant.com* 🕑 *No lunch.*

Sansei Seafood Restaurant and Sushi Bar
$$ | **JAPANESE** | **FAMILY** | Creative sushi and contemporary Asian cuisine take center stage at this entertaining restaurant at Queens' MarketPlace, where you can make a meal out of appetizers and sushi rolls or feast on great entrées from both land and sea. Though it has tried-and-true mainstays, the menu is consistently updated to include options such as Hawaiian *moi* (a local fish) sashimi rolls and Japanese yellowtail nori aioli poke. **Known for:** sushi bar specials; panko-encrusted ahi sashimi roll; karaoke on the weekends. [$] *Average main: $20* ✉ *Queens' MarketPlace, 201 Waikoloa Beach Dr., Suite 801, Waikoloa* ☎ *808/886–6286* 🌐 *www.sanseihawaii.com* 🕑 *No lunch.*

Coffee and Quick Bites

Island Fish and Chips
$ | **AMERICAN** | **FAMILY** | Hidden lakeside at the Kings' Shops, this little takeout place is a best-kept secret in the Waikoloa Beach Resort. The combo baskets brim with tempura fresh-catch fish, chicken, shrimp, and more. **Known for:** breakfast options such as loco moco (meat, rice, and eggs smothered in gravy) laden with tempura fish fillet; local ownership since 2000; great fish-and-chips to go. [$] *Average main: $12* ✉ *Kings' Shops, 69-250 Waikoloa Beach Dr., #D3, Waikoloa* ☎ *808/886–0005.*

Hotels

Aston Shores at Waikoloa
$$$ | **RENTAL** | **FAMILY** | Villas with terra-cotta-tile roofs are set amid landscaped lagoons and waterfalls at the edge of the championship Waikoloa Village Golf Course. **Pros:** good prices for the area; great location; kid-friendly option with a pool and in-room kitchens. **Cons:** no restaurants on-site; daily resort fee; older decor in some rooms. [$] *Rooms from: $309* ✉ *69-1035 Keana Pl., Waikoloa* ☎ *808/886–5001, 800/922–7866* 🌐 *www.aquaaston.com* 🛏 *120 suites* 🍴 *No meals.*

Hilton Waikoloa Village
$$$$ | **RESORT** | **FAMILY** | Gondola trams glide by, pint-size guests zoom down the 175-foot waterslide, a bride poses on the grand staircase, a fire-bearing runner lights the torches along the seaside path at sunset—these are some typical scenes at this 62-acre megaresort. **Pros:** family-friendly saltwater lagoon; lots of restaurant and activity options, including two golf courses; close to retail shopping. **Cons:** gigantic and crowded; $45 per night resort fee; restaurants are pricey. [$] *Rooms from: $346* ✉ *69-425 Waikoloa Beach Dr., Waikoloa* ☎ *808/886–1234, 800/445–8667* 🌐 *www.hiltonwaikoloavillage.com* 🛏 *1241 rooms* 🍴 *No meals.*

Kohala Condo Comforts 🍴

Renting a resort condo is a great way to relax near the beach with many of the comforts of home. The upside is that you get all the pluses of being near a resort with all the privacy of your own place. Most condos have kitchens or a place to barbecue, so you'll want to stock up on groceries. The nearest full-service market is **KTA Super Stores** (✉ 68-3916 Paniolo Ave., Waikoloa Village ☎ 808/883–1088), no more than a half hour from the resorts.

Even closer are both the **Kings' Shops** (✉ 250 Waikoloa Beach Dr., Waikoloa ☎ 808/886–8811) and the **Queens' MarketPlace** (✉ 201 Waikoloa Beach Dr., Waikoloa ☎ 808/886–8822) in the Waikoloa Beach Resort. There is a small general store with a liquor department and several nice restaurants at the Kings' Shops. Across the street, Queens' MarketPlace also has a food court and sit-down restaurants, as well as a gourmet market where you can get pizza baked to order.

★ Kolea at Waikoloa Beach Resort

$$$$ | RENTAL | FAMILY | These modern, impeccably furnished condos offer far more high-end amenities than the average condo complex, including both an infinity pool and a sand-bottom children's pool at its oceanside Beach Club; a fitness center; and a hot tub. **Pros:** high design; close to beach and activities; resort amenities of nearby Hilton. **Cons:** pricey for not being directly on the beach; no on-property restaurants; limited view from some units. Ⓢ Rooms from: $400 ✉ Waikoloa Beach Resort, 69-1000 Kolea Kai Circle, Waikoloa ☎ 808/987–4519 ⊕ www.koleavacations.com ⤢ 53 units ⦿l No meals.

★ Lava Lava Beach Club Cottages

$$$$ | RENTAL | FAMILY | Spend the day swimming at the beach just steps away from your private lanai and fall asleep to the sound of the ocean at one of four artfully decorated, one-room cottages on the sandy beach at Anaehoomalu Bay. These cottages are among the few beachfront rentals you will find anywhere on the island. **Pros:** on the beach; fully air-conditioned; fun, Hawaii-themed decor. **Cons:** beach is public, so there may be people in front of cottage; quite

expensive; often booked up. Ⓢ Rooms from: $495 ✉ 69-1081 Kuualii Pl., Waikoloa ☎ 808/769–5282 ⊕ www.lavalavabeachclub.com ⤢ 4 cottages ⦿l No meals.

Waikoloa Beach Marriott Resort and Spa

$$$$ | RESORT | FAMILY | Encompassing 15 acres replete with ancient fishponds, historic trails, and petroglyph fields, the Marriott has rooms with sleek modern beds, bright white linens, Hawaiian art, and private lanai. **Pros:** more low-key than the Hilton Waikoloa; sunset luau Wednesday and Saturday; sand-bottom pool for kids. **Cons:** some rooms lack views; expensive daily parking charge; resort fee of $30 per day. Ⓢ Rooms from: $400 ✉ 69-275 Waikoloa Beach Dr., Waikoloa ☎ 808/886–6789, 800/228–9290 ⊕ www.marriott.com ⤢ 297 rooms ⦿l No meals.

🎭 Performing Arts

LUAU

Legends of Hawaii Luau at Hilton Waikoloa Village

CULTURAL FESTIVALS | FAMILY | Presented outdoors at the Kamehameha Court, this show is aptly subtitled "Our Big Island Story." A delicious buffet offers

Big Island–grown luau choices as well as more familiar fare and tropical drinks. Pay a small fee and upgrade to Alii seating for a front-row vantage; unlimited cocktails, beer, and wine; and your own buffet station. A children's station has kid favorites. Delicious desserts such as *haupia* (with coconut milk) cream puffs and Kona-coffee cheesecake top it all off. ⊠ *Hilton Waikoloa Village, 69-425 Waikoloa Beach Dr., Waikoloa* ☎ *808/886–1234* ⊕ *www. hiltonwaikoloavillage.com/luau* ⌧ *$142.*

Waikoloa Beach Marriott Resort and Spa Sunset Luau

CULTURAL FESTIVALS | Overlooking the white sands of Anaehoomalu Bay, this Polynesian luau includes a spectacular Samoan fire-dance performance as well as traditional music and dances from various Pacific Island cultures. Traditional dishes are served alongside more familiar Western fare, and there's also an open bar. ⊠ *Waikoloa Beach Marriott Resort and Spa, 69-275 Waikoloa Beach Dr., Waikoloa* ☎ *808/886–8111* ⊕ *www. waikoloabeachresort.com* ⌧ *$117.*

● Shopping

ARTS AND CRAFTS
Hawaiian Quilt Collection

CRAFTS | The Hawaiian quilt is a work of art that is prized and passed down through generations. At this store, you'll find everything from hand-quilted purses and bags to wall hangings and blankets. More than likely, a friendly Hawaiian *tutu* (grandma) will be in the shop talking story. You can even get a take-home kit and sew your own Hawaiian quilt. ⊠ *Queens' MarketPlace, 69-201 Waikoloa Beach Dr., #305, Waikoloa* ☎ *808/886–0494* ⊕ *www. hawaiian-quilts.com.*

Island Pearls by Maui Divers

JEWELRY/ACCESSORIES | Among the fine jewelry at this boutique is a wide selection of high-end pearl jewelry, including Tahitian black pearls, South Sea white and golden pearls, and chocolate Tahitian

pearls. Also here are freshwater pearls in the shell, black coral (the Hawaii state gemstone), and diamonds. Prices are high but so is the quality. ⊠ *Queens' MarketPlace, 69-201 Waikoloa Beach Dr., #J-11, Waikoloa* ☎ *808/886–4817* ⊕ *www. mauidivers.com.*

CLOTHING AND SHOES
Blue Ginger

CLOTHING | The Waikoloa branch of this fashion veteran offers really sweet matching aloha outfits for the entire family. There are also handbags, shoes, robes, jewelry, and lotions. ⊠ *Queens' MarketPlace, 69-201 Waikoloa Beach Dr., Waikoloa* ☎ *808/886–0022* ⊕ *www. blueginger.com.*

SHOPPING CENTERS
Kings' Shops at Waikoloa Beach Resort

SHOPPING CENTERS/MALLS | Stores here include Martin & MacArthur, featuring koa furniture and accessories, and Tori Richard, which offers upscale resort wear, as well as high-end chains Coach, Tiffany, and Michael Kors. Gourmet offerings include Roy's Waikoloa Bar and Grill, A-Bay's Island Grill, and Island Fish and Chips. Stock your hotel fridge with fresh local produce from the Kings' Shops Farmers Market, held Wednesday 8:30 to 2:30. ⊠ *Waikoloa Beach Resort, 250 Waikoloa Beach Dr., Waikoloa* ☎ *808/339–7145* ⊕ *www.kingsshops.com.*

Queens' MarketPlace

SHOPPING CENTERS/MALLS | The largest shopping complex on the Kohala Coast houses fashionable clothing stores, jewelry boutiques, galleries, gift shops, and restaurants, including Sansei Seafood Restaurant and Sushi Bar; Daylight Mind; and Romano's Macaroni Grill. Island Gourmet Markets and Starbucks are also here, as is an affordable food court. Waikoloa Luxury Cinemas offers the ultimate movie experience and includes a restaurant called Bistro at the Cinemas. ⊠ *Waikoloa Beach Resort, 201 Waikoloa Beach Dr., Waikoloa* ☎ *808/886–8822* ⊕ *www.queensmarketplace.net.*

Mauna Lani

8 miles north of Waikoloa.

Mauna Lani is known for its expensive resorts, but fortunately it's so much more. In addition to cooling trade winds, black lava landscapes, and turquoise seas, the region has numerous historical sites, including ancient fishponds, petroglyphs, and historical trails that invite lovers of history and culture to explore numerous spots along this coast.

Sights

Holoholokai Beach Park and Petroglyph Trail
BEACH—SIGHT | While mostly rocky topography makes swimming and snorkeling a bit difficult here, this little park is still scenic and relaxing. Take the short trail over to the petroglyph trail; interpretive signs will guide you. There are showers, picnic tables, and restrooms. ✉ *Holoholokai Beach Park Rd., Mauna Lani* ✣ *Near the end of N. Kaniku Dr.* ☎ *808/657–3293* 🎟 *Free.*

Restaurants

Binchotan Bar and Grill
$$$ | **ASIAN FUSION** | In a sophisticated setting that includes open-air patio seating, this new restaurant offers contemporary Asian dishes made with meats, prawns, peppers, and more grilled over an open flame in the traditional style. Blending locally sourced ingredients with Japanese and Hawaiian influences, Chef Justin Kalaluhi creates a menu that pays homage to multiple cultures. **Known for:** Robatayaki Experience (chef's selection of grilled items); okonomiyaki (savory Japanese-style pancakes) featuring Kona lobster and macadamia nut shrimp; shared plates. [$] *Average main: $28* ✉ *Fairmont Orchid Hawaii, 1 N. Kaniku Dr., Mauna Lani* ☎ *808/885–5778* 🌐 *www.fairmont.com* 🕒 *Closed Tues. and Wed. No lunch.*

Brown's Beach House at the Fairmont Orchid Hawaii
$$$$ | **MODERN HAWAIIAN** | Sitting right on the resort's sandy bay, Brown's Beach House offers beautiful sunset dining and innovative cuisine. Attention to detail is evident in the sophisticated menu, which may include crab-crusted Kona *kampachi* or other dishes with sea fish, roasted duck breast, or Kona coffee–crusted venison, as well as locally grown produce. **Known for:** Dungeness crab and lobster tail; tiki torches and live Hawaiian music beneath starry skies; vegetarian and gluten-free options. [$] *Average main: $40* ✉ *Fairmont Orchid Hawaii, 1 N. Kaniku Dr., Mauna Lani* ☎ *808/885–2000* 🌐 *www.fairmont.com* 🕒 *No lunch.*

★ CanoeHouse at the Mauna Lani, Auberge Resorts Collection
$$$$ | **MODERN HAWAIIAN** | One of the most romantic settings on the Kohala Coast, this landmark, oceanfront restaurant showcases traditional Hawaiian flavors, artful presentations, and locally grown or raised products. The progressive menu spotlights standout entrées such as roasted beef tenderloin, lamb, fish caught locally, shellfish, island-fresh greens, and local goat cheese. **Known for:** memorable sunsets with tiki torches; good choice of wines by the glass; customized dining program by the chef offered at the Captain's Table. [$] *Average main: $48* ✉ *Mauna Lani, Auberge Resorts Collection, 68-1400 Mauna Lani Dr., Mauna Lani* ☎ *808/885–6622* 🌐 *www.maunalani.com* 🕒 *No lunch.*

Shiono at Mauna Lani
$$ | **JAPANESE** | With three locations and a fourth coming up, this very popular Japanese establishment does not disappoint. At this location especially, high-end fish and meats (some flown in daily from Japan) highlight an eclectic menu of handcrafted sushi, combination platters, and entrées. **Known for:**

outstanding omakase (chef chooses the food) experience; fresh ingredients, both local and imported; fine collection of premium sakes. $ *Average main: $25* ✉ *The Shops at Mauna Lani, 68-1330 Mauna Lani Dr., Suite 111 (2nd fl.), Mauna Lani* ☎ *808/881–1111* 🌐 *www.sushishiono.com/mauna-lani* 🕒 *No lunch.*

Tommy Bahama Restaurant and Bar
$$$$ | **MODERN HAWAIIAN** | **FAMILY** | This breezy, open-air restaurant, located upstairs at the Shops at Mauna Lani, offers an excellent roster of appetizers, including seared-scallop sliders and coconut-crusted crab cakes, as well as meat and fish mains and decadent desserts. The chef here has freedom to cook up his own daily specials, and the seared ahi is a standout. **Known for:** the chain's reliable cuisine and relaxed vibe; popular cocktail bar and lounge; house-baked breads and specialty butters. $ *Average main: $38* ✉ *The Shops at Mauna Lani, 68-1330 Mauna Lani Dr., Suite 102, Mauna Lani* ☎ *808/881–8686* 🌐 *www.tommybahama.com.*

Hotels

★ Fairmont Orchid Hawaii
$$$ | **RESORT** | **FAMILY** | This first-rate resort overflows with tropical gardens, cascading waterfalls, a sandy beach cove, beautiful wings with "open sesame" doors, a meandering pool, and renovated rooms with all the amenities. **Pros:** oceanfront location; excellent pool; aloha hospitality. **Cons:** central pool can get very crowded; 40-minute drive to Kailua-Kona; not the best beach among Kohala Coast resorts. $ *Rooms from: $269* ✉ *1 N. Kaniku Dr., Mauna Lani* ☎ *808/885–2000, 800/845–9905* 🌐 *www.fairmont.com* 🛏 *540 rooms* 🍴 *No meals.*

★ Mauna Lani, Auberge Resorts Collection
$$$$ | **RESORT** | Popular with honeymooners and anniversary couples for decades, this elegant Kohala Coast classic is still one of the most beautiful resorts on the island, highlighted by a breathtaking, open-air lobby with cathedral-like ceilings, Zen-like koi ponds, and illuminated sheets of cascading water. **Pros:** beautiful design; award-winning spa; many Hawaiian cultural programs. **Cons:** no luau; limited dining selection on-site; 26 miles from airport. $ *Rooms from: $579* ✉ *68-1400 Mauna Lani Dr., Mauna Lani* ☎ *808/885–6622, 808/657–3293* 🌐 *aubergeresorts.com/maunalani* 🛏 *338 rooms* 🍴 *No meals.*

Mauna Lani Point and the Islands at Mauna Lani
$$$$ | **RENTAL** | Surrounded by the emerald greens of a world-class oceanside golf course, the private, independent, luxury condominiums at Islands at Mauna Lani offer spacious two-story suites, while Mauna Lani Point's villas are closer to the beach. **Pros:** friendly front desk; stellar views; extra-large units. **Cons:** quite pricey; individually owned units vary in decor and amenities; some units are a distance from the barbecue/pool area. $ *Rooms from: $665* ✉ *Mauna Lani Point, 68-1050 Mauna Lani Point Dr., Mauna Lani* ☎ *808/885–5022, 800/642–6284* 🌐 *www.classicresorts.com* 🛏 *66 units* 🍴 *No meals.*

Nightlife

BARS

Luana Lounge
BARS/PUBS | The contemporary lounge in the Fairmont Orchid has a large terrace and an impressive water view. Bartenders are skilled at mixology, and service is impeccable. The crowd is mellow, so it's a nice place for an early evening cocktail or after-dinner liqueur. Happy hour is from 5 to 6, and live music begins at sunset and continues until 9. ✉ *Fairmont Orchid Hawaii, 1 N. Kaniku Dr., Mauna Lani* ☎ *808/885–2000* 🌐 *www.fairmont.com.*

🎭 Performing Arts

LUAU

Hawaii Loa Luau

CULTURAL FESTIVALS | Slickly produced and well choreographed, this gorgeous show incorporates both traditional and contemporary music and dance, along with an array of beautiful costumes. It tells the tale of Hawaiiloa, the great navigator from Tahiti, and of the celestial object—*Hokulea*, "Star of Gladness"—that guided him to the islands later named Hawaii. Presented under the stars at the Fairmont Orchid Hawaii on Saturdays, the meal offers several stations with a variety of Hawaiian and Hawaii regional cuisine dishes, and there's a full bar for mai tais and other tropical libations. ⊠ *Fairmont Orchid Hawaii, 1 N. Kaniku Dr., Mauna Lani* 🕿 *808/885–2000, 808/326–4969* ⊕ *www.gatheringofthekings.com* 🖃 *$131.*

👜 Shopping

SHOPPING CENTERS

The Shops at Mauna Lani

SHOPPING CENTERS/MALLS | The best part about this complex is its roster of restaurants, which includes coffee, smoothie, and sandwich shops; Tommy Bahama Restaurant and Bar; Ruth's Chris Steakhouse; and Under the Bodhi Tree café (gourmet vegetarian options). You can find tropical apparel at Jams World, high-end housewares at Oasis Lifestyle, and original art at a number of galleries. ⊠ *68-1330 Mauna Lani Dr., Mauna Lani* 🕿 *808/885–9501* ⊕ *www.shopsatmaunalani.com.*

Mauna Kea and Hapuna

6 miles north of Mauna Lani.

Every visitor to the Big Island should put Hapuna Beach State Recreation Area on an itinerary, especially if you're not staying at the Westin Hapuna Beach Resort,

located beachfront. This glorious white-sand beauty will not fail to take your breath away, no matter what the season or time of day. Sheer enchantment also defines the luminous waters and curve of white sand at Kaunaoa, also called Mauna Kea Beach, but it's more difficult to access due to the Mauna Kea Beach Hotel's control of the parking area.

🏖 Beaches

★ Hapuna Beach State Recreation Area

BEACH—SIGHT | FAMILY | One of Hawaii's finest beaches, Hapuna is a ½-mile-long stretch of white perfection. The turquoise water is calm in summer, so it's good for kids, with just enough rolling waves to make body surfing and body boarding fun. Watch for the undertow; in winter it can be rough. There is excellent snorkeling around the jagged rocks that border the beach on either side, but high surf brings strong currents. Known for awesome sunsets, this is one of the best places on the island to see the "green flash" as the sun dips below a clear horizon.

The north end of the beach fronts the Westin Hapuna Beach Resort, which rents water-sports equipment and has a food concession with shaded picnic tables. There is ample parking, although the lot can fill up by midday and the beach can get crowded on holidays. Lifeguards, on duty during peak hours, cover the state park section, not areas north of the rocky cliff that juts out near the middle of the beach. **Amenities:** food and drink; lifeguards; parking (fee); showers; toilets; water sports. **Best for:** sunset; surfing; swimming; walking. ⊠ *Hwy. 19 near mile marker 69, Mauna Kea* ✛ *Just south of the Westin Hapuna Beach Resort* 🕿 *808/961–9544* ⊕ *dlnr.hawaii.gov* 🖃 *$5 per vehicle.*

★ Kaunaoa Beach *(Mauna Kea Beach)*

BEACH—SIGHT | FAMILY | Hands down one of the most beautiful beaches on the

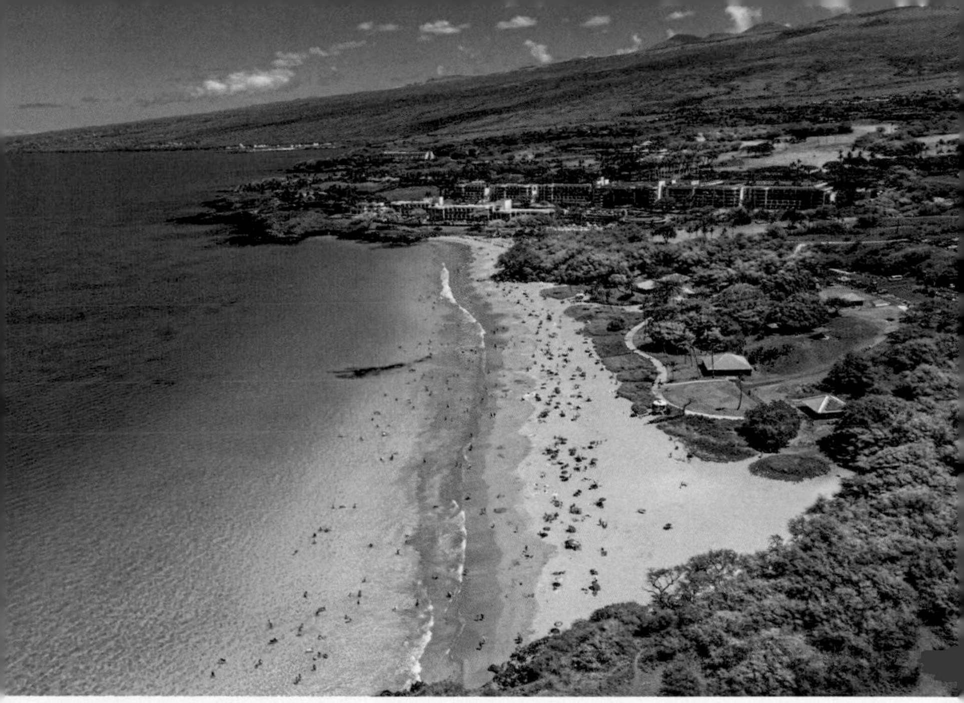

Hapuna Beach State Recreation area protects the island's largest white-sand beach. At the northern end sits the Westin Hapuna Beach Resort.

island, if not the whole state, Kaunaoa features a long crescent of pure white sand framed by coco palms. The beach, which fronts the Mauna Kea Beach Hotel, slopes very gradually, and there's great snorkeling along the rocks. Classic Hawaii postcard views abound, especially in winter, when snow tops Maunakea to the east. When conditions permit, waves are good for body- and board surfing also. Currents can be strong in winter, so be careful. Get a cocktail at the beach cabana and enjoy the sunset. **■ TIP→ Public parking is limited to a few spaces, so arrive before 10 am or after 4 pm. If the lot is full, head to nearby Hapuna Beach, where there's a huge parking lot ($5 per vehicle). Try this spot again another day—it's worth it! Amenities:** parking (no fee); showers; toilets; water sports. **Best for:** snorkeling; sunset; swimming; walking. ✉ *62-100 Mauna Kea Beach Dr., Mauna Kea* ✣ *Entry through gate to Mauna Kea Beach Hotel.*

🍴 Restaurants

Hau Tree

$$$ | MODERN HAWAIIAN | Though it sits on a patio by the pool, this beachside restaurant and beach bar is not just for *pupus* (appetizers) and cocktails. The island-infused dinner menu features excellent entrées, such as the grass-fed Kulana beef tenderloin brochettes, plus plentiful seafood dishes and greens from local farms. **Known for:** famous Fredrico cocktail; great sunset views; Saturday clambake. [$] *Average main: $27* ✉ *Mauna Kea Beach Hotel, 62-100 Mauna Kea Beach Dr., Mauna Kea* ☎ *808/882–5707* 🌐 *www.maunakeabeachhotel.com.*

★ Manta at the Mauna Kea Beach Hotel

$$$$ | MODERN HAWAIIAN | Perched on the edge of a bluff overlooking the sparkling waters of Kaunaoa Beach, the resort's flagship restaurant is a compelling spot for a romantic meal at sunset, especially at one of the outside tables. The culinary team's take on Hawaii regional cuisine highlights locally sourced, sustainable fish, chicken, and beef. **Known for:** beachfront balcony dining; exhibition kitchen; Sunday brunch with prime rib, smoked salmon, and omelet station. $ *Average main: $40* ✉ *Mauna Kea Beach Hotel, 62-100 Mauna Kea Beach Dr., Mauna Kea* ☎ *808/882–5707* 🌐 *www.maunakeabeachhotel.com* 🕒 *No lunch.*

Hotels

Mauna Kea Beach Hotel, Autograph Collection
$$$$ | **RESORT** | The grande dame of the Kohala Coast has long been regarded as one of the state's premier vacation resort hotels, and it borders one of the world's finest white-sand beaches, Kaunaoa. **Pros:** good dining options; premier tennis center; no resort fees. **Cons:** some oceanfront rooms are noisy; $30 daily valet parking fee; 27 miles from airport. $ *Rooms from: $629* ✉ *62-100 Mauna Kea Beach Dr., Mauna Kea* ☎ *808/882–7222, 866/977–4589* 🌐 *www.maunakeabeachhotel.com* 🛏 *252 rooms* 🍴 *No meals.*

The Westin Hapuna Beach Resort
$$$$ | **RESORT** | **FAMILY** | Slightly more affordable than its neighbor resorts and with direct access to the Big Island's largest white-sand beach, this massive hotel has enormous columns and a terraced, open-air lobby with rotunda ceiling, curved staircases, and skylights. **Pros:** extra-large rooms, all ocean-facing; direct access to one of island's best beaches; resort has 18-hole championship golf course. **Cons:** fitness center a five-minute walk from the hotel; $30 daily resort fee; 30 miles from Kailua-Kona. $ *Rooms from: $539* ✉ *62-100 Kaunaoa Dr., Mauna Kea* ☎ *808/880–1111, 866/774–6236* 🌐 *www.marriott.com* 🛏 *249 rooms* 🍴 *No meals.*

Performing Arts

LUAU

Mauna Kea Beach Hotel Clambake
CULTURAL FESTIVALS | The weekly clambake near the sand at Hau Tree beach restaurant features an extensive menu with oysters on the half shell, Manila clams, Dungeness crab legs, mussels, sashimi, and "all-you-can-eat" Keahole lobster. There's even prime rib and a dessert station. Live Hawaiian music is often accompanied by a graceful hula dancer. ✉ *Mauna Kea Beach Hotel, 62-100 Mauna Kea Beach Dr., Mauna Kea* ☎ *808/882–5707* 🌐 *maunakeabeachhotel.com* 🎟 *$122.*

Kawaihae

6 miles north of Hapuna.

This no-frills industrial harbor, where in 1793 the first cattle landed in Hawaii, is a hub of commercial and community activity, including interisland transports. It's also where King Kamehameha and his men launched their canoes when they set out to conquer the neighboring islands. It's especially busy on weekends, when paddlers, surfers, tourist charters, and local fishing boats share the waters. Second in size only to Hilo Harbor, the port serves interisland cargo carriers and often shelters the *Makalii,* one of three traditional Hawaiian sailing canoes. Kawaihae Village has several restaurants with nice sunset views.

Sights

★ Puukohola Heiau National Historic Site
HISTORIC SITE | Quite simply, this is one of the most historic and commanding sites in all of Hawaii. It was here in 1810, on top of Puukohola (Hill of the Whale), that Kamehameha the Great built the war *heiau,* or temple, that would serve to unify the Hawaiian Islands, ending 500 years of almost continual warring chiefdoms.

The oceanfront, fortresslike site is foreboding and impressive. A paved ½-mile, looped trail runs from the visitor center to the main temple sites. An even older temple, dedicated to the shark gods, lies submerged just offshore, where sharks can be spotted swimming, usually first thing in the morning. A museum displays ancient Hawaiian weapons, including clubs, spears, a replica of a bronze cannon that warriors dragged into battle on a Hawaiian sled, and three original paintings by artist Herb Kane. Rangers are available to answer questions, or you can take a free audio tour on your own smartphone. Plan about an hour to see everything. ✉ *62-3601 Kawaihae Rd., Kawaihae* ☎ *808/882–7218* 🌐 *www.nps.gov/puhe* 🎫 *Free.*

Beaches

Spencer Park at Ohaiula Beach

BEACH—SIGHT | **FAMILY** | This white-sand beach is popular with local families because of its reef-protected waters. **■ TIP→ It's probably the safest beach in West Hawaii for young children.** It's also safe for swimming year-round, which makes it a reliable spot for a lazy day at the beach. There is a little shade, plus a volleyball court and pavilion, and the soft sand is perfect for sand castles. It does tend to get crowded with families and campers on weekends, but the beach is generally clean. Although you won't see a lot of fish if you're snorkeling here, in winter you can often catch sight of a breaching whale or two. The beach park lies just below Puukohola Heiau National Historic Park, site of the historic war temple built by King Kamehameha the Great in 1810 after uniting the Islands. **Amenities:** lifeguards (weekends and holidays only); parking (no fee); showers; toilets. **Best for:** sunset; swimming. ✉ *Hwy. 270, Kawaihae* ✥ *Toward Kawaihae Harbor, just after road forks from Hwy. 19* ☎ *808/961–8311.*

Restaurants

★ Seafood Bar and Grill

$$ | **SEAFOOD** | Upstairs in a historical building, this seafood tiki bar has been a hot spot for years, serving up a dynamite and well-priced bar menu with tasty *pupus* (appetizers), signature seafood dishes such as the coconut shrimp or poke burger, and even a prime rib special on Tuesdays. Don't let the funky appearance deter you; this place is frequented by legacy celebrities whose names you know or whose records you've bought. **Known for:** funky tiki theme; seafood quesadilla; two nightly happy hours. [$] *Average main: $23* ✉ *61-3642 Kawaihae Harbor (Hwy. 270), Kawaihae* ☎ *808/880–9393* 🌐 *www.seafoodbarandgrill.com.*

Shopping

GALLERIES

Harbor Gallery

ART GALLERIES | Since 1990, this gallery has been enticing visitors with a vast collection of paintings and sculptures by more than 200 Big Island artists. There are also antique maps and prints, wooden bowls, paddles, koa furniture, jewelry, and glasswork. The shop hosts two annual wood shows. ✉ *Kawaihae Harbor Shopping Center, 61-3665 Akoni Pule Hwy., Kawaihae* ☎ *808/882–1510* 🌐 *www.harborgallery.biz.*

SHOPPING CENTERS

Kawaihae Harbor Shopping Center

SHOPPING CENTERS/MALLS | This almost-oceanfront shopping plaza houses the exquisite Harbor Gallery, which represents many Big Island artists. Try the Big Island–made ice cream and shave ice (the best in North Hawaii) at local favorite Anuenue. Also here are Mountain Gold Jewelers and Kohala Divers. ✉ *61-3665 Akoni Pule Hwy., Kawaihae.*

Hawi and Kapaau

18 miles north of Kawaihae.

Near the birthplace of King Kamehameha, these North Kohala towns thrived during the plantation days, once bustling with hotels, saloons, and theaters—even a railroad. They took a hit when "Big Sugar" left the island, but both towns are blossoming once again, thanks to strong local communities, tourism, athletic events, and an influx of artists keen on honoring the towns' past. They are full of lovingly restored vintage buildings housing fun and funky shops and galleries, as well as eateries worth a stop for a quick bite. Hawi is internationally known as the turnaround point for the cycling portion of the Ironman triathlon event.

⊙ Sights

Keokea Beach Park

NATIONAL/STATE PARK | A renovated pavilion (it was damaged in a 2006 quake) welcomes visitors to this 7-acre beach park fronting the rugged shore in North Kohala. This is a popular local spot for picnics, fishing, and surfing. ⚠ **Enjoy the scenery, but don't try to swim here—the water is very rough. Be careful on the hairpin curve going down.** ⊠ *Hwy. 270, Kapaau* ✛ *On the way to Pololu Valley, near mile marker 27* ⊜ *Free.*

Lapakahi State Historical Park

HISTORIC SITE | A self-guided, 1-mile walking tour leads through the ruins of the once-prosperous fishing village Koaie, which dates as far back as the 15th century. Displays illustrate early Hawaiian fishing and farming techniques, salt gathering, games, and legends. Because the shoreline near the state park is an officially designated Marine Life Conservation District (and part of the site itself .is considered sacred), swimming, swim gear, and sunscreen are not allowed in the water. Portable restrooms are available but not drinking water. ⚠ **Gates close promptly at 4 pm, and they mean business!** ⊠ *Hwy. 270 at mile marker 14, between Kawaihae and Mahukona, Kapaau* ☎ *808/327–4958* ⊕ *www.hawaiistateparks.org* ⊜ *Free.*

Mookini Heiau

ARCHAEOLOGICAL SITE | This isolated National Historic Landmark within Kohala Historical Sites State Monument is so impressive in size and atmosphere that it's guaranteed to give you what locals call "chicken skin" (goose bumps). Dating as early as AD 480, the parallelogram-shape structure is a stunning example of a *luakini heiau*, used for ritualized human sacrifice to the Hawaiian war god Ku. The place feels haunted, and even more so if you are the only visitor and the skies are dark and foreboding. Visit with utmost care and respect. Nearby is Kapakai Royal Housing Complex, the birthplace of Kamehameha the Great. Although it is now under the care of the National Park Service, the site is still watched over by family descendants. ⚠ **Don't drive out here if it's been raining; even with a four-wheel drive, you could easily get stuck.** ⊠ *Coral Reef Pl./Upolu Point Rd., off Upolu Airport Rd. and Hwy. 270 (Akoni Pule Hwy.), Hawi* ✛ *Turn at sign for Upolu Airport, near Hawi, and hike or drive 1½ miles southwest* ☎ *808/961–9540* ⊕ *www.nps.gov* ⊜ *Free* ⊘ *Closed Wed.*

⊙ Beaches

Pololu Valley Beach

BEACH—SIGHT | On the North Kohala peninsula, this is one of the Big Island's most scenic beaches. After about 8 miles of lush, winding road past Hawi Town, Highway 270 ends at the overlook of Pololu Valley. Snap a few photos of the stunning view, then take the 15-minute hike down (allow twice as long to go back up) to the beach. The trail is steep and rocky; it can also be muddy and slippery, so watch your step. The beach itself is a wide expanse of fine gray sand

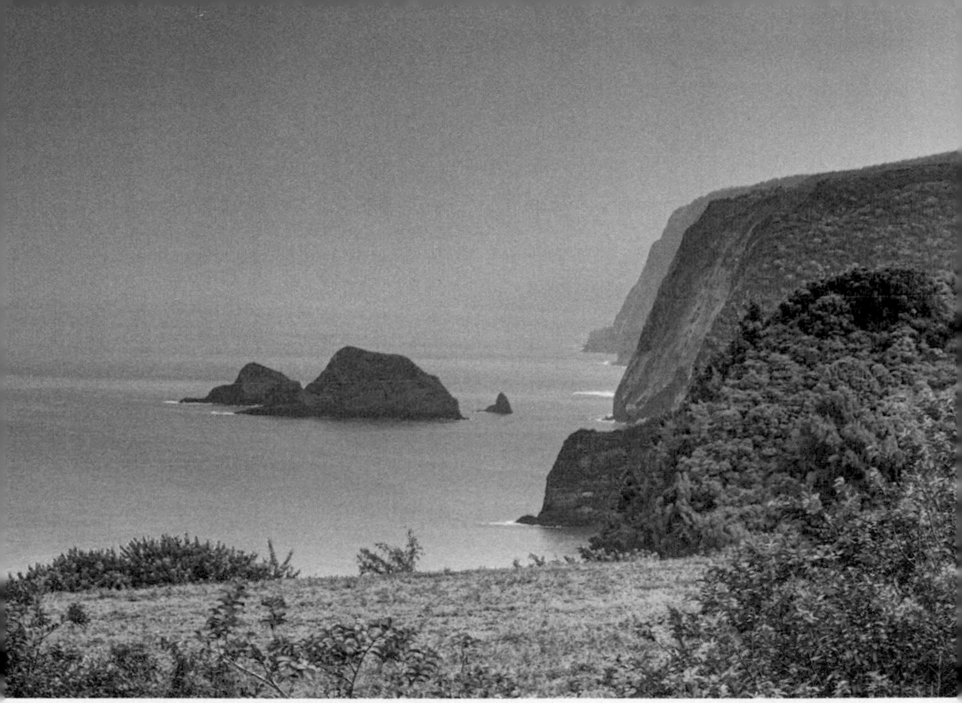

Pololu Valley Beach is one of the island's most beautiful, but you may want to enjoy it from the lookout at the top; it's a steep, 15-minute climb down to reach the light gray sand.

with piles of large, round boulders and driftwood. It's surrounded by sheer green cliffs and backed by high dunes and ironwood trees. A gurgling stream leads to the beach from the back of the valley. ⚠ **This is not a safe swimming beach even though locals do swim, body board, and surf here. Dangerous rip currents and usually rough surf pose a real hazard.** Because this is a remote, isolated area far from emergency help, extreme caution is advised. **Amenities:** none. **Best for:** solitude. ✉ *Hwy. 270 at end of road, Kapaau.*

🍴 Restaurants

★ Sushi Rock

$$$ | **JAPANESE** | Located in historic Hawi Town, Sushi Rock isn't big on size—its narrow dining room is brightly painted and casually decorated with Hawaiian and Japanese knickknacks—but discerning locals and *akamai* (in-the-know) visitors come here for some of the island's best sushi. The restaurant prides itself on using local ingredients like grass-fed beef tenderloin, goat cheese, macadamia nuts, and mango in the Islands-inspired sushi rolls. **Known for:** well-priced trios with beef, poke, and other choices; cone sushi; extensive salad menu. [$] *Average main: $33* ✉ *55-3435 Akoni Pule Hwy., Hawi* ☎ *808/889–5900* 🌐 *sushirockrestaurant.net.*

☕ Coffee and Quick Bites

Kohala Coffee Mill and Tropical Dreams

$ | **CAFÉ** | If you're looking for something sweet—or savory—this busy café in downtown Hawi serves great local coffee, breakfast (bagels, espresso machine–steamed eggs), and lunch (hot dogs, burgers, chili, salads, vegan soup) until 6. Sit outside and watch the world go by as you enjoy locally made ice cream that is *ono* (delicious), as well as other sweet treat specialties. **Known for:** great ice cream; sometimes crowded; outstanding coffee. [$] *Average main: $4* ✉ *55-3412 Akoni Pule Hwy., Hawi* ☎ *808/889–5577* 🕒 *No dinner.*

Hotels

★ Hawaii Island Retreat at Ahu Pohaku Hoomaluhia

$$$$ | **B&B/INN** | Here, above the sea cliffs in North Kohala's Hawi, sustainability meets luxury without sacrificing comfort: the resort generates its own solar and wind-turbine power, harnesses its own water, and grows much of its own food. **Pros:** stunning location; emphasis on organic food; affordable yurts are one lodging option. **Cons:** somewhat isolated and not within walking distance of restaurants; yurts don't have in-unit showers; four-night minimum. [$] *Rooms from: $425* ✉ *250 Maluhia Rd., Kapaau* ✣ *Off Hwy. 270 in Hawi* ☎ *808/889–6336* 🌐 *www.hawaiiislandretreat.com* 🛏 *20 rooms* 🍴 *Free breakfast.*

★ Puakea Ranch

$$$ | **RENTAL** | **FAMILY** | Four beautifully restored ranch houses and bungalows occupy this historic country estate in Hawi, where guests enjoy their own private swimming pools, horseback riding, round-the-clock concierge availability, and plenty of fresh fruit from the orchards. **Pros:** charmingly decorated; beautiful bathrooms; private swimming pools. **Cons:** 15 minutes to the beach; spotty cell-phone coverage; sometimes windy. [$] *Rooms from: $289* ✉ *56-2864 Akoni Pule Hwy., Hawi* ☎ *808/315–0805* 🌐 *www.puakearanch.com* 🛏 *4 houses* 🍴 *No meals.*

Shopping

ARTS AND CRAFTS

Elements Jewelry and Fine Crafts

CRAFTS | The beautiful little shop carries lots of original jewelry handmade by local artists, as well as carefully chosen gifts, including unusual ceramics, paintings, prints, glass items, baskets, fabrics, bags, and toys. ✉ *55-3413 Akoni Pule Hwy., Hawi* ✣ *Next to Bamboo Restaurant* ☎ *808/889–0760* 🌐 *www.elements-jewelryandcrafts.com.*

CLOTHING AND SHOES

As Hawi Turns

CLOTHING | This landmark North Kohala shop, housed in the 1932 Toyama Building, stocks sophisticated resort wear made of hand-painted silk in tropical designs by local artists. There are also plentiful vintage treasures, jewelry, gifts, hats, bags, and toys, plus handmade ukuleles by local luthier David Gomes. ✉ *55-3412 Akoni Pule Hwy., Hawi* ☎ *808/889–5023.*

GALLERIES

Ackerman Fine Art Gallery

ART GALLERIES | Kapaau-based, this multiple-gallery/café is truly a family affair. Local artist Gary Ackerman's wife, Yesan, runs Ackerman Fine Art Gallery, featuring Gary's original oil paintings, fused glass art, and glass sculpture, plus works from other local artists. Down the street, Gary's daughter, Alyssa, and her husband, Ronnie, run Ackerman Gift Gallery, which showcases fine art, photography, and gifts, and their own King's View Cafe, located across from the historic King Kamehameha statue. ✉ *54-3878 Akoni Pule Hwy., Kapaau* ☎ *808/889–5138 Ackerman Fine Art Gallery* 🌐 *www.ackermangalleries.com.*

Rankin Gallery

ART GALLERIES | Watercolorist and oil painter Patrick Louis Rankin showcases his own work at his shop in a restored plantation store next to the bright-green Chinese community and social hall, on the way to Pololu Valley. The building sits right at a curve in the road, at the first gulch past Kapaau. ✉ *53-4380 Akoni Pule Hwy., Kapaau* ☎ *808/889–6849* 🌐 *www.patricklouisrankin.net.*

Waimea

Waimea is 40 miles northeast of Kailua-Kona and 10 miles east of the Kohala Coast.

Thirty minutes over the mountain from Kohala, Waimea (sometimes called "Kamuela" to distinguish it from the similarly named places on Kauai and Oahu) offers a completely different experience than the rest of the island. Rolling green hills, large open pastures, light rain, cool evening breezes and morning mists, along with abundant cattle, horses, and regular rodeos, are just a few of the surprises you'll stumble upon here in *paniolo* (cowboy) country. Parker Ranch, one of the largest privately held cattle ranches in the United States, surrounds this attractive little town.

Waimea is also where some of the island's top Hawaii regional cuisine chefs practice their art using local ingredients, which makes it an ideal place to find yourself at dinnertime. In keeping with the recent restaurant trend toward featuring local farm-to-table ingredients, a handful of Waimea farms and ranches supply most of the restaurants on the island, and many sell to the public as well. With its galleries, coffee shops, brewpubs, restaurants, beautiful countryside, and *paniolo* culture, Waimea is well worth a stop if you're heading to Hilo or Maunakea. ■ **TIP→ The short highway, or mountain road, that connects Waimea to North Kohala (Highway 250) affords some of our favorite Big Island views.**

From the Kohala Coast, it's a reasonable drive to Waimea. From the Mauna Kea and Hapuna resorts, it's about 12 miles; from the Waikoloa resorts, it's about 19 miles via Waikoloa Road. You can see most of what Waimea has to offer in one day, but if you're heading up to Maunakea for stargazing—which you should—it could easily be stretched to two. If you stay in Waimea overnight (there are many B&B options), spend the afternoon browsing through town or touring some of the area's ranches and historic sites. Then indulge in a gourmet dinner before heading up the Daniel K. Inouye Highway, also known as the Saddle Road, for world-renowned stargazing on Maunakea. Just gas up and bring water, snacks, and warm clothes with you (there are plenty of gas stations, cafés, and shops in Waimea).

◉ Sights

★ Anna Ranch Heritage Center
FARM/RANCH | This stunning heritage property, on the National and State Registers of Historic Places, belonged to the "first lady" of Hawaii ranching, Anna Lindsey Perry-Fiske. Here is a rare opportunity to see a fully restored cattle ranch compound and learn about the life of this fascinating woman, who butchered cattle by day and threw lavish parties by night. Wander the picturesque grounds and gardens on a self-guided walk, watch a master saddle maker and an ironsmith in action, and take a guided tour (by appointment only) of the historic house, where Anna's furniture, gowns, and elaborate *pau* (parade riding) costumes are on display. The knowledgeable staff shares anecdotes about Anna's life. (Some staff and visitors have even reported strange goings-on in the main house, suggesting that Anna herself may still be "around.") ⊠ *65-1480 Kawaihae Rd., Waimea (Hawaii County)* ☎ *808/885–4426* ⊕ *www.annaranch.org* ✉ *Grounds and Discovery Trail free, historic home tours $10* ☉ *Closed Sat.–Mon.*

Kohala Mountain Road Lookout
VIEWPOINT | The road between North Kohala and Waimea is one of the most scenic drives in Hawaii, passing Parker Ranch, open pastures, rolling hills, and tree-lined mountains. There are a few places to pull over and take in the view; the lookout at mile marker 8 provides a splendid vista of the Kohala Coast

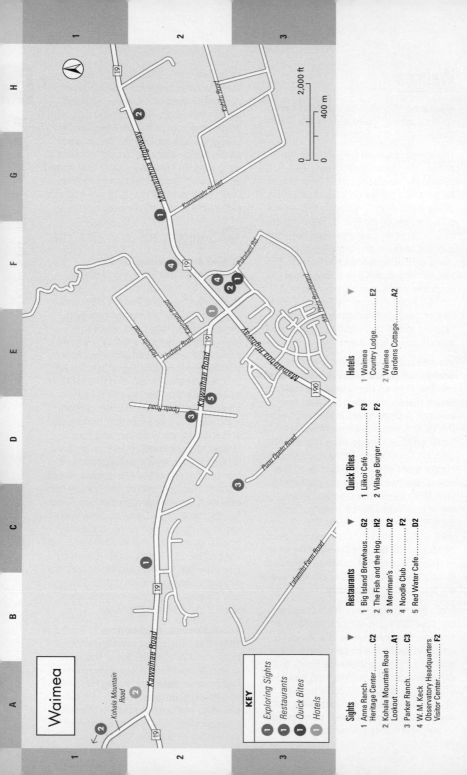

Waimea

KEY

- ① Exploring Sights
- ① Restaurants
- ① Quick Bites
- ① Hotels

Sights ▶

1 Anna Ranch
Heritage Center..............**C2**
2 Kohala Mountain Road
Lookout...........................**A1**
3 Parker Ranch................**C3**
4 W. M. Keck
Observatory Headquarters
Visitor Center................**F2**

Restaurants ▶

1 Big Island Brewhaus......**G2**
2 The Fish and the Hog.....**H2**
3 Merriman's....................**D2**
4 Noodle Club..................**F2**
5 Red Water Cafe.............**D2**

Quick Bites ▶

1 Lilikoi Café...................**F3**
2 Village Burger...............**F2**

Hotels ▶

1 Waimea
Country Lodge...............**E2**
2 Waimea
Gardens Cottage...........**A2**

0   2,000 ft
0   400 m

and Kawaihae Harbor far below. On clear days, you can see well beyond the resorts to Maui, while at other times an eerie mist drifts over the view. ✉ *Kohala Mountain Rd. (Hwy. 250), Waimea (Hawaii County).*

★ Parker Ranch

FARM/RANCH | Exceeding 130,000 acres and regularly running tens of thousands of head of cattle, Parker Ranch is an impressive and compelling backdrop for the scenic town of Waimea. It was established in 1847 by a sailor from Massachusetts, John Palmer Parker, who was permitted by the Hawaiian ruler King Kamehameha I to cull vast herds of out-of-control cattle; thus, the ranch was born. It later grew into the empire it is today, and the foundation started by Parker's descendants supports communityhealthcare and education. In addition to taking self-guided tours of two of the ranch's historic homes—Hale Mana and Puuopelu—free of charge, you can also visit Parker Ranch Center (a shopping and restaurant complex) to peruse gift items in the Parker Ranch Store. ✉ *Parker Ranch Headquarters, 66-1304 Mamalahoa Hwy., Waimea (Hawaii County)* ☎ *808/885–7311* 🌐 *parkerranch.com* 🎟 *Free* 🕒 *Closed weekends.*

W. M. Keck Observatory Headquarters Visitor Center

OBSERVATORY | Although the twin, 10-meter optical/infrared telescopes (among the largest and most scientifically productive in the world) are at the summit of Maunakea, the headquarters and visitor center of the observatory are in downtown Waimea and make a great stop if you want to learn more about the telescopes without making the long journey up the mountain. Top global astronomy teams have used the scopes to make astounding discoveries, thanks in part to their location atop the mountain, far above the turbulence of the atmosphere. Docents at the visitor center offer personalized tours weekdays from 10 am to 2 pm, showing you models of the telescopes and the observatory, as well as one of the original instruments. You can also peruse the exhibits and interpretive infographics at your own pace. About six times per year, highly renowned speakers, including Nobel Prize laureates, give free astronomy talks to the public. ✉ *65-1120 Mamalahoa Hwy., Waimea (Hawaii County)* ✥ *Across from hospital* ☎ *808/885–7887* 🌐 *www.keckobservatory.org* 🎟 *Free* 🕒 *Closed weekends.*

🍴 Restaurants

★ Big Island Brewhaus

$ | **AMERICAN** | A hands-down island favorite, this casual brewpub from owner and veteran brewmaster Tom Kerns churns out premium ales, lagers, and specialty beers from his on-site brewery in Waimea. With a focus on fresh ingredients, the brewpub's menu includes outstanding burgers, grilled steak, poke, fish tacos, burritos, rellenos, and quesadillas fresh to order. **Known for:** coconut-infused White Mountain porter; affordable sampler with six beer choices; amazing grass-fed burgers. [$] *Average main: $12* ✉ *64-1066A Mamalahoa Hwy., Waimea (Hawaii County)* ☎ *808/887–1717* 🌐 *www.bigislandbrewhaus.com.*

The Fish and the Hog

$ | **ECLECTIC** | This casual little restaurant along the highway serves up generous sandwiches, salads, and melt-in-your-mouth barbecue items. Because the owners are fisherpeople, the poke and nightly specials showcase fish caught from their boat. **Known for:** enormous, puffy, onion rings; kiawe-smoked pulled pork, ribs, pork ribs, and brisket; yummy banana cream pie. [$] *Average main: $15* ✉ *64-957 Mamalahoa Hwy. (Hwy. 11), Waimea (Hawaii County)* ☎ *808/885–6268* 🌐 *fishandthehog.com.*

Merriman's

$$$$ | MODERN HAWAIIAN | The signature restaurant of Peter Merriman, one of the pioneers of Hawaii Regional Cuisine, is the home of the original wok-charred ahi: it's seared on the outside, leaving sashimi on the inside. Although lunch prices are reasonable, dinner is "resort pricey," so prepare to splurge. **Known for:** grilled-to-order New York steak; locally raised Kahua Ranch braised lamb; chocolate oblivion torte. $ *Average main: $45 ⊠ Opelo Plaza, 65-1227 Opelo Rd., Waimea (Hawaii County) ☎ 808/885–6822 ⊕ www.merrimanshawaii.com.*

Noodle Club

$ | JAPANESE FUSION | FAMILY | Star Wars toys and action figures line the shelves of Noodle Club, a fun destination with serious food in the Parker Ranch Center. Veteran resort chef Edwin Goto simmers his broths for up to 36 hours to create the noodle, or saimin, dishes such as the savory Bowl of Seoul or the All Things Pork Ramen. **Known for:** homemade pork, beef, and vegetable broths; bao buns with Hamakua Alii mushrooms; delicous desserts, including dairy-free chocolate mousse. $ *Average main: $14 ⊠ Parker Ranch Center, 67-1185 Mamalahoa Hwy., #A106, Waimea (Hawaii County) ☎ 808/885–8825 ⊕ www.noodleclub-waimea.com ☉ Closed Mon.*

Red Water Cafe

$$$$ | ECLECTIC | FAMILY | Chef David Abraham serves Hawaiian café food with a twist and a side of aloha. There's a full sushi menu as well; the Fuji roll is prepared tempura style, and sashimi is served with organic greens. **Known for:** worthy saketini (sake martini); Kansas City rib-eye steak, Berkshire pork chops, and short ribs; good kids' menu. $ *Average main: $36 ⊠ 65-1299 Kawaihae Rd., Waimea (Hawaii County) ☎ 808/885–9299 ⊕ www.redwatercafe.com ☉ No lunch.*

☕ Coffee and Quick Bites

Lilikoi Café

$ | EUROPEAN | FAMILY | Locals love this gem of a café, tucked away in the back of the Parker Ranch Center, in part because it's hard to find and they want to keep its delicious breakfast crepes, freshly made soups, and croissants Waimea's little secret. It's just as good for lunch: owner and chef John Lorda creates an impressive selection of salad choices daily, including chicken curry, beet, fava bean, chicken pesto, and Mediterranean pasta. **Known for:** handpainted murals; Israeli couscous with tomato, red onion, and cranberry; creative sandwiches and hot lunch entrées. $ *Average main: $9 ⊠ Parker Ranch Center, 67-1185 Mamalahoa Hwy. (Hwy. 11), Waimea (Hawaii County) ☎ 808/887–1400 ☉ Closed Sun. No dinner.*

Village Burger

$ | AMERICAN | FAMILY | At this little eatery that brings a whole new meaning to gourmet hamburgers, locally raised, grass-fed, hormone-free beef is ground fresh, hand-shaped daily on-site, and grilled to perfection right before your eyes. Top your burger (be it ahi, veal, Kahua Ranch Wagyu beef, Hamakua mushroom, or Waipio taro) with everything from local avocados, baby greens, and chipotle goat cheese to tomato marmalade. **Known for:** delicious brioche buns baked fresh in nearby Hawi; lots of toppings for burgers; ice cream for milkshakes made fresh in Waimea. $ *Average main: $10 ⊠ Parker Ranch Center, 67-1185 Mamalahoa Hwy. (Hwy. 11), Waimea (Hawaii County) ☎ 808/885–7319 ⊕ www.villageburgerwaimea.com.*

🏨 Hotels

Though it seems a world away, Waimea is only about a 15- to 20-minute drive from the Kohala Coast resorts, which places it considerably closer to the island's best beaches than Kailua-Kona.

Did You Know?

Coffee beans are actually the seeds of a cherry-like fruit, appropriately named coffee cherries. Be sure to sample some Kona brew while you're in the area.

Yet few visitors think to book lodging in this pleasant upcountry ranching community, where you can enjoy cool mornings and evenings after a day spent basking in the sun. To the delight of residents and visitors, there are some very good restaurants. Sightseeing is easy from here, too: Maunakea is a short drive away, and Hilo and Kailua-Kona are about an hour away. There aren't as many condos and hotels here, but there are some surprisingly good B&B and cottage options—as well as some great deals, especially considering their vantage point. Many have spectacular views of Maunakea, the ocean, and the beautiful green hills of Waimea.

Waimea Country Lodge

$ | HOTEL | In the heart of cowboy country, this quaint ranch house–style lodge offers views of the green, rolling slopes of Waimea and distant view of Maunakea. **Pros:** beautiful views; kitchenettes in some rooms; free coffee in morning. **Cons:** not near the beach; no pool; no on-site restaurant. [$] *Rooms from: $109* ✉ *65-1210 Lindsey Rd., Waimea (Hawaii County)* ☎ *808/885-4100, 800/367-5004* 🌐 *www.waimeacountrylodge.com* 🛏 *22 rooms* 🍴 *No meals.*

Waimea Gardens Cottage

$$ | RENTAL | Surprisingly luxe yet cozy and quaint, the three charming country cottages and one suite at this historical Hawaiian homestead are surrounded by flowering private gardens and a backyard stream. **Pros:** charming, self-contained units; manicured gardens; cascading stream. **Cons:** 50% deposit within two weeks of booking and payment in full six weeks before arrival; only personal or bank checks accepted; 3-night minimum stay. [$] *Rooms from: $205* ✉ *Waimea (Hawaii County)* ✣ *Located off Kawaihae Rd., 2 miles from Waimea Town* ☎ *808/885-8550* 🌐 *www.waimeagardens.com* 💳 *No credit cards* 🛏 *4 units* 🍴 *Free breakfast.*

Performing Arts

THEATER

Kahilu Theatre

ARTS CENTERS | The intimate theater regularly hosts internationally acclaimed performers and renowned Hawaiian artists such as Jake Shimabukuro, Kealii Reichel, and the Brothers Cazimero. They share the calendar with regional and national modern-dance troupes, community theater and dance groups, ukulele festivals, and classical music performances. The theater also supports the community by welcoming local artists to exhibit in its lobby, which doubles as a gallery. ✉ *Parker Ranch Center, 67-1185 Mamalahoa Hwy., Waimea (Hawaii County)* ☎ *808/885-6868* 🌐 *kahilutheatre.org.*

Shopping

ARTS AND CRAFTS

★ Gallery of Great Things

ART GALLERIES | You might lose yourself exploring the trove of fine art and collectibles in every price range at this gallery, which represents hundreds of local artists and has a low-key, unhurried atmosphere. The "things" include hand-stitched quilts, ceramic sculptures, vintage kimonos, original paintings, koa-wood bowls and furniture, etched glassware, Niihau shell lei, and feather art by local artist Beth McCormick. ✉ *Parker Square, 65-1279 Kawaihae Rd., Waimea (Hawaii County)* ☎ *808/885-7706* 🌐 *www.galleryofgreatthingshawaii.com.*

Wishard Gallery

ART GALLERIES | A Big Island–born artist whose verdant landscapes, sea views, and *paniolo* (cowboy)-themed paintings have become iconic throughout the Islands, Harry Wishard showcases his original oils at this gallery, along with works by other renowned local artists like Kathy Long, Edward Kayton, and Lynn Capell. ✉ *55-498 Hawi Rd., Hawi* ☎ *808/731-6556* 🌐 *www.wishardgallery.com.*

FOOD AND WINE

Kamuela Liquor Store

WINE/SPIRITS | From the outside it doesn't look like much, but this store sells the best selection of premium spirits, wines, and gourmet items on the island. Alvin, the owner, is a collector of fine wines, as evidenced by his multiple cellars. Wine tastings take place Friday afternoon from 3 to 6 and Saturday at noon. ⊠ *64-1010 Mamalahoa Hwy., Waimea (Hawaii County)* ☎ *808/885–4674.*

★ Waimea General Store

HOUSEHOLD ITEMS/FURNITURE | Since 1970, this Waimea landmark at Parker Square has been a favorite of locals and visitors alike. Although specialty kitchenware takes center stage, the shop brims with local gourmet items, books, kimonos, and Hawaiian gifts and souvenirs. ⊠ *Parker Square, 65-1279 Kawaihae Rd., Suite 112, Waimea (Hawaii County)* ☎ *808/885–4479* ⊕ *www.waimeageneralstore.com.*

SHOPPING CENTERS

Parker Ranch Center

SHOPPING CENTERS/MALLS | With a snazzy ranch-style motif, this shopping hub includes a supermarket, some great local eateries (Village Burger, Noodle Club, and Lilikoi Café), a coffee shop, a natural foods store, galleries, and clothing boutiques. The Parker Ranch Store and Parker Ranch Visitors Center and Museum are also here. ⊠ *67-1185 Mamalahoa Hwy. (Hwy. 11), Waimea (Hawaii County)* ⊕ *parkerranchcenter.com.*

Parker Square

SHOPPING CENTERS/MALLS | Although the Gallery of Great Things, known for art and collectibles, is this center's star attraction, it's also worth looking in at the Waimea General Store; Sweet Wind, for books, chimes, and beads; Sassafras, which sells locally crafted Hawaiian jewelry; and Hula Moon, for upscale women's fashions. Waimea Coffee Company satisfies with salads, sandwiches, and Kona coffee. ⊠ *65-1279 Kawaihae Rd., Waimea (Hawaii County).*

The Hamakua Coast with Maunakea

The Hamakua Coast is about 25 miles east of Waimea.

The spectacular waterfalls, mysterious jungles, emerald fields, and stunning ocean vistas along Highway 19 northwest of Hilo are collectively referred to as the Hilo–Hamakua Heritage Coast. Brown signs featuring a sugarcane tassel reflect the area's history: thousands of former acres of sugarcane sat idle after "King Sugar" left the island in the early 1990s, but today diversified agriculture is growing.

This is a great place to wander off the main road and see "real" Hawaii—untouched valleys, overgrown banyan trees, tiny coastal villages, and little plantation towns such as Honomu, Laupahoehoe, and Honokaa. Some small communities are still hanging on quite nicely, well after the demise of the big sugar plantations that first engendered them. They have homey cafés, gift shops, galleries, and a way of life from a time gone by. And today, plenty of farmers use premium agricultural lands serviced by the network of former cane roads and the restored and repaired Hamakua Ditch, growing crops such as Hamakua mushrooms, sweet potatoes, tomatoes, vanilla, coffee, and lettuce.

The dramatic Akaka Falls is only one of hundreds of waterfalls here, many of which tumble into a series of cascading pools. The falls may expand or retract depending on inclement weather. The pristine Waipio Valley was once a favorite getaway spot for Hawaiian royalty. The isolated valley floor has maintained the ways of old Hawaii, with taro patches, wild horses, and a handful of homes. The view from the lookout is breathtaking.

Before you head out to the coast, consider taking a side trip to Maunakea, the tallest peak in the Hawaiian Islands, and home to 11 powerful telescopes, co-managed by a consortium of nations, universities, and researchers. You can go with a licensed guide to the summit (recommended) or just drive up to the visitor center at 9,200 feet to peruse exhibits and check out the stars above for yourself.

GETTING HERE AND AROUND

Most visitors to the Hamakua Coast fly into Ellison Onizuka Kona International Airport on the west side, which is about 1 hour, 15 minutes, away.

A car is by far the best and most efficient way to see this coastline. You will want the freedom to leisurely stop off at various lookouts to take in the scenery or pause in a little town to grab a snack or lunch.

TOURS

A guided tour from a locally owned and operated company is one of the best (and easiest) ways to see Waipio Valley. You can walk down and up the steep, narrow road yourself, but you need to be in good shape and you may not see as much. And as locals say, it's 15 minutes to walk down but about 45 minutes to walk back up. The cost for a tour depends on both the company and the transport mode.

Waipio Naalapa Stables

GUIDED TOURS | Friendly horses and friendly guides take guests on tours of the valley floor. The 2½-hour tours run Monday through Saturday (the valley rests on Sunday), with check-in times of 9 and 12:30. Riders meet at Waipio Valley Artworks, near the lookout, where they are transported to the valley floor in a four-wheel-drive van. ⊠ Waipio Valley Artworks Bldg., 48-5416 Kukuihaele Rd., Kukuihaele ☎ 808/775–0419 ⊕ www. naalapastables.com ⊠ From $110.

Waipio on Horseback

GUIDED TOURS | This outfit offers guided, 2½-hour horseback-riding tours on the Waipio Valley floor. Riders experience lush tropical foliage, curving rivers (Waipio means "curved water" in Hawaiian), flowering trees, a scenic beach, tranquil streams, and 3,000-foot-tall cliff walls. Local paniolo (cowboy) guides share the history, culture, and mythology of this magical valley and also give you a sneak peek into a traditional family farm where the owners tend Hawaiian staples such as taro. You'll also get to see the stunning Naalapa Falls. ⊠ Hwy. 240 at mile marker 7.5, Honokaa ✛ Northwest of Honokaa ☎ 808/775–7291, 877/775–7291 ⊕ www. waipioonhorseback.com ⊠ From $105.

Waipio Valley Shuttle

GUIDED TOURS | Not up for hiking in and out of the valley on foot? These informative, 1½- to 2-hour, four-wheel-drive tours do the driving for you, exploring the valley with lots of stops Monday through Saturday. The windows on the van are removed, allowing you to snap unobstructed photos. You have the option to stay at the beach for two to four hours and come back up with the next tour. ⊠ 48-5416 Kukuihaele Rd., Kukuihaele ☎ 808/775–7121 ⊕ www.waipiovalley-shuttle.com ⊠ From $65.

Waipio Valley

24 miles east and then north of Waimea.

Bounded by 3,000-foot cliffs, the "Valley of the Kings" was once a favorite retreat of Hawaiian royalty. Waterfalls drop thousands of feet feet from the North Kohala watershed to the Waipio Valley floor. The lush valley is breathtaking in every way and from every vantage: tropical foliage, abundant flowers, wild horses, misty pastures, curving rivers, and stands of ironwood trees combine with a wide, gray, boulder-strewn shore to make it one of the most picturesque spots in all of Hawaii. Though almost completely off the grid today, Waipio was once a center of Hawaiian life; somewhere between 4,000 and 20,000 people made it their home between the 13th and

17th centuries. In addition, it is a highly historic and culturally significant area, as it housed *heiau* (temples) and *puuhonua* (places of refuge) in addition to royal residences. King Kamehameha the Great launched a great naval battle from here, which marked the start of his unification (some would say conquest) and reign of the Hawaiian Islands. To preserve this pristine part of the island, commercial-transportation permits are limited—only a few outfitters offer organized valley floor trips.

A treacherous paved road leads down from the Waipio Valley Lookout, but no car-rental companies on the island allow their cars to be driven down. You can walk it, and you should if you can. The distance is actually less than a mile from the lookout point—just keep in mind that the climb back gains 1,000 feet in elevation and is highly strenuous, so bring water and a walking stick. Area landowners do not look kindly on public trespassing to access Hiilawe Falls at the back of the valley, so stick to the front by the beach. Hike all the way to the end of the beach for a glorious vantage point. Swimming, surfing, and picnics are all popular activities here, conditions permitting. You can also take the King's Trail from the end of the beach to access another waterfall not far down the trail. (Waterfalls can come and go depending on the level of recent rains.) If you do visit here, respect this area, as it is considered highly sacred to Hawaiians and is still home to several hundred full-time residents who cultivate taro on family farms.

◉ Sights

★ Waipio Valley Lookout
VIEWPOINT | If you are looking for an easily accessible access point to see the beauty of the Waipio Valley, this is it, offering a stunning view of the valley and the high cliffs that surround it. Not surprising, it's a very popular spot, but there's plenty

of parking to handle the cars on most days; the park at the top is maintained by Hawaii County. A treacherous paved roads leads down (Big Island car-rental companies don't usually allow their cars to be driven down because it's so steep, but you can walk down if you wish, though it's 1,000 feet back up). Your best bet to reach the valley floor is with a guided four-wheel-drive tour. ⊠ *Hwy. 240, 8 miles west of Honokaa, Kukuihaele.*

Shopping

ART GALLERIES
Waipio Valley Artworks
ART GALLERIES | In this quaint gallery in a vintage home, you can find finely crafted wooden bowls, koa furniture, paintings, and jewelry—all made by local artists. There's also a great little café where you can pick up a sandwich or homemade ice cream before descending into Waipio Valley. ⊠ *48-5416 Kukuihaele Rd., Kukuihaele* ☎ *808/775–0958* ⊕ *www. waipiovalleyartworks.com.*

Honokaa

8 miles east of Waipio Valley Lookout, 15 miles northeast of Waimea.

This quaint, cliff-top village fronting the ocean was built in the 1920s and 1930s by Japanese and Chinese workers who quit the nearby plantations to start businesses that supported the sugar economy. The intact historical character of the buildings, bucolic setting, and friendliness of the merchants provide a nice reason to stop and stroll. Cool antiques shops, a few interesting galleries, funky gift shops, and good cafés abound. There's even a vintage theater that often showcases first-rate entertainment. Most restaurants close by 8.

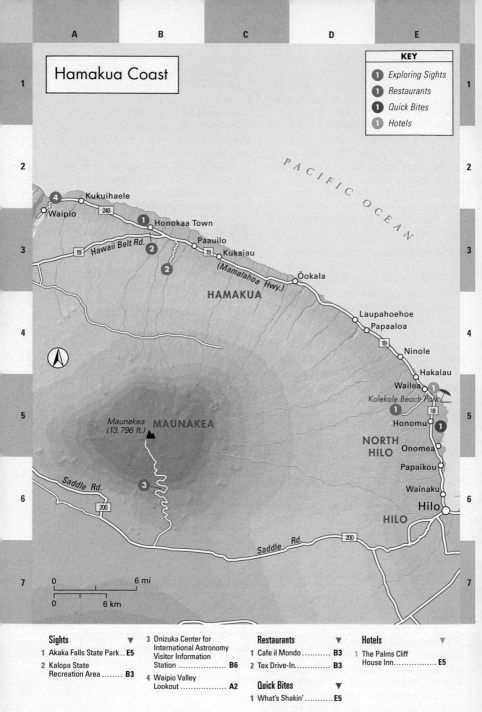

Hamakua Coast

KEY
- 1 Exploring Sights
- 1 Restaurants
- 1 Quick Bites
- 1 Hotels

PACIFIC OCEAN

Kukuihaele

Waipio

240

1 Honokaa Town

Hawaii Belt Rd.

2 Paauilo

19 Kukaiau

2 (Mamalahoa Hwy.)

Ōokala

HAMAKUA

Laupahoehoe

Papaaloa

19 Ninole

Hakalau

Wailea

Kolekole Beach Park

1 Honomu

1

NORTH HILO

Onomea

Papaikou

Maunakea
(13,796 ft.)   MAUNAKEA

Wainaku

Hilo

3

Saddle Rd.

200

HILO

Saddle Rd.

200

0   6 mi
0   6 km

A   B   C   D   E

1   2   3   4   5   6   7

Sights ▼
1 Akaka Falls State Park .. **E5**
2 Kalopa State Recreation Area **B3**

3 Onizuka Center for International Astronomy Visitor Information Station **B6**
4 Waipio Valley Lookout **A2**

Restaurants ▼
1 Cafe il Mondo **B3**
2 Tex Drive-In............. **B3**

Quick Bites ▼
1 What's Shakin' **E5**

Hotels ▼
1 The Palms Cliff House Inn................. **E5**

Sights

★ Kalopa State Recreation Area

NATIONAL/STATE PARK | FAMILY | North of the old plantation town of Paauilo, at a cool elevation of 2,000 feet, lies this sweet 100-acre state park. There's a lush forested area with picnic tables and restrooms, as well as an easy ¾-mile loop trail with additional paths in the adjacent forest reserve. Small signs identify some of the plants, including the Gothic-looking native ohia and the rare loulu palm. It's chilly and damp here, making it a good escape from the heat at sea level. Three campground areas with full-service kitchens, as well as four cabins, can be reserved online. ✉ *44-3375 Kalopa Mauka Rd., Honokaa* ✣ *12 miles north of Laupahoehoe and 3 miles inland off Hwy. 19* ☎ *808/775–8852* 🌐 *hawaiistateparks.org* 🎫 *Free.*

Restaurants

★ Cafe il Mondo

$ | ITALIAN | Unquestionably the fanciest spot in Honokaa, this cozy Italian bistro known for its pizza and more feels like you've taken a step into Florence. Wood details, a full bar, travertine finishes, antique furnishings, pendant lighting, and a fantastic stone pizza oven combine to create a thoroughly welcoming ambience. **Known for:** variety of homemade calzones; pasta primavera; Paauilo penne. [$] *Average main: $11* ✉ *3580 Mamane St., Honokaa* ☎ *808/775–7711.*

★ Tex Drive-In

$ | DINER | A local institution, this casual place is famous for its *malasadas,* the puffy, doughy, deep-fried Portuguese doughnuts without a hole, best eaten hot; there are also cream-filled versions, including vanilla, chocolate, and coconut. For more than a snack, go for the Hawaiian burger, with a fat, juicy slice of sweet pineapple on top, the overstuffed burrito, or some decent homemade pizza. **Known for:** the island's best malasadas; food cooked to order; long waits. [$] *Average main: $6* ✉ *45-690 Pakalana St., at Hwy. 19, Honokaa* ☎ *808/775–0598* 🌐 *www.texdriveinhawaii.com.*

Laupahoehoe

19 miles east of Honokaa.

After the devastating events of 1946, in which a tsunami raged ashore and 24 people were killed, the once-thriving railway town of Laupahoehoe was relocated to higher ground. Now all that's there is a small museum, convenience store, and beach park. It's a quick turn off the highway and well worth it to see the memorial to the schoolteachers and children who died here.

Honomu

12 miles southeast of Laupahoehoe.

Bordering Akaka Falls State Park, this tiny town did not die when sugar did. Its sugar-plantation past is reflected in its wooden boardwalks and metal-roofed buildings. It's fun to browse through old, dusty shops filled with little treasures such as antique bottles. But you can also check out homemade baked goods, have an espresso, or browse the local art at one of the fine galleries.

Sights

★ Akaka Falls State Park

BODY OF WATER | A paved, 10-minute loop trail (approximately ½ mile) takes you to the best spots to see the spectacular cascades of Akaka. The majestic upper Akaka Falls drops more than 442 feet, tumbling far below into a pool drained by Kolekole Stream amid a profusion of fragrant white, yellow, and red torch ginger and other tropical foliage. Another 400-foot falls is on the lower end of the trail. Restroom facilities are available but no drinking water. The park is 4 miles inland, and vehicle parking closes at 6. **■ TIP→ A series of steps along parts of the trail may prove challenging for some visitors.** ✉ *875 Akaka Falls Rd., Honomu* ✥ *At the end of Akaka Falls Rd. (Hwy. 220)* ☎ *808/974–6200* 🌐 *dlnr.hawaii.gov/dsp/parks/hawaii/akaka-falls-state-park/* 🎫 *$5 per vehicle.*

Coffee and Quick Bites

What's Shakin'

$ | VEGETARIAN | A cute vintage shack, painted a cheery yellow, is the home of the best smoothies and shakes on the Hamakua Coast. Order at the counter and take away, or sit awhile under the canopy while you indulge in a Mango Tango, Lava Java, Bananarama, or any of about 15 selections of creative smoothies; you can pair it with tasty turkey, fish, or chicken roll-ups and other wraps. **Known for:** healthy vegetarian and vegan wraps; smoothies made from fruit grown on location; one of the few places to stop on the way to Honokaa. [$] *Average main: $10* ✉ *27-999 Old Mamalahoa Hwy., Pepeekeo* ☎ *808/964–3080* 🌐 *whatsshakinbigisland.com* 🕘 *No dinner.*

Hotels

The Palms Cliff House Inn

$$$ | B&B/INN | About 15 minutes north of downtown Hilo and a few minutes from Akaka Falls, this handsome Victorian-style mansion is perched on the sea cliffs 100 feet above the crashing surf of the tropical coast. **Pros:** stunning oceanfront views; coffee and fresh fruit plate with breakfast every morning; all rooms have private outdoor entrances. **Cons:** no pool; remote location means driving 13 miles to Hilo for dinner; 50% booking deposit required. [$] *Rooms from: $299* ✉ *28-3514 Mamalahoa Hwy., Honomu* ☎ *808/963–6076* 🌐 *www.palmscliffhouse.com* 🛏 *8 rooms* 🍴 *Free breakfast.*

Shopping

ARTS AND CRAFTS

Glass from the Past

ANTIQUES/COLLECTIBLES | A fun place to shop for a quirky gift or just to poke around before or after a visit to Akaka Falls, the store is chock-full of old Hawaiian bottles, antiques, vintage clothing, Japanese collectibles, and interesting ephemera. There's often even a "free" table out front to add to the discovery. ✉ *28-1672 Old Mamalahoa Hwy., Honomu* ☎ *808/963–6449.*

GALLERIES

Woodshop Gallery

ART GALLERIES | Run by local artists Peter and Jeanette McLaren, this Honomu gallery showcases their woodwork and photography collections along with beautiful ceramics, photography, glass, and paintings from other Big Island artists. The historical building still has a working soda fountain dating from 1935. ✉ *28-1690 Old Government Rd., Honomu* ☎ *808/963–6363* 🌐 *www.woodshopgallery.com.*

Maunakea

Maunakea's summit is 18 miles southeast of Waimea and 34 miles northwest of Hilo.

Maunakea ("white mountain") offers the antithesis of the typical tropical island experience. Freezing temperatures and arctic conditions are common at the summit, and snow can fall year-round. You can even snowboard or ski up here. Seriously. But just because you can doesn't mean you'll want to. You should be in very good shape and a close-to-expert boarder or skier to get down the slopes near the summit and then up again in the thin air with no lifts. During the winter months, lack of snow is usually not a problem.

Winter sports, however, are the least of the reasons that most people visit this

starkly beautiful mountain, a dormant volcano. From its base below the ocean's surface to its summit, Maunakea is the tallest island mountain on the planet. It's also home to little Lake Waiau, one of the highest natural lakes in the world, though lately, the word "pond" is closer to the truth.

GETTING HERE AND AROUND

Maunakea's summit—at 13,796 feet—is the world's best place for viewing the night sky. For this reason, the summit is home to the largest and most productive astronomical observatories in the world—and $1 billion (with a "B") worth of equipment. Research teams from 11 different countries operate 11 telescopes on Maunakea, several of which are record holders: the world's largest optical-infrared telescopes (the dual Keck telescopes), the world's largest dedicated infrared telescope (UKIRT), and the largest submillimeter telescope (the JCMT). The still-larger Thirty Meter Telescope (TMT) had been cleared for construction and was slated to open its record-breaking eye to the heavens until it got delayed by protests in 2019.

Maunakea is tall, but there are higher mountains in the world, so what makes this spot so superb for astronomy? It has more to do with atmosphere than with elevation. A tropical-inversion-cloud layer below the summit keeps moisture from the ocean and other atmospheric pollutants down at the lower elevations. As a result, the air around the Maunakea summit is extremely dry, which helps in the measurement of infrared and submillimeter radiation from stars, planets, and the like. There are also rarely clouds up here; the annual number of clear nights here blows every other place out of the water. And, because the mountain is far away from any interfering artificial lights (not a total coincidence—in addition to the fact that the nearest town is nearly 30 miles away, there's an official ordinance limiting certain kinds of streetlights on the island), skies are dark for the astronomers' research. To quote the staff at the observatory, astronomers here are able to "observe the faintest galaxies that lie at the very edge of the observable universe."

Teams from various nations and universities around the world must submit proposals years in advance to get the chance to use the telescopes on Maunakea. They have made major astronomical discoveries, including several about the nature of black holes, new satellites around Jupiter and Saturn, new Trojans (asteroids that orbit, similar to moons) around Neptune, new moons and rings around Uranus, and new moons around Pluto. Their studies of galaxies are changing the way scientists think about time and the evolution of the universe.

What does all this mean for you? A visit to Maunakea is a chance to see more stars than you've likely ever seen before and an opportunity to learn more about mind-boggling scientific discoveries in the very spot where these discoveries are being made. Only the astronomers, though, are allowed to use the telescopes and other equipment, but the scenery is available to all. (You must leave the summit before dark for your safety.) For you space geeks, a trip to Maunakea may just be the highlight of your trip. We recommend you go with a licensed summit tour company that takes care of the details for you. All take you to the summit for sunset and then present a star talk at about 11,000 feet, where the elevation is more comfortable.

If you're in Hilo, be sure to visit the Imiola Astronomy Center, which is near the University of Hawaii at Hilo. It offers presentations and planetarium films about the mountain and the science being conducted there, as well as exhibits describing the deep knowledge of the heavens possessed by the ancient Hawaiians. You can also visit the W. M. Keck Observatory Headquarters Visitor Center in Waimea to

The world's largest optical and infrared telescopes are located at the Keck Observatory on Maunakea's summit.

learn about the important work astronomers are conducting on the summit.

The summit of Maunakea isn't terribly far, but the drive takes about 90 minutes from Hilo and an hour from Waimea thanks to the steep road. Between the ride there, sunset on the summit, and stargazing, allot at least five hours for a Maunakea visit.

To reach the summit, you must take Saddle Road (Highway 200, now known as the Daniel K. Inouye Highway), which has been rerouted and is a beautiful shortcut across the middle of the island. At mile marker 28, John A. Burns Way, the access road to the visitor center (9,200 feet), is fine, but the road from there to the summit is a lot more precarious because it's unpaved washboard and very steep. Only four-wheel-drive vehicles with low range should attempt this journey. Two-wheel-drive cars are unsafe, especially in winter conditions. Unsuitable cars may experience engine failure as a result of the low oxygen levels. Legislation is pending regarding a total

ban of anything but four-wheel-drive vehicles on the summit. And if you're driving back down in the dark, slow and cautious is the name of the game. △ **Most rental car companies will not permit you to drive to the summit of Maunakea. Driving there without permission will void your contract and leave you responsible for damages. This happens more often than you'd think.**

If you haven't rented a four-wheel-drive vehicle from Harper or Big Island Jeep Rentals—the only rental companies that allow their vehicles on the summit—and don't want to deal with driving to the summit, or don't want to wait in line to use the handful of telescopes at the visitor center, the best thing to do is book a commercial tour. Operators provide transportation to and from the summit along with expert guides; some also provide parkas, gloves, telescopes, dinner, hot beverages, and snacks. All give their own star talks a few thousand feet below the summit. Companies that offer summit tours are headquartered in both Hilo and Kona.

Also remember that Maunakea's extreme altitude can cause altitude sickness, leading to disorientation, headaches, and light-headedness. Keeping hydrated is crucial. Scuba divers must wait at least 24 hours before traveling to the summit. Children under 16, pregnant women, and those with heart, respiratory, or weight problems should not go higher than the visitor center. While you can park at the visitor center and hike to the summit if you are in good shape, the trip takes approximately seven hours one way, and no camping is allowed. That means you must leave in the predawn hours to be back before dark; a permit is also required for this hike.

The last potential obstacle to visiting the summit: it's cold—as in freezing—usually with significant wind chill, ice, and snow. Winds have been clocked exceeding 135 miles per hour. Be advised this is a wilderness area and there are no services or rangers, except in an absolute emeergency.

TOURS

Arnott's Lodge and Hiking Adventures

SPECIAL-INTEREST | This outfitter takes you to the summit for sunset and then stops along the way down the mountain, where guides give visual lectures (dependent on clear skies) using lasers. They focus on major celestial objects and Polynesian navigational stars. The excursion departs from Hilo and includes parkas and hot beverages. Pickup is available from Hilo hotels. The company also offers a traveler's lodge and a number of volcano park and Puna eruption site adventure hikes. ⊠ *98 Apapane Rd., Hilo* ☏ *808/339–0921* ⊕ *www.arnottslodge. com* ⌨ *From $199.*

★ Hawaii Forest and Trail

SPECIAL-INTEREST | The ultra-comfortable, highly educational Summit and Stars tour packs a lot of fun into a few hours. Guides are knowledgeable about astronomy and Hawaii's geologic and cultural history, and the small group size (max of 14) encourages camaraderie. Included in the tour are dinner at an old ranching station, catered by a favorite local restaurant; sunset on the summit; and a fantastic private star show midmountain. The company's powerful 11-inch Celestron Schmidt-Cassegrain telescope reveals many interesting celestial objects, including seasonal stars, galaxies, and nebulas. Everything from water bottles, parkas, and gloves to hot chocolate and brownies is included.

The company's Maunakea Sunrise tour begins in the wee hours before the sun comes up and includes a hike among the endangered silverswords as well as breakfast at the visitor center. And of course, the main event—a spectacular sunrise on the summit. The company also offers a daytime version of the summit tour. ⊠ *73-5593 Olowalu St., Kailua-Kona* ☏ *808/331–8505, 800/464–1993* ⊕ *www. hawaii-forest.com* ⌨ *From $225.*

Mauna Kea Summit Adventures

SPECIAL-INTEREST | As the first company to specialize in tours to the mountain, Mauna Kea Summit Adventures is a small outfit that focuses on stars. Cushy vans with panoramic windows journey first to the visitor center, where participants enjoy a hearty lasagna dinner on the lanai and acclimatize for 45 minutes before donning hooded arctic-style parkas and ski gloves for the sunset trip to the 14,000-foot summit. With the help of knowledgeable guides, stargazing through a powerful Celestron telescope happens midmountain, where the elevation is more comfortable and skies are just as clear. The tour includes dinner, hot cocoa and biscotti, and west-side pickup; it runs 364 days a year, weather permitting. ■TIP➔ **Book at least one month prior, as these tours sell out fast.** ⊠ *Kailua-Kona* ☏ *808/322–2366, 888/322–2366* ⊕ *www. maunakea.com* ⌨ *From $259.*

Sights

Onizuka Center for International Astronomy Visitor Information Station

INFO CENTER | At 9,200 feet, this excellent amateur observation site has a handful of telescopes and a knowledgeable staff. Open daily from 9 am to 6 pm, the center is currently not offering stargazing activities at night, but this could change in the future. It's a good place to stop to acclimatize yourself to the altitude if you're heading for the summit. Fortunately, it's a pleasure to do so. Sip hot chocolate and peruse the gift shop and exhibits about ancient Hawaiian celestial navigation, the mountain's significance as a quarry for the best basalt in the Hawaiian Islands, and Maunakea as a revered spiritual destination. You'll also learn about modern astronomy and ongoing projects at the summit. Nights are clear 90% of the year, so the chances are good of seeing some amazing sights in the sky. ■**TIP→ Keep in mind that no summit telescope facilities are open to the public, so this is a great way to get the sense of the observatory work without going all the way to the top.** ✉ *Maunakea* ☎ *808/934–4550 visitor center, 808/935–6268 current road conditions* ⊕ *www.ifa.hawaii.edu/info/vis* 🎫 *Free, donations welcome.*

Hilo

Hilo is 55 miles southeast of Waimea, 95 miles northeast of Kailua-Kona, and just north of the Hilo Airport.

In comparison to Kailua-Kona, Hilo is often deemed "the old Hawaii." With significantly fewer visitors than residents, more historic buildings, and a much stronger identity as a long-established community, this quaint, traditional town does seem more authentic and local.

The town stretches from the banks of the Wailuku River to Hilo Bay, where a few hotels line stately Banyan Drive. The vintage buildings that make up Hilo's downtown have been spruced up as part of a revitalization effort. Nearby, the 30-acre Liliuokalani Gardens, a formal Japanese garden with arched bridges, stepping-stones and waterways, were created in the early 1900s to honor the area's Japanese sugar plantation laborers. The garden also became a safety zone after a devastating tsunami swept away businesses and homes on May 22, 1960, killing 61 people.

With a population of almost 50,000 in the entire district, Hilo is the fourth-largest city in the state and home to the University of Hawaii at Hilo. Although it is the center of government and commerce for the island, Hilo is clearly a residential town. Mansions with yards of lush tropical foliage share streets with older, single-walled plantation-era houses with rusty corrugated roofs. It's a friendly community, populated primarily by descendants of the contract laborers—Japanese, Chinese, Filipino, Puerto Rican, and Portuguese—brought in to work the sugarcane fields during the 1800s.

One of the main reasons visitors have tended to steer clear of the east side of the island is its weather. With an average rainfall of 130 inches per year, it's easy to see why Hilo's yards are so green and its buildings so weatherworn. Outside of town, the Hilo District boasts scenic beach valleys, rain forests, and waterfalls, a terrain unlike the hot and dry white-sand beaches of the Kohala Coast. But when the sun does shine—usually part of nearly every day—the town sparkles, and, during winter, the snow glistens on Maunakea, 25 miles in the distance. Best of all is when the mists fall and the sun shines at the same time, leaving behind the colorful arches that earn Hilo its nickname: the City of Rainbows.

For a week every year in April, Hilo becomes the epicenter of the hula world when the Merrie Monarch Festival

Did You Know?

Hilo, on the east side of Big Island, is appropriately nicknamed "The City of Rainbows," as it's surrounded by rain forests and gets about 130 inches of rain per year.

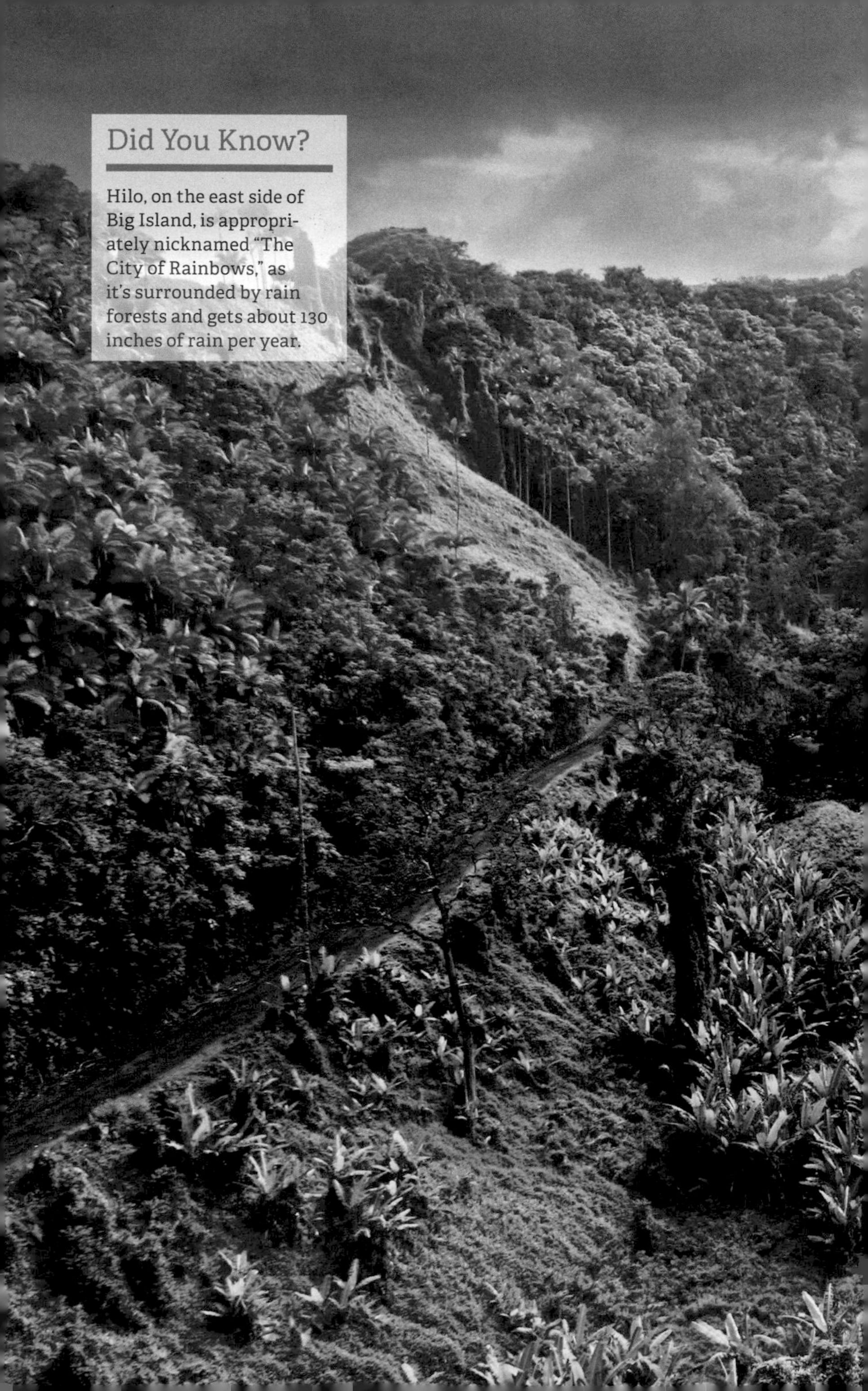

attracts tens of thousands of people to the renowned international event, steeped in traditions that represent the essence of Hilo's pioneering spirit. If you're planning a stay in Hilo during this time, be sure to book your room and car rentals at least eight months in advance.

GETTING HERE AND AROUND

Hilo International Airport is one of the island's two international airports, although flights to and from Kailua-Kona are more frequent. Still, this is the best airport to fly into if your main goal is to visit Hilo and Hawaii Volcanoes National Park.

Hilo is a great base for exploring the eastern and southern parts of the island, including Hawaii Volcanoes National Park; just be sure to bring an umbrella for sporadic—and sometimes torrential—showers. If you're passing through town or making a day-trip from either side of the island, you can focus your itinerary on the downtown area's museums, shops, and historical buildings. Street parking is relatively easy to find, and downtown is best experienced on foot.

There are plenty of gas stations and restaurants in the area. Hilo is a good spot to load up on food and supplies—just south of downtown there are several large budget retailers. If you're here on Wednesday or Sunday, be sure to stop by the expansive Hilo Farmers Market to peruse stalls and stalls of produce, flowers, baked goods, coffee, honey, and more.

Downtown

Visitors to downtown Hilo might wonder why the bayfront shops and businesses are located such a distance from the actual bayfront. That's because the devastating tsunamis of 1946 and 1960 decimated the populated shoreline areas of Hilo's former downtown center. Still, local flavor abounds downtown, where vintage homes are the norm and businesses occupy older buildings, some historic. The Hilo Farmers Market, in full swing on Wednesday and Saturday, is a must-see here.

⊙ Sights

Lyman Museum and Mission House

MUSEUM | Built in 1839 by a missionary couple from New England, Sarah and David Lyman, the beautifully restored Lyman Mission House is the oldest wood-frame building on the island. On display are household utensils, artifacts, tools, and furniture used by the family, giving visitors a peek into the day-to-day lives of Hawaii's first missionaries. The Lymans hosted such literary dignitaries as Isabella Bird and Mark Twain here. The home is on the State and National Registers of Historic Places. Docent-guided tours are offered. An adjacent museum houses wonderful exhibits on volcanoes, island formation, island habitats and wildlife, marine shells, and minerals and gemstones. It also showcases native Hawaiian culture and immigrant ethnic groups. On permanent exhibit is a life-size replica of a traditional 1930s Korean home. The gift shop sells great Hawaiian-made items. ⊠ 276 Haili St., Hilo ☎ 808/935–5021 ⊕ www.lymanmuseum. org ⊠ $10 ⊙ Closed Sun.

Mokupapapa Discovery Center for Hawaii's Remote Coral Reefs

ZOO | FAMILY | This is a great place to learn about the stunning Papahanaumokuakea Marine National Monument, which encompasses nearly 140,000 square miles in the northwestern Hawaiian Islands and is the only mixed UNESCO World Heritage Site (meaning one that has both natural and cultural significance) in the United States. Giant murals, 3-D maps, and hands-on interactive kiosks depict the monument's extensive wildlife, including millions of birds and more than 7,000 marine species, many of which are found only in the Hawaiian archipelago. Knowledgeable staff and volunteers are on hand to answer questions. A 3,500-gallon aquarium and short films give insight into the unique features of the monument, as well as threats to its survival. Located in the refurbished F. Koehnen Building, the center is worth a stop just to get an up-close look at its huge stuffed albatross with wings outstretched or the monk seal exhibit. The price is right, too. ✉ *F. Koehnen Bldg., 76 Kamehameha Ave., Hilo* ☎ *808/933–8180* 🌐 *www.papahanaumokuakea.gov/education/center.html* 🎟 *Free* 🕒 *Closed Sun. and Mon.*

🍴 Restaurants

★ Bears' Coffee

$ | DINER | FAMILY | A fixture downtown since the late 1980s, this favorite, cozy breakfast spot is much loved for its fresh-fruit waffles and tasty morning coffee. For lunch the little diner serves up huge deli sandwiches and decent entrée-size salads, plus specials like hearty meat loaf, roasted chicken, and pot roast. **Known for:** reliable breakfasts; bear wallpaper and decor; specialty coffee such as the iced toddy cold brew. [$] *Average main: $10* ✉ *106 Keawe St., Hilo* ☎ *808/935–0708* 🕒 *No dinner.*

Café Pesto

$$ | ITALIAN | Located in a beautiful high-ceiling venue in the historical S. Hata building, Café Pesto offers creative pizzas with ingredients such as fresh Hamakua mushrooms, artichokes, and Gorgonzola. **Known for:** use of local farm produce; wood-fired pizza; happy hour from 2 pm. [$] *Average main: $20* ✉ *308 Kamehameha Ave., Hilo* ☎ *808/969–6640* 🌐 *www.cafepesto.com.*

Moon and Turtle

$$$ | INTERNATIONAL | This sophisticated, intimate restaurant in a bayfront building offers a classy selection of international fare with the focus on locally sourced meats, produce, and seafood. The menu changes daily (see the Facebook page), but mushroom pappardelle is a highlight, along with seafood chowder, spicy *kajiki* (marlin) tartare, and crispy whole-fried *moi* (Pacific threadfin). **Known for:** smoky ahi sashimi; lychee martinis infused with Hawaiian influences; high prices for Hilo. [$] *Average main: $30* ✉ *51 Kalakaua St., Hilo* ☎ *808/961–0599* 🕒 *Closed Sun. and Mon.*

Ocean Sushi

$ | JAPANESE | FAMILY | What this casual restaurant lacks in ambience, it certainly makes up for in quality and value. We're talking about light and crispy tempura; tender, moist teriyaki chicken; and about 25 specialty sushi rolls, all at unbeatable prices. **Known for:** bento plates; hospital roll with shrimp tempura, cream cheese, and spicy ahi; good kids' menu. [$] *Average main: $12* ✉ *235 Keawe St., Hilo* ☎ *808/961–6625* 🕒 *Closed Sun.*

Pineapples

$ | AMERICAN | FAMILY | If you expect that a restaurant named Pineapples would serve tropical beverages in hollowed-out pineapples, you'd be exactly correct. Always packed, this open-air bistro looks like a tourist trap, but there is a fine-dining component to the menu, which includes fresh catch, *kalbi* ribs (grilled, Korean-style), teriyaki flank steak, burgers, wraps, and sandwiches. **Known for:** surprisingly inventive island cuisine; great pineapple salsa; live entertainment nightly. [$] *Average main: $14* ✉ *332 Keawe St, Hilo* ☎ *808/238–5324* 🕒 *Closed Mon.*

🛏 Hotels

The Bay House Bed and Breakfast

$$ | B&B/INN | Overlooking Hilo Bay and just steps away from the Singing Bridge near Hilo's historical downtown area, this small, quiet B&B is vibrantly decorated, with Hawaiian-quilted beds and private lanai in each of the three rooms. **Pros:** oceanfront lanai in each room; cliffside hot tub; Hilo Bay views. **Cons:** only two

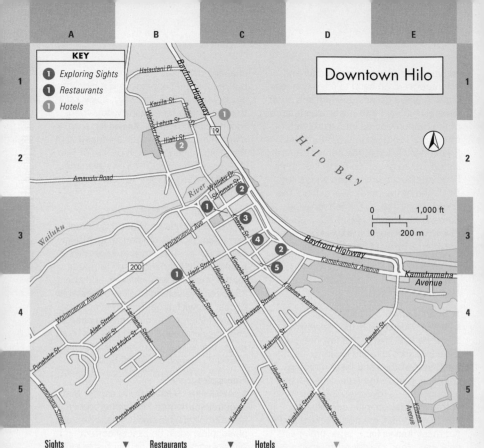

Downtown Hilo

KEY
- 1 Exploring Sights
- 1 Restaurants
- 1 Hotels

Hilo Bay

0 ——— 1,000 ft
0 ——— 200 m

Sights ▼	Restaurants ▼	Hotels ▼
1 Lyman Museum and Mission House **B4**	1 Bears' Coffee............. **C3**	1 The Bay House Bed and Breakfast....... **C1**
2 Mokupapapa Discovery Center for Hawaii's Remote Coral Reefs **C2**	2 Café Pesto................ **C3**	2 Dolphin Bay Hotel **B2**
	3 Moon and Turtle **C3**	
	4 Ocean Sushi.............. **C3**	
	5 Pineapples................ **C3**	

people per room; occasional street noise; no twin beds. $ *Rooms from: $189* ⊠ *42 Pukihae St., Hilo* ☏ *888/235–8195, 808/961–6311* ⊕ *www.bayhousehawaii. com* ⇆ *3 rooms* ⏐◯⏐ *Free breakfast.*

Dolphin Bay Hotel

$ | **HOTEL** | **FAMILY** | Units in this circa-1950s motor lodge are modest but charming, as well as clean and inexpensive; a glowing lava flow sign marks the office and bespeaks owner John Alexander's passion for the volcano. **Pros:** great value; full kitchens in all units; helpful and pleasant staff. **Cons:** no pool; no phones in the rooms; dated decor. $ *Rooms from: $129* ⊠ *333 Iliahi St., Hilo* ☏ *808/935–1466* ⊕ *www.dolphinbayhotel.com* ⇆ *18 rooms* ⏐◯⏐ *No meals.*

ⓨ Nightlife

BARS

Cronies Bar and Grill

BARS/PUBS | A sports bar by night and a good hamburger joint by day, Cronies is a local favorite. When the lights go down, the bar gets packed. ⊠ *11 Waianuenue Ave., Hilo* ☏ *808/935–5158* ⊕ *www. cronieshawaii.com.*

ⓢ Shopping

CLOTHING AND SHOES

Sig Zane Designs

CLOTHING | The acclaimed boutique sells distinctive island wearables with bold colors and motifs designed by the legendary Sig Zane, known for his artwork honoring native flora and fauna. All apparel is handcrafted in Hawaii and is often worn by local celebrities and businesspeople. ⊠ *122 Kamehameha Ave., Hilo* ☏ *808/935–7077* ⊕ *www.sigzane.com.*

FOOD

★ Sugar Coast Candy

FOOD/CANDY | Located on the bayfront in downtown Hilo, this beautifully decorated candy boutique is a blast from the past, featuring an amazing array of nostalgic candies, artisan chocolates, and wooden barrels overflowing with saltwater taffy and other delights. ⊠ *274 Kamehameha Ave., Hilo* ☏ *808/935–6960.*

Two Ladies Kitchen

FOOD/CANDY | This hole-in-the-wall confections shop has made a name for itself thanks to its pillowy mochi. The proprietors are best known for their huge ripe strawberries wrapped in a white mochi covering, which won't last as long as a box of chocolates—most mochi items are good for only two or three days. To guarantee you get your fill, call and place your order ahead of time. ⊠ *274 Kilauea Ave., Hilo* ☏ *808/961–4766.*

MARKETS

★ Hilo Farmers Market

OUTDOOR/FLEA/GREEN MARKETS | The 200 vendors here—stretching a couple of blocks at the bayfront—sell a profusion of tropical flowers, locally grown produce, aromatic honey, tangy goat cheese, hot breakfast and lunch items, and fresh baked specialties at extraordinary prices. This colorful, open-air market—the largest and most popular on the island—opens for business Wednesday and Saturday from 6 am to 4 pm. A smaller version on the other days features more than 30 vendors. ⊠ *Kamehameha Ave. and Mamo St., Hilo* ☏ *808/933–1000* ⊕ *www.hilofarmersmarket.com.*

Liliuokalani Gardens and Reeds Bay

The hotel district near Banyan Drive is within walking distance of nearby scenic Liliuokalani Gardens. To its east, Reeds Bay is small and idyllic, surrounded by a tiny sand beach and some parks with picnic tables. There's a lot of local activity here, including kayaking, fishing, swimming, and stand-up paddleboarding. Several bayside restaurants are within walking distance of the hotels, some with spectacular bayfront views.

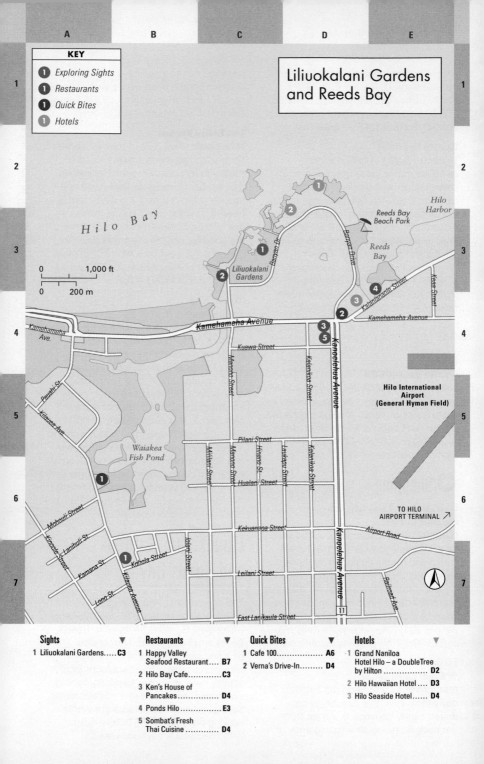

Liliuokalani Gardens and Reeds Bay

KEY

- 1 Exploring Sights
- 1 Restaurants
- 1 Quick Bites
- 1 Hotels

Hilo Bay

Hilo Harbor

Reeds Bay Beach Park

Reeds Bay

Liliuokalani Gardens

0   1,000 ft
0   200 m

Hilo International Airport (General Hyman Field)

Waiakea Fish Pond

TO HILO AIRPORT TERMINAL ↗

Kamehameha Avenue

Kamehameha Ave.

Banyan Dr.

Banyan Drive

Kalanianaole Street

Keeo Street

Kamehameha Avenue

Kuawa Street

Kaiulani Street

Kaiulani Street

Kalanikoa Street

Kanoelehua Avenue

Manono Street

Mililani Street

Manono Street

Pilani Street

Hinano St.

Laukapu Street

Hualani Street

Kekuanaoa Street

Airport Road

Leilani Street

Railroad Ave.

East Lanikaula Street

Pauahi St.

Kilauea Ave.

Mahaoli Street

Kinoole Street

Lanihuli St.

Kamana St.

Kilauea Avenue

Kohala Street

Iolani Street

Lono St.

11

Sights ▼

1 Liliuokalani Gardens..... **C3**

Restaurants ▼

1 Happy Valley Seafood Restaurant.... **B7**

2 Hilo Bay Cafe............. **C3**

3 Ken's House of Pancakes................ **D4**

4 Ponds Hilo **E3**

5 Sombat's Fresh Thai Cuisine **D4**

Quick Bites ▼

1 Cafe 100.................. **A6**

2 Verna's Drive-In......... **D4**

Hotels ▼

1 Grand Naniloa Hotel Hilo – a DoubleTree by Hilton **D2**

2 Hilo Hawaiian Hotel **D3**

3 Hilo Seaside Hotel...... **D4**

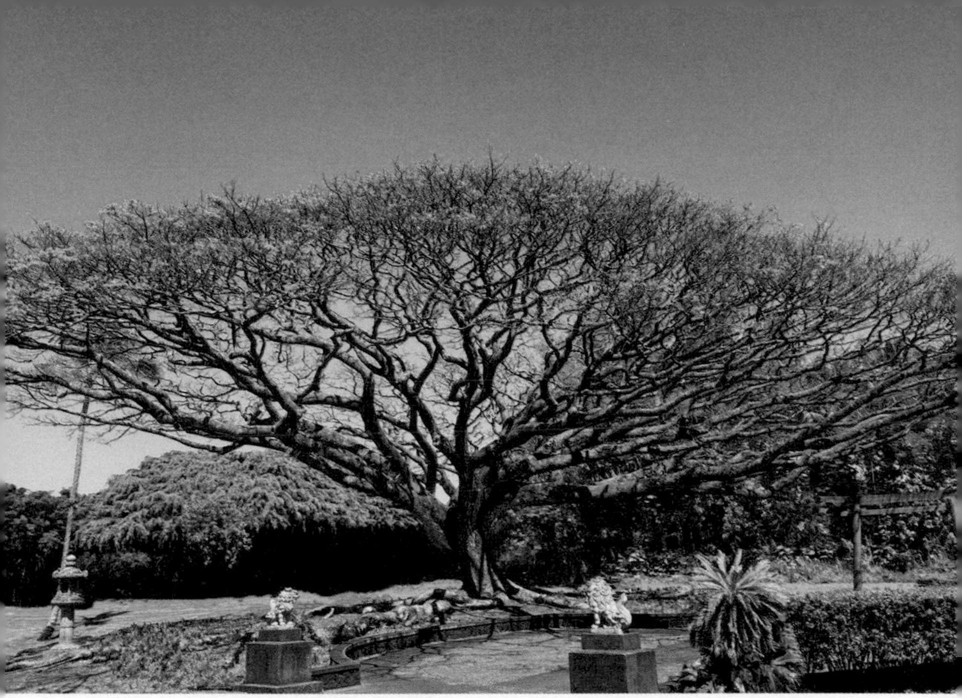

Liliuokalani Gardens, the largest ornamental Japanese garden outside of Japan, was built in 1917 to honor the island's first Japanese immigrants.

Sights

Liliuokalani Gardens

GARDEN | Designed to honor Hawaii's first Japanese immigrants and named after Hawaii's last reigning monarch, Liliuokalani Gardens' 30 acres of fish-filled ponds, stone lanterns, half-moon bridges, elegant pagodas, and a ceremonial teahouse make it a favorite Sunday destination. You'll see weddings, picnics, and families as you stroll. The surrounding area, once a busy residential neighborhood on Waiakea peninsula, was destroyed by a 1960 tsunami that caused widespread devastation and killed 61 people. ✉ *Banyan Dr., at Lihiwai St., Hilo* 🎟 *Free.*

Restaurants

Happy Valley Seafood Restaurant

$ | **CHINESE** | Don't let the name fool you: though Hilo's best Chinese restaurant does specialize in seafood, it also offers many other Cantonese treats, including salt-and-pepper pork, Mongolian lamb, and vegetarian specialties like garlic eggplant and crispy green beans. The food is good, portions are large, and the price is right, but don't come here expecting any ambience—this is a funky, cheap Chinese restaurant, with a few random pieces of artwork tacked up here and there. **Known for:** authentic Cantonese Chinese food; salt-and-pepper prawns; good soups. [$] *Average main: $12* ✉ *1263 Kilauea Ave., Suite 320, Hilo* ☎ *808/933–1083.*

★ **Hilo Bay Cafe**

$$ | **AMERICAN** | Overlooking Hilo Bay from its towering perch on the waterfront, this popular, upscale restaurant has a sophisticated second-floor dining room that looks like it's straight out of Manhattan. A sushi bar complements the excellent selection of fresh fish, pork, beef, and vegan options. **Known for:** excellent bayside views; Blue Bay burger with shoestring fries; most upscale restaurant in Hilo. [$] *Average main: $22*

✉ *123 Lihiwai St., Hilo* ☎ *808/935–4939* 🌐 *www.hilobaycafe.com* 🕒 *Closed Sun.*

★ Ken's House of Pancakes

$ | **DINER** | **FAMILY** | For years, this 24-hour diner near Banyan Drive between the airport and the hotels has been a gathering place for Hilo residents and visitors. Breakfast is the main attraction: Ken's serves 11 types of pancakes, plus all kinds of fruit waffles (banana, peach) and popular omelets, like the Da Bradda, teeming with meats. **Known for:** local landmark with old-fashioned vibe; extensive menu of Hawaiian and diner fare; weekly special nights like Sunday spaghetti and Tuesday tacos. [$] *Average main: $15* ✉ *1730 Kamehameha Ave., Hilo* ☎ *808/935–8711* 🌐 *www.kenshouseofpancakes.com.*

Ponds Hilo

$$ | **HAWAIIAN** | **FAMILY** | Perched on the waterfront overlooking a serene and scenic pond, this restaurant has the look and feel of an old-fashioned, harborside steak house and bar. The menu features a good range of burgers and salads, steak, and seafood. **Known for:** Thursday lobster night; excellent fish and chips; popular Sunday brunch. [$] *Average main: $20* ✉ *135 Kalanianaole Ave., Hilo* ☎ *808/934–7663* 🌐 *www.pondshilo.com.*

★ Sombat's Fresh Thai Cuisine

$$ | **THAI** | There's a reason why locals flock to this hideaway for the best Thai cuisine in Hilo. Fresh local ingredients highlight proprietor Sombat Saenguthai's menu (many of the herbs come from her own garden) to create authentic and tasty Thai treats like coconut curries, fresh basil rolls, eggplant stir-fry, and green papaya salad. **Known for:** famous pad Thai sauce available for purchase; friendly service; single owner and chef. [$] *Average main: $17* ✉ *Waiakea Kai Plaza, 88 Kanoelehue Ave., Hilo* ✥ *Close to Ken's House of Pancakes* ☎ *808/969–9336* 🌐 *www.sombats.com* 🕒 *Closed Sun. No lunch.*

Coffee and Quick Bites

Cafe 100

$ | **HAWAIIAN** | **FAMILY** | Established in 1948, this family-owned restaurant is famous for its tasty *loco moco* (meat, rice, and eggs smothered in gravy), prepared in more than three dozen ways (with different meats, chicken, vegetables, and fish), and its low-priced breakfast and lunch specials. The word "restaurant," or even "café," is used loosely—you order at a window and eat on one of the outdoor benches provided—but you come here for the food, prices, and authentic, old-Hilo experience. **Known for:** local flavor; the Super Loco Moco; generous portions. [$] *Average main: $6* ✉ *969 Kilauea Ave., Hilo* ☎ *808/935–8683* 🌐 *www.cafe100.com* 🕒 *Closed Sun.*

Verna's Drive-In

$ | **HAWAIIAN** | Verna's is tried and true among locals, who come for the juicy homemade burgers and filling plate lunches, and the price is right with a burger combo that includes fries and a drink. If you're hungry for more, try the traditional Hawaiian plate with either *laulau*, beef stew, chicken long rice, or lomilomi salmon. **Known for:** local grindz 24/7 with outdoor seating; smoked meat plate lunch; superlow prices. [$] *Average main: $6* ✉ *1765 Kamehameha Ave., Hilo* ☎ *808/935–2776.*

Hotels

Grand Naniloa Hotel Hilo–a DoubleTree by Hilton

$ | **HOTEL** | **FAMILY** | Hilo isn't known for its fancy resort hotels, but the Grand Naniloa, built in 1939, attempts to remedy that situation in grand fashion, paying homage to hula, Hawaiian culture, and Big Island adventures. **Pros:** walking distance to botanical park and Coconut Island; rental kayaks, bikes, and SUPs; free golf at adjacent 9-hole course and driving range. **Cons:** some rooms don't have ocean views; limited parking spaces; small swimming pool. $ *Rooms from: $149* ⊠ *93 Banyan Dr., Hilo* ☎ *808/969–3333* ⊕ *www.grandnaniloahilo.com* ⤴ *388 rooms* ⦿ *No meals.*

Hilo Hawaiian Hotel
$ | **HOTEL** | **FAMILY** | This landmark hotel has large bayfront rooms offering spectacular views of Maunakea and Coconut Island on Hilo Bay; street-side rooms overlook the golf course, and the hotel is within walking distance to the botanical park. **Pros:** Hilo Bay views; private lanai in most rooms; free parking. **Cons:** pricey breakfast buffet; older hotel; lacks amenities. $ *Rooms from: $129* ⊠ *71 Banyan Dr., Hilo* ☎ *808/935–9361, 800/367–5004 from mainland, 800/272–5275 interisland* ⊕ *www.castleresorts.com* ⤴ *286 rooms* ⦿ *No meals.*

Hilo Seaside Hotel
$ | **HOTEL** | Ten minutes from the airport, this local-flavor destination is a friendly, laid-back, and otherwise peaceful place, with tropical rooms that have private lanai. **Pros:** private lanai; friendly staff; budget friendly with frequent specials. **Cons:** not walking distance to historic bayfront; hotel is a little dated; no restaurant. $ *Rooms from: $99* ⊠ *126 Banyan Way, Hilo* ☎ *808/935–0821, 800/560–5557* ⊕ *www.hiloseasidehotel.com* ⤴ *133 rooms* ⦿ *No meals.*

🎭 Performing Arts

FESTIVALS
★ **Merrie Monarch Festival**
CULTURAL FESTIVALS | The mother of all Hawaii festivals, the world-class Merrie Monarch celebrates all things hula for one fantastic week every April in Hilo with competitions, activities, parades, and more. The esteemed event honors the legacy of King David Kalakaua, the man responsible for reviving fading Hawaiian cultural traditions including hula. The three-day hula competition is staged at the Edith Kanakaole Multi-Purpose Stadium during the first week

following Easter Sunday. Hula *halau* (studios) worldwide come to perform both *kahiko* (ancient) and *auana* (modern) dance styles, both solo and in groups. ■**TIP→** You should reserve accommodations and rental cars up to a year in advance. Ticket requests must be mailed and postmarked after December 1 of the preceding year. ⊠ *Edith Kanakaole Multi-Purpose Stadium, 350 Kalanikoa St., Hilo* ☎ *808/935–9168* ⊕ *www.merriemonarch.com.*

🛍 Shopping

BOOKS AND MAGAZINES
★ **Basically Books**
BOOKS/STATIONERY | The legendary shop stocks one of Hawaii's largest selections of maps, including topographical and relief maps, and Hilo's largest selection of Hawaiian music (feel free to ask for advice about your selection). Of course, it also has a wealth of books about Hawaii, including great choices for children. If you're in need of an umbrella on a rainy Hilo day, this bookstore has plenty of them. ⊠ *1672 Kamehameha Ave., Hilo* ✛ *Near Ken's House of Pancakes* ☎ *808/961–0144* ⊕ *www.basicallybooks.com.*

Greater Hilo

Sights beyond the downtown area spread out in every direction and are often amid or between residential neighborhoods and industrial parks. Be sure to check out Panaewa Rainforest Zoo with its Hawaiian animals and hundreds of species of tropical plants. Above the University of Hilo campus, the Imiloa Astronomy Center has a planetarium and gift shop. For other things to do, Big Island Candies is a must-visit destination for world-class confections. Heading toward Hamakua, there are beaches, surf spots, a botanical garden, small towns, and the famed Akaka Falls (at the beginning of the Hamakua coast).

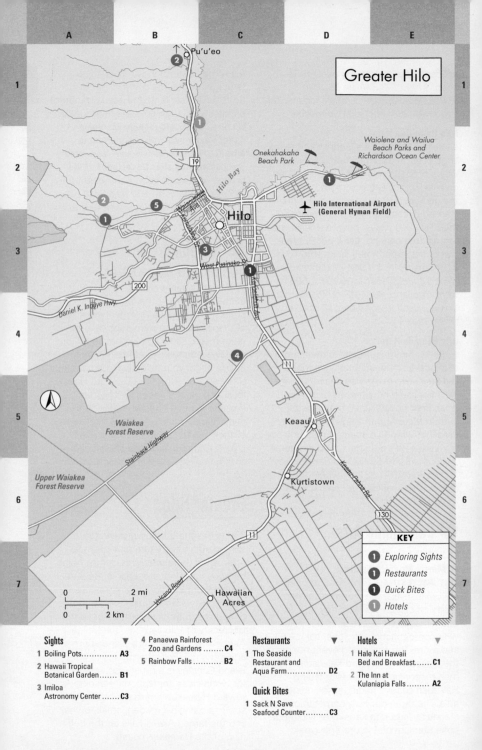

Greater Hilo

Sights ▼

1 Boiling Pots............... **A3**

2 Hawaii Tropical
Botanical Garden........ **B1**

3 Imiloa
Astronomy Center **C3**

4 Panaewa Rainforest
Zoo and Gardens **C4**

5 Rainbow Falls **B2**

Restaurants ▼

1 The Seaside
Restaurant and
Aqua Farm............... **D2**

Quick Bites ▼

1 Sack N Save
Seafood Counter......... **C3**

Hotels ▼

1 Hale Kai Hawaii
Bed and Breakfast....... **C1**

2 The Inn at
Kulaniapia Falls **A2**

KEY

- 1 Exploring Sights
- 1 Restaurants
- 1 Quick Bites
- 1 Hotels

Sights

Boiling Pots

BODY OF WATER | Four separate streams fall into a series of circular pools here, forming the Peepee Falls. The resulting turbulent action—best seen after a good rain—has earned this scenic stretch of the Wailuku River the nickname Boiling Pots. There's no swimming allowed at Peepee Falls or anywhere in the Wailuku River, due to extremely dangerous currents and undertows. The falls are 3 miles northwest of Hilo off Waianuenue Avenue; keep to the right when the road splits and look for the sign. The gate opens at 7 am and closes at 6 pm. **⚠ You may be tempted, as you watch others ignore the signs and climb over guardrails, to jump in, but resist. Swimming is expressly prohibited and unsafe, and people have died here.** You may want to combine a drive to this site with a visit to Rainbow Falls, a bit closer to downtown. ⊠ *Wailuku River State Park, Off Waianuenue Ave., Hilo* ⊕ *dlnr.hawaii.gov/dsp/parks/hawaii/wailuku-river-state-park* 🖃 *Free.*

Hawaii Tropical Botanical Garden

GARDEN | Stunning coastline views appear around each curve of the 4-mile scenic jungle drive that accesses this privately owned nature preserve next to Onomea Bay. Paved pathways in the 17-acre botanical garden lead past ponds, waterfalls, and more than 2,000 species of plants and flowers, including palms, bromeliads, ginger, heliconia, orchids, and ornamentals. The garden is well worth a stop, and your entry fee helps the nonprofit preserve plants, seeds, and rain forests for future generations. Trails can get slippery when it's raining. ⊠ *27-717 Old Mamalahoa Hwy., Papaikou* ⊹ *8 miles north of downtown Hilo* 🕾 *808/964–5233* ⊕ *www.htbg.com* 🖃 *$25.*

★ Imiloa Astronomy Center

OBSERVATORY | Part Hawaiian cultural center, part astronomy museum, this center provides an educational and cultural complement to the research being conducted atop 14,000-foot Maunakea. Although visitors are welcome at Maunakea, its primary function is as a research facility—not observatory, museum, or education center. Those roles have been taken on by Imiloa in a big way. With its interactive exhibits, full-dome planetarium shows, and regularly scheduled talks and events, the center is a must-see for anyone interested in the stars, the planets, or Hawaiian culture and history. Five minutes from downtown Hilo, near the University of Hawaii at Hilo, the center also provides an important link between the scientific research being conducted at Maunakea and its history as a sacred mountain for the Hawaiian people. Admission includes one planetarium show and an all-day pass to the exhibit hall, which features more than 100 interactive displays. The lunch buffet at the adjoining Sky Garden Restaurant is popular and affordable. ⊠ *University of Hawaii at Hilo Science and Technology Park, 600 Imiloa Pl., off Nowelo and Komohana, Hilo* 🕾 *808/969–9700* ⊕ *www.imiloahawaii.org* 🖃 *$17.50* ⊘ *Closed Mon.*

★ Panaewa Rainforest Zoo and Gardens

ZOO | **FAMILY** | Billed as "the only natural tropical rain forest zoo in the United States," this sweet zoo features native Hawaiian species such as the state bird, the nene goose, and the *io* (hawk), as well as lots of other rare birds, monkeys, sloths, and lemurs. Two Bengal tigers are also part of the collection. The white-faced whistling tree ducks are a highlight. There's a petting zoo on Saturdays from 1:30 to 2:30. It's a joy to stroll the grounds, which are landscaped with hundreds of species of lush and unusual tropical plants. To get here, turn left on Mamaki off Highway 11; it's just past the "Kulani 19, Stainback Hwy." sign. ⊠ *800 Stainback Hwy., Hilo* 🕾 *808/959–7224* 🖃 *Free, donations encouraged.*

Rainbow Falls

BODY OF WATER | After a hard rain, these impressive falls thunder into the Wailuku River gorge, often creating magical rainbows in the mist. Rainbow Falls, sometimes known as the "Hilo Town Falls," are located just above downtown Hilo. Take Waianuenue Avenue west for a mile; when the road forks, stay right and look for the Hawaiian warrior sign. They remain open during daylight hours. If you're visiting the falls, you can also drive to the Boiling Pots, also inside the park but a bit farther from downtown. At this site, four streams fall into a series of turbulent pools. ✉ *Wailuku River State Park, Rainbow Dr., Hilo* 🌐 *dlnr.hawaii.gov/dsp/parks/hawaii* 🎟 *Free.*

Beaches

Onekahakaha Beach Park

BEACH—SIGHT | **FAMILY** | Shallow, rock-wall-enclosed tide pools and an adjacent grassy picnic area make this park a favorite among Hilo families with small children. The protected pools are great places to look for Hawaiian marine life like sea urchins and anemones. There isn't much white sand, but access to the water is easy. The water is usually rough beyond the line of large boulders protecting the inner tide pools, so be careful if the surf is high. This beach gets crowded on weekends. **Amenities:** lifeguards (weekends, holidays, and summer only); parking (no fee); showers; toilets. **Best for:** swimming. ✉ *Onekahakaha Rd. and Kalanianaole Ave., via Kanoelehua St., Hilo* ✣ *3 miles east of Hilo* ☎ *808/961–8311.*

Waiolena and Wailua Beach Parks and Richardson Ocean Center

BEACH—SIGHT | **FAMILY** | Just east of Hilo, almost at the end of the road, three adjacent parks make up one beautiful spot with a series of bays, protected inlets, lagoons, and pretty parks. This is one of the best snorkeling sites on this side of the island, as rocky outcrops provide shelter for schools of reef fish and sea turtles. Resist the urge to get too close to turtles or disturb them; they are protected from harassment by federal and state law. Local kids use the small black-sand pocket beach for body boarding. The shaded grassy areas are great for picnics. Be warned: this place is very crowded on weekends. **Amenities:** lifeguards (weekends, holidays, and summer only); parking (no fee); showers; toilets. **Best for:** snorkeling; walking. ✉ *2349 Kalanianaole Ave., Hilo* ✣ *4 miles east of Hilo* ☎ *808/961–8311.*

Restaurants

The Seaside Restaurant and Aqua Farm

$$ | **SEAFOOD** | **FAMILY** | Owned and operated by the Nakagawi family since the early 1920s, this landmark restaurant features three separate dining rooms that overlook a 30-acre natural brackish fishpond, making this one of the most interesting places to eat in Hilo. Along wth *paniolo* (cowboy) prime rib, New York steak, and shrimp scampi, the menu highlights *aholehole* (Hawaiian flagtail) raised in the pond. **Known for:** authentic local experience; ocean and pond views at sunset; fried aholehole (young Hawaiian flagtail). [$] *Average main: $23* ✉ *1790 Kalanianaole Ave., Hilo* ☎ *808/935–8825* 🌐 *www.seasiderestauranthilo.com* 🕓 *Closed Mon. No lunch.*

Coffee and Quick Bites

Sack N Save Seafood Counter

$ | **HAWAIIAN** | **FAMILY** | It may sound strange, but the takeout seafood counter tucked in the back of this grocery store serves some of the finest poke in Hilo. For $10 a bowl, you get enough seafood on a steaming pile of rice to feed two people. **Known for:** variety of fresh, Hawaiian-style poke offerings; house-made sauces; affordable grab-and-go lunch spot. [$] *Average main: $10* ✉ *Puainako Center, 2100 Kanoelehua Ave., Suite 101,*

Hilo ☎ *808/959–5831* ⊕ *www.foodland.com/stores/sack-n-save-puainako.*

🛏 Hotels

Hale Kai Hawaii Bed and Breakfast

$$ | B&B/INN | On a bluff above Honolii surf beach, this modern 5,400-square-foot home is 2 miles from downtown Hilo and features four rooms—each with patio, deluxe bedding, and grand ocean views within earshot of the surf. **Pros:** delicious hot breakfast; panoramic views of Hilo Bay; smoke-free property. **Cons:** no kids under 13; just outside walking distance to downtown Hilo; occasional coqui frog noise. ⓢ *Rooms from: $187* ✉ *111 Honolii Pl., Hilo* ☎ *808/935–6330* ⊕ *www.halekaihawaii.com* 🛏 *4 rooms* ⦿ *Free breakfast.*

The Inn at Kulaniapia Falls

$$ | B&B/INN | Overlooking downtown Hilo and the ocean beyond, this inn sits next to a 120-foot waterfall that tumbles into a 300-foot-wide natural pond—ripe for swimming, conditions permitting. **Pros:** waterfalls on property; delicious full breakfast; eco-friendly option. **Cons:** isolated location away from Hilo sights; dark road challenging to navigate at night; no air-conditioning. ⓢ *Rooms from: $199* ✉ *100 Kulaniapia Dr., Hilo* ☎ *808/935–6789* ⊕ *www.waterfall.net* 🛏 *11 rooms* ⦿ *Free breakfast.*

🛍 Shopping

ARTS AND CRAFTS
Most Irresistible Shop in Hilo
GIFTS/SOUVENIRS | This place lives up to its name by stocking unique gifts from around the Pacific, be it pure Hawaiian ohia lehua honey, Kau coffee, aloha wear, or tinkling wind chimes. ✉ *256 Kamehameha Ave., Hilo* ☎ *808/935–9644.*

FOOD
★ Big Island Candies
FOOD/CANDY | A local legend in the cookie- and chocolate-making business, Big Island Candies is a must-see for connoisseurs of fine chocolates. The packaging is first-rate, which makes these world-class confections the ideal gift or souvenir. Enjoy a free cookie sample and a cup of Kona coffee as you watch through a window as sweets are being made. The store has a long list of interesting and tasty products, but it is best known for its chocolate-dipped shortbread cookies. The classy showroom is festive during holidays. ✉ *585 Hinano St., Hilo* ☎ *808/935–8890* ⊕ *www.bigislandcandies.com.*

SHOPPING CENTERS
Prince Kuhio Plaza
SHOPPING CENTERS/MALLS | The Big Island's most comprehensive mall has indoor shopping, entertainment (a multiplex), and dining, including KFC, Hot Dog on a Stick, Cinnabon, Genki Sushi, IHOP, and Maui Tacos. The kids might like the arcade (near the food court), while you enjoy the stores, anchored by Macy's and Old Navy. ✉ *111 E. Puainako St., Hilo* ☎ *808/959–3555* ⊕ *www.princekuhioplaza.com.*

Hawaii Volcanoes National Park, Puna, and Kau

Dynamic, dramatic, and diverse, Hawaii Volcanoes National Park encompasses 333,308 acres across two active shield volcanoes: Kilauea and Mauna Loa. The sparsely populated districts of Puna and Kau surround the park to the northeast and southwest, respectively.

One of the state's most popular visitor destinations, Hawaii Volcanoes National Park, a UNESCO World Heritage Site and International Biosphere Reserve, beckons visitors to explore the sacred home of the fire goddess Pele, whose active presence shapes the primordial landscape. The area has recovered from the damaging events of the 2018 Kilauea eruption that rocked the region for months, beginning with the collapse of the Puu Oo Vent in the Lower East Rift Zone. The famed lava lake at Halemaumau Crater, known for its nighttime glow, is no more, having drained completely from view after sending hot liquid magma through underground lava channels to Lower Puna, where lava flows destroyed more than 700 homes and farms. At the summit, hundreds of earthquakes per day rocked the area for several months as Halemaumau Crater increased in volume to nearly 14 times its original size. The seismic events at the summit caused permanent damage to the Jaggar Museum and the Hawaii Volcano Observatory facility that overlooked the crater; both are closed.

Today the park has returned to normal, and visitors can explore most of the sights and trails that were open to the public prior to the eruption. Although the dramatic changes to Halemaumau Crater are evident to anyone who visited the park before the eruption, many of the park's favorite attractions have survived, including Thurston Lava Tube, Devastation Trail, and Kilauea Iki Trail. The park now has no active surface lava flows or eruptions, nor is any activity expected in the near future. Still, there are plenty of activities such as hiking, biking, and picnicking. And with attractions from incomparable scenic vistas to fascinating geological features including wide expanses of *aa* (rough) and *pahoehoe* (smooth) lava, Hawaii Volcanoes National Park is a must-see destination, whether for a half-day trek or a week-long deep dive into this unique place.

Located just outside of Hawaii Volcanoes National Park, the artsy, forested enclave of Volcano Village features fine-art galleries, glass-blowing studios, cozy cafés, restaurants, boutiques, and a Sunday farmers' market with breakfast items as well as crafts. The plentiful accommodations here include inns, bed-and-breakfasts, vacation cottages, and cabins. When staying in Volcano Village, you can partake in wine tastings and tours at a local winery, play golf at an 18-hole course, go bird-watching, or ride a bike along quiet, flat streets through rain forest neighborhoods. Nearby but inside the park, the Kilauea Military Camp has an arcade, bowling alley, a general store, and the Lava Lounge cocktail bar, all open to the public. And of course, you can just take in the starry nighttime sky or the ever-changing daytime skies with their random rain showers, rainbows, rolling clouds, and crystal-clear skies.

The districts of Kau and Puna lie adjacent to each other and are big and sparse, requiring lots of drive time to get to places of the most interest. The area is known for its wide-open spaces, vast desert regions, rugged coastline, dense macadamia groves, and windswept ranchlands.

GETTING HERE AND AROUND
The 27-mile drive on Highway 19 from Hilo to Volcano (all through Upper Puna) takes about 40 minutes. From Kailua-Kona, the drive requires traversing Saddle Road to Hilo and then heading up to Volcano; the one-way drive takes approximately 2½ hours. The park itself is easy to drive around, as there are only two main roads: Chain of Craters Road and Crater Rim Drive. Because of recent events at Kilauea Caldera, part of Crater Rim Drive remains closed to the public.

TOURS
Volcano Art Center
SPECIAL-INTEREST | Volcano Art Center offers a free Monday morning forest tour where visitors can learn about rare native Hawaiian rain forests. These hour-long walks take place on easily traversed gravel trails, rain or shine. No reservations are required, but they are recommended for groups of five or more. The center offers additional customized rain

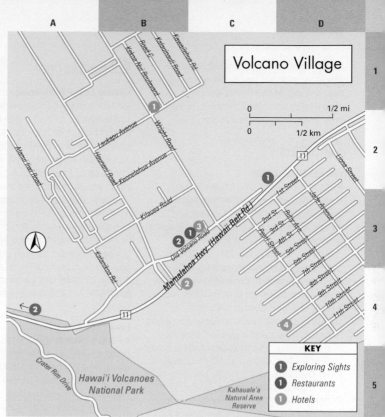

Sights ▼

1 Volcano Garden Arts.......... **C2**
2 Volcano Winery **A4**

Restaurants ▼

1 Kilauea Lodge Restaurant.. **C3**
2 Lava Rock Cafe **B3**

Hotels ▼

1 Chalet Kilauea Rainforest Hotel.......... **B1**
2 Hale Ohia Cottages **C4**
3 Kilauea Lodge........ **C3**
4 Volcano Mist Cottage...... **D4**

Volcano Village

KEY

1 *Exploring Sights*
1 *Restaurants*
1 *Hotels*

forest tours, as well as forest restoration activities. ☎ 866/967–8222 for administration, 808/967–7565 for gallery ⊕ www. volcanoartcenter.org 🖃 From $10.

VISITOR INFORMATION

The park is open 24/7. When you arrive at the park entrance during normal visiting hours, you'll receive a complimentary, detailed map and brochure about the park. The entrance fee (good for seven days) is $30 per vehicle, $15 per pedestrian, and $25 per motorcycle. Inside the Kilauea Vistor Center, trail guide booklets written by park geologists are available for less than $3 each. Operated by Hawaii Pacific Parks, the park store features educational materials, apparel, gifts, books, and art. A small theater plays educational films about the history of the park, and park rangers are available to answer questions. There is always a

roster of ranger-led activities. ■TIP→ Purchase the Hawaii Tri-park Annual Pass for $55, which allows full access to Hawaii Volcanoes National Park and Puuhonua O Honaunau National Historical Park on the Big Island and Haleakala National Park on Maui.

Volcano Village

Located right outside the park boundary and surrounded by rain forest, Volcano Village is a residential neighborhood that offers vacation rental accommodations, B&B inns, a gas station, a post office, an art school, galleries, shops, a general store, and a fun Sunday farmers' market. The immediate area also has a country club and golf course, along with the popular Volcano Winery. Next door to the winery, the Keauhou Bird Conservation

Center is not open to the public, but if you listen closely, you may be able to hear the call of the highly endangered *alala* (Hawaiian raven), which is being bred in captivity at the center.

Sights

Volcano Garden Arts

MUSEUM | Located on beautifully landscaped grounds dotted with intriguing sculptures, this delightful gallery and garden lend credence to Volcano Village's reputation as an artists' haven. The charming complex includes an eclectic gallery representing more than 100 artists, an excellent organic café housed in redwood buildings built in 1908, and a cute, one-bedroom artist's cottage, available for rent. If you're lucky, you'll get to meet the eccentric owner/"caretaker" of this enclave, the multitalented Ira Ono, known for his whimsical art, recycled trash creations, and friendly personality. ✉ *19-3834 Old Volcano Rd., Volcano* ☎ *808/985–8979* 🌐 *www.volcanogardenarts.com* 🎟 *Free* ⏲ *Garden closed Sun. and Mon.*

Volcano Winery

WINERY/DISTILLERY | Not all volcanic soils are ideal for the cultivation of grapes, but this winery grows its own grapes and produces some interesting vintages. The Macadamia Nut Honey wine is a nutty, very sweet after-dinner drink. The Infusion pairs estate-grown black tea with South Kona's fermented macadamia nut honey for a smooth concoction perfect for brunch through early evening. Though this isn't Napa Valley, the vintners take their wine seriously, and the staff is friendly and knowledgeable. Wine tasting is available; you can also get wine and cheese to eat in the picnic area, and a gift store has a selection of local crafts. ✉ *35 Pii Mauna Dr., Volcano* ✣ *Past entrance to Hawaii Volcanoes National Park, by golf course* ☎ *808/967–7772* 🌐 *www.volcanowinery.com.*

Restaurants

Kilauea Lodge Restaurant

$$$ | **HAWAIIAN** | The koa-wood tables and intimate lighting are in keeping with the ambience of this cozy lodge in the heart of Volcano Village, built in 1937 as a YMCA camp and still retaining the Fireplace of Friendship, embedded with coins and plaques from around the world. The fare ranges from grass-fed Big Island beef burgers and Niihau lamb burgers to a chicken pasta, catch of the day, and farm-fresh salads. **Known for:** gourmet burgers; fine dining with prices to match; popular Sunday brunch. [$] *Average main: $30* ✉ *19-3948 Old Volcano Rd., Volcano* ☎ *808/967–7366* 🌐 *www.kilauealodge.com.*

Lava Rock Cafe

$ | **DINER** | **FAMILY** | This is an affordable place to grab a sandwich or a coffee and check your email (Wi-Fi is free with purchase of a meal) before heading to Hawaii Volcanoes National Park. The homey, sit-down diner caters to families, serving up heaping plates of pancakes and French toast for breakfast; on the lunch menu, burgers range from bacon-cheese to turkey and *paniolo* (cowboy) burgers made with Hawaii grass-fed beef. **Known for:** roadhouse atmosphere; live music in evenings; diner-style comfort food. [$] *Average main: $10* ✉ *19-3972 Old Volcano Hwy., Volcano* ✣ *Next to Kilauea General Store* ☎ *808/967–8526* ⏲ *No dinner Sun. and Mon.*

Hotels

Chalet Kilauea Rainforest Hotel

$ | **B&B/INN** | **FAMILY** | Quirky yet upscale, this accommodation features four artistically distinctive rooms that unveil beautiful views of the rain forest from a great location five minutes from Hawaii Volcanoes National Park. **Pros:** unique decor; friendly front desk; hot tub on property. **Cons:** space heaters; not close to the beach; can get cold at night.

Rooms from: $169 ✉ *19-4178 Wright Rd., Volcano* ☎ *808/967–7786, 800/937–7786* ⊕ *www.volcano-hawaii.com* ⤳ *4 rooms* ⍾ *No meals.*

Hale Ohia Cottages

$ | B&B/INN | FAMILY | A stately and comfortable Queen Anne–style mansion, Hale Ohia was built in the 1930s as a summer home for a wealthy Scotsman (the property is listed on the State Historic Register). **Pros:** unique architecture; free Wi-Fi and parking; private location. **Cons:** no TVs; simple breakfast offerings; 30 minutes from downtown Hilo via car. *$ Rooms from: $149* ✉ *11-3968 Hale Ohia Rd., Volcano* ☎ *808/967–7986, 800/455–3803* ⊕ *www.haleohia.com* ⤳ *15 rooms* ⍾ *Free breakfast.*

Kilauea Lodge

$$ | HOTEL | A mile from the entrance of Hawaii Volcanoes National Park, this lodge was initially built as a YMCA camp in the 1930s; now it is a pleasant inn, tastefully furnished with European antiques, photographs, and authentic Hawaiian quilts. **Pros:** great restaurant; close to volcano; fireplaces in each room. **Cons:** no TV or phone in lodge rooms; 45 minutes to downtown Hilo; few shopping options nearby. *$ Rooms from: $229* ✉ *19-3948 Old Volcano Rd., Volcano* ⌖ *1 mile northeast of national park* ☎ *808/967–7366* ⊕ *www.kilauealodge.com* ⤳ *12 rooms* ⍾ *Free breakfast.*

Volcano Mist Cottage

$$$ | RENTAL | Both rustic and Zen, this magical cottage in the rain forest features cathedral ceilings, spruce walls, cork flooring, and amenities not usually found at Volcano vacation rentals, like bathrobes, a Bose home theater system, and Trek mountain bikes. **Pros:** isolated and private cottage; outdoor Jacuzzi tub; upscale amenities. **Cons:** not large enough for families; 45 minutes from downtown Hilo; limited shopping options nearby. *$ Rooms from: $300* ✉ *11-3932 9th St., Volcano* ☎ *808/895–8359*

⊕ *www.volcanomistcottage.com* ⤳ *1 cottage* ⍾ *Free breakfast.*

Summit Area

In the heart of Hawaii Volcanoes National Park, a primeval landscape unfolds at the summit of Kilauea Volcano, where steam rises continuously from cracks in the earth and volcanic gases create malodorous sulfur banks. Here, Halemaumau Crater has doubled in diameter from the seismic events of the 2018 Kilauea eruption. In addition to the many geological sights, the summit area of the park includes Kilauea Visitor Center, Volcano Art Center Gallery, and Volcano House, a landmark hotel perched above the rim of the massive Kilauea Caldera. This is a good area to begin your visit to the park.

◉ Sights

Devastation Trail

TRAIL | A paved pathway takes visitors across a barren lavascape strewn with chunky cinders that descended from towering lava fountains during the 1959 eruption of nearby Kilauea Iki Crater. The easy 1-mile (round-trip) hike ends at the edge of the Kilauea Iki Crater. This must-see view of the crater could yield such memorable sights as white-tailed tropic birds gliding in the breeze or a rainbow stretching above the crater's rim after a sunlit rain shower. ✉ *Hawaii Volcanoes National Park* ⌖ *4 miles from visitor center at intersection of Crater Rim Dr. and Chain of Craters Rd.* ☎ *808/985–6101* ⊕ *www.nps.gov/havo.*

★ Kilauea Iki Trail

TRAIL | The stunning 4-mile loop hike descends 400 feet into a massive crater via a forested nature trail. As part of this, you hike across the crater floor, walking on a solidified lava lake. Still steaming in places, the crater is dotted with baby ohia trees emerging from the cracks.

Continued on page 402

HAWAII VOLCANOES NATIONAL PARK

Exploring the surface of the world's most active volcano—from the moonscape craters at the summit to the red-hot lava flows on the coast to the kipuka, pockets of vegetation miraculously left untouched—is the ultimate ecotour and one of Hawaii's must-dos.

The park sprawls over 520 square miles and encompasses Kilauea and Mauna Loa, two of the five volcanoes that formed the Big Island nearly half a million years ago. Kilauea, youngest and most rambunctious of the Hawaiian volcanoes, erupted at its summit from the 19th century through 1982. Since then, the top of the volcano had been more or less quiet, frequently shrouded in mist; an eruption in the Halemaumau Crater in 2008 ended this period of relative inactivity.

Kilauea's eastern side sprang to life on January 3, 1983, shooting molten lava four stories high. This eruption has been ongoing, and lava flows are generally steady and slow, appearing and disappearing from view. Over 500 acres have been added to Hawaii's eastern coast since the activity began, and scientists say this eruptive phase is not likely to end anytime soon. However, the famed lava lake at Halemaumau Crater has drained, so for now, there's no flowing lava to see anywhere in the park.

The damaging events of 2018 have now subsided, and you can see the effects of creation elemental—when molten lava meets the ocean, cools, and solidifies into brand-new stretches of coastline. Although you can no longer view flowing lava, you can hike 150 miles of trails and camp amid wide expanses of *aa* (rough) and *pahoehoe* (smooth) lava. There's nothing quite like it.

- 🏠 P.O. Box 52, Hawaii Volcanoes National Park, HI 96718
- ☎ 808/985–6000
- 🌐 www.nps.gov/havo
- 💲 $30 per vehicle; $15 for pedestrians and bicyclists. Ask about passes. Admission is good for seven consecutive days.
- 🕐 The park is open daily, 24 hours. Kilauea Visitor Center: 9 am–5 pm. Volcano Art Center Gallery: 9–5.

(top) Kilauea Iki Trail
(left) Fuming rim of Puu Oo, source of the current eruption

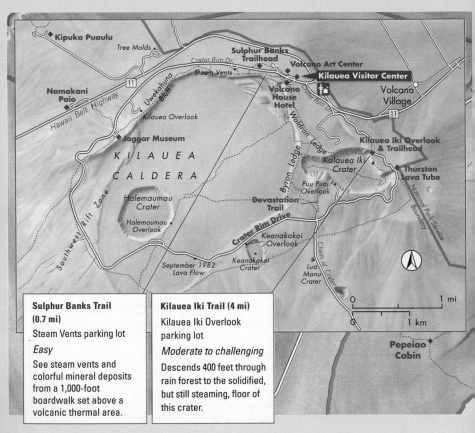

Sulphur Banks Trail (0.7 mi)

Steam Vents parking lot

Easy

See steam vents and colorful mineral deposits from a 1,000-foot boardwalk set above a volcanic thermal area.

Kilauea Iki Trail (4 mi)

Kilauea Iki Overlook parking lot

Moderate to challenging

Descends 400 feet through rain forest to the solidified, but still steaming, floor of this crater.

SEEING THE SUMMIT

The best way to explore the summit of Kilauea is to cruise along Crater Rim Drive to Kilauea Overlook. From Kilauea Overlook you can see all of Kilauea Caldera and Halemaumau Crater, an awesome depression in Kilauea Caldera measuring 3,000 feet across and nearly 300 feet deep. It's a huge and breathtaking view with pluming steam vents. At this writing, there are no active lava flows in the park after the lava lake in Halemaumau Crater drained suddenly and quickly after seismic events in 2018.

Regrettably, the events of 2018 damaged the Thomas A. Jaggar Museum beyond repair, and it is now permanently closed. You can visit the nearby Kilauea Military Camp, with its recreational activities and general store, and the park's star attractions, the Thurston Lava Tube, which you can walk through.

Other Highlights along Crater Rim Drive include sulfur and steam vents, fractures, and gullies along Kilauea's flanks. Kilauea Iki Crater, on the way down to Chain of Crater's Road, is smaller, but just as fascinating when seen from Puu Pai Overlook.

Kipuka Puaulu

SEE LEFT

Kilauea Visitor Center

Volcano Village

Hawaii Belt Hwy.

Kilauea Caldera

Crater Rim Dr.

Lua Manu Crater

Puhimau Crater

Kookoolau Crater

Pauahi Crater

Puu Huluhulu

Kane Nui o HamoLava Shield

Mauna Ulu Lava Shield

Makaopuhi Crater

Napau Crater

EAST RIFT ZONE

Kupaianaha Lava Shield

Puu Oo (Source of Current Eruption)

1983– Present Lava Flow

Cone Crater

Twin Pit Craters

Hawaii Volcanoes National Park

Chain of Craters Rd.

HILINA PALI

Hilina Pali Overlook

End of Road & Mobile Ranger Station

Puu Loa

Holei Sea Arch

Kaena Point

Pacific Ocean

Puu Huluhulu Trail (2.5 mi)
Mauna Ulu parking lot
Moderate
Great view of the ocean, Mauna Kea, Mauna Loa, Kilauea, and Puu Oo cinder cone from atop this cinder cone formed 400 years ago.

Puu Loa Petroglyphs Trail (1.5 mi)
Puu Loa Petroglyphs parking lot
Easy to moderate
Spotlighted here: ancient petroglyphs the Hawaiians created on smooth lava flows to ensure the health and safety of their children.

SEEING LAVA

Lava flows have never been guaranteed, and at this writing there is no flowing lava in the park. But you can still see steam vents and sulfur banks, as well as the effects of millennia of past lava flows.

There are three guarantees about lava flows in HVNP. First: They constantly change. Second: Because of that, you can't predict when and where you'll be able to see them. Third: New land formed when lava meets the sea is highly unstable and can collapse at any time. Never go into areas that have been closed.

■TIP➔ **Even without flowing lava, Chain of Craters Road is a magnificent drive, and the park's best hiking trails how now reopened fully.**

PLANNING YOUR TRIP TO HVNP

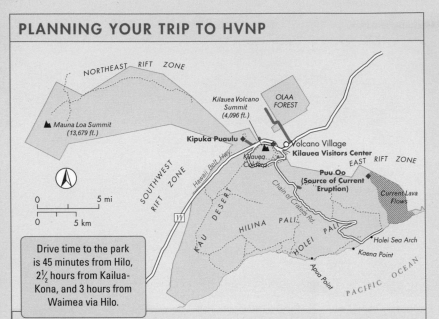

NORTHEAST RIFT ZONE

Kilauea Volcano Summit (4,096 ft.)

OLAA FOREST

Mauna Loa Summit (13,679 ft.)

Kipuka Puaulu ◆

SOUTHWEST RIFT ZONE

Hawaii Belt Hwy.

Kilauea Caldera

Kilauea Visitors Center

Volcano Village

EAST RIFT ZONE

Puu Oo (Source of Current Eruption)

Current Lava Flows

0   5 mi

0   5 km

KAU DESERT

HILINA PALI

HOLEI PALI

Chain of Craters Rd.

Holei Sea Arch

Kaena Point

Apua Point

PACIFIC OCEAN

Drive time to the park is 45 minutes from Hilo, 2½ hours from Kailua-Kona, and 3 hours from Waimea via Hilo.

Lava entering the ocean

WHERE TO START

Begin your visit at the Visitor Center, where you'll find maps, books, and DVDs; information on trails, ranger-led walks, and special events; and current weather, road, and lava-viewing conditions. Free volcano-related film showings, lectures, and other presentations are regularly scheduled.

WEATHER

Weather conditions fluctuate daily, sometimes hourly. It can be rainy and chilly even during the summer; the temperature usually is 14° cooler at the 4,000-foot-high summit of Kilauea than at sea level.

Expect hot, dry, and windy coastal conditions at the end of Chain of Craters Road. Bring rain gear, and wear layered clothing, sturdy shoes, sunglasses, a hat, and sunscreen.

Photographer on lava table filming lava flow into ocean

FOOD
It's a good idea to bring your own favorite snacks and beverages; stock up on provisions in Volcano Village, 1½ miles away. Kilauea Military Camp, near the summit, has a general store as well as casual dining options, and all are open to the public.

PARK PROGRAMS
Rangers lead daily walks at 10:30 and 1:30 into different areas; check with the Visitor Center for details as times and destinations depend on weather conditions and eruptions.

Over 60 companies hold permits to lead hikes at HVNP. Good choices are Hawaii Forest & Trail (www.hawaii-forest.com), Hawaiian Walkways (www.hawaiianwalkways.com), and Native Guide Hawaii (www.nativeguidehawaii.com).

CAUTION
"Vog" (volcanic smog) can cause headaches; breathing difficulties; lethargy; irritations of the skin, eyes, nose, and throat; and other health problems. Pregnant women, young children, and people with asthma and heart conditions are most susceptible, and should avoid areas such as Halemaumau Crater where fumes are thick.

Wear long pants and boots or closed-toe shoes with good tread for hikes on lava. Stay on marked trails and step carefully. Lava is composed of 50% silica (glass) and can cause serious injury if you fall.

Carry at least 2 quarts of water on hikes. Temperatures near lava flows can rise above 100°F, and dehydration, heat exhaustion, and sunstroke are common consequences of extended exposure to intense sunlight and high temperatures.

Remember that these are active volcanoes, and eruptions can cause parts of the park to close at any time. Check the park's website or call ahead for last-minute updates before your visit.

Volcanologists inspecting a vent in the East Rift Zone

In recent years, Kilauea's lava flows (now ceased) have produced some of the newest land on the face of the Earth.

Venture across the crater floor to the Puu Puai cinder cone that was formed by spatter from a towering lava fountain during the 1959 Kilauea Iki eruption. There are three different trailheads for Kilauea Iki; the main one, which takes two or three hours, begins at the Kilauea Iki Overlook parking lot off Crater Rim Drive. You can also access the crater from Devastation Trail or Puu Puai on the other side. ■ **TIP→ Bring water, snacks, a hat, sunscreen, and hooded rain gear, as weather can change at a moment's notice.** ✉ *Crater Rim Dr., Hawaii Volcanoes National Park ✛ 2 miles from visitor center* ☎ *808/985–6101* ⊕ *www.nps.gov/havo.*

Kilauea Military Camp

COMMERCIAL CENTER | FAMILY | Located inside the park, Kilauea Military Camp offers visitor accommodations to members of the military and their families but also has places open to the public, including an arcade, bowling alley, diner, buffet, general store, and gas station. In addition, the Lava Lounge cocktail bar features live music on weekends.

✉ *99-252 Crater Rim Dr., Hawaii Volcanoes National Park* ☎ *808/967–8333* ⊕ *www.kilaueamilitarycamp.com.*

Kilauea Visitor Center

INFO CENTER | Rangers and volunteers greet people and answer all questions at this visitor center, located just beyond the park entrance. There are lots of educational murals and displays, maps, and guidebooks. Also check out the daily itinerary of ranger-led activities and plan to sign up for some. The gift shop operated by the Hawaii Pacific Park Association stocks plenty of excellent art, books, apparel, and more. A small theater plays documentaries about the park. ✉ *1 Crater Rim Dr., Hawaii Volcanoes National Park* ☎ *808/985–6000* ⊕ *www.nps.gov/havo.*

Steam Vents and Sulfur Banks

VOLCANO | A short walk from the Kilauea Visitor Center leads to the smelly yet fascinating sulfur banks, where gases composed of hydrogen sulfide produce a smell akin to rotten eggs. Most of the rocks surrounding the vents have been dyed yellow due to constant gas exposure. Throughout the surrounding landscape, dozens of active steam vents emit white, billowing vapors that originate from groundwater heated by volcanic rocks. Located on the caldera's edge, Steaming Bluff is a short walk from a nearby parking area. ■ TIP➔ The best steam vents are across the road from the main steam vent parking area; they vary in size and are scattered alongside the dirt trails. ⊠ Crater Rim Dr., Hawaii Volcanoes National Park ✣ Within walking distance of Kilauea Visitor Center ☎ 808/ 985–6101 ⊕ www.nps.gov/havo.

Thurston Lava Tube (Nahuku)

NATURE SITE | One of the star attractions in the park, the Thurston Lava Tube (named "Nahuku" in Hawaiian) spans 600 feet underground. The massive cave-like tube, discovered in 1913, was formed by hot molten lava traveling through the channel. To reach the entrance of the tube, visitors descend a series of stairs surrounded by lush foliage and the sounds of native birds. The Kilauea eruption of 2018 resulted in an almost two-year closure of the Thurston Lava Tube as engineers surveyed for potential structural damage. Long-term safety monitoring of the cave resulted in an "all clear" from engineers and specialists in March 2020. During the closure, the drainage system was improved to reduce standing water on the cave's floor, and electrical lines were replaced. Visitors should not touch the walls or delicate tree root systems that grow down through the ceiling. ■ TIP➔ Parking is limited near the tube; if the lot is full, you can park at the Kilauea Iki Overlook parking lot a ½ mile away. ⊠ Crater Rim Dr., Hawaii Volcanoes National Park ✣ 1½ miles from the park entrance ☎ 808/985–6101 ⊕ www.nps.gov/havo.

🍴 Restaurants

The Rim at Volcano House

$$ | HAWAIIAN | FAMILY | This fine-dining restaurant overlooks the rim of Kilauea Caldera and the expansive Halemaumau Crater. Featuring two bars (one of which is adjacent to a lounge) and live entertainment nightly, the restaurant highlights island-inspired cuisine and locally sourced ingredients. Known for: views of Halemaumau Crater; Hilo coffee–rubbed rack of lamb; well-priced Taste of Hawaii lunch special. $ Average main: $25 ⊠ Volcano House, 1 Crater Rim Dr., Hawaii Volcanoes National Park ☎ 808/756–9625 ⊕ www.hawaiivolcanohouse.com.

🛏 Hotels

★ Volcano House

$$$ | HOTEL | Hawaii's oldest hotel—and the only one in Hawaii Volcanoes National Park—is committed to sustainable practices and promoting local Hawaiian culture and history through its locally sourced restaurants, artisan-crafted decor, and eco-focused guest programs. Pros: unbeatable location; views of crater; sense of place and history. Cons: basic facilities; books up quickly; some rooms have parking lot views. $ Rooms from: $285 ⊠ 1 Crater Rim Dr., Hawaii Volcanoes National Park ☎ 808/756–9625 ⊕ www.hawaiivolcanohouse.com ⇥ 33 rooms ⦿ No meals.

Greater Park Area

Spanning landscapes from sea level to the summits of two of the most active volcanoes in the world, Hawaii Volcanoes National Park boasts a diverse landscape with rain forests, rugged coastlines, surreal lava fields, and sacred cultural sites. There's also a sense of peace and tranquility here, despite the upheavals of nature. A drive down Chain of Craters Road toward the ocean allows you to access the greater area of the park, affording opportunities for exploration beyond the summit destinations. Along the way are birding trails, backcountry hikes, two campgrounds, pit craters, and a dramatic sea arch at the coast.

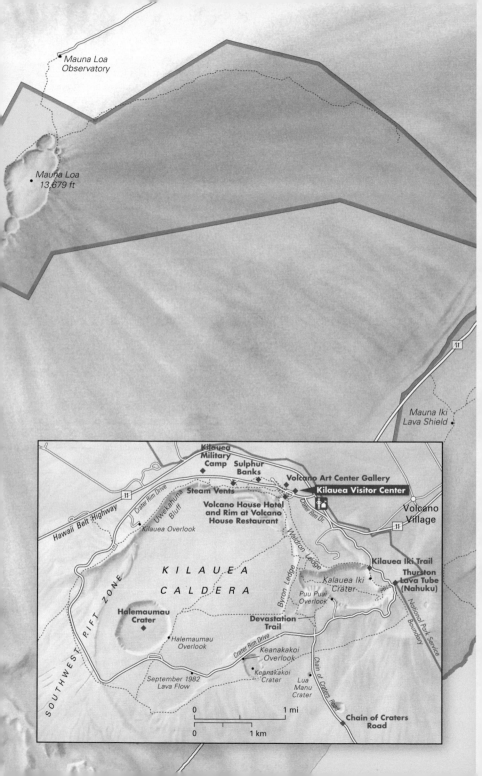

Mauna Loa
Observatory

Mauna Loa
13,679 ft

Mauna Iki
Lava Shield

Kilauea
Military
Camp

Sulphur
Banks

Volcano Art Center Gallery

Kilauea Visitor Center

Steam Vents

Volcano House Hotel
and Rim at Volcano
House Restaurant

Volcano
Village

Hawaii Belt Highway

Crater Rim Drive

Uwekahuna
Bluff

Kilauea Overlook

Waldron Ledge

Kilauea Iki Trail

Thurston
Lava Tube
(Nahuku)

Byron Ledge

Kalauea Iki
Crater

K I L A U E A
C A L D E R A

Puu Puai
Overlook

Devastation
Trail

National Park Service Boundary

Halemaumau
Crater

Halemaumau
Overlook

Crater Rim Drive

Keanakakoi
Overlook

September 1982
Lava Flow

Keanakakoi
Crater

Lua
Manu
Crater

Chain of Craters Road

SOUTHWEST RIFT ZONE

Chain of Craters Road

0   1 mi

0   1 km

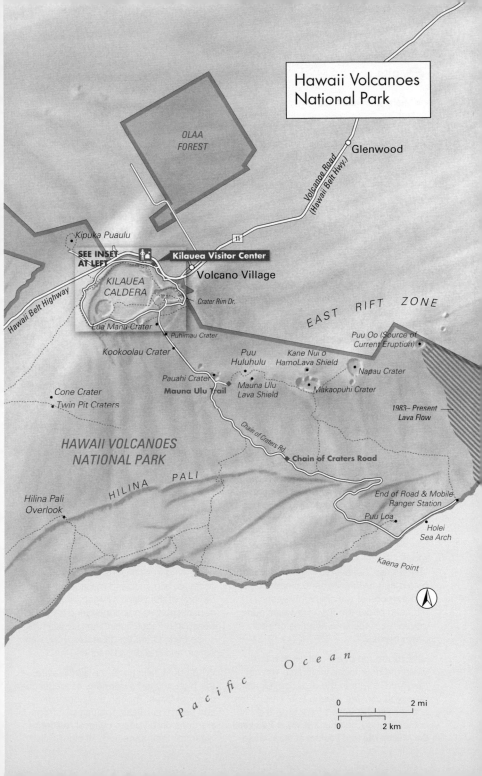

Sights

★ Chain of Craters Road

SCENIC DRIVE | The coastal region of Hawaii Volcanoes National Park is accessed via scenic Chain of Craters Road, which descends 18.8 miles to sea level. You could drive it without stopping, but it's well worth spending a few hours or a day exploring the various stops and trails. Winding past ancient craters and modern eruption sites, this scenic road was realigned in 1979 after parts of it were buried by the Mauna Ulu eruption.

Marked stops along the way include Lua Manu Crater, Hilina Pali Road, Pauahi Crater, the Mauna Ulu eruption site, Kealakomo Lookout, and Puu Loa Petroglyphs. As you approach the coast, panoramic ocean vistas prevail. The last marked stop features views of the striking natural Holei Sea Arch from an overlook. In recent years, many former sights along the coast have been covered in lava, including a black-sand beach and the old campground. ⊠ *Hawaii Volcanoes National Park* ☎ *808/ 985–6101* ⊕ *www. nps.gov/havo.*

★ Mauna Ulu Trail

TRAIL | The Mauna Ulu lava flow presents an incredible variety of geological attractions within a moderate, 2½-mile round-trip hike. The diverse lava landscape was created during the spectacular 1969–74 Mauna Ulu flow, which featured enormous "lavafalls" the size of Niagara Falls. Visitors can see everything from lava tree molds and fissure vents to cinder cones and portions of the old highway still exposed under the flow. Hawaiian nene geese roam the area, feeding on ripe ohelo berries.

Hike to the top of a small hill that survived the flow for an incredible view of the Puu Oo Vent in the distance. On clear days, you can see Mauna Loa, Maunakea, and the Pacific Ocean from atop this hill, known as Puu Huluhulu. ■**TIP**➔ **Purchase the Mauna Ulu trail booklet at the Kilauea** Visitor Center for under $3. This excellent resource includes descriptions of trailside attractions, trail maps, history, eyewitness accounts, and photographs. ⊠ *Chain of Craters Rd., Hawaii Volcanoes National Park* ✛ *7 miles from Kilauea Visitor Center* ☎ *808/985–6101* ⊕ *www.nps.gov/havo.*

Puna

Puna is about 6 miles south of Hilo.

The Puna District is wild in every sense of the word. The jagged black coastline is changing all the time; the albizzia trees grow out of control, forming canopies over the few paved roads; the residential areas are remote; and the people—well, there's something about living in an area that could be destroyed by lava at any moment (as Kalapana was in 1990, or Kapoho in 1960, or parts of Pahoa Town in 2014, or Kapoho Vacationland in 2018) that makes the norms of modern society seem silly. Vets, surfers, hippies, yoga teachers, and other free spirits abound. And also a few ruffians. So it is that Puna has its well-deserved reputation as an "outlaw" region of the Big Island.

That said, it's well worth a detour, especially if you're near this part of the island anyway. Some mighty fine people-watching opportunities exist in Pahoa, a funky little town that the "Punatics" call home.

This is also farm country for an array of agricultural products. Local farmers grow everything from orchids and anthuriums to papayas, bananas, and macadamia nuts. Several of the island's larger, rural, residential subdivisions are nestled between Keaau and Pahoa, including Hawaiian Paradise Park, Orchidland Estates, Hawaiian Acres, and Hawaiian Beaches.

When dusk falls here, the air fills with the high-pitched symphony of thousands of coqui frogs. Though they look cute and seem harmless, the invasive frogs are considered pests by local residents weary of their shrieking, all-night calls.

The sprawling Puna District stretches northeast down to the coast. If you're staying in Hilo for the night, driving around Lower Puna is a great way to spend a morning.

◉ Sights

Kilauea Caverns of Fire

CAVE | This way-out adventure explores the underbelly of the world's most active volcano via the Kazamura Lava Tube system. The longest lava tube system in the world—more than 40 miles long, with sections up to 80 feet wide, and 80 feet tall—it is 500 to 700 years old and filled with bizarre lava formations and mind-blowing colors. Tours are customized to groups' interest and skill level; tours focus on conservation and education and take visitors through the fascinating and beautiful lava caves unlike any others in the world. Tours are by reservation only and are well worth the extra detour (about 40 minutes off the main highway) and planning. At the time you make your reservation, you will be given detailed directions to the location. Equipment is included. ✉ *Hawaiian Acres, off Hwy. 11, between Kurtistown and Mountain View* ☎ *808/217–2363* ⊕ *www.kilaueacavernsoffire.com* ✑ *$29 for one-hour walking tour, $89 for three-hour adventure tour.*

Lava Tree State Monument

NATIONAL/STATE PARK | Tree molds that rise like blackened smokestacks formed here in 1790, when a lava flow swept through the ohia forest. Some reach as high as 12 feet. A meandering trail provides closeup looks at some of Hawaii's tropical plants and trees. There are restrooms and a couple of picnic pavilions and tables. In 2018, the park narrowly avoided getting swallowed by lava flows that came within a couple hundred feet of it. ⚠ **Mosquitoes live here in abundance, so come prepared.** ✉ *Hwy. 132, Pahoa* ☎ *808/974–6200* ✑ *Free.*

Pahoa Town

TOWN | This eclectic little town is reminiscent of the Wild West, with its wooden boardwalks and vintage buildings—not to mention a reputation as a pot growers' haven. Founded originally to serve the sugar plantation community, Pahoa today is a free-spirited throwback to the 1960s and '70s. You'll see plenty of hippies, vets, survivalists, woofers (workers on organic farms), yoga students, and other colorful characters pursuing alternative lifestyles. Secondhand stores, tie-dye/ hemp clothing boutiques, smoke shops, and art/antiques galleries add to the "trippy" experience. In 2014, lava flows from Kilauea almost intruded into the town, nearly overrunning the transfer station and cemetery and destroying a couple of buildings. Residents began saying goodbye to their town and packed up as smoke from the flows billowed in the near distance and the flows glowed after dark. Then it all abruptly stopped within 500 yards of Pahoa Village Road, once again ensuring the town's status as a survivor—until 2018 when Pahoa became command central for disaster assistance, civil defense, and media reporters covering the nearby dramatic eruption of Kilauea in real time. Pahoa's funky main street—with buildings dating from 1910—boasts a handful of excellent, local-style eateries. (In 2017, a fire swept through parts of the boardwalk and buildings, which are still being rebuilt.) To get here, turn southeast onto Highway 130 at Keaau, and drive 11 miles and follow signs to the Village. ✉ *Pahoa.*

❿ Restaurants

Kaleo's Bar and Grill

$ | AMERICAN | Pahoa Town isn't necessarily known for gourmet dining choices, but Kaleo's is pretty sophisticated for a small-town restaurant and remains a local favorite with very good food. Hawaiian-inspired fare blends the gamut of island ethnic influences with such choices as tempura ahi rolls, grilled burgers, and banana spring rolls. **Known for:** sophisticated menu; nightly entertainment; kalua (baked in an earth oven) pork wontons. $ *Average main: $15 ✉ 15-2969 Pahoa Village Rd., Pahoa ☎ 808/965–5600 ⊕ www.kaleoshawaii.com.*

Luquin's Cantina

$ | MEXICAN | Long an island favorite for tasty, albeit greasy, Mexican grub, this landmark is making a comeback in the funky town of Pahoa after a tragic fire burned the original restaurant to the ground in 2017. Tacos are great (go for crispy), especially when stuffed with grilled, seasoned local fish on occasion. **Known for:** longtime Pahoa restaurant; affordable fare; delicious huevos rancheros. $ *Average main: $9 ✉ 15-1448 Kahakai Blvd., Pahoa ☎ 808/965–9990 ⊕ www.luquins.com.*

Hotels

Your Hawaiian Retreat

$ | RENTAL | A collection of three little rentals deep in the heart of Puna and well off the beaten path comprise this exotic destination on an organic farm. **Pros:** affordable whole house rental options; breakfast items stocked for Mango and Avocado House; Ohana House good for groups. **Cons:** remote; not on the beach; three-night minimum stay. $ *Rooms from: $100 ✉ 13-809 Kamaili Rd., Pahoa ✛ 6 miles south of Pahoa ☎ 808/965–7088 ⊕ www.yourhawaiianretreat.org ⇗ 3 units ⁙⃝ No meals.*

Kau

South Point is 50 miles south of Kailua-Kona.

Perhaps the most desolate region of the island, Kau is nevertheless home to some spectacular sights. Mark Twain wrote some of his finest prose here, where macadamia nut farms, remote green-sand beaches, and tiny communities offer rugged, largely undiscovered beauty. The drive from Kailua-Kona to windswept South Point winds away from the ocean through a surreal moonscape of lava plains and patches of scrub forest. Coming from Volcano, as you near South Point, the barren lavascape gives way to lush vistas from the ocean to the hills.

At the end of the 12-mile, two-lane road to South Point, you can park and hike about an hour to Papakolea (Green Sands Beach). Back on the highway, the coast passes verdant cattle pastures, sheer cliffs, and the village of Naalehu on the way to the black-sand beach of Punaluu, a common nesting place of the Hawaiian hawksbill turtle.

Kau is usually combined with a quick trip to Hawaii Volcanoes National Park from Kona. This is probably cramming too much into one day, however. Visiting the volcano fills up at least a day (two is better), and the sights of this southern end of the island are worth more than a cursory glance.

Instead, make Green Sands Beach or Punaluu a full beach day, and see some of the other sights on the way there or back. Bring sturdy shoes, water, and a sun hat if Green Sands Beach is your choice (reaching the beach requires a hike). You can pay some enterprising locals $5 a head to give you a ride in their pickups to the beach. And be careful in the surf here. Don't go in unless you're used to ocean waves. There are no lifeguards at this remote beach. It's decidedly calmer and you can sometimes snorkel at Punaluu, but use caution at these and all Hawaii beaches.

Sights

Hawaii Volcanoes National Park: Kahuku Unit

NATIONAL/STATE PARK | Located off Highway 11 at mile marker 70.5, the Kahuku section of the park takes visitors

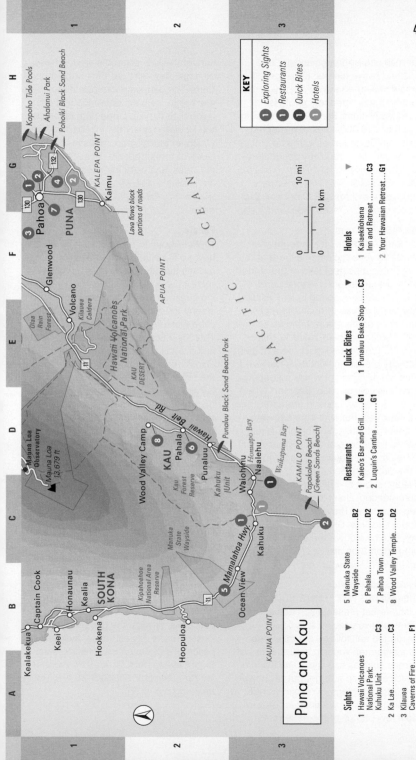

Puna and Kau

Sights ▶

1 Hawaii Volcanoes
National Park:
Kuhuku Unit...............**C3**
2 Ka Lae..................**C3**
3 Kilauea
Caverns of Fire.........**F1**
4 Lava Tree
State Monument.........**G1**
5 Manuka State
Wayside................**B2**
6 Pahala.................**D2**
7 Pahoa Town............**G1**
8 Wood Valley Temple.....**D2**

Restaurants ▶

1 Kaleo's Bar and Grill......**G1**
2 Luquin's Cantina **G1**

Quick Bites ▶

1 Punaluu Bake Shop **C3**

Hotels ▶

1 Kaiaekilohana
Inn and Retreat **C3**
2 Your Hawaiian Retreat....**G1**

KEY

1 Exploring Sights
1 Restaurants
1 Quick Bites
1 Hotels

SOUTH
KONA

PUNA

KAU

PACIFIC OCEAN

Mauna Loa
Observatory
▲ Mauna Loa
13,679 ft

Hawaii Volcanoes
National Park

Kilauea
Caldera

KAU
DESERT

Olaa
Rain
Forest

Kau
Forest
Reserve

Manuka
State
Wayside

Kipahoehoe
National Area
Reserve

Kahuku
Unit

Hawaii Belt Rd

Mamalahoa Hwy.

Kapoho Tide Pools
Ahalanui Park
Pohoiki Black Sand Beach

KALEPA POINT

APUA POINT

Punaluu Black Sand Beach Park

Honuapo Bay

Waikapuna Bay

KAMILO POINT

Papokolea Beach
(Green Sands Beach)

KAUNA POINT

Lava flows block
portions of roads

Kealakekua
Keei
Captain Cook
Honaunau
Kealia
Hookena
Hoopuloa

Glenwood
Volcano

Pahoa
Kaimu

Wood Valley Camp
Pahala
Punaluu
Waiohinu
Naalehu
Kahuku
Ocean View

0   10 mi
0   10 km

409

over many trails through ancient lava flows and native forests. Endangered plants and animals are on display in this beautiful but isolated region of Hawaii Volcanoes National Park, encompassing more than 116,000 acres of protected parklands. Guided hikes with knowledgeable rangers are a regularly scheduled highlight. ⊠ *Hwy. 11 at mile marker 70.5, Kahuku* ☎ *808/985–6101* ⊕ *www.nps. gov/havo/index.htm* ⊠ *$30 per car, $15 for pedestrian* ⊘ *Closed Mon. and Tues.*

Ka Lae (*South Point*)

NATIONAL/STATE PARK | It's thought that the first Polynesians came ashore at this southernmost point of land in the United States, also a National Historic Landmark. Old canoe-mooring holes, visible today, were carved through the rocks, possibly by settlers from Tahiti as early as AD 750. To get here, drive 12 miles down the turnoff road, past rows of giant electricity-producing windmills powered by the nearly constant winds sweeping across this coastal plain. Bear left when the road forks, and park in the lot at the end. Walk past the boat hoists toward the little lighthouse. South Point is just past the lighthouse at the southernmost cliff. You may see brave locals jumping off the cliffs and then climbing up rusty old ladders, but swimming here is not recommended. Don't leave anything of value in your car. The area is isolated and without services. Green Sands Beach is a 40-minute hike down the coast. ⊠ *South Point Rd. off Mamalahoa Hwy., near mile marker 70, Naalehu* ⊠ *Free.*

Manuka State Wayside

NATIONAL/STATE PARK | **FAMILY** | This lowland forest preserve spreads across several relatively recent lava flows. A semirugged trail follows a 2-mile loop past a pit crater, winding around interesting trees such as hau and *kukui* (candlenut). It's a nice spot to get out of the car and stretch your legs—you can wander through the well-maintained arboretum, snap a few photos of the eerie forest,

and let the kids scramble around trees so large they can't get their arms around them. The pathways can get muddy and rough, so bring appropriate shoes if you plan to hike. Large populations of the Hawaiian hoary bat inhabit the area, which, in totality, encompasses 25,000 acres of forest reserve. Restrooms, picnic areas, and camping sites (by permit) are available. ⊠ *Hwy. 11, north of mile marker 81, Pahala* ☎ *808/974–6200* ⊕ *dl-nr.hawaii.gov/dsp/parks/hawaii* ⊠ *Free.*

Pahala

TOWN | About 16 miles east of Naalehu, beyond Punaluu Beach Park, Highway 11 passes directly by this little town. You'll miss it if you blink. Pahala, once a booming sugar plantation company town, is sleepy today but still inhabited by retired cane workers and their descendants. There is a Longs Pharmacy, a gas station, and a small supermarket, but not much else in terms of conveniences. Beyond the town past a wide, paved cane road, is Wood Valley, once a prosperous community, now just a peaceful area heavily scented by eucalyptus trees, coffee blossoms, and night-blooming jasmine and often laden in mist. ⊠ *Pahala.*

Wood Valley Temple (*Nechung Temple*)

RELIGIOUS SITE | Behind the remote town of Pahala, this serene and beautiful Tibetan Buddhist temple, established in 1973, has hosted more than 50 well-known lamas, including the Dalai Lama on two occasions. Known as Nechung Dorje Drayang Ling (Immutable Island of Melodious Sound), this peaceful place welcomes all creeds. You can visit and meditate, leave an offering, walk the lush gardens shared by strutting peacocks, browse the gift shop, or stay in the temple's guesthouse, available for peaceful, nondenominational retreats taught by masters. ⊠ *96-2285 Wood Valley Rd., Pahala* ☎ *808/928–8539* ⊕ *www. nechung.org* ⊠ *$5.*

Beaches

You shouldn't expect to find sparkling white-sand beaches on the rugged and rocky coasts of Kau, and you won't. What you will find is something a bit rarer and well worth the visit: black- and green-sand beaches. And there's the chance to see the endangered hawksbill or Hawaiian green sea turtles close up.

Papakolea Beach (*Green Sands Beach*)
BEACH—SIGHT | Tired of the same old gold-, white-, or black-sand beach? Then how about a green-sand beach? You'll need good hiking shoes or sneakers to get to this olive-green crescent, one of the most unusual beaches on the island. It lies at the base of Puu O Mahana, at Mahana Bay, where a cinder cone formed during an early eruption of Mauna Loa. The greenish tint is caused by an accumulation of olivine crystals that form in volcanic eruptions. The dry, barren landscape is totally surreal but stunning, as aquamarine waters lap on green sand against reddish cliffs. ⚠ **The surf is often rough and swimming can be hazardous due to strong currents, so caution is advised**. Drive down to South Point; at the end of the 12-mile paved road, take the road to the left and park at the end. To reach the beach, follow the 2¼-mile coastal trail, which ends in a steep and dangerous descent down the cliffside on an unimproved trail. The hike takes about two hours each way and it can get hot and windy, so bring lots of drinking water. Four-wheel-drive vehicles are no longer permitted on the trail. **Amenities:** none. **Best for:** solitude; walking. ✉ *Hwy. 11, Naalehu* ✣ *2½ miles northeast of South Point.*

★ Punaluu Black Sand Beach Park
BEACH—SIGHT | A must-do on a south–southeast–bound trip to the volcano, this easily accessible black-sand beach is backed by low dunes, brackish ponds, and tall coco palms. The shoreline is jagged, reefed, and rocky. Most days, large groups of sea turtles nap on the sand—a stunning sight. Resist the urge to get too close or disturb them; they're protected by federal and state law, and fines for harassment can be hefty. Removing black sand is also prohibited. ⚠ **Extremely strong rip currents prevail, so only experienced ocean swimmers should consider getting in the water here.** A popular stop for locals and tour buses alike, this beach park can get very busy, especially on weekends (the north parking lot is usually quieter). Shade from palm trees provides an escape from the sun, and at the northern end of the beach, near the boat ramp, lie the ruins of Kaneeleele Heiau, an old Hawaiian temple. The area was a sugar port until the 1946 tsunami destroyed the buildings. Developers tried to bring a huge resort experience here in the early 1990s, but that has mostly failed. **Amenities:** parking (no fee); showers; toilets. **Best for:** walking. ✉ *Hwy. 11, between mile markers 55 and 56, Naalehu* ✣ *27 miles south of Hawaii Volcanoes National Park* ☎ *808/961–8311.*

Coffee and Quick Bites

Punaluu Bake Shop
$ | CAFÉ | Billed as the southernmost bakery in the United States, it's a good spot to grab a snack, and the heavenly smell alone is worth the stop. Local-style plate lunches and sandwiches on the bakeshop's famous sweetbread buns go well with Kau coffee. **Known for:** plate lunches and sandwiches; goods all baked on-site; lilikoi-glazed malasada (Portuguese doughnuts). [$] *Average main: $8* ✉ *5642 Mamalahoa Hwy., Naalehu* ☎ *808/929–7343* 🌐 *www.bakeshophawaii.com.*

Hotels

Kalaekilohana Inn and Retreat
$$$$ | B&B/INN | You wouldn't really expect to find a top-notch B&B in Kau, but just up the road from South Point, this grand residence offers large private suites with

locally harvested hardwood floors, private lanai with ocean and mountain views, and big, comfy beds with high-thread-count sheets and fluffy down comforters. **Pros:** luxurious beds; beautiful decor reminscent of old Hawaii; delicious complimentary breakfast. **Cons:** not for children under 12; no pool; very limited nearby shopping. [$] *Rooms from: $349* ✉ *94-2152 South Point Rd., Naalehu* ☎ *808/939–8052* 🌐 *www.kau-hawaii.com* 🛏 *4 suites* 🍴 *Free breakfast.*

Activities and Tours

With the Big Island's predictably mild year-round climate, it's no wonder you'll find an emphasis on outdoor activities. After all, this is the home of the annual Ironman World Championship triathlon. Whether you're an avid hiker or a beginning bicyclist, a casual golfer or a tennis buff, you'll find plenty of activities to lure you away from your resort or condo.

You can explore by bike, helicopter, ATV, zipline, or horse, or you can put on your hiking boots and use your own horsepower. No matter how you get around, you'll be treated to breathtaking backdrops along the Big Island's 266-mile coastline and within its 4,028 square miles (and still growing!). Aerial tours take in the latest eruption activity and lava flows, as well as the island's gorgeous tropical valleys, gulches, and coastal plains. Trips into the backcountry wilderness explore the rain forest, private ranchlands, and coffee farms, while sleepy sugar plantation villages offer a glimpse of Hawaii's bygone days.

Golfers will find acclaimed championship courses at the Kohala Coast resorts—Mauna Kea Beach Hotel, Autograph Collection; the Westin Hapuna Beach Resort; Mauna Lani, Auberge Resorts Collection; and Waikoloa Beach Resort, among others. During the winter, if snow conditions allow, you can even go skiing on top of Maunakea (elevation: 13,796 feet). It's a skiing experience unlike any other.

The ancient Hawaiians, who took much of their daily sustenance from the ocean, also enjoyed playing in the water, so it's no wonder that visitors want to get out onto the water as well. In fact, surfing was the sport of kings. Though it's easy to be lulled into whiling away the day baking in the sun on a white-, gold-, black-, or green-sand beach, getting into or onto the water is a highlight of most trips.

All of the Hawaiian Islands are surrounded by the Pacific Ocean, and blessed with a temperate latitude, making them some of the world's greatest natural playgrounds. But certain experiences are even better on the Big Island: nighttime diving trips to see manta rays; deep-sea fishing in Kona's fabled waters, where dozens of Pacific blue marlin of 1,000 pounds or more have been caught; and kayaking in pristine bays, to name a few.

From almost any point on the Big Island, the ocean is nearby. Whether it's body boarding and snorkeling or kayaking and surfing, there is a water sport for everyone. For most activities, you can rent gear and go it alone. Or book a group excursion with an experienced guide, who offers convenience and security, as well as special insights into Hawaiian marine life and culture. Want to try surfing? Contrary to what you may have heard, there *are* waves on the Big Island. You can take lessons from pros who promise to have you standing the first day out.

The Kona and Kohala Coasts of West Hawaii boast the largest number of ocean sports outfitters and tour operators. They operate from the small-boat harbors and piers in Kailua-Kona, Keauhou, Kawaihae, and at the Kohala Coast resorts. There are also several outfitters in the East Hawaii and Hilo areas.

As a general rule, the waves are gentler here than on the other Islands, but there are a few things to be aware of. First, don't turn your back on the ocean. It's unlikely, but if conditions are right, a wave could come along and push you face-first into the sand or drag you out to sea. Second, when the Big Island does experience high surf, dangerous conditions prevail and can change rapidly. Watch the ocean for a few minutes before going out to scan for waves, which arrive in sets. If it looks rough, don't chance it. Third, realize that ultimately you must keep yourself safe. We strongly encourage you to obey lifeguards and high surf advisories, and heed the advice of outfitters from whom you rent equipment, and even from locals on shore. It could save your trip or even your life.

Aerial Tours

There's nothing quite like the aerial view of a waterfall crashing down a couple of thousand feet into cascading pools, or watching lava flow to the ocean as exploding clouds of steam billow into the air. You can get this bird's-eye view from a helicopter or a fixed-wing small plane. All operators pay strict attention to safety. So how to get the best experience for your money? ■ TIP➜ **Before you choose a company, be a savvy traveler and ask the right questions. What kind of aircraft do they fly? What is their safety record?**

Big Island Air Tours
FLYING/SKYDIVING/SOARING | This small company, in business since the 1980s, offers fixed-wing tours of the island, including a circle island tour, Kilauea sunset tour, or Maui–Big Island tour. It also features charters between all the major islands. This is a good alternative to the pricier helicopter tours. ☎ 808/329–4868 ⊕ www.bigislandair.com ✈ From $297.

Blue Hawaiian Helicopters
FLYING/SKYDIVING/SOARING | Hawaii Island's premier aerial tour is on Blue Hawaiian's roomy Eco-Star helicopters—so smooth and quiet you hardly realize you're taking off. There are no worries about what seat you get because each has great views. Pilots are also State of Hawaii–certified tour guides, so they are knowledgeable and experienced but not overly chatty. In the breathtaking Waimanu Valley, the helicopter hovers amazingly close to 2,600-foot cliffs and cascading waterfalls. The two-hour Big Island Spectacular also takes in the incredible landscapes of Hawaii Volcanoes National Park, as well as the stunning valleys; you can even choose an optional waterfall landing as part of it. Most tours leave from Blue Hawaiian's Waikoloa heliport, but the 50-minute Circle of Fire tour, the 15-minute Hilo Holoholo tour, and the fun Craters and Coffee tour all depart from Hilo. ✉ Waikoloa Heliport, Hwy. 19, Waikoloa ☎ 808/961–5600 ⊕ www.bluehawaiian. com ✈ From $99 (15-minute tour).

★ Paradise Helicopters
FLYING/SKYDIVING/SOARING | Even when the volcano is not actively flowing, there's still plenty to see from the air, with great options from this locally owned and operated company. Opt for the Doors-Off Kohala Valleys and Waterfalls tour departing from the Waimea-Kohala Airport, which takes you soaring deep into the heart of the spectacular Kohala Valleys to view 2,500-foot waterfalls and sheer cliff walls. Or take the Doors-Off Lava and Rainforests Adventure, departing from Hilo, to see Hilo's rain forests and Rainbow Falls, as well as Puna's 2018 eruption site. You'll marvel at the incredible 8-mile river of frozen lava stretching from Fissure 8 to the Pacific Ocean; the newest black-sand beaches on earth; and the spectacular craters of Kilauea Volcano. Pilots, many of whom have military backgrounds, are fun and knowledgeable. ■ TIP➜ **The only helicopter company in Hawaii certified by the**

Hawaii Ecotour Association, Paradise offers you the option to offset your tour's carbon footprint by having a tree planted in Hawaii for each ride you take. ☎ *808/969–7392, 866/876–7422* ⊕ *www.paradisecopters. com* 🖃 *From $274.*

Biking

The Big Island's biking trails and road routes range from easy to moderate coastal rides to rugged backcountry wilderness treks that challenge the most serious cyclists. You can soak up the island's storied scenic vistas and varied geography—from tropical rain forest to rolling ranch country, from high-country mountain meadows to dry lava deserts. It's dry, windy, and hot on Kona's and Kohala's coastal trails, mountainous through South Kona, and cool, wet, and muddy in the upcountry Waimea and Volcano areas, as well as in lower Puna. There are long distances between towns, few bike lanes, narrow single-lane highways, and scanty services in the Kau, Puna, South Kona, and Kohala Coast areas, so plan accordingly for your weather, water, food, and lodging needs before setting out. ■TIP→ **Your best bet is to book with an outfitter who has all the details covered.**

EQUIPMENT AND TOURS

There are rental shops in Kailua-Kona and a couple in Waimea and Hilo. Many resorts rent bicycles that can be used around the properties. Most outfitters can provide a bicycle rack for your car, and all offer reduced rates for rentals longer than one day. All retailers offer excellent advice about where to go; they know the areas well.

BikeVolcano.com

BICYCLING | This outfitter leads three- or five-hour bike rides through Hawaii Volcanoes National Park, mostly downhill, that take in fantastic sights from rain forests to craters. The company also coordinates and leads a cool ride to the 2018 eruption site in Puna. Equipment, support van, and food are included; pickup locations are in Hilo and Volcano (and Kona by request). Cruise passengers are welcome. ⊠ *Hilo* ☎ *808/934–9199, 888/934–9199* ⊕ *www.bikevolcano.com* 🖃 *From $135.*

Mid Pacific Wheels

BICYCLING | The oldest bike shop on the Big Island, this community-oriented shop near the university carries a full line of bikes and accessories and rents mountain bikes for exploring the Hilo area. The friendly staff provides expert advice on where to go and what to see and do on a self-guided tour. They also carry a large selection of cycling accesssories, bikes, and repair parts. ⊠ *1133C Manono St., Hilo* ☎ *808/935–6211* ⊕ *www.midpacificwheelsllc.com* 🖃 *From $35/day.*

Body Boarding and Body Surfing

According to the movies, in the Old West there was always friction between cattle ranchers and sheep ranchers. A somewhat similar situation exists between surfers and body boarders (and between surfers and stand-up paddleboarders). That's why they generally keep to their own separate areas. Often the body boarders, who lie on their stomachs on shorter boards, stay closer to shore and leave the outside breaks to the board surfers. Or the board surfers may stick to one side of the beach and the body boarders to the other. The truth is, body boarding (often called "boogie boarding," in homage to the first commercial manufacturer of this slick, little, flexible-foam board) is a blast. Most surfers also sometimes carve waves on a body board, no matter how much of a purist they claim to be. ■TIP→ **Novice body boarders should catch shore-break waves only. Ask lifeguards or locals for the best spots.** You'll need a pair of short fins to get out to the bigger waves offshore (again, not recommended for newbies). As for body surfing, just catch a wave and make like Superman going faster than a speeding bullet.

BEST SPOTS

Hapuna Beach State Recreation Area. Often considered one of the top 10 beaches in the world, Hapuna Beach State Recreation Area offers fine white sand, turquoise water, and easy rolling surf on most days, making it great for body surfing and body boarding at all levels. Ask the lifeguards—who only cover areas south of the rocky cliff that juts out near the middle of the beach—about conditions before heading into the water, especially in winter. Sometimes northwest swells create a dangerous undertow. ⊠ *Hwy. 19, near mile marker 69, just south of Mauna Kea Hotel, Kohala Coast* ⊕ *dlnr.hawaii.gov/dsp/parks/hawaii/hapuna-beach-state-recreation-area.*

Honolii Cove. North of Hilo, this is the best body-boarding spot on the east side of the island. ⊠ *Off Hwy. 19, near mile marker 4, Hilo.*

Magic Sands Beach Park (White Sands Beach). This white-sand, shore-break cove is great for beginning to intermediate body surfing and body boarding. Sometimes in winter, much of the sand here washes out to sea and forms a sandbar just offshore, creating fun wave conditions. Also known as White Sands, it's popular and can get crowded with locals, especially when school is out. Watch for nasty rip currents at high tide. ■TIP→ **If you're not using fins, wear reef shoes for protection against sharp rocks.** ⊠ *Alii Dr., just north of mile marker 4, Kailua-Kona.*

EQUIPMENT

Equipment-rental shacks are located at many beaches and boat harbors, along the highway, and at most resorts. Bodyboard rental rates are around $12–$15 per day and around $60 per week. Ask the vendor to throw in a pair of fins—some will for no extra charge.

★ **Orchidland Surfboards and Surf Shop**
WATER SPORTS | This venerable shop in historic downtown Hilo—in business since 1972—carries a wide variety of surf and other water sports equipment for sale or rent. It stocks professional custom surfboards, body boards, and surf apparel. Owner Stan Lawrence, famous for his "Drainpipe" legacy, was one of the last people to surf that famous break before lava flows claimed the Kalapana area. Old photos and surf posters on the walls add to the nostalgia. Through the shop, he hosts surf contests and does the daily surf report for local radio stations. This surf shop is as authentic as they get. ⊠ *262 Kamehameha Ave., Hilo* ☎ *808/935–1533* ⊕ *www.orchidlandsurf.com* ⌨ *From $15 body board/day, $25 surfboard/day.*

★ **Pacific Vibrations**
SURFING | Family-owned, this surf shop—in business since 1978—holds the distinction of being the oldest, smallest surf shop in the world. Even at a compact, sub-500 square feet, this place stocks tons of equipment, surf wear and gear, sunglasses, and GoPro cameras. Located oceanfront in downtown Kailua Town, it is tucked away in a vintage building, and is worth a stop just for the cool Hawaii surf vibe and to talk story with the friendly owners. The owners are activists in protecting local surf spots from development. ⊠ *75-5702B Likana La., at Alii Dr., Kailua-Kona* ☎ *808/329–4140.*

Caving

The Kanohina Lava Tube system is about 1,000 years old and was used by the ancient Hawaiians for water collection and for shelter. More than 56 miles of braided lava tubes have been mapped so far in the Kau District of the Big Island, near Ka Lae (South Point). About 45 miles south of Kailua-Kona, these lava tubes are a great experience for cavers of all age levels and abilities.

★ Kula Kai Caverns

SPELUNKING | Expert cave guides lead groups into the fantastic underworld of these caverns near South Point. The braided lava-tube system attracts scientists from around the world, who come to study and map them (more than 56 miles so far). Tours range from the Lighted Trail (in the lighted show cave, which is easy walking) to the Two Hour, a deep-down-under spelunking adventure that often takes closer to three hours and allows you to see archaeological evidence of the ancient Hawaiians. Longer, customized tours are also available; all gear is provided. Tours start at an Indiana Jones–style expedition tent and divulge fascinating details about the caves' geologic and cultural history. Reservations are required. ⊠ *Kula Kai Estates, Lauhala Dr. at Kona Kai Blvd.* ☎ *808/929–9725* ⊕ *www.kulakaicaverns.com* 🖃 *From $28.*

Deep-Sea Fishing

The Kona Coast has some of the world's most exciting "blue-water" fishing. Although July, August, and September are peak months, with the best fishing and a number of tournaments, charter fishing goes on year-round. You don't have to compete to experience the thrill of landing a Pacific blue marlin or other big-game fish. Some 60 charter boats, averaging 26 to 58 feet, are available for hire, all of them out of **Honokohau Harbor,** north of Kailua-Kona.

The Kona Coast is world-famous for the presence of large marlin, particularly the Pacific blue. In fact, it's also known as "Grander Alley" for the fish caught here that weigh more than 1,000 pounds. The largest blue marlin on record was caught in 1984 and weighed 1,649 pounds. In total, more than 60 Granders have been reeled in here by top sportfishing teams.

For an exclusive charter, prices generally range from $600 to $950 for a half-day trip (about four hours) and $800 to $1,600 for a full day at sea (about eight hours). For share charters, rates are about $100 to $140 per person for a half day and $200 for a full day. If fuel prices increase, expect charter costs to rise. Most boats are licensed to take up to six passengers, in addition to the crew. Tackle, bait, and ice are furnished, but you usually have to bring your own lunch. You won't be able to keep your catch, although if you ask, many captains will send you home with a few fillets.

Honokohau Harbor's Fuel Dock

FISHING | Show up around 11 am and watch the weigh-in of the day's catch from the morning charters, or around 3:30 for the afternoon charters, especially during the summer tournament season. Weigh-ins are fun when the big ones come in, but these days, with most of the marlin being released, it's not a sure thing. ■ **TIP→ In the foyer of the Kona Inn, look for some of the "granders" on display.** ⊠ *Honokohau Harbor, Kealakehe Pkwy. at Hwy. 11, Kailua-Kona.*

BOATS AND CHARTERS
Bwana Sportfishing

FISHING | Full-, half-, three-quarter-day, and overnight charters are available on the 46-foot *Bwana.* The boat features the latest electronics, top-of-the-line equipment, and air-conditioned cabins. You get outstanding, quality tackle and lots of experience here. Captain Teddy comes from a fishing family; father Pete was a legend on Kona waters for decades. ⊠ *Honokohau Harbor, Slip H-17, 74-381 Kealakehe Pkwy., Kailua-Kona* ✛ *Just south of Kona airport* ☎ *808/936–5168* 🖃 *From $1,250.*

Charter Locker

FISHING | Half- and full-day charter fishing trips on 36- to 53-foot vessels are offered by this experienced company. Featured boats include *Kona Blue, JR's Hooker, Strong Persuader,* and *Kila Kila.* Rates

Most of the Big Island's top golf courses are located on the sunny Kona Coast.

depend on the boat. ⊠ *Honokohau Harbor, 74-381 Kealakehe Pkwy., #16, Kailua-Kona* ✛ *Just south of Kona airport* ☎ *808/326–2553* ⊕ *www.charterlocker. com* ✉ *From $395.*

Humdinger Sportfishing

FISHING | This father-son team brings more than five decades of fishing experience in Kona waters, and the expert crew are marlin specialists. Their 37-foot Rybovich, the *Humdinger,* features the latest in electronics and top-line rods and reels. ■ TIP→ **They will let you keep your catch (except for billfish) and will even fillet it for you.** Book online for discounts and specials; they sell out quickly, so plan ahead. ⊠ *Honokohau Harbor, 74-381 Kealakehe Pkwy., Slip B-4, Kailua-Kona* ☎ *808/425– 9225, 800/926–2374, 808/425–9228 boat phone* ⊕ *www.humdingersportfishing. com* ✉ *From $399.*

Jeff Rogers Charters

FISHING | One of Kona's friendliest "old salts," Captain Jeff has been leading personalized big game and other fishing charters since 1982. Using a few tricks of the trade (including targeting the bottom), he's able to find the right fish in the right place, nearly without fail. You may ask him to fillet part of your catch. Holder of six world records and six state records, Jeff has caught his share of marlin granders (over 1,000 pounds). Guests (no more than two) may share a charter to save costs through his special program, so check online for the list of available shares. ⊠ *73-4345 Oneone St., Kailua-Kona* ☎ *808/895–1852* ⊕ *www. fishinkona.com* ✉ *From $375.*

Golf

For golfers, the Big Island is a big deal—starting with the Mauna Kea Golf Course, which opened in 1964 and remains one of the state's top courses. Black lava and deep blue sea are the predominant themes on the island. In the roughly 40 miles from the Kona Country Club to the Mauna Kea resort, nine courses are carved into sunny seaside lava plains, with four more in the hills above. Indeed, most of the Big Island's best courses are concentrated along the Kohala Coast, statistically the sunniest spot in Hawaii. Vertically speaking, although the majority of courses are seaside or at least near sea level, three are located above 2,000 feet, another one at 4,200 feet. This is significant because in Hawaii temperatures drop 3°F for every 1,000 feet of elevation gained.

Green Fee: Green fees listed here are the highest course rates per round on weekdays for U.S. residents. Courses with varying weekend rates are noted in the individual listings. (Some courses charge non–U.S. residents higher prices.) ■TIP➔ **Discounts are often available for resort guests and for those who book tee times online, as well as for those willing to play in the afternoon. Twilight rates are also usually offered.**

Hapuna Golf Course

GOLF | Hapuna's challenging play and environmental sensitivity make it one of the island's most unusual courses. Designed by Arnold Palmer and Ed Seay, it is nestled into the natural contours of the land from the shoreline to about 700 feet above sea level. There are spectacular views of mountains and sea (Maui is often visible in the distance). Holes wind through kiawe scrub, beds of jagged lava, and tall fountain grasses. Hole 12 is favored for its beautiful views and challenging play. ✉ *62-100 Kanunaoa Dr., Waimea (Hawaii County)* ☎ *808/880–3000* ⊕ *www.hapunabeachresort.com/golf* 💲 *$175, $125 after 1 pm* ⛳ *18 holes, 6875 yards, par 72.*

Hilo Municipal Golf Course

GOLF | Hilo Muni is proof that you don't need sand bunkers to create a challenging course. Trees and several meandering creeks are the danger here. The course, which offers views of Hilo Bay from most holes, has produced many of the island's top players over the years. Taking a divot reminds you that you're playing on a volcano—the soil is dark black crushed lava.

✉ *340 Haihai St., Hilo* ☎ *808/959–7711* ⊕ *www.hawaiicounty.gov/pr-golf* 💲 *$38 weekdays, $45 weekends; $20 cart* ⛳ *18 holes, 6325 yards, par 71.*

Makani Golf Club

GOLF | Set 2,000 feet above sea level on the slopes of Hualalai, this course is out of the way but well worth the drive. In 1997, Pete and Perry Dye created a gem that plays through upland woodlands—more than 2,500 trees line the fairways. On the par-5 16th, a giant tree in the middle of the fairway must be avoided with the second shot. Five lakes and a meandering natural mountain stream bring water into play on nine holes. The most dramatic is the par-3 17th, where Dye created a knockoff of his infamous 17th at the TPC at Sawgrass. ✉ *71-1420 Hawaii Belt Rd., Kailua-Kona* ☎ *808/325–5044* ⊕ *makanigolfclub.com* 💲 *$119 with cart, bottled water* ⛳ *18 holes, 7075 yards, par 72.*

★ Mauna Kea Golf Course

GOLF | Originally opened in 1964, this golf course is one of the most revered in the state. It underwent a tee-to-green renovation by Rees Jones, son of the original architect, Robert Trent Jones Sr. Hybrid grasses were planted, the number of bunkers increased, and the overall yardage expanded. The par-3 third is one of the world's most famous holes—and one of the most photographed. You play from a cliffside tee across a bay to a cliffside green. Getting across the ocean is just half the battle because the green is surrounded by seven bunkers, each one large and undulated. The course is a shot-maker's paradise and follows Jones's "easy bogey, tough par" philosophy. ✉ *62-100 Kaunaoe Dr., Waimea (Hawaii County)* ☎ *808/882–5400* ⊕ *www.maunakeagolf.com* 💲 *$295, $225 after 11 am, $175 after 1:30 pm* ⛳ *18 holes, 7250 yards, par 72.*

★ Mauna Lani Golf Courses

GOLF | Black lava flows, lush green turf, white sand, and the Pacific's multihues of blue define the 36 holes at Mauna Lani. The **South Course** includes the par-3 15th across a turquoise bay, one of the most photographed holes in Hawaii. But it shares "signature hole" honors with the seventh, a long par 3, which plays downhill over convoluted patches of black lava, with the Pacific immediately to the left and a dune to the right. The **North Course** plays a couple of shots tougher. Its most distinctive hole is the 17th, a par 3 with the green set in a lava pit 50 feet deep. The shot from an elevated tee must carry a pillar of lava that rises from the pit and partially blocks a view of the green. ⊠ *68-1310 Mauna Lani Dr., Waimea (Hawaii County)* ☎ *808/885–6655* ⊕ *www.mau-nalani.com* ✉ *From $259, but dynamic pricing means greens fee fluctuates* ⅄ *South Course: 18 holes, 6025 yards, par 72. North Course: 18 holes, 6057 yards, par 72.*

★ Waikoloa Beach Resort

GOLF | Robert Trent Jones Jr. built the Beach Course at Waikoloa (1981) on an old flow of crinkly *aa* lava, which he used to create holes that are as artful as they are challenging. The par-5 12th hole is one of Hawaii's most picturesque and plays through a chute of black lava to a seaside green. At the Kings' Course (1990), Tom Weiskopf and Jay Morrish built a links-esque track. It turns out lava's natural humps and declivities replicate the contours of seaside Scotland. But there are a few island twists—such as seven lakes. This is "option golf," as Weiskopf and Morrish provide different risk-reward tactics on each hole. ■**TIP→ Resort guests receive a lower rate.** ⊠ *600 Waikoloa Beach Dr., Waikoloa* ☎ *808/886–7888* ⊕ *www.waikoloabeach-golf.com* ✉ *From $150, including cart* ⅄ *Beach Course: 18 holes, 6566 yards, par 70. Kings' Course: 18 holes, 7074 yards, par 72.*

Volcano Golf and Country Club

GOLF | Just outside Hawaii Volcanoes National Park—and barely a stone's throw from Halemaumau Crater—this is by far Hawaii's highest course. At 4,200 feet elevation, shots tend to fly a bit farther than at sea level, even in the often cool, misty air. Because of the elevation and climate, this Hawaii course features Bermuda and seashore paspalum grass putting greens. The course is mostly flat, and holes play through stands of ohia lehua (flowering evergreen trees) and multitrunk hau trees. The uphill par-4 15th doglegs through a tangle of hau. ⊠ *99-1621 Pii Mauna Dr., off Hwy. 11, Volcano* ☎ *808/967–7331* ⊕ *www.volcanogolf-shop.com* ✉ *$62 with cart* ⅄ *18 holes, 6106 yards, par 72.*

Hiking

Department of Land and Natural Resources, State Parks Division

HIKING/WALKING | The division provides information on all the Big Island's state parks and jurisdictions. Check online for the latest additions, information, and advisories. ⊠ *75 Aupuni St., Hilo* ☎ *808/961–9544* ⊕ *www.dlnr.hawaii.gov/dsp/parks/hawaii.*

BEST SPOTS

Hawaii Volcanoes National Park. Perhaps the Big Island's premier area for hikers, the park has more than 155 miles of trails providing close-up views of fern and rain forest environments, cinder cones, craters, steam vents, lava fields, rugged coastline, and current eruption activity. Day hikes range from easy to moderately difficult, and from one or two hours to a full day. For a bigger challenge, consider an overnight or multiday backcountry hike with a stay in a park cabin (available en route to the remote coast, in a lush forest, or atop frigid Mauna Loa). To do so, you must first obtain a permit at the backcountry office in the Visitor Emergency Operations Center. ■**TIP→ Daily guided hikes are led by knowledgeable, friendly park rangers.** The bulletin boards outside Kilauea Visitor Center and inside

Hawaii Volcanoes National Park's 155 miles of trails offer easy to moderately difficult day hikes.

Jaggar Museum have the day's schedule. Perhaps the Big Island's premier area for hikers, the park has 150 miles of trails providing close-up views. ⊠ *Hwy. 11, 30 miles south of Hilo, Hawaii Volcanoes National Park* ☎ *808985–6000* ⊕ *www. nps.gov/havo/index.htm.*

Kekaha Kai State Park. A 1.8-mile unimproved road leads to Mahaiula Bay, a gorgeous little piece of paradise, while on the opposite end of the park is lovely Kua Bay. Connecting the two is the 4½-mile Ala Kahakai historic coastal trail. Midway between the two white-sand beaches, you can hike to the summit of Puu Kuili, a 342-foot-high cinder cone with an excellent view of the coastline. Mahaiula has picnic tables and vault toilets. It's dry and hot with no drinking water, so pack sunblock, hats, and extra water. Gates close at 7 pm sharp. ⊠ *Trailhead on Hwy. 19, About 2 miles north of Kona airport, Kailua-Kona* ⊕ *dlnr.hawaii.gov/dsp/parks/ hawaii.*

Muliwai Trail. On the western side of mystical Waipio Valley, this trail leads to the back of the valley, then switchbacks up through a series of gulches, and finally emerges at Waimanu Valley. Only very experienced hikers should attempt the very remote entire 18-mile trail, the hike of a lifetime. It can take two to three days of backpacking and camping, which requires camping permits from the Division of Forestry and Wildlife in Hilo. ⊠ *Trailhead at end of Hwy. 240, Honokaa* ☎ *808/974–4221* ⊕ *hawaiitrails.ehawaii. gov.*

Onomea Bay Trail. This short but beautiful trail is packed with stunning views of the cliffs, bays, and gulches of the Hamakua Coast, on the east side of the island. The trail is just under a mile and fairly easy, with access down to the shore if you want to dip your feet in, although we don't recommend swimming in the rough waters. Unless you pay the $15 entry fee to the nearby botanical garden, entering its gates (even by accident) will send one of the guards running after you to nicely but firmly point you back to the trail. ✉ *Trailhead on Old Hawaiian Belt Rd., just before botanical garden.* ⊕ *hawaiitrails. ehawaii.gov.*

GOING WITH A GUIDE

Ecologically diverse, Hawaii Island has four of the five major climate zones and eight of 13 subclimate zones—a lot of variation for one island—and you can experience almost all of them on foot. The ancient Hawaiians cut trails across the lava plains, through the rain forests, and up along the mountain heights. Many of these paths are still in use today. Part of the King's Trail at Anaehoomalu winds through a field of lava rock covered with ancient petroglyphs. Many other trails—historic and modern—crisscross the huge Hawaii Volcanoes National Park and other parts of the island. Plus, the serenity of certain remote beaches is accessible only to hikers. Check the statewide trail system website at ⊕ *hawaiitrails.ehawaii.gov* for up-to-date trail information.

★ Hawaii Forest and Trail

HIKING/WALKING | Since 1993, this locally owned and operated outfit has built a reputation for outstanding nature tours and eco-adventures. Sustainability, cultural sensitivity, and forging island connections are company missions. They have access to thousands of acres of restricted or private lands and employ expert, certified guides who are entertaining and informative. Choose an Endangered Native Habitats bird-watching tour, or journey deep into the Hakalau Forest National Wildlife Refuge. Other tours include a Hidden Craters adventure that leads you along private hiking trails on Hualalai Volcano, a Kohala waterfall trip, or the Kohala Canopy Zipline adventure. Their Summit and Stars adventure is a crowd favorite, but book well in advance. ✉ *73-5593A Olowalu St., Kailua-Kona* ☎ *808/331–8505, 800/464–1993* ⊕ *www. hawaii-forest.com* ⌖ *From $149.*

★ KapohoKine Adventures

HIKING/WALKING | **FAMILY** | One of the largest outfitters on the island, locally owned KapohoKine Adventures offers a number of excellent hiking tours that depart from both Hilo and Kona. The epic full-day Elite Volcano Hike hits all the great spots, including now-quiet areas in Puna impacted by the 2018 eruption. Hikers will encounter a 40-foot wall of lava and follow it to the sea and an enormous black-sand beach. Also included are Kalapana, the Kaumana Caves, the Steaming Bluffs, and a tour of Hawaii Volcanoes National Park. The final stop at Volcano Winery features a wine tasting and Hawaiian barbecue dinner. Lunch is also included.

For highly advanced hikers, the company offers a private tour (minimum 7 guests) that takes you on a 20-mile, 10-hour hike into the Waimanu Valley, a remote location north of Waipio. The price is $3,385 and includes taxes, shuttles, gratuity, trail permits, meals, guides, and support gear. ✉ *Grand Nanilola Hotel Hilo, 93 Banyan Dr., Hilo* ☎ *808/964–1000* ⊕ *www.kapohokine.com* ⌖ *From $259.*

Horseback Riding

With its *paniolo* (cowboy) heritage and the ranches it spawned, the Big Island is a great place for equestrians. Riders can gallop through upcountry green pastures or saunter through Waipio Valley for a taste of old Hawaii.

TOURS

Paniolo Adventures

HORSEBACK RIDING | Paniolo Adventures offers an open-range horseback ride on a working Kohala Mountain cattle ranch, spectacular views of three volcanoes and the coastline, and an authentic *paniolo* (cowboy) experience from 3,000 feet up. You don't ride nose-to-tail and can spread out and trot or canter if you wish: this is an 11,000-acre ranch, so there's room to roam. The company caters to beginning and experienced riders and offers special private rides as well. ⊠ *Kohala Mountain Rd. (Hwy. 250) at mile marker 13.2, Waimea (Hawaii County)* ☎ *808/889–5354* ⊕ *www.panioloadventures.com* ☒ *From $69.*

Kayaking

The leeward (west coast) areas of the Big Island are protected for the most part from the northeast trade winds, making for ideal near-shore kayaking conditions. There are miles and miles of uncrowded Kona and Kohala coastline to explore, presenting close-up views of stark, raw, lava-rock shores and cliffs; lava-tube sea caves; pristine, secluded coves; and deserted beaches. There's even guided kayaking in a hand-built irrigation ditch dating from the early 1900s.

Ocean kayakers can get close to shore—where the commercial snorkel and dive cruise boats can't reach. This opens up all sorts of possibilities for adventure, such as near-shore snorkeling among the expansive coral reefs and lava rock formations that teem with colorful tropical fish and Hawaiian green sea turtles. You can pull ashore at a quiet cove for a picnic and a plunge into turquoise waters. With a good coastal map and some advice from the kayak vendor, you might paddle by ancient battlegrounds, burial sites, bathing ponds for Hawaiian royalty, or old villages.

Kayaking can be enjoyed via a guided tour or on a self-guided paddling excursion. Either way, the kayak outfitter can brief you on recommended routes, safety, and how to help preserve and protect Hawaii's ocean resources and coral reef system.

BEST SPOTS

Hilo Bay. This is a favorite kayak spot. The best place to put in is at **Reeds Bay Beach Park.** Parking is plentiful and free at the bayfront. Most afternoons you'll share the bay with local paddling clubs. Stay inside the breakwater unless the ocean is calm (or you're feeling unusually adventurous). Conditions range from extremely calm to quite choppy. ⊠ *Banyan Way and Banyan Dr., 1 mile from downtown Hilo.*

Kailua Bay and Kamakahonu Beach. The small sandy beach that fronts the Courtyard King Kamehameha's Kona Beach Hotel is a nice place to rent or launch kayaks. You can unload in the cul-de-sac and park in nearby free or paid lots. The water here is especially calm, and the surroundings are historical and scenic. ⊠ *Alii Dr., next to Kailua Pier, Kailua-Kona.*

Kealakekua Bay State Historical Park. The excellent snorkeling and likelihood of seeing dolphins (morning is best) make Kealakekua Bay one of the most popular kayaking spots on the Big Island. An ocean conservation district, the bay is usually calm and tranquil. (Use caution and common sense during surf advisories.) Tall coral pinnacles and clear visibility surrounding the monument also make for stupendous snorkeling. Regulations permit only a few operators to lead kayak tours in the park. ⊠ *Napoopoo Rd. and Manini Bch. Rd., Captain Cook* ⊕ *dlnr. hawaii.gov/dsp/parks/hawaii.*

Oneo Bay. Right downtown, this is usually a placid place to kayak. It's fairly easy to get to. If you can't find parking along the road, there's a free lot across the street from the library and farmers' market. ⊠ *Alii Dr., Kailua-Kona.*

EQUIPMENT, LESSONS, AND TOURS

There are several rental outfitters on Highway 11 between Kainaliu and Captain Cook, but only a few are specially permitted to lead kayak trips in Kealakekua Bay.

Aloha Kayak Co.

KAYAKING | This outfitter is one of the few permitted to guide kayaking tours to the stunningly beautiful Kealakekua Bay, leaving from Napoopoo, including about 1½ hours at the Captain Cook Monument. The 3½-hour morning and afternoon tours include snacks and drinks, while the five-hour tour includes lunch. Local guides discuss the area's cultural, historical, and natural significance. You may see dolphins, but you must observe them from a distance only, as this is a protected marine reserve. Keauhou Bay tours are also available, including a two-hour evening manta ray tour. ⊠ 82-5674 Kahau Pl., Captain Cook ☎ 808/322–2868 ⊕ www.alohakayak.com ⊠ Tours from $99.

★ Kona Boys

KAYAKING | On the highway above Kealakekua Bay, this full-service, environmentally conscious outfitter handles kayaks, body boards, surfboards, stand-up paddleboards, and snorkeling gear. Single-seat and double kayaks are offered. Surfing and stand-up paddleboarding lessons are available for private or group instruction.

One of the few companies permitted to lead tours in Kealakekua Bay, Kona Boys offer their Morning Magic and Midday Meander tours, two half-day guided kayaking and snorkeling trips with gear, lunch, snacks, and beverages. They also run a beach shack fronting the Courtyard King Kamehameha's Kona Beach Hotel, with everything for the beachgoer such as rentals of beach mats, chairs, and other gear. ■TIP→ The Kailua-Kona location offers Hawaiian outrigger canoe rides and SUP lessons. ⊠ 79-7539 Mamalahoa Hwy., Kealakekua ☎ 808/328–1234 Kealakekua location, 808/329–2345 Kailua-Kona location ⊕ www.konaboys.com ⊠ Rentals from $74.

Ocean Safari's Kayak Adventures

KAYAKING | On the guided, 3½-hour morning sea-cave tour that begins in Keauhou Bay, you can visit lava-tube sea caves along the coast, then swim ashore for a snack. The kayaks are already on the water, so you won't have the hassle of transporting them. They also offer stand-up paddleboard lessons. ■TIP→ Book online for best availabilty. ⊠ End of Kamehameha III Rd., Kailua-Kona ✛ Next to Sheraton Kona Resort and Spa at Keauhou Bay ☎ 808/326–4699 ⊕ www.oceansafariskayaks.com ⊠ From $49.

Sailing

For old salts and novice sailors alike, there's nothing like a cruise on the Kona or Kohala Coast. Calm waters, serene shores, and the superb scenery of Maunakea, Mauna Loa, and Hualalai, the Big Island's primary volcanic peaks, make for a great sailing adventure. You can drop a line over the side and try your luck at catching dinner, or grab some snorkel gear and explore when the boat drops anchor in one of the quiet coves and bays. A cruise may well be the most relaxing and adventurous part of a Big Island visit.

Honu Sail Charters

SAILING | The fully equipped 32-foot cutter-rigged sloop Honu (Hawaiian for sea turtle) carries six passengers on full-day, half-day, and sunset sailing excursions along the scenic Kona Coast, which include time to snorkel in clear waters over coral reefs during the day tours and heavy pupus (appetizers) for the sunset excursion. This friendly outfitter allows passengers to get some hands-on sailing experience or just to kick back and relax. There are plenty of cushions and lots of shade. ⊠ Honokohau Harbor, Kailua-Kona ☎ 808/896–4668 ⊕ www.sailkona.com ⊠ Tours from $100.

Kohala Blue LLC

SAILING | Based at the Kawaihae South Small Boat Harbor, this company offers day sailing, sunset cruises, and humpback whale-watching (in season) aboard the 34-foot *Riva*. Owned and operated by Captain Steve Turner, the company focuses on sharing the wonders of the Kawaihae area, including the impressive Puukohola Heiau National Historic Site, the Puako reef, and views of Big Island volcanoes and even Maui's Haleakala. Private charters for up to six are available. ⊠ *Kawaihae Harbor South, Slip #8, 61-3527 Kawaihae Rd., Kawaihae* ☎ *808/895–1781* ⊕ *kohalablue.net* 🖃 *From $125.*

Scuba Diving

The Big Island's underwater world is the setting for a dramatic diving experience. With generally warm and calm waters, vibrant coral reefs and rock formations, and plunging underwater drop-offs, the Kona and Kohala coasts offer premier scuba diving. There are also some good dive locations in East Hawaii, not far from the Hilo area. Divers find much to occupy their time, including marine reserves teeming with tropical reef fish, Hawaiian green sea turtles, an occasional and critically endangered Hawaiian monk seal, and even some playful spinner dolphins. On special night dives to see manta rays, divers descend with bright underwater lights that attract plankton, which in turn attract these otherworldly creatures. The best spots to dive are all on the west coast.

BEST SPOTS

Garden Eel Cove. Accessible only by boat, this is a great place to see manta rays somersaulting overhead as they feast on a plankton supper. It's also home to hundreds of tiny garden eels darting out from their sandy homes. There's a steep drop-off and lots of marine life. ⊠ *Rte. 19, near the Kona Airport, Kailua-Kona.*

Manta Village. Booking with a night-dive operator is required for the short boat ride to this area, one of Kona's best night-dive spots. If you're a diving or snorkeling fanatic, it's well worth it to experience manta rays drawn by the lights of the hotel. ■TIP➔ If night swimming isn't your cup of tea, you can catch a glimpse of the majestic creatures from the Sheraton's viewing areas. (No water access is allowed from the hotel's property.) ⊠ *78-128 Ehukai St., off Sheraton Kona Resort & Spa at Keauhou Bay, Kailua-Kona.*

Pawai Bay Marine Perserve. Clear waters, abundant reef life, and interesting coral formations make protected Pawai Bay Marine Preserve ideal for diving. Explore sea caves, arches, and lava rock formations and dive into lava tubes. An easy, boat-only dive spot is ½ mile north of Old Airport. (No shoreline access to protected Pawai Bay is available due to its cultural and environmental significance.) ⊠ *Kuakini Hwy., north of Old Kona Airport Park, Kailua-Kona.*

Puako. Just south of Hapuna Beach State Recreation Area, beautiful Puako offers easy entry to some fine reef diving. Deep chasms, sea caves, and rock arches abound with varied marine life. ⊠ *Puako Rd., off Hwy. 19, Kailua-Kona.*

EQUIPMENT, LESSONS, AND TOURS

There are quite a few good dive shops along the Kona Coast. Most are happy to take on all customers, but a few focus on specific types of trips. Trip prices vary, depending on whether you're already certified and whether you're diving from a boat or from shore. Instruction with PADI, SDI, or TDI certification in three to five days costs $600 to $850. Most instructors rent dive equipment and snorkel gear, as well as underwater cameras. Most organize otherworldly manta ray dives at night and whale-watching cruises in season.

Big Island Divers

DIVING/SNORKELING | This company offers several levels of certification as well as numerous excursions, including night dives, two-tank charters, and in-season whale-watching. ⊠ *74-5467 Kaiwi St., Kailua-Kona* ☎ *808/329–6068* ⊕ *bigislanddivers.com* ☲ *From $149.*

Jack's Diving Locker

SCUBA DIVING | Good for novice and intermediate divers, Jack's has trained and certified tens of thousands of divers since 1981, with classrooms and a dive pool for instruction. Four boats that accommodate up to 18 divers and six snorkelers visit more than 80 established dive sites along the Kona Coast, yielding sightings of turtles, manta rays, garden eels, and schools of barracuda. They even take you lava tube diving. Snorkelers can accompany their friends on the dive boats or take guided morning trips and manta night trips, and dolphin-watch and reef snorkels. Combined sunset/night manta ray dives are offered as well. ■TIP➔ **Kona's best deal for scuba newbies is Jack's pool and shore dive combo.** ⊠ *75-5813 Alii Dr., Kailua-Kona* ☎ *808/329–7585, 800/345–4807* ⊕ *www. jacksdivinglocker.com* ☲ *Tours from $155 certified divers, $275 intro divers.*

Nautilus Dive Center

SCUBA DIVING | Across from Hilo Bay, Nautilus Dive Center is the oldest and most experienced dive shop on the island. It offers a broad range of services for both beginners and experienced divers. Owner Bill De Rooy, with his calm, reassuring manner, has been diving around the Big Island since 1982, personally certifying more than 2,000 divers. He's known for helping nervous guests feel comfortable in the water. He can provide you with underwater maps and show you the best dive spots in Hilo, and also offers PADI instruction, one- and two-tank dives, and snorkeling tours. ⊠ *382 Kamehameha Ave., Hilo* ☎ *808/935–6939* ⊕ *www.nautilusdivehilo.com* ☲ *Certification from $480.*

Snorkeling

A favorite pastime on the Big Island, snorkeling is perhaps one of the easiest and most enjoyable water activities for visitors. By floating on the surface, peering through your mask, and breathing through your snorkel, you can see lava rock formations, sea arches, sea caves, and coral reefs teeming with colorful tropical fish. While the Kona and Kohala coasts boast more beaches, bays, and quiet coves to snorkel, the east side around Hilo and at Kapoho are also great places to get in the water.

BEST SPOTS

Kahaluu Beach Park. Since ancient times, the waters around Kahaluu Beach have provided traditional throw net–fishing grounds. With super-easy access, the bay offers good swimming and outstanding snorkeling, revealing turtles, angelfish, parrotfish, needlefish, puffer fish, and many types of tang. ■TIP➔ **Stay inside the breakwater and don't stray too far, as dangerous and unpredictable currents swirl outside the bay.** ⊠ *Alii Dr., Kailua-Kona.*

Kapoho Tide Pools. Here you'll find the best snorkeling on the Hilo side. Fingers of lava from the 1960 flow that destroyed the town of Kapoho jut into the sea to form a network of tide pools. Conditions near the shore are excellent for beginners, while farther out is challenging enough for experienced snorkelers. ⊠ *End of Kapoho-Kai Rd., off Hwy. 137, Hilo.*

Kealakekua Bay State Historical Park. This protected Marine Life Conservation District is hands-down one of the best snorkeling spots on the island, thanks to clear visibility, fabulous coral reefs, and generally calm waters. Pods of dolphins can be abundant, but they're protected under federal law and may not be disturbed or approached. Access to the area is restricted, but a few companies are permitted to escort tours to the bay.

The Kona Coast's relatively calm waters and colorful coral reefs are excellent for scuba diving.

■ **TIP➔ Overland access is difficult, so opt for one of the guided snorkel cruises permitted to moor here.** ✉ *Napoopoo, at end of Beach Rd. and Hwy. 160, Kailua-Kona.*

Magic Sands Beach Park. Also known as White Sands or Disappearing Sands Beach Park, this is a great place for beginning and intermediate snorkelers. In winter, it's also a prime spot to watch for whales. ✉ *Alii Dr., Kailua-Kona.*

Puako Tide Pools. There's a large shelf of extensive reef and tide pools at this sleepy beach town along the Kohala Coast, where you'll find fantastic snorkeling as long as conditions are calm. ✉ *South end of Puako Beach Rd., off Hwy. 11.*

EQUIPMENT, LESSONS, AND TOURS
Body Glove Cruises
SNORKELING | FAMILY | A good choice for families, this operator has a waterslide and high-dive platform that kids love. On the daily Snorkel and Dolphin Watch Adventure, the 65-foot catamaran sets off for stunning Red Hill in uncrowded South Kona from Kailua-Kona pier. The morning snorkel cruise includes breakfast and a barbecue burger lunch, with vegetarian options. A three-hour historical dinner cruise to Kealakekua Bay is a great way to relax, watch the sunset, and learn about Kona's history. It includes a Hawaiian-style buffet, complimentary cocktail, and live music. (A lunch version is also available.) Seasonal whale-watch cruises and all dolphin snorkel cruises guarantee you will see the featured mammals or you can go again for free; the company implements a NOAA-approved Dolphin SMART policy on all of their cruises. Children under five are always free. ✉ *75-5629 Kuakini Hwy., Kailua-Kona* ☎ *808/326–7122, 800/551–8911* ⊕ *www. bodyglovehawaii.com* 🎟 *From $138.*

★ Fair Wind Cruises
SNORKELING | FAMILY | In business since 1971, Fair Wind offers morning and afternoon snorkel trips into breathtaking Kealakekua Bay. Great for families with small kids, the custom-built, 60-foot

catamaran has two 15-foot waterslides, freshwater showers, and a staircase descending directly into the water for easy access. Snorkel gear is included, along with flotation equipment and prescription masks. The 4½-hour cruise is known for its delicious meals; 3½-hour snack cruises are offered, too. For ages seven and older, the company also operates the *Hula Kai* snorkel cruise, a 55-foot luxury hydrofoil catamaran that takes guests to several remote South Kona locations. Their five-hour morning snorkel cruise includes a gourmet breakfast buffet and barbecue lunch. ⊠ *Keauhou Bay, 78-7130 Kaleiopapa St., Kailua-Kona* ☎ *808/322–2788, 800/677–9461* ⊕ *www.fair-wind.com* 🖅 *From $149.*

Sea Quest

SNORKELING | Careful stewardship of the Kona Coast and its sea life is a major priority for this company, which offers catamaran charters and other snorkeling excursions. Trips leave from Keauhou Bay and head to Captain Cook Monument and other points south. ∎**TIP**→ **Book five days in advance for $10 off.** ⊠ *78-7138 Kaleiopapa St., Kailua-Kona* ☎ *808/329–7238* ⊕ *www.seaquesthawaii.com* 🖅 *From $88.*

Stand-Up Paddling

Stand-up paddleboarding (or SUP for short), a sport with roots in the Hawaiian Islands, has grown popular worldwide in recent years. It's available for all skill levels and ages, and even novice stand-up paddleboarders can get up, stay up, and have a great time paddling around a protected bay or exploring the gorgeous coastline. All you need to get started is a large body of calm water, a board, and a paddle. The workout tests your core strength as well as your balance and offers an unusual vantage point from which to enjoy the beauty of island and ocean.

BEST SPOTS

Anaehoomalu Bay Beach (A-Bay). In this well-protected bay, even when surf is rough on the rest of the island, it's usually fairly calm here, though trades pick up heartily in the afternoon. Boards are available for rent at the north end, and the safe area for stand-up paddling is marked by buoys. ⊠ *Off Waikoloa Beach Dr., south of Waikoloa Beach Marriott, Kohala Coast.*

Hilo Bay. At this favorite among locals, the best place to put in is at **Reeds Bay Beach Park.** Most afternoons you'll share the bay with local paddling clubs. Stay inside the breakwater unless the ocean is calm (or you're feeling unusually adventurous). Conditions range from extremely calm to quite choppy. ⊠ *Banyan Way and Banyan Dr., 1 mile from downtown Hilo.*

Kailua Bay and Kamakahonu Beach. The small sandy beach that fronts the Courtyard King Kamehameha's Kona Beach Hotel is great for kids; the water here is especially calm and gentle. If you're more daring, you can easily paddle out of the bay and along the coast for some great exploring. ⊠ *Alii Dr., next to Kailua Pier, Kailua-Kona.*

EQUIPMENT AND LESSONS

★ **Hypr Nalu Hawaii**

WATER SPORTS | SUP master Ian Foo is the king of the stand-up paddleboard in downtown Kailua-Kona. At his small oceanfront shop across from the pier, a family affair, he stocks surfboards and paddleboards, all beautifully custom-made with veneer finishes and gorgeous hardwoods such as rosewood and applewood. Hypr also offers OC1 (outrigger canoe, one person) lessons, rentals, active ocean gear, and a great line of logo apparel. Foo and his fitness-minded family are serious and enthusiastic about ocean sports and are awesome teachers. If you rent or take a lesson, there's a very good chance you will fall in love with one of their iconic boards; luckily, they ship worldwide. Rentals for surfboards and paddleboards are weekly only, and rates vary by type. ⊠ *75-5663 Palani Rd., Unit K, Kailua-Kona* ☎ *808/960–4667* ⊕ *www. hyprnalu.com* ✉ *Instruction from $110; 2-hour outrigger rentals from $95 for OC1 and $135 for OC2.*

Ocean Sports

WATER SPORTS | This outfitter at the Waikoloa Beach Marriott rents equipment, offers lessons, and has the perfect location for easy access to the bay. Ocean Sports also operates rental shacks at the Whale Center Kawaihae, Queens' MarketPlace, and Anaehoomalu Bay. They can also set you up with cruises, dives, and charters elsewhere on the island. ⊠ *Waikoloa Beach Marriott, 69-275 Waikoloa Beach Dr., Waikoloa* ☎ *808/886–6666* ⊕ *www.hawaiioceansports.com* ✉ *SUP rental $50/hr, body board $5/hr, snorkel gear $25/day.*

Submarine Tours

Atlantis Submarines

TOUR—SPORTS | FAMILY | Want to stay dry while exploring the tropical undersea world? Climb aboard the 48-passenger *Atlantis X* submarine, anchored off Kailua Pier, across from Courtyard King Kamehameha's Kona Beach Hotel. A large glass dome in the bow and 13 viewing ports on each side allow clear views of the aquatic world more than 100 feet down. They take you to a pristine, 25-acre coral garden brimming with sea creatures of all kinds. This is a great trip for kids and nonswimmers. ■**TIP➜ Book online for discounts and specials.** ⊠ *75-5669 Alii Dr., Kailua-Kona* ☎ *808/326–7939, 800/381–0237* ⊕ *www.atlantisadventures.com* ✉ *$114.*

Surfing

The Big Island does not have the variety of great surfing spots found on Oahu or Maui, but it does have decent waves and a thriving surf culture. Local kids and avid surfers frequent a number of places up and down the Kona and Kohala coasts of West Hawaii; some have become famous surf champions. Expect high surf in winter and much calmer activity during summer. The surf scene is much more active on the Kona side.

EQUIPMENT AND LESSONS
★ **Hawaii Lifeguard Surf Instructors**
SURFING | This family-owned, lifeguard-certified school helps novices become wave riders at Kahaluu Beach Park and offers lessons for more experienced riders at Kona's top surf spots. A two-hour introductory lesson has one instructor per two to four students, and is gentle and reassuring. Private instruction is available as well. If the waves are on the smaller side, the school converts to stand-up paddleboard lessons for the same prices as surfing. ⊠ *75-5909 Alii Dr., Kailua-Kona* ☎ *808/324–0442, 808/936–7873* ⊕ *www. surflessonshawaii.com* ✉ *From $75.*

Ocean Eco Tours Surf School
SURFING | Family owned and operated, Kona's oldest surf school emphasizes the basics and specializes in beginners. It's one of a handful of operators permitted to conduct business in Kaloko-Honokohau National Historical Park, which gets waves even when other spots on the west side are flat. All lessons are taught by certified instructors, and the school guarantees that you will surf. If you're hooked, sign up for a three-day package. There's an authentic soul surfer's vibe to this operation, and they are equally diehard about teaching you about the ocean and having you standing up riding waves on your first day. Group, private, and semiprivate lessons available. ⊠ *Courtyard King Kamehameha's Kona Beach Hotel, 75-5660 Palani Rd., Suite 304, Kailua-Kona* ☎ *808/324–7873* ⊕ *www. oceanecotours.com* ✉ *From $99.*

Whale-Watching

Each winter, some two-thirds of the North Pacific humpback whale population (about 4,000–5,000 animals) migrate over 3,500 miles from the icy Alaska waters to the warm Hawaiian ocean to mate and, the following year, give birth to and nurse their calves. Recent reports indicate that the whale population is on the upswing—a few years ago one even ventured into the mouth of Hilo Harbor, which marine biologists say is quite rare. Humpbacks are spotted here from early December through the end of April, but other species, like sperm, pilot, and beaked whales as well as spinner, spotted, and bottlenose dolphins, can be seen year-round. ■TIP→ **If you take a morning cruise, you're more likely to see dolphins.** *In addition to the outfitters listed below, see Snorkeling for more outfitters that offer whale- and dol-phin-watching cruises.*

TOURS
Captain Dan McSweeney's Whale Watch Learning Adventures
WHALE-WATCHING | Captain Dan McSweeney, self-described whale researcher and conservationist, offers three-hour trips on his double-deck-er, 40-foot cruise boat. In addition to humpbacks (in winter), he'll try to show you dolphins and some of the six other whale species that live off the Kona Coast throughout the year. McSweeney guarantees you'll see whales or he'll take you out again for free. ⊠ *Honokohau Harbor, 74-381 Kealakehe Pkwy., Kailua-Kona* ☎ *808/322–0028, 888/942–5376* ⊕ *www.ilovewhales.com* ☜ *$120.*

Hawaii Nautical
WHALE-WATCHING | A NOAA-designated "Dolphin SMART" operator, this compa-ny practices strict guidelines for viewing protected marine animals, including dolphins and whales. You can be assured that you'll enjoy a wonderful ocean tour, see plenty of animals, and not be a part of harming or impacting the animals' activities or habitats. Excursions include affordable powerboat cruises, catamaran snorkel sails, and even a pampering yacht adventure that takes a maximum of six guests to Pawai Bay or Makalawena. Private charters are also available, but prepare to splurge. ⊠ *74-425 Kealakehe Pkwy., Slip I-10, Kailua-Kona* ☎ *808/234–7245* ⊕ *www.hawaiinautical.com* ☜ *From $79.*

Zipline Tours

Kohala Zipline
ZIP LINING | Located in the canopy of the Halawa Gulch in North Kohala, this tour features nine zips and five suspension bridges for a thrilling, within-the-canopy adventure in the forest. You'll bounce up to the site in a six-wheel-drive, mili-tary-style vehicle. Two certified guides accompany each small group. Designed for all ability levels, the Kohala Zipline focuses on fun and safety, offering a dual line for efficient, confident braking. You'll soar more than 100 feet above the ground and feel like a pro by the last platform. A quickie lesson in rappelling is included. Zip and Dip tours (combining zipline, nature walk, lunch, snacks, and waterfall swim) are available. ⊠ *54-3676 Akoni Pule Hwy., Kapaau* ☎ *808/331–3620, 800/464–1993* ⊕ *www.kohala-zipline.com* ☜ *From $189.*

Chapter 6

KAUAI

Updated by Joan Conrow,
Charles E. Roessler,
and Mary F. Williamson

👁 **Sights**
★★★★★

🍴 **Restaurants**
★★★☆☆

🏨 **Hotels**
★★★☆☆

🛍 **Shopping**
★★★☆☆

🍸 **Nightlife**
★★☆☆☆

WELCOME TO KAUAI

TOP REASONS TO GO

★ **Napali Coast:** On foot, by boat, or by air—explore what is unarguably one of the most beautiful stretches of coastline in all Hawaii.

★ **Kalalau Trail:** Hawaii's ultimate adventure hike will test your endurance but reward you with lush tropical vegetation, white-sand beaches, and unforgettable views.

★ **Kayaking:** Kauai is a hub for kayakers, with four rivers plus the spectacular coastline to explore.

★ **Waimea Canyon:** Dramatic, colorful rock formations and frequent rainbows make this natural wonder one of Kauai's most stunning features.

★ **Scenic Drives:** The North Shore's Highway 560 and the West Side's Waimea Canyon Drive are picture-perfect bliss.

1 North Shore. Dreamy beaches, green mountains, breathtaking scenery, and abundant rain, waterfalls, and rainbows characterize the North Shore, which includes the communities of Kilauea, Princeville, and Hanalei.

2 East Side. This is Kauai's commercial and residential hub, dominated by the island's largest town, Kapaa. The airport, harbor, and government offices are found in the county seat of Lihue.

3 South Shore. Peaceful landscapes, sunny weather, and beaches that rank among the best in the world make the South Shore the resort capital of Kauai. The Poipu resort area is here, along with the small towns of Koloa, Lawai, and Kalaheo.

4 West Side. Dry, sunny, and sleepy, the West Side includes the historic towns of Hanapepe, Waimea, and Kekaha. This area is ideal for outdoor adventurers because it's the entryway to the Waimea Canyon and Kokee State Park, and the departure point for most Napali Coast boat trips.

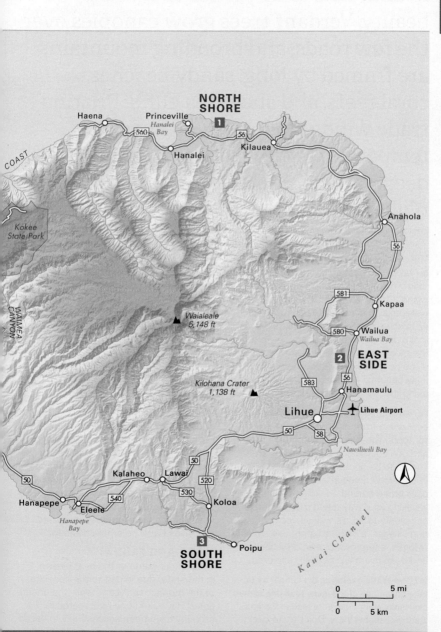

NORTH SHORE 1

Haena

Princeville
Hanalei Bay

560

Hanalei

56

Kilauea

NA PALI COAST

Kokee State Park

WAIMEA CANYON

Anahola

56

581

Kapaa

580

Wailua
Wailua Bay

Waialeale 5,148 ft

EAST SIDE 2

583

56

Hanamaulu

Kilohana Crater 1,138 ft

Lihue

Lihue Airport

50

58

Nawiliwili Bay

Kalaheo

Lawai

50

520

530

Koloa

Hanapepe

50

Eleele

540

Hanapepe Bay

3 SOUTH SHORE

Poipu

Kauai Channel

0 5 mi

0 5 km

Even a nickname like "The Garden Island" fails to do justice to Kauai's beauty. Verdant trees grow canopies over the few roads, and brooding mountains are framed by long, sandy beaches, coral reefs, and sheer sea cliffs. Pristine trade winds moderate warm daily temperatures while offering comfort for deep, refreshing sleep through gentle nights.

The main road tracing Kauai's perimeter takes you past much more scenery than would seem possible on one small island. Chiseled mountains, thundering waterfalls, misty hillsides, dreamy beaches, lush vegetation, and small towns make up the physical landscape. Perhaps the most stunning piece of scenery is a place no road will take you—breathtakingly beautiful Napali Coast, which runs along the northwest side of the island.

For adventure seekers, Kauai offers everything from difficult hikes to helicopter tours. The island has top-notch spas and golf courses, and its beaches are known to be some of the most beautiful in the world. Even after you've spent days lazing around drinking mai tais or kayaking your way down a river, there's still plenty to do, as well as see: plantation villages, a historic lighthouse, wildlife refuges, a fern grotto, a colorful canyon, and deep rivers are all easily explored.

■TIP➔ While exploring the island, try to take advantage of the many roadside scenic overlooks and pull over to take in the constantly changing view. Don't try to pack too much into one day. Kauai is small, but travel is slow. The island's sights are divided into four geographic areas, in clockwise order: the North Shore, the East Side, the South Shore, and the West Side.

GEOLOGY

Kauai is the oldest and northernmost of the main Hawaiian Islands. Five million years of wind and rain have worked their magic, sculpting fluted sea cliffs and whittling away at the cinder cones and caldera that prove its volcanic origin. Foremost among these is Waialeale, one of the wettest spots on Earth. Its approximate 450-inch annual rainfall feeds the mighty Wailua River, the only navigable waterway in Hawaii. The vast Alakai Swamp soaks up rain like a sponge, releasing it slowly into the watershed that gives Kauai its emerald sheen.

FLORA AND FAUNA

Kauai offers some of the best birding in the state, due in part to the absence of the mongoose. Many nene (the endangered Hawaiian state bird) reared in captivity have been successfully released here, along with an endangered forest bird called the puaiohi. The island is also home to a large colony of migratory nesting seabirds and has two refuges protecting endangered Hawaiian waterbirds. Kauai's most noticeable fowl, however, is the wild chicken. A cross between jungle fowl (*moa*) brought by the Polynesians and domestic chickens and fighting cocks that escaped during the last two hurricanes, they are everywhere, and the roosters crow when they feel like it, not just at dawn. Consider yourself warned.

HISTORY

Kauai's residents have had a reputation for independence since ancient times. Called "The Separate Kingdom," Kauai alone resisted King Kamehameha's charge to unite the Hawaiian Islands. In fact, it was only by kidnapping Kauai's king, Kaumualii, and forcing him to marry Kamehameha's widow that the Garden Island was joined to the rest of Hawaii. That spirit lives on today as Kauai residents try to resist the lure of tourism dollars captivating the rest of the Islands. Local building tradition maintains that no structure be taller than a coconut tree, and Kauai's capital, Lihue, is still more small town than city.

LEGENDS AND MYTHOLOGY: THE MENEHUNE

Although all of the islands have a few stories about the Menehune—magical, tiny people who accomplished great feats—Kauai is believed to be their home base. The Menehune Fishpond, above Nawilwili Harbor, is a prime example of their work. The story goes that the large pond (initially 25 miles in diameter) was built in one night by thousands of Menehune passing stones from hand to hand. A spy disrupted their work in the middle of the night, leaving two gaps that are still visible today (drive to the pond on Hulemalu Road, or kayak up Huleia Stream).

LUAU

Although the commercial luau experience is a far cry from the backyard luau thrown by local residents to celebrate a wedding, graduation, or baby's first birthday, they're nonetheless entertaining and a good introduction to the Hawaiian food that isn't widely sold in restaurants. With many, you can watch a roasted pig being carried out of its *imu,* a hole in the ground used for cooking meat with heated stones. Besides the feast, and free mai tais, there's often an exciting dinner show with Polynesian-style music and dancing. It all makes for a fun evening that's suitable for couples, families, and groups, and the informal setting is conducive to meeting other people. Every luau is different, reflecting the cuisine and tenor of the host facility, so compare prices, menus, and entertainment before making your reservation. Most luau on Kauai are offered only on a limited number of nights each week, so plan ahead to get the luau you want. We tend to prefer those *not* held on resort properties, because they feel a bit more authentic.

Planning

Getting Here and Around

AIR

On Kauai, visitors fly into Lihue Airport, on the East Side of the island. Visitor information booths are outside each baggage-claim area. Visitors will also find news- and lei stands, an HMS Host restaurant, and a Travel Traders gift shop at the airport.

Alaska Airlines has a daily Seattle–Lihue flight. American Airlines offers a daily, nonstop Los Angeles–Lihue flight, in addition to its service into Honolulu, Maui, and the Big Island. Delta has a Los Angeles–Lihue flight and also serves Oahu (Honolulu) and Maui. United

Great Itineraries

As small as Kauai may be, you still can't do it all in one day: hiking Kalalau Trail, kayaking Wailua River, showering in a waterfall, watching whales at Kilauea Lighthouse, waking to the sunrise above Kealia, touring underwater lava tubes at Tunnels, and shopping for gifts at Koloa Town shops. Rather than trying to check everything off your list in one fell swoop, we recommend choosing your absolute favorite and devoting a full day to the experience.

A Bit of History

Hawaiian beliefs are traditionally rooted in nature. If you're interested in archaeological sites where sacred ceremonies were held, focus on the Wailua River area. Your best bet is to take a riverboat tour—it's full of kitsch, but you'll definitely walk away with a deeper understanding of ancient Hawaii. Then, head to Lihue's Kauai Museum, where you can pick up a memento of authentic Hawaiian artistry at the gift shop. End your day at Gaylord's restaurant and meander through the historic Kilohana Plantation sugar estate.

Adventure Galore

For big-time adventure, kayak Napali Coast or skydive over the ocean and island for a once-in-a-lifetime experience. For those whose idea of adventure is a good walk, take the flat, coastal trail along the East Side—you can pick it up just about anywhere starting at the southern end of Lydgate Park, heading north. It'll take you almost all the way to Anahola, if you desire. After it's all over, recuperate with a massage by the ocean—or in the comfort of your own room, so you can crash immediately afterward.

A Day on the Water

Start your day before sunrise and head west to Port Allen Marina. Check in with one of the tour-boat operators—who will provide you with plenty of coffee to jump-start your day—and cruise Napali Coast before heading across the Kaulakahi Channel to snorkel the fish-rich waters of Niihau. Slather up with sunscreen and be prepared for a long—and sometimes big—day on the water; you can enjoy a couple of mai tais on the return trip. Something about the sun and the salt air conspires to induce a powerful sense of fatigue—so don't plan anything in the evening. The trip also helps build a huge appetite, so stop at Port Allen Sunset Grill & Bar on the way home.

Coastal Drives

If you're staying on the East Side or North Shore, the best drive for ocean vistas is, hands down, Highway 560, which begins at Princeville on the main highway where Highway 56 ends. Stop at the first lookout overseeing Hanalei River valley for a few snapshots; then head down the hill, across the one-lane bridge—taking in the taro fields—and through the town of Hanalei and on to the end of the road at Kee Beach. If you're up for it, enjoy a bit of unparalleled hiking on the Kalalau Trail, go snorkeling at Kee, or simply soak up the sun on the beach, if it's not too crowded. If you're staying on the South Shore or West Side, follow Highway 50 west. You'll start to catch distant ocean vistas from the highway as you head out of the town of Kalaheo and from the coffee fields of Kauai Coffee. Stop here for a sample. You'll come closer to the ocean—and practically reach out and touch it—after you pass through Waimea en route to Kekaha. Although this isn't great swimming water—it's unprotected, with no reef—there is a long stretch of beach here perfect for walking, running, or simply meandering. Once the paved road ends—if you're brave and your car-rental agreement allows—keep going and you'll eventually come to Polihale, a huge, deserted beach. It'll feel like the end of the world here, so it's a great place to spend a quiet afternoon and witness a spectacular sunset. Just be sure to pack plenty of food, water, and sunscreen before you depart Kekaha—and gas up the car.

Shop 'Til You Drop
You could actually see a good many of the island's sights by browsing in our favorite island shops. Of course, you can't see the entire island, but this itinerary will take you through Kapaa and north to Hanalei. A mile north of the grocery stores in Waipouli, Kela's Glass has great art pieces. From there, a leisurely drive north will reveal a rural side of Kauai. If you enjoy tea, sake, or sushi, stop at Kilauea's Kong Lung, where you can stock up on complete place settings for each. Then, head down the road to Hanalei. If you're inspired by surf, stop in Hanalei Surf Company. Our favorite for one-of-a-kind keepsakes—actually antiques and authentic memorabilia—are the shops in Hanalei Center.

Relax Kauai-Style
If you're headed to Kauai for some peace and quiet, you'll want to start your day with yoga at Yoga Hanalei (⊕ www.yogahanalei.com) or Kapaa's Golden Lotus Studio (⊕ www.golden-lotuskauai.org). If you're staying on the South Shore, try yoga on the beach

(actually a grassy spot just off the beach) with longtime yoga instructor Antonia Joy (⊕ www.kauaioceanfrontyoga.com). If it happens to be the second or last Sunday of the month, you might then head to the Lawai International Center (⊕ www.lawaicenter.org) for an afternoon stroll among 88 Buddhist shrines. On the North Shore, Limahuli Gardens is the perfect place to wander among native plants. Then watch the sun slip into the sea on any west-facing beach and call it a day with a glass of wine.

Have a Little Romance
We can't think of a better way to ensure a romantic vacation than to pop a bottle of champagne and walk the Mahaulepu shoreline at sunset, hand in hand with a loved one. Make this a Sunday and take a sunrise walk followed by brunch at the Grand Hyatt. Then spend the afternoon luxuriating with facials, body scrubs, and massage in the Hyatt ANARA Spa's Garden Treatment Village, in a private, thatched hut just for couples. That'll put you in the mood for a wedding ceremony or renewal of vows on the beach followed by a sunset dinner overlooking the ocean at the Beach House restaurant. Can it get any more romantic than this?

Airlines provides direct service to Lihue Airport from Denver, Los Angeles, and San Francisco. The carrier also flies into Honolulu, Maui, and the Big Island. Hawaiian offers a daily, nonstop Los Angeles–Lihue flight; all other mainland flights require a connection in Honolulu except Southwest Airlines, which has limited direct flights to Lihue from Oakland.

CAR

Unless you plan to stay strictly at a resort or do all of your sightseeing as part of guided tours, you'll need a rental car. There is bus service on the island, but the bumpy buses tend to run limited hours.

You most likely won't need a four-wheel-drive vehicle anywhere on the island, so save yourself the money. And although convertibles look like fun, the frequent, intermittent rain showers and intense tropical sun make hardtops a better (and cheaper) choice.

If possible, avoid the "rush" hours when the local workers go to and from their jobs. Kauai has some of the highest gas prices in the Islands.

Ride-share companies Uber and Lyft are somewhat recent arrivals on the island, but you can still expect to pay around $75–$80 for a ride from the airport to Princeville (approximately 30 miles).

ISLAND DRIVING TIMES

It might not seem as if driving from the North Shore to the West Side, say, would take much time, as Kauai is smaller than Oahu, Maui, and certainly the Big Island. But it will take longer than you'd expect, and Kauai roads are subject to some heavy traffic, especially going through Kapaa and Lihue.

Driving Times

Haena to Hanalei	5 miles/15 mins
Hanalei to Princeville	4 miles/10 mins
Princeville to Kilauea	5 miles/10 mins
Kilauea to Anahola	8 miles/12 mins
Anahola to Kapaa	5 miles/10 mins
Kapaa to Lihue	10 miles/20 mins
Lihue to Poipu	13 miles/25 mins
Poipu to Kalaheo	8 miles/15 mins
Kalaheo to Hanapepe	4 miles/8 mins
Hanapepe to Waimea	7 miles/10 mins

Beaches

Kauai may be nicknamed the Garden Island, but with more sandy beaches per mile of coastline than any other Hawaiian Island, it could easily be called the Sandy Island as well. Totaling more than 50 miles, Kauai's beaches make up 44% of the island's shoreline—almost twice that of Oahu, second on this list.

It is, of course, because of Kauai's age as the eldest sibling of the inhabited Hawaiian Islands, allowing more time for water and wind erosion to break down rock and coral into sand.

But not all of Kauai's beaches are the same. Each beach is unique unto itself. Conditions and scenery can change throughout the day and certainly throughout the year, transforming, say, a tranquil, lakelike ocean setting in summer into monstrous waves drawing internationally ranked surfers from around the world in winter.

There are sandy beaches, rocky beaches, wide beaches, narrow beaches, skinny beaches, and alcoves. Generally speaking, surf kicks up on the North Shore in winter and the South Shore in summer, although summer's southern swells aren't nearly as frequent or as big as the northern winter swells that attract those surfers. Kauai's longest and widest beaches are found on the North Shore and West Side and are popular with beachgoers, although during winter's rains, everyone heads to the drier South Shore and West Side. The East Side beaches tend to be narrower and have onshore winds less popular with sunbathers, yet fishers abound. Smaller coves are characteristic of the South Shore and attract all kinds of water lovers year-round, including monk seals.

In Hawaii, all beaches are public, but their accessibility varies greatly. Some require an easy ½-mile stroll, some require a four-wheel-drive vehicle, others require boulder-hopping, and one takes an entire day of serious hiking. And then there are those "drive-in" beaches adjacent to parking areas. Kauai is not Disneyland, so don't expect much signage to help you along the way. One of the top-ranked beaches in the whole world—Hanalei— doesn't have a single sign in town directing you to the beach. Furthermore, most of the beaches on Kauai's vast coastline are remote, offering no facilities. It's important to note that drownings are common on Kauai, in part because many beaches have no lifeguards and tricky ocean conditions. When in doubt, stay out. ■TIP→ **If you want the convenience of restrooms, picnic tables, lifeguards, and the like, stick to county beach parks.**

Hotels

The Garden Island has lodgings for every taste, from swanky resorts to rustic cabins, and from family-friendly condos to romantic bed-and-breakfasts. The savvy traveler can also find inexpensive places that are convenient, safe, and accessible to Kauai's special places and activities.

Kauai may seem small on a map, but because it's circular with no through roads, it can take more time than you think to get from place to place. If at all possible, stay close to your desired activities. This way, you'll save time to squeeze in all the things you'll want to do.

Time of year is also a factor. If you're here in winter or spring, consider staying on the South Shore, as the surf on the North Shore and East Side tends to be rough, making many ocean beaches dangerous for swimming or water sports.

Before booking accommodations, think hard about what kind of experience you want to have for your island vacation. There are several top-notch resorts to choose from, and Kauai also has a wide variety of condos, vacation rentals, and bed-and-breakfasts. The Kauai Visitors Bureau provides a comprehensive listing of accommodation choices to help you decide.

If you want to golf, play tennis, or hang at a spa, stay at a resort. You'll also be more likely to find activities for children at resorts, including camps that allow parents a little time off. The island's hotels tend to be smaller and older, with fewer on-site amenities. One of the swankiest places to stay is the Grand Hyatt Kauai on the South Shore.

Condos and vacation rentals on Kauai tend to run the gamut from fabulous luxury estates to scruffy little dives. It's buyer-beware in this totally unregulated sector of the visitor industry. If you're planning to stay at a vacation rental, be sure it's one that is properly permitted by the county. The permit number should be prominent on the ads and signs outside the house.

The island's limited bed-and-breakfasts allow you to meet local residents and more directly experience the aloha spirit. Some have oceanfront settings and breakfasts with everything from tropical fruits and juices, Kauai coffee, and macadamia-nut waffles to breads made with local bananas and mangoes. Some have pools, hot tubs, services such as *lomilomi* massage, and breakfasts delivered to your lanai. Some properties have stand-alone units on-site. *Hotel reviews have been shortened. For full information, visit Fodors.com.*

Restaurants

Kauai's cultural diversity is apparent in its restaurants, which offer authentic Chinese, Korean, Japanese, Thai, Mexican, Italian, Vietnamese, and Hawaiian specialties. Less specialized restaurants cater to the tourist crowd, serving standard American fare—burgers, pizza, sandwiches, surf-and-turf combos, and so on. Poipu and Kapaa offers the best selection of restaurants, with options for a variety of tastes and budgets; most fast-food joints are in Lihue.

Parents will be relieved to encounter a tolerant attitude toward children, even if they're noisy. Men can leave their jackets and ties at home; attire tends toward informal. But if you want to dress up, you can. Reservations are accepted in most places and required at some of the top restaurants.

If you're lucky enough to win an invitation to a potluck, baby luau, or beach party, don't think twice—just accept. The best grinds (food) are homemade, and so you'll eat until you're full, then rest, eat some more, and make a plate to take home, too.

But even if you can't score a spot at one of these parties, don't despair. Great local-style food is easy to come by at countless low-key places around the island. As an extra bonus, these eats are often inexpensive, and portions are generous. Expect plenty of meat—usually deep-fried or marinated in a teriyaki sauce and grilled *pulehu*-style (over an open fire)—and starches. Rice is standard, even for breakfast, and it's often served alongside potato–macaroni

salad, another island specialty. Another local favorite is *poke,* made from chunks of raw tuna or octopus seasoned with sesame oil, soy sauce, onions, and pickled seaweed. It's a great *pupu* (appetizer) when paired with a cold beer.

What It Costs in U.S. Dollars			
$	$$	$$$	$$$$
RESTAURANTS			
Under $18	$18–$26	$27–$35	Over $35
HOTELS			
Under $180	$180–$260	$261–$340	Over $340

Nightlife

Kauai has never been known for its nightlife. It's a rural island, where folks tend to retire early, and the streets are dark and deserted well before midnight. The island does have its nightspots, though, and the after-dark entertainment scene keeps expanding, especially in areas frequented by tourists. All bars and clubs that serve alcohol must close at 2 am, except those with a cabaret license, which allows them to close at 4 am.

Most of the island's dinner and luau shows are held at hotels and resorts. Hotel lounges are a good source of live music, often with no cover charge, as are a few bars and restaurants around the island.

Check the local newspaper, the *Garden Island,* for listings of weekly happenings. Free publications such as *Kauai Gold, This Week on Kauai,* and *Essential Kauai* also list entertainment events. You can pick them up at Lihue Airport near the baggage claim area, as well as at numerous retail areas on the island.

Where to Stay in Kauai

	Local Vibe	Pros	Cons
The North Shore	Properties here have the "wow" factor with ocean and mountain beauty; laid-back Hanalei and Princeville set the high-end pace.	When the weather is good (summer) this side has it all. Epic winter surf, gorgeous waterfalls, and verdant vistas create some of the best scenery in Hawaii.	Frequent winter rain (being green has a cost) means you may have to travel south to find the sun; expensive restaurants and shopping offer few deals.
The East Side	The most reasonably priced area to stay for the practical traveler; lacks the pizzazz of expensive resorts on North and South shores; more traditional beach hotels.	The best travel deals show up here; more direct access to the local population; plenty of decent restaurants with good variety, along with delis in food stores.	Beaches aren't the greatest (rocky, reefy) at many of the lodging spots; congested traffic at times; some crime issues in parks.
The South Shore	Resort central; plenty of choices where the consistent sunshine is perfect for those who want to do nothing but play golf or tennis and read a book by the pool.	Beautiful in its own right; many enchanted evenings with stellar sunsets; summer surf a bit easier for beginners to handle.	Though resorts are lush, surrounding landscape is desert-like with scrub brush; construction can be brutal on peace of mind.
The West Side	There are few options for lodging in this mostly untouristed setting, with contrasts such as the extreme heat of a July day in Waimea to a frozen winter night up in Kokee.	A gateway area for exploration into the wilds of Kokee or for boating trips on Napali Coast; main hub for boat and helicopter trips; outstanding sunsets.	Least convenient side for most visitors; daytime is languid and dry; river runoff can ruin ocean's clarity.

6

Kauai PLANNING

Shopping and Spas

There aren't a lot of shops and spas on Kauai, but what you will find here are a handful of places very much worth checking out for the quality of their selection of items sold and services rendered. Many shops now make an effort to sell as many locally made products as possible. When buying an item, ask where it was made or even who made it.

Often you will find that a product handcrafted on the island may not be that much more expensive than a similar product made overseas. You can also look for the purple "Kauai Made" sticker many merchants display.

Along with one major shopping mall, a few shopping centers, and a growing number of big-box retailers, Kauai has some delightful mom-and-pop shops and specialty boutiques with lots of character. The Garden Island also has a large and talented community of artisans and fine artists, with galleries all around the island showcasing their creations. You can find many island-made arts and crafts in the small shops, and it's worthwhile to stop in at crafts fairs and outdoor markets to look for bargains and mingle with island residents.

If you're looking for a special memento of your trip that is unique to Kauai County, check out the distinctive Niihau shell lei. The tiny shells are collected from beaches on Kauai and Niihau, pierced, and strung into beautiful necklaces, chokers, and earrings. It's a time-consuming and exacting craft, and these items are much in demand, so don't be taken aback by the high price tags. Those made by Niihau residents will have certificates of authenticity and are worth collecting. You often can find cheaper versions made by non-Hawaiians at crafts fairs.

Kauai is often touted as the healing island, and local spas try hard to fill that role. With the exception of the Hyatt's ANARA Spa, the facilities aren't as posh as some might want, but it's in the human element that Kauai excels. Many island residents are known for their warmth, kindness, and humility, and you can often find all these attributes in the massage therapists and technicians who work long hours at the resort spas. These professionals take their therapeutic mission seriously; they genuinely want you to experience the island's relaxing, restorative qualities. Private massage services abound on the island, and your spa therapist may offer the same services at a much lower price outside the resort, but if you're looking for a variety of health-and-beauty treatments, an exercise workout, or a full day of pampering, a spa will prove most convenient.

Though most spas on Kauai are associated with resorts, none is restricted to guests only. And there's much by way of healing and wellness to be found on Kauai beyond the traditional spa—or even the day spa. More and more retreat facilities are offering what some would call alternative healing therapies. Others would say there's nothing alternative about them; you can decide for yourself.

Stores are typically open daily from 9 or 10 am to 5 pm, although some stay open until 9 pm, especially those near resorts. Don't be surprised if the posted hours don't match the actual hours of operation at the smaller shops, where owners may be fairly casual about keeping to a regular schedule.

Tours

Guided tours are convenient; you don't have to worry about finding a parking spot or getting admission tickets. Certified tour guides have taken special classes in Hawaiian history and lore. On the other hand, you won't have the freedom to proceed at your own pace, nor will you have the ability to take a detour trip if something else catches your attention.

Kauai ATV / Aloha Kauai Tours

EXCURSIONS | FAMILY | You get *way* off the beaten track on these excursions. Choose from several options, including an ATV tour leading from the haul-cane roads behind the locked gates of Grove Farm Plantation to a waterfall, and another exploring the archaeology and ecosystem of Makauwahi Cave. The tour center, adjacent to a lively food truck scene, is also the place to book with SeaFun Ocean Adventures, for a four-hour snorkeling excursion; Koloa Zipline, for the chance to zip over Waita Reservoir; and Koloa Bass Fishing. ⊠ *3477A Weliweli Rd. (for check-in), Koloa* ☎ *808/742–2734* ⊕ *www.kauaiatv.com.*

Roberts Hawaii Tours

BUS TOURS | The Round-the-Island Tour, sometimes called the Waimea Canyon–Fern Grotto Tour, gives a good overview of half the island, including Fort Elizabeth and Opaekaa Falls. Guests are transported in air-conditioned, 25-passenger minibuses. The $110 trip includes a boat ride up the Wailua River to the Fern Grotto and a visit to the lookouts above Waimea Canyon. Roberts also offers a Kauai Movie Tour for $109. ⊠ *3-4567 Kuhio Hwy., Hanamaulu* ☎ *808/245–9101, 800/831–5541* ⊕ *www.robertshawaii. com/kauai* ☑ *From $110.*

Waimea Historic Walking Tour

WALKING TOURS | The West Kauai Visitor Center offers special group tours of historic Waimea Town by appointment only, as well as maps for self-guided tours. ⊠ *9565 Kaumualii Hwy., Waimea (Kauai County)* ☎ *808/338–1332* ⊕ *www. westkauaivisitorcenter.org* ☑ *Donation.*

Visitor Information

For information about hiking and camping permits and rules and regulations for Napali Coast visit the Division of State Parks section of the ⊕ *hawaii.gov* website.

CONTACTS **Division of State Parks.** ⊠ *3060 Eiwa St., Suite 306, Lihue* ☎ *808/274–3444* ⊕ *dnlr.hawaii.gov.* **West Kauai Visitor Center.** ⊠ *West Kauai Technology and Visitor Center Building, 9565 Kaumualii Hwy, Waimea (Kauai County)* ☎ *808/338–1332* ⊕ *www.westkauaivisitorcenter.org.*

The North Shore

The North Shore of Kauai includes the environs of Kilauea, Princeville, Hanalei, and Haena. Traveling north on Route 56 from the airport, the coastal highway crosses the Wailua River and the busy towns of Wailua and Kapaa before emerging into a decidedly rural and scenic landscape, with expansive views of the island's rugged interior mountains. As the two-lane highway turns west and narrows, it winds through spectacular scenery and passes the posh resort community of Princeville before dropping down into Hanalei Valley. Here it narrows further and becomes a federally recognized scenic roadway, replete with one-lane bridges (the local etiquette is for six or seven cars to cross at a time), hairpin turns, and heart-stopping coastal vistas. The road ends at Kee, where the ethereal rain forests and fluted sea cliffs of the Napali Coast Wilderness State Park begin.

In winter Kauai's North Shore receives more rainfall than other areas of the island. Don't let this deter you from visiting. The clouds drift over the mountains of Namolokama creating a mysterious mood and then, in a blink, disappear, rewarding you with mountains laced with a dozen waterfalls or more. The views of the mountain—as well as the sunsets over the ocean—from Hanalei Bay and Kee Beach are fantastic.

The North Shore attracts all kinds—from celebrities to surfers. In fact, the late Andy Irons, three-time world surfing champion, along with his brother Bruce and legend Laird Hamilton, grew up riding waves along the North Shore.

Hanalei, Haena, and West

Haena is 40 miles northwest of Lihue; Hanalei is 5 miles southeast of Haena.

Crossing the historic one-lane bridge into Hanalei reveals old-world Hawaii, including working taro farms, poi making, and evenings of throwing horseshoes at Black Pot Beach Park—found unmarked (as many places are on Kauai) at the east end of Hanalei Bay Beach Park. Although the current real-estate boom on Kauai has attracted mainland millionaires to build estate homes on the few remaining parcels of land in Hanalei, there's still plenty to see and do. It's *the* gathering place on the North Shore. Restaurants, shops, and people-watching here are among the best on the island, and you won't find a single brand name, chain, or big-box store around—unless you count surf brands like Quiksilver and Billabong.

The beach and river at Hanalei offer swimming, snorkeling, body boarding, surfing, and kayaking. Those hanging around at sunset often congregate at the Hanalei Pavilion, where a husband-and-wife slack-key-guitar-playing combo makes impromptu appearances. There's an old rumor, since quashed by the local newspaper, the *Garden Island*, that says Hanalei was the inspiration for the song "Puff the Magic Dragon," performed by the 1960s singing sensation Peter, Paul and Mary. Even with the newspaper's clarification, some tours still point out the shape of the dragon carved into the mountains encircling the town.

Once you pass through Hanalei Town, the road shrinks even more as you skirt the coast and pass through Haena. Blind corners, quick turns, and one-lane bridges force slow driving along this scenic stretch across the Lumahai and Wainiha valleys.

There is only one road leading beyond Princeville to Kee Beach at the western end of the North Shore: Route 560. Hanalei's commercial stretch fronts this route, and you'll find parking at the shopping compounds on each side of the road. After Hanalei, parking is restricted to two main areas, Haena Beach Park and a new lot at Haena State Park, and there are few pullover areas along Route 560. Traffic and especially parking have become major concerns as the North Shore has gained popularity, so be prepared to be patient.

◉ Sights

★ Hanalei Valley Overlook
VIEWPOINT | Dramatic mountains and a patchwork of neat taro farms bisected by the wide Hanalei River make this one of Hawaii's loveliest sights, even with the flood damage it sustained in 2018. The fertile Hanalei Valley has been planted with taro since perhaps AD 700, save for an 80-year-long foray into rice that ended in 1960. (The historic Haraguchi Rice Mill is all that remains of that era.) Many taro farmers lease land within the 900-acre Hanalei National Wildlife Refuge, helping to provide wetland habitat for four species of endangered Hawaiian water birds. ⊠ *Rte. 56, across from Foodland, Princeville.*

Limahuli Garden
GARDEN | Narrow Limahuli Valley, with its fluted mountain peaks and ancient stone taro terraces, creates an unparalleled setting for this botanical garden and nature preserve. Dedicated to protecting native plants and unusual varieties of taro, it represents the principles of conservation and stewardship held by its founder, Charles "Chipper" Wichman. Limahuli's primordial beauty and strong *mana* (spiritual power) eclipse the extensive botanical collection. It's one of the most

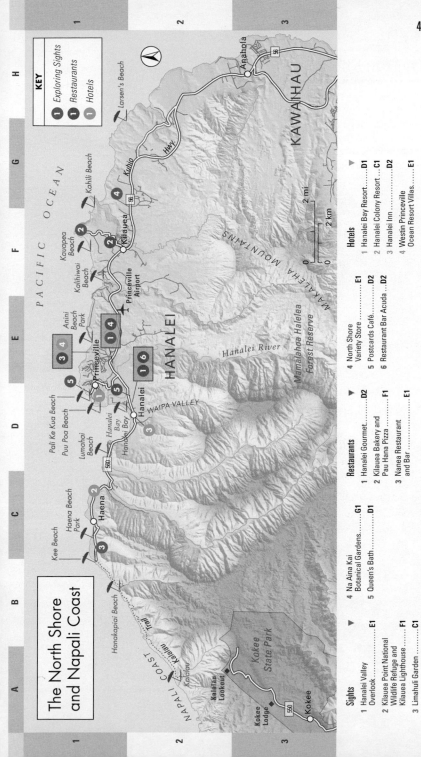

The North Shore and Napali Coast

KEY
- Exploring Sights
- Restaurants
- Hotels

PACIFIC OCEAN

Larsen's Beach
Kahili Beach
Kawapea Beach
Kalihiwai Beach
Anini Beach Park
Pali Ke Kua Beach
Puu Poa Beach
Lumahai Beach
Kee Beach
Haena Beach Park
Hanakapiai Beach
Hanalei Bay

Anahola
Kilauea
Princeville Airport
Princeville
Hanalei
Haena
Kokee

KAWAIHAU
HANALEI
WAIPA VALLEY
MAKALEHA MOUNTAINS
Mamalahoa Halelea Forest Reserve
Hanalei River
NAPALI COAST
Kalalau Trail
Kokee State Park
Kalalau Lookout
Kokee Lodge

Hanalei Valley Overlook

0   2 mi
0   2 km

445

6

Kauai THE NORTH SHORE

Sights ▸
1 Hanalei Valley Overlook E1
2 Kilauea Point National Wildlife Refuge and Kilauea Lighthouse F1
3 Limahuli Garden C1
4 Na Aina Kai Botanical Gardens G1
5 Queen's Bath D1

Restaurants ▸
1 Hanalei Gourmet D2
2 Kilauea Bakery and Pau Hana Pizza F1
3 Nanea Restaurant and Bar E1
4 North Shore Variety Store E1
5 Postcards Café D2
6 Restaurant Bar Acuda ... D2

Hotels ▸
1 Hanalei Bay Resort D1
2 Hanalei Colony Resort ... C1
3 Hanalei Inn D2
4 Westin Princeville Ocean Resort Villas E1

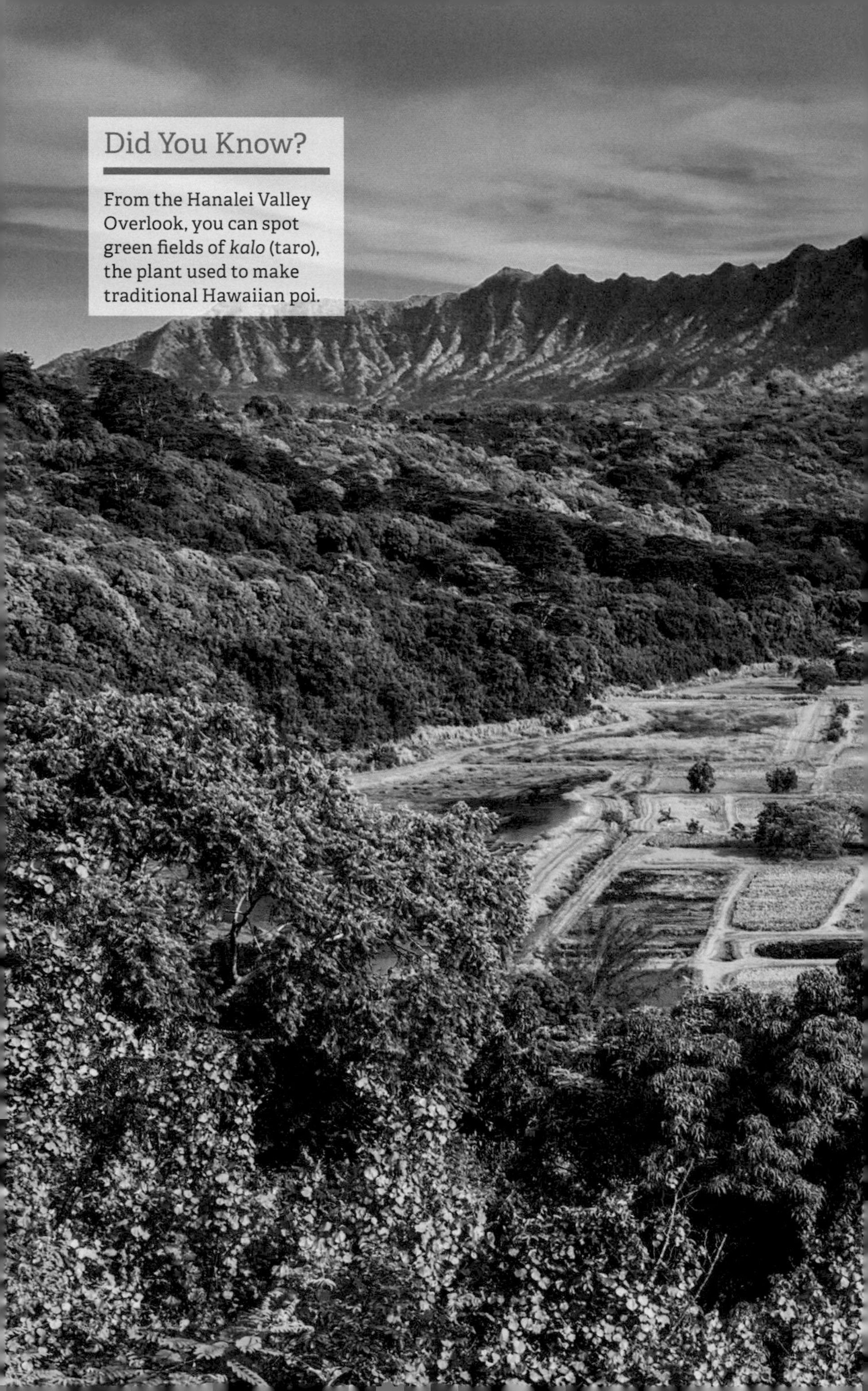

Did You Know?

From the Hanalei Valley Overlook, you can spot green fields of *kalo* (taro), the plant used to make traditional Hawaiian poi.

gorgeous spots on Kauai and the crown jewel of the National Tropical Botanical Garden, which Wichman now heads. Call ahead to reserve a guided tour, or tour on your own. A reservation is now required to park here, though North Shore Shuttle riders are exempt. Be sure to check out the quality gift shop and revolutionary compost toilet, and be prepared to walk a somewhat steep hillside. ⊠ 5-8291 Kuhio Hwy., Hanalei ☎ 808/826–1053 ⊕ www. ntbg.org ⊠ Self-guided tour $20, guided tour $40 (reservations required).

⏱ Beaches

If you've ever dreamed of Hawaii—and who hasn't—you've dreamed of Kauai's North Shore. "Lush," "tropical," and "abundant" are just a few words to describe this rugged and dramatic area. And the views to the sea aren't the only attraction—the inland views of velvety-green valley folds and carved mountain peaks will take your breath away. Rain is the reason for all the greenery on the North Shore, and winter is the rainy season. Not to worry, though; it rarely rains *everywhere* on the island at one time. ■TIP➜ The rule of thumb is to head south or west when it rains in the north.

The waves on the North Shore can be big—and we mean huge—in winter, drawing crowds to witness nature's spectacle. By contrast, in summer the waters can be completely serene.

★ Haena Beach Park
BEACH—SIGHT | This is a drive-up beach park popular with campers year-round. The wide bay here—named Makua—is bordered by two large reef systems creating favorable waves for skilled surfers during peak winter conditions. In July and August, waters at this same beach are usually as calm as a lake. Entering the water can be dangerous in winter when the big swells roll in. ■TIP➜ During the summer months only, this is a premier snorkeling site on Kauai. It's not unusual to find a food vendor parked here selling sandwiches and drinks out of a converted bread van. **Amenities:** food and drink; lifeguards; parking; showers; toilets. **Best for:** snorkeling; surfing; walking. ⊠ Near end of Rte. 560, across from "Dry Cave", Haena.

★ Hanalei Bay
BEACH—SIGHT | FAMILY | This 2-mile crescent beach cradles a wide bay in a setting that is quintessential Hawaii. The sea is on one side, and behind you are the mountains, often ribboned with waterfalls and changing color in the shifting light. In winter, Hanalei Bay boasts some of the biggest onshore surf breaks in the state, attracting world-class surfers, and the beach is plenty wide enough for sunbathing and strolling. In summer, the bay is transformed—calm waters lap the beach, sailboats moor in the bay, and outrigger-canoe paddlers ply the sea. Pack the cooler, haul out the beach umbrellas, and don't forget the beach toys, because Hanalei Bay is worth scheduling for an entire day, maybe two. Several county beach parks, some with pavilions, can be found along the bay. **Amenities:** lifeguards; parking; showers; toilets. **Best for:** sunset; surfing; swimming; walking. ⊠ Weke Rd., Hanalei.

★ Kalalau
BEACH—SIGHT | Located at the end of the trail with the same name, Kalalau is a remote beach in spectacular Napali Coast State Wilderness Park. Reaching it requires an arduous 11-mile hike along sea cliff faces, through steaming tropical valleys, and across sometimes-raging streams. Another option is to paddle a kayak to the beach—summer only, though, or else the surf is way too big. The beach is anchored by a *heiau* (a stone platform used as a place of worship) on one end and a waterfall on the other. The safest time to come is summer, when the trail is dry and the beach is wide, cupped by low, vegetated sand dunes and a large walk-in cave on the

western edge. Day hikes into the valley offer waterfalls, freshwater swimming pools, and wild, tropical fruits. Though state camping permits are required, the valley often has a significant illegal crowd, which has strained park facilities and degraded much of its former peaceful solitude. Helicopter overflights are near-constant in good weather. **Amenities:** none. **Best for:** sunset; walking; solitude. ✉ *Trailhead starts at end of Rte. 560, 7 miles west of Hanalei* ⊕ *www.hawaiistateparks.org.*

★ Kee Beach
BEACH—SIGHT | Highway 560 on the North Shore literally dead-ends at this beach, pronounced "kay-eh." This is also the start of the famous Kalalau Trail and a culturally significant area to Native Hawaiians, who still use an ancient *heiau* dedicated to hula. (It's not appropriate to hang out on the grass platform or leave offerings there.) The setting is gorgeous, with Makana (a prominent peak that Hollywood dubbed "Bali Hai" in the blockbuster musical *South Pacific*) dramatically imposing itself on the lovely coastline and lots of lush tropical vegetation. The small beach is protected by a reef—except during high surf—creating a small sandy-bottom lagoon that's a popular snorkeling spot. There can be a strong current in winter. Beach-area amenities were greatly improved after repairs from flooding in 2018. There is now a mandatory permit system that limits guests and prevents overcrowding. The new parking area is 1/3 of a mile from the beach on a path partially on a boardwalk so be prepared to lug your beach gear. It's a great place to watch the sunset lighting up Napali Coast. **Amenities:** lifeguards; parking; showers; toilets. **Best for:** snorkeling; sunset; swimming; walking. ✉ *End of Rte. 560, 7 miles west of Hanalei.*

Lumahai Beach
BEACH—SIGHT | Famous as the beach where Nurse Nellie washed that man right out of her hair in *South Pacific,*

Lumahai's setting is picturesque, with a river and ironwood grove on the western end and stands of hala (pandanus) trees and black lava rock on the eastern side. In between is a long stretch of thick olivine-flecked sand that can be wide or narrow, depending on surf. It can be accessed in two places from the highway; one involves a steep hike from the road. The ocean can be very dangerous here, with a snapping shore break year-round and monster swells in the winter. The current can be strong near the river. Parking is very limited, along the road or in a rough dirt lot near the river. **Amenities:** none. **Best for:** solitude; sunset; walking. ✉ *On winding section of Rte. 560, near mile marker 5, Hanalei.*

🍽 Restaurants

Because of the North Shore's isolation, restaurants have enjoyed a captive audience of visitors who don't want to make the long, dark trek into Kapaa town for dinner. As a result, dining in this region has been characterized by expensive fare that isn't especially tasty, either. Fortunately, the situation is slowly improving as new restaurants open and others change hands or menus.

Still, dining on the North Shore can be pricier than other parts of the island, and it's not especially family friendly. Most of the restaurants are found either in Hanalei town or the Princeville resorts. Consequently, you'll encounter delightful mountain and ocean views, but just one restaurant with oceanfront dining.

Hanalei Gourmet
$$ | **AMERICAN** | This spot in Hanalei's restored old schoolhouse offers dolphin-safe tuna, low-sodium meats, fresh-baked breads, and homemade desserts as well as a casual atmosphere where both families and the sports-watching crowd can feel equally comfortable. Lunch and dinner menus feature sandwiches, burgers, hearty salads, a variety

Best Beaches

He says "to-mah-toe," and she says "to-may-toe." When it comes to beaches on Kauai, the meaning behind that axiom holds true: people are different. What rocks one person's world wreaks havoc for another's. Here are some additional tips on how to choose a beach that's right for you.

Best for Families

Lydgate State Park, East Side. The kid-designed playground, the protected swimming pools, and Kamalani Bridge guarantee you will not hear these words from your child: "Mom, I'm bored."

Poipu Beach Park, South Shore. The *keiki* (children's) pool and lifeguards make this a safe spot for kids. The near-perpetual sun isn't so bad, either.

Best Stand-Up Paddling

Anini Beach Park, North Shore. The reef and long stretch of beach give beginners a calm place to try stand-up paddling. You won't get pummeled by waves here.

Wailua Beach, East Side. On the East Side, the Wailua River bisects the beach and heads inland 2 miles, providing stand-up paddlers with a long and scenic stretch of water before they have to figure out how to turn around.

Best Surfing

Hanalei Bay Beach Park, North Shore. In winter, Hanalei Bay offers a range of breaks, from beginner to advanced. Surfing legends Laird Hamilton and the Irons Brothers grew up surfing the waters of Hanalei.

Waiohai Beach, South Shore. Surf instructors flock to this spot with their students for its gentle, near-shore break. Then, as students advance, they can paddle out a little farther to an intermediate break—if they dare.

Best Sunsets

Kee Beach, North Shore. Even in winter, when the sun sets in the south and out of view, you won't be disappointed here, because the "golden hour," as photographers call the time around sunset, paints Napali Coast with a warm gold light. Plan ahead and have your visitor permit at hand when you arrive. ⊕ *www.gohaena.com*

Polihale State Park, West Side. This due-west-facing beach may be tricky to get to, but it does offer the most unobstructed sunset views on the island. The fact that it's so remote means you won't have strangers in your photos, but you will have Niihau, the Forbidden Island. Also, you will want to depart right after sunset or risk getting spooked in the dark.

Best for Celeb Spotting

Haena Beach Park, North Shore. Behind those gated driveways and heavily foliaged yards that line this beach live—at least, part-time—some of the world's most celebrated music and movie moguls.

Hanalei Bay Beach Park, North Shore. We know we tout this beach often, but it deserves the praise. It's a mecca for everyone—regular joes, surfers, fishers, young people, old folks, locals, visitors, and, especially, the famous. You may also recognize Hanalei Bay from the movie *The Descendants*.

of pupus, and nightly specials of fresh local fish. **Known for:** friendly bar; consistently good food; fresh bread. $ *Average main: $25 ⊠ Hanalei Center, 5-5161 Kuhio Hwy., Hanalei ☎ 808/826–2524 ⊕ www.hanaleigourmet.com.*

Postcards Café

$$$ | AMERICAN | This plantation-cottage restaurant has a menu full of seafood but also offers additive-free vegetarian and vegan options. Top menu picks include taro fritters, scallops over squid-ink linguini, and Wagyu strip steak. **Known for:** meat-free menu; cozy dining room; historic setting. $ *Average main: $35 ⊠ 5-5075A Kuhio Hwy., Hanalei ☎ 808/826–1191 ⊕ postcardscafe.com* ☾ *No lunch.*

★ Restaurant Bar Acuda

$$$$ | TAPAS | This hip and pricey tapas bar is a top place in Hanalei in terms of flavor and creativity, with food that's often organic and consistently remarkable. The dining room is supercasual but chic, with a welcoming bar and a nice porch for outdoor dining. **Known for:** sophisticated cuisine; innovative specials; eclectic menu. $ *Average main: $40 ⊠ Hanalei Center, 5-5161 Kuhio Hwy., Hanalei ☎ 808/826–7081 ⊕ www.restaurantbaracuda.com.*

🛏 Hotels

The North Shore is mountainous and wet, which accounts for its rugged, lush landscape. Hanalei, a bay-side town in a broad valley, has a smattering of hotel rooms and numerous vacation rentals, many within walking distance of the beach. Prices tend to be high in this resort area. If you want to do extensive sightseeing on other parts of the island, be prepared for a long drive—one that's very dark at night.

Hanalei Colony Resort

$$$$ | RESORT | The only true beachfront resort on Kauai's North Shore, Hanalei Colony is a laid-back, go-barefoot kind of resort sandwiched between towering mountains and the sea. **Pros:** oceanfront setting; private, quiet property; well-maintained units with Hawaiian-style furnishings. **Cons:** weak cell-phone reception; damp in winter; isolated location. $ *Rooms from: $375 ⊠ 5-7130 Kuhio Hwy., Haena ☎ 808/826–6235, 800/628–3004 ⊕ www.hcr.com* ➟ *48 units* ❖ *No meals.*

Hanalei Inn

$ | RENTAL | If you're looking for lodgings that won't break the bank a block from gorgeous Hanalei Bay, look no further, as this is literally the only choice among the town's pricey vacation rentals. **Pros:** quick walk to beach, bus stop, and shops; full kitchen; coin-operated laundry on-site. **Cons:** strict cancellation policy; daytime traffic noise; older property. $ *Rooms from: $179 ⊠ 5-5468 Kuhio Hwy., Hanalei ☎ 808/826–9333, 888/773–4730 ⊕ www.hanaleiinn.net* ➟ *4 studios* ❖ *No meals.*

🍸 Nightlife

Hanalei Gourmet

BARS/PUBS | The sleepy North Shore stays awake—until 10:30, that is—each evening in this small, convivial deli and bar inside Hanalei's restored old school building. There's local live Hawaiian, jazz, rock, and folk music on Saturday and Sunday evening. ⊠ *Hanalei Center, 5-5161 Kuhio Hwy., Hanalei ☎ 808/826–2524 ⊕ www.hanaleigourmet.com.*

Tahiti Nui

BARS/PUBS | This venerable and funky institution in sleepy Hanalei still offers its famous luau at 5 on Wednesday evenings, although the bar is the big attraction. The spirits of locals and visitors alike are always high at this popular hangout, which features live nightly entertainment and Hawaiian slack-key guitar music on Friday evenings. It's open until 1 am on weekends. ⊠ *5-5134 Kuhio Hwy., Hanalei ☎ 808/826–6277 ⊕ www.thenui.com.*

🎭 Performing Arts

Hanalei Slack-Key Concerts

MUSIC | Relax to the instrumental music form created by Hawaiian *paniolo* (cowboys) in the early 1800s. Shows are Wednesday in Kapaa at All Saints Church and Tuesday at the Princeville Community Center. If you're looking for a scenic setting, head to Hale Halawai Ohana O Hanalei on Friday and Sunday; it's *mauka* (toward the mountains) down a dirt access road across from St. William's Catholic Church (Malolo Road) and then left down another dirt road. ✉ *5-5299 Kuhio Hwy., Hanalei* ☎ *808/826–1469* ⊕ *www.hawaiianslackkeyguitar.com* 💲 *From $10.*

🛍 Shopping

The North Shore has three main shopping areas, all in towns off the highway. Hanalei has two shopping centers directly across from each other, which offer more than you would expect in a remote, relaxed town.

Ching Young Village

SHOPPING CENTERS/MALLS | This popular shopping center has its roots in the Chinese immigrants who came to Hawaii in the early 19th century. Hanalei's only full-service grocery store is here along with a number of other shops useful to locals and visitors, such as a music shop selling ukulele and CDs, jewelry stores, art galleries, a surf shop, variety store, and several smallish restaurants. ✉ *5-5190 Kuhio Hwy., near mile marker 2, Hanalei* ⊕ *chingyoungvillage.com.*

Hanalei Center

SHOPPING CENTERS/MALLS | Once an old Hanalei schoolhouse, the Hanalei Center is now a bevy of boutiques and restaurants. You can dig through '40s and '50s vintage memorabilia, find Polynesian artifacts, or search for that unusual gift. Buy beach gear as well as island wear and women's clothing. Find a range of fine

jewelry and paper art jewelry. There are a full-service salon and a yoga studio in the two-story modern addition to the center, which also houses a small natural foods grocery. ✉ *5-5161 Kuhio Hwy., near mile marker 2, Hanalei* ☎ *808/826–7677.*

Princeville, Kilauea, and Around

Princeville is 4 miles northeast of Hanalei; Kilauea is 5 miles east of Princeville.

Built on a bluff offering gorgeous sea and mountain vistas, including Hanalei Bay, Princeville is the creation of a 1970s resort development. The area is anchored by a few large hotels, world-class golf courses, and lots of condos and time-shares.

Five miles down Route 56, a former plantation town, Kilauea maintains its rural flavor in the midst of unrelenting gentrification encroaching all around it. Especially noteworthy are its historic lava-rock buildings, including **Christ Memorial Episcopal Church** on Kolo Road and, on Keneke and Kilauea Road (commonly known as Lighthouse Road), the Kong Lung Company, which is now an expensive shop.

There is only one main road through the Princeville resort area, so maneuvering a car here can be a nightmare. If you're trying to find a smaller lodging unit, be sure to get specific driving directions. Parking is available at the Princeville Shopping Center at the entrance to the resort. Kilauea is about 5 miles east on Route 56. There's a public parking lot in the town center as well as parking at the end of Kilauea Road for access to the lighthouse.

Kilauea Point Lighthouse is located in the Kilauea Point National Wildlife Refuge, a sanctuary for seabirds.

⊙ Sights

★ Kilauea Point National Wildlife Refuge and Kilauea Lighthouse

LIGHTHOUSE | A beacon for sea traffic since it was built in 1913, this National Historic Landmark celebrated its centennial in 2013 and has the largest clamshell lens of any lighthouse in the world. It's within a national wildlife refuge, where thousands of seabirds soar on the trade winds and nest on the steep ocean cliffs. It's well worth the modest entry fee to see endangered nene geese, white- and red-tailed tropic birds, and more (all identifiable by educational signboards) as well as native plants, dolphins, humpback whales, huge winter surf, and gorgeous views of the North Shore. The gift shop has a great selection of books about the island's natural history and an array of unique merchandise, with all proceeds benefiting education and preservation efforts. ⊠ *Kilauea Lighthouse Rd., Kilauea* ☎ *808/828–0384* ⊕ *www.kilaueapoint. org, www.fws.gov/kilaueapoint* ⊠ *$10, under 15 free.*

★ Na Aina Kai Botanical Gardens

GARDEN | Joyce and Ed Doty's love for plants and art spans 240 acres and includes many different gardens, a hardwood plantation, an *ahupuaa* (a Hawaiian land division), a re-created Navajo compound, an Athabascan village, a Japanese teahouse, a hedge maze, a waterfall, and access to a sandy beach. Throughout are more than 200 bronze sculptures, one of the nation's largest collections. One popular feature is a children's garden with a 16-foot-tall Jack and the Beanstalk bronze sculpture, gecko maze, tree house, kid-size train, and, of course, a tropical jungle. Located in a residential neighborhood and hoping to maintain good neighborly relations, the gardens, a nonprofit organization, limits tours (guided only). Tour lengths vary widely, from 1½ to 5 hours. Reservations are required. ⊠ *4101 Wailapa Rd., Kilauea* ☎ *808/828–0525* ⊕ *www.naainakai.org* ⊠ *From $35.*

Queen's Bath

HOT SPRINGS | A tropical path tucked away in a North Shore neighborhood winds its way down to the oceanfront, where a large tide pool has been carved into the dark lava rock creating nature's version of an infinity pool. It's a pretty sight to see when the surf is calm, but we do not recommend descending all the way down (it takes some dexterity and reef shoes to get there, and the path can be muddy and slippery) or diving into this pool, as big surf can be dangerous. ⚠ **Be careful: October through May brings big surf, and people have been swept off the rocks and have drowned. If you choose to go, always heed warning signs.** ✉ *Kapiolani Rd., Princeville.*

⓵ Beaches

Anini Beach Park

BEACH—SIGHT | FAMILY | A great family park, Anini features one of the longest and widest fringing reefs in all Hawaii, creating a shallow lagoon that is good for snorkeling and kids splashing about. It is safe except when surf is raging outside the reef and strong currents are created. A rip current exists between the two reefs where the boats enter and exit the beach ramp, so avoid swimming there. The entire reef follows the shoreline for some 2 miles and extends 1,600 feet offshore at its widest point. There's a narrow ribbon of sandy beach and lots of grass and shade, as well as a county campground at the western end and a small boat ramp. **Amenities:** lifeguard; parking; showers; toilets. **Best for:** sunrise; swimming; walking. ✉ *Anini Rd., off Rte. 56, Princeville.*

Kalihiwai Beach

BEACH—SIGHT | A winding road leads down a cliff face to picture-perfect Kalihiwai Beach, which fronts a bay of the same name. It's another one of those drive-up beaches, so it's very accessible. Most people park under the grove of ironwood trees, near the stream, where young kids like to splash and older kids like to body board. Though do beware: the stream carries leptospirosis, a potentially lethal bacteria that can enter through open cuts. In winter months, beware of a treacherous shore break. Summer is the only truly safe time to swim. There's a local-favorite winter surf spot off the eastern edge of the beach, for advanced surfers only. The toilets here are the portable kind, and there are no showers. **Amenities:** parking; toilets. **Best for:** solitude; surfing; swimming; walking. ✉ *Kalihiwai Rd., on Kilauea side of Kalihiwai Bridge, Kilauea.*

Kauapea Beach (*Secret Beach*)

BEACH—SIGHT | This beach was relatively unknown—except by local fishermen, of course—for a long time, hence the common reference to it as "Secret Beach." You'll understand why once you stand on the coarse white sands of Kauapea and see the solid wall of rock that runs the length of the beach, making it fairly inaccessible. For the hardy, there is a steep hike down the western end. From there, you can walk for a long way in either direction in summer. During winter, big swells cut off access to sections of the beach. You may witness dolphins just offshore, and it's a great place to see seabirds, as the Kilauea Point National Wildlife Refuge and its historic lighthouse lie at the eastern end. Nudity is not uncommon, though it is illegal in Hawaii. A consistent onshore break makes swimming here typically very dangerous. On big-surf days, don't go near the shoreline. **Amenities:** parking. **Best for:** solitude; sunrise; walking. ✉ *Kalihiwai Rd., just past turnoff for Kilauea, Kilauea.*

ⓤ Restaurants

A rough couple of years have diminished the restaurant selection in the Princeville and Kilauea areas, starting in 2018 with massive flooding and continuing through 2020 with widespread closures due to COVID-19. Restaurants at the former St.

Regis, under renovation to become a 1 Hotel, have also closed. Though it may not offer what it once did, this area still has a number of good spots—after all, people need to eat no matter what. You'll find everything from inexpensive holes-in-the-wall to relatively sophisticated and expensive establishments.

Kilauea Bakery and Pau Hana Pizza

$$ | AMERICAN | FAMILY | Open from 6:30 am, the bakery serves coffee drinks, delicious fresh pastries, bagels, and breads in the morning. Late risers beware: breads and pastries sell out quickly. **Known for:** its starter of Hawaiian sourdough made with guava; specialty pizzas topped with eclectic ingredients; fresh chocolate chip cookies made in-house daily. $ *Average main: $20* ⊠ *Kong Lung Center, 2484 Keneke St., Kilauea* ☎ *808/828–2020* ⊕ *www.kilaueabakery. com.*

Nanea Restaurant and Bar

$$$ | HAWAIIAN | FAMILY | This is the signature restaurant of the Westin Princeville Ocean Resort Villas, and its casual, open-air seating is the perfect compliment to an island-style menu that is sure to please a wide range of diners. The grilled rib eye is served with bacon and sour cream mashed potatoes, while the half-chicken—smoked kalua style—is accompanied by Molokai sweet potatoes. **Known for:** kids eat free; inventive cocktails; local ingredients. $ *Average main: $35* ⊠ *Westin Princeville Ocean Resort Villas, 3838 Wyllie Rd., Princeville* ☎ *808/827–8808* ⊕ *www.westinprinceville.com.*

North Shore Variety Store

$ | AMERICAN | Attached to a gas station and small items store, this classic hole-in-the-wall has the best deals for a pick-up lunch on the North Shore. Darron's local-beef burgers have a loyal following, and you may have to get in line for his lunch-time favorite, chili-pepper chicken. **Known for:** chili-pepper chicken; burgers; food truck at Anini Beach on weekdays.

$ *Average main: $8* ⊠ *Princeville Shopping Center, 5-4280 Kuhio Hwy., Princeville* ☎ *808/826–7992.*

🛏 Hotels

Posh resorts and condominiums await you at Princeville, a community with dreamy views, excellent golf courses, and lovely sunsets. It maintains the lion's share of North Shore accommodations—primarily luxury hotel rooms and condos built on a plateau overlooking the sea.

Hanalei Bay Resort

$$ | RESORT | FAMILY | The nicest feature of this condominium resort overlooking Hanalei Bay and Napali Coast is its upper-level pool, with authentic lava-rock waterfalls, an open-air hot tub, and a kid-friendly sand beach. **Pros:** beautiful views; pool, tennis courts, and fitness center on property; lively lounge. **Cons:** steep walkways; long walk to beach. $ *Rooms from: $215* ⊠ *5380 Honoiki Rd., Princeville* ☎ *808/826–6522, 877/507–1428* ⊕ *www.hanaleibayresort. com* ⇌ *134 units* ⟨🍽⟩ *No meals.*

★ Westin Princeville Ocean Resort Villas

$$$$ | RESORT | FAMILY | Spread out over 18½ acres on a bluff above Anini Beach, this Westin property marries the comforts of spacious condominium living with the top-notch service and amenities of a luxurious hotel resort. **Pros:** on-site minimarket; ocean views; kids' program. **Cons:** path to the nearby beach is a steep six- to seven-minute walk; whirlpool tub is small; units can be far from parking. $ *Rooms from: $356* ⊠ *3838 Wyllie Rd., Princeville* ☎ *808/827–8700* ⊕ *www. westinprinceville.com* ⇌ *366 units* ⟨🍽⟩ *No meals.*

🍸 Nightlife

★ Happy Talk Lounge

BARS/PUBS | Want to sip an umbrella cocktail while you gaze at the original Bali Hai? Open on two sides, Happy Talk Lounge offers breezy views across Hanalei Bay to plush emerald mountains. If you think the scene looks familiar, maybe you've seen the classic movie *South Pacific*, filmed here. The Hollywood version of Bali Hai is actually Kauai's Mount Makana. Order a tropical cocktail and *pupu* (Hawaiian hors d'oeuvres) and enjoy a truly enchanting evening as the sun sets over the sparkling waters. ■TIP→ **Nearby Tunnels Beach (aka Haena Beach and Makua) is often called Nurses' Beach, where Mitzi Gaynor sang about washing that man right outta her hair; Hanalei Bay is where Bloody Mary sang "Bali Hai."** ✉ *Hanalei Bay Resort, 5380 Honoiki Rd., Princeville* ☎ *808/431–4084* ⊕ *www.happytalk-lounge.com.*

🛍 Shopping

Princeville Shopping Center is a bustling little mix of businesses, necessities, and some unique, often pricey, shops. Kilauea is a bit more spread out and offers a charming, laid-back shopping scene with a neighborhood feel.

Kong Lung Co
GIFTS/SOUVENIRS | Sometimes called the Gump's of Kauai, this store sells elegant clothing, glassware, books, gifts, and artwork—all very lovely and expensive. The shop is housed in a beautiful 1892 stone building in the heart of Kilauea. It's the showpiece of the pretty little Kong Lung Center, where everything from handmade soaps to hammocks can be found. A great bakery and pizzeria round out the offerings, along with an exhibit of historical photos. ✉ *2484 Keneke St., Kilauea* ☎ *808/828–1822* ⊕ *www.konglungkauai.com.*

Princeville Shopping Center
SHOPPING CENTERS/MALLS | The big draws at this small center are a full-service grocery store and a hardware store, but there's also a fun toy store, a bar, a mailing service, a very nice sandal boutique, women's clothing, and an ice-cream shop. This is also the last stop for gas and banking when you're heading to the North Shore. ✉ *5-4280 Kuhio Hwy., near mile marker 28, Princeville* ☎ *808/826–9497* ⊕ *www.princevillecenter.com.*

Napali Coast

Napali Coast is considered the jewel of Kauai, and for all its greenery, it would surely be an emerald. After seeing the coast, many are at a loss for words, because its beauty is so overwhelming. Others resort to poetry. Pulitzer Prize–winning poet W. S. Merwin wrote a book-length poem, *The Folding Cliffs*, based on a true story set in Napali. *Napali* means "the cliffs," and while it sounds like a simple name, it's quite an apt description. The coastline is cut by a series of small valleys, like fault lines, running to the interior, with the resulting cliffs seeming to bend back on themselves like an accordion-folded fan made of green velvet. More than 5 million years old, these sea cliffs rise thousands of feet above the Pacific, and every shade of green is represented in the vegetation that blankets their lush peaks and folds. At their base there are caves, secluded beaches, and waterfalls to explore.

Let's put this in perspective: even if you had only one day on Kauai, we'd still recommend heading northwest to the Napali Coast. Once you're there, you'll soon realize why no road traverses this series of folding-fan cliffs. That leaves three ways to experience the coastline—by air, by water, or on foot. We recommend all three, in this order: air, water, foot. Each one gets progressively more sensory.(⇨ *See the Napali feature in the chapter.*) A helicopter tour is your best bet if you're strapped for time. We recommend Jack Harter Helicopters or Safari Helicopters. Boat tours are great for family fun; and hiking, of course, is the most budget-friendly option.

Whatever way you choose to visit Napali, you might want to keep this awe-inspiring fact in mind: at one time, thousands of Hawaiians lived self-sufficiently in these valleys.

Napali Coast runs 15 miles from Kee Beach, one of Kauai's more popular snorkeling spots, on the island's North Shore to Polihale State Park, the longest stretch of beach in the state, on the West Side of the island.

How do you explore this gorgeous stretch of coastline? You can't drive to it, through it, or around it. You can't see Napali from a scenic lookout. You can't even take a mule ride to it. The only way to experience its magic is from the sky, the ocean, or the trail. The Kalalau Trail can be hiked from the "end of the road" at Kee Beach where the trailhead begins in Haena State Park at the northwest end of Kuhio Highway (Route 56). There's no need to hike the entire 11 miles to get a full experience, especially if you just hike the first 2 miles into Hanakapiai Beach and another 2 miles up that valley.

⊛ Beaches

Kee Beach State Park
BEACH—SIGHT | This stunning beach marks the start of majestic Napali Coast. The 11-mile **Kalalau Trail** begins near the parking lot, drawing day hikers and backpackers. Permits are required to take the entire trek, but day-trippers can head 2 miles into Hanakapiai Beach for a dollar. Another path leads from the sand to a stone hula platform dedicated to Laka, the goddess of hula, which has been in use since ancient times. This is a sacred site that should be approached with respect; it's inappropriate for visitors to leave offerings at the altar, which is tended by students in a local hula *halau* (school). Local etiquette suggests observing from a distance. Most folks head straight for the sandy beach and its dreamy lagoon, which is great for snorkeling when the sea is calm. ⊠ *Western end of Rte. 560, Haena.*

The East Side

Location, location, location. The East Side, encompassing Lihue, Wailua, and Kapaa, is a good centralized home base if you want to see and do it all. It. This is one of the few resort areas on Kauai where you can actually walk to the beach, restaurants, and stores from your condo, hotel, or vacation-rental unit. It's not only convenient, but comparatively cheap. You pay less for lodging, meals, services, merchandise, and gas here—mainly because much of the coral-reef coastline isn't as ideal as the sandy-bottom bays that front the fancy resorts. We think the shoreline is just fine. There are pockets in the reef to swim in, and the coast is uncrowded and boasts spectacular views. All in all, it's a good choice for families because the prices are right, and there's plenty to keep everyone happy and occupied.

The East Side is known as the Coconut Coast, as there was once a coconut plantation where today's aptly named Coconut Marketplace is located. A small grove still exists on both sides of the highway. *Mauka,* a fenced herd of goats keeps the grass tended; on the *makai* side, you can walk through the grove, although it's best not to walk directly under the trees—falling coconuts can be dangerous. Lihue is the county seat, and the whole East Side is the island's center of commerce, so early-morning and late-afternoon drive times can get very congested. (Because there's only one main road, if there's a serious traffic accident the entire roadway may be closed, with no way around. Not to worry; it's a rarity.)

Kapaa and Wailua

Kapaa is 16 miles southeast of Kilauea; Wailua is 3 miles southwest of Kapaa.

Old Town Kapaa was once a sugar and pineapple plantation town, which is no surprise—most of the larger towns on Kauai once were. Old Town Kapaa is made up of a collection of wooden-front shops, some built by plantation workers and still run by their progeny today. Kapaa houses two of the biggest grocery stores on the island, side by side: Foodland and Safeway. It also offers plenty of dining options for breakfast, lunch, and dinner, and gift shopping. If the timing is right, plan to cruise the town on the first Saturday evening of each month when the bands are playing and the town's wares are on display. To the south, Wailua comprises a few restaurants and shops, a few mid-range resorts along the coastline, and a local housing community *mauka* (toward the mountains).

Turn to the right out of the airport at Lihue for the road to Wailua. Careful, though—the zone between Lihue and Wailua has been the site of many car accidents. Two bridges—under which the very culturally significant Wailua River gently flows—mark the beginning of Wailua. It quickly blends into Kapaa; there's no real demarcation. Pay attention, and drive carefully, always knowing where you are going and when to turn off.

👁 Sights

★ Ke Ala Hele Makalae Path

TRAIL | Running from the southern end of Lydgate Park to Donkey Beach, between Kealia and Anahola, this seaside path is a favorite of visitors and locals alike. Sea breezes, gorgeous ocean views, smooth pavement, and friendly smiles from everyone as they bike, walk, skate, and run can be seen on the trail. The path has many entry points, and you'll have your choice of bike shops just off the trail.

✉ *1121 Moanakai Rd., Kapaa* ⊕ *www. kauaipath.org/kauaicoastalpath.*

Opaekaa Falls

BODY OF WATER | FAMILY | The mighty Wailua River produces many dramatic waterfalls, and Opaekaa (pronounced "oh-pie-kah-ah") is one of the best. It plunges hundreds of feet to the pool below and can be easily viewed from a scenic overlook with ample parking. Opaekaa means "rolling shrimp," which refers to tasty native crustaceans that were once so abundant they could be seen tumbling in the falls. Do not attempt to hike down to the pool. ■**TIP→ Just before reaching the parking area for the waterfall, turn left into a scenic pullout for great views of the Wailua River valley and its march to the sea.** ✉ *Kuamoo Rd., Wailua (Kauai County)* ✛ *From Rte. 56, turn mauka onto Kuamoo Rd. and drive 1½ miles.*

★ Poliahu Heiau

ARCHAEOLOGICAL SITE | Storyboards near this ancient *heiau* (sacred site) recount the significance of the many sacred structures found along the Wailua River. It's unknown exactly how the ancient Hawaiians used Poliahu Heiau—one of the largest pre-Christian temples on the island—but legend says it was built by the Menehune because of the unusual stonework found in its walled enclosures. From this site, drive downhill toward the ocean to *pohaku hanau,* a two-piece birthing stone said to confer special blessings on all children born there, and *pohaku piko,* whose crevices were a repository for umbilical cords left by parents seeking a clue to their child's destiny, which reportedly was foretold by how the cord fared in the rock. Some Hawaiians feel these sacred stones shouldn't be viewed as tourist attractions, so always treat them with respect. Never stand or sit on the rocks or leave any offerings. ✉ *Rte. 580, Kuamoo Rd., Wailua (Kauai County).*

Continued on page 468

NAPALI COAST: EMERALD QUEEN OF KAUAI

If you're coming to Kauai, Napali ("the cliffs" in Hawaiian) is a major must see. More than 5 million years old, these sea cliffs rise thousands of feet above the Pacific, and every shade of green is represented in the vegetation that blankets their lush peaks and folds. At their base, there are caves, secluded beaches, and waterfalls to explore.

The big question is how to explore this gorgeous stretch of coastline. You can't drive to it, through it, or around it. You can't see Napali from a scenic lookout. You can't even take a mule ride to it. The only way to experience its magic is from the sky, the ocean, or the trail.

FROM THE SKY

If you've booked a helicopter tour of Napali, you might start wondering what you've gotten yourself into on the way to the airport. Will it feel like being on a small airplane? Will there be turbulence? Will it be worth all the money you just plunked down?

Your concerns will be assuaged on the helipad, once you see the faces of those who have just returned from their journey: Everyone looks totally blissed out. And now it's your turn.

Climb on board, strap on your headphones, and the next thing you know the helicopter gently lifts up, hovers for a moment, and floats away like a spider on the wind—no roaring engines, no rumbling down a runway. If you've chosen a flight with music, you'll feel as if you're inside your very own IMAX movie.

Pinch yourself if you must, because this is the real thing. Your pilot shares history, legend, and lore. If you miss something, speak up: pilots love to show off their island knowledge. You may snap a few pictures (not too many or you'll miss the eyes-on experience!), nudge a friend or spouse, and point at a whale breeching in the ocean, but mostly you stare, mouth agape. There is simply no other way to take in the immensity and greatness of Napali but from the air.

(left) The Napali Coast is a breathtaking stretch of Kauai coastline lined by sea cliffs rising thousands of feet into the sky. (bottom) Helicopter tour over Napali Coast

GOOD TO KNOW

Helicopter companies depart from the north, east, and west sides of the island. Most are based in Lihue, near the airport.

If you want more adventure—and air—choose one of the helicopter companies that flies with the doors off.

Some companies offer flights without music. Know the experience you want ahead of time. Some even sell a DVD of your flight, so you don't have to worry about taking pictures.

Wintertime rain grounds some flights; plan your trip early in your stay in case the flight gets rescheduled.

IS THIS FOR ME?

Taking a helicopter trip is the most expensive way to see Napali—as much as $300 for an hour-long tour.

Claustrophobic? Choose a boat tour or hike. It's a tight squeeze in the helicopter, especially in one of the middle seats.

Short on time? Taking a helicopter tour is a great way to see the island.

WHAT YOU MIGHT SEE

■ Nualolo Kai (an ancient Hawaiian fishing village) with its fringed reef

■ The 300-foot Hanakapiai Falls

■ A massive sea arch formed in the rock by erosion

■ The 11-mile Kalalau Trail threading its way along the coast

■ The amazing striations of aa and pahoehoe lava flows that helped push Kauai above the sea

FROM THE OCEAN

Napali from the ocean is two treats in one: spend a good part of the day on (or in) the water, and gaze up at majestic green sea cliffs rising thousands of feet above your head.

There are three ways to see it: a mellow pleasure-cruise catamaran allows you to kick back and sip a mai tai; an adventurous raft (Zodiac) tour will take you inside sea caves under waterfalls, and give you the option of snorkeling; and a daylong outing in a kayak is possible in the summer.

Any way you travel, you'll breathe ocean air, feel spray on your face, and see pods of spinner dolphins, green sea turtles, flying fish, and, if you're lucky, a rare Hawaiian monk seal.

Napali stretches from Kee Beach in the north to Polihale beach on the West Side. You'll be heading towards the lush Hanakapiai Valley, where within a few minutes, you'll see caves and waterfalls galore. About halfway down the coast just after the Kalalau Trail ends, you'll come to an immense arch—formed where the sea eroded the less dense basaltic rock—and a thundering 50-foot waterfall. And as the island curves near Nualolo State Park, you'll begin to notice less vegetation and more rocky outcroppings.

(left and top right) Kayaking on Napali Coast
(bottom right) Dolphin on Napali Coast

GOOD TO KNOW

If you want to snorkel, choose a morning rather than an afternoon tour—preferably during a summer visit—when seas are calmer.

If you're on a budget, choose a non-snorkeling tour.

If you want to see whales, take any tour, but be sure to plan your vacation for December through March.

You can only embark from the North Shore in summer. If you're staying on the South Shore, it might not be worth your time to drive to the north, so head to the West Side.

IS THIS FOR ME?

Boat tours are several hours long, so if you have only a short time on Kauai, a helicopter tour is a better alternative.

Even on a small boat, you won't get the individual attention and exclusivity of a helicopter tour.

Prone to seasickness? A large boat can be surprisingly rocky, so be prepared. Afternoon trips are rougher because the winds pick up.

WHAT YOU MIGHT SEE

■ Hawaii's state fish—the humuhumunukunukuapuaa—otherwise known as the reef triggerfish

■ Waiahuakua Sea Cave, with a waterfall coming through its roof

■ Tons of marine life, including dolphins, green sea turtles, flying fish, and humpback whales, especially in February and March

■ Waterfalls—especially if your trip is after a heavy rain

FROM THE TRAIL

If you want to be one with Napali—feeling the soft red earth beneath your feet, picnicking on the beaches, and touching the lush vegetation—hiking the Kalalau Trail is the way to do it.

Most people hike only the first 2 miles of the 11-mile trail and turn around at Hanakapiai. This 4-mile round-trip hike takes three to four hours. It starts at sea level and doesn't waste any time gaining elevation. (Take heart—the uphill lasts only a mile and tops out at 400 feet; then it's downhill all the way.) At the half-mile point, the trail curves west and the folds of Napali Coast unfurl.

Along the way you might share the trail with feral goats and wild pigs. Some of the vegetation is native; much is introduced.

After the 1-mile mark the trail begins its drop into Hanakapiai. You'll pass a couple of streams of water trickling across the trail, and maybe some banana, ginger, the native uluhe fern, and the Hawaiian ti plant. Finally the trail swings around the eastern ridge of Hanakapiai for your first glimpse of the valley and then switchbacks down the mountain. You'll have to boulder-hop across the stream to reach the beach. If you like, you can take a 4-mile, round-trip fairly strenuous side trip from this point to the gorgeous Hanakapiai Falls.

(left) Awaawapuhi mountain biker on razor-edge ridge
(top right) Feral goats in Kalalau Valley
(bottom right) Napali Coast

GOOD TO KNOW

Wear comfortable, amphibious shoes. Unless your feet require extra support, wear a self-bailing sort of shoe (for stream crossings) that doesn't mind mud. Don't wear heavy, waterproof hiking boots.

During winter the trail is often muddy, so be extra careful; sometimes it's completely inaccessible.

Don't hike after heavy rain—flash floods are common.

If you plan to hike the entire 11-mile trail (most people do the shorter hike described at left) you'll need a permit to go past Hanakapiai.

IS THIS FOR ME?

Of all the ways to see Napali (with the exception of kayaking the coast), this is the most active. You need to be in decent shape to hit the trail.

If you're vacationing in winter, this hike might not be an option due to flooding—whereas you can take a helicopter year-round.

WHAT YOU MIGHT SEE

■ Big dramatic surf right below your feet

■ Amazing vistas of the cool blue Pacific

■ The spectacular Hanakapiai Falls; if you have a permit don't miss Hanakoa Falls, less than 1/2 mile off the trail

■ Wildlife, including goats and pigs

■ Zany-looking hala trees, with aerial roots and long, skinny serrated leaves known as lau hala. Early Hawaiians used them to make mats, baskets, and canoe sails.

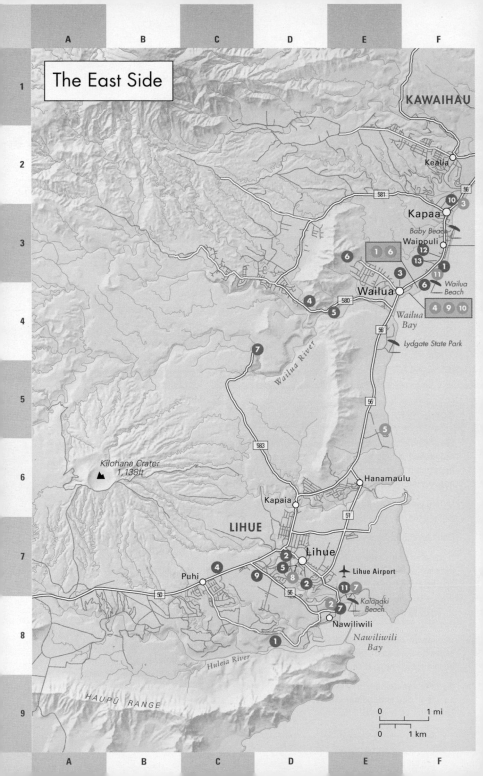

Kealia Beach

PACIFIC OCEAN

KEY

1 *Exploring Sights*

1 *Restaurants*

1 *Hotels*

Sleeping Giant

MOUNTAIN—SIGHT | Although its true name is Nounou, this landmark mountain ridge is better known as the Sleeping Giant because of its resemblance to a very large man sleeping on his back. Legends differ on whether the giant is Puni, who was accidentally killed by rocks launched at invading canoes by the Menehune, or Nunui, a gentle creature who has not yet awakened from the nap he took centuries ago after building a massive temple and enjoying a big feast. ⊠ *Rte. 56, Kapaa* ✛ *About 1 mile north of Wailua River.*

★ Wailua Falls

BODY OF WATER | FAMILY | You may recognize this impressive cascade from the opening sequences of the *Fantasy Island* television series. Kauai has plenty of noteworthy waterfalls, but this one is especially gorgeous, easy to find, and easy to photograph. To reach it, drive north from Lihue following Maalo Road in Hanamaulu, then travel uphill for 3 miles. ⊠ *Maalo Rd., off Rte. 580, Lihue.*

🏖 Beaches

The East Side of the island is considered the "windward" side, a term you'll often hear in weather forecasts. It simply means the side of the island receiving onshore winds. The wind helps break down rock into sand, so there are plenty of beaches here. Unfortunately, only a few of those beaches are protected, so many are not ideal for beginning ocean goers, though they are perfect for long sunrise ambles. On superwindy days, kiteboarders sail along the east shore, sometimes jumping waves and performing acrobatic maneuvers in the air.

Baby Beach

BEACH—SIGHT | FAMILY | There aren't many safe swimming beaches on Kauai's East Side; however, this one usually ranks highly with parents because there's a narrow, lagoonlike area between the beach and the near-shore reef perfect for small children. In winter, watch for east and northeast swells that would make this not such a safe option. There are no beach facilities—no lifeguards—so watch your babies. There is an old-time shower spigot (cold water only) along the roadside available to rinse off the salt water. **Amenities:** parking; showers. **Best for:** sunrise; swimming. ⊠ *Moanakai Rd., Kapaa.*

Kealia Beach

BEACH—SIGHT | A half mile long and adjacent to the highway heading north out of Kapaa, Kealia Beach attracts body boarders and surfers year-round. It's a favorite with locals and visitors alike. Kealia is not generally a great beach for swimming, but it's a place to sunbathe and enjoy the beach scene. The safest area to swim is at the far north end of the beach, protected by a lava rock sea wall. The waters are often rough and the waves crumbly due to an onshore break (no protecting reef) and northeasterly trade winds. A scenic lookout on the southern end, accessed off the highway, is a superb location for saluting the morning sunrise or spotting whales during winter. A level, paved section of the Ke Maka Hele Makalae bike path with small, covered pavilions runs along the coastline here and is very popular for walking and biking. **Amenities:** lifeguard; parking; showers; toilets. **Best for:** sunrise; surfing; swimming; walking. ⊠ *Rte. 56, at mile marker 10, Kealia.*

Lydgate State Park

BEACH—SIGHT | FAMILY | This is by far the best family beach park on Kauai. The waters off the beach are protected by a hand-built breakwater, creating two boulder-enclosed saltwater pools for safe swimming and snorkeling most of the year. Heavy rains upriver do occasionally deposit driftwood, clogging the pools. The smaller of the two pools is perfect for *keiki* (children). Behind the beach is Kamalani Playground; children of all ages—that includes you—enjoy the

Did You Know?

Wailua Falls is best known for appearing in the opening credits of *Fantasy Island*.

swings, lava-tube slides, tree house, and open field. Picnic tables abound in the park, and pavilions for day use and overnight camping are available by permit. The Kamalani Kai Bridge is a second playground, south of the original. (The two are united by the Ke Ala Hele Makalae bike and pedestrian coastal path.) ■**TIP→ This park system is perennially popular; the quietest times to visit are early mornings and weekdays.** **Amenities:** lifeguards; parking; showers; toilets. **Best for:** partiers; sunrise; swimming; walking. ✉ *Leho Dr., just south of Wailua River, Wailua (Kauai County).*

🍴 Restaurants

Because the East Side is the island's largest population center, it makes sense that it should boast a wide selection of restaurants. It's also a good place to get both cheaper meals and the local-style cuisine that residents favor. In recent years, the most affordable, hip new eateries on the island have opened in Kapaa. Unlike the resort-dominated South and North Shores, Kapaa is local, fun, and eclectic, with food trucks on the side of the road, vegetarian venues, and bars serving up artful appetizers. Diversity is the key to this area; there is something for everyone, especially those on a budget.

Bull Shed

$$$ | **STEAKHOUSE** | The A-frame structure makes this popular restaurant look distinctly rustic from the outside, but inside, light colors and a full wall of glass highlight an ocean view that is one of the best on Kauai. The food is simple, but they know how to do surf and turf. **Known for:** views of the surf crashing on the rocks; unlimited salad bar; quiet bar. [$] *Average main: $35* ✉ *796 Kuhio Hwy.* ☎ *808/822–3791* 🌐 *www.bullshedrestaurant.com* 🕒 *No lunch.*

Eat Healthy Kauai

$$ | **VEGETARIAN** | A restored plantation cottage surrounded by tropical foliage is the casual setting for this island café. The menu emphasizes local and organic products, with many vegan, vegetarian, and gluten-free options including nori wraps and tofu-based entrées. **Known for:** outdoor seating in the vine-covered garden; delicious food with healthy ingredients; smoothies like Chocolate Coffee Kiss and I Heart Blueberries. [$] *Average main: $24* ✉ *4-369 Kuhio Hwy., Wailua (Kauai County)* ☎ *808/822–7990* 🌐 *eathealthykauai.com* 🕒 *No dinner Sun. and Mon.*

★ Hukilau Lanai

$$ | **AMERICAN** | Relying heavily on super-fresh island fish and local meats and produce, this restaurant offers quality food that is competently and creatively prepared. The nightly fish specials—served grilled, steamed, or sautéed with succulent sauces—shine here. **Known for:** nightly fish specials; gluten-free options; delicious desserts. [$] *Average main: $25* ✉ *Kauai Coast Resort, Coconut Marketplace, 520 Aleka Loop, Wailua (Kauai County)* ☎ *808/822–0600* 🌐 *www.hukilaukauai.com* 🕒 *Closed Mon.*

★ JO2 Restaurant

$$$ | **ECLECTIC** | The creation of Jean-Marie Josselin, the renowned chef who brought Hawaii regional cuisine to Kauai in 1990, reflects his growth as a chef. The food is very imaginative, with its French, Japanese, and Islands influences, and it's served with flair in a chic yet casual dining room that's tucked away in a nondescript strip mall. **Known for:** the $35 prix fixe 5–6 pm; inventive cuisine; excellent service. [$] *Average main: $35* ✉ *4-971 Kuhio Hwy., Kapaa* ☎ *808/212–1627* 🌐 *www.jotwo.com.*

Kountry Kitchen

$ | **AMERICAN** | **FAMILY** | If you like a hearty breakfast, try this family-friendly restaurant with its cozy, greasy-spoon atmosphere and friendly service; it's a great spot for omelets, banana pancakes, waffles, and eggs Benedict in two sizes. Lunch selections include sandwiches, burgers, and *loco mocos* (a popular local rice, beef, gravy, and eggs concoction). **Known for:** all day breakfast; takeout options; hearty portions. $ *Average main: $14* ✉ *1485 Kuhio Hwy., Kapaa* ☎ *808/822–3511* ⊕ *www.kountrystyle-kitchen.com* ◷ *No dinner.*

Lemongrass Grill

$$ | **ASIAN FUSION** | The inside of Kapaa's Lemongrass Grill may remind you of a Pacific Rim–theme rustic tavern, with its stained wood interior, numerous paintings and carvings, and eclectic Asian-influenced menu. There's something for everybody here: salads, poultry, steaks and ribs, vegetarian fare, and, of course, a wide selection of seafood, all with an island flair. **Known for:** curries and satays; live acoustic music; fresh fish. $ *Average main: $25* ✉ *4-871 Kuhio Hwy., Kapaa* ☎ *808/821–2888* ⊕ *www.lemongrassha-waii.com* ◷ *No lunch.*

Shivalik Indian Cuisine

$ | **INDIAN** | This eatery provides a refreshing alternative to the typical surf-and-turf offerings at most of Kauai's restaurants. Boasting no particular Indian regional style, this small-plaza hideaway turns out delectable biryani and tandoori, light and flavorful naan, many vegetarian items, as well as curries and chicken and lamb dishes. **Known for:** Wednesday and Friday night all-you-can-eat buffet; tandoor oven; extensive menu. $ *Average main: $17* ✉ *4-771 Kuhio Hwy., Wailua (Kauai County)* ☎ *808/821–2333* ⊕ *www.shivalikindi-ancuisines.com* ◷ *Closed Tues.*

Tiki Tacos

$ | **MEXICAN** | Tiki Tacos is a notch above most Kauai taco joints, with excellent authentic Mexican food at reasonable prices. The meals are made from quality ingredients, many of them organic and locally sourced. **Known for:** large portions; good value; friendly service. $ *Average main: $8* ✉ *4-971 Kuhio Hwy., Kapaa* ☎ *808/823–8226.*

🛏 Hotels

Since Kapaa is the island's major population center, this area, including Waipouli and Wailua, has a lived-in, real-world feel. This is where you'll find some of the best deals on accommodations and a wider choice of inexpensive restaurants and shops than in the resort areas. The beaches here are so-so for swimming but nice for sunbathing, walking, and watching the sun- and moonrise.

The Wailua area is rather compact and much of it can be accessed from a coastal walking and biking path. The resorts here are attractive to middle-class travelers seeking a good bang for their buck. Wailua had a rich cultural significance for the ancient Hawaiians. Their royalty lived here, and ancient sacred grounds, called *heiau*, are clearly marked.

Aston Islander on the Beach

$$ | **HOTEL** | A low-rise, Hawaii-plantation-style design gives this 6-acre beachfront property a pleasant, relaxed feeling. **Pros:** convenient location; free airport shuttle; online rate deals. **Cons:** smallish pool; no restaurant on the property; no resort amenities. $ *Rooms from: $189* ✉ *440 Aleka Pl., Wailua (Kauai County)* ☎ *808/822–7417, 866/774–2924* ⊕ *www.aquaaston.com* ⤳ *200 rooms* ⦿ *No meals.*

Hotel Coral Reef

$$ | **HOTEL** | **FAMILY** | In business since 1956, this small hotel is something of a Kauai beachfront landmark, with clean, comfortable rooms, some with great ocean views, and a large pool that overlooks the water; expect great sunrises. **Pros:** free parking; oceanfront setting; convenient location. **Cons:** located in a busy section of Kapaa; ocean swimming is marginal; traffic noise. $ *Rooms from: $219* ✉ *4-1516 Kuhio Hwy., Kapaa* ☎ *808/822–4481, 800/843–4659* ⊕ *www.hotelcoralreefresort.com* ⤳ *27 rooms* ⦿ *Free Breakfast.*

Kapaa Sands

$ | **RENTAL** | An old rock etched with *kanji* (Japanese characters) reminds you that the site of this condominium gem was once occupied by a Shinto temple. **Pros:** discounts for extended stays; walking distance to shops, restaurants, and beach; turtle and monk seal sightings common. **Cons:** no-frills lodging; small bathrooms; traffic noise in rear units. [$] *Rooms from: $179* ✉ *380 Papaloa Rd., Wailua (Kauai County)* ☎ *808/822–4901, 800/222–4901* 🌐 *www.kapaasands.com* 🛏 *24 units* 🍴 *No meals.*

★ Kauai Coast Resort at the Beachboy

$$ | **RENTAL** | **FAMILY** | Fronting an uncrowded stretch of beach, this three-story primarily time-share resort is convenient and a bit more upscale than nearby properties. **Pros:** central location; nice sunrises; free parking. **Cons:** beach is narrow; ocean not ideal for swimming; daily housekeeping fee. [$] *Rooms from: $215* ✉ *520 Aleka Loop, Wailua (Kauai County)* ☎ *808/822–3441, 866/729–7182* 🌐 *www.shellhospitality.com* 🛏 *108 units* 🍴 *No meals.*

Kauai Shores

$ | **HOTEL** | This oceanfront inn has been transformed into an affordable boutique hotel, thanks to a much-needed renovation of its guest rooms and public spaces. **Pros:** convenient location; free Wi-Fi and rate discounts for LGBTQ+ travelers; great sunrises. **Cons:** coral reef makes ocean swimming marginal; modest property; minimal amenities but still has a daily hospitality fee. [$] *Rooms from: $158* ✉ *420 Papaloa Rd., Wailua (Kauai County)* ☎ *808/822–4951, 800/560–5553* 🌐 *www.kauaishoreshotel.com* 🛏 *202 rooms* 🍴 *No meals.*

Outrigger at Lae Nani

$$$ | **RENTAL** | Ruling Hawaiian chiefs once returned from ocean voyages to this spot, now host to comfortable condominiums. **Pros:** nice beach; walking distance to playground; attractively furnished. **Cons:** third floor is walk-up; no Wi-Fi; cleaning fee. [$] *Rooms from: $339* ✉ *410 Papaloa Rd., Wailua (Kauai County)* ☎ *808/823–1401, 866/956–4262* 🌐 *www.outrigger.com* 🛏 *84 units* 🍴 *No meals.*

Sheraton Kauai Coconut Beach Resort

$$ | **RESORT** | This popular hotel, one of the few true oceanfront properties on Kauai, sits on a ribbon of sand in Kapaa with bright, spacious rooms that face the ocean or pool. **Pros:** convenient location; close to ocean; pleasant grounds. **Cons:** coastline not conducive to swimming; small pool; high daily parking fee. [$] *Rooms from: $224* ✉ *650 Aleka Loop, Wailua (Kauai County)* ☎ *808/822–3455, 800/760–8555* 🌐 *www.marriott.com* 🛏 *311 rooms* 🍴 *No meals.*

Nightlife

★ Hukilau Lanai

BARS/PUBS | This open-air bar and restaurant is on the property of the Kauai Coast Resort but operates independently. Trade winds waft through the modest little bar, which looks out onto a coconut grove. If the mood takes you, go on a short walk to the sea, or recline in big, comfortable chairs in Wally's Bar in the lobby while listening to mellow jazz or Hawaiian slack-key guitar. Live music plays from 6 to 9 every night, but the restaurant and bar are closed on Monday. Poolside happy hour runs from 3 to 5. Freshly infused tropical martinis—perhaps locally grown lychee and pineapple or a Big Island vanilla bean infusion—are house favorites. ✉ *520 Aleka Loop, Wailua (Kauai County)* ☎ *808/822–0600* 🌐 *www.hukilaukauai.com* ☞ *Closed Mon.*

Trees Lounge

BARS/PUBS | This cool bar and restaurant hosts live music nightly that gets people out on the tiny dance floor. It's behind the Coconut Marketplace and next to the Kauai Coast Resort in Kapaa. ✉ *440 Aleka Pl., Kapaa* ☎ *808/823–0600* 🌐 *www.treesloungekauai.com* ☞ *Closed Sun.*

⏯ Performing Arts

★ Smith's Tropical Paradise Luau

THEMED ENTERTAINMENT | A 30-acre tropical garden on the Wailua River provides the lovely setting for this popular luau, which begins with the traditional blowing of the conch shell and *imu* (pig roast) ceremony, followed by cocktails, an island feast, great music, and an international show in the amphitheater overlooking a torch-lighted lagoon. It's fairly authentic and a better deal than the pricier resort events. ⊠ *174 Wailua Rd., Kapaa* ☎ *808/821–6895* ⊕ *www.smithskauai. com* ⤶ *$108.*

🛍 Shopping

Kapaa is the most heavily populated area on Kauai, so it's not surprising that it has the most diverse shopping opportunities on the island. Unlike the North Shore's retail scene, shops here are not neatly situated in centers; they are spread out along a long stretch of road, with many local retail gems tucked away that you may not find if you're in a rush.

Deja Vu Surf Hawaii: Kapaa

CLOTHING | This family operation has a great assortment of surf wear and clothes for outdoors fanatics, including tank tops, visors, swimwear, and Kauai-style T-shirts. They also carry body boards and water-sports accessories. Good deals can be found at sidewalk sales. ⊠ *4-1419 Kuhio Hwy., Kapaa* ☎ *808/320–7108* ⊕ *www.dejavusurf.com.*

Jim Saylor Jewelers

JEWELRY/ACCESSORIES | Jim Saylor and his team of jewelers have been designing beautiful keepsakes on Kauai since 1976. Gems from around the world, including black pearls, diamonds, and more, appear in his unusual settings. ⊠ *4-1318 Kuhio Hwy., Kapaa* ☎ *808/822–3591* ⊕ *www.jimsaylorjewelers.com* ⊗ *Closed Sun.*

Kauai Village Shopping Center

SHOPPING CENTERS/MALLS | The buildings of this Kapaa shopping village are in the style of a 19th-century plantation town. **ABC Discount Store** sells sundries; **Safeway** carries groceries and alcoholic beverages; **Papaya's** has health foods and a minimalist café. There's also a small bakery, **Ross Dress for Less,** and a **UPS store.** Other shops sell jewelry, art, and home decor. Restaurants include Chinese and Vietnamese options, and there's also a **Starbucks** and a bar. ⊠ *4-831 Kuhio Hwy., Kapaa* ☎ *808/822–3777.*

Kela's Glass Gallery

ART GALLERIES | The colorful vases, bowls, and other fragile items sold in this distinctive gallery, now expanded into a new, larger space, are definitely worth viewing if you appreciate quality handmade glass art. It's expensive, but if something catches your eye, they'll happily pack it for safe transport home. They also ship worldwide. ⊠ *4-1400 Kuhio Hwy., Kapaa* ☎ *808/822–4527* ⊕ *www. glass-art.com.*

Kinipopo Shopping Village

SHOPPING CENTERS/MALLS | Kinipopo is a tiny little center on Kuhio Highway. **Korean Barbeque** fronts the highway, as does **Goldsmith's Kauai Gallery,** which sells handcrafted Hawaiian-style gold jewelry. There's also a clothing shop, beauty salon, bakery, cake shop, and a healing-arts center. ⊠ *4-356 Kuhio Hwy., Kapaa* ⊕ *www.kinipopovillage.com.*

Vicky's Fabric Shop

GIFTS/SOUVENIRS | This small store is packed full of tropical and Hawaiian prints, silks, slinky rayons, soft cottons, and other fine fabrics. A variety of sewing patterns and notions are featured as well, making it a must-stop for any seamstress and a great place to buy unique island-made gifts. Check out the one-of-a-kind selection of purses, aloha wear, and other quality hand-sewn items. ⊠ *4-1326 Kuhio Hwy., Kapaa* ☎ *808/822–1746* ⊕ *www.vickysfabrics.com* ⊗ *Closed Sun.*

Lihue

7 miles southwest of Wailua.

The commercial and political center of Kauai County, which includes the islands of Kauai and Niihau, Lihue is home to the island's major airport, harbor, and hospital. This is where you can find the state and county offices that issue camping and hiking permits and the same fast-food eateries and big-box stores that blight the mainland.

Route 56 leads into Lihue from the north and Route 50 comes here from the south and west. The road from the airport (where Kauai's car rental agencies are) leads to the middle of Lihue. Many of the area's stores and restaurants are on and around Rice Street, which also leads to Kalapaki Bay and Nawiliwili Harbor.

◉ Sights

★ Alekoko (Menehune) Fishpond

ARCHAEOLOGICAL SITE | No one knows just who built this intricate aquaculture structure in the Huleia River. Legend attributes it to the Menehune, a mythical—or real, depending on who you ask—ancient race of people known for their small stature, industrious nature, and superb stoneworking skills. Volcanic rock was cut and fit together into massive walls 4 feet thick and 5 feet high, forming a centuries-old enclosure for raising mullet and other freshwater fish. ⊠ *Hulemalu Rd., Niumalu.*

★ Kauai Museum

MUSEUM | Maintaining a stately presence on Rice Street, the historic museum building is easy to find. It features a permanent display, "The Story of Kauai," which provides a competent overview of the Garden Island and Niihau, tracing the Islands' geology, mythology, and cultural history. Local artists are represented in changing exhibits in the second-floor Mezzanine Gallery. The expanded gift shop alone is worth a visit, with a fine collection of authentic Niihau shell lei, feather hatband lei, hand-turned wooden bowls, reference books, and other quality arts, crafts, and gifts—many of them locally made. ⊠ *4428 Rice St., Lihue* ☎ *808/245–6931* ⊕ *www.kauaimuseum. org* ⊠ *$15.*

🏖 Beaches

Kalapaki Beach

BEACH—SIGHT | FAMILY | Five minutes south of the airport in Lihue, you'll find this wide, sandy-bottom beach fronting the Kauai Marriott. It's almost always safe from rip currents and undertows because it's around the back side of a peninsula, in its own cove. There are tons of activities here, including all the usual water sports—beginning and intermediate surfing, body boarding, body surfing, and swimming—plus, there are two outrigger canoe clubs paddling in the bay and the Nawiliwili Yacht Club's boats sailing around the harbor. Kalapaki is the only place on Kauai where double-hulled canoes are available for rent (at Kauai Beach Boys, which fronts the beach next to Duke's Canoe Club restaurant). Visitors can also rent snorkel gear, surfboards, body boards, and kayaks from Kauai Beach Boys. A volleyball court on the beach is often used by a loosely organized group of local players; visitors are always welcome. **■TIP→ Avoid the stream on the south side of the beach; it often has high bacteria counts.** Duke's Canoe Club restaurant is one of only a couple of restaurants on the island actually on a beach; the restaurant's lower level is casual—even welcoming beach attire and sandy feet—making it perfect for lunch or an afternoon cocktail. **Amenities:** food and drink; lifeguard; parking; showers; toilets; water sports. **Best for:** partiers; surfing; swimming; walking. ⊠ *Off Rice St., Lihue* ⊕ *www.kauai.com/kalapaki-beach.*

🍴 Restaurants

You will probably find yourself in Lihue at least a few times during your stay. When it comes to dining, Lihue isn't especially outstanding. There are some decent restaurants and some good low-cost eateries that feed locals and the business-lunch crowd—but nothing really stellar. If you are in town for lunch, don't pass up some of the authentic local spots.

Dani's Restaurant

$ | **HAWAIIAN** | **FAMILY** | Kauai residents frequent this eatery near the Lihue Fire Station for hearty, local-style food at breakfast and lunch; it's a good place to try traditional luau cuisine without commercial luau prices. You can order Hawaiian-style *laulau* (pork and taro leaves wrapped in ti leaves and steamed) or kalua pig, slow roasted in an underground oven. **Known for:** local-style dining; low prices; casual setting. *[$] Average main: $8 ✉ 4201 Rice St., Lihue ☎ 808/245–4991 🕒 Closed Sun. No dinner.*

Gaylord's

$$$ | **ECLECTIC** | Located in what was once Kauai's most expensive plantation estate, Gaylord's pays tribute to the elegant dining rooms of 1930s high society—candlelit tables sit on a cobblestone patio that surrounds a fountain and overlooks a wide lawn. The menu is eclectic, ranging from tender seared scallops served in a fennel cream to grilled filet mignon. **Known for:** lavish Sunday brunch buffet; quiet dining; delightful outdoor seating. *[$] Average main: $30 ✉ Kilohana Plantation, 3-2087 Kaumualii Hwy., Puhi ☎ 808/245–9593 🌐 www.gaylordskauai.com.*

★ Hamura Saimin

$ | **ASIAN** | Folks just love this old plantation-style diner—locals and tourists stream in and out all day long, and neighbor islanders stop in on their way to the airport to pick up takeout orders to bring home. Their famous *saimin* soup is the big draw, and each day the Hiraoka family dishes up about 1,000 bowls of the steaming broth and homemade noodles topped with a variety of garnishes. **Known for:** classic Kauai experience; grilled chicken and beef sticks; counter-style dining. *[$] Average main: $7 ✉ 2956 Kress St., Lihue ☎ 808/245–3271 💳 No credit cards.*

JJ's Broiler

$$$ | **AMERICAN** | This spacious, low-key restaurant has a great ocean view and serves hearty fare, with dinner specials such as lobster and Slavonic steak, a broiled sliced tenderloin dipped in buttery wine sauce, and local-style kalua pig and cabbage; you can save money by ordering from the lunch menu at dinner time. On sunny afternoons, ask for a table on the lanai overlooking Kalapaki Bay and try one of the generous salads or appetizers and a drink. **Known for:** one of the best ocean views in Lihue; great place for a drink; friendly service. *[$] Average main: $30 ✉ Anchor Cove, 3416 Rice St., Nawiliwili ☎ 808/246–4422 🌐 www.jjsbroiler.com.*

Kalapaki Joe's

$$ | **AMERICAN** | Both locations—in Lihue's Kukui Grove and in Poipu—appeal to sports fans who like a rip-roaring happy hour. The appetizer menu is extensive, and you can also choose from burgers, salads, sandwiches, fish tacos, steaks, ribs, and fresh fish specials. **Known for:** wide-ranging menu; boisterous bar; affordable, casual dining. *[$] Average main: $20 ✉ 3-2600 Kaumualii Hwy., Lihue ☎ 808/245–6366 🌐 www.kalapakijoes.com.*

Kukui's Restaurant and Bar

$$ | **ECLECTIC** | **FAMILY** | The meals at Kukui's feature Hawaiian, Asian, and contemporary American influences, and the open-air setting makes it a pleasant place to dine. It's very spacious and not as busy and noisy as the other eateries at the Marriott, making it well suited to

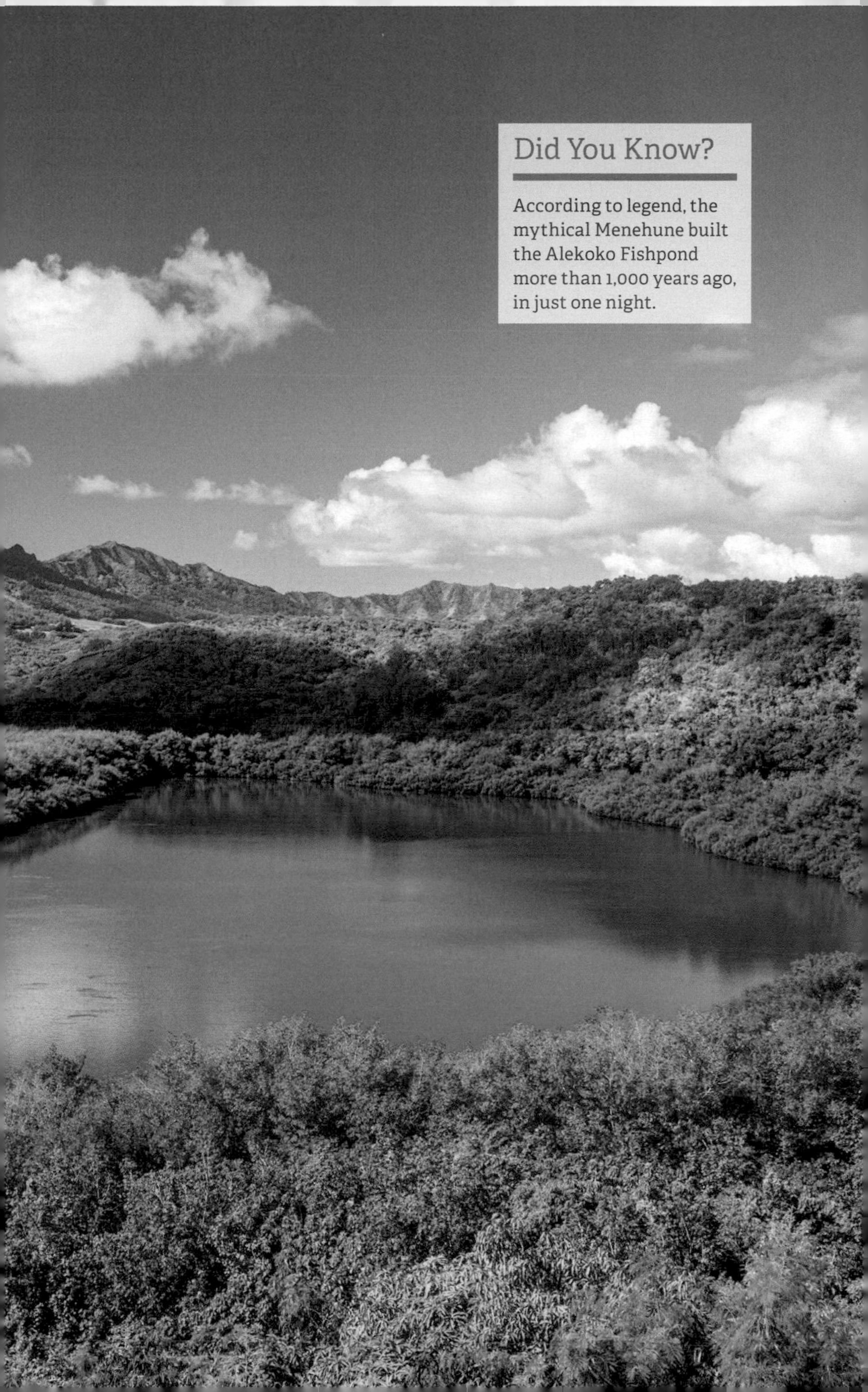

Did You Know?

According to legend, the mythical Menehune built the Alekoko Fishpond more than 1,000 years ago, in just one night.

families and those who want a relaxed setting. **Known for:** garden setting; lavish buffets; evening entertainment. $ *Average main: $25* ⊠ *Kauai Marriott Resort & Beach Club, 3610 Rice St., Kalapaki Beach, Lihue* ☏ *808/245–5042* ⊕ *www.marriott.com.*

🛏 Hotels

Lihue is not the most desirable place to stay on Kauai in terms of scenic beauty, although it does have its advantages, including easy access to the airport. Restaurants and shops are plentiful, and there's lovely Kalapaki Bay for beachgoers. Aside from the Marriott and the Kauai Beach Resort, most of the limited lodging possibilities are smaller and aimed at the cost-conscious traveler.

Garden Island Inn

$$ | **HOTEL** | Budget travelers love this three-story inn near Kalapaki Bay and Anchor Cove shopping center as it's clean, offers free Wi-Fi, and the innkeepers are friendly, sharing fruit, flowers, and beach gear. **Pros:** walk to beach, restaurants, and shops; good for extended stays and budget travel; air-conditioning. **Cons:** some traffic noise; near a busy harbor; no pool. $ *Rooms from: $185* ⊠ *3445 Wilcox Rd., Kalapaki Beach, Lihue* ☏ *808/245–7227, 800/648–0154* ⊕ *www.gardenislandinn.com* ⤴ *21 rooms* ⋈ *No meals.*

Kauai Beach Resort

$$$ | **RESORT** | This plantation-style hotel provides a relaxing, upscale experience close to the airport, but without the noise. **Pros:** unique sand-bottom pool with 12-foot waterfall; shuttle service to airport; resort amenities. **Cons:** not a good swimming beach; windy at times; no nearby restaurants or resorts. $ *Rooms from: $279* ⊠ *4331 Kauai Beach Dr., Hanamaulu* ☏ *808/246–5576* ⊕ *www.kauaibeachresortandspa.com* ⤴ *350 rooms* ⋈ *No meals.*

Kauai Marriott Resort on Kalapaki Beach

$$$ | **RESORT** | **FAMILY** | An elaborate tropical garden, waterfalls right off the lobby, Greek statues and columns, and an enormous 26,000-square-foot swimming pool characterize the grand—and grandiose—scale of this resort on Kalapaki Beach, which looks out at the dramatic Haupu Ridge. **Pros:** oceanfront setting; numerous restaurants; convenient location and airport shuttle. **Cons:** airport noise; ocean water quality can be poor at times; located near an industrial area. $ *Rooms from: $339* ⊠ *3610 Rice St., Kalapaki Beach, Lihue* ☏ *808/245–5050, 800/220–2925* ⊕ *www.kauaimarriott.com* ⤴ *367 rooms* ⋈ *Free Breakfast.*

Kauai Palms Hotel

$ | **HOTEL** | Not only is this low-cost alternative close to the airport, but it's also a great base for day trips to all sides of the island. **Pros:** friendly staff; inexpensive; centrally located. **Cons:** bare-bones amenities; smallish rooms; traffic noise. $ *Rooms from: $114* ⊠ *2931 Kalena St., Lihue* ☏ *808/246–0908* ⊕ *www.kauaipalmshotel.com* ⤴ *33 rooms* ⋈ *No meals.*

▼ Nightlife

Duke's Barefoot Bar

BARS/PUBS | This is one of the liveliest bars in Nawiliwili. Contemporary Hawaiian music is usually performed at this beachside bar and restaurant every day but Tuesday during "Aloha Hours" from 4 to 6 pm. On Saturday nights, live music is held from 8:30 to 10:30 pm. ⊠ *Kalapaki Beach, 3610 Rice St., Lihue* ☏ *808/246–9599* ⊕ *www.dukeskauai.com.*

Rob's Good Times Grill

BARS/PUBS | Let loose at this popular restaurant and sports bar, which has live music Monday through Thursday from 4 to 6 pm. Tuesday offers swing dancing from 7:30 to 10 pm, Friday features live

Continued on page 484

HAWAII'S PLANTS 101

Tropical Hibiscus

Hawaii is a bounty of rainbow-colored flowers and plants. The evening air is scented with their fragrance. Just look at the front yard of almost any home, travel any road, or visit any local park and you'll see a spectacular array of colored blossoms and leaves. What most visitors don't know is that many of the plants they are seeing are not native to Hawaii; rather, they were introduced during the last two centuries as ornamental plants, or for timber, shade, or fruit.

Hawaii boasts nearly every climate on the planet, excluding the two most extreme: arctic tundra and arid desert. The Islands have wine-growing regions, cactus-speckled ranchlands, icy mountaintops, and the rainiest forests on earth.

Plants introduced from around the world thrive here. The lush lowland valleys along the windward coasts are predominantly populated by non-native trees including yellow- and red-fruited **guava**, silvery-leafed **kukui**, and orange-flowered **tulip trees.**

The colorful **plumeria flower**, very fragrant and commonly used in lei making, and the giant multicolored **hibiscus flower** are both used by many women as hair adornments, and are two of the most common plants found around homes and hotels. The umbrella-like **monkeypod tree** from Central America provides shade in many of Hawaii's parks including Kapiolani Park in Honolulu. Hawaii's largest tree, found in Lahaina, Maui, is a giant **banyan tree**. Its canopy and massive support roots cover about two-thirds of an acre. The native **ohia tree**, with its brilliant red brush-like flowers, and the **hapuu**, a giant tree fern, are common in Hawaii's forests and are also used ornamentally in gardens.

Naupaka, Limahuli Garden

Bougainvillea

Guava

Monkeypod

Banyan

Ohia Lehua*

Tulip Tree

Plumeria

Pandanus

Hibiscus

Anthurium

Kukui

Hapuu

*endemic to Hawaii

DID YOU KNOW?

More than 2,200 plant species are found in the Hawaiian Islands, but only about 1,000 are native. Of these, 320 are so rare, they are endangered. Hawaii's endemic plants evolved from ancestral seeds arriving in the Islands over thousands of years as baggage with birds, floating on ocean currents, or drifting on winds from continents thousands of miles away. Once here, these plants evolved in isolation, creating many new species known nowhere else in the world.

music until midnight, Saturday has late-night club dancing with a DJ, while Sunday through Thursday go full-on karaoke until closing. Lunch is a good choice, too. ✉ *4303 Rice St., Lihue* ☎ *808/246–0311* ⊕ *www.kauaisportsbarandgrill.com.*

🎭 Performing Arts

Kauai Community College Performing Arts Center

ARTS CENTERS | The main venue for island entertainment hosts a concert music series, visiting musicians, dramatic productions, and special events such as educational forums. ✉ *3-1901 Kaumualii Hwy., Lihue* ☎ *808/245–8311* ⊕ *www. kauai.hawaii.edu/pac.*

Kauai Concert Association

MUSIC | This group offers a seasonal program at the Kauai Community College Performing Arts Center that features well-known classical musicians, including soloists and small ensembles. ✉ *3-1901 Kaumualii Hwy., Lihue* ☎ *808/245–7464* ⊕ *www.kauai-concert.org* 🎟 *From $30.*

Luau Kalamaku

THEMED ENTERTAINMENT | Set on historic sugar-plantation land, this luau bills itself as the only "theatrical" luau on Kauai. The luau feast is served buffet style, there's an open bar, and the performers aim to both entertain and educate about Hawaiian culture. Guests sit at tables around a circular stage; tables farther from the stage are elevated, providing unobstructed views. Additional packages offer visitors the opportunity to watch the show only, tour the 35-acre plantation via train, or enjoy special romantic perks like a lei greeting and champagne. ✉ *Kilohana Plantation, 3-2087 Kaumualii St., Lihue* ☎ *877/622–1780* ⊕ *www.luaukalamaku. com* 🎟 *From $57.*

🛍 Shopping

Lihue is the business area on Kauai, as well as home to all the big-box stores (Costco, Home Depot, etc.) and the only real mall. Make no mistake, though: this town isn't lacking in rare finds. Lihue is steeped in history and diversity while simultaneously welcoming new trends and establishments.

Hilo Hattie, The Store of Hawaii

CLOTHING | This is the big name in aloha wear for tourists throughout the Islands, and Hilo Hattie has only one store on Kauai. Located a mile from Lihue Airport, come here for cool, comfortable aloha shirts and muumuu in bright floral prints, as well as other souvenirs. Also, be sure to check out the line of Hawaii-inspired home furnishings. ✉ *3252 Kuhio Hwy., Lihue* ☎ *808/245–3404* ⊕ *www.hilohattie. com.*

★ Kapaia Stitchery

GIFTS/SOUVENIRS | Hawaiian quilts made by hand and machine, a beautiful selection of fabrics, quilting kits, handmade aloha shirts, and unique fabric arts fill Kapaia Stitchery, a cute little red plantation-style building a mile outside of Lihue. There are also many locally made gifts and quilts for sale in this locally owned store. The staff is friendly and helpful, even though a steady stream of customers keeps them busy. ✉ *3-3551 Kuhio Hwy., Lihue* ☎ *808/245–2281* ⊕ *kapaiastitchery. com* 🕐 *Closed Sun.*

★ Kauai Community Market

OUTDOOR/FLEA/GREEN MARKETS | FAMILY | This is the biggest and best farmers' market on Kauai, sponsored by the Kauai Farm Bureau at the community college in Lihue and held on Saturday mornings. You'll find fresh produce and flowers, as well as packaged products like breads, goat cheese, pasta, honey, coffee, soaps, lotions, and more, all made locally. Seating areas are available to grab a snack or lunch from the food booths or the lunch wagons that set up here. ✉ *3-1901*

Kauai: Undercover Movie Star

Though Kauai has played itself in the movies, starring in *The Descendants* (2011), much of its screen time has been as a stunt double for a number of tropical paradises. The island's remote valleys portrayed Venezuelan jungle in Kevin Costner's *Dragonfly* (2002) and a Costa Rican dinosaur preserve in Steven Spielberg's *Jurassic Park* (1993). Spielberg was no stranger to Kauai, having filmed Harrison Ford's escape via seaplane from Menehune Fishpond in *Raiders of the Lost Ark* (1981).

The fluted cliffs and gorges of Kauai's rugged Napali Coast play the misunderstood beast's island home in *King Kong* (1976), and a jungle dweller of another sort, in *George of the Jungle* (1997), also frolicked on Kauai. Harrison Ford returned to the island for 10 weeks during the filming of *Six Days, Seven Nights* (1998), a romantic adventure set in French Polynesia. Part-time Kauai resident Ben Stiller used the island as a stand-in for the jungles of Vietnam in *Tropic Thunder* (2008), and Johnny Depp came here to film some of *Pirates of the Caribbean: On Stranger Tides* (2011). But these are all relatively contemporary movies. What's truly remarkable is that Hollywood discovered Kauai in 1933 with the making of *White Heat*, which was set on a sugar plantation and—like *South Pacific* (also filmed on Kauai)— dealt with an interracial love story.

Then, it was off to the races, as Kauai saw no fewer than a dozen movies filmed on the island in the 1950s, though not all of them were Oscar contenders. Rita Hayworth starred in *Miss Sadie Thompson* (1953), and

no one you'd recognize starred in the tantalizing *She Gods of Shark Reef* (1956).

The movie that is still immortalized on the island in the names of restaurants, real estate offices, a hotel, and even a sushi item is *South Pacific* (1957). (You guessed it, right?) That mythical place called Bali Hai is never far away on Kauai.

In the 1960s, Elvis Presley filmed *Blue Hawaii* (1961) and *Girls! Girls! Girls!* (1962) on the island. A local movie tour likes to point out the stain on a hotel carpet where Elvis's jelly doughnut fell.

Kauai has welcomed a long list of Hollywood's A-List: John Wayne in *Donovan's Reef* (1963); Jack Lemmon in *The Wackiest Ship in the Army* (1961); Richard Chamberlain in *The Thorn Birds* (1983); Gene Hackman in *Uncommon Valor* (1983); Danny DeVito and Billy Crystal in *Throw Momma from the Train* (1987); and Dustin Hoffman, Morgan Freeman, Renee Russo, and Cuba Gooding Jr. in *Outbreak* (1995).

Kauai has also appeared on a long list of TV shows and made-for-TV movies, including *Gilligan's Island, Fantasy Island, Starsky & Hutch, Baywatch Hawaii*—even reality TV shows *The Bachelor* and *The Amazing Race 3*.

For the record, just because a movie did some filming here doesn't mean the entire movie was filmed on Kauai. *Honeymoon in Vegas* filmed just one scene here, while the murder mystery *A Perfect Getaway* (2009) was set on the famous Kalalau Trail and featured beautiful Kauaian backdrops, but was shot mostly in Puerto Rico.

Kaumualii Hwy., Lihue ☎ *808/855–5429* ⊕ *www.kauaicommunitymarket.com.*

Kauai Fruit and Flower Company

FOOD/CANDY | At this shop near Lihue and five minutes away from the airport, you can buy fresh Hawaii Gold pineapple, sugarcane, ginger, tropical flowers, coconuts, local jams, jellies, and honey, plus papayas, bananas, and mangoes from Kauai. (Note that some of the fruit sold here cannot be shipped out of state.) ⊠ *3-4684 Kuhio Hwy., Lihue* ☎ *808/245–1814* ⊕ *www.kauaifruit.com* ⊗ *Closed Sat. afternoon and Sun.*

★ Kauai Museum

GIFTS/SOUVENIRS | The gift shop at the museum sells some fascinating books, maps, and prints, as well as lovely authentic Niihau shell jewelry, handwoven *lau hala* hats, and koa wood bowls. Also featured at the Kauai Museum are tapa cloth, authentic *tikis* (hand-carved wooden figurines), as well as other good-quality local crafts and books at reasonable prices. ⊠ *4428 Rice St., Lihue* ☎ *808/245–6931* ⊕ *www.kauaimuseum.org* ⊗ *Closed Sun.*

Kilohana Plantation

SHOPPING CENTERS/MALLS | This 16,000-square-foot Tudor mansion contains art galleries, a jewelry store, and the restaurant Gaylord's. Kilohana Plantation is filled with antiques from its original owner, and the restored outbuildings house a craft shop and a Hawaiian-style clothing shop. Train rides on a restored railroad are available, with knowledgeable guides recounting the history of sugar on Kauai. The site is also now the home of Luau Kalamaku and Koloa Rum Company. ⊠ *3-2087 Kaumualii Hwy., Lihue* ☎ *808/245–5608* ⊕ *www.kilohanakauai.com.*

Kukui Grove Center

SHOPPING CENTERS/MALLS | This is Kauai's only true mall. Anchor tenants are Longs Drugs, Macy's, Ross, Kukui Grove Cinemas, and Times Supermarket. The mall's stores offer women's clothing, surf wear, art, toys, athletic shoes, jewelry, a hair salon, and locally made crafts. Restaurants range from fast food and sandwiches to sushi and Korean, with a popular Starbucks and Jamba Juice. The center stage often has entertainment, especially on Friday night, and there is a farmers' market on Monday afternoon. ⊠ *3-2600 Kaumualii Hwy., Lihue* ☎ *808/245–7784* ⊕ *www.kukuigrovecenter.com.*

Two Frogs Hugging

HOUSEHOLD ITEMS/FURNITURE | At Two Frogs Hugging, you'll find lots of interesting housewares, accessories, knickknacks, and hand-carved collectibles, as well as baskets and furniture from Indonesia, the Philippines, and China. The shop occupies expansive quarters in the Lihue Industrial Park. ⊠ *3094 Aukele St., Lihue* ☎ *808/246–8777* ⊕ *www.twofrogshugging.com* ⊗ *Closed Sun.*

The South Shore

As you follow the main road south from Lihue, the landscape becomes lush and densely vegetated before giving way to drier conditions that characterize Poipu, the South Side's major resort area. Poipu owes much of its popularity to a steady supply of sunshine and a string of sandy beaches, although the beaches are smaller and more covelike than those on the West Side. With its extensive selection of accommodations, services, and activities, the South Shore attracts more visitors than any other area of Kauai. It also attracted developers with big plans for the onetime sugarcane fields that are nestled in this region and enveloped by mountains. There are few roads in and out, and local residents are concerned about increased traffic as well as noise and dust pollution as a result of chronic construction. If you're planning to stay on the South Side, be sure to ask if your hotel, condo, or vacation rental will be impacted by the development during your visit.

Both Poipu and nearby Koloa (site of Kauai's first sugar mill) can be reached via Route 520 (Maluhia Road) from the Lihue area. Route 520 is known locally as Tree Tunnel Road, due to the stand of eucalyptus trees lining the road that were planted at the turn of the 20th century by Walter Duncan McBryde, a Scotsman who began cattle ranching on Kauai's South Shore. The canopy of trees was, quite literally, ripped to shreds twice—in 1982 during Hurricane Iwa and again in 1992 during Hurricane Iniki. And, true to Kauai, both times the trees grew back into an impressive tunnel. It's a distinctive way to announce, "You are now on vacation," for there's a definite feel of leisure in the air here. There's still plenty to do—snorkel, bike, walk, horseback ride, take an ATV tour, surf, scuba dive, shop, and dine—everything you'd want on a tropical vacation. From the west, Route 530 (Koloa Road) slips into downtown Koloa, a string of fun shops and restaurants, at an intersection with the only gas station on the South Shore.

Koloa

11 miles southwest of Lihue.

Hawaii's lucrative foray into sugar was born in this sleepy town, where the first sugar was milled back in 1830. You can still see the mill's old stone smokestack. Little else remains, save for the charming plantation-style buildings that have kept Koloa from becoming a tacky tourist trap for Poipu-bound visitors. The original small-town character has been preserved by converting historic structures along the main street into boutiques, restaurants, and shops. Placards describe the original tenants and life in the old mill town. Look for Koloa Fish Market, which offers poke and sashimi takeout, and Progressive Expressions, a popular local surf shop.

◉ Sights

★ Old Koloa Town

HISTORIC SITE | Koloa's first sugar mill opened in 1835, ushering in an era of sugar production throughout the islands, with more than 100 plantations established by 1885. Many of the workers came from the Philippines, Japan, China, Korea, and Portugal, creating Hawaii's multiethnic mélange. Today, many of Koloa's historic buildings beneath the shade of ancient monkeypod trees have been converted into fun shops and restaurants. You'll just want to stroll and take it all in; favorites include Island Soap and Candleworks, Crazy Shirts, and Lappert's, Hawaiian-inspired ice cream made daily in nearby Hanapepe. Try the Kauai Pie or Luau Delight flavors, after a food truck lunch in nearby Knudsen Park. ■TIP→ **Be sure to approach Old Koloa Town via the Tree Tunnel, a romantic canopy of eucalyptus trees planted more than a century ago along a stretch of Maluhia Road.** ✉ *Koloa Rd., Koloa* ⊕ *www.oldkoloa.com.*

🍴 Restaurants

Most eateries in Koloa are come-as-you-are casual, family-friendly, and modestly priced. Food trucks gather by the old sugar monument and in a lot behind the main street. Finer dining, sometimes with a view, can be found in Poipu, closer to the sea.

Monkeypod Jam

$ | HAWAIIAN | Part shop and part bistro, the highway storefront of Monkeypod Jam serves up healthy takeaway sandwiches, quiche, soup, baked goodies, and smoothies, and its shelves are packed with award-winning jams, curds, and chutneys made from tropical fruits. Travel-friendly samplers are available. **Known for:** preserves; quick lunches; cooking workshops. ⓢ *Average main: $10* ✉ *2-3687 Kaumualii Hwy., Lawai* ✛ *next to Lawai Post Office* ☎ *808/378–4208*

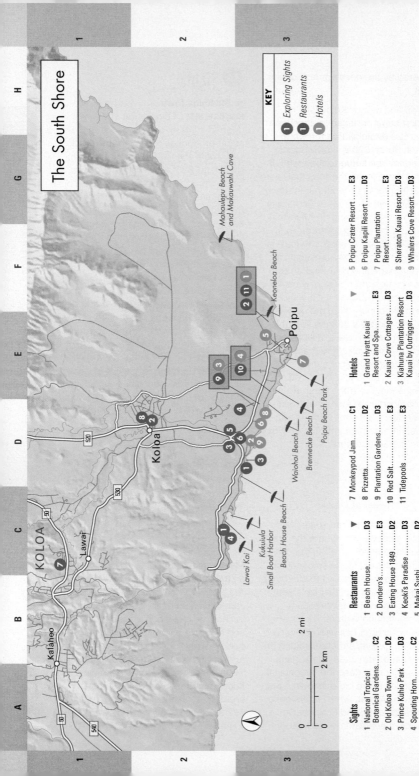

The South Shore

KEY

- ① Exploring Sights
- ① Restaurants
- ① Hotels

▶

Sights

1. National Tropical
   Botanical Gardens........**C2**
2. Old Koloa Town.........**D2**
3. Prince Kuhio Park.......**D3**
4. Spouting Horn............**C2**

▶

Restaurants

1. Beach House..............**D3**
2. Dondero's...................**E3**
3. Eating House 1849......**D2**
4. Keoki's Paradise.........**D3**
5. Makai Sushi...............**D2**
6. Merriman's
   Fish House................**D2**
7. Monkeypod Jam.........**C1**
8. Pizzetta.....................**D2**
9. Plantation Gardens......**D3**
10. Red Salt...................**E3**
11. Tidepools..................**E3**

▶

Hotels

1. Grand Hyatt Kauai
   Resort and Spa.........**E3**
2. Kauai Cove Cottages....**D3**
3. Kiahuna Plantation Resort
   Kauai by Outrigger......**D3**
4. Koa Kea
   Hotel and Resort.........**E3**
5. Poipu Crater Resort......**E3**
6. Poipu Kapili Resort.......**D3**
7. Poipu Plantation
   Resort.......................**E3**
8. Sheraton Kauai Resort...**D3**
9. Whalers Cove Resort....**D3**

🌐 *www.monkeypodjam.com* 🕒 *Closed Sun.*

Pizzetta
$ | ITALIAN | FAMILY | This family-style Italian restaurant has an open-air deck where hearty portions of pasta, calzones, and thin-crust pizza are served, along with kalua pork and cabbage, grilled fish, and barbecue ribs, all of which can find their way into pizza toppings. Gluten-free crust and pasta are available. **Known for:** neighborhood delivery service; attentive wait staff; fresh, house-made bread. [$] *Average main: $17* ✉ *5408 Koloa Rd., Koloa* ☎ *808/742–8881.*

Shopping

Warehouse 3540
LOCAL SPECIALTIES | An old warehouse to the west of Koloa in Lawai has new life as a marketplace for a dozen creative entrepreneurs and as a hub for food trucks. Hand-sewn and hand-printed clothing, authentic *lau hala* hats, boho chic jewelry, letterpressed cards, specialty food products, and locally crafted soaps are offered at the permanent micro-shops. These are joined by craft vendors, farmers, takeout food cooks, and musicians on Fridays and second Saturday evenings. Locals and visitors mingle at a large indoor library or enjoy communal seating outside. ✉ *3540 Koloa Rd., Kalaheo* 🌐 *www.warehouse3540.com* 🕒 *Closed Sun.*

Poipu

2 miles southeast of Koloa.

Thanks to its generally sunny weather and a string of golden-sand beaches dotted with oceanfront lodgings, Poipu is a top choice for many visitors. Beaches are user-friendly, with protected waters for *keiki* (children) and novice snorkelers, lifeguards, restrooms, covered pavilions, and a sweet coastal promenade ideal for leisurely strolls. Some experts have even ranked Poipu Beach Park number one in the nation. It depends on your preferences, of course, though it certainly does warrant high accolades.

Poipu is the one area on Kauai where you could get by without a car, though that could mean an expensive taxi ride from the airport and limited access to other parts of the island. To reach Poipu by car, follow Poipu Road south from Koloa. After the traffic circle, the road curves to follow the coast, leading to some of the popular South Shore beaches.

Sights

National Tropical Botanical Gardens (*NTBG*)
GARDEN | Tucked away in Lawai Valley, these gardens include lands and a cottage once used by Hawaii's Queen Emma for a summer retreat. Trams depart frequently to transport people from the visitor center to the gardens. The rambling 252-acre McBryde Garden has exhibits and easy trails to help visitors learn about biodiversity and plants collected throughout the tropics, including the Canoe Garden that features plants originally brought to Hawaii by early Polynesian voyagers. The 100-acre Allerton Garden, which can be visited only on a guided tour, artfully displays statues and water features originally developed as part of a private estate. Reservations and closed-toe shoes are required for all tours. The visitor center has a high-quality gift shop and a grab-and-go cafe. Besides propagating rare and endangered plants from Hawaii and elsewhere, NTBG functions as a scientific research and education center. The organization also operates gardens in Limahuli, on Kauai's North Shore, in Hana, on Maui's east shore, and in Florida. ✉ *4425 Lawai Rd., Poipu* ☎ *808/742–2623* 🌐 *www.ntbg.org* 🎟 *McBryde self-guided tour $30, Allerton guided tour $60.*

Prince Kuhio Park

CITY PARK | A triangle of grass next to the Prince Kuhio condominiums honors the birthplace of Kauai's beloved Prince Jonah Kuhio Kalanianaole. Known for his kind nature and tireless work on behalf of the Hawaiian people, he lost his chance at the throne when Americans staged an illegal overthrow of Queen Liliuokalani in 1893 and toppled Hawaii's constitutional monarchy. He served as a delegate to the U.S. Congress for 19 years after Hawaii became a territory in 1900. An annual commemoration is held in March. This is a great place to watch wave riders surfing a popular break known as PKs or to watch the sun sink into the Pacific. ⊠ *Lawai Rd., Poipu.*

★ Spouting Horn

LOCAL INTEREST | When conditions are right, a natural blowhole in the rocky shoreline behaves like Old Faithful, shooting salt water high into the air and making a hollow, echoing sound. It's most dramatic during big summer swells, which jam large quantities of water through an ancient lava tube with great force. Most sidewalk vendors hawk inexpensive souvenirs, but a few carry locally set South Sea pearls or rare Niihau-shell creations, with prices ranging from affordable up to several thousand dollars. Look for green sea turtles bobbing in the adjacent cove. ⊠ *End of Lawai Rd., Poipu* ⊕ *www.kauai.com/spouting-horn.*

⚓ Beaches

The South Shore's primary access road is Highway 520, a tree-lined, two-lane, windy road. As you drive along it, there's a sense of tunneling down a rabbit hole into another world, à la Alice. And the South Shore is certainly a wonderland. On average, it rains only 30 inches per year, so if you're looking for fun in the sun, this is a good place to start. The beaches, with their powdery-fine sand, are consistently good year-round, except during high surf, which, if it hits at all, will be in summer. If you want solitude, this isn't it; if you want excitement—well, as much excitement as quiet Kauai offers—this is the place for you.

Brennecke Beach

BEACH—SIGHT | This beach is synonymous on Kauai with board surfing and body surfing, thanks to its shallow sandbar and reliable shore break. Because the beach is small and often congested, surfboards are prohibited near shore. The water on the rocky eastern edge of the beach is a good place to see the endangered green sea turtles noshing on plants growing on the rocks. **Amenities:** food and drink; parking. **Best for:** sunset; surfing. ⊠ *Hoone Rd., off Poipu Rd., Poipu.*

Keoneloa Beach (*Shipwreck Beach*)

BEACH—SIGHT | The Hawaiian name for this stretch of beach, Keoneloa, means "long sand," but many refer to this beach fronting the Grand Hyatt Kauai Resort and Spa by its common name: Shipwreck Beach. Both make sense. It is a long stretch of crescent beach punctuated by stunning sea cliffs on both ends, and, yes, a ship once wrecked here. With its rough onshore break, the waters off Shipwreck are best for body-boarding and body-surfing experts; however, the beach itself is plenty big for sunbathing, sand-castle building, Frisbee throwing, and other beach-related fun. The eastern edge of the beach is the start of an interpretive cliff and dune walk (complimentary) held by the hotel staff; check with the concierge for days and times, and keep an eye out for snoozing monk seals below. **Amenities:** food and drink; parking; showers; toilets. **Best for:** sunrise; surfing; walking. ⊠ *Ainako Rd., continue on Poipu Rd. past Hyatt, turn makai on Ainako Rd., Poipu.*

Lawai Kai

BEACH—SIGHT | One of the most spectacular beaches on the South Shore is inaccessible by land unless you tour the National Tropical Botanical Garden's Allerton Garden, which we highly

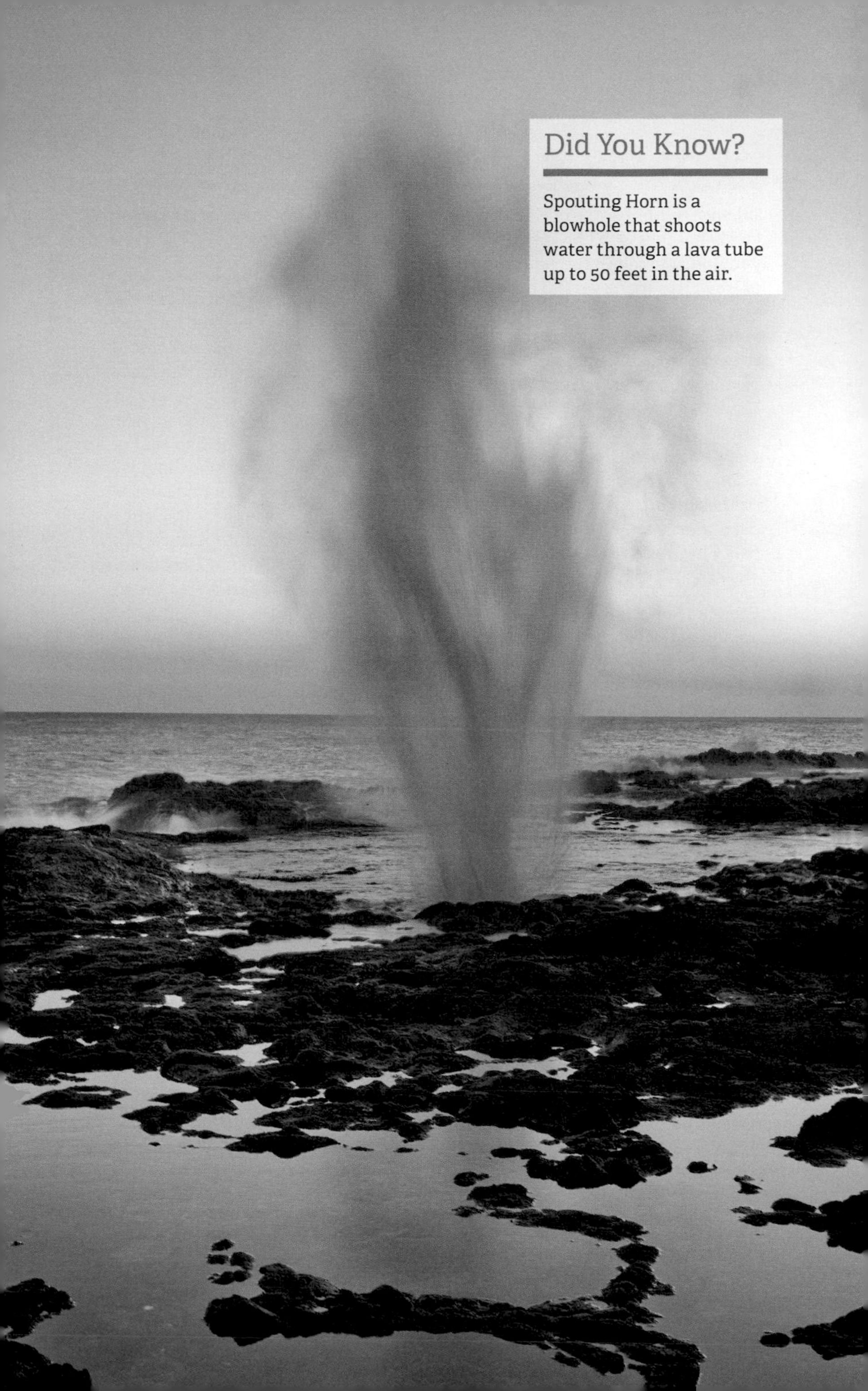

Did You Know?

Spouting Horn is a blowhole that shoots water through a lava tube up to 50 feet in the air.

Seal-Spotting on the South Shore 👁

When strolling on one of Kauai's lovely beaches, don't be surprised if you find yourself in the rare company of Hawaiian monk seals. These are among the most endangered of all marine mammals, with perhaps fewer than 1,400 remaining. They primarily inhabit the northwestern Hawaiian Islands, although more are showing their sweet faces on the main Hawaiian Islands, especially on Kauai. They're fond of hauling out on the beach for a long snooze in the sun, particularly after a night of gorging on fish. They need this time to rest and digest, safe from predators.

Female seals regularly birth their young on the beaches around Kauai, where they stay to nurse their pups for upward of six weeks. It seems the seals enjoy particular beaches for the same reasons we do: the shallow, protected waters.

If you're lucky enough to see a monk seal, keep your distance and let it be. Although they may haul out near people, they still want and need their space. Stay several hundred feet away, and forget photos unless you've got a zoom lens. It's illegal to do anything that causes a monk seal to change its behavior, with penalties that include big fines and even jail time. In the water, seals may appear to want to play. It's their curious nature. Don't try to play with them. They are wild animals—mammals, in fact, with teeth.

If you have concerns about the health or safety of a seal, or just want more information, contact the **Hawaiian Monk Seal Conservation Hui** (☎ 808/651–7668).

recommend. On the tour, you'll see the beach, but you won't step on the sand. The only way to legally access the beach on your own is by paddling a kayak 1 mile from Kukuiula Harbor. However, you have to rent the kayaks elsewhere and haul them on top of your car to the harbor. Also, the wind and waves usually run westward, making the in-trip a breeze but the return trip a workout against Mother Nature. ■**TIP**→ **Do not attempt this beach in any manner during a south swell. Amenities:** none. **Best for:** solitude; sunset. ✉ *4425 Lawai Rd., off Poipu Rd.* ☎ *808/742–2623 for tour information at the National Tropical Botanical Garden's Allerton Garden* ⊕ *www.ntbg.org.*

★ **Mahaulepu Beach and Makauwahi Cave**
BEACH—SIGHT | This 2-mile stretch of coast, with its sand dunes, limestone hills, sinkholes, and the Makauwahi Cave, is unlike any other on Kauai. Remains of a large, ancient settlement, evidence of great battles, and the discovery of a now-underwater petroglyph field indicate that Hawaiians lived in this area as early as AD 700. Mahaulepu's coastline is unprotected and rocky, which makes venturing into the ocean hazardous. There are three beach areas with bits of sandy-bottom swimming; however, the best way to experience Mahaulepu is simply to roam, especially in the morning, along the sand or heritage trail. Pack water and sun protection. ■**TIP**→ **Access to this beach is via private property. Before driving or hiking here, check conditions as the unpaved road can be closed due to weather, grading, or movie filming. Access is during daylight hours only, so be sure to depart before sunset or risk getting locked in for the night. Amenities:** parking. **Best for:** solitude; sunrise; walking. ✉ *Poipu*

Rd., Poipu ✣ past Hyatt Hotel and CJM Stables 🌐 www.cavereserve.org.

★ Poipu Beach Park

BEACH—SIGHT | FAMILY | The most popular beach on the South Shore is Poipu Beach Park. During calm seas, the snorkeling and swimming are good, and when the surf's up, the body boarding and surfing are good, too. Frequent sunshine, grassy lawns, play equipment, and easy access add to the appeal, especially with families. The beach is frequently crowded and great for people-watching. Even the endangered Hawaiian monk seal often makes an appearance. Take a walk west on a path fronting numerous resorts. **Amenities:** food and drink; lifeguards; parking; showers; toilets. **Best for:** partiers; snorkeling; sunbathing; swimming. ✉ *Hoone Rd., off Poipu Rd., Poipu* ☎ *808/742–7444.*

Waiohai Beach

BEACH—SIGHT | The first hotel built in Poipu in 1962 overlooked this beach, adjacent to Poipu Beach Park. Actually, there's little to distinguish where this one ends and the other begins, other than a crescent reef at the eastern end of Waiohai Beach. That crescent, however, is important. It creates a small, protected bay—good for snorkeling and beginning surfers. However, when a summer swell kicks up, the near-shore conditions become dangerous; offshore, there's a splendid surf break for experienced surfers. The beach itself is narrow and, like its neighbor, gets very crowded in summer. **Amenities:** parking. **Best for:** snorkeling; sunset; surfing; swimming. ✉ *Hoone Rd., off Poipu Rd., Poipu.*

🍴 Restaurants

Most South Shore restaurants are more upscale and located within the Poipu resorts. If you're looking for a gourmet meal in a classy setting, the South Shore is where you'll find it. Poipu has a number of excellent restaurants in dreamy settings and decidedly fewer family-style, lower-price eateries.

Beach House

$$$$ | MODERN HAWAIIAN | This busy restaurant has a dreamy ocean view, making it a good setting for a special dinner or a cocktail and appetizer while the sun sinks into the glassy blue Pacific and surfers slice the waves. The prices have gone up, but you can still find satisfaction in the pork belly appetizer or fresh catch of the day served with *lilikoi* (passion fruit) lemongrass beurre blanc. **Known for:** gluten-free and vegan entrees; small bar with a big view; indoor-outdoor dining. [$] *Average main: $40* ✉ *5022 Lawai Rd., Poipu* ☎ *808/742–1424* 🌐 *www.the-beach-house.com.*

★ Dondero's

$$$$ | ITALIAN | With a beautiful setting, good food, stunning ocean view, and impeccable service by career waiters, Dondero's is one of Kauai's better restaurants. The menu features house-made pastas, classics like grilled seafood cioppino and tender veal osso buco, and salad greens cut daily from the hotel's hydroponic farm. **Known for:** Italianate murals and elegant interior; romantic outdoor dining experience; emphasis on local ingredients. [$] *Average main: $38* ✉ *Grand Hyatt Kauai Resort and Spa, 1571 Poipu Rd., Poipu* ☎ *808/240–6456* 🌐 *grandhyattkauai.com* 🕒 *Closed Sun. and Mon. No lunch.*

★ Eating House 1849

$$$ | ASIAN FUSION | Hawaii's culinary superstar, Roy Yamaguchi, moved his signature Hawaiian-fusion-cuisine restaurant on Kauai's South Shore to a shopping village that suits the name and creative fare. Though billed as "plantation cuisine," the hot pot rice bowl, spicy ramen bowl, and burger that's half wild boar are about the only items that might have their roots in the days when sugar was king; otherwise, the menu is classic Asian fusion. **Known for:** innovative cuisine; use of local ingredients; lively atmosphere.

[$] *Average main: $35* ✉ *Shops at Kukuiula, 2829 Ala Kalanikaumaka Rd., No. A-201, Poipu* ☎ *808/742–5000* 🌐 *www.eatinghouse1849.com.*

Keoki's Paradise

$$$ | **ASIAN FUSION** | **FAMILY** | Built to resemble a dockside boathouse, this active, semi-outdoor place fills up quickly at night thanks to a busy lounge and frequent live music. The day's fresh catch is available in various styles and sauces, from appetizers (Thai shrimp sticks) to mains (seafood risotto) to meat-lover options like the *imu*-roasted pork ribs. **Known for:** bustling bar with live music; keiki (kids) menu; fresh fish. [$] *Average main: $30* ✉ *Poipu Shopping Village, 2360 Kiahuna Plantation Dr., Poipu* ☎ *808/742–7534* 🌐 *www.keokisparadise.com.*

★ Makai Sushi

$ | **SUSHI** | The menu is simple—poke bowls and a few types of sushi rolls—but the freshness of the fish and attention to quality preparation set this tiny sushi bar apart from the crowd and make it a star of the Poipu Beach food scene. Tucked into a corner of Kukuiula Market, it attracts a steady stream of customers who watch owner Matthew Oliver or another chef transform spicy ahi, blue crab, avocado, cucumber, and *tobiko* (roe) into the Hapa Roll or mix raw ahi, ono fish, salmon, cucumber, avocado, and sweet Maui onion into the Gorilla Bowl. **Known for:** superfresh fish; friendly sushi chefs; takeout options. [$] *Average main: $15* ✉ *Kukuiula Market, 2728 Poipu Rd., Koloa* ☎ *808/639–7219* 🌐 *makaisushi.com.*

Merriman's Fish House

$$$$ | **MODERN HAWAIIAN** | The regional food served up at chef Peter Merriman's namesake restaurant is enhanced by a sophisticated setting and lovely views from a pretty second-floor dining room. Start at the bar, where fine wines are offered by the glass, and then continue to the dinner menu, which states the origins of the fish, shrimp, lamb, beef, chicken, and veggies. **Known for:** upscale, romantic atmosphere; casual menu downstairs; partnerships with local fishermen and farmers. [$] *Average main: $45* ✉ *2829 Ala Kalanikaumaka St., G-149, Poipu* ☎ *808/742–8385* 🌐 *www.merrimanshawaii.com.*

Plantation Gardens

$$$ | **HAWAIIAN** | A historic plantation manager's home has been converted to a restaurant that serves seafood and meats with a Pacific Rim and Hawaiian influence. Arrive early to stroll through the torch-lit orchid gardens and among lotus-studded koi ponds before settling in to the cozy European-style dining room or tropical veranda. **Known for:** veranda for outdoor dining; unique setting; inspired cocktails and bar menu. [$] *Average main: $30* ✉ *Kiahuna Plantation, 2253 Poipu Rd., Koloa* ☎ *808/742–2121* 🌐 *www.pgrestaurant.com* ⏲ *No lunch.*

★ Red Salt

$$$$ | **ECLECTIC** | Smart, sophisticated decor, attentive and skilled service, and an exceptional menu that highlights Hawaiian seafood make Red Salt a great choice for leisurely fine dining. A breakfast buffet is also served, and the sushi lounge and pool bar offer more of the kitchen's great food at lower prices. **Known for:** dramatic presentation; $79 tasting menu; perfectly grilled meats. [$] *Average main: $48* ✉ *Koa Kea Resort, 2251 Poipu Rd., Poipu* ☎ *808/742–4200* 🌐 *meritagecollection.com/koa-kea.*

Tidepools

$$$$ | **SEAFOOD** | Of the Grand Hyatt's notable restaurants, Tidepools is definitely the most tropical and campy, with grass-thatch huts that seem to float on a koi-filled pond beneath starry skies while torches flicker in the lushly landscaped grounds nearby. The equally distinctive food has an island flavor that comes from the chef's advocacy of Hawaii regional cuisine and extensive use of island-grown products, including fresh herbs from the resort's organic garden. **Known**

for: Hawaii regional cuisine; extensive use of island-grown products; excellent service. [$] *Average main: $50* ✉ *Grand Hyatt Kauai Resort and Spa, 1571 Poipu Rd., Poipu* ☎ *808/240–6380* 🌐 *grandhyattkauai.com* ⏲ *No lunch.*

Hotels

Sunseekers usually head south to the condo-studded shores of Poipu, where three- and four-story complexes line the coast, and the surf is generally ideal for swimming. As the island's primary resort community, Poipu has the bulk of the island's accommodations, and more condos than hotels, with prices in the moderate to expensive range. Although it accommodates many visitors, its extensive, colorful landscaping and low-rise buildings save it from feeling dense and overcrowded, and it has a delightful coastal promenade perfect for sunset strolls. Surprisingly, the South Shore doesn't have as many shops and restaurants as one might expect for such a popular resort region, but the new Kukuiula shopping plaza is doing its best to fill the gaps. **■ TIP→ The area's beaches are among the best on the island for families, with sandy shores, shallow waters, and grassy lawns adjacent to the sand.**

★ Grand Hyatt Kauai Resort and Spa

$$$$ | **RESORT** | **FAMILY** | Dramatically handsome, this classic Hawaiian low-rise is built into the cliffs overlooking an unspoiled coastline; it's taken great strides to reduce its carbon footprint and boasts mouthwatering restaurants, all of which helps to make it Kauai's best mega-resort. **Pros:** fabulous pool; excellent restaurants; Hawaiian ambience. **Cons:** dangerous swimming beach during summer swells; small balconies; $40 daily resort fee. [$] *Rooms from: $424* ✉ *1571 Poipu Rd., Poipu* ☎ *808/742–1234* 🌐 *www.grandhyattkauai.com* 🛏 *604 rooms* 🍴 *No meals.*

Kauai Cove Cottages

$$ | **RENTAL** | Located in a residential neighborhood, this property includes a quaint studio cottage at the mouth of Waikomo Stream, about two blocks from a nice snorkeling cove, as well as a full bedroom suite and a guest room with shared bath in a larger house a few miles away in the resort community at Poipu Kai. The airy tropical-theme studio has a cathedral ceiling, a complete kitchen, and a private patio with a gas grill. **Pros:** walk to shops and restaurants; great snorkeling nearby; quiet neighborhood. **Cons:** not on beach; $60–$90 cleaning fee upon departure; better for couples than families. [$] *Rooms from: $180* ✉ *2672 Puuholo Rd., Poipu* ☎ *808/631–9313 for cottage* 🌐 *www.kauaicove.com* 🛏 *3 units* 🍴 *No meals.*

Kiahuna Plantation Resort Kauai by Outrigger

$$ | **RENTAL** | **FAMILY** | This longtime Kauai condo project consists of 42 plantation-style, low-rise buildings with individually owned one- and two-bedroom units that arc around a large, grassy field leading to a lovely beach. **Pros:** great sunset and ocean views are bonuses in some units; convenient to restaurants and shops; swimmable beach and lawn for picnics and games. **Cons:** no air-conditioning; be prepared for stairs; housekeeping is extra. [$] *Rooms from: $180* ✉ *2253 Poipu Rd., Poipu* ☎ *808/742–6411, 866/994–1588 reservations* 🌐 *www.outrigger.com* 🛏 *333 units* 🍴 *No meals.*

★ Koa Kea Hotel and Resort

$$$$ | **RESORT** | This boutique property offers a stylish, high-end experience without the bustle of many larger resorts, making it a great place to forget it all while relaxing at the spa or lounging by the pool on a honeymoon or babymoon. **Pros:** incredibly comfortable beds; friendly service; perfect romantic getaway. **Cons:** not much for children; all parking is valet, but it feels more like a convenience than a burden; very busy area. [$] *Rooms*

from: $429 ⊠ 2251 Poipu Rd., Poipu
☎ *808/742–4200 general information,*
808/742–4271 reservations ⊕ *www.*
koakea.com ⮧ *121 rooms* ⦿❘ *No meals.*

Poipu Crater Resort

$ | **RENTAL** | Set within an extinct volcanic crater known as Piha Keakua, or "Place of the Gods," these two-bedroom condominium units in South Pacific–style bungalows are fairly spacious, with large windows, high ceilings, and full kitchens. **Pros:** attractive and generally well-kept; lush hilltop crater location; family friendly with ping-pong, pool, and clubhouse. **Cons:** beach isn't good for swimming; few resort amenities; individually owned units means upkeep and decor varies. $ *Rooms from: $150 ⊠ 2330 Hoohu Rd., Poipu* ☎ *808/742-7260* ⮧ *30 units* ⦿❘ *No meals.*

Poipu Kapili Resort

$$$ | **RENTAL** | **FAMILY** | White-frame exteriors and double-pitched roofs complement the tropical landscaping at this resort, which offers spacious one- and two-bedroom condo units—with full kitchens, bedroom air-conditioning, entertainment centers, and garden or ocean views—that are minutes from Poipu's restaurants and across the street from a nice beach. **Pros:** units are roomy and well-spaced; parking is close to the unit; tennis and pickleball on site. **Cons:** units are ocean-view but not oceanfront; a three-night minimum stay is required; minimal amenities. $ *Rooms from: $300 ⊠ 2221 Kapili Rd., Poipu* ☎ *808/742–6449, 800/325–5701* ⊕ *www.poipukapili. com* ⮧ *60 units* ⦿❘ *No meals.*

Poipu Plantation Resort

$ | **B&B/INN** | Plumeria, ti, and other tropical foliage create a lush landscape for this resort, which rents four suites in a bed-and-breakfast–style plantation home and nine one- and two-bedroom cottage apartments. **Pros:** attractively furnished; full breakfast at B&B; air-conditioning and free Wi-Fi. **Cons:** three-night minimum; not on the ocean; no resort amenities.

$ *Rooms from: $165 ⊠ 1792 Pee Rd., Poipu* ☎ *808/742–6757, 800/634–0263* ⊕ *www.poipubeach.com* ⮧ *4 rooms, 9 cottages* ⦿❘ *Free Breakfast.*

★ Sheraton Kauai Resort

$$$ | **RESORT** | The Sheraton is a sprawling resort with rooms that offer views of the ocean and lovely landscaped gardens; it's worth splurging on the ocean-wing accommodations, which are so close to the water you can practically feel the spray of the surf as it hits the rocks below. **Pros:** ocean-view pool; restaurant with spectacular sunset views; good facilities for meetings, events, reunions. **Cons:** parking can be a ways from the room; renovated rooms but some dated infrastructure; $30 daily resort fee. $ *Rooms from: $340 ⊠ 2440 Hoonani Rd., Poipu Beach, Koloa* ☎ *808/742–1661, 888/627–8113* ⊕ *www.sheraton-kauai. com* ⮧ *378 rooms* ⦿❘ *No meals.*

Whalers Cove Resort

$$$$ | **RENTAL** | Perched about as close to the water's edge as they can get, these condos are the most luxurious on the South Shore, available in one-, two-, or three-bedroom units. **Pros:** on-site staff and daily housekeeping; outstanding setting; spacious, with full kitchens. **Cons:** rocky beach not ideal for swimming; no air-conditioning; resort fee, but few amenities (parking, enhanced Wi-Fi). $ *Rooms from: $430 ⊠ 2640 Puuholo Rd., Poipu* ☎ *808/742–7571, 800/225– 2683* ⊕ *www.whalerscoveresort.com* ⮧ *24 units* ⦿❘ *No meals.*

🍸 Nightlife

Grand Hyatt Kauai Luau

THEMED ENTERTAINMENT | **FAMILY** | Excellent unlimited buffet food, an open bar, and exciting dance performances characterize this traditional luau, held twice weekly in a garden setting near majestic Keoneloa Bay. ⊠ *Grand Hyatt Kauai Resort and Spa, 1571 Poipu Rd., Poipu* ☎ *808/240–6320*

⊕ kauai.grand.hyatt.com/en/hotel/dining/
grand-hyatt-kauai-luau.html 🍴 From $135.

Keoki's Paradise
BARS/PUBS | A young, energetic crowd
makes this a lively spot on Friday and
Saturday night. When the dining room
clears out, there's a bit of a bar scene for
singles. Live music every night and two
happy hours—one 3–5 pm and the other
from 9:30 until closing at 10:30 pm—
keep the Bamboo Bar a happening place.
✉ Poipu Shopping Village, 2360 Kiahuna
Plantation Dr., Poipu ☎ 808/742–7534
⊕ www.keokisparadise.com.

🛍 Shopping

Surprisingly, the South Shore doesn't
have as many shops and restaurants
as one might expect for such a popular
resort region. However, it does have
convenient shopping clusters, including
Poipu Shopping Village, the upscale The
Shops at Kukuiula, Koloa Town's main
street, and the hip Warehouse 3540 nearby in Lawai. There are many high-priced
shops but some unique clothing and gift
selections.

Poipu Shopping Village
SHOPPING CENTERS/MALLS | FAMILY | Con-
venient to nearby hotels and condos on
the South Shore, the two dozen shops at
Poipu Shopping Village sell resort wear,
gifts, souvenirs, upscale jewelry, and art.
This complex also has a number of food
choices, from hot-dog or gelato stands to
casual sit-down restaurants. Kauai Juice
Co. has a loyal following. Watch a traditional hula show in the open-air courtyard
Monday and Thursday at 5 pm, and shop
at the bimonthly produce market. ✉ 2360
Kiahuna Plantation Dr., Poipu ☎ 808/742–
2831 ⊕ www.poipushoppingvillage.com.

The Shops at Kukuiula
SHOPPING CENTERS/MALLS | This is the
South Shore's upscale shopping center,
with chic shops, exclusive galleries, several great restaurants, and a gourmet grocery store. The flagship of Malie Organics

bath line, used by many top hotels and
spas, is here. Check out the Kauai Culinary Market on Wednesday from 3:30 to
6 to see cooking demonstrations, listen
to live music, visit the beer and wine
garden, and shop from local vendors.
This attractive open-air, plantation-style
center is at the roundabout as you enter
Poipu. ✉ 2829 Kalanikaumaka St., Poipu
☎ 808/742–9545 ⊕ www.theshopsat-
kukuiula.com.

The West Side

Exploring the West Side is akin to visiting
an entirely different world. The landscape
is dramatic and colorful: a patchwork
of green, blue, black, and orange. The
weather is hot and dry, the beaches are
long, the sand is dark. Niihau, a private
island and the last remaining place in
Hawaii where Hawaiian is spoken exclusively, can be glimpsed offshore. This is
rural Kauai, where sugar is making its last
stand, and taro is still cultivated in the
fertile river valleys. The lifestyle is slow,
easy, and traditional, with many folks
fishing and hunting to supplement their
diets. Here and there modern, industry
has intruded into this pastoral scene:
huge generators turn oil into electricity
at Port Allen; seed companies cultivate
experimental crops of genetically engi-
neered plants in Kekaha and Waimea; the
navy launches rockets at Mana to test
the "Star Wars" missile defense system;
and NASA mans a tracking station in the
wilds of Kokee. It's a region of contrasts
that simply shouldn't be missed.

Heading west from Lihue or Poipu, you
pass through a string of tiny towns,
plantation camps, and historic sites, each
with a story to tell of centuries past.
There's Hanapepe, whose coastal salt
ponds have been harvested since ancient
times; Kaumakani, where the sugar
industry still clings to life; Fort Elisabeth,
from which an enterprising Russian tried
to take over the island in the early 1800s;

and Waimea, where Captain Cook made his first landing in the Islands, forever changing the face of Hawaii.

From Waimea town you can head up into the mountains, skirting the rim of magnificent Waimea Canyon and climbing higher still until you reach the cool, often-misty forests of Kokee State Park. From the vantage point at the top of this gemlike island, 3,200 to 4,200 feet above sea level, you can gaze into the deep, verdant valleys of the North Shore and Napali Coast. This is where the "real" Kauai can still be found: the native plants, insects, and birds that are found nowhere else on Earth.

Hanapepe

15 miles west of Poipu.

In the 1980s, Hanapepe was fast becoming a ghost town, its farm-based economy mirroring the decline of agriculture. Today, it's a burgeoning art colony with galleries, crafts studios, and a lively art-theme street fair on Friday nights. The main street has a new vibrancy enhanced by the restoration of several historic buildings. The emergence of Kauai coffee as a major West Side crop and expanded activities at Port Allen, now the main departure point for tour boats, also gave the town's economy a boost.

Hanapepe, locally known as Kauai's "biggest little town," is just past the Eleele Shopping Center on the main highway (Route 50). A sign leads you to the town center, where street parking is easy, and there's an enjoyable walking tour.

👁 Sights

Hanapepe Swinging Bridge
BRIDGE/TUNNEL | FAMILY | This bridge may not be the biggest adventure on Kauai, but it's enough to make your heart hop. It's considered a historic suspension bridge even though it was rebuilt in 1996

after the original was destroyed—like so much of the island—by Hurricane Iniki. It was also repaired and reopened following severe damages inflicted by flooding in 2019. What is interesting about this bridge is that it's not just for show; it actually provides the only access to taro fields across the Waimea River. If you're in the neighborhood, it's worth a stroll. ⊠ *Off Hanapepe Rd., next to Banana Patch Studios parking lot, Hanapepe* ⊕ *www.kauai.com/ hanapepe-swinging-bridge.*

Hanapepe Valley and Canyon Lookout
VIEWPOINT | This dramatic divide and fertile river valley once housed a thriving Hawaiian community of taro farmers, with some of the ancient fields still in cultivation today. From the roadside lookout, you can take in the farms on the valley floor with the majestic mountains as a backdrop. ⊠ *Rte. 50, Hanapepe.*

🌊 Beaches

The West Side of the island receives hardly enough rainfall year-round to water a cactus, and because it's also the leeward side, there are few tropical breezes. That translates to sunny and hot with long, languorous, and practically deserted beaches. You'd think the leeward waters—untouched by wind—would be calm, but there's no reef system, so the beach drops off quickly and currents are common. Rivers often turn the ocean water murky. ■TIP→ **The best place to gear up for the beaches on the West Side is on the South Shore or East Side.** Although there's some catering to visitors here, it's not much.

Salt Pond Beach Park
BEACH—SIGHT | FAMILY | A great family spot, Salt Pond Beach Park features a naturally made, shallow swimming pond behind a curling finger of rock where *keiki* (children) splash and snorkel. This pool is generally safe except during a large south swell, which usually occurs in

summer, if at all. The center and western edge of the beach is popular with body boarders and body surfers. Pavilions with picnic tables offer shade, and there's a campground that tends to attract a rowdy bunch at the eastern end. On a cultural note, the flat stretch of land to the east of the beach is the last spot in Hawaii where ponds are used to harvest salt in the dry heat of summer. The beach park is popular with locals, and it can get crowded on weekends and holidays. **Amenities:** lifeguard; parking; showers; toilets. **Best for:** sunset; swimming; walking. ✉ *Lolokai Rd., off Rte. 50, Hanapepe.*

🍴 Restaurants

When it comes to dining on the West Side, pickings are mighty slim. Fortunately, the few eateries that are here are generally worth patronizing.

Kalaheo Café & Coffee Co.

$$ | AMERICAN | FAMILY | Folks love this roadside café—especially at breakfast, though it's good for lunch and dinner specials, too—for its casual neighborhood feel. It's frequently busy, especially on weekend mornings. **Known for:** fresh-baked pastries and bread; great local coffee; hearty portions like the Kahili Breakfast or the Longboard sandwich. [$] *Average main: $22* ✉ *2-2560 Kaumualii Hwy. (Rte. 50), Kalaheo* ☎ *808/332–5858* 🌐 *www.kalaheo.com* 🕓 *No dinner Sun. and Mon.*

Little Fish Coffee

$ | CAFÉ | FAMILY | For a wholesome breakfast or lunch on the West Side, this friendly, funky, and fun café—right down to the marking pens that allow you to leave your own graffiti on the bathroom wall—is the spot. The coffee is good, with each cup individually dripped, and the fresh bagels come with house-made cream cheese or a variety of toppings. **Known for:** casual setting; emphasis on wholesome ingredients; smoothies and fresh juices. [$] *Average main: $9* ✉ *3900 Hanapepe Rd., Hanapepe* ☎ *808/335–5000* 🌐 *littlefishcoffee.com* 🕓 *No dinner.*

🛏 Hotels

Kalaheo Inn

$ | B&B/INN | FAMILY | It isn't easy to find good lodgings on the southwest side of the island, but this old-fashioned budget inn with studios or one-, two-, and three-bedroom suites does an adequate, no-frills job in Kalaheo Town. **Pros:** some units have kitchens; walking distance to restaurants; coin-operated laundry on-site. **Cons:** property is a ways from the beach; no air-conditioning; dated furnishings. [$] *Rooms from: $93* ✉ *4444 Papalina Rd., Kalaheo* ☎ *808/332–6023, 888/332–6023* 🌐 *www.kalaheoinn.com* 🛏 *16 units* 🍽 *No meals.*

👜 Shopping

The West Side is years behind the South Shore in development, offering minimal, simple shops with authentic local flavor.

Eleele Shopping Center

SHOPPING CENTERS/MALLS | Kauai's West Side has a scattering of stores, including those at this no-frills strip mall. It has a post office, several banks, a hardware store, a laundromat, and a hair salon, and it's a good place to rub elbows with local folk at Longs Drugs or Big Save Times grocery store. There's a McDonald's, Subway, and a few little local eateries. ✉ *4469 Waialo Rd., Eleele* ☎ *808/245–7238* 🌐 *www.eleeleshoppingcenter.com.*

Kauai Coffee Visitor Center and Museum

FOOD/CANDY | Kauai produces more coffee than any other island in the state. The local product can be purchased from grocery stores or here at the Kauai Coffee Visitor Center and Museum, where a sampling of the nearly two dozen coffees is available. Be sure to try some of the estate-roasted varieties. ✉ *870 Halewili Rd., off Rte. 50, Kalaheo*

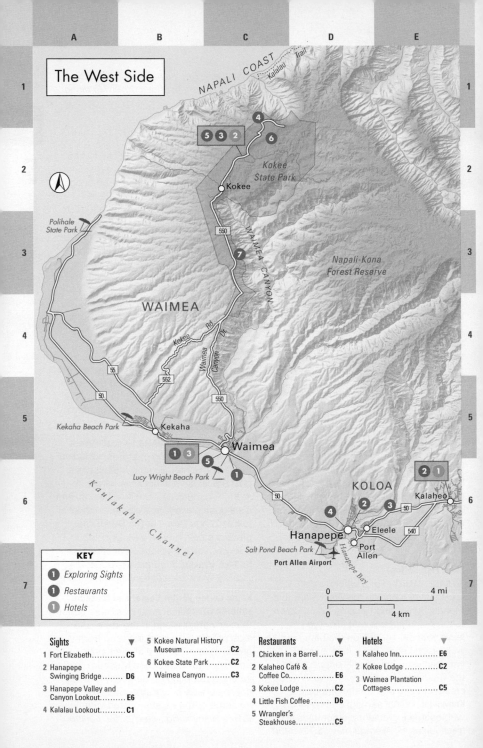

The West Side

Kokee State Park

Napali-Kona Forest Reserve

Polihale State Park

WAIMEA

Kokee

NAPALI COAST

Kalalau Trail

WAIMEA CANYON

Kokee Rd

Waimea Canyon Dr

Kekaha Beach Park

Kekaha

Waimea

Lucy Wright Beach Park

Kaulakahi Channel

KOLOA

Kalaheo

Eleele

Hanapepe

Port Allen

Salt Pond Beach Park

Hanapepe Bay

Port Allen Airport

| 0 | | 4 mi |
| 0 | | 4 km |

KEY

① Exploring Sights

① Restaurants

① Hotels

Sights ▼

1 Fort Elizabeth............**C5**

2 Hanapepe
Swinging Bridge........**D6**

3 Hanapepe Valley and
Canyon Lookout.........**E6**

4 Kalalau Lookout..........**C1**

5 Kokee Natural History
Museum **C2**

6 Kokee State Park........**C2**

7 Waimea Canyon **C3**

Restaurants ▼

1 Chicken in a Barrel **C5**

2 Kalaheo Café &
Coffee Co.................**E6**

3 Kokee Lodge **C2**

4 Little Fish Coffee **D6**

5 Wrangler's
Steakhouse...............**C5**

Hotels ▼

1 Kalaheo Inn...............**E6**

2 Kokee Lodge **C2**

3 Waimea Plantation
Cottages **C5**

Sunshine Markets

If you want to rub elbows with the locals and purchase fresh produce and flowers at (somewhat) reasonable prices, head for Sunshine Markets, also known as Kauai's farmers' markets. These busy markets are held throughout the week, usually in the afternoon, at locations all around the island—just ask any local person. They're good fun, and they support neighborhood farmers. Arrive a little early, bring dollar bills to speed up transactions and your own shopping bags to carry your produce, and be prepared for some pushy shoppers. Farmers are usually happy to educate visitors about unfamiliar fruits and veggies, especially when the crowd thins. For schedules and information on all of the Sunshine Markets, check out Kauai's government website at ⊕ *www.kauai.gov.*

East Side Sunshine Markets
⊠ *Vidinha Stadium, Lihue, ½ mile south of airport on Rte. 51, Friday 3 pm. ⊠ Kapaa, turn mauka on Rte. 581/ Olohena Rd. for 1 block, Wednesday 3 pm.*

North Shore Sunshine Markets
⊠ *Waipa, mauka of Rte. 560 north of Hanalei after mile marker 3, Hanalei, Tuesday 2 pm. ⊠ Kilauea Neighborhood Center, on Keneke St., Kilauea, Thursday 4:30 pm. ⊠ Hanalei Community Center, 5299 Kuhio Hwy, Hanalei, Saturday 9:30 am.*

South Shore Sunshine Markets
⊠ *Ballpark, Koloa, north of intersection of Koloa Rd. and Rte. 520, Monday noon.*

West Side Sunshine Markets ⊠ *Kalaheo Community Center, on Papalina Rd. just off Kaumualii Hwy., Kalaheo, Tuesday 3 pm. ⊠ Hanapepe Park, Hanapepe, Thursday 3 pm. ⊠ Kekaha Neighborhood Center, Elepaio Rd., Kekaha, Saturday 9 am.*

☎ *808/335–0813, 800/545–8605* ⊕ *www. kauaicoffee.com.*

Talk Story Bookstore

BOOKS/STATIONERY | Located in a historic building in quiet Hanapepe Town, this is the only bookstore on Kauai, with some 150,000 titles and a resident cat named Mochi Celeste. The cozy shop becomes a gathering place on busy Friday evenings, when local authors sign their books while live music and food trucks entertain meandering crowds during the weekly art nights. New, used, rare, and out-of-print books are sold here, as well as vinyl records. ⊠ *3785 Hanapepe Rd., Hanapepe* ☎ *808/335–6469* ⊕ *www. talkstorybookstore.com.*

Waimea, Waimea Canyon, and Around

Waimea is 7 miles northwest of Hanapepe; Waimea Canyon is approximately 10 miles northeast of Waimea.

Waimea is a serene, pretty town that has the look of the Old West and the feel of Old Hawaii, with a lifestyle that's decidedly laid-back. It's an ideal place for a refreshment break while sightseeing on the West Side. The town has played a major role in Hawaiian history since 1778, when Captain James Cook became the first European to set foot on the Hawaiian Islands. Waimea was also the place where Kauai's King Kaumualii acquiesced to King Kamehameha's unification drive

You don't have to hike to see sweeping Waimea Canyon vistas. Many overlooks, like the one pictured above, are reachable by car, right off the main road.

in 1810, averting a bloody war. The town hosted the first Christian missionaries, who hauled in massive timbers and limestone blocks to build the sturdy Waimea Christian Hawaiian and Foreign Church in 1846. It's one of many lovely historic buildings preserved by residents who take great pride in their heritage and history.

North of Waimea town, via Route 550, you'll find the vast and gorgeous Waimea Canyon, also known as the Grand Canyon of the Pacific. The spectacular vistas from the lookouts along the road culminate with an overview of Kalalau Valley. There are various hiking trails leading to the inner heart of Kauai. A camera is a necessity in this region.

Route 50 continues northwest to Waimea and Kekaha from Hanapepe. You can reach Waimea Canyon and Kokee State Park from either town—the way is clearly marked. Some pull-off areas on Route 550 are fine for a quick view of the canyon, but the designated lookouts have bathrooms and parking.

◉ Sights

Fort Elizabeth
ARCHAEOLOGICAL SITE | The ruins of this stone fort, built in 1816 by an agent of the imperial Russian government named Anton Scheffer, are a reminder of the days when Scheffer tried to conquer the island for his homeland, or so one story goes. Another claims that Scheffer's allegiance lay with King Kaumualii, who was attempting to regain leadership of his island nation from the grasp of Kamehameha the Great. The crumbling walls of the fort are not particularly interesting, but the signs loaded with historical information are. ⊠ *Rte. 50, Waimea (Kauai County).*

Kalalau Lookout
VIEWPOINT | At the end of the road, high above Waimea Canyon, Kalalau Lookout marks the start of a 1-mile (one-way) hike to **Puu o Kila Lookout.** On a clear day at either spot, you can see a dreamy landscape of gaping valleys, sawtooth ridges, waterfalls, and turquoise seas, where

whales can be seen spouting and breaching during the winter months. If clouds block the view, don't despair—they tend to blow through fast, giving you time to snap that photo of a lifetime. You may spot wild goats clambering on the sheer rocky cliffs, and white-tailed tropic birds. If it's very clear to the northwest, drink in the shining sands of Kalalau Beach, gleaming like golden threads against the deep blue of the Pacific. ⊠ *Waimea Canyon Dr.* ✛ *4 miles north of Kokee State Park.*

Kokee Natural History Museum

MUSEUM | Kokee Natural History Museum is a great place to start your visit to Kokee State Park. The friendly staff is knowledgeable about trail conditions and weather, while informative displays and a good selection of reference books can teach you more about the unique attributes of the native flora and fauna. You may also find that special memento or gift you've been looking for. ⊠ *Rte. 550, Kokee* ☎ *808/335–9975* ⊕ *kokee.org* ✍ *Donations accepted.*

Kokee State Park

NATIONAL/STATE PARK | This 4,345-acre wilderness park is 3,600 feet above sea level, an elevation that affords you breathtaking views and a cooler, wetter climate that's in marked contrast to the beach. You can gain a deeper appreciation of the island's rugged terrain and dramatic beauty from this vantage point. Large tracts of native ohia and koa forest cover much of the land, along with many varieties of exotic plants. Hikers can follow a 45-mile network of trails through diverse landscapes that feel wonderfully remote—until the tour helicopters pass overhead. *Note there's no cell phone service in the park.* ⊠ *Hwy. 50, Kekaha* ✛ *15 miles north of Kekaha* ⊕ *kokee.org.*

★ Waimea Canyon

CANYON | Carved over countless centuries by the Waimea River and the forces of wind and rain, Waimea Canyon is a dramatic gorge nicknamed the "Grand Canyon of the Pacific"—but not by Mark Twain, as many people mistakenly think. Hiking and hunting trails wind through the canyon, which is 3,600 feet deep, 2 miles wide, and 10 miles long. The cliff sides have been sharply eroded, exposing swatches of colorful soil. The deep red, brown, and green hues are constantly changing in the sun, and frequent rainbows and waterfalls enhance the natural beauty. This is one of Kauai's prettiest spots, and it's worth stopping at both the **Puu ka Pele** and **Puu Hinahina** lookouts. Clean public restrooms and parking are at both lookouts. ⊠ *Hwy. 550 (Kokee Rd.), Waimea (Kauai County)* ☎ *808/274–3444* ⊕ *dlnr.hawaii.gov/dsp/parks/kauai/.*

☺ Beaches

Kekaha Beach Park

BEACH—SIGHT | This is one of the premier spots on Kauai for sunset walks and the start of the state's longest beach. We don't recommend much water activity here without first talking to a lifeguard. The beach is exposed to open ocean and has an onshore break that can be hazardous any time of year. However, there are some excellent surf breaks—for experienced surfers only. Or, if you would like to run or stroll on a beach, this is the one—the hard-packed sand goes on for miles, all the way to Napali Coast, but you won't get past the Pacific Missile Range Facility and its post-9/11 access restrictions. Another bonus for this beach is its relatively dry weather year-round. If it's raining where you are, try Kekaha Beach Park. Toilets here are the portable kind. **Amenities:** lifeguards; parking; showers; toilets. **Best for:** sunset; surfing; walking. ⊠ *Rte. 50, near mile marker 27, Kekaha.*

★ Polihale State Park

BEACH—SIGHT | The longest stretch of beach in Hawaii starts in Kekaha and ends west about 15 miles away at the start of Napali Coast. On the far west end is the 5-mile-long, 140-acre Polihale State

Park. In addition to being long, this beach is 300 feet wide in places and backed by sand dunes 50 to 100 feet tall. It is frequently very hot, with minimal shade and scorching sand in summer. Polihale is a remote beach accessed via a very rough and potholed, 5-mile haul-cane road (AWD or four-wheel drive recommended) at the end of Route 50 in Kekaha. **■ TIP→ Be sure to start the day with a full tank of gas and a cooler filled with food and drink.** Though it's a popular camping and day-use beach location, the water here is typically rough and not recommended for recreation. No driving is allowed on the beach. The Pacific Missile Range Facility, operated by the U.S. Navy, is adjacent to the beach, and access to the coastline in front of the base is restricted. **Amenities:** parking; showers; toilets. **Best for:** solitude; sunset; walking. ✉ *Dirt road at end of Rte. 50, Kekaha* ☎ *808/587–0300.*

🍴 Restaurants

Chicken in a Barrel
$ | **BARBECUE** | **FAMILY** | This casual eatery is located in the equally laid-back Waimea Plantation Cottages hotel; it's a great place to sit with a cocktail and watch the sun set or let the kids run around on the lawn. The fare is simple and hearty: barrel-smoked barbecue chicken, pork, brisket, or ribs; plus salads, tacos, and burgers. **Known for:** large portions; kid-friendly dining; great selection of sides. [$] *Average main: $15* ✉ *9400 Kaumualii Hwy., Waimea (Kauai County)* ☎ *808/338–1625* 🌐 *www.coasthotels.com.*

Kokee Lodge
$ | **AMERICAN** | There's only one place to buy breakfast, hot food, drinks, and snacks in Kokee State Park, and that's the rustic Kokee Lodge. It's known for its Portugese bean soup and corn bread, of all things. **Known for:** Portuguese bean soup; pie and coffee; gift shop. [$] *Average main: $12* ✉ *Kokee State Park, 3600 Kokee Rd., mile marker 15, Kokee* ☎ *808/335–6061* 🌐 *kokeelodge.com* 🕒 *No dinner.*

Wrangler's Steakhouse
$$$ | **STEAKHOUSE** | **FAMILY** | Denim-covered seating, decorative saddles, and a stagecoach in a loft helped to transform the historic Ako General Store in Waimea into a West Side steak house where you can eat under the stars on the deck out back or in the old-fashioned, wood-panel dining room. Open weekend evenings, the Saddle Room features a bar menu that includes seven styles of burgers, and there's live music on Saturday night. **Known for:** special lunch (rice, beef teriyaki, and shrimp tempura with kimchi) served in a three-tier kaukau tin; campy setting; local, grass-fed beef. [$] *Average main: $32* ✉ *9852 Kaumualii Hwy., Waimea (Kauai County)* ☎ *808/338–1218* 🌐 *wranglerssteakhousehi.com* 🕒 *Closed Sun. No lunch Sat.*

🛏 Hotels

To do a lot of hiking or immerse yourself in the island's history, find a room in Waimea. You won't find many resorts, restaurants, or shops, but you will encounter quiet days, miles of largely deserted beach, and a rural environment.

Kokee Lodge
$ | **RENTAL** | If you're an outdoors enthusiast, you can appreciate Kauai's mountain wilderness from the 12 rustic cabins—of varying age and quality—that make up this lodge. **Pros:** outstanding setting; more refined than camping; cooking facilities. **Cons:** wood-burning stove is the only heat; no restaurants for dinner; $45 cleaning fee. [$] *Rooms from: $89* ✉ *Kokee State Park, 3600 Kokee Rd., at mile marker 15, Kokee* ☎ *808/652–6852* 🌐 *www.westkauailodging.com/en-us* 🛏 *12 cabins* 🍴 *No meals.*

★ Waimea Plantation Cottages
$$ | **RENTAL** | Originally built in the early 1900s, these relocated and refurbished one- to five-bedroom sugar-plantation

cottages are tucked among coconut trees along a lovely, walkable stretch of beach on the sunny West Side. **Pros:** unique lodging experience; quiet and low-key; lovely grounds. **Cons:** not a good swimming beach; rooms are simple; cottages can be hot in summer. [$] *Rooms from: $209* ✉ *9400 Kaumualii Hwy., Box 367, Waimea (Kauai County)* ☎ *808/338–1923, 800/716–6199* 🌐 *www.coasthotels.com* 🛏 *61 cottages* 🍴 *No meals.*

Shopping

Waimea Canyon Plaza

SHOPPING CENTERS/MALLS | As the last stop for supplies before heading up to Waimea Canyon or out to Polihale Beach, Waimea Canyon Plaza has a Menehune Food Mart with limited groceries, snacks, beverages, fresh and prepared local foods, souvenirs, and island-made gifts for all ages. ✉ *8171 Kekaha Rd., at Rte. 50, Kekaha* ☎ *808/337–1335.*

Activities and Tours

Kauai's outdoor recreation options extend well beyond the sand and surf, with plenty of activities to keep you busy on the ground and even in the air. You can hike the island's many trails, or consider taking your vacation into flight with a treetop zipline. You can have a backcountry adventure in a four-wheel-drive vehicle, or relax in an inner tube floating down the cane-field irrigation canals.

Before booking tours, check with your concierge to find out what the forecast is for water and weather conditions. Don't rely on the Weather Channel for accurate weather reports, as they're often reporting Oahu weather. If you happen to arrive during a North Shore lull in the surf, you'll want to plan to be on the ocean in a kayak or snorkeling on the reef. If it's raining, ATV tours are the activity of choice.

For the golfer in the family, Kauai's spectacular courses are rated among the most scenic, as well as the most technical. Princeville Golf Course has garnered accolades from numerous national publications, and Poipu Bay Golf Course hosted the prestigious season-end PGA Grand Slam of Golf for 13 years, although Tiger (he won a record five-straight tournaments) and company, unfortunately, now head to Bermuda for this tourney.

One of the most popular Kauai experiences is to see the island from the air. In an hour or so, you can see waterfalls, craters, and other places that are inaccessible even by hiking trails (some say that 70% or more of the island is inaccessible). The majority of flights depart from the Lihue airport and follow a clockwise pattern around the island. ■ **TIP→ If you plan to take an aerial tour, it's a good idea to fly when you first arrive, rather than saving it for the end of your trip. It will help you visualize what's where on the island, and it may help you decide what you want to see from a closer vantage point during your stay.** Be prepared to relive your flight in dreams for the rest of your life. The most popular flight is 60 minutes long.

Ancient Hawaiians were water-sports fanatics—they invented surfing, after all—and that propensity hasn't strayed far from today's mind-set. Even if you're not into water sports or sports in general, there's only a slim chance that you'll leave this island without getting out on the ocean, as Kauai's top attraction—Napali Coast—is not to be missed.

For those who can't pack enough snorkeling, fishing, body boarding, or surfing time into a vacation, Kauai has it all—everything except parasailing, that is, as it's illegal to do it here (though not on Maui, the Big Island, or Oahu). If you need to rent gear for any of these activities, you'll find plenty of places with large selections at reasonable prices. And no matter what part of the island you're staying on, you'll have several options for choice spots to enjoy playing in the water.

One thing to note, and we can't say this enough—the waters off the coast of Kauai have strong currents and can be unpredictable, so always err on the side of caution and know your limits. Follow the tagline repeated by the island's lifeguards—"When in doubt, don't go out."

Aerial Tours

If you only drive around Kauai in your rental car, you will not see *all* of Kauai. There is truly only one way to see it all, and that's by air. Helicopter tours are the favorite way to get a bird's-eye view of Kauai—they fly at lower altitudes, hover above waterfalls, and wiggle their way into areas that a fixed-wing aircraft cannot. That said, if you've already tried the helitour, how about flying in the open cockpit of a biplane—à la the Red Baron?

Air Tour Kauai

FLYING/SKYDIVING/SOARING | This company can hold up to six people in its Cessna 207 plane. The flights take off from the less crowded Port Allen Airport and will last 65 to 70 minutes. ⊠ *Port Allen Airport, 3441 Kuiloko Rd., Hanapepe* ☎ *808/639–3446* ⊕ *www.airtourkauai. com* 🖃 *$99 per person.*

Blue Hawaiian Helicopters

TOUR—SPORTS | This multiisland operator flies the latest in helicopter technology, the Eco-Star, costing $1.8 million. It has 23% more interior space for its six passengers, as well as unparalleled viewing and a few extra safety features. As the name implies, the helicopter is also a bit more environmentally friendly, with a 50% noise-reduction rate. Even though flights run a tad shorter than those offered by other companies (50 to 55 minutes instead of 55 to 65 minutes), they feel complete. A DVD of your tour is available for an additional $25. ⊠ *3651 Ahukini Rd., Heliport 8, Lihue*

☎ *808/245–5800, 800/745–2583* ⊕ *www. bluehawaiian.com* 🖃 *$289.*

★ Jack Harter Helicopters

TOUR—SPORTS | Jack Harter was the first company to offer helicopter tours on Kauai. The company flies the six-passenger ASTAR helicopter with floor-to-ceiling windows, and the four-person Hughes 500, which is flown with no doors. The doorless ride can get windy, but it's the best bet for taking reflection-free photos. Pilots provide information on the Garden Island's history and geography through two-way intercoms. The company flies out of Lihue. Tours are 60 to 65 minutes and 90 to 95 minutes. Receive a $30 discount when you book through their website. ⊠ *4231 Ahukini Rd.* ☎ *808/245–3774, 888/245–2001* ⊕ *www.helicopters-kauai.com* 🖃 *From $289.*

Sunshine Helicopter Tours

TOUR—SPORTS | If the name of this company sounds familiar, it may be because its pilots fly on all the main Hawaiian Islands except Oahu. On Kauai, Sunshine Helicopters departs out of two different locations: Lihue and Princeville. They fly the six-passenger FX STAR from Lihue or the super-roomy six-passenger WhisperSTAR birds. ■**TIP→ Discounts can be substantial by booking online and taking advantage of the "early-bird" seating during off-hours.** ⊠ *3416 Rice St., Ste. 203, Lihue* ☎ *808/240–2577, 866/501–7738* ⊕ *www.sunshinehelicopters.com* 🖃 *From $244, Princeville $289.*

ATV Tours

Although all the beaches on the island are public, much of the interior land—once sugar and pineapple plantations—is privately owned. This is really a shame, because the valleys and mountains that make up the vast interior of the island easily rival the beaches in sheer beauty. The good news is some tour operators have agreements with landowners that make exploration possible, albeit a bit bumpy, and unless you have back troubles, that's half the fun. ■**TIP➜ If it looks like rain, book an ATV tour ASAP. That's the thing about these tours: the muddier, the better.**

★ Kauai ATV Tours
TOUR—SPORTS | This is *the* thing to do when it rains on Kauai. Consider it an extreme mud bath. Kauai ATV in Koloa is the originator of the island's all-terrain-vehicle tours. The three-hour Koloa tour takes you through a private sugar plantation and historic haul-cane tunnel. The four-hour waterfall tour visits secluded waterfalls and includes a picnic lunch. This popular option includes a hike to secret WWII bunkers and a swim in a freshwater pool at the base of the falls—to rinse off all that mud. You must be 18 or older to operate your own ATV, but Kauai ATV also offers its four-passenger "Ohana Bug" and two-passenger "Mud Bugs" to accommodate families with kids ages five and older. ✉ *3477A Weliweli Rd., Koloa* ☎ *808/742–2734, 877/707–7088* ⊕ *www.kauaiatv.com* ✍ *From $358 for 2 people.*

Kipu Ranch Adventures
TOUR—SPORTS | This 3,000-acre property extends from the Huleia River to the top of Mt. Haupu. *Jurassic Park* and *Indiana Jones* were filmed here, and you'll see the locations for them on the three-hour Ranch Tour. The four-hour Waterfall Tour includes a visit to two waterfalls and a picnic lunch. Once a sugar plantation, Kipu Ranch today is a working cattle ranch, so you'll be in the company of bovines as well as pheasants, wild boars, and peacocks. If you're not an experienced ATV driver, they also offer guide-driven tour options. ✉ *235 Kipu Rd., off Hwy. 50, Lihue* ☎ *808/246–9288* ⊕ *www.kiputours.com* ✍ *From $148.*

Biking

Kauai is a labyrinth of cane-haul roads that are fun for exploring on two wheels. The challenge is finding roads where biking is allowed and then not getting lost in the maze. Maybe that explains why Kauai is not a hub for the sport—yet. Still, for those who are interested, there are some epic rides, both the adrenaline-rush and the mellower beach-cruiser kind. If you want to grind out some mileage, you could take the main highway that skirts the coastal area, but be careful: there are only a few designated bike lanes, the shoulders are often crowded with invasive guinea grass, and the terrain is hilly. You may find that keeping your eyes on the road rather than the scenery is your biggest challenge. "Cruisers" should head to Kapaa, where the Ke Ala Hele Makalae, a pedestrian and bicycle trail, runs along the East Side of Kauai for miles. You can rent bikes (with helmets) from the activities desks of certain hotels, but these are not the best quality. You're better off renting from Kauai Cycle in Kapaa, Outfitters Kauai in Poipu, or Pedal 'n' Paddle in Hanalei. Ask for the "Go Green Kauai" map for a full description of Kauai biking options.

BEST SPOTS
★ **Ke Ala Hele Makalae** (*coastal path*)
BICYCLING | This county beach park path follows the coastline on Kauai's East Side and is perfect for cruisers. Eventually, the path is projected to run some 20 miles, but an existing 8-mile-long stretch already offers scenic views, picnic pavilions, and restroom facilities along the way—all in compliance with the Americans with Disabilities Act. The path runs from Lydgate Beach Park to secluded Kuna Bay (aka Donkey Beach). An easy way to access the longest completed section of the path is from Kealia Beach. Park here and head north into rural lands with spectacular coastline vistas, or head south into Kapaa for a more immersive

experience. ✉ *Kealia Beach, Kapaa*
⊕ *Trailhead: 1 mile north of Kapaa; park
at north end of Kealia Beach* ⊕ *www.
kauaipath.org/kauaicoastalpath.*

Moalepe Trail

BICYCLING | This trail is perfect for interme-
diate to advanced trail-bike riders. The
first 2 miles of this 5-mile double-track
road wind steeply through pastureland.
The real challenge begins when you
reach the steep and rutted switchbacks,
which during a rainy spell can be hazardous. Moalepe intersects the Kuilau
Trail, which you can follow to its end at
the Keahua Arboretum stream. ✉ *Wailua
(Kauai County)* ⊕ *From Kuhio Hwy. in
Kapaa drive mauka (toward mountains)
on Kuamoo Rd. for 3 miles and turn right
on Kamalu Rd., which dead-ends at Olohena Rd. Turn left and follow until road
veers sharply to right.*

Wailua Forest Management Road

BICYCLING | For the novice mountain biker,
this is an easy ride, and it's also easy to
find. From Route 56 in Wailua, turn *mauka (toward the mountains)* on Kuamoo
Road and continue 6 miles to the picnic
area known as Keahua Arboretum; park
here. The potholed four-wheel-drive road
includes some stream crossings—⚠ **stay
away during heavy rains, because the
streams flood**—and continues for 2 miles
to a T-stop, where you should turn right.
Stay on the road for about 3 miles until
you reach a gate; this is the spot where
the gates in the movie *Jurassic Park*
were filmed, though it looks nothing like
the movie. Go around the gate and down
the road for another mile to a confluence
of streams at the base of Mt. Waialeale.
Be sure to bring your camera. ✉ *Kuamoo
Rd., Kapaa.*

Waimea Canyon Road

BICYCLING | For those wanting a very chal-
lenging road workout, climb this road,
also known as Route 550. After a 3,000-
foot climb, the road tops out at mile 12,
adjacent to Waimea Canyon. From here it
continues several miles (somewhat level)
past the Kokee Museum and ends at
the Kalalau Lookout. It's paved the entire
way, uphill 100%, and curvy. ⚠ **There's
not much of a shoulder on either road—
sometimes none—so be extra cautious.** The
road gets busier as the day wears on, so
you may want to consider a sunrise ride.
We suggest the slightly more moderate
uphill climb on Kokee Road, Route 552,
from Kekaha, which intersects with
Route 550. Bicyclists can park their cars
at Waimea ball park and ride over to
Kekaha to begin the uphill climb. Bicycles
aren't allowed on the hiking trails in and
around Waimea Canyon and Kokee State
Park, but there are miles of wonderful
four-wheel-drive roads perfect for mountain biking. Check at the Kokee Natural
History Museum for a map and conditions. ✉ *Off Rte. 50, near grocery store,
Waimea (Kauai County).*

EQUIPMENT AND TOURS

Kauai Cycle

BICYCLING | This reliable, full-service bike
shop rents, sells, and repairs bikes.
Cruisers, mountain bikes (front and full
suspension), and road bikes are available,
with directions to trails. The Ke Ala Hele
Makalae coastal path is right out the
back door. ✉ *4-934 Kuhio Hwy., across
from Taco Bell, Kapaa* ☎ *808/821–2115*
⊕ *www.kauaicycle.com* ✉ *Rentals from
$15 per day and $110 per wk.*

Outfitters Kauai

BICYCLING | Hybrid "comfort" and moun-
tain bikes (both full suspension and hard-
tails) as well as road bikes are available at
this shop in Poipu. You can ride right out
the door to tour Poipu or get information
on how to do a self-guided tour of Kokee
State Park and Waimea Canyon. The
company also leads sunrise and evening
coasting tours (under the name **Bicycle
Downhill**) from Waimea Canyon past the
island's West Side beaches. Stand-up
paddle tours are also available. ✉ *2827-A
Poipu Rd., near turnoff to Spouting Horn,
Poipu* ☎ *808/742–9667, 888/742–9887*

Bikers who prefer a leisurely cruise can pedal along the Ke Ala Hele Makalae trail, an 8-mile, multiuse path in Kapaa.

⊕ *www.outfitterskauai.com* ✉ *Downhill bike tours $114.*

Pedal 'n' Paddle

BICYCLING | This company in the heart of Hanalei rents old-fashioned, single-speed beach cruisers and hybrid road bikes. This is a great way to cruise the town; the more adventuresome cyclist can head to the end of the road. Be careful, though, because there are no bike lanes on the twisting-and-turning road to Kee Beach. Be sure to obtain the $1 permit before entering the park either on bike or on foot. ✉ *Ching Young Village, 5-5190 Kuhio Hwy., Hanalei* ☎ *808/826–9069* ⊕ *www. pedalnpaddle.com* ✉ *Rentals from $15 per day and $60 per wk.*

Boat Tours

Deciding to see Napali Coast by boat is an easy decision. Choosing the outfitter to go with is not. There are numerous boat-tour operators, and, quite frankly, they all do a good job. Before you even start thinking about who to go out with,

answer these three questions: What kind of boat do I prefer? Where am I staying? Do I want to go in the morning or afternoon? Once you settle on these three, you can easily zero in on the tour outfitter.

First, the boat. The most important thing is to match your personality and that of your group with the personality of the boat. If you like thrills and adventure, the rubber, inflatable rafts—often called Zodiacs, which Jacques Cousteau made famous and which the U.S. Coast Guard uses—will entice you. They're fast, likely to leave you drenched and windswept, and quite bouncy. If you prefer a smoother, more leisurely ride, then the large catamarans are the way to go. The next boat choice is size. Both the rafts and catamarans come in small and large. Again—think smaller, more adventurous; larger, more leisurely. ■ TIP→ **Do not choose a smaller boat because you think there will be fewer people. There might be fewer people, but you'll be jammed together sitting atop strangers.** If you prefer privacy over

Boat Tour Weather Cancellations 👁

If it's raining where you're staying, that doesn't mean it's raining over the water, so don't shy away from a boat tour. Besides, it's not the rain that should concern you—it's the wind and waves. Especially from due north and south, wind creates surface chop and makes for rough riding. Larger craft are designed to handle winter's ocean swells, however, so unless monster waves are out there, your tour should depart without a hitch. If the water is too rough, your boat captain may reroute to calmer waters. It's a tough call to make, but your comfort and safety are always the foremost factor. ■TIP➔ In winter months, North Shore departures are cancelled much more often than those departing the West Side. This is because the waves are often too big for the boats to leave Hanalei Bay, and as a result, some operators only work the summer season. If you want the closest thing to a guarantee of seeing Napali Coast in winter, choose a West Side outfitter. Oh, and even if your tour boat says it cruises the "entire Napali," keep in mind that "ocean conditions permitting" is always implied.

socializing, go with a larger boat, so you'll have more room to spread out. The smaller boats will also take you along the coast at a higher rate of speed, making photo opportunities a bit more challenging. One advantage to smaller boats, however, is that—depending on ocean conditions—some may slip into a sea cave or two. If that sounds interesting to you, call the outfitter and ask their policy on entering sea caves. Some won't, no matter the conditions, because they consider the caves sacred or because they don't want to cause any environmental damage.

Boats leave from three points around the island (Hanalei, Port Allen, and Waimea), and all head to the same spot: Napali Coast. Here's the inside skinny on which is the best: if you're staying on the North Shore, choose to depart out of the North Shore. If you're staying anywhere else, depart out of the West Side. It's that easy. Sure, the North Shore is closer to Napali Coast; however, you'll pay more for less overall time. The West Side boat operators may spend more time getting to Napali Coast; however, they'll spend about the same amount of time along Napali, plus you'll pay less. Finally, you'll also have to decide whether you want to go on a morning tour, which includes a deli lunch and a stop for snorkeling, or an afternoon tour, which does not always stop to snorkel but does include a sunset over the ocean. The morning tours with snorkeling are more popular with families and those who love dolphins, as the animals enjoy the "waves" created by the front of the catamarans and might just escort you down the coast. The winter months will also be a good chance to spot some whales breaching, though surf is much rougher along Napali. You don't have to be an expert snorkeler or even have any prior experience, but if it is your first time, note that although there will be some snorkeling instruction, there might not be much. Hawaiian spinner dolphins are so plentiful in the mornings that some tour companies guarantee you'll see them, though you won't get in the water and swim with them. The afternoon tours are more popular with nonsnorkelers—obviously—and photographers interested in capturing the setting sunlight on the coast. ■TIP➔ No matter which tour you select, book it online whenever possible. Most companies offer Web specials, usually around $10 to $20 off per person.

The best way to see Kauai's rugged coastline is by boat.

CATAMARAN TOURS

★ Blue Dolphin Charters

BOATING | Blue Dolphin operates 65-foot sailing (rarely raised and always motoring) catamarans designed with three decks of spacious seating with great visibility, as well as motorized rafts. ■**TIP→ The lower deck is best for shade seekers.** The most popular is a daylong tour of Napali Coast, which includes a detour across the channel to Niihau for snorkeling and diving. Morning snorkel tours of Napali include a deli lunch. Sunset sightseeing tours include a Hawaiian-style buffet. North Shore and South Shore rafting tours are also available, as are daily sportfishing charters of four to eight hours for no more than six guests. Blue Dolphin promises dolphin sightings and the best mai tais "off the island." Book online for cheaper deals on every tour offered. ⊠ *4353 Waialo Rd., #7B, Eleele* ☎ *808/335–5553, 877/511–1311* ⊕ *www.kauaiboats.com* 🖃 *From $100; 2-hr whale-watching/sunset tours, winter only, $65.*

★ Capt. Andy's Sailing Adventures

BOATING | **FAMILY** | Departing from Port Allen and running 55- and 60-foot sailing catamarans, as well as 24-foot inflatables out of Kikiaola Harbor in Kekaha, Capt. Andy's offers something for every taste, from raft expeditions to Hawaiian yachting. They have several lunch and snorkeling packages and four-hour sunset tours along Napali Coast. The Zodiac rafts have hydrophones to hear whales and other underwater sounds. The longtime Kauai company also operates a snorkel barbecue sail and a dinner sunset sail aboard its *Southern Star* yacht, originally built for private charters. This boat now operates as host for two of Capt. Andy's daily sailing trips for an upgraded feel. ■**TIP→ If the winds and swells are up on the North Shore, this company is usually a good choice—especially if you're prone to seasickness.** ⊠ *4353 Waiola Rd., Suite 1A-2A, Eleele* ☎ *808/335–6833* ⊕ *www. napali.com* 🖃 *From $99.*

Captain Sundown

BOATING | Sundown has one of the few permits to sail from Hanalei Bay and operates the only sailing catamaran there. Captain Bob has been cruising Napali Coast since 1971—six days a week, sometimes twice a day. (And right alongside Captain Bob is his son, Captain Larry.) To say he knows the area is an understatement. Here's the other good thing about this tour: they take a maximum of 17 passengers on the 40-foot boat. The breathtaking views of the waterfall-laced mountains behind Hanalei and Haena start immediately, and then it's around Kee Beach and the magic of Napali Coast unfolds before you. All the while, the captains are trolling for fish, and if they catch any, guests get to reel 'em in. Afternoon sunset sails (summertime only) run three hours and check in around 3 pm—these are BYOB. Cancellations due to rough surf are more frequent in winter. ⊠ *5-5134 Kuhio Hwy., Hanalei* ☎ *808/826–5585* ⊕ *www.captain-sundown.com* 🛥 *From $151.*

Catamaran Kahanu

BOATING | Hawaiian-owned and-operated, Catamaran Kahanu has been in business since 1985 and runs a 40-foot power catamaran with 18-passenger seating. It offers seasonal whale-watching and snorkeling cruises, ranging from two to five hours, and departs from Port Allen. The five-hour, year-round Na Pali Coast tour includes snorkeling at Nualolo Kai, plus a deli lunch and soft drinks. Check-in is at 7 am and the boat returns at approximately 1 pm. The boat is smaller than most and may feel a tad crowded, but the tour feels more personal, with a laid-back, *ohana* (family) style. There's no alcohol allowed. The two-hour whale-watching tour is available from late December through March and begins at 1 pm. ⊠ *4353 Waialo Rd., near Port Allen Marina Center, Eleele* ☎ *808/645–6176, 888/213–7711* ⊕ *www.catamarankahanu. com* 🛥 *From $75.*

HoloHolo Charters

BOATING | Choose between the 50-foot catamaran called *Leila* for a morning snorkel sail to Napali Coast, or the 65-foot *HoloHolo* seven-hour catamaran trip to the "forbidden island" of Niihau. Both boats have large cabins and little outside seating. *HoloHolo* also offers a four-hour seasonal voyage of Napali from Hanalei Bay on its rigid-hull inflatable rafts, specifically for diving and snorkeling. Originators of the Niihau tour, HoloHolo Charters built their 65-foot powered catamaran with a wide beam to reduce side-to-side motion and twin 425 HP turbo diesel engines specifically for the 17-mile channel crossing to Niihau. It's the only outfitter running daily Niihau tours. The *HoloHolo* also embarks on a daily sunset and sightseeing tour of Napali Coast. *Leila* can hold 37 passengers, while her big brother can take a maximum of 47. Check-in is at Port Allen Marina Center. ⊠ *4353 Waialo Rd., Suite 5A, Eleele* ☎ *808/335–0815, 800/848–6130* ⊕ *www.holoholocharters. com* 🛥 *From $139.*

Kauai Sea Tours

BOATING | This company operates the *Lucky Lady,* a 60-foot sailing catamaran designed almost identically to that of Blue Dolphin Charters, with all the same benefits, including great views and spacious seating. Snorkeling tours anchor near Makole (based on the captain's discretion). If snorkeling isn't your thing, try the two-hour, seasonal, whale-watching cruise or the four-hour sunset tour, with beer, wine, mai tais, *pupu* (appetizers), and a hot buffet dinner. Tours of Napali, one with a beach landing, are offered on inflatable rafts. Check in is at Port Allen Marina Center. ⊠ *4353 Waialo Rd., Eleele* ☎ *808/335–5309, 800/733–7997* ⊕ *www. kauaiseatours.com* 🛥 *From $95.*

Liko Kauai Cruises

BOATING | There are many things to like about Liko Kauai Cruises. The 49-foot powered catamaran will enter sea caves,

If you choose to sail by yourself in Kauai, be prepared for strong currents and know your limits.

ocean conditions permitting. Sometimes, Captain Liko himself—a Native Hawaiian—still takes the helm. We particularly like the layout of his boat: most of the seating is in the bow, so there's good visibility. A maximum of 32 passengers make each trip, which lasts five hours and includes snorkeling, food, and soft drinks. Trips usually depart out of Kikiaola Harbor in Waimea, a bit closer to Napali Coast than those leaving from Port Allen. ⊠ 4516 Alawai Rd., Waimea (Kauai County) ☎ 808/338–0333, 888/732–5456 ⊕ www.liko-kauai.com ☎ $135.

RAFT TOURS
Kauai Sea Tours

BOATING | This company holds a special permit from the state to land at Nualolo Kai along Napali Coast, ocean conditions permitting. Here, you'll enjoy a picnic lunch, as well as an archaeological tour of an ancient Hawaiian fishing village, ocean conditions permitting. Kauai Sea Tours operates four 24-foot inflatable rafts—maximum occupancy 14. These are small enough for checking out the insides of

sea caves and the undersides of waterfalls. Four different tours are available, including snorkeling and whale-watching, depending on the season. ⊠ Port Allen Marina Center, 4353 Waialo Rd., Eleele ☎ 808/335–5309, 800/733–7997 ⊕ www.kauaiseatours.com ☎ From $145.

★ Napali Explorer

BOATING | These tours operate out of Kikiaola Harbor, a tad closer to Napali Coast than most of the other West Side tours. The company runs two different sizes of inflatable rubber raft: a 48-foot, 36-passenger craft with an onboard toilet, freshwater shower, shade canopy, and seating in the stern (which is surprisingly smooth and comfortable) and bow (which is where the fun is); and a 26-foot, 14-passenger craft for the all-out fun and thrills of a white-knuckle ride in the bow. The smaller vessel stops at Nualolo Kai and ties up onshore for a tour of the ancient fishing village. Charters are available. ⊠ 9814 Kaumalii Hwy., Waimea (Kauai County) ☎ 808/338–9999 ⊕ www.napaliexplorer.com ☎ From $149.

Napali Riders

BOATING | This tour-boat outfitter distinguishes itself in two ways. First, it cruises the entire Napali Coast, clear to Kee Beach and back. Second, it has a reasonable price because it's a no-frills tour—no lunch provided, just beverages and snacks. The company runs morning and afternoon four-hour snorkeling, sightseeing, and whale-watching trips out of Kikiaola Harbor in Waimea on a 30-foot inflatable raft with a 28-passenger maximum—that's fewer than they used to take, but it can still be a bit cramped. ⊠ *9600 Kaumualii Hwy., Waimea (Kauai County)* ☎ *808/742–6331* ⊕ *www.napaliriders.com* ⌨ *$149*.

Z-Tourz

BOATING | What we like about Z-Tourz is that it's a boat company that makes snorkeling its priority. Its two- and three-hour tours focus solely on the South Shore's abundant offshore reefs. If you want to snorkel with Hawaii's tropical reef fish and turtles (pretty much guaranteed), this is your boat. The craft is a 26-foot rigid-hull inflatable (think Zodiac) with a maximum of 16 passengers. These snorkel tours are guided, so someone actually identifies what you're seeing. Rates include lunch and snorkel gear. ⊠ *3417 Poipu Rd., Poipu* ☎ *808/742–7422, 888/998–6879* ⊕ *www.kauaiztours.com* ⌨ *From $78*.

RIVERBOAT TOURS TO FERN GROTTO

Smith's Motor Boat Services

BOATING | This 2-mile trip up the lush and lovely Wailua River, the only navigable waterway in Hawaii, culminates at the infamous Fern Grotto, a yawning lava tube that is covered with fishtail ferns. During the boat ride, guitar and ukulele players serenade you with Hawaiian melodies and tell the history of the river. It's a kitschy, but fun, bit of Hawaiiana, and the river scenery is beautiful. Flat-bottom, 150-passenger riverboats (that rarely fill up) depart from Wailua Marina at the mouth of the Wailua River. ■TIP→ It's extremely rare, but occasionally after heavy rains the tour doesn't disembark at the grotto; if you're traveling in winter, ask beforehand. Round-trip excursions take 1½ hours, including time to walk around the grotto and environs. Tours run at 9:30, 11, 2, and 3:30 daily. ⊠ *5971 Kuhio Hwy., Kapaa* ☎ *808/821–6895* ⊕ *www.smithskauai.com/fern-grotto* ⌨ *$30*.

Body Boarding and Body Surfing

The most natural form of wave riding is body surfing, a popular sport on Kauai because there are many shore breaks around the island. Wave riders of this style stand waist deep in the water, facing shore, and swim madly as a wave picks them up and breaks. It's great fun and requires no special skills and absolutely no equipment other than a swimsuit. The next step up is body boarding, also called boogie boarding. In this case, wave riders lie with their upper body on a foam board about half the length of a traditional surfboard and kick as the wave propels them toward shore. Again, this is easy to pick up, and there are many places around Kauai to practice. The locals wear short-finned flippers to help them catch waves, which is a good idea to enhance safety in the water. It's worth spending a few minutes watching these experts as they spin, twirl, and flip—that's right—while they slip down the face of the wave. Of course, all beach-safety precautions apply, and just because you see wave riders of any kind in the water doesn't mean the water is safe for everyone. Any snorkeling-gear outfitter also rents body boards.

Some of our favorite body-surfing and body-boarding beaches are **Brennecke, Wailua, Kealia, Kalihiwai,** and **Hanalei.**

Deep-Sea Fishing

Simply step aboard and cast your line for mahimahi, ahi, ono, and marlin. That's about how quickly the fishing—mostly trolling with lures—begins on Kauai. The water gets deep quickly here, so there's less cruising time to fishing grounds, which is nice, since Hawaii's seas are notoriously rough. Of course, your captain may elect to cruise to a hot location where he's had good luck lately.

There are tons of charter fishermen around; most depart from Nawiliwili Harbor in Lihue, and most use lures instead of live bait. Inquire about each boat's "fish policy," that is, what happens to the fish if any are caught. Some boats keep all; others will give you enough for a meal or two, even doing the cleaning themselves. On shared charters, ask about the maximum passenger count and about the fishing rotation; you'll want to make sure everyone gets a fair shot at reeling in the big one. Another option is to book a private charter. Shared and private charters run four, six, and eight hours in length.

BOATS AND CHARTERS
Captain Don's Sportfishing
FISHING | Captain Don is very flexible and treats everyone like family—he'll stop to snorkel or whale-watch if that's what the group (four to six) wants. Saltwater fly fishermen (bring your own gear) are welcome. He'll even fish for bait and let you keep part of whatever you catch, as long as the fish is less than 25 pounds. His *Happy Ryder* is a 39-foot Hatteras boat. ⊠ *Nawiliwili Small Boat Harbor, 2494 Niumalu Rd., Nawiliwili* ☎ *808/639–3012* ⊕ *www.captaindonsfishing.com* ⊠ *From $150 (shared); from $750 (private).*

Kai Bear
FISHING | What's particularly nice about this company are the boats: the 38-foot Bertram, *Kai Bear,* and the 42-foot Bertram, *Grander,* which are well maintained and very roomy. The 41-foot Bertram, *Emma Nalani*, docks in Nawiliwili Small Boat Harbor, which is convenient for those staying on the East Side. The prices are reasonable ($160 per person for the four-hour shared charter or $699 for the eight-hour private charter), and they share the catch. ⊠ *Nawiliwili Small Boat Harbor, 2900 Nawiliwili Rd., Nawiliwili* ☎ *808/652–4556* ⊕ *www.kaibear.com* ⊠ *From $160.*

Golf

For golfers, the Garden Island might as well be known as the Robert Trent Jones Jr. Isle. Four of the island's eight courses, including Poipu Bay—onetime home of the PGA Grand Slam of Golf—are the work of Jones, who maintains a home at Princeville. Combine these four courses with those from Jack Nicklaus, Robin Nelson, and local legend Toyo Shirai, and you'll see that golf sets Kauai apart from the other Islands as much as the Pacific Ocean does. ■TIP➔ **Afternoon tee times at most courses can save you big bucks.**

Anaina Hou Mini Golf & Gardens
GOLF | The island's first miniature-golf course also has a small botanical garden and a new 300-seat theater/arts center. The 18-hole course was designed to be challenging, beautiful, and family-friendly. Replacing the typical clown's nose and spinning wheels are some water features and tropical tunnels. Surrounding each hole is plant life that walks players through different eras of Hawaiian history. The new Porter Pavillion hosts special events such as concerts, plays, private parties, and community meetings. There is also a children's playground made from recycled materials on-site. A gift shop with local products and a concessions counter make it a fun activity for any time of day. On Saturday morning and Monday afternoon, a farmers' market is adjacent to the course with fresh Kauai produce and local goods. ⊠ *5-273 Kuhio*

The Makai course at Princeville Makai Golf Club has consistently been ranked a top course in the U.S.

Hwy., Kilauea ☎ *808/828–2118* ⊕ *www.anainahou.org* ✉ *$18.*

Kiahuna Plantation Golf Course

GOLF | A meandering creek, lava outcrops, and thickets of trees give Kiahuna its character. Robert Trent Jones Jr. was given a smallish piece of land just inland at Poipu, and defends par with smaller targets, awkward stances, and optical illusions. In 2003 a group of homeowners bought the club and brought Jones back to renovate the course (it was originally built in 1983), adding tees and revamping bunkers. The pro here boasts his course has the best putting greens on the island. This is the only course on Kauai with a complete set of junior's tee boxes. ✉ *2545 Kiahuna Plantation Dr., Koloa* ☎ *808/742–9595* ⊕ *www.kiahunagolf.com* ✉ *$105, including cart* 🏌 *18 holes, 6787 yards, par 70.*

Ocean Course Hokuala Golf Club

GOLF | The Jack Nicklaus–designed Ocean Course Hokuala offers a beautiful and distinctly Hawaiian golf experience. With an assortment of plants and tropical birds adding to the atmosphere, this course winds through dark ravines and over picturesque landscape. The fifth hole is particularly striking as it requires a drive over a valley populated by mango and guava trees. The final holes feature unmatched views of Nawiliwili Bay, including the harbor, a lighthouse, and secluded beaches. ✉ *3351 Hoolaulea Way, Lihue* ☎ *808/241–6000, 800/634–6400* ⊕ *www.hokualakauai.com/golf* ✉ *From $150; after 2 pm $126* 🏌 *18 holes, 7156 yards, par 72.*

Poipu Bay Golf Course

GOLF | Poipu Bay has been called the Pebble Beach of Hawaii, and the comparison is apt. Like Pebble Beach, Poipu is a links course built on headlands, not true links land. There's wildlife galore. It's not unusual for golfers to see monk seals sunning on the beach below, sea turtles bobbing outside the shore break, and humpback whales leaping offshore. From 1994 to 2006, the course (designed by Robert Trent Jones Jr.) hosted the annual PGA Grand Slam of Golf. Tiger

Woods was a frequent winner here. Call ahead to take advantage of varying prices for tee times. ✉ *2250 Ainako St., Koloa* ☎ *808/742–8711* ⊕ *www.poipubaygolf. com* ✉ *$209 before noon, $185 after* 🏌 *18 holes, 6127 yards, par 72.*

★ **Princeville Makai Golf Club**

GOLF | The 27-hole Princeville Makai Golf Club was named for its five ocean-hugging front holes. Designed by golf-course architect Robert Trent Jones Jr. in 1971, the 18-hole championship Makai Course has consistently been ranked a top golf course in the United States. ■TIP➜ **Check the website for varying rates as well as other nongolf activities at the facility like the Sunset Golf Cart Tour, where you ride the course, sans clubs, and take in the spectacular ocean views.** ✉ *4080 Lei O Papa Rd., Princeville* ⊕ *www. makaigolf.com* ✉ *$305* 🏌 *18 holes, 7223 yards, par 72; Woods Course: 9 holes, 3445 yards, par 36.*

Wailua Municipal Golf Course

GOLF | Considered by many to be one of Hawaii's best public golf courses, this seaside course provides an affordable game with minimal water hazards, but it is challenging enough to have been chosen to host three USGA Amateur Public Links Championships. It was first built as a nine-holer in the 1930s. The second nine holes were added in 1961. Course designer Toyo Shirai created a course that is fun but not punishing. The trade winds blow steadily on the East Side of the island and provide a game with challenges. An ocean view and affordability make this one of the most popular courses on the island. Tee times are accepted up to seven days in advance and can be paid in cash, traveler's checks, and some credit cards. ✉ *3-5350 Kuhio Hwy., Lihue* ☎ *808/241–6666* ⊕ *www.kauai.gov/golf* ✉ *$48 weekdays, $60 weekends; cart rental $20* 🏌 *18 holes, 6585 yards, par 72.*

Hiking

The best way to experience the *aina*— the land—on Kauai is to step off the beach and hike into the remote interior. You'll find waterfalls so tall you'll strain your neck looking, pools of crystal-clear water for swimming, tropical forests teeming with plant life, and ocean vistas that will make you wish you could stay forever.

■TIP➜ **For your safety, wear sturdy shoes—preferably water-resistant ones.** All hiking trails on Kauai are free, so far. There's a development plan in the works that could turn the Waimea Canyon and Kokee state parks into admission-charging destinations. Whatever it may be, it will be worth it.

BEST SPOTS

Hanalei-Okolehao Trail

HIKING/WALKING | *Okolehao* basically translates to "moonshine" in Hawaiian. This trail follows the Hihimanu Ridge, which was established in the days of Prohibition, when this backyard liquor was distilled from the roots of ti plants. The 2-mile hike climbs 1,200 feet and offers a 360-degree view of Hanalei Bay and Waioli Valley. Your ascent begins at the China Ditch off the Hanalei River. Follow the trail through a lightly forested grove and then climb up a steep embankment. From here the trail is well marked. Most of the climb is lined with hala, ti, wild orchid, and eucalyptus. You'll get your first of many ocean views at mile marker 1. ✉ *Hanalei* ✛ *Follow Ohiki Rd. (north of Hanalei Bridge) 5 miles to U.S. Fish and Wildlife Service parking area. Directly across street is small bridge that marks trailhead.*

★ Kalalau Trail

HIKING/WALKING | Of all the hikes on the island, Kalalau Trail is by far the most famous and in many regards the most strenuous. A moderate hiker can handle the 2-mile trek to Hanakapiai Beach,

Hiking along the 11-mile Kalalau Trail will lead you from Kee Beach to Kalalau Beach.

and for the seasoned outdoorsman, the additional 2 miles up to the falls is manageable. But be prepared to rock-hop along a creek and ford waters that can get waist high during the rain. Round-trip to Hanakapiai Falls is 8 miles. This steep and often muddy trail is best approached with a walking stick. If there has been any steady rain, wait for drier days for a more enjoyable trek. The narrow Kalalau Trail delivers one startling ocean view after another along a path that is alternately shady and sunny. Wear hiking shoes or sandals, and bring drinking water since that in the creeks on the trail is not potable. Plenty of food is always encouraged on a strenuous hike such as this one. If you plan to venture the full 11 miles into Kalalau, you need to acquire a camping permit, either online or at the State Building in Lihue, for $20 per person per night. You should secure a permit well in advance of your trip. ⊹ *Drive north past Hanalei to end of road. Trailhead is directly across from Kee Beach* ⊕ *www. kalalautrail.com* ✉ *$20 per person per night.*

Mahaulepu Heritage Trail

HIKING/WALKING | This trail offers the novice hiker an accessible way to appreciate the rugged southern coast of Kauai. A cross-country trail wends its way along the water, high above the ocean, through a lava field, and past a sacred *heiau* (stone structure) . Walk all the way to Mahaulepu, 2 miles north, for a two-hour round-trip. If conditions are right, you should be able to see dolphins, *honu* (green sea turtles), and whales. ⊹ *Drive north on Poipu Rd., turn right at Poipu Bay Golf Course sign. The street name is Ainako, but sign is hard to see. Drive down to beach and park in lot* ⊕ *www. hikemahaulepu.org.*

Sleeping Giant Trail

HIKING/WALKING | An easily accessible trail practically in the heart of Kapaa, the moderately strenuous Sleeping Giant Trail—or simply Sleeping Giant—gains 1,000 feet over 2 miles. We prefer an early-morning—say, sunrise—hike up the east-side trailhead, with sparkling blue-water vistas, but there are other back-side approaches. At the top you can see a grassy grove with a picnic table. It is a local favorite, with many East Siders meeting here to exercise. ⊠ *Haleilio Rd., off Rte. 56, Wailua (Kauai County).*

Waimea Canyon and Kokee State Park
HIKING/WALKING | This park contains a 50-mile network of hiking trails of varying difficulty that take you through acres of native forests, across the highest-elevation swamp in the world, to the river at the base of the canyon, and onto pinnacles of land sticking their necks out over Napali Coast. All hikers should register at Kokee Natural History Museum, where you can find trail maps, current trail information, and specific directions.

The **Kukui Trail** descends 2,200 feet over 2½ miles into Waimea Canyon to the edge of the Waimea River—it's a steep climb. The **Awaawapuhi Trail,** with 1,600 feet of elevation gains and losses over 3¼ miles, feels more gentle than the Kukui Trail, but it offers its own huffing and-puffing sections in its descent along a spiny ridge to a perch overlooking the ocean.

The 3½-mile **Alakai Swamp Trail** is accessed via the **Pihea Trail** or a four-wheel-drive road. There's one strenuous valley section, but otherwise it's a pretty level trail—once you access it. This trail is a bird-watcher's delight and includes a painterly view of Wainiha and Hanalei valleys at the trail's end. The trail traverses the purported highest-elevation swamp in the world via a boardwalk so as not to disturb the fragile plant and wildlife. It is typically the coolest of the hikes due to the tree canopy, elevation, and cloud coverage.

The **Canyon Trail** offers much in its short trek: spectacular vistas of the canyon and its only dependable waterfall. The easy 2-mile hike can be cut in half if you have a four-wheel-drive vehicle. The late-afternoon sun sets the canyon walls ablaze in color. ⊠ *Kokee Natural History Museum,*

3600 Kokee Rd., Kekaha ☎ *808/335–9975 for trail conditions* ⊕ *www.kokee. org.*

EQUIPMENT AND TOURS
★ **Kauai Nature Tours**
HIKING/WALKING | Father-and-son scientists started this hiking tour business. As such, their emphasis is on education and the environment. If you're interested in flora, fauna, volcanology, geology, oceanography, and the like, this is the company for you. They offer daylong hikes along coastal areas, beaches, and in the mountains. ■TIP→ **If you have a desire to see a specific location, just ask. They will do custom hikes to spots they don't normally hit if there is interest.** Hikes range from easy to strenuous. Transportation is often provided from your hotel. ⊠ *5162 Lawai Rd., Koloa* ☎ *808/742–8305, 888/233–8365* ⊕ *www.kauainaturetours.com* ⊡ *From $155.*

Princeville Ranch Adventures
HIKING/WALKING | This company offers a 4-mile hike that traverses Princeville Ranch, crossing through a rain forest to a five-tier waterfall for lunch and swimming. Moderately strenuous hiking is required. ⊠ *Rte. 56, between mile markers 27 and 28, Princeville* ☎ *808/826–7669, 888/955–7669* ⊕ *www. princevilleranch.com* ⊡ *$129.*

Horseback Riding

Most of the horseback-riding tours on Kauai are primarily walking tours with little trotting and no cantering or galloping, so no experience is required. Zip. Zilch. Nada. If you're interested, most of the stables offer private lessons. The most popular tours are the ones including a picnic lunch by the water. Your only dilemma may be deciding what kind of water you want—waterfalls or ocean. You may want to make your decision based on where you're staying. The "waterfall picnic" tours are on the wetter North

Wailua River, Hanalei River, and Huleia River are Kauai's most scenic spots to river kayak.

Shore, and the "beach picnic" tours take place on the South Side.

★ Princeville Ranch Adventures

HORSEBACK RIDING | A longtime *kamaaina* (resident) family operates Princeville Ranch. They originated the waterfall picnic tour, which runs 3½ hours and includes a short but steep hike down to Kalihiwai Falls, a dramatic three-tier waterfall, for swimming and picnicking. Princeville also has shorter, straight riding tours and private rides. A popular option is the three-hour combination Ride 'N Glide tour with three ziplines. ✉ *Kuhio Hwy., off Kapaka Rd., between mile markers 27 and 28, Princeville* ☎ *808/826–7669* ⊕ *www.princevilleranch. com* ✆ *Ride only from $129; private tours from $189.*

Kayaking

Kauai is the only Hawaiian island with navigable rivers. As the oldest inhabited island in the chain, Kauai has had more time for wind and water erosion to

deepen and widen cracks into streams and streams into rivers. Because this is a small island, the rivers aren't long, and there are no rapids, which makes them generally safe for kayakers of all levels, even beginners, except when rivers are flowing fast from heavy rains.

For more advanced paddlers, there aren't many places in the world more beautiful for sea kayaking than Napali Coast. If this is your draw to Kauai, plan your vacation for the summer months, when the seas are at their calmest. ■TIP➔ **Tour and kayak-rental reservations are recommended at least two weeks in advance during peak summer and holiday seasons.** In general, tours and rentals are available year-round, Monday through Saturday. Pack a swimsuit, sunscreen, a hat, bug repellent, water shoes (sport sandals, aqua socks, old tennis shoes), and motion sickness medication if you're planning on sea kayaking.

RIVER KAYAKING

Tour outfitters operate on the Huleia, Wailua, and Hanalei rivers with guided tours that combine hiking to waterfalls, as in the case of the first two, and snorkeling, as in the case of the third. Another option is renting kayaks and heading out on your own. Each has its advantages and disadvantages, but it boils down as follows:

If you want to swim at the base of a remote 100-foot waterfall, sign up for a five-hour kayak (4-mile round-trip) and hiking (2-mile round-trip) tour of the **Wailua River.** It includes a dramatic waterfall that is best accessed with the aid of a guide, so you don't get lost. ■TIP➜ **Remember— it's dangerous to swim under waterfalls no matter how good a water massage may sound. Rocks and logs are known to plunge down, especially after heavy rains.**

If you want to kayak on your own, choose the **Hanalei River.** It's most scenic from the kayak itself—there are no trails to hike to hidden waterfalls. And better yet, a rental company is right on the river—no hauling kayaks on top of your car.

If you're not sure of your kayaking abilities, head to the **Huleia River;** 3½-hour tours include easy paddling upriver, a nature walk through a rain forest with a cascading waterfall, a rope swing for playing Tarzan and Jane, and a ride back downriver—into the wind—on a motorized, double-hull canoe.

As for the kayaks themselves, most companies use the two-person sit-on-top style that is quite buoyant—no Eskimo rolls required. The only possible danger comes in the form of communication. The kayaks seat two people, which means you'll share the work (good) with a guide, or your spouse, child, parent, or friend (the potential danger part). On the river, the two-person kayaks are known as "divorce boats." Counseling is not included in the tour price.

EQUIPMENT AND TOURS

Kayak Kauai

KAYAKING | This company pioneered kayaking on Kauai. It offers guided tours on the Wailua River, and sea kayak tours in Hanalei Bay and along Napali Coast, in season. It has consolidated operations and is now conveniently located in the Wailua Marina. From there, it can launch kayaks right into the Wailua River for its five-hour Secret Falls hike-paddle tour and three-hour paddle to a swimming hole. Kayak Kauai also offers 12-hour escorted summer sea kayak tours and camping trips on Napali Coast. Stand-up paddleboard instruction and sea-kayak whale-watching tours round out its repertoire. The company will shuttle kayakers as needed, and, for rentals, it provides the hauling gear necessary for your rental car. Snorkel gear, body boards, and stand-up paddleboards also can be rented. ✉ *Wailua Marina, 3-5971 Kuhio Hwy., Wailua (Kauai County)* ☎ *808/826–9844, 888/596–3853* ⊕ *www.kayakkauai.com* 💲 *From $85 (river tours) and $240 (sea tours); kayak rentals from $95 per day.*

Kayak Wailua

KAYAKING | We can't quite figure out how this family-run business offers pretty much the same Wailua River kayaking tour as everyone else—except for lunch and beverages, which are BYO—for the lowest price, but it does. They say it's because they don't discount and don't offer commissions to activities and concierge desks. Their trip, a 4½-hour kayak, hike, and waterfall swim, is offered six times a day, with the last at 1 pm. With the number of boats going out, large groups can be accommodated. No tours are allowed on Wailua River on Sunday. ✉ *4565 Haleilio Rd., behind old Coco Palms hotel, Kapaa* ☎ *808/822–3388* ⊕ *www.kayakwailua.com* 💲 *$60.*

★ Napali Kayak

KAYAKING | A couple of longtime guides ventured out on their own to create this company, which focuses solely on a 17-mile sea-kayaking paddle along Napali Coast from April to October for small groups, or private and honeymoon tours. These guys are highly experienced and still highly enthusiastic about their livelihood—so much so that REI Adventures hires them to run their multiday, multisport tours. If you're an experienced kayaker and want to try camping on your own at Kalalau (you'll need permits), Napali Kayak will provide kayaks outfitted with dry bags, extra paddles, and seat backs, while also offering transportation drop-off and pickup. They also do Napali Coast day tours from Hanalei to Polihale, with a lunch break at Milolii, and rent camping equipment and first-aid kits. ⊠ 5-5075 Kuhio Hwy., next to Postcards Café, Hanalei ☎ 808/826–6900 ⊕ www. napalikayak.com ⊠ From $250.

Outfitters Kauai

KAYAKING | FAMILY | This well-established tour outfitter operates year-round river-kayak tours on the Huleia and Wailua rivers, as well as sea-kayaking tours along Napali Coast in summer and the South Shore in winter. Outfitters Kauai's specialty, however, is the Kipu Safari. This all-day adventure starts with kayaking up the Huleia River and includes a rope swing over a swimming hole, a wagon ride through a working cattle ranch, a picnic lunch by a private waterfall, hiking, and two "zips" across the rain-forest canopy (strap on a harness, clip into a cable, and zip over a quarter of a mile). They then offer a one-of-a-kind Waterzip Zipline at their mountain stream–fed blue pool. The day ends with a ride on a motorized double-hull canoe. It's a great tour for the family, because no one ever gets bored. ⊠ 2827-A Poipu Rd., Poipu ☎ 808/742–9667, 888/742–9887 ⊕ www. outfitterskauai.com ⊠ Kipu Safari $189.

Wailua Kayak & Canoe

KAYAKING | This purveyor of kayak rentals is right on the Wailua River, which means no hauling your kayak on top of your car (a definite plus). Guided waterfall tours

are also offered. This outfitter promotes itself as "Native Hawaiian owned and operated." No Wailua River tours are offered on Sunday. ⊠ 162 Wailua Rd., Kapaa ☎ 808/821–1188 ⊕ www.wailuariverkayaking.com ⊠ $50 for a single, $100 for a double; guided tours from $75.

Mountain Tubing

For the past 40 years, Hawaii's sugarcane plantations have closed one by one. In the fall of 2009, Gay & Robinson announced the closure of Kauai's last plantation, leaving only one in Maui, the last in the state. The sugarcane irrigation ditches remain, striating these islands like spokes in a wheel. Inspired by the Hawaiian auwai, which diverted water from streams to taro fields, these engineering feats harnessed the rain. One ingenious tour company on Kauai has figured out a way to make exploring them an adventure: float inflatable tubes down the route.

Kauai Backcountry Adventures

LOCAL SPORTS | FAMILY | Both zipline and tubing tours are offered. Popular with all ages, the tubing adventure can book up two weeks in advance in busy summer months. Here's how it works: you recline in an inner tube and float down fern-lined irrigation ditches that were built more than a century ago—the engineering is impressive—to divert water from Mt. Waialeale to sugar and pineapple fields around the island. They'll even give you a headlamp so you can see as you float through five covered tunnels. The scenery from the island's interior at the base of Mt. Waialeale on Lihue Plantation land is superb. Ages five and up are welcome. The tour takes about three hours and includes a picnic lunch and a swim in a swimming hole. ■TIP→ You'll definitely want to pack water-friendly shoes (or rent some from the outfitter), sunscreen, a hat, bug repellent, and a beach towel. Tours are offered up to a dozen times daily.

✉ *3-4131 Kuhio Hwy., across from gas station, Hanamaulu* ☎ *808/245–2506, 888/270–0555* ⊕ *www.kauaibackcountry. com* ✉ *$125 per person.*

Scuba Diving

The majority of scuba diving on Kauai occurs on the South Shore. Boat and shore dives are available, although boat sites surpass the shore sites for a couple of reasons. First, they're deeper and exhibit the complete symbiotic relationship of a reef system, and second, the visibility is better a little farther offshore.

The dive operators on Kauai offer a full range of services, including certification dives, referral dives, boat dives, shore dives, night dives, and drift dives. ■TIP→ **As for certification, we recommend completing your confined-water training and classroom testing before arriving on the island.** That way, you'll spend less time training and more time diving.

BEST SPOTS

The best and safest scuba-diving sites are accessed by boat on the South Shore of the island, right off the shores of Poipu. The captain selects the actual site based on ocean conditions of the day. Beginners may prefer shore dives, which are best at **Koloa Landing** on the South Shore year-round and **Makua (Tunnels) Beach** on the North Shore in the calm summer months. Keep in mind, though, that you'll have to haul your gear a ways down the beach.

For the advanced diver, the island of Niihau—across an open ocean channel in deep and crystal-clear waters—beckons and rewards, usually with some big fish. Seasport Divers, Fathom Five, and Bubbles Below venture the 17 miles across the channel in summer when the crossing is smoothest. Divers can expect deep dives, walls, and strong currents at Niihau, where conditions can change rapidly. To make the long journey

worthwhile, three dives and Nitrox are included.

EQUIPMENT, LESSONS, AND TOURS
Bubbles Below

SCUBA DIVING | Marine ecology is the emphasis here aboard the 36-foot, eight-passenger *Kai Manu.* This longtime Kauai company discovered some pristine dive sites on the West Side of the island where white-tip reef sharks are common—and other divers are not. Thanks to the addition of a 32-foot powered catamaran—the six-passenger *Dive Rocket*—the group also runs Niihau, Napali, and North Shore dives year-round (depending on ocean conditions, of course). They're still known for their South Side trips and lead dives at the East Side walls as well, so they truly do circumnavigate the island. A bonus on these tours is the wide variety of food served between dives. Open-water certification dives, check-out dives, and intro shore dives are available upon request. ✉ *Port Allen Small Boat Harbor, 4353 Waialo Rd., Eleele* ☎ *808/332–7333* ⊕ *www.bubblesbelowkauai.com* ✉ *$140 for 2-tank boat dive; $90 for rider/snorkeler; Niihau charter $400.*

Kauai Down Under Dive Team
SCUBA DIVING | This company offers boat dives and specializes in shore diving for beginners, typically at Koloa Landing (year-round). They're not only geared toward beginning divers—for whom they provide a thorough and gentle certification program as well as the Discover Scuba program—but also offer night dives and scooter (think James Bond) dives for certified divers. Their main emphasis is a detailed review of marine biology, such as pointing out rare dragon eel and harlequin shrimp tucked away in pockets of coral. ■TIP→ **Hands down, we recommend Kauai Down Under for beginners, certification (all levels), and refresher dives.** One reason is that their instructor-to-student ratio does not exceed 1:4 for beginners.

For certified divers the ratio can be 6:1. All dive gear is included. ✉ *Sheraton Kauai Resort, 2440 Hoonani Rd., Koloa* ☎ *877/538–3483, 808/742–9534* ⊕ *www. kauaidownunderscuba.com* ✉ *From $155 for a 2-tank certified dive; $550 for certification.*

★ Ocean Quest Watersports/Fathom Five

SCUBA DIVING | This operator offers it all: boat dives, shore dives, night dives, certification dives. They pretty much do what everyone else does with a few twists. First, they offer a three-tank premium charter for those really serious about diving. Second, they operate a Nitrox continuous-flow mixing system, so you can decide the mix rate. Third, they add on a twilight dive to the standard, one-tank night dive, making the outing worth the effort. Fourth, their shore diving isn't an afterthought. Finally, we think their dive masters are pretty darn good, too. They even dive Niihau in the summer aboard their 38-foot *Force*. In summer, book well in advance. ✉ *3450 Poipu Rd., Koloa* ☎ *808/742–6991, 800/972–3078* ⊕ *www.fathomfive.com* ✉ *From $155 for boat dives; from $100 for shore dives; $45 for gear rental, if needed.*

Seasport Divers

SCUBA DIVING | Rated highly by readers of *Scuba Diving* magazine, Seasport Divers' 48-foot *Anela Kai* tops the chart for dive-boat luxury. But owner Marvin Otsuji didn't stop with that. A second boat—a 32-foot catamaran—is outfitted for diving, but we like it as an all-around charter. The company does brisk business, which means it won't cancel at the last minute because of a lack of reservations, like some other companies, although they may book up to 18 people per boat. ■ **TIP→ There are slightly more challenging trips in the morning; mellower dive sites are in the afternoon.** The company runs a good-size dive shop for purchases and rentals, as well as a classroom for certification. Night dives are offered, and Niihau trips are available in summer.

There's also an outlet in Kapaa. ✉ *2827 Poipu Rd., look for yellow submarine in parking lot, Poipu* ☎ *808/742–9303, 808/742–9303* ⊕ *www.seasportdivers. com* ✉ *From $145, plus $37 for gear; $105 1-tank shore dive, plus gear charge.*

Snorkeling

Generally speaking, the calmest water and best snorkeling can be found on Kauai's North Shore in summer and South Shore in winter. The East Side, known as the windward side, has year-round, prevalent northeast trade winds that make snorkeling unpredictable, although there are some good pockets. The best snorkeling on the West Side is accessible only by boat.

A word on feeding fish: don't. As Captain Ted with HoloHolo Charters says, fish have survived and populated reefs for much longer than we have been donning goggles and staring at them. They will continue to do so without our intervention. Besides, fish food messes up the reef and—one thing always leads to another—can eliminate a once-pristine reef environment. As for gear, if you're snorkeling with one of the Napali boat-tour outfitters, they'll provide it; however, depending on the company, it might not be the latest or greatest. If you have your own, bring it. On the other hand, if you're going out with SeaFun or Z-Tourz, the gear is top-notch. If you need to rent, hit one of the "snorkel-and-surf" shops such as Snorkel Bob's in Koloa and Kapaa, Nukumoi in Poipu, or Seasport in Poipu and Kapaa. ■ **TIP→ If you wear glasses, you can rent prescription masks at the rental shops—just don't expect them to match your prescription exactly.**

BEST SPOTS

Just because we say these are good places to snorkel doesn't mean that the exact moment you arrive, the fish will flock—they are wild, after all.

Beach House (Lawai Beach). Don't pack the beach umbrella, beach mats, or cooler for snorkeling at Beach House. Just bring your snorkeling gear. The beach—named after its neighbor the Beach House restaurant—is on the road to Spouting Horn. It's a small slip of sand during low tide and a rocky shoreline during high tide; however, it's right by the road's edge, and its rocky coastline and somewhat rocky bottom make it great for snorkeling. Enter and exit in the sand channel (not over the rocky reef) that lines up with the Lawai Beach Resort's center atrium. Stay within the rocky points anchoring each end of the beach. The current runs east to west. ⊠ *5017 Lawai Rd., makai (ocean) side of Lawai Rd., park on road in front of Lawai Beach Resort, Koloa.*

Kee Beach. Although it can get quite crowded, Kee Beach is quite often a good snorkeling destination if the water conditions are right. Just be sure to come during the off-hours, say early in the morning or later in the afternoon, or you will have difficulty finding a parking spot. ■TIP➔ **Snorkeling here in winter can be hazardous. Summer is the best and safest time, although you should never swim beyond the reef.** During peak times, a parking lot is available back down the road away from the beach. ⊠ *At end of Rte. 560, Haena.*

Lydgate Beach Park. Lydgate Beach Park is typically the safest place to snorkel on Kauai, though not the most exciting. With its lava-rock wall creating a protected swimming pool, it's a good spot for beginners, young and old. The fish are so tame here it's almost like swimming in a saltwater aquarium. There is also a life-guard, a playground for children, plenty of parking, and full-service restrooms with showers. ⊠ *4470 Nalu Rd.* ✛ *Just south of Wailua River, turn makai (towards ocean) off Rte. 56 onto Lehu Dr. and left onto Nalu Rd., Kapaa.*

Niihau. With little river runoff and hardly any boat traffic, the waters off the island of Niihau are some of the clearest in all Hawaii, and that's good for snorkeling and excellent for scuba diving. Like Nualolo Kai, the only way to snorkel here is to sign on with one of the tour boats venturing across a sometimes rough open-ocean channel: Blue Dolphin Charters and HoloHolo.

Nualolo Kai. Nualolo Kai was once an ancient Hawaiian fishpond and is now home to the best snorkeling along Napali Coast (and perhaps on all of Kauai). The only way to access it is by boat, including kayak. Though many boats stop offshore, only a few Napali snorkeling-tour operators are permitted to come ashore. We recommend Napali Explorer and Kauai Sea Tours.

Poipu Beach Park. You'll generally find good year-round snorkeling at Poipu Beach Park, except during summer's south swells (which are not nearly as frequent as winter's north swells). The best snorkeling fronts the Marriott Waiohai Beach Club. Stay inside the crescent created by the sandbar and rocky point, and within sight of the lifeguard tower. The current runs east to west. ⊠ *Hoone Rd.* ✛ *From Poipu Rd., turn right onto Hoone Rd.*

Tunnels (Makua). The search for Tunnels (Makua) is as tricky as the snorkeling. Park at Haena Beach Park and walk east—away from Napali Coast—until you see a sand channel entrance in the water, almost at the point. Once you get here, the reward is fantastic. The name of this beach comes from the many underwater lava tubes, which always attract marine life. The shore is mostly beach rock interrupted by three sand channels. You'll want to enter and exit at one of these channels (or risk stepping on a sea urchin or scraping your stomach on the reef). Follow the sand channel to a drop-off; the snorkeling along here is always full of nice surprises. Expect a current running east to west. Snorkeling here in winter can be hazardous; summer is the best and safest time for snorkeling. ⊠ *Haena Beach Park* ⊹ *Near end of Rte. 560, across from lava-tube sea caves, after stream crossing.*

TOURS

★ SeaFun Kauai

SNORKELING | FAMILY | This guided snorkeling tour, for beginners and intermediates alike, is led by a marine expert who not only provides snorkeling instruction but also actually gets into the water with you and identifies marine life. You're guaranteed to spot tons of critters you'd never see on your own. This is a land-based operation and the only one of its kind on Kauai. (Don't think those snorkeling cruises are guided snorkeling tours—they rarely are. A member of the boat's crew serves as lifeguard, not a marine life *guide*.) A morning or afternoon tour includes all your snorkeling gear—and a wet suit to keep you warm—and stops at one or two snorkeling locations, chosen based on ocean conditions. They will pick up customers at some of the resorts, depending on locale and destination. ⊠ *3477A Weliweli Rd., Koloa* ☎ *808/245–6400, 800/452–1113* ⊕ *www.seafunkauai. com* ✉ *$89.*

Spas

THE NORTH SHORE

Hanalei Day Spa

SPA/BEAUTY | As you travel past tony Princeville, life slows down. The single-lane bridges may be one reason. Another is the Hanalei Day Spa, a boutique day spa on the grounds of the Hanalei Colony Resort in Haena with in-spa and beach-side spa services. Owner Darci Frankel is an Ayurveda practitioner with more than 27 years of experience. Spa treatments include body wraps, scrubs, and packages for individuals and couples. Its specialty is the massage: *lomilomi* (a traditional Hawaiian-style

massage), deep tissue, relaxation, and a special four-hands massage. ⊠ *Hanalei Colony Resort, Rte. 560, Haena* ⊹ *6 miles past Hanalei* ☎ *808/826–6621* ⊕ *www.hanaleidayspa.com* ✉ *Massage from $110* ⊗ *Closed Sun. and Mon.*

THE EAST SIDE

Alexander Day Spa & Salon at the Kauai Marriott

SPA/BEAUTY | This sunny, pleasant spa focuses on body care rather than exercise, so don't expect any fitness equipment or exercise classes, just pampering and beauty treatments. Massages are available in treatment rooms, your room, and on the beach, although the beach locale isn't as private as you might imagine. Wedding-day and custom spa packages can be arranged. ⊠ *Kauai Marriott Resort & Beach Club, 3610 Rice St., Suite 9A, Lihue* ☎ *808/246–4918* ⊕ *www.alexanderspa.com* ✉ *Massage from $130.*

Angeline's Muolaulani Wellness Center

SPA/BEAUTY | It doesn't get more authentic, or rustic, than this. In the mid-1980s Aunty Angeline Locey opened her Anahola home to offer traditional Hawaiian healing practices. Though she passed on, her son and granddaughter carry on the tradition. There's a two-hour treatment ($175) that starts with a steam, followed by a sea-salt-and-clay body scrub and a four-handed massage. The real treat, however, is relaxing on Aunty's open-air garden deck. The center's mission is to promote a healthy body image. Detailed directions are given when you book a treatment. ■TIP→ This is cash only and you need to bring your own towel. ⊠ *Kamalomaloo Pl., Anahola* ☎ *808/822–3235* ⊕ *www.angelineslomikauai.com.*

THE SOUTH SHORE

★ Anara Spa

SPA/BEAUTY | The luxurious Anara Spa has all the equipment and services you expect from a top resort spa, along with a pleasant, professional staff. Best

Winter brings big surf to Kauai's North Shore. You can see some of the sport's biggest celebrities catching waves at Haena and Hanalei Bay.

of all, it has indoor and outdoor areas that capitalize on the tropical locale and balmy weather, further distinguishing it from other hotel spas. Its 46,500 square feet of space includes the lovely Garden Treatment Village, an open-air courtyard with private thatched-roof huts, each featuring a relaxation area, misters, and open-air shower in a tropical setting. Ancient Hawaiian remedies and local ingredients are featured in many of the treatments, such as a pineapple-papaya body hydration and a traditional *lomilomi* massage. The open-air lava-rock showers are wonderful, introducing many guests to the delightful island practice of showering outdoors. The spa, which includes a full-service salon, adjoins the Hyatt's legendary swimming pool. ⊠ *Hyatt Regency Kauai Resort and Spa, 1571 Poipu Rd., Poipu* ☎ *808/240–6440* ⊕ *www.anaraspa. com* ✉ *Massages from $180.*

Stand-Up Paddling

This is an increasingly popular sport that even a novice can pick up—and have fun doing. Beginners start with a heftier surfboard and a longer-than-normal canoe paddle. And, just as the name implies, stand-up paddlers stand on their surfboards and paddle out from the beach—no timing a wave and doing a push-up to stand. The perfect place to learn is a river (think **Hanalei** or **Wailua**) or a calm lagoon (try **Anini** or **Kalapaki**). But this sport isn't just for beginners. Tried-and-true surfers turn to it when the waves are not quite right for their preferred sport, because it gives them another reason to be on the water. Stand-up paddlers catch waves earlier and ride them longer than longboard surfers. In the past couple of years, professional stand-up paddling competitions have popped up, and surf shops and instructors have adapted to its quick rise in popularity.

EQUIPMENT

Not all surf instructors teach stand-up paddling, but more and more are, like Blue Seas Surfing School and Titus Kinimaka Hawaiian School of Surfing *(see Surfing)*.

Back Door Surf Co.

WATER SPORTS | Along with its sister store across the street—Hanalei Surf Shop—Back Door Surf Co. provides just about all the rentals necessary for a fun day at Hanalei Bay, along with clothing and new boards. ⊠ *Ching Young Village, 5-5190 Kuhio Hwy., Hanalei* ☎ *808/826–9000* ⊕ *www.hanaleisurf.com/our-sister-stores.*

Hawaiian Surfing Adventures

WATER SPORTS | This Hanalei location has a wide variety of stand-up boards and paddles for rent, with a few options depending on your schedule. Check in at the storefront and then head down to the beach, where your gear will be waiting. Lessons are also available on the scenic Hanalei River or in Hanalei Bay, and include 30 minutes of ocean safety, paddling, and wave-reading instruction and an hour in the water to practice with the board. This Native Hawaiian–owned company also offers surfboard and kayak rentals and surfing lessons. ⊠ *5134 Kuhio Hwy., Hanalei* ☎ *808/482–0749* ⊕ *www. hawaiiansurfingadventures.com* ⊠ *Paddleboard rental from $30; surfboard rentals from $20; lessons from $65.*

Kauai Beach Boys

WATER SPORTS | This outfitter is right on the beach at Kalapaki, so there's no hauling your gear on your car. Classes are also held at Poipu Beach, at the Marriott Waiohai. In addition to stand-up paddle lessons, they offer sailing and surfing lessons, too. ⊠ *3610 Rice St., Lihue* ☎ *808/246–6333, 808/742–4442* ⊕ *www. kauaibeachboys.com* ⊠ *$79 for 90-min surf or SUP lesson.*

Surfing

Good ol' stand-up surfing is alive and well on Kauai, especially in winter's high-surf season on the North Shore. If you're new to the sport, we highly recommend taking a lesson. Not only will this ensure you're up and riding waves in no time, but instructors will provide the right board for your experience and size, help you time a wave, and give you a push to get your momentum going. ■ **TIP→ You don't need to be in top physical shape to take a lesson. Because your instructor helps push you into the wave, you won't wear yourself out paddling.** If you're experienced and want to hit the waves on your own, most surf shops rent boards for all levels, from beginners to advanced.

BEST SPOTS

Perennial-favorite beginning surf spots include **Poipu Beach** (the area fronting the Marriott Waiohai Beach Club), **Hanalei Bay,** and the stream end of **Kalapaki Beach.** More advanced surfers move down the beach in Hanalei to an area fronting a grove of pine trees known as **Pine Trees,** or paddle out past the pier. When the trade winds die, the north ends of **Wailua** and **Kealia** beaches are teeming with surfers. Breaks off **Poipu** and **Beach House/Lawai Beach** attract intermediates year-round. During high surf, the break on the cliff side of **Kalihiwai** is for experts only. Advanced riders will head to Polihale to face the heavy West Side waves when conditions are right.

EQUIPMENT AND LESSONS

Hanalei Surf Company

SURFING | You can rent boards here and shop for rash guards, wet suits, and some hip surf-inspired apparel. ⊠ *Hanalei Center, 5-5161 Kuhio Hwy., Hanalei* ☎ *808/826–9000* ⊕ *www.hanaleisurf. com.*

On the North Shore, adventure seekers will find a nine-zip line course run by Princeville Ranch Adventures.

Nukumoi Surf Co.

SURFING | Owned by the same folks who own Brennecke's restaurant, this shop arranges surfing lessons and provides board (surfing, body, and stand-up paddle), snorkel, and beach-gear rental, as well as casual clothing. Their primary surf spot is the beach fronting the Sheraton. ⊠ *2100 Hoone Rd., across from Poipu Beach Park, Koloa* ☎ *808/742–8019* ⊕ *www.nukumoi.com* ✉ *$75 for groups for 90 min; $250 for private sessions.*

Progressive Expressions

SURFING | This full-service shop has a choice of rental boards and a whole lotta shopping for clothes, swimsuits, and casual beach wear. ⊠ *5428 Koloa Rd., Koloa* ☎ *808/742–6041* ⊕ *www.progres-siveexpressions.com.*

Tamba Surf Company

SURFING | Kauai's homegrown surf shop is your best East Side bet for surfboard and snorkel gear rentals, new boards, and surfing lessons. Tamba is a big name in local surf apparel. ⊠ *4-1543 Kuhio Hwy., Kapaa* ☎ *808/823–6942* ⊕ *www.tamba. com.*

Titus Kinimaka Hawaiian School of Surfing

SURFING | Famed as a pioneer of big-wave surfing, this Hawaiian believes in giving back to his sport. Beginning, intermediate, and advanced lessons are available at Hanalei, with a maximum of three students. If you want to learn to surf from a living legend, this is the man. Advanced surfers can also take a tow-in lesson with a Jet Ski. ■**TIP➜ He employs other instructors, so if you want Titus, be sure to ask for him. (And good luck, because if the waves are going off, he'll be surfing, not teaching.)** Customers are able to use the board for a while after the lesson is complete. ⊠ *Quicksilver, 5-5088 Kuhio Hwy., Hanalei* ☎ *808/652–1116* ⊕ *www. hawaiianschoolofsurfing.com* ✉ *$75, 90-min group; $250 Jet Ski surf; $130, 90-min stand-up paddle.*

Whale-Watching

Every winter, North Pacific humpback whales swim some 3,000 miles over 30 days, give or take a few, from Alaska to Hawaii. Whales arrive as early as November and sometimes stay through April, though they seem to be most populous in February and March. They come to Hawaii to breed, calve, and nurse their young.

TOURS

Of course, nothing beats seeing a whale up close. During the season, any boat on the water is looking for whales; they're hard to avoid, whether the tour is labeled "whale-watching" or not. Consider the whales a benefit to any boating event that may interest you. If whales are definitely your thing, though, you can narrow down your tour-boat decision by asking a few whale-related questions, like whether there's a hydrophone on board, how long the captain has been running tours in Hawaii, and if anyone on the crew is a marine biologist or trained naturalist.

Several boat operators will add two-hour afternoon whale-watching tours during the season that run on the South Shore (not Napali). Operators include **Blue Dolphin, Catamaran Kahanu, HoloHolo,** and **Napali Explorer** *(see Boat Tours)*. Trying one of these excursions is a good option for those who have no interest in snorkeling or sightseeing along Napali Coast, although keep in mind, the longer you're on the water, the more likely you'll be to see the humpbacks.

One of the more unique ways to (possibly) see some whales is atop a kayak. For such an encounter, try **Outfitters Kauai**'s South Shore kayak trip *(see Kayaking Tours)*. There are a few lookout spots around the island with good land-based viewing: Kilauea Lighthouse on the North Shore, the Kapaa Scenic Overlook just north of Kapaa town on the East Side,

and the cliffs to the east of Keoniloa (Shipwreck) Beach on the South Shore.

Zipline Tours

The latest adventure on Kauai is "zipping," or "ziplining." Regardless of what you call it, chances are you'll scream like a rock star while trying it. Strap on a harness, clip onto a cable running from one side of a river or valley to the other, and zip across. The step off is the scariest part. ■TIP→ **Pack knee-length shorts or pants, athletic shoes, and courage for this adventure.**

Outfitters Kauai

TOUR—SPORTS | This outfitter's most popular adventure, the Kipu Zipline Safari Tour, features an 1,800-foot tandem zip—that's right, you don't have to go it alone. You can also paddle the Wailua River or take the downhill bike ride along the Waimea Canyon road. They also offer The Flyline, the state's longest zipline, which has a "run" of 4,000 feet. ⊠ *2827-A Poipu Rd., Poipu* ☎ *808/742–9667, 888/742–9887* ⊕ *www.outfitterskauai.com* ⊠ *From $109.*

Princeville Ranch Adventures

TOUR—SPORTS | The North Shore's answer to ziplining is a nine-zipline course with a bit of hiking and suspension-bridge-crossing thrown in for a half-day adventure. The 4½-hour Zip 'N Dip tour includes a picnic and swimming at a waterfall pool, while the Zip Express whizzes you through the entire course in three hours. Both excursions conclude with a 1,200-foot tandem zip across a valley. Guides are energetic and fun. This is as close as it gets to flying; just watch out for the albatross. ⊠ *Rte. 56, between mile markers 27 and 28, Princeville* ☎ *808/826–7669, 888/955–7669* ⊕ *www.princevilleranch.com* ⊠ *From $139.*

Chapter 7

MOLOKAI

7

Updated by Laurie
Lyons-Makaimoku

◉ Sights   🍴 Restaurants   🛏 Hotels   💼 Shopping   🍸 Nightlife
★★★★★   ★★★★☆   ★★★☆☆   ★★★★☆   ★☆☆☆☆

WELCOME TO MOLOKAI

TOP REASONS TO GO

★ **Kalaupapa Peninsula:** Hike or take a mule ride down the world's tallest sea cliffs, or take a plane to a fascinating historic community that still houses a few former Hansen's disease patients and learn more about the people who have been hidden away from the world.

★ **A waterfall hike in Halawa:** A fascinating guided (intermediate) hike through private property takes you past ancient ruins, restored taro patches, and a sparkling cascade.

★ **Deep-sea fishing:** Sport fish are plentiful in these waters, as are gorgeous views of several islands. Fishing is one of the island's great adventures.

★ **Closeness to nature:** Deep valleys, sheer cliffs, endless rainbows, and the untamed ocean are the main attractions on Molokai.

★ **Papohaku Beach:** This 3-mile stretch of golden sand is one of the most sensational beaches in all of Hawaii. Sunsets and barbecues are perfect here.

Molokai is about 10 miles wide on average and four times that long. It comprises east, west, and central regions, plus the Kalaupapa Peninsula and the Kalaupapa National Historic Park. The north shore thrusts up from the sea to form the tallest sea cliffs on Earth, while the south shore slides almost flat into the water, then fans out to form the largest shallow-water reef system in the United States. Kaunakakai, the island's main town, has most of the stores and restaurants. Surprisingly, the highest point on Molokai rises to only 4,970 feet.

1 **West Molokai.** The most arid part of the island, known as the west end, has two inhabited areas: the coastal stretch includes a few condos and luxury homes, along with the largest beaches on the island; nearby is the fading hilltop hamlet of Maunaloa, a former plantation town, whose backdrop is the dormant volcano that shares its name. Papohaku Beach, one of the remote beaches found here, is the Hawaiian Islands' second-longest white-sand beach.

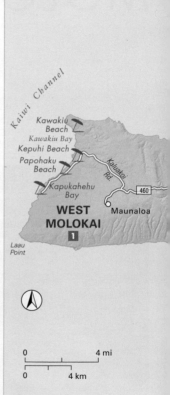

2 **Central Molokai.** The island's only true town, Kaunakakai, with its mile-long wharf, is here. Nearly all the island's eateries and stores are in or close to Kaunakakai. Highway 470 crosses the center of the island, rising to the top of the sea cliffs and the Kalaupapa overlook. At the base of the cliffs is Kalaupapa National Historical Park, a top attraction.

3 Kalaupapa Peninsula.
One of the most remote areas in the entire Hawaiian Islands is currently accessible only by air. It is typically accessible by foot or on a mule, but as of late 2019 the path is closed indefinitely due to a landslide. It's a place of stunning beauty with a tragic history.

4 East Molokai. The
scenic drive on Route 450 around this undeveloped area, also called the east end, passes through the green pastures of Puu O Hoku Ranch and climaxes with a descent into Halawa Valley. As you continue east, the road becomes increasingly narrow and the island ever more lush.

With sandy beaches to the west, sheer sea cliffs to the north, and a rainy, lush eastern coast, Molokai offers a bit of everything, including a peek at what the Islands were like 50 years ago. Large tracts of land from Hawaiian Homeland grants have allowed the people to retain much of their traditional lifestyle. A favorite expression is "Slow down, you're on Molokai." Exploring the great outdoors and visiting the historic Kalaupapa Peninsula, where Saint Damien and Saint Marianne Cope helped people with Hansen's disease, are attractions for visitors.

Molokai is generally thought of as the last bit of "real" Hawaii. Tourism has been held at bay by the island's unique history and the pride of its predominantly Native Hawaiian population. Only 38 miles long and 10 miles wide at its widest point, Molokai is the fifth-largest island in the Hawaiian archipelago. Eight thousand residents call Molokai home, nearly 60% of whom are Hawaiian.

Molokai is a great place to be outdoors. There are no tall buildings, no traffic lights, no streetlights, no stores bearing the names of national chains, and nothing at all like a resort. You will, however, find 15 parks and more than 100 miles of shoreline to play on. At night the whole island grows dark, creating a velvety blackness and a wonderful rare thing called silence.

The first thing to do on Molokai is to drive everywhere. It's a feat you can accomplish comfortably in two days. Depending on where you stay, spend a day exploring the west end andanother exploring the east end. Basically you have one 40-mile west–east highway (two lanes, no stoplights) with three side trips: the nearly deserted little west-end town of Maunaloa, the Highway 470 drive (just a few miles) to the top of the north shore and the overlook of Kalaupapa Peninsula, and the short stretch of shops in Kaunakakai town. After you learn the general lay of the land, you can return to the places that interest you most. Directions on the island—as throughout Hawaii—are often given as *mauka* (toward the mountains) and *makai* (toward the ocean).

■ TIP→ **Most Molokai establishments cater to the needs of locals, not tourists, so you may need to prepare a bit more than if you were going to a more popular destination. Pick up a disposable cooler in Kaunakakai town, and then buy supplies in local markets. Don't forget to carry some water, and bring sunscreen and mosquito repellent to the island with you.**

GEOGRAPHY

Molokai was created when two large volcanoes—Kamakou in the east and Maunaloa in the west—broke the surface of the Pacific Ocean to create an island. Afterward, a third section of the island emerged when a much smaller caldera, Kauhako, popped up to form the Kalaupapa Peninsula. But it wasn't until an enormous landslide sent much of Kauhako Mountain into the sea that the island was blessed with the sheer sea cliffs—the world's tallest—that make Molokai's north shore so spectacularly beautiful.

HISTORY

Molokai is named in chants as the child of the moon goddess Hina. For centuries the island was occupied by native people, who took advantage of the reef fishing and ideal conditions for growing taro.

When leprosy broke out in the Hawaiian Islands in the 1840s, the Kalaupapa Peninsula, surrounded on three sides by the Pacific and accessible only by a steep trail, was selected as the place to exile people suffering from the disease. The first patients were thrown into the sea to swim ashore as best they could, and left with no facilities, shelter, or supplies. In 1873, a missionary named Father Damien arrived and began to serve the peninsula's suffering inhabitants. He died in 1889 from leprosy and was canonized

as a saint by the Catholic Church in 2009. In 1888, a nun named Mother Marianne Cope moved to Kalaupapa to care for the dying Father Damien and continue his vital work. Mother Marianne stayed at Kalaupapa until her death in 1918; she was canonized in 2012.

Although leprosy, known now as Hansen's disease, is no longer contagious and can be remitted, the buildings and infrastructure created by those who were exiled here still exist, and some longtime residents have chosen to stay in their homes. Today the area is Kalaupapa National Historical Park. Visitors are welcome but must book a tour in advance.

THE BIRTHPLACE OF HULA

Tradition has it that, centuries ago, Lailai came to Molokai and lived on Puu Nana at Kaana. She brought the art of hula and taught it to the people, who kept it secret for her descendants, making sure the sacred dances were performed only at Kaana. Five generations later, Laka was born into the family and learned hula from an older sister. She chose to share the art and traveled throughout the Islands teaching the dance, although she did so without her family's consent. The yearly Ka Hula Piko Festival, held on Molokai in May, celebrates the birth of hula at Kaana.

Planning

When to Go

If you're keen to explore Molokai's beaches, coral beds, or fishponds, summer is your best bet for nonstop calm seas and sunny skies. The weather mimics that of the other Islands: low to mid-80s year-round, slightly rainier in winter. As you travel up the mountainside, the weather changes with bursts of downpours. The strongest storms occur in winter, when winds and rain shift to come in from the south.

For a taste of Hawaiian culture, plan your visit around a festival. In January, islanders and visitors compete in ancient Hawaiian games at the Ka Molokai Makahiki Festival. The Molokai Ka Hula Piko, an annual daylong event in May, draws premier hula troupes, musicians, and storytellers. Long-distance canoe races from Molokai to Oahu are in late September and early October. Although never crowded, the island is busier during these events—book accommodations and transportation six months in advance.

Getting Here and Around

AIR

If you're flying in from the mainland United States, you must first make a stop in Honolulu, Oahu; Kahului, Maui; or Kailua-Kona, the Big Island. From any of those, Molokai is just a short hop away. Molokai's transportation hub is Molokai Airport, a tiny airstrip 8 miles west of Kaunakakai and about 18 miles east of Maunaloa. An even smaller airstrip serves the little community of Kalaupapa on the north shore.

From Molokai Airport, it takes about 10 minutes to reach Kaunakakai and 25 minutes to reach the west end of the island by car. There's no public bus. A taxi will cost about $27 from the airport to Kaunakakai with Hele Mai Taxi. Shuttle service costs about $25 per person from Molokai Airport (sometimes called Hoolehua Airport) to Kaunakakai; call Molokai Tours. Keep in mind, however, that it's difficult to visit the island without a rental car.

AIRPORT CONTACTS Molokai Airport (MKK). ✉ 3980 Airport Loop, Hoolehua ☎ 808/567–9660 ⊕ www.airports.hawaii. gov/mkk.

TAXI CONTACTS Hele Mai Taxi. ☎ 808/336–0967, 808/646–0608 ⊕ www.molokaitaxi.com. **Molokai Day Tours.** ✉ 1300 Kamehameha V Hwy., Kaunakakai ☎ 808/660–3377 ⊕ www. molokaidaytours.com.

CAR

If you want to explore Molokai from one end to the other, you must rent a car. With just a few main roads to choose from, it's a snap to drive around here. The gas stations are in Kaunakakai. Ask your rental agent for a free *Molokai Drive Guide*.

Alamo maintains a counter at Molokai Airport. Make arrangements in advance, because the number of rental cars on Molokai is limited. Be sure to check that the vehicle's four-wheel drive is working before you depart from the agency. Off-road driving is not allowed; beware of fees for returning the car dirty. If Alamo is fully booked, check out Molokai Car Rental.

CONTACTS Alamo Rent a Car. ✉ 3980 Airport Loop, Building 2, Hoolehua ☎ 808/567–6381 ⊕ www.alamo.com. **Molokai Car Rental.** ✉ 109 Ala Malama St., Kaunakakai ☎ 808/336–0670 ⊕ www. molokaicars.com.

Beaches

Molokai's unique geography gives the island plenty of drama and spectacle along the shorelines but not so many places for seaside basking and bathing. The long north shore consists mostly of towering cliffs that plunge directly into the sea and is inaccessible except by boat, and even then only in summer. Much of the south shore is enclosed by a huge reef, which stands as far as a mile offshore and blunts the action of the waves. Within this reef you can find a thin strip of sand, but the water here is flat, shallow, and at times clouded with silt. This reef area is best suited to wading, pole fishing, kayaking, and paddleboarding.

The big, fat, sandy beaches lie along the west end. The largest of these—the second largest in the Islands—is Papohaku Beach, which fronts a grassy park shaded by a grove of *kiawe* (mesquite) trees. These stretches of west-end sand are generally unpopulated. At the east end, where the road hugs the sinuous shoreline, you encounter a number of pocket-size beaches in rocky coves, good for snorkeling. Don't venture too far out, however, or you can find yourself caught in dangerous currents. The island's east-end road ends at Halawa Valley with its unique double bay, which is not recommended for swimming.

If you need snorkeling gear, head to Molokai Fish & Dive at the west end of Kaunakakai's only commercial strip, or rent beach chairs, surfboards, or umbrellas from Beach Break, 4 miles west of Kaunakakai. To rent kayaks contact Molokai Outdoors.

Hotels

Molokai appeals most to travelers who appreciate genuine Hawaiian ambience rather than swanky digs. Most hotel and condominium properties range from adequate to funky. Visitors who want to lollygag on the beach should choose one of the condos or home rentals in West Molokai. Travelers who want to immerse themselves in the spirit of the island should seek out a condo or cottage, the closer to East Molokai the better.

Note: Maui County has regulations concerning vacation rentals; to avoid disappointment, always contact the property manager or the owner and ask if the accommodations have the proper permits and are in compliance with local ordinances.

The coastline along Molokai's west end has ocean-view condominium units and luxury homes available as vacation rentals. Central Molokai offers seaside condominiums. The only lodgings on the east end are some guest cottages in magical settings and the cottages and ranch lodge at Puu O Hoku. Note that room rates do not include the 13.42% sales tax.

Hotel reviews have been shortened. For full information, visit Fodors.com.

WHAT IT COSTS			
$	$$	$$$	$$$$
HOTELS			
under $181	$181– $260	$261– $340	over $340

Molokai Vacation Properties

HOTEL—SIGHT | FAMILY | This company handles condo rentals and can arrange a rental car for you during your stay. There is a three-night minimum on all properties, and options for weekly and monthly rates are available. Private rental properties, from beach cottages to large estates, are also available. ✉ *130 Kamehameha V Hwy., Kaunakakai* ☎ *800/367–2984, 808/553–8334* ⊕ *www. molokaivacationrental.com.*

Restaurants

Dining on Molokai is simply a matter of eating—there are no fancy restaurants, just pleasant low-key places to dine. Paddlers Restaurant and Bar and Hiro's Ohana Grill currently have the best dinner offerings. Other options include burgers, plate lunches, pizza, coffee shop-style sandwiches, and make-it-yourself fixings.

During a week's stay, you might easily hit all the dining spots worth a visit and then return to your favorites for a second round. The dining scene is fun, because it's a microcosm of Hawaii's diverse cultures. You can find locally grown vegetarian foods, spicy Filipino cuisine, or Hawaiian fish with a Japanese influence—such as tuna, mullet, and moonfish that's grilled, sautéed, or mixed with seaweed to make *poke* (salted and seasoned raw fish).

Most eating establishments are on Ala Malama Street in Kaunakakai. If you're heading to West Molokai for the day, be sure to stock up on provisions, as there is no place to eat there. If you are on the east end, stop by **Manae Goods & Grindz** (☎ *808/558–8186*) near mile marker 16 for good local seafood plates, burgers, and ice cream.

WHAT IT COSTS			
$	$$	$$$	$$$$
RESTAURANTS			
under $18	$18–$26	$27–$35	over $35

Nightlife

Local nightlife consists mainly of gathering with friends and family, sipping a few cold ones, strumming ukuleles and guitars, singing old songs, and talking story. Still, there are a few ways to kick up your heels. Pick up a copy of the weekly *Molokai Dispatch* and see if there's a concert, church supper, or dance.

Shopping

Molokai has one main commercial area: Ala Malama Street in Kaunakakai. There are no department stores or shopping malls, and the clothing is typical island wear. A small number of family-run businesses defines the main drag of Maunaloa, a rural former plantation town, and there are a couple of general stores

and other random stores throughout the island. Most stores in Kaunakakai are open Monday–Saturday 10 am–6 pm, but posted hours are sometimes just a suggestion. If you find that a store isn't open at the posted time, grab a coffee, shop at a couple of other spots, then circle back around. Almost everything shuts down on Sundays, so be sure to plan ahead.

Visitor Information

CONTACTS Destination Molokai Visitors Bureau. ✉ *3980 Airport Loop, Hoolehua* ☎ *808/553–5221* ⊕ *www.gohawaii.com/molokai*.

West Molokai

Papohaku Beach is 17 miles west of the airport; Maunaloa is 10 miles west of the airport.

The remote beaches and rolling pastures on Molokai's west end are presided over by Maunaloa, a dormant volcano, and a sleepy little former plantation town of the same name. Papohaku Beach, the Hawaiian Islands' second-longest white-sand beach, is one of the area's biggest draws.

GETTING HERE AND AROUND

The sometimes winding paved road through West Molokai begins at Highway 460 and ends at Kapukahehu Bay. The drive from Kaunakakai to Maunaloa is about 30 minutes.

◉ Sights

Kaluakoi

TOWN | Although the mid-1970s Kaluakoi Hotel and Golf Club is closed and forlorn, some nice condos and a gift shop are operating nearby. Kepuhi Beach, the white-sand beach along the coast, is worth a visit. ✉ *Kaluakoi Rd., Maunaloa*.

Lava ridges make Kepuhi Beach beautiful, but swimming here is difficult unless the water is calm.

Maunaloa

TOWN | Built in 1923, this quiet community at the western end of the highway once housed workers for the island's pineapple plantation. Many businesses have closed, but it's the last place you can buy supplies when exploring the nearby beaches. If you're in the neighborhood, stop at Maunaloa's Big Wind Kite Factory. You'll want to talk with Uncle Jonathan, who has been making and flying kites here for more than three decades. There's not much in Maunaloa anymore, but it's not every day that you can see something this close to a ghost town. ⊠ *Maunaloa Hwy., Maunaloa.*

🏖 Beaches

Molokai's west end looks across a wide channel to the island of Oahu. This crescent-shape cup of coastline holds the island's best sandy beaches as well as the sunniest weather. Remember: all beaches are public property, even those that front developments, and most have public access roads. *Beaches in this section are listed from north to south.*

Kawakiu Beach

BEACH—SIGHT | Seclusion is yours at this remote, beautiful, white-sand beach, accessible by four-wheel-drive vehicle (through a gate that is sometimes locked) or a 45-minute walk (wear close-toed shoes as you may find yourself in a thorny situation). To get here, drive to Paniolo Hale off Kaluakoi Road and look for a dirt road off to the right. Park here and hike in or, with a four-wheel-drive vehicle, drive along the dirt road to the beach. ⚠ **Rocks and undertow make swimming extremely dangerous at times, so use caution. Amenities:** none. **Best for:** solitude. ⊠ *Off Kaluakoi Rd., Maunaloa.*

Kepuhi Beach

BEACH—SIGHT | The Kaluakoi Hotel is closed, but its half mile of ivory sand is still accessible. The beach shines against the turquoise sea, black outcroppings of lava, and magenta bougainvillea blossoms. When the sea is perfectly

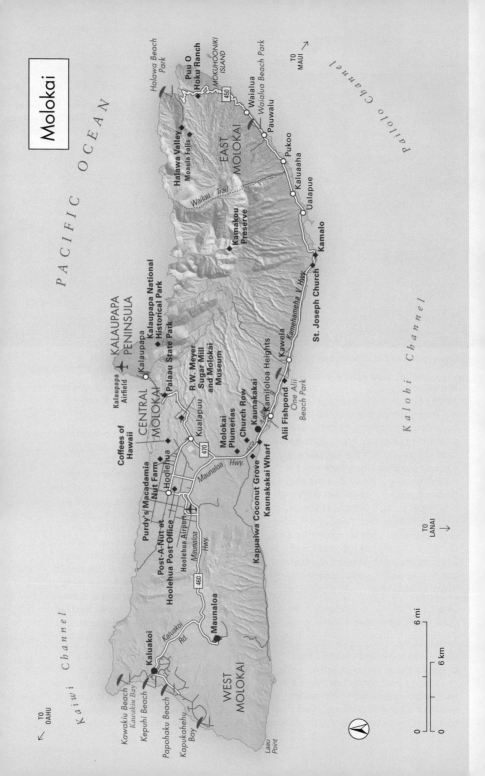

calm, lava ridges in the water make good snorkeling spots. With any surf at all, however, the water around these rocky places churns and foams, wiping out visibility and making it difficult to avoid being slammed into the jagged rocks. Stick to the northern part of the beach to avoid as many of the rocks as possible. If the surf is too big for snorkeling, there's a nice bench up the path that lets you relax and take it all in. **Amenities:** none. **Best for:** snorkeling; walking. ✉ *Kaluakoi Rd., Maunaloa.*

★ Papohaku Beach

BEACH—SIGHT | One of the most sensational beaches in Hawaii, Papohaku is a 3-mile-long strip of light golden sand, the longest of its kind on the island. There's so much sand here that Honolulu once purchased bargeloads of the stuff to replenish Waikiki Beach. A shady beach park just inland is the site of the Ka Hula Piko Festival, held each year in May. The park is also a great sunset-facing spot for a rustic afternoon barbecue. A park ranger patrols the area periodically. **■ TIP→ Swimming is not recommended, as there's a dangerous undertow except on exceptionally calm summer days.** **Amenities:** showers; toilets. **Best for:** sunset; walking. ✉ *Kaluakoi Rd., Maunaloa* ✣ *2 miles south of the former Kaluakoi Hotel.*

Kapukahehu Bay

BEACH—SIGHT | This sandy protected cove is usually completely deserted on weekdays but can fill up when the surf is up. The water in the cove is clear and shallow with plenty of well-worn rocky areas. These conditions make for excellent snorkeling, swimming, and body boarding on calm days. Locals like to surf in a break called Dixie's or Dixie Maru. **Amenities:** none. **Best for:** snorkeling; surfing; swimming. ✉ *End of Kaluakoi Rd., 3½ miles south of Papohaku Beach, Maunaloa.*

Beach Safety

Unlike protected shorelines like Kaanapali on Maui, the coasts of Molokai are exposed to rough sea channels and dangerous rip currents. The ocean tends to be calmer in the morning and in summer. No matter what the time, however, always study the sea before entering. Unless the water is placid and the wave action minimal, it's best to stay on shore, even though locals may be in the water. Don't underestimate the power of the ocean. Protect yourself with sunblock; cool breezes make it easy to underestimate the power of the sun as well.

Hotels

If you want to stay in West Molokai so you'll have access to unspoiled beaches, you can choose from condos or vacation homes. Note that units fronting the abandoned Kaluakoi golf course present a bit of a dismal view.

Ke Nani Kai

$ | RENTAL | These pleasant, spacious one- and two-bedroom condos near the beach—each with a washer, dryer, and a fully equipped kitchen—have ocean views and nicely maintained tropical landscaping. **Pros:** on island's secluded west end; uncrowded pool; beach across the road. **Cons:** amenities vary from unit to unit; far from commercial center; some units overlook abandoned golf course. [$] *Rooms from: $135* ✉ *50 Kepuhi Pl., Maunaloa* ☎ *800/490–9042* 🌐 *www.molokai-vacation-rental.net* 🛏 *120 units* 🍴 *No meals.*

★ **Paniolo Hale**

$ | **RENTAL** | Perched high on a ridge overlooking a favorite local surfing spot, this is Molokai's best condominium property and boasts mature tropical landscaping and a private serene setting. **Pros:** close to beach; quiet surroundings; perfect if you are an expert surfer. **Cons:** amenities vary; far from shopping; golf course units front abandoned course. [$] *Rooms from: $125* ✉ *100 Lio Pl., Kaunakakai* ☎ *808/553–8334, 800/367–2984* 🌐 *www.molokai-vacation-rental.net* 🛏 *77 units* 🍴 *No meals.*

Shopping

ARTS AND CRAFTS

★ **Big Wind Kite Factory and Plantation Gallery**

CRAFTS | The factory has custom-made kites you can fly or display. Designs range from Hawaiian flags to Hawaiian animals like *pueo* (owls) with a little bit of mermaid fun in between. Also in stock are paper kites, mini kites, and wind socks. Ask to go on the factory tour, or take a free kite-flying lesson. The adjacent gallery carries an eclectic collection of merchandise, including locally made crafts, Hawaiian books and CDs, jewelry, handmade batik sarongs, and an elegant line of women's linen clothing. ✉ *120 Maunaloa Hwy., Maunaloa* ☎ *808/552–2364* 🌐 *www.bigwindkites.com.*

FOOD

Maunaloa General Store

FOOD/CANDY | Stocking meat, produce, beverages, and dry goods, this shop is a convenient stop if you're planning a picnic at one of the west-end beaches. Stop for other treats as well—they've got ice cream, beer, and other snacks. ✉ *200 Maunaloa Hwy., Maunaloa* ☎ *808/552–2346.*

Central Molokai

Kaunakakai is 8 miles southeast of the airport.

Most residents live centrally, near the island's one and only true town, Kaunakakai. It's just about the only place on the island to get food and supplies—it *is* Molokai. Go into the shops along and around Ala Malama Street to shop and talk with the locals. Take your time, and you'll really enjoy being a visitor. On the north side is Coffees of Hawaii, a 500-acre coffee plantation, and the Kalaupapa National Historical Park, one of the island's most notable sights.

GETTING HERE AND AROUND

Central Molokai is the hub of the island's road system, and Kaunakakai is the commercial center. Watch for kids, dogs, and people crossing the street downtown.

Sights

Church Row

RELIGIOUS SITE | Standing together along the highway are seven houses of worship with primarily native-Hawaiian congregations. Notice the unadorned, boxlike architecture so similar to missionary homes. ✉ *Rte. 460, Kaunakakai* ✣ *5½ miles south of airport.*

Coffees of Hawaii

FARM/RANCH | Visit the headquarters of a 500-acre Molokai coffee plantation. There's a small gift shop that sells all things coffee, and live music and hula are performed on the covered lanai every Tuesday at lunchtime. Don't expect a full coffee experience, though, as the espresso bar has shut down at this location and only operates at the airport. ✉ *1630 Farrington Hwy., off Rte. 470, Kualapuu* ☎ *808/567–9490* 🌐 *www.coffeesofhawaii.com* 🕒 *Closed Sun.*

Kapuaiwa Coconut Grove in Central Molokai is a survivor of royal plantings from the 19th century.

Kapuaiwa Coconut Grove

HISTORIC SITE | From far away this spot looks like a sea of coconut trees. Closer up you can see that the tall stately palms are planted in long rows leading down to the sea. This is a remnant of one of the last surviving royal groves planted for Prince Lot, who ruled Hawaii as King Kamehameha V from 1863 until his death in 1872. Watch for falling coconuts. ⊠ *30 Mauna Loa Hwy., Kaunakakai.*

Kaunakakai

TOWN | Central Molokai's main town looks like a classic 1940s movie set. Along the one-block main drag is a cultural grab bag of restaurants and shops, and many people are friendly and willing to supply directions or just "talk story." Preferred dress is shorts and a tank top, and no one wears anything fancier than a cotton skirt or aloha shirt. ⊠ *Rte. 460, 3 blocks north of Kaunakakai Wharf, Kaunakakai.*

Kaunakakai Wharf

TRANSPORTATION SITE (AIRPORT/BUS/FER-RY/TRAIN) | Once bustling with barges exporting pineapples, these docks now host visiting boats and the twice-weekly barge from Oahu. The wharf, the longest in the state, is also the starting point for fishing, sailing, snorkeling, whale-watching, and scuba-diving excursions. It's a nice place at sunset to watch fish rippling the water. To get here, take Kaunakakai Place, which dead-ends at the wharf. ⊠ *Rte. 450, at Ala Malama St., Kaunakakai.*

Molokai Plumerias

GARDEN | The sweet smell of plumeria surrounds you at this 10-acre orchard containing thousands of these fragrant trees. Purchase a lei to go, or for $25 owner Dick Wheeler will give you a basket, set you free to pick your own blossoms, then teach you how to string your own lei. Whether purchasing a lei or making your own, it's best to call first for an appointment or to order your lei in advance. ⊠ *1342 Maunaloa Hwy., Kaunakakai* ☎ *808/553–3391* ⊕ *www. molokaiplumerias.com.*

Kaule O Nanahoa at Palaau State Park

★ Palaau State Park

ARCHAEOLOGICAL SITE | FAMILY | One of the island's few formal recreation areas, this 233-acre retreat sits at a 1,000-foot elevation. A short path through an ironwood forest leads to **Kalaupapa Lookout,** a magnificent overlook with views of the town of Kalaupapa and the 1,664-foot-high sea cliffs protecting it. Informative plaques have facts about leprosy, Saint Damien, and the colony. The park is also the site of **Kaule O Nanahoa** (Phallus of Nanahoa), where women in old Hawaii would come to the rock to enhance their fertility; it is said some still do. Because the rock is a sacred site, be respectful and don't deface the boulders. The park is well maintained, with trails, camping facilities, restrooms, and picnic tables. ⊠ *Rte. 470, Kaunakakai* ✛ *Take Hwy. 460 west from Kaunakakai and then head mauka (toward the mountains) on Hwy. 470, which ends at the park* ☎ *808/567–6923* ⊕ *dlnr. hawaii.gov/dsp/parks/molokai/palaau-state-park* ☒ *Free.*

Post-A-Nut at Hoolehua Post Office

GOVERNMENT BUILDING | At this small, rural post office you can mail a coconut anywhere in the world. Postmaster Gary Lam provides the coconuts and colored markers. You decorate and address your coconut, and Gary affixes eye-catching stamps on it from his extensive collection. Costs vary according to destination, but for domestic addresses they start around $10. ⊠ *69-2 Puupeelua Ave., Hoolehua* ☎ *808/567–6144* ⊙ *Closed weekends.*

Purdy's Macadamia Nut Farm

FARM/RANCH | Molokai's only working macadamia nut farm is open for educational tours hosted by the knowledgeable and entertaining owner. A family business in Hoolehua, the farm takes up 1½ acres with a flourishing grove of 50 original trees that are more than 90 years old, as well as several hundred younger trees. The nuts taste delicious right out of the shell, home roasted, or dipped in macadamia-blossom honey.

Look for Purdy's sign behind Molokai High School. ⊠ *Lihi Pali Ave., Hoolehua* ☎ *808/567–6601* ⊕ *www.molokai-aloha. com/macnuts* ⊠ *Free* ⊙ *Sun. and holidays by appointment only.*

★ R. W. Meyer Sugar Mill and Molokai Museum

MUSEUM | Built in 1877, the fully restored, three-room sugar mill has been reconstructed as a testament to Molokai's agricultural history. It is located next to the Molokai Museum and is usually included in the museum tour. Several interesting machines from the past are on display, including a mule-driven cane crusher and a steam engine. The museum contains changing exhibits on the island's early history and has a gift shop. Currently (and for the foreseeable future) the museum is home to an incredible photography exhibit that showcases the people of and life in Kalaupapa; attending the exhibit and speaking with docents is a great way to learn more about the community if you aren't able to visit. Be sure to step into the gift shop for some unique, locally-made items. ⊠ *Rte. 470, Kualapuu* ✛ *2 miles southwest of Palaau State Park* ☎ *808/567–6436* ⊠ *$5* ⊙ *Closed Sun.*

🏖 Beaches

The south shore is mostly a huge, reef-walled expanse of flat saltwater edged with a thin strip of gritty sand and stones, mangrove swamps, and the amazing system of fishponds constructed by the chiefs of ancient Molokai. From this shore you can look out across glassy water to see people standing on top of the sea—actually, way out on top of the reef—casting fishing lines into the distant waves. This is not a great area for swimming beaches, but it is a good place to snorkel or wade in the shallows.

One Alii Beach Park

BEACH—SIGHT | Clear, close views of Maui and Lanai across the Pailolo Channel

Hawaii's First Saint 👁

A long-revered figure on Molokai and in Hawaii, Father Damien, who cared for the desperate patients at Kalaupapa, was elevated to sainthood in 2009. Refurbishment of the three churches in the Catholic parish is currently under way. Visitors who cannot visit Kalaupapa can find information on Saint Damien at the Damien Center in Kaunakakai and may worship at Our Lady of Seven Sorrows (just west of Kaunakakai) or at St. Vincent Ferrer in Maunaloa.

dominate One Alii Beach Park (*One* is pronounced "o-nay," not "won"), the only well-maintained beach park on the island's south-central shore. Molokai folks gather here for family reunions and community celebrations; the park's tightly trimmed expanse of lawn could almost accommodate the entire island's population. Swimming within the reef is perfectly safe, but don't expect to catch any waves. Nearby is the restored One Alii fishpond (it is appropriate only for Native Hawaiians to fish here). **Amenities:** playground, showers; toilets. **Best for:** parties; swimming. ⊠ *Rte. 450, Kaunakakai* ✛ *east of Hotel Molokai.*

🍴 Restaurants

★ Hiro's Ohana Grill

$$$ | MODERN HAWAIIAN | Located in Hotel Molokai, the island's only oceanfront restaurant is also its fanciest and best place to grab a drink or watch the game on TV. Enjoy pasta, steak, shrimp, or fish while watching the sunset and listening to live music, and don't be surprised if the couple you saw hiking is seated at the

table right next to you. **Known for:** shrimp pesto over linguini; live music and hula; whale-watching from your table in winter. $ *Average main: $27* ✉ *Hotel Molokai, 1300 Kamehameha V Hwy., Kaunakakai* ☎ *808/660–3400* ⊕ *www.hirosohana-grill.com* ☞ *Breakfast available on the weekends.*

Kamoi Snack-n-Go

$ | AMERICAN | The old school interior at this "Molokai rest stop" feels a bit like a time warp, making it the perfect place to try one (or two) of the 30 or more flavors of Dave's Hawaiian Ice Cream; it's the only place that serves it on the island. Sit in the refreshing breeze on one of the benches outside to enjoy your cone, pick up snacks, crack seed, water, and cold drinks. **Known for:** tropical flavors of Dave's Hawaiian Ice Cream; milkshakes; grab-n-go snacks and drinks. $ *Average main: $6* ✉ *28 Kamoi St., Kaunakakai* ☎ *808/553–3742* ⊕ *www.facebook.com/kamoisnack.*

★ Kanemitsu's Bakery and Coffee Shop

$ | CAFÉ | Stop at this James Beard–nominated Molokai institution for morning coffee, a loco moco, and some Molokai bread—a sweet, pan-style white loaf that makes excellent cinnamon toast. By night, the famous "Hot Bread Lane" is a Molokai institution—sniff your way down the alley behind the store around 7:30 pm to find the hidden bakery window and grab a loaf of tomorrow's bread right out of the oven. **Known for:** Molokai sweet bread; poi donuts. $ *Average main: $9* ✉ *79 Ala Malama St., Kaunakakai* ☎ *808/553–5855* ◷ *Closed Tues.*

Kualapuu Cookhouse

$ | HAWAIIAN | Across the street from Kualapuu Market, this laid-back diner is a local favorite set in a classic, refurbished, green-and-white plantation house that's decorated with local photography and artwork and accented with a shady lanai. Typical fare at Kualapuu's only restaurant

is a plate of chicken, pork, or hamburger steak served with rice, but there's also the more expensive spicy crusted ahi at dinner. **Known for:** chicken katsu; BYOB; laid-back atmosphere. $ *Average main: $13* ✉ *102 Farrington Ave., 1 block west of Rte. 470, Kualapuu* ☎ *808/567–9655* ⊟ *No credit cards* ◷ *Closed for dinner Sun. and Mon.*

Manae Goods & Grindz

$ | HAWAIIAN | The best place to grab a snack or picnic supplies is this store, 16 miles east of Kaunakakai. It's the only place on the east end where you can find essentials such as ice and bread, and not-so-essentials such as seafood plate lunches, bentos, burgers, shakes, and refreshing smoothies. **Known for:** only place to get food on the east end; hearty portions; loco moco and plate lunches. $ *Average main: $9* ✉ *8615 Kamehameha V Hwy., Kaunakakai* ☎ *808/558–8498* ◷ *Lunch counter closed Wed.; no dinner.*

Molokai Burger

$ | BURGER | Clean and cheery, Molokai Burger offers both drive-through and eat-in options. This is the island's version of fast food, and the tasty burger buns and super crispy fries help to elevate this past a typical experience. **Known for:** affordable burgers; convenient and quick; air-conditioning and Wi-Fi. $ *Average main: $7* ✉ *20 W. Kamehameha V Hwy., Kaunakakai* ☎ *808/553–3533* ◷ *Closed Sun.*

Molokai Pizza Cafe

$ | AMERICAN | This is a popular gathering spot for local families and a good place to pick up food for a picnic. Pizza, sandwiches, salads, pasta, and fresh fish are simply prepared and served without fuss. **Known for:** games for kids; linguine alfredo; open Sundays. $ *Average main: $15* ✉ *15 Kaunakakai Pl. , at Wharf Rd., Kaunakakai* ☎ *808/553–3288* ⊟ *No credit cards.*

★ Paddlers Restaurant and Bar
$$ | **AMERICAN** | New owners breathed new life—and a new menu—into this popular Molokai standout, and the result is a laid-back setting and a fusion of gourmet cuisine that stays true to the island's roots, with tacos carne asada, and heaping plates of loco moco. The bar has the island's only draft beer, there's live music and dancing most nights, and produce is locally sourced when available—especially with daily fish specials. **Known for:** an umami explosion in the Paddler Fries; Tomato Jam burger; live performance by Na Kupuna on Friday from 4 to 6 pm. *Average main: $18 ✉ 10 S. Mohala St., Kaunakakai ☎ 808/553–3300 🌐 www.paddlersrestaurant.com ⏲ Closed Sun.*

Sundown Deli
$ | **DELI** | A Molokai staple for more than 20 years, this small deli focuses on freshly made takeout food. Sandwiches come on a half dozen types of bread, and the homemade soups are outstanding. **Known for:** homemade soups; kimchi as a sandwich add-on. *Average main: $8 ✉ 145 Puali Pl., Kaunakakai ☎ 808/553–3713 🌐 www.sundowndeli.com ⏲ Closed weekends. No dinner.*

Hotels

Hotel Molokai is the closest thing to a resort that can be found on the island, with a pool, on-site dining, activities desk, and more. In addition, there are two condo properties in this area, one close to shopping and dining in Kaunakakai, and the other on the way to the east end.

★ Hotel Molokai
$$ | **HOTEL** | **FAMILY** | At this local favorite, Polynesian-style bungalows are scattered around the nicely landscaped property, many overlooking the reef and distant Lanai. **Pros:** five minutes to town; some units have kitchenettes; authentic Hawaiian entertainment. **Cons:** Wi-Fi can be somewhat spotty; lower-priced rooms are small and plain; evening live music can be loud. *Rooms from: $199 ✉ 1300 Kamehameha V Hwy., Kaunakakai ☎ 808/660–3408, 877/553–5347 Reservations only 🌐 www.hotelmolokai.com 40 rooms No meals.*

Molokai Vibes

Molokai is one of the last places in Hawaii where most of the residents are living an authentic rural lifestyle and wish to retain it. Many oppose developing the island for visitors or outsiders, so you won't find much to cater to your needs, but if you take time and talk to the locals, you will find them hospitable and friendly. Some may even invite you home with them. It's a safe place, but don't interrupt private parties on the beach or trespass on private property. Consider yourself a guest in someone's house, rather than a customer.

Molokai Shores
$ | **RENTAL** | Many of the units in this three-story condominium complex have a view of the ocean and Lanai in the distance, and there's a chance to see whales in season. **Pros:** convenient location; some units upgraded; near water. **Cons:** three-night minimum stay for most units; units close to highway can be noisy; beach is narrow and water is too shallow for swimming. *Rooms from: $150 ✉ 1000 Kamehameha V Hwy., Kaunakakai ☎ 808/553–8334, 800/367–2984 🌐 www.molokai-vacation-rental.net 100 units No meals.*

Wavecrest
$ | **RENTAL** | This 5-acre oceanfront condominium complex is convenient if you want to explore the east side of the island—it's 13 miles east of Kaunakakai,

with access to a beautiful reef, excellent snorkeling, and kayaking. **Pros:** convenient location for exploring the east end; good value; nicely maintained grounds. **Cons:** amenities vary; far from shopping; area sometimes gets windy. [$] *Rooms from: $125* ✉ *7148 Kamehameha V Hwy., near mile marker 13, Kaunakakai* ☎ *800/367–2984, 808/553–8334* 🌐 *www.molokai-vacation-rental.net* 🛏 *126 units* 🍴 *No meals.*

Nightlife

Nightlife on Molokai may not be exactly what you think of for a typical night on the town, but that's what makes it special. It's easy to get to know locals and other travelers when you're singing karaoke, tasting island-brewed beers or enjoying the sounds of the ukulele at sunset.

Hiro's Ohana Grill

BARS/PUBS | The bar at Hiro's Ohana Grill at Hotel Molokai is always a good place to drink, with a rotating lineup of local musicians adding ambiance to stunning sunset views. ✉ *1300 Kamehameha V Hwy., Kaunakakai* ☎ *808/660–3400* 🌐 *www.hirosohanagrill.com.*

★ Kanemitsu Bakery & Coffee Shop

CAFES—NIGHTLIFE | For something truly unique, stop in at Kanemitsu Bakery on Ala Malama Street in Kaunakakai for the nightly hot bread sale (Tuesday–Sunday beginning at 7:30 pm). Follow your nose down the alley to the little bread window. While you wait you can talk story with the locals and returning visitors who know not to miss this treat. Take some hot bread home for a late-night or early morning snack. ✉ *79 Ala Malama St., Kaunakakai* ☎ *808/553–5855.*

★ Paddlers Restaurant and Bar

BARS/PUBS | Paddlers Restaurant and Bar offers the most diverse nightlife on the island, with music and dancing most nights of the week. Start off with happy hour from 2 to 5 pm Monday through Saturday, then stick around for the fun. To catch a showing of Na Kupuna, a group of accomplished *kupuna* (old-timers) with guitars and ukuleles, visit on Fridays from 4 to 6 pm. Karaoke nights happen most Saturdays, and if you're looking for a football game or UFC fight, this is the place for it. ✉ *10 Mohala St., Kaunakakai* ☎ *808/553–3300* 🌐 *www.paddlersrestaurant.com.*

Shopping

GIFTS

Blue Monkey

GIFTS/SOUVENIRS | **FAMILY** | This fun and funky store near the airport is great for supplies for a day in the sun including sunscreen, fins, masks, and more. The real draw here is to stock up on souvenirs, jewelry, books, and more from their variety of fun items (they also have a nice kids corner), and maybe even choose a ukulele to bring home. ✉ *1630 Farrington Ave., Kualapuu* ☎ *808/567–6776* 🌐 *www.bigwindkites.com/bluemonkey* 🕒 *Closed Sun.*

Imports Gift Shop

JEWELRY/ACCESSORIES | You'll find soaps and lotions, a small collection of 14-karat-gold chains, rings, earrings, and bracelets, and a jumble of Hawaiian quilts, pillows, books, and postcards at this local favorite. The shop also helps to create custom orders (takes approximately one week) for Hawaiian heirloom jewelry, inspired by popular Victorian pieces and crafted in the islands since the late 1800s. These pieces are created on Oahu and shipped. ✉ *82 Ala Malama St., Kaunakakai* ☎ *808/553–5734.*

ARTS AND CRAFTS

Molokai Art from the Heart

CRAFTS | A small downtown shop, this arts and crafts co-op has locally made folk art like dolls, clay flowers, silk sarongs, and children's items. The shop also carries original art by Molokai artists and Giclée prints, jewelry, locally produced music, and Saint Damien keepsakes. ⊠ *64 Ala Malama St., Kaunakakai* ☎ *808/553–8018* ⊕ *www.molokaigallery. com.*

CLOTHING AND SHOES
★ Hawaii's Finest

CLOTHING | FAMILY | One of Hawaii's better-known clothing lines for contemporary aloha apparel, Hawaii's Finest sells just that, and at fair prices. Their only boutique outside of Honolulu, this shop on the Ala Malama shopping strip fits in with the Hawaiian pride that permeates Molokai's culture. Their modern designs and bold colors adorn light cotton fabrics and accessories, and the apparel comes in a variety of sizes. ⊠ *75B Ala Malama Ave., Kaunakakai* ☎ *808/553–5403* ⊕ *www.hifinest.com* ۞ *Closed Sun.*

★ Something for Everybody Molokai

CLOTHING | This vibrant shop on the Ala Malama strip sells quirky souvenirs like funny T-shirts and local products. They have a café counter offering sandwiches, smoothies, and salads. The owners act as informal area guides, helping visitors find their way around and arrange services that they may need. ⊠ *61 Ala Malama Ave., Unit 3, Kaunakakai* ☎ *808/553–3299* ⊕ *www.allthingsmolokai.com* ۞ *Closed Sun.*

FOOD
Friendly Market Center

CONVENIENCE/GENERAL STORES | The best-stocked supermarket on the island has a slogan ("Your family store on Molokai") that is truly credible. Sun-and-surf essentials keep company with fresh produce, meat, groceries, and liquor. Locals say the food is fresher here than at the other major supermarket. ⊠ *90 Ala Malama St., Kaunakakai* ☎ *808/553–5595* ۞ *Closed Sun.*

Kualapuu Market

CONVENIENCE/GENERAL STORES | This small market that's been open since 1938 has a little bit of everything and is a good stop for provisions, drinks, and other goodies before visiting the western or northern part of the island. This multi-generational mom-and-pop store is run by the same family as Molokai Wines and Spirits. ⊠ *311 Farrington Hwy., Kualapuu* ☎ *808/567–6223* ⊕ *kualapuumarket. wixsite.com/kmltd* ۞ *Closed Sun.*

Kumu Farms

FOOD/CANDY | The most diverse working farm on Molokai is *the* place to purchase fresh produce, herbs, and gourmet farm products. ⊠ *Hua Ai Rd., off Mauna Loa Hwy., near Molokai Airport, Kaunakakai* ☎ *808/351–3326* ⊕ *www.kumufarms. com* ۞ *Closed Sat.–Mon.*

Molokai Wines and Spirits

WINE/SPIRITS | Don't let the name fool you; along with a surprisingly good selection of fine wines and liquors, the store also carries cheeses and snacks. ⊠ *77 Ala Malama St., Kaunakakai* ☎ *808/553–5009.*

SPORTING GOODS
Molokai Bicycle

SPORTING GOODS | This bike shop rents and sells mountain and road bikes as well as helmets, racks, and jogging strollers. It supplies maps and information on biking and hiking and will pick up and drop off equipment nearly anywhere on the island. Be sure to make arrangements ahead of time, as the shop hours are very limited. ⊠ *80 Mohala St., Kaunakakai* ☎ *808/553–5740, 800/709–2453* ⊕ *www. mauimolokaibicycle.com.*

★ Molokai Fish & Dive

SPORTING GOODS | This is the source for your sporting needs, from snorkel rentals to free and friendly advice. Other island essentials like high-quality sunglasses and wide-brimmed hats are also for sale. This is also a good place to pick up original-design Molokai T-shirts, water sandals, books, and gifts. ⊠ *53 Ala Malama St., Kaunakakai* ☎ *808/553–5926* ⊕ *www.molokaifishanddive.com.*

Kalaupapa Peninsula

The Kalaupapa Airport is in the town of Kalaupapa.

One of the more remote areas in the Hawaiian Islands is a place of stunning natural beauty coupled with a tragic past. It's here that residents of Hawaii who displayed symptoms of Hansen's disease were permanently exiled beginning in 1866. Today, the peninsula is still isolated. But a day spent here is, without a doubt, a profound, once-in-a-lifetime experience.

GETTING HERE AND AROUND

Unless you fly (through Makani Kai Air on-island or Mokulele Airlines off-island), the only way into Kalaupapa National Historical Park is to travel down a dizzy-ing switchback trail, either on foot or by mule. Going down on foot takes at least an hour, but you must allow 90 minutes for the return; going down by mule is even slower, taking two hours down, and the same to travel back up. The switch-backs are numbered—26 in all—and descend 1,700 feet to sea level in just under 3 miles. The steep trail is more of a staircase, and most of the trail is shaded. However, the footing is uneven, and there is little to keep you from pitching over the side. If you don't mind heights, you can stare straight down to the ocean for most of the way. It's strenuous regardless of which method you choose.

The Kalaupapa Trail and Peninsula are all part of Kalaupapa National Historical Park (☎ *808/567–6802* ⊕ *www.nps.gov/kala*), which is open every day but Sunday for tours only. Keep in mind there are no public facilities (except an occasional restroom) anywhere in the park. Pack your own food and water, as well as light rain gear, sunscreen, and bug repellent. As of this writing, the Kalaupapa Trail is closed due to landslides.

TOURS
Mokulele Airlines

AIR EXCURSIONS | To fly into Kalaupapa from another island your only option is Mokulele Airlines (they'll make a layover at the Molokai Airport). As with other ways of traveling into the area, you'll need to arrange a tour so that they can secure permits for you—all visitors must have a sponsor and may not roam around Kalaupapa freely; your tour company serves as your sponsor. Mokulele will require sponsor information before booking. Mokulele Airlines is now part of Southern Airways. ⊠ *Kalaupapa* ☎ *866/260–7070 Reservations only.*

◉ Sights

Kalaupapa National Historical Park

NATIONAL/STATE PARK | For 100 years, this remote strip of land was "the loneliest place on Earth," a beautiful yet feared place of exile for those suffering from leprosy (now known as Hansen's disease). Today, visitors to Molokai's **Kalaupapa Peninsula,** open every day but Sunday, can admire the tall sea cliffs, rain-chiseled valleys, and tiny islets along the coast. The park tells a poignant human story, as the Kalaupapa Peninsula was once a community of about 1,000 people who were banished from their homes in Hawaii. It also recounts the wonderful work of Father Damien, a Belgian missionary who arrived in 1873 to work with the patients. He died in 1889 from leprosy and was canonized as a saint by the Catholic Church in 2009. Mother Marianne Cope, who continued St. Damien's work after his death, was canonized in 2012.

Today there are about eight patients still living in Kalaupapa—now by choice, as the disease is treatable. Out of respect

The Truth About Hansen's Disease

■ A cure for leprosy has been available since 1941. Multidrug therapy, a rapid cure, has been available since 1981.

■ With treatment, none of the disabilities traditionally associated with leprosy need occur.

■ Most people have a natural immunity to leprosy. Only 5% of the world's population is even susceptible to the disease.

■ There are still more than 200,000 new cases of leprosy each year; the majority are in India.

■ All new cases of leprosy are treated on an outpatient basis.

■ The term "leper" is offensive and should not be used. It is appropriate to say "a person is affected by leprosy" or "by Hansen's disease."

to these people, visitors must be at least 16 years old, cannot stay overnight, and must be on a guided tour or invited by a resident. Photographing patients without their permission is forbidden. There are no public facilities (except an occasional restroom) anywhere in the park. Pack your own food and water, as well as light rain gear, sunscreen, and bug repellent.

✉ Hwy. 470, Kualapuu ☎ 808/567–6802 ⊕ www.nps.gov/kala.

East Molokai

Halawa Valley is 36 miles northeast of the airport.

On the beautifully undeveloped east end of Molokai you can find ancient fishponds, a magnificent coastline, splendid ocean views, and a fertile valley that's been inhabited for 14 centuries. The eastern uplands are flanked by Mt. Kamakou, the island's highest point at 4,970 feet and home to the Nature Conservancy's Kamakou Preserve. Mist hangs over waterfall-filled valleys, and ancient lava cliffs jut out into the sea.

GETTING HERE AND AROUND

Driving the east end is a scenic adventure, but the road narrows and becomes curvy after the 20-mile marker. Take your time, especially in the seaside lane, and watch for oncoming traffic. Driving at night is not recommended.

◉ Sights

★ Alii Fishpond

ARCHAEOLOGICAL SITE | With its narrow rock walls arching out from the shoreline, Alii is typical of the numerous fishponds that define southern Molokai. Many were built around the 13th century under the direction of powerful alii (chiefs), who were typically the only ones allowed to eat the harvest from the ponds. This early type of aquaculture, particular to Hawaii, exemplifies the ingenuity of Native Hawaiians. One or more openings were left in the wall, where gates called makaha were installed. These gates allowed seawater and tiny fish to enter the enclosed pond but kept larger predators out. The tiny fish would then grow too big to get out. At one time there were 62 fishponds around Molokai's coast. ✉ Kamehameha V Hwy., Kaunakakai ✛ 1/4 mile past Hotel Molokai.

Halawa Valley is an iconic site in Molokai.

★ Halawa Valley

ARCHAEOLOGICAL SITE | The Solatorio *ohana* (family) leads hikes through the valley, the oldest recorded habitation on Molokai. It is home to two sacrificial temples and many historic sites. Inhabitants grew taro and fished from 650 until the 1960s, when an enormous flood wiped out the taro patches and forced old-timers to abandon their traditional lifestyle. Now, a new generation of Hawaiians has begun the challenging task of restoring the taro fields. Much of this work involves rerouting streams to flow through carefully engineered level ponds called *loi*. Taro plants, with their big, dancing leaves, grow in the submerged mud of the loi, where the water is always cool and flowing. Hawaiians believe that the taro plant is their ancestor and revere it both as sustenance and as a spiritual necessity. The 3.4-mile round-trip valley hike, which goes to **Moaula Falls,** a 250-foot cascade, is rated intermediate to advanced and includes two moderate river crossings (so your feet will get wet).

A $60 fee per adult supports restoration efforts. ⌧ *Eastern end of Rte. 450* ☎ *808/542–1855* ⊕ *www.halawavalley-molokai.com* ⌧ *$60.*

Kamakou Preserve

NATURE PRESERVE | Tucked away on the slopes of Mt. Kamakou, Molokai's highest peak, this 2,774-acre rain-forest preserve is a dazzling wonderland full of wet *ohia* forests (hardwood trees of the myrtle family, with red blossoms called *lehua*), rare bogs, and native trees and wildlife. Free guided educational tours (donations welcome), limited to eight people, are held one Saturday each month March–October. Hikers must be 10 years or older. Reserve well in advance, as these excursions fill up several months in advance. ⌧ *23 Pueo Pl., Kualapuu* ☎ *808/553–5236* ⊕ *www. nature.org* ⌧ *Free.*

Kamalo

BODY OF WATER | A natural harbor used by small cargo ships during the 19th century and a favorite fishing spot for locals,

Kamalo Harbor is a quick stop worth making to take in the quiet calm and hang out with shore birds; look for the "Drive Slow" signs just before the highway bends. This area is also the location of **St. Joseph Church,** a tiny white church built by Saint Damien of the Kalaupapa colony in the 1880s. ⊠ *Rte. 450, Kaunakakai* ⊹ *11 miles east of Kaunakakai.*

Puu O Hoku Ranch

FARM/RANCH | A 14,000-acre private ranch in the highlands of East Molokai, Puu O Hoku was developed in the 1930s by wealthy industrialist Paul Fagan. Route 450 ambles right through this rural treasure with its pastures and grazing horses and cattle. As you drive slowly along, enjoy the splendid views of Maui and Lanai. The small island off the coast is Mokuhooniki, a favorite spot among visiting humpback whales and nesting seabirds. The ranch is also a retreat center and organic farm, and it offers limited accommodations. ⊠ *Rte. 450, mile marker 25, Kaunakakai* ⊹ *25 miles east of Kaunakakai* ☎ *808/558–8109* ⊕ *www. puuohoku.com.*

St. Joseph Church

HISTORIC SITE | At this small, white church, a quick stop off the highway, you can learn more about Father Damien and his work. It's a state historic site and place of pilgrimage. The door is often open; if it is, slip inside, sign the guest book, and make a donation. The congregation keeps the church in beautiful condition. ⊠ *Kamehameha V Hwy., Kaunakakai* ☎ *808/558–0109* ⊕ *www.damienchurchmolokai.org.*

🌀 Beaches

The east end unfolds as a coastal drive with turnouts for tiny cove beaches— good places for snorkeling, shore fishing, or scuba exploring. Rocky little Mokuhooniki Island marks the eastern point of the island and serves as a nursery for humpback whales in winter, nesting seabirds in spring, and hammerhead sharks in the fall. The road loops around the east end, then descends and ends at Halawa Valley.

Halawa Beach Park

BEACH—SIGHT | The vigorous water that gouged the steep, spectacular Halawa Valley also carved out two adjacent bays. Accumulations of coarse sand and river rock have created some protected pools that are good for wading or floating around. You might see surfers, but it's not wise to entrust your safety to the turbulent open ocean along this coast. Most people come here to hang out and absorb the beauty of Halawa Valley. The valley itself is private property, so do not wander without a guide. **Amenities:** toilets. **Best for:** solitude. ⊠ *End of Rte. 450, Kaunakakai.*

Waialua Beach Park

BEACH—SIGHT | Also known as Twenty Mile Beach, this arched stretch of sand leads to one of the most popular snorkeling spots on the island. The water here, protected by the flanks of the little bay, is often so clear and shallow that even from land you can watch fish swimming among the coral heads. Watch out for traffic when you enter the highway. ■**TIP→** This is a pleasant place to stop on the drive around the east end. **Amenities:** none. **Best for:** snorkeling; swimming. ⊠ *Rte. 450 near mile marker 20.*

🛏 Hotels

Two unique lodging options await on the remote, far east end of the island. Dunbar Beachfront Cottages, which lives up to its name as it's just steps from the sand, is great for families. Puu O Hoku Ranch, an active ranch and retreat facility, offers on-site ocean and waterfall views.

★ Dunbar Beachfront Cottages

$$ | RENTAL | FAMILY | Perfect for a comfortable base in the country, think of these two oceanfront, plantation-style cottages as your own private beach home on Molokai's east end; each has a full kitchen, washer and dryer, and ocean-facing lanai. **Pros:** oceanfront location; full kitchen and amenities; convenient location to east end beaches. **Cons:** isolated and far from town; credit cards not accepted, only checks; additional cleaning fee. [$] *Rooms from: $210* ✉ *9750 Kamehameha V Hwy., Kaunakakai* ✣ *Just past mile marker 18* ☎ *808/336–0761* 🌐 *www.molokaibeachfrontcottages.com* 🛏 *2 cottages* 🍴 *No meals* 💳 *No credit cards.*

Puu O Hoku Ranch

$$ | **B&B/INN** | At the east end of Molokai, these ocean-view accommodations are on 14,000 isolated acres of pasture and forest—a remote and serene location for people who want to get away from it all or meet in a retreat atmosphere. **Pros:** ideal for large groups; authentic working ranch; great hiking. **Cons:** on remote east end of island; road to property is narrow and winding; very high cleaning fee. [$] *Rooms from: $250* ✉ *Rte. 450 near mile marker 25, Kaunakakai* ☎ *808/558-8109* 🌐 *www.puuohoku.com* 🛏 *3 cottages, 1 lodge* 🍴 *No meals.*

Activities

Molokai's shoreline topography limits opportunities for water sports. Sea cliffs dominate the north shore; the south shore is largely encased by a huge, taming reef. ■ **TIP→ Open-sea access at west-end and east-end beaches should be used only by experienced ocean swimmers, and even then with caution as seas are rough, especially in winter.** Generally speaking, there's no one around—certainly not lifeguards—if you are in need of assistance. For this reason alone, guided excursions are recommended. At the very least, be sure to ask for advice from outfitters or residents. Two kinds of water activities predominate: kayaking within the reef area and open-sea excursions on charter boats, most of which tie up at Kaunakakai Wharf.

Activity vendors in Kaunakakai are a good source of information on outdoor adventures on Molokai. For a mellow round of golf, head to the island's only golf course, Ironwood Hills, where you'll likely share the greens with local residents. Molokai's steep and uncultivated terrain offers excellent hikes and some stellar views. Although the island is largely wild, most land is privately owned, so get permission before hiking.

BIKING

Cyclists who like to eat up the miles love Molokai, because its few roads are long, straight, and extremely rural. You can really go for it—there are no traffic lights and (most of the time) no traffic.

Molokai Bicycle

BICYCLING | You can rent a bike here for the day; prices depend on the model, with reductions for additional days or weeklong rentals. Bike trailers (for your drinks cooler, perhaps), including doubles for the kids, are also available. Hours are limited due to the owner's teaching schedule, but drop-offs and pickups are available for free at certain locations and for $25 at the airport. ✉ *80 Mohala St., Kaunakakai* ☎ *808/553–5740* 🌐 *www.mauimolokaibicycle.com* 🎟 *Bikes from $25 per day, bike trailers from $15 per day.*

BODY BOARDING AND BODY SURFING

You rarely see people body boarding or body surfing on Molokai, and the only surfing is for advanced wave riders. The best spots for body boarding when conditions are safe (occasional summer mornings) are the west-end beaches. Another option is to seek out waves at the east end around mile marker 20.

St. Joseph's Church is one of Molokai's most historic sites.

DEEP-SEA FISHING

For Molokai people, as in days of yore, the ocean is more of a larder than a playground. It's common to see residents fishing along the shoreline or atop South Shore Reef, using poles or lines. Deep-sea fishing by charter boat is a great Molokai adventure. The sea channels here, though often rough and windy, provide gorgeous views of several islands. Big fish are plentiful in these waters, especially mahimahi, marlin, and various kinds of tuna. Generally speaking, boat captains will customize the outing to your interests, share a lot of information about the island, and let you keep some or all of your catch.

EQUIPMENT

Molokai Fish & Dive

FISHING | If you'd like to try your hand at fishing, you can rent or buy equipment, book a trip, and ask for advice from the friendly staff here. They also host snorkel, scuba, and whale-watching tours. ✉ 53 Ala Malama St., Kaunakakai ☎ 808/553–5926 ⊕ www.molokaifishanddive.com.

BOATS AND CHARTERS

Alyce C.

FISHING | This 31-foot cruiser runs excellent sportfishing excursions in the capable hands of Captain Joe. Full-day, half-day, ¾-day, and full around-the-island trips are available upon the six-passenger boat; gear is provided. It's a rare day when you don't snag at least one memorable fish. Whale-watching trips are also available. ✉ Kaunakakai Wharf, Kaunakakai Pl., Kaunakakai ☎ 808/558–8377 ⊕ www.alycecsportfishing.com 🚤 From $450.

Fun Hogs Sportfishing

FISHING | Trim and speedy, the 27-foot flybridge boat named Ahi offers four-hour, six-hour, and eight-hour sportfishing excursions, either near-shore or deep-sea. Skipper Mike Holmes also provides one-way or round-trip fishing expeditions to Lanai, as well as sunset cruises and whale-watching trips in winter. ✉ Kaunakakai Wharf, Kaunakakai Pl., Kaunakakai ☎ 808/336–0047 ⊕ www.molokaifishing.com 🚤 From $450.

Molokai Action Adventures

FISHING | Walter Naki has traveled (and fished) all over the globe. He will create customized fishing expeditions and gladly share his wealth of experience. He will also take you to remote beaches for a day of swimming. If you want to explore the north side under the great sea cliffs, this is the way to go. His 21-foot Boston Whaler is usually seen in the east end at the mouth of Halawa Valley. ⊠ *Kaunakakai* ☎ *808/558–8184* ⊞ *From $300.*

GOLF

Molokai is not a prime golf destination, but the sole 9-hole course makes for a pleasant afternoon.

Ironwood Hills Golf Course

GOLF | Like other 9-hole plantation-era courses, Ironwood Hills is in a prime spot, with basic fairways and not always manicured greens. It helps if you like to play laid-back golf with locals and can handle occasionally rugged conditions. On the plus side, most holes offer views of the ocean, as well as those of peaks of Oahu and Molokai's sea cliffs. Fairways are *kukuya* grass and run through pine, ironwood, and eucalyptus trees. Clubs are rented on the honor system; there's not always someone there to assist you and you should bring your own water. Access is via a bumpy, unpaved road. ⊠ *Kalae Hwy., Kualapuu* ☎ *808/567–6000* ⊞ *$20 for 9 holes* 🏌 *9 holes, 3088 yards, par 34.*

HIKING

Rural and rugged, Molokai is an excellent place for hiking. Roads and developments are few. The island is steep, so hikes often combine spectacular views with hearty physical exertion. Because the island is small, you can come away with the feeling of really knowing the place. And you won't see many other people around. Much of what may look like deserted land is private property, so be careful not to trespass—seek permission or use an authorized guide.

BEST SPOTS
Kalaupapa Trail

HIKING/WALKING | You can hike down to the Kalaupapa Peninsula and back via this 3-mile, 26-switchback route. The trail is often nearly vertical, traversing the face of the high sea cliffs. You can reach Kalaupapa Trail off Highway 470 near Kalaupapa Overlook. Only those in excellent shape should attempt it. You must have made prior arrangements with Kekaula (Mule Ride) Tours in order to access Kalaupapa via this trail. ⊠ *Off Hwy. 470, Kualapuu* ☎ *808/567–6088 Kekaula Tours* ⊕ *www.nps.gov/kala.*

GOING WITH A GUIDE
★ **Halawa Valley Falls Cultural Hike**

HIKING/WALKING | This gorgeous, steep-walled valley was carved by two rivers and is rich in history. Site of the earliest Polynesian settlement on Molokai, Halawa is a sustained island culture with its ingeniously designed *loi,* or taro fields. Because of a tsunami in 1948 and changing cultural conditions in the 1960s, the valley was largely abandoned. The Solatorio *ohana* (family) is restoring the loi and taking visitors on guided hikes through the valley, which includes two of Molokai's *luakini heiau* (sacred temples), many historic sites, and the trail to **Moaula Falls,** a 250-foot cascade. Bring water, food, a *hookupu* (small gift or offering), insect repellent, and wear sturdy shoes that can get wet. The 3½-mile round-trip hike is rated intermediate to advanced and includes two moderate river crossings. ⊠ *14777 Kamehameha V Hwy., Kaunakakai* ✛ *Guide will meet you at the Halawa Beach Park pavilion* ☎ *808/542–1855* ⊕ *www.halawavalley-molokai.com* ⊞ *$60.*

KAYAKING

Molokai's south shore is enclosed by the largest reef system in the United States—an area of shallow, protected sea that stretches over 30 miles. This reef gives inexperienced paddlers an

Bikers on Molokai can explore the north-shore sea cliffs overlooking the Kalaupapa Peninsula.

unusually safe, calm environment for shoreline exploring. ■TIP→ **Outside the reef, Molokai waters are often rough, and strong winds can blow you out to sea. Kayakers out here should be strong, experienced, and cautious.**

BEST SPOTS
South Shore Reef
KAYAKING | This reef's area is superb for flat-water kayaking any day of the year. Get out in the morning before the wind picks up and paddle east, exploring the ancient Hawaiian fishponds. When you turn around, the wind will usually give you a push home. ■TIP→ **For a kayak or paddleboard lessons, contact Molokai Outdoors.** ⊠ *Kaunakakai.*

EQUIPMENT, LESSONS, AND TOURS
Molokai Outdoors
KAYAKING | For guided kayak and paddleboard tours, this longtime Molokai activity company offers guided 3-, 5-, and 8½-mile downwind runs along Molokai's southern coast. ⊠ *1529 Kamehameha V Hwy, Kaunakakai* ☎ *808/633–8700, 855/208–0811* ⊕ *www.molokai-outdoors. com* ✉ *From $99 per person.*

SCUBA DIVING
Molokai Fish & Dive is the only PADI-certified dive company on Molokai. Shoreline access for divers is extremely limited, even nonexistent in winter. Boat diving is the way to go. Without guidance, visiting divers can easily find themselves in risky situations with wicked currents. Proper guidance, however, opens an undersea world rarely seen.

SNORKELING
During the times when swimming is safe—mainly in summer—just about every beach on Molokai offers good snorkeling along the lava outcroppings in the island's clean and pristine waters. Although rough in winter, Kepuhi Beach is a prime spot in summer. Certain spots inside the South Shore Reef are also worth checking out.

BEST SPOTS

During the summer, **Kepuhi Beach,** on Molokai's west end, offers excellent snorkeling opportunities. The ½-mile-long stretch has plenty of rocky nooks that swirl with sea life. Take Kaluakoi Road all the way to the west end, park at the now-closed Kaluakoi Resort, and walk to the beach. Avoid Kepuhi Beach in winter, as the sea is rough here.

At **Waialua Beach Park,** on Molokai's east end, you'll find a thin curve of sand that rims a sheltered little bay loaded with coral heads and aquatic life. The water here is shallow—sometimes so shallow that you bump into the underwater landscape—and it's crystal clear. Pull off the road near mile marker 20.

EQUIPMENT AND TOURS

Rent snorkel sets from Molokai Fish & Dive in Kaunakakai. Rental fees are nominal ($7–$10 per day). All the charter boats carry snorkel gear and include dive stops.

Fun Hogs Sportfishing

SNORKELING | Mike Holmes, captain of the 27-foot *Ahi,* knows the island waters intimately, likes to have fun, and is willing to arrange any type of excursion—for example, one dedicated entirely to snorkeling. His two-hour snorkel trips leave early in the morning and explore rarely seen fish and turtle sites outside the reef. ⊠ *Kaunakakai Wharf, Kaunakakai Pl., Kaunakakai* ☎ *808/336–0047* ⊕ *www. molokaifishing.com* ⊠ *From $75 per person.*

Molokai Fish & Dive

SNORKELING | Climb aboard a 31-foot twin-hull PowerCat for a snorkeling trip to Molokai's pristine barrier reef. Trips include equipment, water, and soft drinks. ⊠ *53 Ala Malama St., Kaunakakai* ☎ *808/553–5926* ⊕ *www.molokaifishand-dive.com* ⊠ *From $89 per person.*

SPAS

Molokai Acupuncture & Massage

SPA—SIGHT | This relaxing retreat offers acupuncture, massage, herbal remedies, wellness treatments, and private yoga sessions by appointment only. ⊠ *40 Ala Malama St., Suite 206, Kaunakakai* ☎ *808/553–3930* ⊕ *www.molokai-well-ness.com.*

Molokai Lomi Massage

SPA—SIGHT | Allana Noury of Molokai Lomi Massage has studied natural medicine for nearly 40 years and is a licensed massage therapist, master herbalist, and master iridologist. She will come to your hotel or condo by appointment. ☎ *808/553–8034* ⊕ *www.molokaimas-sage.com.*

WHALE-WATCHING

Although Maui gets all the credit for the local wintering humpback-whale population, the big cetaceans also come to Molokai December–April. Mokuhoon-iki Island at the east end serves as a whale nursery and courting ground, and the whales pass back and forth along the south shore. This being Molokai, whale-watching here will never involve floating amid a group of boats all ogling the same whale.

BOATS AND CHARTERS

Alyce C.

WHALE-WATCHING | Although this six-passenger sportfishing boat is usually busy hooking mahimahi and marlin, the captain will gladly take you on a three-hour excursion to admire the humpback whales. ■ **TIP→ The price is based on the number of people in your group.** ⊠ *Kaunakakai Wharf, Kaunakakai Pl., Kaunakakai* ☎ *808/558–8377* ⊕ *www. alycecsportfishing.com* ⊠ *From $75 per person.*

Ama Lua and Coral Queen

WHALE-WATCHING | Molokai Fish & Dive offers two boats for whale-watching. The *Ama Lua* is a 31-foot dive boat that holds up to 12 passengers, while the Coral Queen is a 38-footer that holds up to 25 passengers. On both boats the crew is respectful of the whales and the laws that protect them. A two-hour whale-watching trip departs from Kaunakakai Wharf at 7 am daily (as long as minimum passenger requirements are met), December–April. ⊠ *Molokai Fish & Dive, 53 Ala Malama St., Kaunakakai* ☎ *808/553–5926* ⊕ *www.molokaifishand-dive.com* ✉ *From $79 per person.*

Fun Hogs Sportfishing

WHALE-WATCHING | The *Ahi*, a flybridge sportfishing boat, takes you on 2½-hour whale-watching trips in the morning, December–April. ∎**TIP**→ **No food or drink is provided.** ⊠ *Kaunakakai Wharf, Kaunakakai Pl., Kaunakakai* ☎ *808/336–0047* ⊕ *www.molokaifishing.com* ✉ *From $75 per person.*

Chapter 8

LANAI

Updated by
Lehia Apana

8

👁 Sights	🍽 Restaurants	🛏 Hotels	💼 Shopping	🍸 Nightlife
★★★★★	★★★☆☆	★★★☆☆	★★★☆☆	★☆☆☆☆

WELCOME TO LANAI

TOP REASONS TO GO

★ **Seclusion and serenity:** Lanai is small; local motion is slow motion. Get into the spirit, and go home rested.

★ **Keahiakawelo (Garden of the Gods):** Walk amid the eerie red-rock spires at what Hawaiians still believe to be a sacred spot. The ocean views are magnificent, too; sunset is a good time to visit.

★ **Diving at Cathedrals:** Explore underwater pinnacle formations and mysterious caverns illuminated by shimmering rays of light.

★ **Dole Park:** Hang out in the shade of the Cook pines in Lanai City and talk story with the locals for a taste of old-time Hawaii.

★ **Hulopoe Beach:** This beach may have it all— good swimming, a shady park for perfect picnicking, great reefs for snorkeling, and sometimes schools of spinner dolphins.

1 Lanai City. Quaint and quiet, this historic plantation town is home to most of the island's residents, restaurants, shops, and businesses. Dole Park, with its stately Cook pines and picnic benches, sits in the middle of the action.

2 Manele Bay. Rest and relaxation characterize this coastal area, home to Manele Harbor, Four Seasons Resort Lanai, iconic Puu Pehe, and the golden sands of Hulopoe Beach.

3 Windward Lanai. This area is the long white-sand beach at the base of Lanaihale. Now uninhabited, it was once occupied by thriving Hawaiian fishing villages and a sugarcane plantation.

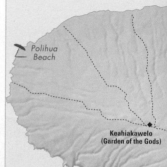

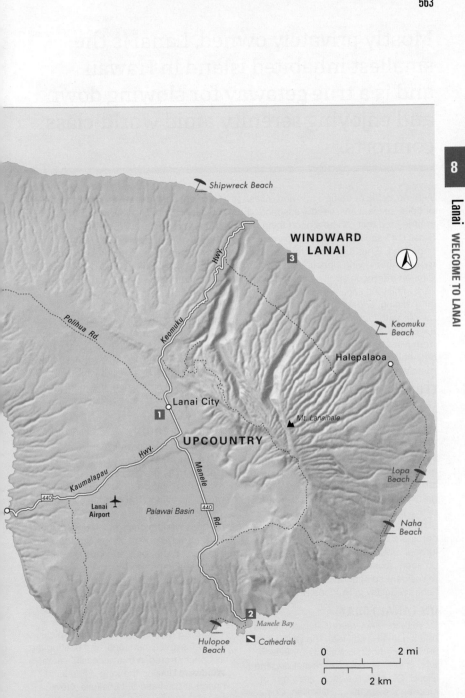

Shipwreck Beach

**WINDWARD
LANAI**

3

*Keomuku
Beach*

Polihua Rd

Keomuku Hwy.

Halepalaoa

Lanai City

1

▲ *Mt. Lanaihale*

UPCOUNTRY

Lopa
Beach

Kaumalapau Hwy.

440

**Lanai
Airport**

Palawai Basin

Manele Rd

440

Naha
Beach

2

Manele Bay

*Hulopoe
Beach*

◼ *Cathedrals*

0		2 mi
0		2 km

Mostly privately owned, Lanai is the smallest inhabited island in Hawaii and is a true getaway for slowing down and enjoying serenity amid world-class comforts.

With no traffic or traffic lights and miles of open space, Lanai seems suspended in time, and that can be a good thing. Small (141 square miles) and sparsely populated, it has just 3,500 residents, most of them living Upcountry in Lanai City. An afternoon strolling around Dole Park in historic Lanai City offers shopping, dining, and the opportunity to mingle with locals. Though it may seem a world away, Lanai is only separated from Maui and Molokai by two narrow channels and is easily accessed by commercial ferry from Maui.

FLORA AND FAUNA
Lanai bucks the "tropical" trend of the other Hawaiian Islands with African kiawe trees, Cook pines, and eucalyptus in place of palm trees, and deep blue sea where you might expect shallow turquoise bays. Abandoned pineapple fields are overgrown with drought-resistant grasses, Christmas berry, and lantana; native plants *aalii* and *ilima* are found in uncultivated areas. Axis deer from India dominate the ridges, and wild turkeys lumber around the resorts. Whales can be seen November–May, and a family of resident spinner dolphins rests and fishes regularly in Hulopoe Bay.

ON LANAI TODAY
Despite its fancy resorts, Lanai still has that languid Hawaii feel. The island is 98% owned by billionaire Larry Ellison, who is in the process of revitalizing the island. Old-time residents are a mix of just about everything: Hawaiian, Chinese, German, Portuguese, Filipino, Japanese, French, Puerto Rican, English, Norwegian—you name it. When Dole owned the island in the early 20th century and grew pineapples, the plantation was divided into ethnic camps, which helped retain cultural cuisines. Potluck dinners feature sashimi, Portuguese bean soup, *laulau* (morsels of pork, chicken, butterfish, or other ingredients steamed in *ti* leaves), potato salad, teriyaki steak, chicken *hekka* (a gingery Japanese chicken stir-fry), and Jell-O. The local language is Pidgin English, a mix of words as complicated and rich as the food. Newly arrived residents have added to the cultural mix.

MAJOR REGIONS
Lanai City, Keahiakawelo (Garden of the Gods), and Manele Bay. Cool and serene, Upcountry is graced by Lanai City, towering Cook pine trees, and misty mountain vistas. The historic plantation village of Lanai City is inching into the modern world. Locals hold conversations in front of Dole Park shops and from their pickups on the road, and kids ride bikes in colorful impromptu parades. Six miles north of Lanai City, Keahiakawelo (nicknamed "Garden of the Gods") is a stunning rocky plateau. The more developed beach side of the island, Manele Bay is where it's happening: swimming, picnicking, off-island excursions, and boating are all concentrated in this accessible area. **Windward Lanai** is the long white-sand beach at the base of Lanaihale. Now

uninhabited, it was once occupied by thriving Hawaiian fishing villages and a sugarcane plantation

Planning

When to Go

Lanai has an ideal climate year-round, hot and sunny at the sea and a few delicious degrees cooler Upcountry. In Lanai City and Upcountry, the nights and mornings can be almost chilly when fog or harsh trade winds settle in. Winter months are known for *slightly* rougher weather— periodic rain showers, occasional storms, and higher surf.

Because higher mountains on Maui capture the trade-wind clouds, Lanai receives little rainfall and has a near-desert ecology. Consider the wind direction when planning your day. If it's blowing a gale on the windward beaches, head for the beach at Hulopoe or check out Keahiakawelo (Garden of the Gods). Overcast days, when the wind stops or comes lightly from the southwest, are common in whale season. At that time, try a whale-watching trip or the windward beaches.

Whales are seen off Lanai's shores November–May (peak season January– March). A Pineapple Festival on the July 4 Saturday in Dole Park features traditional entertainment, a pineapple-eating contest, and fireworks. Buddhists hold their annual outdoor Obon Festival, honoring departed ancestors with joyous dancing, local food, and drumming, in early July. During hunting-season weekends, mid-February–mid-May and mid-July– mid-October, watch out for hunters on dirt roads even though there are designated safety zones. On Sundays, many shops and restaurants have limited hours or are closed altogether.

Getting Here and Around

AIR

Hawaiian Airlines is the only commercial airline routinely serving Lanai City. Direct flights are available from Oahu; if you're flying to Lanai from any other Hawaiian island, you'll make a stop in Honolulu. Mokulele Airlines offers charter flights; guests of the Four Seasons Resort Lanai can arrange private charters from Honolulu on Lanai Air, which is operated by Mokulele Airlines.

If you're staying at the Four Seasons Resort Lanai, or renting a vehicle from Lanai City Service, you'll be met at the airport or ferry dock by a bus that shuttles between the resort and Lanai City (and there may be an additional fee).

AIRLINE CONTACTS Hawaiian Airlines. ☎ 800/367–5320 ⊕ www.hawaiianairlines.com. **Mokulele Airlines.** ☎ 866/260–7070 ⊕ www.mokuleleairlines.com.

AIRPORT CONTACTS Lanai Airport (LNY). ☎ 808/565–7942 ⊕ www.airports.hawaii.gov/lny.

CAR

It's always good to carry a cell phone. Lanai has only 30 miles of paved roads; its main road, Highway 440, refers to both Kaumalapau Highway and Manele Road. Keomuku Highway starts just past the Lodge at Koele and runs northeast to the dirt road that goes to Kaiolohia (aka Shipwreck Beach) and Lopa Beach. Manele Road (Highway 440) runs south down to Manele Bay, the Four Seasons Resort Lanai, and Hulopoe Beach. Kaumalapau Highway (also Highway 440) heads west to Kaumalapau Harbor. The rest of your driving takes place on bumpy dusty roads that are unpaved and unmarked. Driving in thick mud is not recommended, and the rental agency will charge a stiff cleaning fee. Watch out for blind curves on narrow roads. Take a map, be sure you have a full tank, and bring a snack and plenty of water.

Renting a four-wheel-drive vehicle is expensive but almost essential if you'd like to explore beyond the resorts and Lanai City. Make reservations far in advance of your trip, because Lanai's fleet of vehicles is limited. Lanai City Service, where you'll find a branch of Dollar Rent A Car, is open daily 7 am–7 pm. Ask the rental agency or your hotel's concierge about road conditions before you set out.

Stop from time to time to find landmarks and gauge your progress. Never drive or walk to the edge of lava cliffs, as rock can give way under you. Directions on the island are often given as *mauka* (toward the mountains) and *makai* (toward the ocean).

If you're visiting for the day, Rabaca's Limousine Service will take you wherever you want to go.

CONTACT Rabaca's Limousine Service. ✉ *552 Alapa St., Lanai City* ☎ *808/559–0230.*

FERRY
Ferries operated by Expeditions cross the channel five times daily between Lahaina on Maui to Manele Bay Harbor on Lanai. The crossing takes 45 minutes and costs $30. Be warned: passage can be rough, especially in winter.

CONTACT Expeditions. ☎ *808/661–3756, 800/695–2624* ⊕ *www.go-lanai.com.*

SHUTTLE
A shuttle transports you to your hotel from the harbor or the airport (a nominal fee may apply). If you're renting a vehicle from Lanai City Service, their shuttle will pick you up at the harbor or airport for a nominal fee.

Restaurants

Lanai has a wide range of choices for dining, from simple plate-lunch local eateries to gourmet resort restaurants.

Lanai's own version of Hawaii regional cuisine draws on the fresh bounty provided by local farmers and fishermen, combined with the skills of well-regarded chefs. The upscale menus at the Four Seasons Resort Lanai encompass European- and Asian-inspired cuisine as well as innovative preparations of international favorites and vegetarian delights. All Four Seasons Resort restaurants offer children's menus. Lanai City's eclectic ethnic fare runs from construction-worker-size local plate lunches to *poke* (raw fish), pizza, and pasta. ■TIP➔ **Lanai "City" is really a small town; restaurants sometimes close their kitchens early, and only a few are open on Sunday.**

Hotels

The good news is that you're sure to escape the crowds on this quaint island. The bad news is that Lanai has limited accommodation options, including the pricey Four Seasons Resort Lanai, or the relatively budget-friendly Hotel Lanai.

Hotel reviews have been shortened. For full information, visit Fodors.com.

WHAT IT COSTS in U.S. Dollars			
$	$$	$$$	$$$$
RESTAURANTS			
under $18	$18–$26	$27–$35	over $35
HOTELS			
under $181	$181–$260	$261–$340	over $340

Beaches

Lanai offers miles of secluded white-sand beaches on its windward side, plus the moderately developed Hulopoe Beach, which is adjacent to the Four Seasons Resort Lanai. Hulopoe is accessible by car or hotel shuttle bus; to reach the

Ocean views provide a backdrop to the eroded rocks at Keahiakawelo (aka Garden of the Gods).

windward beaches you need a four-wheel-drive vehicle. Reef, rocks, and coral make swimming on the windward side problematic, but it's fun to splash around in the shallow water. Expect debris on the windward beaches due to the Pacific convergence of ocean currents. Driving on the beach itself is illegal and can be dangerous.

Biking

Many of the same red-dirt roads that invite hikers are excellent for biking, offering easy, flat terrain and long clear views. There's only one hitch: you will have to bring your own bike, as there are no rentals or tours available.

A favorite biking route is along the fairly flat red-dirt road northward from Lanai City through the old pineapple fields to Keahiakawelo (Garden of the Gods). Start your trip on Keomuku Highway in town. Take a left just before the Lodge

at Koele's (closed for renovation) tennis courts, and then a right where the road ends at the fenced pasture, and continue on to the north end and the start of Polihua and Awalua dirt roads. If you're really hardy, you could bike down to Polihua Beach and back, but it would be a serious all-day trip. In wet weather these roads turn to mud and are not advisable. Go in the early morning or late afternoon, because the sun gets hot in the middle of the day. Take plenty of water, spare parts, and snacks.

For the exceptionally fit, it's possible to bike from town down the Keomuku Highway to the windward beaches and back, or to bike the Munro Trail (⇨ see Hiking). Experienced bikers also travel up and down the Manele Highway from Manele Bay to town.

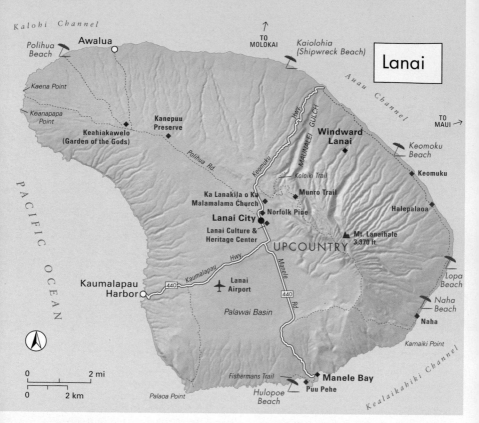

Lanai City

Lanai City is 3 miles northeast of the airport; Manele Bay is 9 miles southeast of Lanai City; Keahiakawelo (Garden of the Gods) is 6 miles northwest of Lanai City.

A tidy plantation town, built in 1924 by Jim Dole to accommodate workers for his pineapple business, Lanai City is home to old-time residents, resort workers, and second-home owners. With its charming plantation-era shops and restaurants having received new paint jobs and landscaping, Lanai City is worthy of whiling away a lazy afternoon.

You can easily explore Lanai City on foot. In its center, Dole Park is surrounded by small shops and restaurants and is a great spot for sitting, strolling, and talking story. Try a picnic lunch in the park and visit the Lanai Culture & Heritage Center in the Old Dole Administration Building to glimpse this island's rich past, purchase historical publications and maps, and get directions to anywhere on the island.

Manele Bay is an ocean lover's dream: Hulopoe Beach offers top-notch snorkeling, swimming, picnicking, tide pools, and sometimes spinner dolphins. Off-island ocean excursions depart from nearby Manele Small Boat Harbor. Take the short but rugged hike to the Puu Pehe (Sweetheart Rock) overlook, and you'll enjoy a bird's-eye view of this iconic Lanai landmark.

GETTING HERE AND AROUND
Lanai City serves as the island's hub, with roads leading to Manele Bay, Kaumalapau Harbor, and windward Lanai.

Keahiakawelo (Garden of the Gods) is usually possible to visit by car, but beyond that you will need four-wheel drive.

⊙ Sights

Kanepuu Preserve

FOREST | Hawaiian sandalwood, olive, and ebony trees characterize Hawaii's largest example of a rare native dryland forest. Thanks to the efforts of volunteers at the Nature Conservancy and a native Hawaiian land trust, the 590-acre remnant forest is protected from the axis deer and mouflon sheep that graze on the land beyond its fence. More than 45 native plant species can be seen here. A short, self-guided loop trail, with eight signs illustrated by local artist Wendell Kahoohalahala, reveals this ecosystem's beauty and the challenges it faces. The reserve is adjacent to the sacred hill, Kane Puu, dedicated to the Hawaiian god of water and vegetation. ⊠ *Polihua Rd., Lanai City ⊹ 4.8 miles north of Lanai City.*

★ Keahiakawelo (Garden of the Gods)

NATURE SITE | This preternatural plateau is scattered with boulders of different sizes, shapes, and colors, the products of a million years of wind erosion. Time your visit for sunset, when the rocks begin to glow—from rich red to purple—and the fiery globe sinks to the horizon. Magnificent views of the Pacific Ocean, Molokai, and, on clear days, Oahu, provide the perfect backdrop for photographs.

The ancient Hawaiians shunned Lanai for hundreds of years, believing the island was the inviolable home of spirits. Standing beside the oxide-red rock spires of this strange raw landscape, you might be tempted to believe the same. This lunar savanna still has a decidedly eerie edge, but the shadows disappearing on the horizon are those of mouflon sheep and axis deer, not the fearsome spirits of lore. According to tradition, Kawelo, a Hawaiian priest, kept a perpetual fire burning on an altar here, in sight of the island of Molokai. As long as the fire burned, prosperity was assured for the people of Lanai. Kawelo was killed by a rival priest on Molokai, and the fire went out. The Hawaiian name for this area is Keahiakawelo, meaning the "fire of Kawelo." ⊠ *Off Polihua Rd., Lanai City ⊹ 6 miles north of Lanai City.*

★ Lanai Culture & Heritage Center

MUSEUM | Small and carefully arranged, this historical museum features artifacts and photographs from Lanai's varied and rich history. Plantation-era clothing and tools, ranch memorabilia, old maps, precious feather lei, poi pounders, and family portraits combine to give you a good idea of the history of the island and its people. Postcards, maps, books, and pamphlets are for sale. The friendly staff can orient you to the island's historical sites and provide directions. This is the best place to start your explorations of the island. ■**TIP→** The Heritage Center's **Lanai Guide app is a trove of information—both practical and historical—on the island's sites.** ⊠ *730 Lanai Ave., Lanai City* ☎ *808/565–7177* ⊕ *www.lanaichc. org* ⊠ *Free* ⊗ *Closed weekends.*

Manele Bay

MARINA | The site of a Hawaiian village dating from 900 AD, Manele Bay is flanked by lava cliffs hundreds of feet high. Ferries from Maui dock five times a day, and visiting yachts pull in here, as it's the island's only small boat harbor. Public restrooms, grassy lawns, and picnic tables make it a busy pit stop—you can watch the boating activity as you rest. Just offshore to the west is Puu Pehe, an isolated 80-foot-high islet steeped in romantic Hawaiian lore; it's often called Sweetheart Rock. ⊠ *Hwy. 440, Manele, Lanai City.*

Norfolk Pine

GARDEN | Considered the "mother" of all the pines on the island, this 160-foot-tall tree was planted here, at the former site of the ranch manager's house, in 1875.

The Story of Lanai

Rumored to be haunted by hungry ghosts, Lanai was sparsely inhabited for many centuries. Most of the earliest settlers lived along the shore and made their living from fishing the nearby waters. Others lived in the Upcountry near seasonal water sources and traded their produce for seafood. The high chiefs sold off the land bit by bit to foreign settlers, and by 1910 the island was owned by the Gay family.

When the Hawaiian Pineapple Company purchased Lanai for $1.1 million in 1922, it built the town of Lanai City, opened the commercial harbor, and laid out the pineapple fields. Field workers came from overseas to toil in what quickly became the world's largest pineapple plantation. Exotic animals and birds were imported for hunting. Cook pines were planted to catch the rain, and eucalyptus windbreaks anchored the blowing soil.

Everything was stable for 70 years, until the plantation closed in 1992. When the resorts opened their doors, newcomers arrived, homes were built, and other ways of life set in. Today, most of the island is owned by billionaire Larry Ellison, and vast areas remain untouched and great views abound. Although the ghosts may be long gone, Lanai still retains its ancient mysterious presence.

Almost 30 years later, George Munro, the manager, observed how, in foggy weather, water collected on its foliage, dripping off rain. This led Munro to supervise the planting of Cook pines along the ridge of Lanaihale and throughout the town in order to add to the island's water supply. This majestic tree is just in front of the Four Seasons Hotel Lanai at Koele. ⊠ *Four Seasons Hotel Lanai at Koele, 1 Keomuku Hwy., Lanai City.*

Puu Pehe

LOCAL INTEREST | Often called Sweetheart Rock, this isolated 80-foot-high islet is steeped in romantic Hawaiian lore. The rock is said to be named after Pehe, a woman so beautiful that her husband kept her hidden in a sea cave. One day, the surf surged into the cave, and she drowned. Her grief-stricken husband buried her on this rock and jumped to his death. It is also believed that the enclosure on the summit is a shrine to birds, built by bird-catchers. Protected shearwaters nest in the nearby sea cliffs July–November. ⊠ *Hwy. 440, Manele, Lanai City.*

Beaches

★ Hulopoe Beach

BEACH—SIGHT | FAMILY | A short stroll from the Four Seasons Resort Lanai, Hulopoe is one of the best beaches in Hawaii. The sparkling crescent of this Marine Life Conservation District beckons with calm waters safe for swimming almost year-round, great snorkeling reefs, tide pools, and sometimes spinner dolphins. A shady, grassy beach park is perfect for picnics. If the shore break is pounding, or if you see surfers riding big waves, stay out of the water. In the afternoon, watch Lanai High School students heave outrigger canoes down the steep shore break and race one another just offshore. To get here, take Highway 440 south to the bottom of the hill and turn right. The road dead-ends at the beach's parking lot. **Amenities:** parking (no fee); showers; toilets. **Best for:** snorkeling; surfing; swimming. ⊠ *Off Hwy. 440, Lanai City.*

Kaiolohia (Shipwreck Beach)

BEACH—SIGHT | The rusting World War II tanker abandoned off this 8-mile stretch of sand adds just the right touch to an already photogenic beach. Strong trade winds have propelled vessels onto the reef since at least 1824, when the first shipwreck was recorded. Beachcombers come to this fairly accessible beach for shells and washed-up treasures, and photographers take great shots of Molokai, just across the Kalohi Channel. A deserted plantation-era fishing settlement adds to the charm. It's still possible to find glass-ball fishing floats as you wander along. Kaiolohia, its Hawaiian name, is a favorite local diving spot. Beyond the beach, about 200 yards up a trail past the Shipwreck Beach sign, are the Kukui Point petroglyphs, marked by reddish-brown boulders. ■**TIP➔ An offshore reef and rocks in the water mean that it's not for swimmers, though you can play in the shallow water on the shoreline.** To get here, take Highway 440 to its eastern terminus, then turn left onto a dirt road and continue to the end. **Amenities:** none. **Best for:** solitude; windsurfing. ⊠ *Off Hwy. 440, Lanai City.*

Lopa Beach

BEACH—SIGHT | A difficult surfing spot that tests the mettle of experienced locals, Lopa is also an ancient fishpond. With majestic views of West Maui and Kahoolawe, this remote white-sand beach is a great place for a picnic. ⚠ **Don't let the sight of surfers fool you: the channel's currents are too strong for swimming.** Take Highway 440 to its eastern terminus, turn right onto a dirt road, and continue south for 7 miles. **Amenities:** none. **Best for:** solitude; sunrise; walking. ⊠ *On dirt road off Hwy. 440.*

Polihua Beach

BEACH—SIGHT | This often-deserted beach features long wide stretches of white sand and unobstructed views of Molokai. The northern end of the beach ends at a rocky lava cliff with some interesting tide

The Coastal Road 👁

Road conditions can change overnight and become impassable due to rain in the Upcountry. The car-rental agency will give you an update before you hit the road. Some of the spur roads leading to the windward beaches from the coastal dirt road cross private property and are closed off by chains. Look for open spur roads with recent tire marks (a fairly good sign that they are safe to drive on). It's best to park on firm ground and walk in to avoid getting your car mired in the sand.

pools and sea turtles that lay their eggs in the sand. (Do not drive on the beach and endanger their nests.) However, the dirt road leading here has deep sandy places that are difficult in dry weather and impassable when it rains. In addition, strong currents and a sudden drop in the ocean floor make swimming dangerous, and strong trade winds can make walking uncomfortable. Thirsty wild bees sometimes gather around your car. To get rid of them, put out water some distance away and wait. The beach is in windward Lanai, 11 miles north of Lanai City. To get here, turn right onto the marked dirt road past Keahiakawelo (Garden of the Gods). **Amenities:** none. **Best for:** solitude; sunrise; walking. ⊠ *East end of Polihua Rd., Lanai City.*

🍴 Restaurants

In Lanai City you can enjoy everything from local-style plate lunches to upscale gourmet meals. For a small area, there are a number of good places to eat and drink, but remember that Lanai City mostly closes down on Sunday.

Blue Ginger Café

$ | **ECLECTIC** | This cheery Lanai City institution offers simply prepared, consistent, tasty food. Local paintings and photos line the walls inside, while townspeople parade by the outdoor tables. **Known for:** authentic local cuisine; comfort food; fresh-baked bread and pastries. $ *Average main: $12* ⊠ *409 7th St., Lanai City* ☎ *808/565–6363* ⊕ *www.bluegingercafelanai.com* ▭ *No credit cards.*

Café 565

$ | **ECLECTIC** | Named after the oldest telephone prefix on Lanai, Café 565 is a convenient stop for plate lunches, sandwiches on freshly baked focaccia, pizza, or platters of local-style favorites to take along for an impromptu picnic. Bring your own beer or wine for lunch or dinner, and request a table on the patio, which is kid-friendly. **Known for:** local-style plate lunch meals; friendly service; quick take-out meals. $ *Average main: $11* ⊠ *408 8th St., Lanai City* ☎ *808/565–6622* ☾ *Closed Sun.*

Coffee Works

$ | **AMERICAN** | A block from Dole Park, this Northern California–style café offers an umbrella-covered deck where you can sip cappuccinos and get in tune with the slow pace of life. Bagels with lox, deli sandwiches, and pastries are served, while blended espresso shakes and gourmet ice cream complete the coffeehouse vibe. **Known for:** casual atmosphere; comfortable outside seating; varied drink selection. $ *Average main: $8* ⊠ *604 Ilima St., Lanai City* ☎ *808/565–6962* ☾ *Closed Sun.*

★ Lanai City Bar & Grille

$$$ | **AMERICAN** | This neighborhood restaurant is a magnet for locals and visitors alike. Friendly service and a casual atmosphere provide the backdrop for a menu featuring fresh island ingredients prepared with bold flavors. **Known for:** farm-to-table cuisine; live music; al fresco dining. $ *Average main: $32* ⊠ *Hotel Lanai, 828 Lanai Ave., Lanai City* ☎ *808/565–7212* ⊕ *www.lanaicitybarandgrille.com* ☾ *Closed Sun.–Mon.*

No Ka Oi Grindz Lanai

$ | **HAWAIIAN** | **FAMILY** | A local favorite, this lunchroom-style café has picnic tables in the landscaped front yard where diners can watch the town drive by, plus five more tables in the no-frills interior. The menu includes local favorites like kimchi fried rice and massive plate lunches, plus daily specials. **Known for:** local comfort food; large portions; reasonable prices. $ *Average main: $10* ⊠ *335 9th St., Lanai City* ☎ *808/565–9413.*

Pele's Other Garden

$$ | **ITALIAN** | Small and colorful, Pele's is a deli and bistro all in one. For lunch, sandwiches or daily hot specials satisfy hearty appetites; at night, it's transformed into a busy bistro, with an intimate backroom bar where entertainers often drop in for impromptu jam sessions. **Known for:** Italian cuisine; quaint atmosphere; good beer and wine selection. $ *Average main: $19* ⊠ *811 Houston St., Lanai City* ☎ *808/565–9628* ⊕ *www.pelesothergarden.com* ☾ *Closed Sun.*

🛏 Hotels

★ Four Seasons Resort Lanai

$$$$ | **RESORT** | **FAMILY** | With stunning views of Hulopoe Bay and the astonishing rocky coastline, this sublime retreat offers beachside urban chic decor with meticulously curated artwork from across Polynesia, Micronesia, and Hawaii and manicured grounds that feature an array of native Hawaiian plants and species. **Pros:** nearby beach; outstanding restaurants and high-tech amenities; rental vehicles available on property. **Cons:** 20 minutes from town; need a car to explore the area; not all guest rooms have coast views. $ *Rooms from: $1150* ⊠ *1 Manele Bay Rd., Manele, Lanai City* ☎ *808/565–2000, 800/321–4666* ⊕ *www.fourseasons.com/lanai* ⇗ *213 rooms* ⦿ *No meals.*

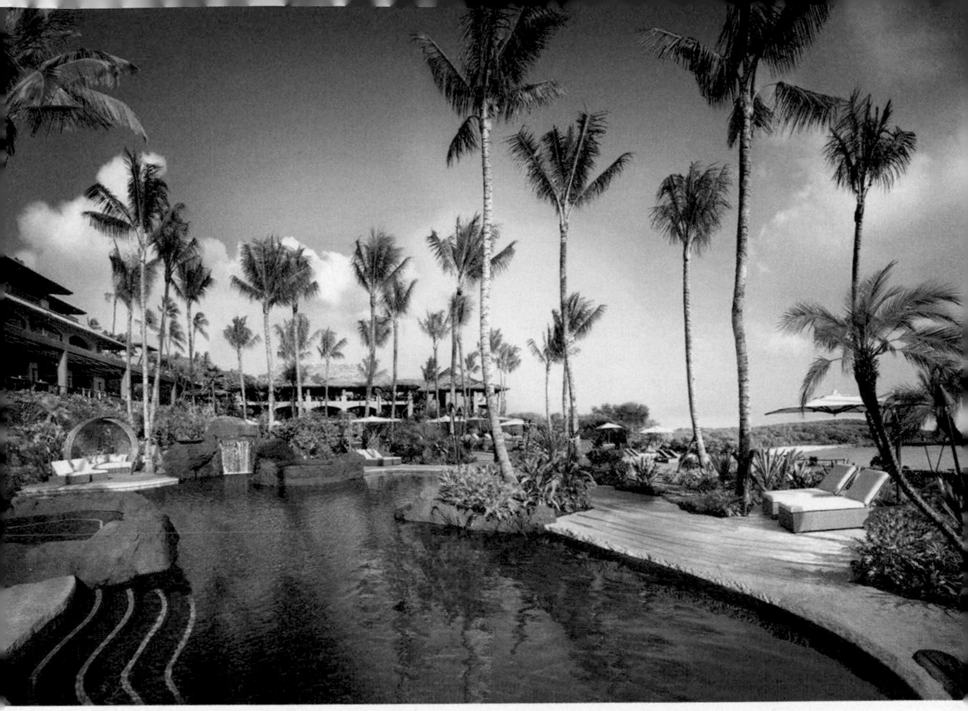

One of the pools at the Four Seasons Resort Lanai.

Hotel Lanai

$$$ | **HOTEL** | Built in 1923 to house visiting pineapple executives, this historic inn is like new following a massive renovation. **Pros:** porches attached to several rooms; walking distance to town; excellent on-site restaurant. **Cons:** far from beach; noisy at dinnertime; small rooms. [$] *Rooms from: $300* ✉ *828 Lanai Ave., Lanai City* ☎ *808/999–0892,* 🌐 *www.hotellanai.com* 🛏 *10 rooms, 1 cottage* 🍴 *Breakfast.*

Nightlife

Lanai's nightlife offerings are fairly limited. The Sports Bar at the Four Seasons Resort Lanai at Manele Bay features a lively sophisticated atmosphere in which to take in ocean views while noshing with your favorite libations.

Hale Keaka (Lanai Theater)

THEATER | **FAMILY** | Modern and comfortable, Hale Keaka's two 93-seat theaters and green room screen recent movie releases throughout the week. ✉ *465 7th St., Lanai City* ☎ *808/565-7511* 🌐 *www.lanai96763.com.*

Lanai City Bar and Grill

BARS/PUBS | A visit to this small, lively bar within Hotel Lanai lets you chat with locals and find out more about the island. Enjoy performances by local and visiting musicians on Friday and Saturday. Get here early—last call is at 9:30. ✉ *Hotel Lanai, 828 Lanai Ave., Lanai City* ☎ *808/565–7211* 🌐 *www.lanaicitybarandgrille.com.*

Shopping

A cluster of Cook pines in the center of Lanai City surrounded by small shops and restaurants, Dole Park is the closest thing to a mall on Lanai. Except for high-end resort boutiques and pro shops, it's the island's only shopping option. A morning or afternoon stroll around the park offers an eclectic selection of gifts and clothing, plus a chance to chat with friendly shopkeepers. Well-stocked general stores are reminiscent of the 1920s, and galleries and a boutique have original art and fashions for everyone.

CLOTHING

★ The Local Gentry

CLOTHING | Spacious and classy, this store has clothing for every need, from casual men's and women's beachwear to evening resort wear, shoes, jewelry, and hats. There are fancy fashions for tots as well. A selection of original Lanai-themed clothing is also available, including the signature "What happens on Lanai everybody knows" T-shirts. Proprietor Jenna Gentry Majkus will mail your purchases. ⊠ 363 7th St., Lanai City ☎ 808/565–9130.

FOOD

Pine Isle Market

FOOD/CANDY | One of Lanai City's two all-purpose markets, Pine Isle stocks everything from beach toys and electronics to meats and vegetables. The staff is friendly, and it's the best place around to buy fresh fish. ⊠ 356 8th St., Lanai City ☎ 808/565–6488.

Richard's Market

FOOD/CANDY | Along with fresh meats, fine wines, and imported gourmet items, Richard's stocks everything from camping gear to household items. ⊠ 434 8th St., Lanai City ☎ 808/565–3780.

GALLERIES

Lanai Art Center

ART GALLERIES | Local artists display their work at this dynamic center staffed by volunteers. Workshops in pottery, photography, woodworking, and painting welcome visitors. The gift shop sells Lanai handicrafts and special offerings like handmade Swarovski crystal bracelets, the sale of which underwrites children's art classes. There are occasional concerts and special events. ⊠ 339 7th St., Lanai City ☎ 808/565–7503 ⊕ www.lanaiart.org ⊗ Closed Sun.

★ Mike Carroll Gallery

ART GALLERIES | The dreamy, soft-focus oil paintings of award-winning painter Mike Carroll are inspired by island scenes. His work is showcased along with those of other local artists and visiting plein air painters. You can also find handcrafted jewelry and other accessories. ⊠ 443 7th St., Lanai City ☎ 808/565–7122 ⊕ www.mikecarrollgallery.com.

GENERAL STORES

International Food and Clothing Center

CONVENIENCE/GENERAL STORES | One of Lanai's oldest stores, this old-fashioned emporium stocks everything from fishing and camping gear to fine wine and imported beer. ⊠ 833 Ilima Ave., Lanai City ☎ 808/565–6433 ⊗ Closed Sat.

Lanai City Service

CONVENIENCE/GENERAL STORES | Lanai's only gas station is a convenient stop to fill your belly, too. The on-site Plantation Deli is famous for its massive sandwiches packed with quality ingredients, as well as tasty salads and soups. Snacks, beer, and souvenirs round out the selection. ⊠ 1036 Lanai Ave., Lanai City ☎ 808/565–7227.

🏃 Activities

HIKING

Only 30 miles of Lanai's roads are paved, but red-dirt roads and trails, ideal for hiking, will take you to sweeping overlooks, isolated beaches, and shady forests. Take a self-guided walk through Kane Puu, Hawaii's largest native dryland forest. You can also explore the Munro Trail over Lanaihale with views of plunging canyons, hike along an old coastal fisherman trail, or head out across Koloiki Ridge. Wear hiking shoes, a hat, and sunscreen, and carry a windbreaker, cell phone, and plenty of water.

Koloiki Ridge

HIKING/WALKING | This marked trail starts behind the Four Seasons Resort Lanai at Koele and takes you along the cool and shady Munro Trail to overlook the windward side, with impressive views of Maui, Molokai, Maunalei Valley, and Naio

Gulch. The average time for the 5-mile round trip is two hours. Bring snacks, water, and a windbreaker; wear good shoes; and take your time. *Moderate.* ⊠ *Lanai City.*

Lanai Fisherman Trail

HIKING/WALKING | Local anglers still use this trail to get to their favorite fishing spots. The trail takes about 1½ hours and follows the rocky shoreline below the Four Seasons Resort Lanai. The marked trail entrance begins at the west end of Hulopoe Beach. Keep your eyes open for spinner dolphins cavorting offshore and the silvery flash of fish feeding in the pools below you. The condition of the trail varies with weather and frequency of maintenance; it can be slippery and rocky. Take your time, wear a hat and enclosed shoes, and carry water. *Moderate.* ⊠ *Manele, Lanai City.*

★ Munro Trail

HIKING/WALKING | This is the real thing: a strenuous 12.8-mile trek that begins behind the Four Seasons Hotel Lanai at Koele and follows the ridge of Lanaihale through the rain forest. The island's most demanding hike, it has an elevation gain of 1,400 feet and leads to a lookout at the island's highest point, Lanaihale. It's also a narrow dirt road; watch out for careening four-wheel-drive vehicles. The trail is named after George Munro, who supervised the planting of Cook pine trees and eucalyptus windbreaks. Mules used to wend their way up the mountain carrying the pine seedlings. Unless you arrange for someone to pick you up at the trail's end, you have a 3-mile hike back through the Palawai Basin to return to your starting point. The summit is often cloud-shrouded and can be windy and muddy, so check conditions before you start. *Difficult.* ⊠ *Keomuku Hwy., Lanai City.*

Puu Pehe Trail

HIKING/WALKING | Beginning to the left of Hulopoe Beach, this trail travels a short distance around the coastline, and then climbs up a sharp rocky rise. At the top, you're level with the offshore stack of Puu Pehe and can overlook miles of coastline in both directions. The trail is not difficult, but it's hot and steep. Be aware of nesting seabirds and don't approach their nests. ⚠ **Stay away from the edge, as the cliff can easily give way.** The hiking is best in the early morning or late afternoon, and it's a perfect place to look for whales in season (November–May, peak season January–March). Wear a hat and enclosed shoes, and take water so you can spend some time at the top admiring the view. *Moderate.* ⊠ *Manele, Lanai City.*

HORSEBACK RIDING

Lanai Ranch at Koele

HORSEBACK RIDING | The subtle beauty of the high country slowly reveals itself to horseback riders. Two-hour adventures traverse leafy trails with scenic overlooks. Well-trained horses take riders (must be under 200 pounds) of all skill levels. Prices are $175 for a 90-minute group ride and $225 for a two-hour private ride. A four person carriage ride is $350 an hour. Lessons are also available. Operated by Four Seasons Resort Lanai, these activities are open to anyone, although prices are slightly higher for nonguests. ⊠ *1 Keomuku Hwy., Lanai City* ☎ *808/565–2072,* ⊕ *www.fourseasons.com/lanai.*

SCUBA DIVING

When you have a dive site such as Cathedrals—with eerie pinnacle formations and luminous caverns—it's no wonder that scuba-diving buffs consider exploring the waters off Lanai akin to a religious experience.

Cathedrals

SCUBA DIVING | Just outside Hulopoe Bay, Cathedrals is the best cavern dive site in Lanai. Shimmering light makes the many openings resemble stained-glass windows. A current generally keeps the water crystal clear, even if it's turbid outside. In these unearthly chambers, large *ulua* (Giant trevally) and small reef sharks add to the adventure. Tiger sharks may appear in certain seasons. ⊠ *Manele, Lanai City.*

Sergeant Major Reef

SCUBA DIVING | Off Kamaiki Point, Sergeant Major Reef is named for big schools of yellow- and black-striped *manini* (sergeant major fish) that turn the rocks silvery as they feed. There are three parallel lava ridges separated by rippled sand valleys, a cave, and an archway. Depths range 15–50 feet. Depending on conditions, the water may be clear or cloudy. ⊠ *Lanai City.*

SNORKELING

Snorkeling is the easiest ocean sport available on the island, requiring nothing but a snorkel, mask, fins, and good sense. Borrow equipment from your hotel or purchase some in Lanai City if you didn't bring your own. Wait to enter the water until you are sure no big sets of waves are coming, and observe the activity of locals on the beach. If little kids are playing in the shore break, it's usually safe to enter. ■TIP→ **To get into the water safely, always swim in past the breakers, and in the comparative calm put on your fins, then mask and snorkel.**

The best snorkeling on Lanai is at **Hulopoe Beach** and **Manele Small Boat Harbor.** Hulopoe, which is an exceptional snorkeling destination, has schools of manini that feed on the coral and coat the rocks with flashing silver. You can also easily view *kala* (unicorn fish), *uhu* (parrot fish), and *papio* (small trevally) in all their rainbow colors. Beware of rocks and surging waves. At Manele Harbor, there's a wade-in snorkel spot beyond the break wall. Enter over the rocks, just past the boat ramp. ■TIP→ **Do not enter if waves are breaking.**

Lanai Ocean Sports

SNORKELING | Take in the beauty of towering sea cliffs, playful spinner dolphins, and crystal-clear waters as you sail along Lanai's coastline before arriving at Kaunolu, where King Kamehameha challenged his Hawaiian warriors to show their courage by cliff jumping. This intimate trip includes snorkel equipment, wetsuit tops, and stand-up paddleboards, plus a gourmet picnic lunch. ⊠ *Manele Small Boat Harbor, Manele Rd., Manele, Lanai City* ☎ 808/866–8256 ⊕ *www. lanaioceansports.com* 🖃 *From $149.*

SPAS

Hawanawana Spa

SPA/BEAUTY | No two experiences are alike at Hawanawana Spa, where every treatment is tailored to your individual desires. Spa and salon services—like the Ocean Ritual or Lanai Tai Signature Scrub—feature locally inspired ingredients and techniques. The spa's Zen aesthetic is complimented with soothing colors of natural sands, ocean textures, and whimsical touches from beneath the sea. Massages are available in couples' suites; limited selection available poolside. ⊠ *Four Seasons Resort Lanai, 1 Manele Bay Rd., Manele, Lanai City* ☎ 808/565–2088 ⊕ *www.fourseasons. com/lanai* ☞ *$240–$360 for 60–90 min massage, Ocean Ritual $460 per person for two hours.*

SURFING

Surfing on Lanai can be truly enjoyable. Quality, not quantity, characterizes this isle's few breaks. Be considerate of the locals, and they will be considerate of you—surfing takes the place of megaplex theaters and pool halls here, serving as one of the island's few recreational luxuries.

Lanai Surf School & Safari

SURFING | Nick Palumbo offers the only surf instruction on the island. The Lanai native is a former Hawaii State Surfing Champion, so you're in good hands. Experienced riders can rent boards overnight, which can be delivered. Palumbo also has the only paddleboard permit for

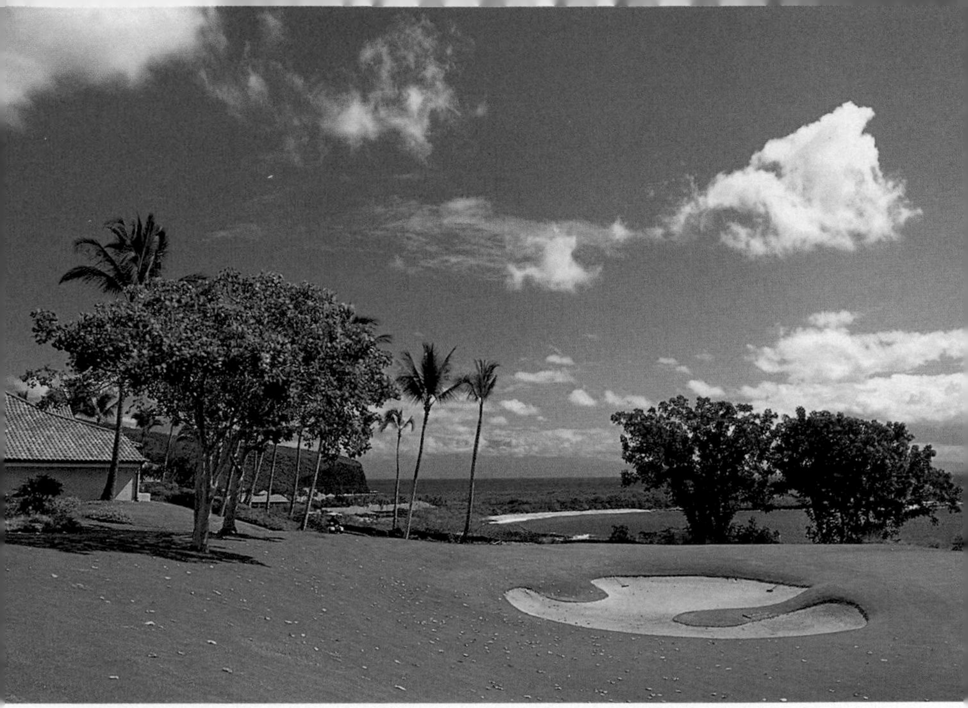

Some holes at the Manele Golf Course use the Pacific Ocean as a water hazard.

Hulopoe Bay, and gives lessons and rents equipment. You can also rent skimboards, boogie boards, and kayaks. He will pick you up at your hotel or at the ferry dock. ✉ *Lanai City* ☎ *808/649–0739* 🌐 *www.surfinglanai.com* 🎟 *Lessons from $200.*

Manele Bay

🍴 Restaurants

Dining at Manele Bay offers the range of options provided by the Four Seasons Resort Lanai, from informal poolside meals to relaxed eclectic dining.

Nobu Lanai

$$$$ | JAPANESE | Chef Nobuyuki "Nobu" Matsuhisa offers his signature new-style Japanese cuisine in this open-air, relaxed luxury venue that features a lounge, teppanyaki stations, and a sushi bar. This is fine dining without the stress, as black-clad waiters present dish after dish of beautifully seasoned, raw and lightly cooked seafood from local waters, or flown in directly from Alaska and Japan. **Known for:** omakase (chef's choice) mul ticourse menu; pricey menu; fresh fish. [$] *Average main: $50* ✉ *Four Seasons Resort Lanai, 1 Manele Bay Rd., Lanai City* ☎ *808/565–2832* 🌐 *www.noburestaurants.com/lanai* 🕓 *No lunch.*

One Forty

$$$$ | AMERICAN | Named after the island's 140 square miles, this ocean-view restaurant serves prime cuts of beef and the freshest local fish in airy comfort on a terrace that overlooks the wide sweep of Hulopoe Bay. Retractable awnings provide shade on sunny days, and comfy rattan chairs, potted palms, and tropical decor create an inviting setting. **Known for:** steak and seafood; ocean views; superb service. [$] *Average main: $45* ✉ *Four Seasons Resort Lanai, 1 Manele Bay Rd., Lanai City* ☎ *808/565–2290* 🌐 *www.fourseasons.com/lanai* 🕓 *No lunch.*

Views at Manele Golf Course

$$ | AMERICAN | A stunning view of the legendary Puu Pehe rock only enhances the imaginative fare of this open-air restaurant, which also has great views of frolicking dolphins from its terrace. Tuck into a Hulopoe Bay prawn BLT, the crispy battered fish-and-chips with Meyer lemon tartar sauce, or any one of the tempting salad options. **Known for:** ocean views; superb service; fish tacos. [$] *Average main: $25* ✉ *Four Seasons Resort Lanai, 1 Manele Bay Rd., Manele, Lanai City* ☎ *808/565–2230* 🌐 *www.fourseasons.com/lanai* 🕒 *No dinner.*

Activities

GOLF

Manele Golf Course

GOLF | You'll need to be a Four Seasons Resort Lanai guest to play at this renowned course. Designed by Jack Nicklaus in 1993, it sits right over the water of Hulopoe Bay. Built on lava outcroppings, it features three holes on cliffs that use the Pacific Ocean as a water hazard. The five-tee concept challenges the best golfers—tee shots over natural gorges and ravines must be precise. Unspoiled natural terrain provides a stunning backdrop, and every hole offers ocean views. Early-morning tee times are recommended to avoid the midday heat. Another reason to start early: morning golfers can enjoy a complimentary continental breakfast at Views. ✉ *Four Seasons Resort Lanai, Challenge Dr., Manele, Lanai City* ☎ *808/565–2222* 🌐 *www.fourseasons.com/lanai* 🎫 *$350 for resort guests* ⛳ *18 holes, 7039 yards, par 72.*

Windward Lanai

9 miles northeast of the Lodge at Koele to end of paved road.

The eastern shore of Lanai is mostly deserted. A few inaccessible *heiau,* or temples, rock walls and boulders marking old shrines, and a restored church at Keomuku reveal traces of human habitation. Four-wheel-drive vehicles are a must to explore this side of the isle. Pack a picnic lunch, a hat and sunscreen, and plenty of drinking water. A mobile phone is also a good idea.

GETTING HERE AND AROUND

Once you leave paved Keomuku Highway and turn left toward Kaiolohia (Shipwreck Beach) or right to Naha, the roads are dirt and sand; conditions vary with the seasons. Mileage doesn't matter much here, but figure on 20 minutes from the end of the paved road to Shipwreck Beach, and about 45 minutes to Lopa Beach.

Sights

Halepalaoa

ARCHAEOLOGICAL SITE | Named for the whales that once washed ashore here, Halepalaoa, or the "House of Whale Ivory," was the site of the wharf used by the short-lived Maunalei Sugar Company in 1899. Some say the endeavor failed because the sacred stones of nearby **Kahea Heiau** were used for its construction of the cane railroad. The brackish well water turned too salty, forcing the sugar company to close in 1901, after just two years. The remains of the *heiau,* once an important place of worship for the people of Lanai, are now difficult to find through the kiawe overgrowth. There's good public-beach access here and clear shallow water for swimming, but no other facilities. Take Highway 440 (Keomuku Highway) to its eastern terminus, then turn right on the dirt road and continue south for 5½ miles. ✉ *On dirt road off Hwy. 440, Lanai City.*

Keomuku

ARCHAEOLOGICAL SITE | There's a peaceful beauty about the former fishing village of Keomuku. During the late 19th century, this small Lanai community served as the headquarters of the Maunalei Sugar Company. After the company failed, the land was abandoned. Although there are no other signs of previous habitation, its church, **Ka Lanakila O Ka Malamalama,** built in 1903, has been restored by volunteers. Visitors often leave some small token, a shell or lei, as an offering. Take Highway 440 to its eastern terminus, then turn right onto a dirt road and continue south for 5 miles. The church is on your right in the coconut trees. ⊠ *On dirt road off Hwy. 440.*

Munro Trail

SCENIC DRIVE | This 12.8-mile four-wheel-drive trail along a fern- and pine-clad narrow ridge was named after George Munro, manager of the Lanai Ranch Company, who began a reforestation program in the 1950s to restore the island's much-needed watershed. The trail climbs **Lanaihale** (House of Lanai), which, at 3,370 feet, is the island's highest point; on clear days you'll be treated to a panorama of canyons and almost all the Hawaiian Islands. ■ **TIP→ The road gets very muddy, and trade winds can be strong. Watch for sheer drop-offs, and keep an eye out for hikers.** You can also hike the Munro Trail although it's steep, the ground is uneven, and there's no water. From the Four Seasons Hotel Lanai at Koele, head north on Highway 440 for 1¼ miles, then turn right onto Cemetery Road. Keep going until you're headed downhill on the main dirt road. It's a one-way road, but you may meet jeeps coming from the opposite direction. ⊠ *Cemetery Rd., Lanai City.*

Naha

ARCHAEOLOGICAL SITE | An ancient rock-walled fishpond—visible at low tide—lies where the sandy shore ends and the cliffs begin their rise along the island's shores. Accessible by four-wheel-drive vehicle, the beach is a frequent dive spot for local fishermen. ■ **TIP→ Treacherous currents make this a dangerous place for swimming.** Take Highway 440 to its eastern terminus, then turn right onto a sandy dirt road and continue south for 11 miles. The shoreline dirt road ends here. ⊠ *On dirt road off Hwy. 440, Lanai City.*

Index

Photo Credits

Notes

Notes

Fodor's ESSENTIAL HAWAII

Publisher: Stephen Horowitz, *General Manager*

Editorial: Douglas Stallings, *Editorial Director*; Jill Fergus, Jacinta O'Halloran, Amanda Sadlowski, *Senior Editors*; Kayla Becker, Alexis Kelly, Rachael Roth, *Editors*

Design: Tina Malaney, *Director of Design and Production*; Jessica Gonzalez, *Graphic Designer;* Mariana Tabares, *Design and Production Intern*

Production: Jennifer DePrima, *Editorial Production Manager;* Elyse Rozelle, *Senior Production Editor;* Monica White, *Production Editor*

Maps: Rebecca Baer, *Senior Map Editor*; Mark Stroud (Moon Street Cartography); David Lindroth, *Cartographers*

Photography: Viviane Teles, *Senior Photo Editor;* Namrata Aggarwal, Ashok Kumar, Carl Yu, *Photo Editors;* Rebecca Rimmer, *Photo Intern*

Business and Operations: Chuck Hoover, *Chief Marketing Officer*; Robert Ames, *Group General Manager*; Devin Duckworth, *Director of Print Publishing*; Victor Bernal, *Business Analyst*

Public Relations and Marketing: Joe Ewaskiw, *Senior Director Communications and Public Relations*; Esther Su, *Senior Marketing Manager*

Fodors.com: Jeremy Tarr, *Editorial Director;* Rachael Levitt, *Managing Editor*

Technology: Jon Atkinson, *Director of Technology;* Rudresh Teotia, *Lead Developer*; Jacob Ashpis, *Content Operations Manager*

Writers: Karen Anderson, Kristina Anderson, Lehia Apana, Powell Berger, Marla Cimini, Joan Conrow, Cheryl Crabtree, Tiffany Hill, Trina Kudlacek, Laurie Lyons-Makaimoko, Charles E. Roessler, Anna Weaver, Mary F. Williamson

Editors: Rachael Roth (lead editor), Kayla Becker, Doug Stallings

Production Editor: Jennifer DePrima

3rd edition

ISBN 978-1-64097-316-9

ISSN 2471–9048

Library of Congress Control Number 2018950373

All details in this book are based on information supplied to us at press time. Always confirm information when it matters, especially if you're making a detour to visit a specific place. Fodor's expressly disclaims any liability, loss, or risk, personal or otherwise, that is incurred as a consequence of the use of any of the contents of this book.

SPECIAL SALES

This book is available at special discounts for bulk purchases for sales promotions or premiums. For more information, e-mail SpecialMarkets@fodors.com.

PRINTED IN THE UNITED STATES OF AMERICA

10 9 8 7 6 5 4 3

About Our Writers

 Karen Anderson is a Kona resident who enjoys horseback riding in the hills of the Big Island. She is the managing editor of *At Home, Living with Style in West Hawaii* and has written for a variety of publications including *West Hawaii Today, Big Island Weekly, Hawaii* magazine, and the Kona-Kohala Chamber of Commerce. She's also the best-selling author of *The Hawaii Home Book, Practical Tips for Tropical Living*, which received an award of excellence from the Hawaii Book Publishers Association. Her monthly editor's column and chef/restaurant profiles are known throughout West Hawaii. Karen updated Hilo, and Hawaii Volcanoes National Park, Puna & Kau on Big Island.

 Kristina Anderson has been writing professionally for more than 25 years. After working as an advertising copywriter and creative director in Southern California for more than a decade, she moved to Hawaii in 1992, freelancing copy and broadcast for Hawaii agencies. Since 2006, she's written for national and regional publications, most notably for *At Home in West Hawaii* magazine, which profiles a variety of homes—from coffee shacks to resort mansions—and for USAToday. com Travel Tips. She also fills in here and there as a substitute teacher, which keeps her busy, as does being a single mom to two teenage boys. When there's time, she paddles outrigger canoes competitively and plays tennis very noncompetitively. For this book, Kristina updated Kailua-Kona & the Kona Coast, The Kohala Coast & Waimea, The Hamakua Coast with Maunakea, and Activities & Tours on Big Island.

 Born and raised on Maui, **Lehia Apana** is an island girl with a wandering spirit. She has lived in Chicago, Rome, and Sydney, but she always finds her way back home. Lehia has been writing about Maui for more than a decade, and has served as an editor at *The Maui News* and *Maui Nō Ka ʻOi Magazine*. Find out more at ⊕ *lehiaapana. com*.

Marla Cimini is an award-winning writer with a passion for travel, beaches, music, and culinary adventures. As an avid globetrotter and frequent Oahu visitor, she has covered topics such as Hawaii's luxury hotels, fascinating and fun surf culture, and the innovative restaurant scene on the islands. She appreciates Oahu's unique dichotomy, and enjoys the bustling Waikiki neighborhood as much as exploring the island's quieter beaches. And she's always up for surfing or an outrigger canoe ride in Waikiki! Marla's articles have appeared in numerous publications worldwide, including *USA Today* and many others. Marla's website is ⊕ *www.marlacimini.com*. She updated Waikiki and Diamond Head on Oahu for this edition.

Powell Berger lives in the heart of Honolulu's Kakaako neighborhood, where she's ever in search of the best poke bowl. Her wanderlust has taken her to more than 50 countries around the world, and her writing appears in numerous state and regional publications, AAA magazines, *The Atlantic,* and various websites, in addition to Fodor's.

 Joan Conrow is an independent journalist who splits her time between Kauai and New Mexico. She has written about Hawaii politics, culture, environment, and lifestyles for many regional and national publications. She

About Our Writers

helped write the original Fodor's guide to Kauai and updated the West Side section of Kauai for this edition.

Cheryl Crabtree first visited Hawaii as a kindergartner, a trip that sparked a life-long passion for the islands and led to frequent visits. She spends months at a time in residence on the North Shore and updated The North Shore and West (Leeward) & Central Oahu sections of Oahu for this edition. Cheryl has also contributed to *Fodor's California* for nearly two decades and is a regular updater for *Fodor's National Parks of the West*. She also contributes to numerous regional and national publications.

Tiffany Hill grew up on Oahu and has lived on both the Leeward and Windward sides, but today she calls Portland, Oregon, home. She specializes in travel, culture, and business. Her work is regularly published in regional and national publications, as well as online. When she's not on assignment, you can find her playing roller derby. Tiffany updated parts of Oahu wrote the features in the Experience chapter.

Trina Kudlacek fell in love with Hawaii while on vacation 20 years ago. She now has the best of all possible worlds as she splits her time between her home in Hawaii, where she is a lecturer at the University of Hawaii, and Italy, where she is a tour guide.

Laurie Lyons-Makaimoku relocated to Hawaii Island from Austin in 2016, looking for a temporary change of pace. After falling in love with the island (and one of its inhabitants), she ended up permanently relocating. Since then she's spent time developing an

appreciation for Hawaii's places, culture, and people, focusing her travel writing on the island chain, always working to strike a balance between sharing the islands with the world and trying to ensure that tourism is sustainable and ethical. She now shares her home with her husband, toddler, stepdaughter, and 20 animals and continues to write about culture, sustainability, environmentalism, plant-based living, and more.

Charles E. Roessler is a longtime Kauai resident who was an editor for the *Japan Times* and the *Buffalo News* after teaching English and journalism for 10 years. He contributes to the *New York Times* as a stringer/freelancer and loves Kauai, especially playing tennis and swimming at Anini Beach. Charles updated the North Shore, the East Side, and Activities sections of Kauai for this guide.

Writer and multimedia journalist **Anna Weaver** is a sixth-generation *kamaaina*, born and raised in Kailua, Oahu. She can never get enough Spam *musubi, malassadas*, or hiking time in her home state. Anna has written for *Slate, Simplemost*, and such Hawaii publications as the *Honolulu Advertiser* (now *Star-Advertiser*), *Honolulu Magazine*, and *Pacific Business News*.

Mary F. Williamson grew up in Honolulu and lives on Kauai, where her husband's family moved in the late 1800s. A former nonprofit director, she now organizes bicycle races and helps small businesses and organizations with public communication and events. She updated the South Shore section of Kauai for this guide. About Our Writers